CALIFORNIA
CONQUERED

CALIFORNIA CONQUERED

The Annexation of a Mexican Province
1846–1850

NEAL HARLOW

UNIVERSITY OF CALIFORNIA PRESS

BERKELEY · LOS ANGELES · LONDON

University of California Press

Berkeley and Los Angeles, California

University of California Press, Ltd.

London, England

© 1982 by

The Regents of the University of California

Printed in the United States of America

First Paperback Printing 1989

2   3   4   5   6   7   8   9

Library of Congress Cataloging in Publication Data

Harlow, Neal.
    California conquered.

    Bibliography: p.
    Includes index.
    1. California—History—1846-1850.   I. Title.
F864.H295   979.4'03   81-7588
ISBN 0-520-06605-7   AACR2

SOMETHING like a connected history of the war in California will be a very desirable object, and although there are others who could perform the task more satisfactorily than ourselves, we find that such persons are unwilling to undertake the task. . . .

ROBERT SEMPLE IN THE MONTEREY *CALIFORNIAN*, MARCH 13, 1847

~ Contents ~

ders from Washington when he thought they would work, bending them often in the people's direction, sometimes inauspiciously for his own good.

ANNEXATION

Maps and Illustrations

Aviso

THE CONQUEST OF CALIFORNIA by the United States was probably inevitable, given the unbridled energy of a young nation and an open continent stretching to the Pacific. But the schemes to obtain it were not made in heaven. Rather, they were conspicuously human in motivation and achievement. A lust for land, a quest for independence beyond the frontier, trade and profit, the vision of a nation from sea to sea, fear of foreign deterrence: these stirred the spirits of countless Americans. Official exploring expeditions spied out the land, but independent trappers, traders, farmers, and adventurers were drawn westward as into a mighty vacuum, followed by the U.S. Army and Navy. *Manifest destiny* heralded the invasion—the American people were *destined* to subdue the continent. Yet, the United States could not await events; Mexico's hold upon California was uncertain, and England must not snatch it from her weakening grasp. We must be first!

Mexican and American interests clashed along a common border from Louisiana to the Pacific. Americans moved into adjacent Texas, drove wagon trains to Santa Fé, made the long passage to California. When Texas sought admission to the American Union and was in time annexed, Mexico threatened hostilities. Whereupon President Polk, driven by an urgent desire to acquire California and unable to obtain it by negotiation or purchase, impelled an already belligerent neighbor into outright war. The United States Navy on both coasts was alerted; and as the southern march into Mexico began, General Kearny moved overland to New Mexico and California with the Army of the West.

The conquering force thus had two divisions, one to overthrow the Mexican government that there might be victor's spoils, the other to take and hold California and New Mexico, the predetermined prize. That much of the conflict in California was unwarranted, even inimical to the American cause, was perceived by some at the time. A none too scrupulous Frémont drove the inhabitants into an early and unnecessarily hostile opposition. An egotistical and domineering Stockton further alienated the populace by a brave if bumptious belligerence. The valorous but irritable Gillespie incited the revolt in Los Angeles; and Mervine's losses, Kearny's debacle at San Pasqual, and the battles of San Gabriel and the Mesa were the gratuitous aftermath. Polk's favored strategy to bring California into the Union with a minimum of upheaval was frustrated by the failure of his agents to conciliate and hold the country "if possible . . . without any strife" until the war ended. Had Captain Dupont and not the blustering Stockton succeeded Commodore Sloat in command, the Navy might have occupied only the California ports and Los Angeles and awaited the treaty of peace, as he and some of the Californians suggested. History, like fiction, is much indebted to individuals; and this is the story of what, instead, happened.

The conquest of California differed both in scale and character from the war in central Mexico. It involved fewer people and was on a more intimate level. The Californians were almost without an army (though with supernumerary officers) and depended for their defense upon reluctant volunteers. Though the conquerors were not required to subdue the enemy, only to be "in possession" when the war ended, they nonetheless proved actively hostile. Yet, in the face of American belligerence, the Californians yielded more to circumstances than to force. Proud of their hospitality to strangers, they accepted many foreigners as their friends. Individualistic and quarrelsome among themselves, they disliked being ruled by others, particularly Mexicans. Many saw the conquest as inevitable, even desirable, and, always ambivalent in their relations with Mexico, were ready to join the invader or await the outcome of more distant and decisive battles. Famous horsemen, masters of the guerrilla tactic of attack and withdrawal, and ferocious fighters when conditions warranted, they were the victims of their own irresolution.

The Americans of the conquest are not so remote from the present that they cannot be understood. Stoutly they defended their rights and liberties. Freedom of speech and press, the right of self-government, security of persons and possessions, attachment to land, patriotism, capitalism, and Christianity were all loudly acclaimed. Subsequent events have vastly affected man's relations and dealings, but the twentieth century bears the marks of its predecessor at its core. Time and distance lend new perspectives, and alien ways seem as ever obscure, but anyone familiar with American character will recognize Larkin, Gillespie, Stockton, Kearny, and Riley (if not Frémont) at the first encounter.

Unlike its neighbors, California was an organized state before it joined the Union and, never having been a Territory, accrued no pre-statehood records. This book began as a venture to collect official and unofficial documents relating to the interval of American military rule. There proved to be thousands, the writings of Presidents, executive officers, and congressmen, naval and military personnel, governors, settlers, and citizens—routine, familiar, wheedling, seductive, blustering, commanding. As the quantity grew, they seemed eager to be heard. But the documents exhibit the traits of their makers. Containing neither the whole truth nor nothing but the truth, they offer many-sided versions of what people believed or wanted others to accept; they must be taken with a grain of salt. Long, sometimes garbled, and always incomplete, the record requires assessment, a referee to appraise the evidence and form his own imperfect conclusions. And any curious or dissenting reader may, by consulting the numerous cited sources, make his own interpretations. References, whenever possible, have been made to materials in some printed form, leading an inquirer to a vast array of historical evidence.

Everything herein happened, or so the record tells, and if an assumption has been made, it is that men, issues, and events can be interesting in their own right, without exaggeration. "To exaggerate," a knowing urban child recently observed, "means you put in something to make it more exciting" (Los Angeles *Times*, Dec. 10, 1978).

ACKNOWLEDGMENTS

The cumulation of documents began in the 1930s, and a first, brief narrative was prepared under the direction of Dr. John Walton Caughey at U.C.L.A. (published as "War and Peace in California" in the *Westerners Brand Book*, Los Angeles, 1950, pp. 23–31). Other matters intervened until 1971, and since that time much new material has accrued, with many debts of gratitude, chiefly to The Huntington Library in San Marino, California; the University of California Research Library at Los Angeles; The Bancroft Library at the University of California, Berkeley; the Library of the University of Southern California, Los Angeles; the California State Archives and the California State Library, Sacramento; and the National Archives in Washington, D.C. Dr. Doyce B. Nunis, Jr., has been generous with his private resources. August Frugé contributed much-needed critical guidance, Marian Harlow gave assistance, endurance, and support. Edwin H. Carpenter and Diane Killou read the text with scrupulous care. The author's obligations to other writers is documented in the list of sources at the end of this work.

Neal Harlow

APPROACHES

❧ 1 ❧

Dress Rehearsal—
Jones' War (1842)

I IMAGINE you have never had a Correspondent from the 'Far West,'"
Thomas O. Larkin wrote from Monterey in February 1843, initiating a
correspondence with James G. Bennett of the New York *Herald*. In fact,
the editor had not yet discovered where the "Far-famed 'Far West'" really
was. But with the delivery of this letter from Upper California, Larkin
genially added, "You now know, and so does Com. Thomas ap C. Jones,
and the officers of his squadron."[1]

It was about Commodore Jones' exploits that merchant Larkin was
particularly writing, hoping to use this international incident to stir up
American interest in Mexico's California domain. With the precipitous
seizure—and just as abrupt surrender—of Monterey by vessels of the
U.S. Pacific squadron the past October, at least the commodore had acquired a close personal awareness of this remote place. And now that he
and the warships had departed, the Californians could resume their leisurely ways; and local Americans, embarrassed, could brood over what
might be the aftermath.

Commodore Thomas ap Catesby Jones had been dispatched by the
U.S. Secretary of the Navy at the end of 1841 to command the U.S. Pacific squadron[2]—flagship *United States*, sloops-of-war *Cyane*, *Dale*, and
Yorktown, schooner *Shark*, and storeship *Relief*, totaling 116 guns.
Jones' expressed instructions had been to protect American commerce,
improve the discipline of his men by affording active service, and collect
useful information. Although it was not mentioned in his orders, rumors
concerning the ultimate fate of California had long been circulating in the

United States, based upon speculation that this out-of-the-way province would one day fall or be plucked from the Mexican bough. The principal heirs-apparent were England, France, and the United States, the first being regarded by the Americans with the greatest apprehension. Englishmen had large claims against the Mexican government (calculated at about £15,000,000), and rumors that a "good portion of the Californias" was being assigned to England in partial settlement of these debts were being bandied about in the popular press.[3] As for France, it was a Latin and Catholic power and held a privileged position in relation to Mexico and a common aversion to English and American ways. Meanwhile, in the United States there was a growing conviction that California—at the other end of the American continent—belonged by some "natural right" to the Republic, and although time and western migration might be on its side, no chances were to be taken.

As early as 1806 the contingency had been envisaged in which American troops might be used in the conquest of California;[4] and John Quincy Adams, as Secretary of State in 1819, believed the whole North American continent was the proper dominion of the United States.[5] In 1822 Joel R. Poinsett, an agent sent to Mexico by President Monroe, had proposed a new boundary giving Texas, New Mexico, and California, with other northern Mexican territory, to the United States.[6] And in 1835 President Andrew Jackson had authorized his chargé d'affaires in Mexico to attempt to buy a large chunk of that country to the west with the "great object of securing the bay of San Francisco."[7] Mexican intractability, excitement over Texas, two decades of Anglo-American indecision over Oregon, and repeated changes of administration in all the interested countries left California in the 1840s still a tantalizing issue. So it was that the Secretary of the Navy in 1841 warned Jones that "Nothing but the necessity of prompt and effective protection to the honor and interests of the United States will justify you in either provoking hostility or committing any act of violence toward a belligerent . . . especially a state with which our country is at peace."[8]

Immediately upon Jones' arrival in the Pacific he learned, at Callao, that a "formidable" French fleet had in March 1842 sailed from Valparaiso to a destination altogether unknown; it might, he thought, be California.[9] Then, on September 5, after his return from a training cruise and before any new instructions had arrived from Washington, three English vessels under Rear Admiral Thomas left Callao, also on a secret mission.[10] At the same time a message from the U.S. consul at Mazatlán was put into his hands, announcing the imminence of war with Mexico over Texas.[11]

With such an accumulation of portents, Jones again put to sea on September 7, accompanied by the *Cyane* and *Dale*, leaving a note for the absent *Yorktown* to follow him to the coast of California.[12] Next day he polled his officers, who agreed that if war had indeed been declared, they were bound to seize and hold every California port and point.[13] They would uphold the Monroe Doctrine by forestalling their great commercial rival, England, and supplanting the Mexican flag at San Francisco and other points in the territory said to have been recently ceded by secret treaty to Great Britain. While the *Dale* proceeded to Panama to obtain news from Washington and learn the movements of the British squadron, the *United States* and *Cyane* made all sail for California.[14]

Jones put great store in the virtues of discipline and preparedness, and he exercised the guns all the way to Monterey, firing at a barrel two miles away and letting go the whole broadside at once, a "rather noisy" performance.[15] Cutlasses were ground and swords sharpened, and Midshipman Jackson thought never were vessels so well prepared for action. A head wind drove them almost as far west as the Sandwich Islands, and not until the night of October 18 did they sight land, some fifteen miles south of Monterey. Beating their way up the coast, at noon the following day they encountered a Mexican vessel, the *Joven Guipuzcoana*, and, after hoisting British colors, boarded her; but Captain Joseph Snook (an Englishman, naturalized in California) knew nothing of hostilities between the two countries.[16]

Flying their own proper flags, the Americans quietly rounded Point Pinos to find no English or French squadron in the harbor, only the American ship *Fama* and some Mexican vessels which were promptly taken as prizes of war.[17] They anchored at 2:45 p.m. under the old fort. After a considerable delay, during which Jones fruitlessly awaited a visit from some American or neutral on shore,[18] two California officers diffidently approached in a boat, and they too professed no knowledge of war. But their manifest nervousness and what looked like preparations for defense on shore intensified the commodore's apprehensions. The mate of the *Fama*, summoned on board, said that reports of war were current in Honolulu, and he had heard that England was to take possession of the country. Meanwhile, the stir on land had become general, the guns of the fort were being manned, and horsemen were gathering. Although the commodore was acquainted with no Americans at Monterey,

Commodore Thomas ap Catesby Jones learned at Callao that a formidable French fleet had sailed to a destination altogether unknown—it might be California.

he knew there should be several, and that none appeared seemed to him a suspicious circumstance.

Though Jones had assured Washington he would not act precipitously—nor shirk his responsibility[19]—he had told his men as they approached the coast that they must strike the Mexican flag at Monterey "and hoist in its place our own." And he had carefully instructed them in their procedures and behavior.[20] On-the-spot observations now convinced him that the time for action had come; another day might bring Admiral Thomas with a superior force, or California's new governor-general might appear to defend his capital. If he took possession of the country and there was war, all would be well. But he might be wrong, and by his action forfeit all he had acquired in thirty-seven years of devotion to his country's service.[21]

Having calculated the risk but believing his duty clear, he hoisted the flag of truce on both ships and, at 4 p.m. October 19, sent Captain James Armstrong, commander of the *United States*, ashore to demand surrender. The summons was signed by the expansive commodore as "Commander-in-chief of the United States naval forces on the Pacific station, and of the naval and military expedition for the occupation of Old and New California, &c.," a usage newly embraced.[22] To avoid delay, he enclosed a form of capitulation.[23] Addressed to the governor and military commandant, and demanding compliance by 9 a.m. the following day, the documents were delivered to Juan B. Alvarado, who excitedly disclaimed holding the positions named. (His successor, General Manuel Micheltorena, had arrived in Los Angeles in August, but Alvarado would continue as civil governor until the end of the year.)[24]

Replying to a pro-forma inquiry, the local captain of artillery, Mariano Silva, said his defenses consisted of twenty-nine soldiers and twenty-five others without military instruction, eleven pieces of cannon which were nearly useless, and the fortification, which was "of no consequence, as everyone knows."[25] A consultation of officials and citizens recognized that resistance against 800 men and eighty pieces of cannon was impossible. So, not waiting until the next day, a commission came on board before midnight of the 19th to arrange terms of surrender (getting the commodore out of bed), with Thomas O. Larkin co-opted as interpreter.[26] Some changes were made in the articles: civil and military officers were to be transported to Mexico; the area surrendered was the district of Monterey, from San Juan Bautista to San Luis Obispo (hardly all of the Californias); and a final clause, for official Mexican perusal, set down that Alvarado had been induced to capitulate from motives of humanity, his small force being no match for the power brought against him.

Perhaps being early risers, the Mexican commissioners, José Abrego and Pedro Narváez, came on board at 7:30 instead of 9 a.m. on the 20th to sign the document,[27] "as if impatient to surrender the country." Then, in mid-morning, three divisions of Jones' "Stormers" and all the marines, 150 men, went ashore and marched six abreast up the hill to the fort. In keeping with the terms of surrender, the Californians marched out with colors flying and the Americans moved in, while the naval bands briskly played "Yankee Doodle" and "The Star-Spangled Banner" and a thirty-six-gun salute was fired from the frigate and answered on shore. Some of the fort's long brass and iron guns were re-positioned to oppose Gov-

ernor Micheltorena's reported approach by land, and—naming their stronghold Fort Catesby—the captors began to settle in.[28]

A proclamation (in English and Spanish) was indispensable.[29] "Although I come in arms, as a representative of a powerful nation," said the commodore, who had given it some attention, "I come not to spread desolation." The inhabitants had only to remain peaceably in their homes to secure their lives and property against the rigors of an unjust war into which Mexico had suddenly plunged them. He proclaimed civil liberty and promised that private property would not be taken without compensation and that those who wished to leave the country might do so without hindrance. "The stars and stripes . . . now float triumphantly before you, and, henceforth and forever, will give protection and security."

"Forever" is a presumptuous term, and Larkin, during his midnight visit to the fleet, had some questions about the reputed hostilities. He asked which side had declared war and said that late papers on shore did not mention difficulties between the two countries. But the commodore did not trust this American who had not earlier come aboard and did not the next morning bring the Mexican papers as requested—particularly with the new Mexican *comandante* on the march with 600 troops and a vessel with military stores and cannon hourly expected.[30] When Jones went ashore for an inspection on the 21st, he was again informed that the news from Mexico was late and pacific. Unopened Mexican papers as late as August 4 and private commercial letters of August 22 (his own intelligence was dated June 4)[31] were turned up in a local office by the commodore's secretary and chaplain which not only reflected friendly relations but contradicted the rumored transfer of the province to England. The Monroe Doctrine was even cited as an obstacle to the transaction should Mexico have thought it desirable, which was denied.[32]

Jones was never irresolute. The same day he wrote to Alvarado and Silva that he would restore everything as it was on the 19th, which was promptly done.[33] And he dispatched explanatory notes to Micheltorena, inquiring when they could meet "to cultivate the relations which ought to subsist between military chiefs of neighboring nations" when far from their respective capitals.[34] Alvarado and Silva likewise transmitted the joyful news.[35]

←――――――

On the morning of October 20, 1842, three divisions of Commodore Jones' "Stormers" and all the marines went ashore at Monterey and marched six abreast up the hill to the fort.

California's new Mexican governor, Manuel Micheltorena, wished himself a thunderbolt to fly and annihilate the invaders.

Micheltorena did not hear of the retrocession until October 26, and he had meanwhile sent orders to Alvarado and the military commanders at Sonoma, Santa Barbara, and Los Angeles.[36] They were to foment public opposition to the invader, drive all cattle from the coast, and prepare the people to take up arms, "for we are attacked in the most tender points of man—his religion, his independence, and his property." He did not fear the enemy (a hundred leagues away), but all should partake of the pleasures of victory. Writing to the Secretary of War and Marine,[37] he wished himself "a thunderbolt, to fly and annihilate the invaders." He did indeed march two hours, when a courier brought news of the evacuation, which cut short his ecstatic prospect of triumph.

The American force was just beginning to feel comfortable and "quite at home" when orders came to decamp and go on board, as Midshipman Jackson lamented.[38] So, with all due ceremony, late in the afternoon of the 21st the Americans retired to their vessels, a salute was fired in honor of the Mexican flag, and visits of courtesy were exchanged. Although some of the tars tended to disparage all things Mexican, Jones could afterwards report that, with 150 seamen on shore for thirty hours, no private house was entered, nor was the slightest disrespect shown to any individual. No public property was destroyed, except the powder burned in the salutes, which Jones said was returned fourfold;[39] and a Monterey storekeeper was amazed when a marine made a purchase and paid for what he bought.[40] As the ships remained at anchor, the men continued to spend their leisure ashore, "hunting wild Deer or dancing with tame Dear," both being plentiful in and around Monterey. With the flagship's splendid band, there were as many balls as there were Sundays, with "Waltzes, Quadrilles, Hotas, Sons, Arabes, Bolero with the castaneta, Etc."—some who had never danced before "danced here."[41]

A long day of war was ended, and Jones had taken an unwarranted precaution. In the process the squadron had seen a bit of action, and the discipline of the men had proved to be superb. Except for the new governor's wordy reprisals, relations between conqueror and conquered remained singularly cordial. Although the commodore and some of the foreign residents were nervous about retaliation,[42] no incidents occurred (cynic John Coffin Jones fearing the worst, and trader Spear at San Francisco fretting that the people seemed to think hoisting the flag had canceled all debts). An aura of unreality hung over the whole action, both the seizure and restoration, but the exercise had clearly confirmed what the United States or any other similarly qualified power might do and that the U.S. did not mean to be outmaneuvered. Some supposed the Americans thought that having flown their flag for twenty-four hours might "avail them something hereafter."[43]

Jones reported faithfully to the Secretary of the Navy, and two days after the restitution penned a long rationalization, which he forwarded to Washington with the supporting poll of his officers.[44] A shorter explanation went off to Waddy Thompson, U.S. minister in Mexico, hoping to "quiet" that government until amends could be made.[45]

Micheltorena responded to the commodore's overtures that the law forbade relationships with his country's enemies; but since the Mexican flag had been restored, his hostile march upon the capital would be suspended.[46] Because Jones' violation of the national honor had been public, however, his reparation must be publicly made, and he was invited to Los Angeles under guarantees of security. Jones quickly accepted but delayed departing until news of peaceful if continuing gloomy relations between the two countries was brought by the *Dale* on December 15. While in Mexico the affair understandably rankled and was denounced as an act "peculiar to the sixteenth century,"[47] in California the commodore and some of his officers dined with the new governor in Los Angeles and attended a ball in their honor.

It was a resplendent affair of archaic proportions.[48] Arriving in the *Cyane* at San Pedro on January 17, the commodore was met by a six-seated carriage, a new "oak-ark-barouche," drawn by three horses and accompanied by "five and twenty lancers." There were cooks in the retinue, and before the cavalcade returned to the pueblo, a sumptuous repast, with champagne, was served on shore. Then Jones and his staff, surrounded by outriders and a military escort, flew to town at the lively rate of ten or twelve miles an hour, the horses being changed regularly without slowing,* and were received at Abel Stearns' mansion, the finest in town. Dinner was announced at 10 p.m., when the governor and his officers appeared in rich embroidery on dark blue cloth, and Micheltorena himself wore an elegant laced cocked hat with splendid white feathers.

At noon the next day all met at the governor's quarters, where "short speeches or long toasts" were delivered, after which the governor read the articles of a convention for which he wished Jones' approval.[49] These demanded indemnity for outrages upon the Mexican flag: 1,500 complete infantry uniforms ruined in an imagined march upon Monterey, a full set of musical instruments likewise damaged, and $15,000 in general compensation. The commodore, astounded, asked for a written translation. There was a ball at 9 p.m. (in spite of a drenching rain), then supper and dancing until the rising sun. Governor Micheltorena "is a Mexican," Jones concluded after reading his proposition, "a descendant of the once proud and haughty Castillians, so celebrated for bombast in diplomacy, demanding everything and *insisting* on nothing but the privilege of using high toned and unmeaning words"; and his articles were "preposterous." The document was returned on the 20th, with a note saying it had been read with the most respectful consideration. The commodore was constrained, he said, not to sign the paper, first because he had no power from his government, and second, "the articles themselves are *objectionable*." And there the matter ended.

---

*Three horses running abreast, not harnessed together but attached by ropes from their saddles to the tongue and fore axletree, could be readily relieved by riders of fresh mounts taking over the tug ropes; downhill, the outside riders fell to the rear to restrain the vehicle's forward push.

Jones remained in Los Angeles until the following day to receive the governor's dispatches, which he had offered to carry to Mazatlán. At 1 p.m. the cavalcade was again under way, its departure heralded by the beat of drums, firing of cannon, and ringing of bells. By 5 o'clock they were at San Pedro, whence the *Cyane* sailed south to join the vessels which had preceded it.

The commodore would be recalled by an embarrassed but not too reproving government, which would acknowledge his ardent zeal and devotion to what he deemed to be his duty regardless of personal consequences.[50] He would be seen in California again.

"I felt at home when I went on board," Larkin recollected in mid-February, and after the proud ship and companions had departed, he was conscious of the void they had left behind. The Yankee merchant was also left, he complained, with $800 to $1,000 worth of potatoes and other perishable produce for which he had received orders from the navy.[51] More momentous for himself and his adopted country, he would soon be appointed U.S. consul at Monterey.[52]

~2~

Alta California

HE AMERICAN Thomas O. Larkin had arrived at Monterey aboard
the *Newcastle* in April 1832, by way of Cape Horn and the Sandwich Islands, the usual route of approach. This Mexican town, the capital of Alta California, had been founded by Spain over sixty years before
and by the 1830s was a settlement of nearly six hundred souls: two hundred men, fewer women, more children, two dozen Indians, and twenty-
five to thirty *extranjeros*.[1] Richard Henry Dana said in the spring of 1835
that it was "decidedly the pleasantest and most civilized-looking place in
California."[2] At the center was an open space, surrounded by one-story
buildings, harboring a half-dozen cannon (some mounted, some not)—
the presidio. As everywhere in California, the houses were of adobe,
often whitewashed, the better ones with red tiled roofs. Perhaps a hundred of them were dotted about at random, there being no streets and
few fences, their tones of red and white contrasting with the greenness of
the spring lawn and echoing the colors of the Mexican flag flying at
its core. Except for the scattering of adobes, the aspect of the place,
set against the wooded backdrop of the Santa Lucía Mountains, had
changed but little since the beginning.

Larkin, a New Englander, had come to this "jumping off place of the
world" to seek his fortune, after having failed in a similar venture in
North Carolina.[3] Though hesitant to quit the United States and settle
among a people for whom he had expressed an aversion, he had been
drawn to California by reports from a half-brother, Juan B. R. Cooper, a
prominent resident of Monterey and naturalized Mexican citizen who
had come out from Boston in 1823 and prospered. Cooper had not been
the earliest American settler in the country, another Bostonian, Thomas

Doak, having deserted the *Albatross* in 1816 and made a permanent home. Ebenezer Dorr, master of the Boston ship *Otter*, had brought the first American vessel to the coast in 1796; and the first American to set foot on California soil was probably John Kendrick, commander of the Spanish frigate *Aranzazu* from Nootka, who anchored in Monterey Bay in 1794.⁴ The number of foreign residents in California had risen from none in 1810 to 13 in a decade, 146 by 1830 (mostly Americans, Scots, and Englishmen), and 300 by 1835.⁵ Larkin was a latecomer even among foreigners.

California had been ceremoniously received into the Mexican empire (later republic) in 1822 and was no longer subject to the viceroy of New Spain and a succession of Spanish kings. Occupied by Spain in 1769, the country had been miraculously preserved from earlier seizure through Spanish neglect and its own elusiveness since it had last been visited by Europeans in 1602. Before that, only scattered landings had been made along its wild coast. California itself came late to world attention.

DISCOVERY

For eons California's existence had been more obscure, because unexpected, than the far side of the moon. The exploration of the New World, of which California proved to be one of the most remote and inaccessible parts, was waged by Europeans bent upon reaping the wealth of the Indies by sailing west. The push began in 1492, and only gradually was it realized that a great land mass intervened, not anticipated by the ancients. Balboa saw the Pacific from Panamá in 1513; Magellan determined the southern extent of the continent in 1520; and in that year some of Cortés' men, having conquered the Aztec capital, reached the west coast of Mexico. Later, Cortés heard of an island off the coast, "inhabited by women," and an expedition of 1533 discovered the tip of Baja California and spread stories about its wealth in pearls.⁶ In 1539 the land was found to be a peninsula,⁷ and two years later a little harbor at its tip was christened California.⁸ This fanciful name—derived from a popular thriller relating that on the "right hand of the Indies there is an island called California," rich in gold, diamonds, and pearls, and peopled by black women living as Amazons⁹—spread irresistibly northward.

The first passage along the Upper California shore was made in 1542 by Juan Rodríguez Cabrillo, who may have sighted Point Reyes and took refuge in the Bahía de Pinos (Monterey).¹⁰ In 1579 Francis Drake, preying

Burt sc

*Yankee Thomas O. Larkin arrived at Monterey
aboard the* Newcastle *in April 1832, coming to this
jumping–off place of the world to seek his fortune.*

upon Spain's lucrative Philippine trade in forbidden waters, found a
"conuenient and fit harborough" on the remote north coast in which to
repair his ship and took possession, calling the place New Albion.[11] Ma-
nila galleons examined the coast for a suitable haven, Pedro de Unamuno
in 1587 halting at Morro Bay and making a brief *jornada* inland,[12] and
Sebastian Rodríguez Cermeño capsizing in a little harbor under Point
Reyes in 1595 and naming it San Francisco.[13] Not to hazard more trea-
sure ships, Sebastian Vizcaíno was sent in 1602 on the same business, and
his excessive praise of the port of Monterey, "sheltered from all winds,"
"all that can be desired," made a lasting impression upon viceroy and
king.[14] A failure to occupy that place in 1606 as ordered delayed California's settlement a hundred and sixty years.

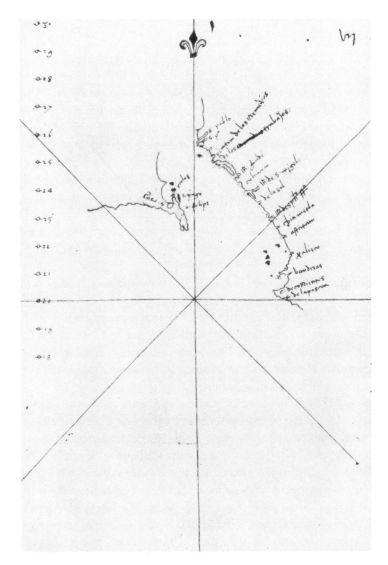

Cortés heard of an island off the coast, inhabited by women, and an expedition of 1533 discovered the tip of Baja California.

OCCUPATION

By the mid-eighteenth century, Russian explorers were making their way down the Alaskan coast, and long-nurtured fears of British entry into the Pacific by a "not universally denied" waterway across North America seemed to threaten the territories of Spain. Another Russian expedition was reported in 1764, and in 1768 Charles III and his representatives in New Spain took protective action.[15] Between January and May 1769 the domineering visitor-general, José de Gálvez, dispatched both land and sea expeditions from the peninsula to Upper California. Much reduced by disease and exhaustion, they reached San Diego by the end of June, and the first Franciscan mission was established in mid-July. But Monterey had been the prized objective, and it was occupied the following May. Meantime, the great inland Bay of San Francisco had been discovered.[16]

Because the voyage from San Blas was slow and treacherous, a desert route from Sonora in northern Mexico was opened by 1774. The following year soldiers, settlers, and friars came that way, and a fort and mission were founded at San Francisco in 1776.[17]

Spain's conquest had spread from Mexico to Alta California, and the Spanish political, military, and religious establishment set about exploiting the land and its indigenous people.

The year 1769 is significant in California history if of no great moment elsewhere. Spain had planted a slight and uncertain colony on the northwest coast, a token of her property rights in that direction. It caused no great commotion—in Mexico the solemn ringing of church bells and publication the following year of an *Estracto de noticias del puerto de Monterey* extolling the achievement.[18] It was a lightly manned and slenderly sustained enterprise, in no way self-supporting, but dependent upon government in every detail: manpower, food, equipment, finance, transportation, organization, protection. Given that, the durability of the distant colony would depend upon how well the trinity of Spanish colonial management—state, army, and church—carried out their interdependent functions and upon the disposition of the inhabitants to participate. The Californias as a symbol of Spanish sovereignty cost some 90,000 pesos a year,[19] which was not unfalteringly forthcoming. And after the closure of the Sonora road by the Yuma Indians in 1781,[20] the country remained remote in space and marginal in respect to profit, hardly ever useful in promoting national aspirations, and increasingly disaffected (though not disloyal) by reason of neglect and local ambition.

Upper California was not extensively occupied under Spanish and Mexican rule.[21] Although expeditions penetrated its great interior (perhaps as far north as Red Bluff), disciplining Indians, recovering stolen animals, seeking mission sites, and checking rumors of foreign intrusion, the Californians stayed rooted in their coastal presidios, pueblos, and ranchos. Hedged in by the Sonora crossing at one end and Sonoma at the other, the spacious inland valleys and far-off Sierra were left to American and English trappers and the likes of John A. Sutter. Of the trappers, Jedediah Smith came first in 1826 and men of the Hudson's Bay Company shortly after, followed by many another.[22] And the Swiss adventurer erected his fort at New Helvetia on the Sacramento River in 1839, creating at that far outpost a rallying point for transient foreigners and the end of the trail for an oncoming American immigration.[23]

UNDER SPAIN

As an emanation of Spain's monarchical system, Spanish California society was necessarily hierarchical and authoritarian. The governor, appointed in Mexico, was both military and political head, uniting in himself executive, legislative, and judicial powers. Though theoretically subservient to Spanish superiors, time, distance, and the attention span of viceroy, *comandante-general*, and *audiencia* rendered his authority essentially absolute. Under him, captains of presidios and civil *comisionados* exercised local jurisdiction. Only in the missions was his power curtailed, and there (except for a corporal's guard) the father-president was sovereign. Nominally responsible to authorities in Mexico, the religious often utilized their Mexican connections to resist military and civil encroachments, and relationships between secular and ecclesiastical interests were commonly awkward. The family, too, was characteristically patriarchal, sons of whatever age deferring to the father's station and will, and the stratification of society was aristocratic. The law, for the guidance of rulers, derived from a *reglamento provisional* of 1773, instructions to governors, and Felipe de Neve's detailed *reglamento* of 1781.[24]

The military, religious, and civil components of California society were embodied in the presidio, mission, pueblo, and rancho. Presidios were indispensable to the Spanish conquest. Though only four in number and poorly provisioned, they held thousands of Indians in check and were the symbol of Spanish power, deterring foreign incursions.[25] Monterey, the residence of the governor, was preeminent, but the establishments at San Francisco, Santa Barbara, and San Diego likewise served as centers of Spanish California life, being the only settlements at the beginning to accommodate families. Initially dependent upon the San Blas ships for their existence, they were supplied during the wars of independence against Spain (1810–1821) through patently illicit trade with foreign vessels, paid for with mission produce for which the padres received unredeemable drafts upon the Spanish treasury.

The missions were to turn native peoples into citizens and Christians and keep them in their place.[26] Admittance was nominally voluntary, that is, by persuasion, but once in, discipline was strict, penalties severe, and there was no legal escape. Although, in theory, the missions belonged to the Indians, the indigenes' role was to attend Christian services and engage in whatever employment was allotted—agriculture, tending flocks, carpentry, masonry, cooperage, saddlery, making leather, shoes, soap, and pottery; and, for women, spinning and weaving, cooking, washing, knitting, and embroidery. Contemporaries charged the system with enslaving Indians in this life to save them in the next.[27] Often diligent preachers, teachers, traders, and managers, the missionaries controlled the best land, raised the most crops, had the largest herds, acquired the greatest wealth, and provided the economic base of the province. Intended to last no longer than ten years, the missions would endure until the country could do without them.

Missions and presidios were insufficient instruments of permanent settlement. A population of "Spaniards" who could become self-supporting and create a civilian economy was essential. Neve's *reglamento* provided for civil towns, or *pueblos*, the recruitment and support of settlers, and granting land for residence and cultivation. In exchange, colonists were expected to raise crops, maintain livestock, sell surplus produce to the presidios, build houses, dig irrigation ditches, till the public lands, and stand ready for military service. Two such communities, San José and Los Angeles, proved to be durable, but were not soon successful, perhaps because of ineffective colonists, the climate of restraint, and the missionaries' opposition to troublesome and competing settlers adjacent to Indian communities.[28] Towns would also develop at presidios and missions, and other communities would ultimately achieve the status of pueblos. Some would be entitled to elect *ayuntamientos*, or town councils. Municipal officers, initially appointed by the governor, were elective, but resi-

John A. Sutter, the Swiss adventurer, erected a fort at New Helvetia on the Sacramento River in 1839 which would become an outpost for foreigners and the end of the trail for an oncoming American immigration.

dent *comisionados* or prefects extended the provincial hierarchy to the local level.

Title to land was vested in the king, though he actually held only presidial grounds and such areas as were required for the royal service. Theoretically, the Indians owned whatever was necessary for their sustenance, the missions administering it while readying them to take possession, and the residue could be used for Spanish settlement. Instructions of 1773 permitted the distribution of land both to Indians and to *pobladores* who would devote themselves to agriculture or stock-raising. Formal allotments were made to the pueblos of San José and Los Angeles in 1782 and 1786 and to individual applicants beginning in 1784. By 1795 some sixteen private ranchos had been (provisionally) granted. Increasing to six hundred by 1840, they became the most prominent feature of California society.[29]

Upper California's period of establishment may be said to have ended with Governor Neve's term in 1782, and the era which followed has been called, with some extravagance, the "romantic" period of its history. It was a "great country," the able and genial Governor Borica (1794–1800) wrote, "climate healthful . . . good bread, excellent meat, tolerable fish. . . . Plenty to eat . . . the most peaceful and quiet country in the world." So good was the climate, he said, they were all getting to look like Englishmen! Soon foreign ships began to appear, adding to the excitement, and after the turn of the century most of them were American, some engaging in contraband trade. Russians burst into San Francisco Bay in 1806, seeking food for a desperate Sitka colony, and six years later erected a base at Fort Ross, just north of the Spanish harbor.[30]

The wars of independence in Spanish America began in 1810, interrupting communication with the mother country. Remote and unenlightened, the Californians remained loyal to the king, even when insurgents from Buenos Aires raided the coast in 1818, seeking recruits and striking a blow for liberty. But when news of independence reached Monterey in January 1822, a half-century of Spanish rule came impassively to an end.[31]

MEXICAN RULE

Upper California declared its allegiance to Mexico with few reservations, except among the clergy. But while it accepted Mexican forms, received appointed governors, and maintained an implicit loyalty, its own sense of independence and identity grew.[32] The territory had always been remote from the home government and became more isolated and neglected during the Mexican regime. A succession of contending officials in Mexico found little time and fewer resources to devote to an unprofitable border province, and it was not easy to recruit settlers for that far-off place. For a time California was utilized as a penal colony, a hundred and fifty convicts being transported there between 1825 and 1830,[33] followed by a still larger number of artisans, professionals, and farmers in 1834.[34] Even the soldiery was often picked up in Mexican jails and, being usually unpaid and larcenous, was feared and despised by class-conscious and affronted citizens. As time passed, imported ideas and personal ambitions bred unrest, expressed in rivalries between the military and civil authorities, north and south, and increased antipathy to outside rule. Mexico sent a series of governors, four of whom were shortly expelled, and dispensed laws, many of which proved to be irrelevant, inappropriate, or simply inconvenient and were consequently ignored, tempered, or supplanted by local initiative.

Under the Mexican constitution of 1824 (patterned upon that of the United States), authority was more dispersed, or at least such was the presumption. But there were both liberals and conservatives in Mexico (Federalists representing the revolution, and Centralists the army and church), and these had adherents in far-off California, though they might

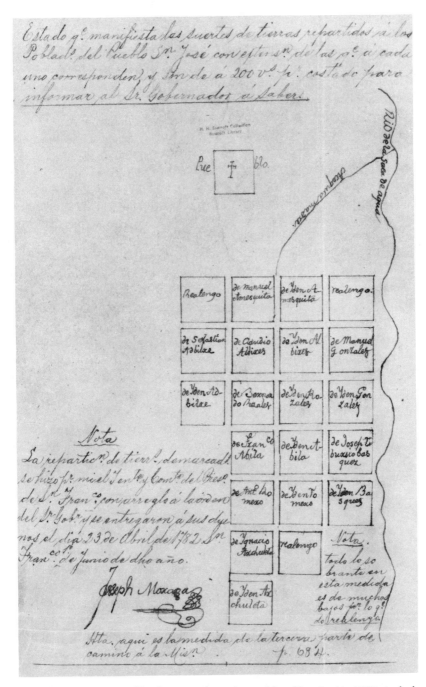

A formal allotment of land was made to the pueblo of San José in 1782, including building lots around the plaza and garden plots.

be fickle. Government under Spain had been military, and this combination of political and military power endured. Initially suspected of being a hotbed of Spanish reaction, California in 1822 received a Mexican commissioner who maneuvered a native, Luis Argüello, into the interim office of civil and military chief in lieu of the ranking Spaniard.[35] Through two layers of electors, a legislature, or *diputación*, was for the first time chosen. Always the traditional *junta* (normally composed of the governor, captains of military companies, and representatives of the missions and of the district of Los Angeles) could be summoned to meditate upon "grave matters." *Ayuntamientos* persisted at the pueblos, and the office of *comisionado* was suppressed, then replaced in 1836 by resident prefects. As before, civil judgments could be appealed from alcalde to *comandante*, then to the governor, while criminal cases were tried by court-martial without further recourse.[36] Trade was open to all comers who would pay the stiff government impost (25 to 42.5 percent); and until secularization, the missions would not only support the presidios but pay a substantial tax as well.[37]

Mexican California was, then, tentatively republican in form, tempered by deep-seated hierarchical and military traditions. Law and justice were elementary, one depending upon the caprice of the governor and legislature (there being no common law or lawyers), the other upon the whim and vitality of local officials. While ties with the mother country were traditional and reassuring, the Californians shied away from Mexican tutelage and authority, even from a Mexican *presence*, preferring their own schemes and devices. They were well enough content with their slow-paced and pleasantly backward condition, though aware that conflict between their ways and those of the intruder must one day be joined. Generosity (they did not love money), complaisance, and ambivalence toward restraint made them susceptible to foreign encroachment.

The Californians, not an industrial or hardly an agricultural people, comprised a classed but fairly cohesive society. The system was late medieval (it has been styled ante-bellum Southern), based upon blood (Spanish), property, and position, and the labor of subservients. The gentry, vaunting some trace of Spanish inheritance and usually intermarrying, held the chief military and civil offices, much of the land and property, and a prejudice against things Mexican. Beneath them in rank, and much greater in number, were the troops, artisans, and retainers, and the *pobladores* of the pueblos, often from Sinaloa and Sonora, many of them illiterate, darker in visage, speaking a different dialect, and married to

Indian women. At the bottom were the Indians, peons if not slaves, laborers, domestics, and menials, cut off from their ancient culture, herded into the missions, farmed out to presidial companies, impressed to toil on the ranchos—the cheap labor of the country.[38]

Among the *gente de razón*,* position was more to be desired than riches, leisure than labor, and individual freedom, even laxity and license, than discipline. Wealth meant lands and cattle, the first initially of small value and virtually free for the asking, the latter, as hides and tallow, providing almost the only free capital and medium of exchange. Juan Bandini, one of the gentry, said in 1828 that most of them did nothing.[39] Richard Henry Dana, a Brahmin Yankee, noted in the 1830s that the men of the country were thriftless, proud, extravagant, and very much given to gaming.[40] In 1842, settler John Bidwell wrote, "It is a proverb here . . . that a Spaniard will not do any thing which he cannot do on horseback"—"perfect centaurs" a later visitor called them—and they did not work perhaps a month a year.[41] Dashing and demonstrative, they were also dilatory and idle, all labor except military service (which was hardly demanding) and herding cattle (not seen as ignoble) being regarded as essentially menial.

As for the California women, they were universally declared by admiring foreigners to be far more industrious than the men.[42] Their humanity and charity were beyond praise, and indeed they were a much more estimable race of beings than their lords and masters, by whom they were held in close subjection. Almost every visitor noted the great number of very handsome ladies in the country. Men and women, a consummate hospitality characterized the people.

As a "race," Bayard Taylor would say in 1849, the native Californians were vastly superior to the Mexicans, with larger frames, stronger muscle, and fresh, ruddy complexions unlike the sallow skins of the warmer states or the swarthy features of the Sonorans.[43] Even the California soldiers, he was informed, because of their physical distinction, were called by the Mexicans "Americans." Although formal schooling was uncommon, a few of the natives were educated, even cultured, being taught individually by the padres (who did not favor public education) or in occasional schools,[44] while some were sent to the Hawaiian Islands or the United States for instruction. Certain families, Taylor noted, possessed a

*European Spaniards, Creoles, and people of mixed blood, to differentiate them from the native Indians, as defined by Miguel Costansó in 1794 (SERVIN 226).

natural refinement of manner which would grace the most polished society; though they claimed to "grow as the trees, with the form and character that Nature gives them," uncultured nature in California wore all the ripeness of maturity of older lands. And he cited Doña Angustias Jimeno of Monterey, sister of Pablo de la Guerra, whose character, intellect, and instincts and her acquaintance with Spanish literature, as well as with Scott and Cooper (in translation), would have given her a position of supremacy in society even in Europe and the United States. Such views were echoed by other observers. Though Californians were often criticized by outsiders for not improving their opportunities, a percipient editor would assert that no one had a right to complain when they "dwelt upon the soil after their own fashion; for it was their own land."[45]

As word about California spread, the number and importance of foreigners grew. Traders, trappers, and ex-sailors multiplied. A number adapted gainfully to their new environment and earned the natives' good will—among them Larkin, J. J. Warner, Abel Stearns, and Jacob P. Leese—some becoming naturalized citizens and Catholics and marrying daughters of the country. Engaging in trade, acquiring land, and performing useful (or even questionable) functions, they became influential by reason of their energy and accomplishments. In time, many, by lending the support of their rifles to partisan causes, created obligations which could not easily be denied. When, in 1840, some of the more obstreperous (Isaac Graham being the most prominent) became arrogant and threatening, about fifty Americans and British were shipped to Mexico in irons.[46] Overland visitors from the United States were greeted with the greatest suspicion; and when, in 1841, the first of the wagon parties came over the Sierra and landed at John Marsh's rancho near Mt. Diablo, *Comandante* Mariano Vallejo, for one, was apprehensive of invasion.[47]

Mexican rule *was* more exciting than what went before. There were twelve governors and fifteen administrations between 1822 and 1846, matching the instability of budding Spanish American republics to the south.[48] Captain Luis Argüello's provisional government, in 1822–1825, recognized the new order and adopted a tentative *plan* for its organization (California's first "constitution"). The first Mexican governor, Lieutenant Colonel José María Echeandía, arrived in 1825, and by fixing his residence first at San Diego engendered lasting discord between north and south. He it was who affirmed the secularization of the missions and, unauthorized, appointed agents to manage the estates. He also experienced the first revolt against ordained authority, in the north, but weathered the gale.

A second governor appeared in 1831, Lieutenant Colonel Manuel Victoria. A soldier with little sympathy for political opponents or republican ways, he freely meted out the death sentence and suspended the *diputación*, greatly offending the Californians. This time southerners arose, Echeandía among them, and though the insurgents were routed, the wounded governor retired to Mexico. In his absence, Pío Pico, senior member of the *diputación*, became the legal *jefe* and was favored in the south. But Monterey backed Agustín V. Zamorano, the former governor's secretary, and since Echeandía would not accept Pico, Zamorano and Echeandía held office each in his own region until a successor came.

The next Mexican leader was Brevet Brigadier General José Figueroa, formerly governor of Sonora and Sinaloa, at the beginning of 1833. One of California's most qualified governors, he arrived during a period of general anarchy and confusion. In accordance with a decision in Mexico, it became his lot to begin breaking up the missions and to contend with the Híjar–Padres colonization scheme, which was related. Recognizing the radical effect of secularization upon society, particularly the Indians, he devised a gradual plan beginning with ten missions, but his death in 1835 left it in other hands.

Figueroa had named a Californian, José Castro, civil governor, but under Mexican pressure the civil and military offices were united under Lieutenant Colonel Nicolás Gutiérrez, a Spaniard who had come with Figueroa. Still another Mexican ruler arrived in May 1836, Colonel Mariano Chico, but intolerant, conceited, and tactless (and with a mistress passing as his niece), he retired after three months, surrendering the government to his predecessor.

The Californians had had enough. At the end of 1836 a liberal young *montereño*, Juan B. Alvarado, rose in revolt, allied with José Castro, some Indians, and a number of foreigners under Isaac Graham. By striking the governor's residence with their one cannon ball, it is said, they induced Gutiérrez to surrender and board ship for Mexico. Winning was easier than ruling; but with his influential uncle, Mariano Vallejo, now *comandante general*, Alvarado persuaded the *diputación* to proclaim California a free and sovereign state until centralism, recently triumphant in Mexico, was abjured.[49]

Again the south was annoyed. By a maneuver in 1835, Los Angeles

In 1836, a young montereño, *Juan B. Alvarado,*
supported by José Castro and a number of foreigners,
rose in revolt.

had been made the capital, which the north would not abide; and southern sentiment opposed independence and deplored the recurring interference of adventurous foreigners. A quick march south by Alvarado
tempered these views. But while Los Angeles vaguely accepted Alvarado
and federalism (they all favored home rule), it soon joined San Diego in
adopting the 1836 Mexican centralist constitution—when Alvarado
artfully switched to the same plan. So much confusion was not enough.
Veteran schemer José Antonio Carrillo (who had won Los Angeles the
capital) now obtained his brother's appointment as governor. In another
sectional confrontation the north prevailed, but not until Alvarado and
Vallejo were provisionally confirmed by Mexico in 1838 as governor and
comandante was the strife curtailed.

Under the new centralist constitution, Alta and Baja California were
reunited,[50] and, best of all, the governor was henceforth to be chosen

Disenchanted with the civil government, Mariano Guadalupe Vallejo, comandante general in 1841, feared for his country.

from a list of local names submitted to Mexico by the *diputación*. Alvarado, in an interval of peace, turned his attention to finance, the disintegrating missions, Indian depredations, and reorganization—though his interest in public affairs, like that of other officers, began to wane. It was he who rounded up a body of unsavory foreigners in 1840 and bundled them off to San Blas.

Disenchanted with the civil government, *Comandante* Vallejo feared for his country. Politicians were unreliable; families were arriving overland from the United States; an American squadron in 1841 surveyed the Sacramento and San Joaquin rivers (Wilkes); the Hudson's Bay Company had established a foothold at Yerba Buena; and Sutter, acquiring the Russian properties at Fort Ross, paraded in the north as the governor of New Helvetia. What was needed, Vallejo wrote to Mexico, were fewer civil officers, more Mexican colonists, two hundred soldiers assured of their pay, and a unified military and civil command free from local entangle-ments.[51] Even Alvarado was uneasy.

Mexico responded, and in August 1842 a new governor and *coman-dante*, Brigadier General Manuel Micheltorena, with three hundred men, reached Los Angeles. On the way to Monterey, he learned at San Fer-nando of Commodore Jones' seizure of the capital, a contretemps amica-bly adjusted. But Micheltorena's ill-chosen conscripts soon aroused the people by their unbridled thievery. Alvarado and Castro again raised the banner of revolt, and Micheltorena, capitulating near San José, agreed to send his *cholos* back to Mexico. Whereupon Sutter, hoping for more land, marched to his aid, and the accord was repudiated. When, at Ca-huenga, foreign contingents in both camps agreed among themselves not to fight, Micheltorena's cause collapsed. A new treaty named Pío Pico governor and José Castro *comandante*, and it was the fate of California's last imported governor, in March 1845, to be shipped ingloriously to San Blas.[52]

With two aspiring leaders, the governor and capital at Los Angeles and the *comandante* and customhouse at Monterey, California was un-equivocally divided. As the chiefs jockeyed for position, an American lieutenant came over the Sierra in December 1845 with a well-armed top-ographical corps. Warnings having been received from Mexico since July 1844 of the imminence of war with the United States over the expected annexation of Texas, Frémont's advent was ominous. Castro, ordering him away from the settled parts of the country, notified an unfriendly governor of the danger and invoked his aid. Only in retreat would the Californians unite uneasily against a common foe.

California by Sea—
Alien Advances

B Y 1786 California's brief season as an exclusive Spanish community was almost ended. With specific instructions to visit California, the Frenchman Jean François Galaup de la Pérouse came down the
foggy northwest coast to Monterey in September, bringing the first foreign vessels (since Drake) into a California port.[1] Sent out by his government to observe opportunities for French commerce and settlement and
to collect scientific data, he was carefully to note the strength of the Spanish establishments and the potential for French trade in furs. Since California's governor had been directed to treat the ships as if they were of
his own nation, they were hospitably received, and the Latin confrères
freely exchanged information. Although la Pérouse was enthusiastic about
California, its air, its fertile land, and the abundance of all kinds of peltries, he noticed the lack of settlers and thought "a certain portion of liberty and property," with free trade, would be more favorable to population. His untimely death in the New Hebrides, revolution in France, and
delay in publishing his findings brought little profit to the French nation
from his revelations.

The next visitor was an Englishman, George Vancouver, in 1792. Having sailed as midshipman with Captain James Cook on his third voyage
to the Pacific in 1776–1780 (which did not touch in California), he was
now charged with extending the earlier hydrographic surveys. On the
coast of what he was pleased to call New Albion, he was also commissioned to settle a boundary dispute involving British and Spanish interests at Nootka (on Vancouver Island) and in this capacity was warmly

received at San Francisco and Monterey on his first call. Before he returned in 1793 and 1794, however, the Californians were warned to guard against English vessels, particularly to prevent their discovering the weakness of Spanish defenses, and he thus met an unexpectedly cool reception. In his published *Voyage*, he nevertheless called attention to the inability of the Californians to resist invasion, "an event which is by no means improbable."[2] And he marveled that so much country should be subjugated, then turned to no account—a view amply sustained by the Spanish engineer Miguel Costansó, who reminded the viceroy in 1794 of the territory's continuing backwardness, want of laborers, shipping, and trade.[3]

The scramble for furs in the New World—which began on the St. Lawrence in the late sixteenth century[4] and advanced westward to Hudson Bay and across the continent—suddenly proved, by Cook's discovery of sea otter on the northwest coast, to be most lucrative in the north Pacific, with an open road to China. Cook's *Voyage*, published in 1784, widely advertised this find, and an English trader, James Hannah, was in 1785 the first to follow in his wake. The earliest of the "Boston" men were John Kendrick and Robert Gray in the *Columbia* and *Lady Washington* in 1788. Meanwhile, Russians had crossed to Alaska in 1741, hunting sable, and in 1783 set up a permanent station at Kodiak off the North American shore. Soon others, mostly Americans, but including English, Russian, French, Portuguese, and Spanish vessels, joined in this profitable if hazardous pursuit. By the 1790s it had spread to California waters.[5]

Fur traders made their first appearance in California in 1796 in the person of Ebenezer Dorr, an American, who put into Monterey in the *Otter* for supplies.[6] Foreign commerce was strictly forbidden, but he was hospitably received; and though he apparently did not engage in contraband trade, as would his many successors, he left ten crewmen on shore, much against the governor's orders. By the end of the century, the far north coast was fairly swarming with ships; and sharpened competition, together with the rising hostility of the Indians, made California a tempting resort for peltries and supplies before crossing to the Sandwich Islands and Asia and returning for another load. But so restrictive were Spanish regulations and so risky the trade that one of the Boston men thought to avoid the California authorities by teaming up with the Russians—they to provide Aleut hunters, he the transportation—with the profits divided between them. This contract system flourished from 1803 to 1812, while the Russians worked their own way down the coast as far as San Pedro and in the latter year opened a station at Fort Ross just north of San Francisco Bay.[7]

Although relations between the Russians and Californians proved to be mutually beneficial, all foreign operations close to California were regarded as intrusive; and the unwillingness of Spain and then Mexico to acquiesce spelled eventual failure for the Russian enterprise and the territorial aspirations which it envisioned. Nikolai Petrovich Rezánof, an imperial inspector in 1806, had hoped to advance gradually toward San Francisco, then use "any favorable turn in European politics" to add California to the Russian possessions.[8]

The revolution against Spain, which seethed in Spanish America for a decade up to 1821 and finally broke political ties with the mother country, brought only neglect to Mexico's northernmost province. The supply ships did not arrive every year, resulting in an acute scarcity of goods and funds and greater readiness to purchase from foreign vessels. With changing times, even the missionaries, who had a vested interest in Spanish royalty and the deterrence of foreign incursion, discreetly bartered with alien traders. Sometimes the laws against trade were strictly enforced, sometimes not, but "never had so many Yankees been locked in Spanish jails."[9]

The wars took an operatic turn in California. From Buenos Aires, a hot spot of the revolution, privateering craft were dispatched during the years 1816–1819 to seize loyalist ports, foment revolution, and prey upon Spanish commerce from Peru to New Spain. A warning reached California in 1816, but not until 1818 did the blow fall. Captain Hippolyte Bouchard in the *Argentina* and Peter Corney* in the *Santa Rosa*, bearing some sixty guns and three hundred men, arrived at Monterey on October 6 "to cruise against the Spaniards." Asking for supplies and being disposed toward plunder, the insurgents were met not by hospitality but by widespread alarm, a show of force, and blusters of defiance. With superior strength and Corney's acquaintance with the coast and ports (he had sailed earlier on the *Columbia*),[10] Bouchard's men leisurely sacked and burned Monterey, repeated the performance at the Ortega Refugio rancho (near Gaviota), exchanged prisoners at Santa Barbara, spilled the wine and spirits they could not drink at San Juan Capistrano, and departed without converts. These "heretics, schismatics, excom-

---

* Corney was also known as Pedro Conde or Covale.

municated persons, heathen, and a few Moors" left behind them an American (Joseph Chapman), a Scotsman, two blacks, a South American, and a barrage of charges and countercharges among the inhabitants impugning their conduct during the emergency.[11]

Seven years afterwards, a British scientific expedition continuing Vancouver's and Cook's investigations made several stops in California. Coming down from the Arctic, Frederick William Beechey anchored at San Francisco in November 1826 and at Monterey in December, returning in October 1827. Allowed to carry out a wholly new survey of San Francisco Bay, his resulting chart was made readily accessible by the British Hydrographic Office in 1833 (and would serve well into the American period). Beechey extolled California's resources but thought an industrious population was needed to end the obscurity in which the country had long slept. If the indifference continued, the province would fall into other hands, for California was too important to remain long in its neglected state.[12]

One of the most industrious California observers was the French trader, Auguste Duhaut-Cilly, who arrived at San Francisco in January 1827, two weeks after Beechey's first departure. With an assortment of goods for sale or barter, he negotiated for hides and tallow, visited ten of the missions from Sonoma to San Diego and all of the towns, being one of the few outsiders to reach Los Angeles. He wrote well and with an eye to the realities of California existence.[13] The "creoles" (as this civilized Latin called the Californians) were hospitable but vain and easily offended; and he rated their mixture of Spanish, English, Mexican, and Indian customs as "dull . . . without life and character." Although large, handsome, and well-formed, the men, he noticed, were awkward when not on horseback and were lazy, ruined by gambling, and degraded by drunkenness. The women too were large and strong and, though "ludicrously dressed," could "pass for beautiful" were they less careless about their complexions, feet, and hands. This enviable country, he intimated, was wasted on its inhabitants.

Another Englishman, Sir Edward Belcher, who had sailed with Beechey, returned to California in 1837 and 1839 to complete his predecessor's observations of the western coasts and islands. After exploring the Sacramento River some hundred and fifty miles to the head of navigation (no chart was issued), he stopped at several ports from Bodega to San Diego and concluded that "Another fate attends this country." The inhabitants were harassed by Indians, pestered by deserters from whalers and merchant ships, and, from want of spirit, unable to protect them-selves. "To Great Britain their hopes are directed," more from fear and want of energy than any friendly feeling.[14]

Two Frenchmen were also in California. Abel Dupetit-Thouars, in the *Vénus*, stopped at Monterey in 1837, examining the Pacific whale fish-eries and other commercial opportunities for France;[15] and Cyrille Pierre Théodore Laplace touched at San Francisco, Monterey, and other points in the *Artémise* on a similar mission two years later.[16] Dupetit-Thouars issued an informative account in 1840–1844, while the report by Laplace did not come out until after the Gold Rush.

Through his surgeon, Laplace apparently saved Governor Alvarado's life; and he warned him against the hostile intentions of the United States, and advocated a French protectorate.

An attaché of the French embassy in Mexico, Eugène Duflot de Mo-fras, was also sent to the northwest coast in 1840–1841 to learn—"inde-pendently of a political point of view"—what advantages might be of-fered to commerce in a region little known to France. Reaching Monterey on the *Ninfa* in May 1841, and carrying letters of introduction, he proba-bly visited every mission and settlement in the country. An intelligent and able if somewhat excitable and not overly diligent observer, he gave a de-scription of California, its history, and condition, based upon the writ-ings of others as well as his own researches. "England and the United States flatter themselves alike with the idea of taking California," he noted; and it was evident to him that the country would belong "to what-ever nation chooses to send there a man-of-war and 200 men." He doubted that England could outdistance its rival, and he preferred to see it belong to the United States if not to France. His book, published in Paris in 1844[17] and including several charts of the California coast, was more comprehensive than the only comparable volume, by an English-man, Alexander Forbes.[18] Forbes, who had never visited California, was through his work more responsible than any other for making it known to the English-speaking world. His final chapter dealt with "Upper Cal-ifornia as a field for foreign colonization."

Concurrently with Duflot de Mofras came the first scientific expedi-tion from the United States, under Charles Wilkes, and he too was in-structed to visit and chart San Francisco Bay. Although as far back as 1825 President John Quincy Adams had proposed to fit out a ship to explore "the whole northwest coast," a nation more concerned with trade than with knowledge did not get around to it until 1838. Thomas ap Catesby Jones had first been appointed commander but resigned after years of controversy and delay,[19] and Wilkes was in charge when the U.S. Exploring Expedition, with six vessels, sailed upon its circumnavigation. The *Vincennes* reached San Francisco from the Columbia on August 14, 1841, and explored the Bay and the Sacramento River beyond its junction with the Feather. A land party meanwhile descended the Sacramento Valley, arriving at San Francisco in October, where Wilkes had appeared a few days before. The five volumes of Wilkes' *Narrative* had little good to say about California, but he believed the country would separate from Mexico before many years, perhaps uniting with Oregon.[20] Possessed as it must be by the Anglo-Norman race, it was "destined to fill a large space in the world's future history." The visit is said to have made the Californians uneasy, temporarily reconciled some of their local differences, and convinced them that the United States was something more than a myth.

Independent Mexico had discarded Spain's mercantile system in 1822, and foreigners were permitted to trade openly in California, though stiff import duties and restrictions upon ports of entry did little to discourage smuggling.[21] At the same time the Russians began to exclude competitors from failing otter fields in the north, thus further spurring commerce with the Mexican province. In 1823, Luis Argüello, California's first provisional governor, regularized the surreptitious hunting of otter by the Russians, permitting them to take furs on shares; and limited licenses were granted by his successor. In the 1830s hunting was reserved by law to Mexican citizens, but American trappers from the interior used their deadly rifles either as employees under Mexican licenses or as naturalized citizens.[22] Their chief rivals were also Americans, *contrabandistas* who outfitted warlike vessels and prodigally slaughtered otters on the offshore islands.[23] By the 1840s, when hides and tallow ("the money of the country") and whaling exceeded the dwindling commerce in furs,[24] most of the import-export business had fallen to Americans, who outfitted hunters, collected produce, and carried on a wholesale and retail trade as true merchant-adventurers. California came to depend upon the Boston ships for both supplies and revenue, and Governor Micheltorena took steps to encourage them, including an 1844 decree (disregarding Mexican law) forbidding the import of foreign goods from Mexico without payment of duty.[25]

Few foreign men-of-war appeared on the California coast before 1840. The first may have been the U.S. sloop-of-war *Peacock*, which called at Monterey in October 1836, checking on reports in the Hawaiian Islands

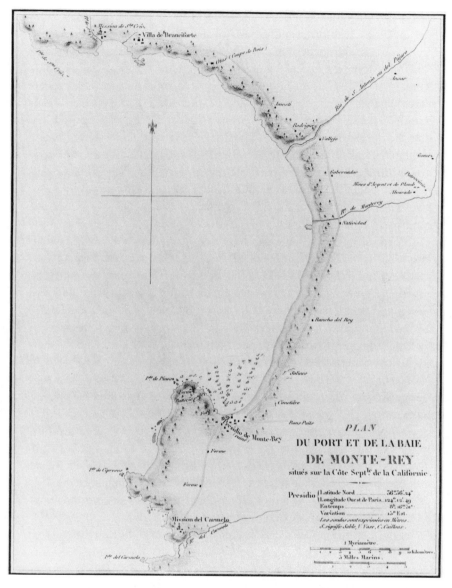

An attaché of the French embassy in Mexico, Eugène Duflot de Mofras, arrived at Monterey on the Ninfa in May 1841 and probably visited every mission and settlement in California; a chart of the port of Monterey appeared in his published atlas.

of outrages against American seamen and commerce.[26] However, with the arrest by California authorities of a large number of foreigners in 1840, and the shipment of many of them to Mexico, a stream of warships sailed to Monterey to make inquiry.[27] The French sloop-of-war *Danaïde* came in June 1840; but, finding no countrymen implicated, the officers and men spent twenty agreeable days on the town. Two days later Commander French Forrest in the U.S. man-of-war *St. Louis* appeared, demanded an explanation (from an absent governor), interviewed a few claimants, and departed. In November 1841 the British warship *Curaçao* arrived in the bay, and a settlement affecting the English exiles was apparently made. A second U.S. man-of-war, the *Yorktown*, paid a hasty call two weeks later, but the impatient captain left with his compatriots' claims still outstanding.

In order to protect American interests on the western coast, particularly the "considerable settlements" in California, the U.S. Secretary of the Navy in December 1841 recommended a large increase in the Pacific squadron, up to twice its current complement.[28] In midyear he had sent Commander Forrest to cruise the California coast and on December 10 gave Commodore Jones his sailing directions. By May, Jones was at Callao, Peru, eyeing the British and French fleets and fretting about their undisclosed intentions.[29] Battleships were still something of a novelty at Monterey in October 1842 when he brought the *United States* and *Cyane* around Point Pinos and anchored below the fort. After his precipitate landing and withdrawal,[30] several U.S. war vessels remained on the coast until January, and no fewer than five were in California waters during 1844 and 1845. An English man-of-war came in 1843, and both English and French ships two years later. When in November 1845, Commodore John Drake Sloat arrived at Mazatlán to command the U.S. squadron, he brought with him explicit instructions to take possession of San Francisco should Mexico declare war.[31]

Of the California watchers, the Americans seemed the most attentive.[32]

~4~

California by Land— Americans West

FROM INITIAL LANDFALLS, tentative beachheads, and dogged fc holds on the eastern shore of North America, emissaries of m nations—explorers, adventurers, developers, and settlers—fashioned tle empires which in time became English colonies and eventually, sc from New England, an independent United States. From there, mo westward, more than a hundred thousand people poured over the ge passes of the Appalachians into the fertile valleys of the Mississippi fore 1800. Beyond, along, and at the end of the great river stretched Sp ish Louisiana.

"Louisiana," first claimed for France in 1682, had been ceded we the Mississippi to Spain in 1762 and east of the river to England in 1 The early American settlers had thus inherited the east bank and con regard the neighboring Spaniards as their natural enemy. Then la 1800 Napoleon, aspiring to raise up a New France in the western of North America, induced the Spanish government to re-cede U and Lower Louisiana (west of the river) to him. Whereupon Pres Thomas Jefferson, fearing the Mississippi might be closed to Ame traffic, sought to gain control by buying New Orleans. To everyone tonishment, Napoleon was ready to part with all of Louisiana in orc finance a war with England in which he might in any event lose his A ican holdings. The deal was soon consummated.¹ This Louisiana Purchase of 1803 had no specified boundary, being described only as having the "same extent" as when bartered back and forth between its former owners (and Napoleon believed that if it "was not somewhat vague already, it would perhaps be politic to make it so").² The acquisition doubled the existing area of the United States and would provide a handy stratagem in bargaining with England over the Oregon country and with Mexico over Texas and California.

As soon as the treaty was signed, President Jefferson did not hesitate in sending Meriwether Lewis (his secretary) and William Clark up the wide and navigable Missouri to explore it to its source, "even to the western ocean." By discovering passes over the Rocky Mountains to the Columbia River, the expedition opened a route with the longest approach on a navigable stream, the narrowest stretch of desert, and the shortest distance to the great bend of the Columbia where canoe transportation began.³ Unfortunately, the portages were long and difficult, the Indians hostile, and the continent much broader than had been imagined. But the venture had established the "image of a highway across the continent" in the minds of the American people.⁴

Many geographical details were filled in by traders who followed in Lewis and Clark's tracks, notably trappers of Astor's American and Pacific Fur Company and the British Northwest Company. Not until 1823 or 1824 did members of the Rocky Mountain Fur Company utilize the great opening in the range called South Pass. When it was demonstrated that wagons could be driven through this broad, gently sloping, and treeless gap, it became the practical road over which most of the emigrant trains later streamed to Oregon and California. By comparison, the northern passes were "scarcely ways, they were rather obstacles."⁵

Among the other explorers sent out by the United States was Zebulon Montgomery Pike. Working his way southwestward of St. Louis in 1806, he ascended the Arkansas River to the site of modern Pueblo, Colorado, discovered Pike's Peak, and headed south to the Rio Grande. Here, captured on Spanish territory (by accident or design), he was conducted to Santa Fé, El Paso, and Chihuahua, then returned by way of Texas to the Mississippi.⁶ Pike's account of New Mexico revealed much that had been carefully concealed and was of the utmost importance in fostering the Santa Fé trade and American penetration of the Southwest. He precipitated the establishment of the trail from St. Louis to Santa Fé; and this

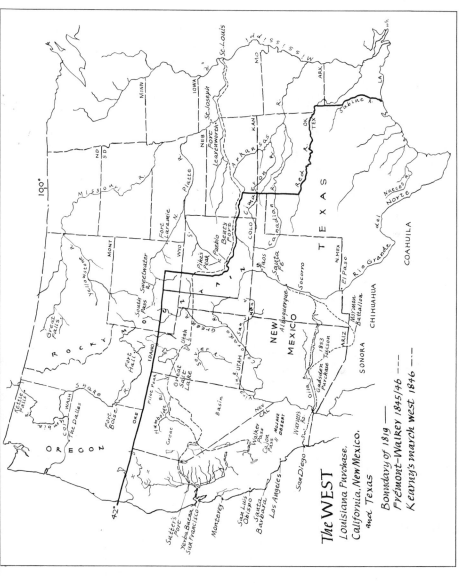

Map of the Louisiana Purchase, California, New Mexico, and Texas, showing the U.S.–Mexican boundary of 1819, Frémont's route from St. Louis to California in 1845, and Kearny's march from Santa Fé to San Diego.

terminus proved to be the beginning of the southwestern routes to the Pacific. From that ancient New Mexican town, the Gila trail followed down the Río Grande to the Gila River, along that stream to the Colorado, and across southern California and Warner's Pass to San Diego. The Spanish trail led from Taos northwestward, over the Green and Sevier rivers to the Virgin and Colorado, and by way of the Mohave Desert to the Cajón Pass and Los Angeles.[7]

Between the Northwest and New Mexico lay an immense basin encompassing some two hundred thousand square miles, walled in by the Rocky Mountains and Sierra Nevada on the east and west.[8] Once filled upon otherwise empty maps by a huge "Sea of the West" and later by streams flowing north and west directly into the Pacific, it did not appear as a distinct basin until depicted by Albert Gallatin and H. S. Tanner in 1836.[9] The Great Basin (as it would be called by Frémont) was visited by the Spaniards Escalante and Domínguez in 1776, seeking a way to California; by British fur traders as early as 1819 (Peter Skene Ogden discovering the west-flowing Mary's River a decade later);[*] and by Americans, of whom James Bridger, in the winter of 1824–1825, probably first saw the Great Salt Lake. From a post established by the Rocky Mountain Fur Company at the south end of that lake, Jedediah Smith crossed the desert to southern California in 1826—the earliest overland visitor—and, upon his return eastward, the first to scale the Sierra Nevada.[10]

In 1833, Joseph Walker, with a party from Captain Bonneville's fur-trading expedition beyond the Rockies, explored northwest from the Great Salt Lake. Following and verifying the practicability of the Humboldt River as a guide and source of water, wood, and grass across the arid Basin, he climbed the Sierra just north of Yosemite Valley (which he was the first to see) and continued to Monterey. Returning, he circumvented the snowy peaks by discovering Walker's Pass near the range's southern extremity.[11] Beginning with the Bidwell–Bartleson party in 1841 (and followed by railroads and highways thereafter), emigrant trains without number would cross the Basin by way of the Humboldt to one of the Sierra passes.

Now it became John Charles Frémont's role to travel, describe, and consolidate information about the Far West in a series of expeditions

---

* First called the Unknown, then Mary's, sometimes the Barren, Ogden's, and finally the Humboldt, it would become the main route to the gold fields (GILBERT 133; 544–5 9–10; WHEAT 2:116–17).

which attracted wide public attention.[12] It was on his second in 1843–1844 that he approached the Basin via South Pass and followed Bear River to Great Salt Lake, all of which he carefully observed and mapped.[13] Since he was to examine the country between South Pass and the mouth of the Columbia, including the Oregon Trail, and connect his survey with Charles Wilkes' on the Pacific, he followed the Snake River to Fort Boise and the Columbia, reaching The Dalles and Fort Vancouver. Turning south in November 1843, he wandered through western Nevada, encountered Pyramid Lake, and concluded (belatedly) that the "Buenaventura River" did not exist.[14] Deciding abruptly that his horses were unfit to cross the desert eastward, he made an almost disastrous transit of the Sierra in February, "rock upon rock—snow upon snow." Ascending the Carson River and passing south of Lake Tahoe (which he and Charles Preuss were the first to view), he crossed the summit and descended the south fork of the American River to meet Captain Sutter near his fort in March 1844.[15] With 130 horses and mules and 30 head of cattle, he left California in April over the Tehachapi, followed the Spanish trail to the Virgin River, turned north to Utah Lake, and crossed the Rocky Mountains.[16]

Less than a year after returning from his second expedition, Frémont embarked in June 1845 upon a third. His official instructions, insofar as known, did not specify entry into Mexican California, although he himself stated before departing that he would examine the country between the Rocky Mountains and the Pacific (and the President and Senator Benton would note in October his intention to visit California before his return).[17] Plausibly, he meant to fill in large gaps left by his earlier crossings, joining his explorations toward Oregon with those of the great rivers and Basin, and all of these with coastal California, which was of lively concern to some members of the government in Washington.

Detaching a small party at Bent's Fort to explore the southern Rockies, as directed, Frémont, with some sixty well-armed men, ascended the Arkansas River to its source in the Rocky Mountains, crossed westward to the Utah and Great Salt lakes, skirted Pilot Peak, and came to the river which he now named the Humboldt. Here the party divided, to meet at Walker Lake near the base of the Sierra Nevada. Separating there again, Frémont and fifteen men scaled the Sierra in December, this time, by chance, ahead of the snows, while the main party crossed the range to the south through Walker Pass. Once more, on December 10, 1845, Frémont descended to the friendly hospitality of Sutter's Fort.[18]

In California this time, Frémont—pioneer scientific explorer, lieutenant of topographical engineers, son-in-law of the powerful expansionist Senator Thomas Hart Benton, and adventurer—soon involved himself in the preliminaries which led to the conquest of California by the United States. Spanning a continent, American initiative confronted a remnant of Spain's imperial domain.

5

Antecedents to Conquest

CALIFORNIA'S FORTUNES were entangled in a web of confusing relationships, most of which were remote from her land and people. Commodore Jones had demonstrated in 1842 that any overt hostility between Mexico and the United States would be crucial to her destiny; and the open war between the two countries which he envisioned would not be averted.

There were many sources of antagonism. Conspicuous among them were the claims of U.S. citizens against Mexico, a long quarrel over the common boundary, and the perennial yearning in Washington for neighboring lands. Buttressing these were a growing sense of "manifest destiny" among the American people, aggressive Americans in the Mexican borderlands, and agitation in the United States over the "re-annexation" of Texas. Other aggravations included the foibles of several U.S. representatives to the Mexican government, unstable Mexican leadership, national and racial antipathies, slavery, religion, politics, and yet less conspicuous *casus belli*. Always there was apprehension in the United States that Britain or France might interfere, particularly that England might interpose in the Texas dispute or grab California before the United States could intervene. And in Mexico there was the overriding fear that the Yankee nation could not be trusted.

CLAIMS

Venturesome Americans, caught in Mexican turmoils, had for years been making financial claims against Mexico—real, dubious, and fraudulent—and although international tribunals recognized many of them as legal in 1839 and 1843, they were never liquidated by a characteristically evanescent and bankrupt government. After an intensive effort to obtain payment, President Andrew Jackson had declared to Congress in 1836 that Mexico's attitude "would justify in the eyes of all nations immediate war," though that body did not concur. Mexico agreed in 1843 to liquidate the adjudicated debts in twenty quarterly installments, but only three were ever paid, leaving a $3,250,000 grievance to be brought up whenever it was expedient.[1]

TEXAS

The United States early developed expansionist tendencies, a disposition known even to the ancients. In the eighteenth century its people had poured into the Mississippi Valley in droves, and in 1803, by a streak of good fortune, it had acquired 800,000 square miles beyond the River— the Louisiana Purchase.[2] Because the new addition had ill-defined boundaries, there were negotiations, and a settlement in 1819 awarded Texas, New Mexico, and territory south of the 42nd parallel to Spain, while the United States acquired West Florida (east of the Mississippi) and a shadowy title to the Oregon country.[3] With Mexico's independence in 1821, the Southwest became part of its inheritance, and the Sabine River boundary between the United States and Texas was reaffirmed by the two countries in 1828.

Always a sparsely settled area and remote from its successive owners, Texas began to be penetrated by American traders, explorers, and adventurers as far back as 1785, while New Spain looked on with growing anxiety. Nevertheless, assistance rendered by Americans in the Mexican war of independence won valuable land concessions in the region, in return for which Mexico anticipated improved trade and a barrier against trespass by the United States. A neighboring territory became the American state of Louisiana in 1812; Missouri, northward, joined the Union in 1821; and by 1827 some 12,000 Americans were settled upon Texas lands.[4]

This substantial American contingent induced President John Quincy Adams in 1825 to contemplate the purchase of Texas, but Mexico was unwilling even to discuss the matter, and the meddling of U.S. Minister Joel Poinsett in Mexican politics did nothing to improve bargaining conditions.[5] When Adams' successor, Andrew Jackson, offered in 1829 and 1835 to buy the territory—in the latter year extending as far west as the

Pacific—Mexican unwillingness and the incompetence and rascality of another U.S. minister, Anthony Butler, defeated his plan.[6] During President John Tyler's ensuing regime, his minister, Waddy Thompson, believing both Texas and California might be obtained, was cautioned to emphasize Mexico's convenience in paying her debts rather than American ambition.[7] At this time Great Britain's view on the purchase of San Francisco by the United States was solicited, and Lord Aberdeen, as foreign secretary, replied that Her Majesty's government had not the slightest intention to annex territory in that direction.[8] But Jones' seizure of Monterey in 1842 put an end to such maneuvers.

Determined meanwhile to keep her aggressive Americans in hand, Mexico in 1829 and 1830 instituted stricter laws, attempted to disarm the Texans, and united Texas with Coahuila, in which the Americans became a minority. Conventions were held in Texas in 1832 and 1833 to promote separation, and a tentative declaration of independence was proclaimed in November 1835. Though in the famous battles of the Alamo and Goliad the following spring the Texas forces were beaten, absolute independence was nevertheless declared in March 1836; and in a subsequent encounter at San Jacinto the Texans turned a long retreat into a great victory, capturing the Mexican President Santa Anna himself. While the U.S. government probably gave no direct aid to the Texas struggle, wide public support was expressed in the American press and in spontaneous contributions of men and provisions; and when the United States recognized the independence of Texas in 1837, Mexico severed relations.[9]

Texas too had expansionist tendencies and, after the victory at San Jacinto in 1836, considered extending its dominion westward to the Pacific.[10] Indeed, President Jackson urged Texas in 1837 to claim California so that a harbor on the coast might make its annexation more palatable to northern commercial interests. Although it was not thought prudent in 1838 to press such a claim, Texas President Mirabeau Lamar projected a southern line running up the Río Grande to El Paso and on to the Pacific as a starting point for negotiations.[11] After Texas forces failed to seize Santa Fé in 1841, its legislature, undaunted, endorsed annexing the two Californias and half of Mexico as well; and though President Sam Houston vetoed this bill as inexpedient, he envisioned the Lone Star Republic as stretching to the Pacific from Lower California to the Columbia.[12]

The southern boundary of Texas had been established by Spain at the Nueces River as early as 1816, and maps of 1838 still depicted that line.

Even Andrew Jackson, in attempting to buy the territory in 1829, proposed the watershed between the Nueces and the more southern Río Grande del Norte as an acceptable limit. Texas did not begin to claim the Del Norte until 1836, but in December of that year the legislature adopted it unequivocally as the boundary, from its mouth to its source. No limits were specified in a failed attempt at annexation by the United States in 1844, and a joint resolution of Congress for annexation in March 1845 left the boundaries to be settled by the concerned governments. It was President James K. Polk in August 1845 who informed General Zachary Taylor that the "crossing of the Del Norte by a Mexican army in force" would be regarded as an act of war.[13]

Amidst such anxieties, American trade was forbidden by Mexico in 1843, and Americans were to be expelled from Mexican soil. This was followed in August by an announcement that Mexico would regard the annexation of Texas as tantamount to a declaration of war. When, on December 29, 1845, therefore, President Polk signed a joint resolution of Congress admitting Texas as a state, both sides immediately began warlike preparations. U.S. forces moved to the Nueces, and Mexican troops readied themselves to cross the Río Grande.[14]

CALIFORNIA

Not only Texas but California loomed over the horizon. Official U.S. interest in the port of San Francisco was recorded as early as 1818, when an emissary of President James Monroe, writing from Monterey, characterized it as the "most convenient, extensive, and safe in the world, wholly without defense."[15] By 1835 its advantages as a western door for the United States had become well enough recognized that President Jackson's Secretary of State wrote to Butler in Mexico. "It having been represented to the President that the port of St. Francisco . . . would be a most desirable place of resort for our numerous vessels," he was to add to his charge (to purchase Texas) an attempt to acquire "the whole bay" by extending Texas above 37° to the Pacific.[16] Nothing came of this stratagem save increasing Mexican resentment—aggravated by Butler's comportment as a "cantankerous, incompetent rascal," a "national disgrace," and, according to Jackson himself, a "scamp."[17] In continuing to press for the payment of American claims, President Tyler's administration suggested in 1842 that the U.S. minister negotiate for California as part of a pecuniary settlement,[18] and this precedent his successor, Polk, would energetically pursue.

As earlier noted, foreigners, many of them Americans, came unbidden to California, some by sea or from Oregon, a few by the southern desert to San Diego and Los Angeles, fewer still over the high Sierra. Among them were respected merchants and ranchers. Others, on the fringes of society—trappers, traders, squatters, adventurers—occupied themselves in lumbering, tanning, and millwork, distilling whiskey, or living by their rifles, now and then taking sides in local squabbles, and being disrespectful, even contemptuous of Mexican law and customs. By 1840 they numbered about four hundred. The following year overland immigration from the United States unceremoniously began, introducing another alien if scattered band, mainly pioneer farmers from the American West, enticed mostly to Oregon but some to beckoning valleys farther south. A preference for inland agricultural lands, and Mexico's desire to keep them away from the coast, made them difficult to assimilate and control.[19] A United States exploring expedition arrived at San Francisco Bay in 1841, and a year later two warships, without provocation, seized Monterey. In March 1844 Frémont's armed party came over the mountains to Sutter's Fort and departed before the government could learn its business.

It was against such outsiders that interdictions were issued by mother Mexico; their presence was portentous, considering the example of Texas. But these restrictions went for the most part unnoticed or unenforced in California, whose inhabitants had a far stronger disposition to be hospitable than hostile to strangers. It was a lenient society. Mexico was far away and communication slow, and when the gyrations of Mexican politics succeeded the wars of Spanish kings, this frontier province became even more dissociated from the live issues at the center. The Russian threat simmered and cooled; French interest never warmed beyond a faint glow; English attention lacked the indispensable fire kept burning by the home government; and, betimes, American self-interest roiled, sputtered, and came to a rolling boil. The United States had geography and time on its side but was ready to be in a hurry.

OTHER INDUCEMENTS TO CONFLICT

The good will and good manners of Americans and Mexicans were corrupted not only by haggling over Mexican debts and the coveting by the United States of Mexican lands. American attitudes also reflected slavery and religious issues, patriotic excitement to "extend the area of freedom," politics, and the gamy flavor of tangling with an untested and disdained foe.

Many Northerners opposed extending the sphere of slavery under any circumstances, holding that territorial expansion was a slave-owners' conspiracy; but others, being cotton-based industrialists or fearing English machinations, approved.[20] Southerners generally applauded westward expansion, but some demurred, believing that slavery would be unprofitable in the arid Southwest or lead to competition with rapidly depleting soils in the South. Nor was religion without its appropriate rationalization. Some Catholics saw annexation as a means to add large numbers of co-religionists to the fold, while Protestants eyed Mexico as a fertile ground for evangelism and the imposition of a "higher and purer Christian civilization."[21]

There was the great lure of a United States from sea to sea, open to both oceans—a new route to the Indies (five treaty ports were opened in China in 1844). Speculation in Texas lands[22] and a hungering for freedom beyond the frontier bred a belief that the United States should envelop neighboring regions. It was the *destiny* of the Anglo-Saxon race and the mission of the United States to civilize, "Americanize," the continent.[23] If Polk Democrats came to favor war, Whigs formed the opposition. The press played an influential role, though the editor of the New York *Sun* may have stretched the truth a little when he said in 1845, "Texas, owing almost entirely to the influence of this paper, has been annexed, and now, our Editors say, 'Why not California?'"[24]

As for the Mexicans, they were proud, suspicious, overextended, disunited, and greatly burdened by a prevailing personalism among their leaders which spawned almost innumerable changes in government between the constitution of 1824 and 1846. In the latter year, when war was imminent between the nations, an American observer professed to find little enthusiasm for it among the Mexican people,* a strong opposition to army rule, disapproval of the warring leaders, and an aspiration for a government which would, "like the United States," provide security and protection.[25] Mexico at the time, it has been said, was not a republic, hardly a government, but a late stage in the breakdown of the Spanish empire;[26] and certainly it was the scene of a destructive struggle between the monarchical-ecclesiastical tradition and an erupting republicanism. It was President Santa Anna, the father of many of its current woes, who

---

* On the other hand, George Frederick Ruxton, an Englishman wandering in Mexico after the war had begun, wrote in his *Adventures in Mexico* of a great hostility to foreigners, Texans, and Yankees, particularly in the *pulquerías* and barrios of the large towns (RUXTON 40–42, 68–69, 89).

confided to an American diplomat that Mexico needed a foreign war to develop its resources. Mexico's attempts to woo England and France to its side were ineffective; France wavered, and while the British press favored the Mexican cause, the government was not disposed to risk war over issues which did not much affect its basic interests and might seriously impair its trade.[27]

THE BRITISH MENACE

In the 1840s Great Britain was seen as the chief adversary of the United States, at least among expansionists. A monarchy and America's historical enemy, its shape was seen under every bed. Be it in Texas, Mexico, Oregon, or California, the British presence threatened American security; its encroachments must be thwarted. The means would be to incorporate the imperiled frontiers, the justification an exuberant Manifest Destiny and a versatile Monroe Doctrine.[28]

British attention to the Far West had first been paid by Francis Drake in 1579. But any exclusive right to California which might have derived from his visit was extinguished by subsequent Spanish settlement and the Nootka convention of 1790, which permitted access by England only above the area of Spanish occupation.[29] British pretensions to the Oregon country were more defensible, though contested by the United States. While neither nation's claim was irrefutable, Britain's was "a little less absurd" than the American, being based upon earlier and more extensive exploration and trade and more factual possession.[30] When the two governments could not agree upon areas of sovereignty in 1818, a ten-year treaty of joint occupation was made, England believing it had actual possession, the United States counting upon its potential for settlement. A year later the United States and Spain fixed the southern boundary of the Louisiana Purchase in this area at 42° (the California–Oregon line), and a treaty with Russia in 1824 established that country's southernmost border at 54° 40', thus effectively defining the area of controversy between England and the United States.[31]

In December 1823, President James Monroe asserted that the American continents were "henceforth not to be considered as subjects for . . . colonization by any European power." Enunciated on behalf of the new Latin American republics, the policy was also meant to embrace the northwest coast.[32] Such a declaration could not prevent colonization except as it might be enforced by the United States, but the principle was restated in negotiations with England in 1824.[33] When, near the end of joint occupation in 1827, no settlement could be reached, the arrangement was indefinitely renewed, with the privilege of abrogation by either party upon a year's notice. England was primarily interested in the fur trade, an American negotiator noted; and though national pride might prevent abrupt relinquishment of her territorial pretensions, "Great Britain does not seem indisposed to let the country gradually and silently slide into the hands of the United States." [34]

Congress did not soon embrace the Oregon issue. But American fur-trapping increased, colonization was encouraged, missionaries gained a firm foothold, and the government collected and issued reports upon the country.

Polk's campaign in 1844 for the "re-annexation of Texas" and the "re-occupation of Oregon" much heightened the excitement, and as President he at once declared the American title to Oregon to be "clear and unquestionable." He soon recommended that notice be given to terminate the 1827 convention, and a joint resolution of Congress was delivered to the British on May 22, 1846. [35] The Senate prudently invited negotiation; and the English, finding a solution that would satisfy the national honor, made a new offer at the 49th parallel, which was ratified by the Senate on June 18 (war with Mexico having commenced). Thus, peacefully, was the long drama ended, the United States having a more aroused and single-minded leader, and England, esteeming Anglo-American trade above war, finding its interests not worth defending. Only California and the Southwest now remained uncertain.

British trappers had been deployed by the Hudson's Bay Company in California before 1830, with some kind of sanction from Governor Alvarado in 1837. Though asked to withdraw in January 1841 because the settlements "now extended to their hunting grounds," these expeditions continued for several years. [36] When the company's chief factor, James Douglas, came down to Monterey at the beginning of 1841 with an "adventure" of goods, he hoped not only to obtain produce for his Columbia settlements but to pursue "other objects of a political nature" which might or might not succeed "according to circumstances." A trading post was established on San Francisco Bay in August of that year and continued with some success until just prior to the American occupation. [37]

It had been widely reported in 1837 that California would be ceded to England in payment for a large Mexican debt. [38] Scotsman Alexander Forbes of Tepic favored such an arrangement and advocated British colonization. [39] Sir George Simpson, overseas governor of the Hudson's

Bay Company, was another proponent. Visiting California in 1842, he warned that either England would get the country or the United States would inundate it with their "peculiar mixture of helpless bondage and lawless insubordination." Although he believed the Russian title to Fort Ross would have little value unless backed by a force of eighty to a hundred men, he afterwards said he would have purchased that property if he had had the opportunity as a basis for "some claim" the British government might subsequently have made.[40]

Neither the hopes nor the views of British entrepreneurs necessarily represented the policy of the home government. Richard Packenham, British minister in Mexico, indeed suggested to the impulsive foreign minister, Lord Palmerston, in August 1841, that a colony be established in Upper California in exchange for Mexican debts. But Lord Aberdeen, Palmerston's more circumspect successor, replied that England was not eager to acquire distant colonies because of the expense and potential for misunderstanding and collision.[41] A vice-consular office was authorized for Monterey in February 1841, but a resident Englishman, James Alexander Forbes,* was not appointed to the post until December 1842, after Jones' visitation. When Forbes wrote in September 1844 that several Californians were planning a revolt and wondered whether England would extend protection, Lord Aberdeen responded that the consul was "entirely unauthorized" to enter into any such arrangement.[42] He also informed Eustace Barron, Forbes' superior at San Blas, that Her Majesty's government would have nothing to do with insurrection in California, and he was to remain entirely passive, though Britain would disapprove the establishment of a protectorate by any other state.[43] When in September 1845 Mexico was deliberating hostilities against the United States over the Texas issue, the Mexican minister in London inquired whether Great Britain would assume some responsibility for California. The offer had come too late, the Prime Minister answered; the hasty inauguration of such a relationship would appear self-serving.[44]

This is not to say that British consular officers on the west coast were thereafter deaf to news about California, for John Parrott, U.S. consul at Mazatlán, said in 1845 that the British legation was "all alive on such occasions";[45] nor that Forbes, like his French counterparts Louis Gasquet and J. A. Moerenhout at Monterey, did not continue to report regularly

---

* James was known but not related to Alexander Forbes, the author of *California*, 1839 (FORBES,A., 1937 xxi–xxii).

to his superior upon California.[46] Lord Aberdeen indeed counseled vigilance, particularly in respect to U.S. residents. In January 1846, therefore, Forbes urged Agustín Olvera, secretary to Governor Pico, to protest Frémont's arrival in California with "soldiers," but this action too received Aberdeen's disapproval. And the plan of an Irish priest, McNamara, to settle thousands of Irishmen in the San Joaquin Valley, though approved by the California legislature and governor, never received an official acknowledgment from the British government.[47]

While the British squadron in the Pacific was believed to have kept a watchful eye upon California, it apparently had no such instructions. The correspondence of Admiral Thomas during the Jones affair did not mention California, and Admiral Seymour's orders in 1844 were to be aggressive in countering French designs in the Pacific islands, with nothing about the Mexican province. Seymour was indeed induced by the British consul, Barron, to interest himself in California, but he afterwards saw Aberdeen's instructions about passivity in respect to that country. Oregon was a livelier issue, and Seymour requested an increase in his force to guard British interests there and "observe the proceedings of the United States relative to California."[48] He sent Captain Blake in the *Juno* to California in May 1846 to confer with Forbes, obtain a list of British residents, and examine potential landing places near San Francisco but made no move to station a vessel there.[49] At Santa Barbara, Blake received an appeal from the governor for aid against the American invaders but could only counsel against accepting a protectorate from any foreign state.[50]

Finally, his own curiosity thoroughly whetted, Seymour explained to the admiralty on June 13, 1846, that he thought it only proper to proceed to Monterey to ascertain the actual state of affairs. Arriving on July 16 and finding the American flag flying, after courtesies were exchanged, he continued on his way to the Sandwich Islands.[51] When he wrote to London that his principal objective for many months had been to be at hand to prevent or retard the American occupation should he be so directed,[52] it was a testimony both to the admiral's prudence and his government's self-restraint.

THE FRENCH

France too was suspect, but her active interest in the Pacific in the 1840s was in the Marquesas and Society Islands. French agents collected and published information about California;[53] there were French residents in the country; and a consul appeared at Monterey in mid-1845 (with "nothing to do *apparent[l]y*," Larkin dolefully reported, but whatever it was Uncle Sam would learn to his sorrow).[54] José Castro and others may have sometimes favored a French protectorate; and Colonel Iniestra, who was dispatched to California with Mexican troops in 1845 (but never arrived), was rumored to have obtained his military education in France and to be bringing a large number of Frenchmen. The French might have been worthy antagonists had they joined England to interfere in Mexico and Texas, but the two great powers were on uneasy terms, and France tended to be conciliatory toward the American republic. Whatever may have been French hopes for annexing California, this Latin and Catholic country never became a strong contender.

WAR

So many conflicting interests, inclinations, and motivations could hardly produce open relationships and candid agreements among nations. Mexico was suspicious of the United States, and the Americans reciprocated in kind. A rising public fervor in both countries gave affairs momentum, and Polk accepted his election as a mandate for expansion. What he required was a treaty, an agreement for purchase, or a guilt-free justification for war to present to Congress and the people.

After a joint resolution to annex Texas had been signed by President Tyler on March 3, 1845, in the last hours of his administration, war did not come as soon as it might. Mexico did not attack—though immediate warnings reached California, and Polk's Cabinet soon agreed that a Mexican crossing of the Del Norte would constitute an act of war.[55] In May, Polk dispatched Captain Robert F. Stockton of the U.S. Navy to the coast of Texas, anxious to extend protection. With him went confidential agent Charles A. Wickliffe to encourage Texas President Anson Jones, some have supposed, to seize the disputed territory beyond the Nueces and start a war which the United States could enter on Texas' behalf.[56] Whatever the official mission, Jones would not send volunteers into the disputed lands; and when Mexico offered independence if Texas would not attach itself to another nation, he issued a proclamation on June 4 declaring hostilities ended. Texas nevertheless accepted annexation to the United States in July, whereupon Mexico withdrew its mission from Washington. As an earnest of his intention, Polk moved General Taylor to Corpus Christi, on the south side of the Nueces River, just inside the contested land, some 120 miles north of the Río Grande.[57]

Polk would not insist upon war—he hardly meant to have it—if he could achieve his ends by negotiation, purchase, or intimidation.[58] He sent John Slidell to Mexico City in November 1845, hoping to repair severed relations. The emissary had a familiar mission, to negotiate the Texas boundary and collect American claims.[59] Secret instructions also authorized the purchase of Upper California and New Mexico, using the claims as a lever, the price to depend upon the area acquired—though the amount paid "would be of small importance" compared with the gains foreseen.[60] Slidell was to discover whether Mexico meant to cede California to any European power and was to correspond with Consul Larkin at Monterey.

A few weeks before, on October 11, Polk had received from Larkin the alarming speculation that Mexican troops were being sent to California at England's instigation; and the same day a letter from Parrott told of the great interest of the English legation in all things Californian.[61] Polk had already heard from Parrott that the British squadron had been strengthened in the Pacific to take California, should hostilities with Mexico occur, and of the project being promoted by Father McNamara to settle Irish families in that country. Earlier he had also had word from Wickliffe that California was to be transferred to England in case Mexico declared war. Consequently, on October 17, 1845, urgent letters were written to Commodores Sloat and Stockton, stressing preparedness, and one to Larkin appointing him confidential agent at Monterey.[62] Lieutenant Archibald Gillespie was sent across Mexico with the messages and a packet for Frémont. And in November orders went to Slidell to do all that he could to prevent the cession of California to England and to use his best efforts to secure it for the United States.[63]

In January 1846, General Santa Anna (exiled in Cuba) was purported to favor a pecuniary settlement, and his agent* visited President Polk, urging him to make a show of force, under cover of which a deal might be made.[64] Though suspicious, Polk at once adopted a harder line, proposing to the Cabinet that if Slidell was not immediately received, Congress should be asked to demand the payment of claims. If Mexico refused, more aggressive measures would be taken. Meanwhile, Polk told Slidell the United States was willing to "relieve" the Mexican government of any

---

* Colonel A. J. Atocha, a Spaniard, naturalized in the U.S., said to have been expelled from Mexico as being obnoxious to that country.

"pecuniary embarrassment" if the boundary question could be satisfactorily arranged (a bribery attempt carefully concealed).[65]

President Herrera, too, was in trouble. No Mexican leader could talk of dismembering the nation; and he was made more timorous by General Paredes' armed forces in the vicinity. By sending Slidell under these disturbed conditions, Polk was asking that normal relations be renewed, while an apprehensive and convulsive Mexican government wanted only to talk about Texas.[66] On April 7 it was learned that Mexico would not accept Slidell.[67] Paredes, having meanwhile overthrown his predecessor, was ready for war, though the Mexican Congress would not go so far. But General Taylor, upon Polk's direct order,[68] had already set out for the Río Grande on March 8, and General Arista moved his forces northward toward Matamoros, near the mouth of the river.

Polk's Cabinet discussed a declaration of war in April and early May, and his diary makes it clear that the determination to have California, New Mexico, and "perhaps some others of the Northern Provinces" was growing upon him.[69] Though he anticipated a collision between American and Mexican forces, a draft message was prepared for delivery to Congress on May 12, justifying war on the basis of the unpaid claims, refusal to receive Slidell, and other grievances.[70] But on Saturday, May 9, at about 6 o'clock in the evening, dispatches from Taylor arrived, announcing that Mexican troops had crossed the Río Grande on April 25 and captured two companies of U.S. dragoons, with several Americans killed.[71] The war message, with a new preamble dwelling upon the Mexican invasion of U.S. territory and the beguiling claim that the area up to the Río Grande was "within one of our Congressional districts," was delivered to Congress on May 11.[72] (But at Corpus Christi the previous October, West Point graduate John James Peck had recognized they were in Mexico, had "invaded their soil"; and north of the river, across from Matamoros, lay a portion of the common lands of the town.)[73]

A joint resolution of both houses of Congress on May 13 declared that a state of war existed by "an act of the Republic of Mexico," and a war proclamation was signed the same day by the President.[74] Polk would not allow his Secretary of State to assure foreign embassies that it was not a war of conquest, for he would, if practicable, obtain California and such other portions of Mexico as would be sufficient to settle the claims and defray the costs of the conflict.[75]

A single-minded and determined man, the President had set his sights upon specific objectives,[76] all of which he realized in his single term. He was also a hard worker and diligent overseer in everything except, perhaps, war. And the war would often prove to be in the hands of generals and subordinates who were almost beyond his control, or in the lap of Congress, which, with its slender Democratic backing, was never very realistic about its prosecution or prepared to give it full support. Be it also remembered that while pressing Mexico he was openly risking hostilities with England over Oregon, as everyone supposed. Senator Benton would afterwards say that one could not conceive of an administration which was less warlike "or more intriguing."[77] They were men of peace, he said, with objects to be accomplished by war. War was necessary, "but they wanted no more of it than would answer their purposes. They wanted a small war, just enough to require a treaty of peace" (with indemnification) without making military reputations.

CONQUEST

❧ 6 ❧

Incident
at Gavilán

OHN CHARLES FRÉMONT, with fifteen members of his expedition, came down out of the mountains to Sutter's Sacramento Valley outpost on December 10, 1845.[1] Quickly gathering supplies, he was on the 13th headed down the San Joaquín Valley, herding a band of cattle, to succor the main party under Theodore Talbot and Joseph Walker, who approached by a southern route. Riding through open woods of white oak, the men crossed, successively, the Cosumnes, Mokelumne, and Calaveras rivers, then the Stanislaus and Tuolumne, where multitudes of wild fowl "made the night noisy." Fording the Merced, Fresno, and upper San Joaquín, they came on December 22 to the Kings—Frémont's "River of the Lake"—one of the largest and handsomest in the valley. Not finding the party there as expected (they were waiting farther south on the Kern), Frémont and his men ascended the river to its "head springs" in the Sierra Nevada, an extraordinary venture in December. Driving their stock before them, sixteen men on horseback forced their way upward till they stood upon a flat ridge of naked granite which "made the division of the waters," 11,000 feet above sea level.[2] Almost trapped by falling snow, and forced to abandon their cattle, they made their way down to sunshine and spring weather, reaching the valley floor on January 7. Having by this diversion squandered most of their provisions, they turned back to Sutter's Fort, which they reached on the 15th. "Arrd. Capt. Fremont [from] below not having been able to find Capt. Walker," read Sutter's New Helvetia diary; and the Fort's proprietor fired a cannon and gave a big dinner in his honor.[3]

Sutter's launch was sailing to Yerba Buena on January 19, and Frémont, with a Mexican passport in his pocket issued by magistrate Sutter, went with eight of his men to the little village on San Francisco Bay.[4] On board were the U.S. vice-consul, William Leidesdorff; William Hinckley, Yankee captain of the port; and the just-arrived immigrant, carpenter, teacher, and farmer William B. Ide, whom he would meet again. Ever curious about the country around him, Frémont went by water with Captain Hinckley to the pueblo of San José and the newly discovered quicksilver mine at New Almadén. At Yerba Buena he spent a few days with Leidesdorff and his "wife," a "handsome girl-like Russian" from Sitka, enjoying their garden and "bungalow sort of adobe house" with a long piazza facing the Bay for the sunny mornings.[5] Here Frémont wrote his wife, Jessie,[6] describing their trip thus far and his suffering among the heavy snows during his recent escapade in the Sierra. He also told of his intention to make a short journey up the Sacramento to complete his explorations for a new road to Oregon, then finish his surveys in California and return homeward in the proper season.

With Leidesdorff now for company, he set out again on January 24 for Monterey to see the American consul, traveling the main road past Mission Dolores. They stayed the first night at Francisco Sánchez' San Pedro rancho (above Point San Pedro), rode down the wooded western shore of the Bay to Antonio Suñol's house at San José and, by way of San Juan, over the ridge to José Gómez' Los Vergeles rancho at the foot of the Gavilán range (north of Salinas). Another half-day's ride across the Salinas plain, amid herds of horned cattle, brought them on the 27th to Monterey and a welcome by Consul Larkin.[7] Sutter had written Larkin on December 22 of Frémont's arrival, and Larkin had replied that he would be happy to see the captain and please give him his "best offers of assistance as a Consul or Countryman."[8]

Frémont doubtless had an eager listener as he told Larkin of his explorations.[9] He had taken a route, he said with some extravagance, which not only made the distance to California eight or nine hundred miles shorter than heretofore but was "less mountainous, with good pasturage, and well watered." He doubtless mentioned his still-missing party and their needs and reported conditions in the United States as of the previous May. Whatever else may have been revealed, Larkin, who often wrote in guarded phrases, got "the idea, that great plans are meditated to be carried out by certain persons."[10] Responding, the consul surely talked about what was on his mind, local politics, rumors of war with the

John Charles Frémont, with members of his expedition, came down out of the mountains to Sutter's Sacramento Valley outpost on December 10, 1845.

United States over Texas, the thousand troops expected from Mexico, increasing American immigration, the Californians' lenience in admitting foreigners, and of his hopes and fears for the country, based upon reports and observations and colored by his own interests as consul and Yankee merchant.

But Frémont was in a foreign country with an armed party, and the news had reached Manuel Castro, the civil prefect at Monterey.[11] Likewise, the British vice-consul, James Alexander Forbes, wrote from Yerba Buena to the departmental secretary at Los Angeles on January 28[12] that an armed force of U.S. citizens was entering the interior of the country and, though its members did not appear to be regular troops, they were in fact soldiers. Since he knew of no declaration of war or treaty allowing their presence, he was called upon to say that while Britain would not interfere in California's affairs, she would look with dissatisfaction upon the establishment of a protectorate by any other nation (this being authentic British doctrine). Shortly after Frémont's appearance, Manuel Castro inquired of Larkin the "object and commission" with which an officer, now residing in his house, had arrived in the country with troops and advanced as far as the Sacramento River, that he might inform the governor.[13] To this formal query the consul replied that Frémont of the United States Army had been ordered to survey the most practicable route to the Pacific, that he had left his company of fifty hired men (not soldiers) on the frontier to rest themselves and their animals, and had come to Monterey to obtain clothing and funds to purchase animals and provisions. When his party was recruited, he intended to continue his journey to the Oregon country.[14]

Larkin and Frémont then went to see the *comandante general*, José Castro; the prefect, Alcalde Manuel Díaz; and ex-Governor Juan B. Alvarado. "I explained to General Castro the object of my coming into California," Frémont afterwards recorded,[15] emphasizing his geographical, scientific, and commercial aims and that his men were citizens, not soldiers. He wanted permission to winter in the valley of the San Joaquín, where there was plenty of game and no inhabitants to be molested by their presence. He apparently reduced his motives to writing, which, as Larkin explained, "were accepted by Gen. Castro in not answering the letter."[16]

Whatever his intentions and Castro's understanding, Frémont's presence was at least not forbidden. He would say in 1848 that permission was given to continue his explorations south to the Colorado and Gila rivers[17] (and Larkin sent a vessel to Santa Barbara in February with funds and provisions, presumably for this purpose).[18] But the consul wrote the Secretary of State in March that the captain would go to Oregon and return to Monterey in May.[19] The Californians too understood he was headed for Oregon; and when Governor Pico, in Los Angeles, was informed of Frémont's presence and intentions, he only cautioned the prefect to observe whether the party did in fact prepare for a northern journey.[20] Having been treated with every courtesy by the Californians and received $1,800 in funds, heavy jackets and shirts, and other supplies from the merchant-consul,[21] Frémont turned back toward the Santa Clara Valley.

Frémont did not of course know where most of his men were, not hav-

To *José Castro*, comandante general *since Michel-torena's expulsion in February 1845, Frémont ex-plained the object of his coming to California, emphasizing his geographical, scientific, and com-mercial aims.*

ing seen them since their separation at Walker Lake east of the Sierra at the end of December. They were, however, a seasoned party with experi-enced leaders, who, through a misunderstanding involving the identity of the "River of the Lake," had camped from December 28 to January 18 at the forks of the Kern (in the vicinity of Lake Isabella), a hundred miles south of Frémont's rendezvous.[22] When Frémont did not appear by the appointed time, they crossed the Greenhorn Mountains in two and a half feet of snow and reached the sunny "Valley of California" on the 21st.[23] Working their way northward down the San Joaquín Valley, and floun-dering for a day in the tule marshes, they crossed the Kings River and came to the Calaveras on February 6. Near there, Walker met an old mountaineer, William "Le Gros" Fallon, from whom he learned that Frémont was at San José; and while Walker went on to the pueblo, the rest remained on the San Joaquín until fresh horses were received. They all reached San José on the 15th, a place artist Kern noted was in a very dilapidated condition, "showing the slothful habits of the people." Frémont had meanwhile moved on to the Laguna farm, where the forces were again joined. This was the vacant rancho of Laguna Seca, on the main road to Monterey (some sixty miles distant), belonging to William Fisher, a Boston sea captain who had just bought it from Juan Alvires. Here Frémont had determined to rest, refit, and prepare for a new departure.

Some of the Californians brought provisions for sale, and among the foreign visitors was Harvard graduate Dr. John Marsh, whose rancho Los Medanos (or Pulpones) was at the foot of Mount Diablo. Having heard "distant rumors of mighty events," he had come to learn what he could from Frémont; and from Alvires' farm he wrote Larkin on February 15 that "the present year will bring great changes over the face of California." [24] Frémont also had an exchange of letters with Alcalde José Dolores Pacheco of San José about one of Frémont's horses which citizen Sebastian Peralta claimed as his own. Having ordered him out of the camp for trying to obtain animals under false pretenses, Frémont replied to the alcalde that he should have been well satisfied to escape without a severe horsewhipping. [25] "You will readily understand," the uppity visitor continued, "that my duties will not permit me to appear before the magistrates of your towns on the complaint of every straggling vagabond who may chance to visit my camp" (Peralta being a former *regidor* at San José and *majordomo* at Santa Clara Mission). Under public relations may also be cited "some rows our men got into," as set down by Talbot, including one of Frémont's probably inebriate followers who insisted that a daughter of Angel Castro drink with him (the father was sent ten dollars in restitution). [26]

Frémont, who was accustomed to wandering in the wilds wherever his fancy chose, now crossed the Santa Clara Valley toward the west—his road to Oregon lying in the opposite direction—and on February 22 camped on Wildcat Ridge (Cuesta de los Gatos) on the road to Santa Cruz. Once again in the forest, he noted the prevalence of a cyprus (redwood) of extraordinary dimensions, one of which was fourteen feet in diameter. "In California this tree is called the *palo colorado*. It is the king of trees." [27] Thus botanizing, recording temperatures, and determining astronomical positions, Frémont and his men descended on the 25th to the coast near Santa Cruz, losing their fine weather. On March 1, after the rain had ceased, they followed the seacoast southward among spring flowers, then turned inland up the Salinas Valley, passing Monterey, about twenty-five miles distant. They camped on the 3rd at Hartnell's Alisal rancho (east of Salinas), "outside the more occupied parts of the country," as he would later claim. Perhaps he was on the way south to the Río Colorado, as he would say in 1848, or headed for an opening into the San Joaquín Valley, as he would recount forty years after,[28] but his route was circuitous.

Wherever he was going when he got around to it, the country was of course inhabited, as he knew, a province of Mexico, and ruled by California officers whose military seat was at Monterey. To the authorities, Frémont had pleaded necessity in entering California, had stated his purpose to be surveying routes across the continent, and had promised to winter in the San Joaquín Valley, away from the settlements, with the intention of going from there to Oregon. And yet, five weeks later, in March, here he was with a band of fifty or sixty tough and sinister-looking men, armed with "from three to six guns, rifles, and pistols each,"[29] not recuperating in a distant valley but riding openly to the sea and hovering about Monterey. They were not only disobeying California authority and poorly repaying hospitality but, under conditions of potential warfare between Mexico and the United States and recurrent warnings from Mexico to mobilize, were threatening hostilities. Even Larkin did not know what to make of it.[30]

Certainly the *comandante general* was alarmed. Repeated rumors, warnings, and orders had raised apprehensions. It was reported at Sutter's Fort in mid-February that the country was "about to be delivered up to the U. States."[31] Frémont's arrival, Larkin testified, had revived excitement respecting the American immigration and fears that the Californians would lose their country.[32] And José Castro had received specific orders, he said, to drive Frémont away.[33] On March 5, therefore, the *comandante* sent a cavalry officer to the Hartnell rancho with an abrupt order, carefully with a copy to Larkin.[34] "At seven o'clock this morning the Commandant General was given to understand that you and the party under your command have entered the towns of this Department, and such being prohibited by our laws, I find myself obligated to notify you that on the receipt of this you will immediately retire beyond the limits of this same Department, such being the orders of the supreme Government, and the subscriber is obligated to see them complied with." Frémont was told to leave!

Perhaps Frémont and his men were randomly "surveying" or killing time while the snow melted in the northern mountains. The captain gloried in the plants and flowers, collected scientific data, and, by forgoing the pleasures he would have found in society at Monterey, practiced the self-denial, he said, which was their constant virtue. "Having seen nothing," he lamented,[35] "what shall I say now to those who ask me of Hastings account?" *

The same day he also received a letter from the prefect.[36] Manuel Castro wrote, "I have learnt with surprise that you, against the laws of the authorities of Mexico, have introduced yourself into the towns of this Departmental district under my charge with an armed force under a commission which must have been given you by your government only to survey its own proper lands. In consequence, this Prefectura now orders that you will immediately on receipt of this without any pretext return with your people out of the limits of this territory. If not this office will take the necessary measures." Again, Larkin received a punctual copy "in order that so far as it may pertain to you, you may demand of Capt. Fremont compliance with what is ordered." Larkin immediately sent translations of both documents to Frémont to be certain he understood.[37]

Frémont had not only been ordered but *threatened*! These offensive and peremptory orders, he decided, were insulting both to himself and his government, and he would not comply. He "wd leave the country, but wd not be driven out," in Talbot's words;[38] and he returned only a verbal reply.[39] Always edgy when challenged, late on March 5 Frémont instead moved his camp six or eight miles northward and up a wood-road from Gómez' rancho to the highest point in the Gavilán Mountains. A small, wooded flat at the summit afforded fuel, water, and grass; commanded a view of the surrounding country, including the valley of San Juan and the Salinas plain; and, in case of exigency, opened a retreat to the San Joaquín. A rough but strong breastwork of logs was built; and on a tall sapling, amid the cheers of his men, Frémont raised an American flag in a province of Mexico. Negotiations with a nearby rancher brought a steer

---

*The reference is to Lansford W. Hastings' *Emigrants' Guide to Oregon and California*, 1845, a famous but exaggerated and not very useful work meant to attract emigrants to California (BANCROFT 4:396–99).

Looking toward the Gavilán Mountains from Monterey, the customhouse in the foreground.

up the mountain for food. With the glasses, they could see troops gathering at San Juan Bautista below, and on the second day a body of cavalry came up the road but halted before reaching the summit.[40]

Larkin immediately reported the state of affairs to the Secretary of State and enclosed translations of documents for information.[41] As consul, he also addressed the Castros, recognizing that they were bound to protect the interests of the country but observing that Frémont's party must not be unjustly or unnecessarily harassed from causes that might arise from false reports or appearances.[42] He recommended that any force going to the camp be commanded by a trustworthy and experienced officer to avoid any unhappy conclusion. Whereupon Prefect Castro accused Larkin of defending Frémont rather than ordering him away and declared that whether he had come into the department "through Malice [or] error," he must now either blindly obey the authorities or suffer the misfortunes he sought by his crimes. (Larkin noted that he had been misunderstood).[43] The prefect insisted he was acting under repeated orders from the Mexican government, prohibiting the introduction not only of troops but of foreigners without legal passports, instructions the

Californians had but fitfully enforced. General Castro had been reprimanded, he said, for permitting Frémont to enter the country in 1844 and within the last twenty days had received orders to drive him out.[44]

The authorities were not inclined to be rash—the Americans were notoriously well armed and effective fighters. The prefect assured the consul that he would seek the necessary proof and go through the required formalities before inflicting punishment.[45] Some of General Castro's men were sent to observe Frémont's position, and Castro wrote the Mexican Minister of War that he would soon take the field.[46] On the evening of the 6th there were some sixty Californians on the plain around San Juan, and Larkin expected two hundred more.[47] Some of Frémont's company slipped into the valley on the 7th "in search of Torres' party" and to advise ranchers not to join either side; the *comandante* took this as a "declaration."[48]

On March 8 General Castro, with uncommon forbearance, got around to issuing a proclamation to his fellow citizens, calling Frémont's men a band of robbers which "sallies forth, committing depredations and making scandalous skirmishes." He asked his countrymen to volunteer under his orders, else they would lose their liberty and independence.[49]

The same day Larkin dispatched a long letter to Frémont, sending two couriers, one native, one foreign, the former getting through.[50] "It is not for me to point out to you your line of conduct," the punctilious consul said. "You have your Government instructions." But he warned against being taken by surprise, for an attack might not come from persons of responsibility but from a more headstrong class. Whatever happened, it might make trouble for resident Americans, cause an interruption in business. If Frémont could not leave California at present, Larkin believed an arrangement could be made with the general and prefect for him to camp at some greater distance. And he asked for an answer. "I am Yours, very truly in heart."

Delivered on the 9th, the letter received an immediate penciled reply.[51] "I this moment received your letters and without waiting to read them, acknowledge the receipt which the Courier requires instantly." They were making themselves as strong as possible so that if unjustly attacked they could fight to extremity and refuse quarter, trusting their country to avenge their deaths. No one had reached the camp, but with the glass they could see troops mustering at San Juan and preparing cannon. He had in no wise done wrong to the people or the authorities of the country.

As a precaution, Larkin also wrote to John Parrott, U.S. consul at Mazatlán, enclosing copies of recent correspondence and a letter "To the Commander of any American Ship of War in San Blas or Mazatlán."[52] Parrott was to consult with the captain of any naval vessel in port, and it was Larkin's earnest desire that if he was not actually obliged to go elsewhere he would come to Monterey. To the commander he explained that if there should be a fight between the Californians and Frémont, the American residents feared for their safety afterwards. With his usual prudence, Larkin reported at the same time to the Secretary of State.[53] He had at some expense sent two couriers to Frémont's camp ($27.50 for the Californian), and having had over half of his hospital expenses for 1844 disallowed, even his bill for a flag, he did not feel disposed to hazard much expense for government. "Although the life of captain Fremont and party may require it, I hardly know how to act." Only one letter had been received from the Department for the year 1845.

Larkin's California courier, Prudencio Espinosa, had at his own insistence carried the documents to Frémont under a passport issued by Alcalde Díaz of Monterey. Afterwards, Díaz asked for a translation for Manuel Castro, hoping it might help to allay the excitement; and although Larkin was not certain Frémont would approve, copies of both his letter and Frémont's reply were immediately provided.[54] Perhaps, Larkin told Díaz, the officials expected something from him as consul, but Frémont was not to be ordered by the consulate; "yet I would with pleasure allay the present sensation, if in my power." He suggested that General Castro request an hour's conversation with Frémont before any extreme measures were taken. Díaz transmitted the correspondence to the *comandante* and governor,[55] and Larkin sent all the papers to Frémont, thanking him for his note; cautioning his men not to talk to anyone, since "it is magnified"; and fervidly offering his assistance, "not only as your Consul, but your Friend and Countryman."[56]

Watching the growing number of horsemen in the valley, seeing copies of all the correspondence, and perhaps reading between Larkin's lines, Frémont in three days of contemplation and suspense may have begun to have misgivings about his extravagant little farce. He had no warrant from his government; he apparently did not wish to declare himself a filibuster by calling other Americans to his side; the proceedings might afterwards appear more as a personal than a martial action; and he began to remember the "corresponding obligation" he owed the California government for the favors accorded his expedition.[57] Late in the afternoon of the third day the pole bearing the flag fell to the ground, and he took advantage of the incident to tell his men it was an indication they should move their camp. In the middle of the night of March 9–10, therefore, he and his party stole away, Frémont perhaps also explaining, as one of his party suggested,[58] that such were the orders of the consul. The next night they camped, according to General Castro's own witness, only three miles away, and nobody attempted to follow.[59]

The *comandante* knew of the Americans' departure by noon of the 10th and wrote the Mexican Minister of War that he had been ready to attack but that the enemy, taking advantage of the darkness, had abandoned the fortifications, without doubt precipitately.[60] He had felt obliged to stay a few days in the neighborhood, rather than give chase.

Frémont was no more candid in writing to his wife from the Sacramento River.[61] "The Spaniards were somewhat rude and inhospitable below, and ordered us out of the country." His sense of duty had not permitted him to fight, but he had retired slowly and growlingly before a force of three or four hundred men and three pieces of artillery. Without a shadow of cause, the government had suddenly raised the whole country against him, and of course he did not dare to compromise the United States. Though it was in his power to increase his party by many Americans, he had refrained from committing any solitary act of hostility or impropriety. "For my own part, I have become disgusted with everything belonging to the Mexicans." Larkin would say it was well understood that no real attack was contemplated upon Frémont's camp, it all being meant to furnish material for a "high-sounding, flaming dispatch to the central government of Mexico."[62]

General Castro is said to have sent the Englishman John Gilroy to Frémont's camp on the 10th with a message, but the place was abandoned, the fires still burning.[63] Aid was summoned from the north, but the crisis was too soon ended.[64] Still watching at San Juan on the 13th, Castro issued another, somewhat more glorious proclamation.[65] Don J. C. Frémont had abandoned his camp and taken to the Tulares. "Compatriots, the act of unfurling the American flag on the hills, the insults and threats offered to the authorities, are worthy of execration and hatred by Mexicans; prepare then to defend our independence" against those who would "repay with so much ingratitude the favors of our cordiality & benevolence." Larkin could not resist asking, respectfully, for a copy of the document which he had heard was put up in a billiard room (not the usual place). In his full report to the Secretary of State, the consul emphasized that the Americans had not run from the Californians but traveled less distance in three or four days than the natives did in returning to Monterey.[66] That he had retreated at all would rankle in Frémont's soul during the coming months, and the remembrance would serve as a spur and rationale for further action.

Emerging into the valley of the San Joaquín, Frémont and his men found almost a summer temperature and the country "clothed in the floral beauty of spring."

7

First in War

B<small>Y THE MIDDLE</small> of March the whole valley of the San Joaquín was in flower. The evergreen oaks were in bloom and *geranium circutarium* made "on all the uplands a close sward." Frémont and his party were advancing toward the Sacramento again and on the 22nd of March camped at a favorite spot across the American River from Sutter's Fort. Though Sutter noted they were looking out for Californians and thought their actions suspicious, they were only being circumspect while readying themselves for an examination of the Sacramento Valley. Breaking camp on March 24, they moved to Keyser's rancho on Bear River, some thirty miles north. Here the naturalist marveled at the magnificent plants in flower, among them the golden California poppy. "It is the characteristic bloom of *California* at this season, and the Bear River bottoms near the hills were covered with it." Following the Feather River northward, they camped at Theodore Cordua's New Mecklenburg (Marysville) on the Yuba River. They then crossed the Feather and came to Butte Creek, passing some fine ranchos, including that of Samuel Neal, a member of Frémont's expedition of two years before. Fording Pine Creek, on the 30th they reached Peter Lassen's farm on Deer Creek (east of Corning). "The seasons are not yet sufficiently understood," Frémont observed, but Lassen had planted wheat (which "gives large returns"), cotton (experimentally), and a vineyard ("for which the Sacramento Valley is considered to be singularly well adapted"). Here they remained six days. Salmon were abundant in the Sacramento, those they caught being generally three or four feet long.[1]

From Lassen's the party made a week's excursion northward, crossing the Sacramento in canoes on April 6 (probably at Robert Thomes' rancho in Tehama County). The snowy peak of "Shastl" bore directly north, showing high above the other mountains, and towards it they made their way. "It ascends like an immense column upwards of 14,000 feet . . . the summit glistening with snow." Camping beside Cottonwood Creek on April 7, they boated the Sacramento again and came to Cow Creek on the west side, near the head of the Sacramento Valley, encountering many Indian rancherías,[2] wild cattle, and much rain. On April 9 a fierce storm burst upon them, scattering their animals and covering the ground an inch deep with hailstones the size of wild cherries. Whereupon they retraced their steps to Lassen's, arriving on the evening of April 11.

While in the region they held a grand fiesta for a party of American immigrants (and a report seeped into Yerba Buena and Los Angeles that an assembly of armed men, augmented by Indians Frémont would bring from the Columbia, was about to fall upon Monterey).[3] Talbot, who had been sent to Yerba Buena for supplies, rejoined the expedition here, as did Alexis Godey and Tom Martin who had gone to the Tulares to buy animals from the "horse-thief" Indians.[4] Frémont made some astronomical observations, and several of his men joined the settlers in attacking an Indian village (a "perfect butchery" according to Carson).[5] After these diversions, Frémont turned north again on the 24th toward Oregon, intent upon connecting his survey with the line of his 1843–1844 expedition. Leaving the Sacramento River this time at Battle Creek (south of Redding), he skirted Mount Shasta on the right, crossed the Pit River and Big Valley, and on May 6 reached the outlet of Upper Klamath Lake, "a fine, broad stream, not fordable." Ferried across by Indians, they traveled along the east side of the lake for two days and made camp on May 8 at its northern end.[6]

There was no hurry about getting to the Oregon country, if that was what he intended, for there was still snow at the higher levels. He had told both Larkin and Castro that he was headed for Oregon and had written his wife on January 24 and April 1[7] that he would go from Klamath Lake to the "Walamath" Valley, make a reconnaissance of that pass, then return home immediately "by the heads of the Missouri," reaching Westport about the 1st of September. At the beginning of April he had explained to trapper-pioneer James Clyman[8] that his explorations in the Far West were completed, the Californians threatened, and war with Mexico was probable. If peace continued he had no business here; if war ensued he would be outnumbered; and his only option was to make his way eastward with his own company (he was discouraging a merger).

As it happened, he would go no farther than Klamath Lake, though it

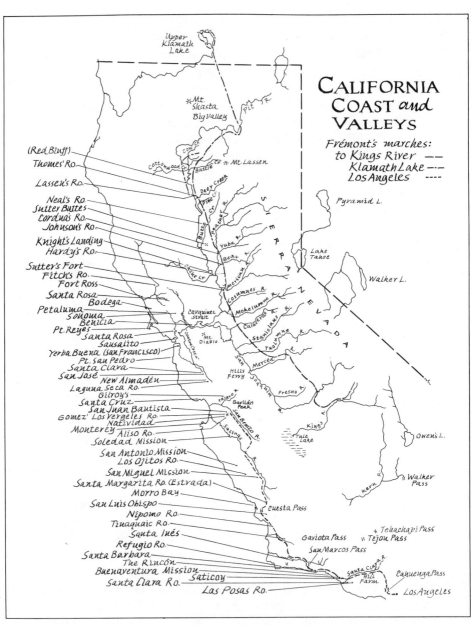

Map of the California coast and valleys, showing mid–nineteenth century place names and Frémont's routes to the Kings River, Klamath Lake, and Los Angeles, 1846–1847.

would not be snow that stood in his way. He did not even mention winter in his letter to Senator Benton of May 24 from the "Sacramento River (Lat. 40°)"[9] but would dwell upon it at the end of July.[10] "Snow was falling steadily and heavily in the mountains . . . in the east, and north, and west, barriers absolutely impassable barred our road . . . I could not bring myself to attempt . . . a passage of these unknown mountains in the dead of winter." (Having already crossed the Cascades in December 1843, surmounted the snow-laden Sierra the following February, and ventured to the 11,000-foot level above the San Joaquín Valley with cattle the past December, he would take even greater risks and more terrible losses in the Rockies in years to follow.)[11]

Late on the day of his arrival, May 8, he caught the faint sound of horses' feet, and two horsemen, Samuel Neal and William Sigler, rode into the circle of firelight. "How fate pursues a man!" They reported that a U.S. officer was two days behind with dispatches and that they were being followed by hostile Indians, whom they had just eluded. In the early dawn, Frémont with ten of his men and the couriers hastened south and at nightfall met Lieutenant Archibald H. Gillespie of the U.S. Marines, who had been trailing him from Sutter's Fort since April 29.[12]

Gillespie, already suspected by the Californians of being a spy, had left New York in the *Petersburgh* with his black servant on November 16, 1845.[13] He bore a dispatch from the President to Consul Larkin[14] and had had private conversations with Polk and the Secretary of State and been appointed special and confidential agent for California to cooperate with Larkin in carrying out his instructions.[15] At the request of Secretary of the Navy Bancroft,[16] he had been given a letter of introduction from the Boston firm of William Appleton & Company to their California agent, Henry Mellus, so that if he were examined en route, the paper would show that he was journeying upon private business. Posing as an invalid merchant traveling for his health, he had reached Vera Cruz on December 10, crossed overland to Mexico City, where he was delayed a month by the Paredes revolution, and continued via Guadalajara and Tepic to Mazatlán on the west coast. There he had been picked up on February 22 by order of Commodore Sloat and taken in the *Cyane* via Honolulu to Monterey,[17] arriving after a stormy passage on April 17 (a month later than planned). From the ship he had written to Larkin, "I send you a letter of introduction which I doubt not you will understand," though it identified him only as a gentleman about to visit the northwest coast on business and bespoke the consul's attention.[18] He had important dispatches, he said, and other sealed packages.

The important letter to Larkin, which Gillespie had memorized, thrown overboard the night before reaching Vera Cruz, then rewritten for delivery,[19] was from the Secretary of State. His other packet—intended as late as October 27 to have gone by the ordinary Mexican mail[20]—was for Frémont and other members of his party.[21] It included letters from the captain's wife, Senator Benton, and James Buchanan, the latter a note of introduction. Though the dispatch to Larkin was highly confidential (and would be so regarded by the State Department forty years after),[22] Frémont's letters proved in the long run to be far more secret, and therefore piquant, since their contents were never revealed. They did not, however, include special instructions from Buchanan, as by some afterwards supposed, for Frémont made this clear to Benton on May 24: "Your letter led me to expect some communication from him, but I *received nothing*."[23]

Larkin's message from the Secretary of State, dated October 17, 1845, had been written soon after Buchanan had received the consul's report of July 10 that Britain was meddling in California's affairs.[24] It had been six months in coming (and the original, entrusted to Commodore Stockton, would not arrive until mid-June).[25] Although not unlike other contemporary letters written by the Secretaries of War and Navy to principals in the conquest, it would have key political consequences. It appointed Larkin Polk's confidential agent for California (in addition to his duties as consul), and his instructions were much like those of John the Baptist, to prepare the way. He was expected to discover and defeat any attempts by foreign powers to gain control of the country; warn the Californians to resist European approaches as ruinous to their interests and freedom; encourage them in their love of liberty and independence; and say that if the people should desire to unite their destiny with that of the United States, "they would be received as brethren" whenever it could be done without just cause of complaint by Mexico. (It was the latter phrase which would remain classified during the next four decades.)[26]

The United States had no ambitions to gratify, the Secretary insisted, and the exercise of compulsion would be repugnant to the principles and inclinations of the American government. Indeed, the true policy for the moment was to let events take their course unless England or France should intervene. For it was clear to the government that immigration from the United States would soon render any European takeover impossible. In short, the Polk administration was prepared to use force against European intervention but would in the meantime conciliate the people toward accepting peaceful annexation or American occupation in case of war. The new agent would receive six dollars a day for his services, plus traveling expenses—a consul was without salary—and Gillespie was to cooperate with him in carrying out his instructions. (Larkin would suggest in return that his remuneration be fixed at $5,000 a year and be assured during Polk's term.)[27]

Larkin had in fact been doing all of these things from the start. This was in effect his normal approach to the Californians as a Boston merchant and consul, and in the process he had become a dependable and respected figure, though an alien, and one who could disarm antagonism with plainness and win allies through soberness and reliability. It had been his boast that he had never made the California government an unreasonable request and therefore never expected a denial and that he had for many years found them well disposed towards him.[28] An American patriot, Larkin, like many other Americans in the country, accepted that whatever favored the United States—or indeed himself—benefited California. Since becoming consul he had already turned over his retail business to Talbot H. Green[29] (though not his credit, land, and brokerage interests) and spent a good deal of time collecting useful information, being observant, conciliating the Californians, communicating with the Secretary of State, and promoting California and his version of the United States' interest. To the editor of the New York *Herald* he wrote that he wished "to keep this country (perhaps my hobby) continually before the public."[30]

It had been a streak of good fortune for the United States that the government had conferred upon Larkin this "delicate and important trust," and he accepted it with unfeigned satisfaction.[31] "I find our Consul," Gillespie reported to the Secretary of the Navy,[32] in "every way worthy of the confidence reposed in him" (though he would afterwards change his stand). On the day his new appointment was received, Larkin straightway wrote letters to three well-known American friends, now Mexican citizens, Jacob P. Leese, J. J. Warner, and Abel Stearns, expressing his views concerning the country's future and soliciting their interest and cooperation.[33] He could now carry on his life's work in collusion with the President of the United States. To celebrate, he gave a grand ball honoring

Gillespie, inviting the elect of the community—one of whom could not believe an American warship would be sent to Monterey just to deliver a "young invalid."[34]

Gillespie's arrival in Monterey aboard a man-of-war caused so much excitement and speculation that he was unable to talk confidentially with many of the people. He did, however, converse with Larkin and two other well-established merchants, Henry Mellus (of William Appleton & Company) and "a very worthy Scotchman," David Spence—and he quickly dispatched to Washington the news that Captain Frémont had pursued a high-minded, honorable course (at Gavilán) and that Don José Castro was a treacherous, cowardly knave.[35] Gillespie had been told by Buchanan that he would probably meet Frémont on the Sacramento and should confer with him and request his aid.[36] So he now wrote Washington that he hoped to overtake Frémont in four days, and if he learned anything of importance would dispatch a courier across the country as directed.[37] He went by horse to Yerba Buena, arriving on the 24th. In his pocket were letters from Larkin to Vice-Consul Leidesdorff, one an introduction, another requesting his attention and best room and accommodation for the visitor.[38] Gillespie was identified as a "Gentleman of much information" who wished to travel through California, had some personal acquaintance with Frémont, and might wish to see him. (But the marine and vice-consul had already met in April 1844, when the *Brandywine*, with Gillespie in command of the marine guard, had visited San Francisco.)[39]

At Yerba Buena, Gillespie received another communication from Larkin,[40] telling of the arrival of the U.S. sloop-of-war *Portsmouth* at Monterey under Captain John B. Montgomery (in response to Larkin's urgent behest of March 9). It also brought news that government officials at Mazatlán were said to have left the town, taking the archives, and that a U.S. naval blockade might be declared the following day. If true, Larkin believed that within a week Commodore Sloat would have a declaration by the United States against Mexico, in which case "we shall see him in a few days to take the Country"! The news was to be forwarded to Sutter's if the lieutenant had already left.[41] Gillespie set out in a whale-boat for the Sacramento on the 25th, horses being too expensive. It will be "Glorious news for Capt Freemont," Leidesdorff wrote the consul, "I thinck I se him smile."[42] The Californians too had received some intelligence, for the prefect, according to the vice-consul, was busy dispatching couriers to "different parts of the country."

William A. Leidesdorff, U.S. vice-consul at Yerba Buena, had met Gillespie in 1844 when the Brandywine, *with the marine aboard, had visited San Francisco Bay.*

Gillespie reached Sutter's Fort on April 28 and departed the following day, with a guide, for the valley above.[43] "He wanted that nobody shall know that he was an officer," Sutter wrote Leidesdorff;[44] but the Swiss had read his name in a list of officers of a man-of-war in a Sandwich Islands newspaper, and his clerk, William Loker, remembered seeing him often in the Navy yard in Washington. Gillespie claimed to have only family letters for Frémont, but Sutter supposed they might be more important, else "Mr. G would not go so far." As a Mexican officer, Sutter also wrote to Castro that Gillespie was a U.S. agent with important dispatches for Frémont, whom he perhaps intended to recall from the northern frontier.[45] And he recommended that the general station a garrison at the fort before the arrival of immigrants in September (he was hoping to sell his establishment to the government).

Gillespie reached Lassen's rancho on May 1, to learn that Frémont was still eight days ahead, and next morning, despite warnings of hostile Indians, he, his servant, and four others set out to overtake him.[46] As earlier noted, they met Frémont at the southern end of Klamath Lake on May 8—three weeks, not four days from Monterey—and the party camped there. After dark, sitting on some "soft stones" around a campfire, Gillespie showed his letter of introduction from Buchanan, addressed to "J. C. Fremont, Esq., Oregon."[47] Like the one to Larkin, it testified to his worth and responsibility but, unlike it, deemed it improbable the two would meet. After delivering Benton's sealed packages, Gillespie gave Frémont a duplicate of Buchanan's instructions to Larkin and acquainted him with their principal objects: "to ascertain the disposition of the California people, to conciliate their feelings in favor of the United States, and to find out, with a design to counteracting, the designs of the British government upon that country."[48]

Gillespie may also have brought across Mexico instructions from the U.S. Secretary of War to Commodore Sloat and been, as Frémont would afterwards say, purposely made acquainted with their import. This would have been Bancroft's letter of October 17, 1845, the same date as Larkin's instructions.[49] In it the Secretary told Sloat that in the event of "actual hostilities" (revising his original order requiring a declaration of war)[50] he was, as earlier directed, to take San Francisco Bay and blockade or occupy such other ports as his forces warranted. Otherwise, he was carefully to avoid anything which might be construed as an act of aggression. He was to keep in touch with Larkin (there was no mention of Frémont), discover any English and French designs, ascertain the temper and disposition of the people, and do everything proper to conciliate the most friendly regard of the people of California. Except for the provisions respecting hostilities—which were in the province of Navy and War, not State—the instructions from Polk through his Cabinet members were essentially identical.

So Frémont and Gillespie talked about whatever two just-over-30 co-adventurers would find most engrossing at such a dramatic time in their newly entwined careers, away out there in the Oregon wilds at so critical a period in their country's history. Frémont, while at the Alvires–Fisher rancho in February, had already intimated to an American settler, John

John A. Sutter, a Mexican magistrate, wrote to General Castro that Gillespie was a U.S. agent with important dispatches for Frémont.

Marsh, that the present year would bring "great changes." [51] Gillespie's news from Larkin that Mexican officials had left Mazatlán with the archives presumed the imminence of war, and that Commodore Sloat might soon arrive was electrifying. Larkin had told Castro, he said, that in his opinion "our Flag may fly here in thirty days" (though he preferred the change to be peaceful), and he believed the leaders of California were fast preparing themselves for coming events. [52] As for Gillespie's own advices, he must have spoken of Mexico's notorious inattention to California and of its failure to avenge the ousting of Micheltorena in 1845, in his view "leaving California apparently independent." [53] Though he had left Washington and Mazatlán before hostilities had commenced, he must have given assurance of Polk's interest in California; mentioned the troop movements he had observed in Mexico;[54] noted the presence of British and French squadrons in the Pacific; and reported, as he had to Bancroft, that British cruisers were constantly watching the movements of American vessels.[55] And he had been delighted to hear Americans at San José volunteer that they were "very decidedly in favor of a change."[56] What Benton's letter revealed has never been disclosed; but among other matters of "friendship and family details," Frémont found passages which he would characterize in 1848 as "enigmatical and obscure" but which he studied out to mean he should discover any foreign schemes and counteract them.[57] Bancroft's letter to Sloat (if known to Gillespie) was itself an augury of war. The talk around the fire could have been heady.

However it was that dark Oregon night, the future appeared so bright to the captain and lieutenant that Frémont, sitting late by the fire cherishing the letters from home and perhaps fretting over the lack of a direct communication from Buchanan, did not post a guard. Indians had followed Gillespie's steps for a couple of days, showing signs of friendship, but they were now lurking in the wings, waiting for the firelight to die down. About midnight, after Frémont had taken to his blankets beneath cedar branches reaching almost to the ground, they attacked, killing three of his men with tomahawks and arrows (one of them Frémont's long-time companion and follower, Canadian trapper Basil Lajeunesse).[58] Next day the small party joined the main company on the lake,[59] turned the northern end, and headed south toward Lassen's—indiscriminately revenging themselves upon the Indians by killing and burning whenever opportunity offered.[60]

Long years afterward Frémont would assert that through the Bentons he had been made thoroughly familiar with the government's intentions and been given discretion to act.[61] "I knew that the men who understood the future of the country . . . regarded the California coast as the boundary fixed by nature to round off our national domain." He had left Washington with full knowledge of their wishes and was called upon to do whatever he could to further their designs.[62] In retrospect, he contended that the information brought by Gillespie absolved him from his responsibility as an explorer and left him to do his duty as an officer of the American Army.[63] And he had the knowledge, on the authority of the Secretary of the Navy, that the government intended to take California.[64]

Looking away back, at the end of his career, Frémont construed his "private" instructions to have been, if needed, to foil England by carrying the war with Mexico into California. Whereupon he had decided that the orders to conciliate the Californians were no longer practicable, and he and Gillespie dropped the idea from their minds. "Then I knew my hour had come," he recalled dramatically. "I resolved . . . to return forthwith to the Sacramento Valley and bring all the influence I could command. This decision was the first step in the conquest of California." [65]

While President Polk only said of his interview with Gillespie that his "secret instructions & the letter to Mr. Larkin . . . will explain the object of his mission," [66] it is reasonable to infer that the two charges were not contradictory. If Gillespie's orders were more belligerent than all the rest, that they were not communicated to the Navy and the American consul—assuring Frémont some cooperation and protection and putting other U.S. agents on the *qui vive*—is at least perplexing. Gillespie would tell a Senate committee in 1848 that he had been instructed to watch over the interests of the United States, counteract the influence of foreign agents, conciliate the feelings of the people, and acquaint Frémont with his and Larkin's instructions. [67] To the same inquiry Frémont would respond in a similar vein, then state plainly that the revolutionary movement had been without expressed authority from the United States, having been carried out in self-defense. [68] In another context, and stressing the importance of secret instructions, he would declare that in giving them their "broadest interpretation," it was probable that he "did more, & more promptly, than had been expected" [69] (a hero never plays second-best).

Telling his men that he had orders from the United States to return to California, [70] Frémont turned toward Peter Lassen's farm, which he reached on May 24 "from an excursion to the Upper Sacramento," as his *Geographical Memoir* to Congress laconically recites. [71] From here Gillespie notified Larkin of their whereabouts, sending the news by Samuel Neal and asking for the same, particularly inquiring about vessels of war, specifically the *Congress*. [72] There had been "too much snow upon the mountains to cross," he explained, and Frémont "goes home from here." The same day Frémont wrote Senator Benton [73] a guarded note, he afterwards said, that he would proceed directly home by the Colorado. But the burden of his letter was the presence of a British post on the Umpqua River (the trade in furs would not justify it) and the relations of these people with the Indians, who were "unfriendly to us." He wanted Benton to remind Buchanan that in case of war with England they must be driven out.

As Larkin had informed Gillespie, the *Portsmouth* had arrived at

Monterey on the 22nd, with instructions to protect American citizens and conciliate the natives.[74] Now, with Gillespie's letter of May 24 in hand, he asked Captain Montgomery to take the vessel to San Francisco, where it arrived with Neal aboard by June 3.[75] Neal brought more letters from Larkin to Gillespie and Frémont, carrying the latest news: of a proposed *junta* of Californians at Santa Barbara, the widening breach between Castro and Pico, and an allusion to an English agent promoting a British protectorate.[76]

Knowing that potential aid was at hand, Frémont moved south to Neal's ranch on Deer Creek and sent Gillespie to Montgomery with a requisition for supplies, prefacing it with a note—in case the Navy was reluctant—that they would materially aid the surveys and expedite his return to the States.[77] The order included a very respectable war chest of 300 pounds of American rifle lead, a keg of powder, and 8,000 percussion caps, plus camp supplies; and Montgomery would send the aid, including $1,500 in cash, "all I required."[78] Gillespie set out from Deer Creek on May 28, left Cordua's on the Feather River the following day in a canoe, and arrived at Sutter's that night, traveling hard. Here he learned of an expected attack by Castro upon the Americans,[79] but it was not so imminent a peril that he could not sail on June 1. Delayed by contrary winds, he did not reach the *Portsmouth* until the 7th or return to Sutter's landing until the 12th (two days after the Americans' first strike).

From away back the California government had been apprehensive if exceedingly tolerant of foreigners in the country (1840 and the "Graham affair" having been the year of exasperation).[80] But repeated warnings of war with the United States and Frémont's ominous extravaganza on Gavilán had made the presence of aliens, particularly Americans, a matter of grave concern. It would probably have been the greatest cause of anxiety had not the chronic struggles for power and precedence among the factions interfered, but the dissensions Californians were heir to—betwixt military and civil authorities, north and south, and competing leaders—had become endemic.[81] After Micheltorena and his unruly *paisanos* had been expelled in March 1845, Pío Pico and José Castro had become civil and military chiefs (as earlier noted). The governor and capital were thus settled in Los Angeles, while the *comandante* and customhouse, with the funds, were at Monterey—and most of the country's antagonisms were neatly lined up on two irreconcilable sides. (If there were no customhouse, Larkin observed, there would be no revolution, and everyone could "get his own living.")[82]

A Californian, Pío Pico, became civil governor after the expulsion of Micheltorena and moved the capital from Monterey to Los Angeles.

The all-southern legislative assembly* began meeting in Los Angeles on March 2, 1846,[83] and at the end of the month (with Frémont ambling toward Oregon) Castro called a military *junta* at Monterey.[84] Each leader pressed the other to meet him, always at a place suited to the proponent's convenience. The governor proclaimed the supremacy of the civil arm, his right under Mexican law to two-thirds of the revenue, and his power to command the military. The general declared the country's prime concern to be foreign invasion and security a military function. Both sent representatives to Mexico to solicit fiscal and military aid and lodge mutual complaints.

A report was received in Los Angeles on April 15 of General Castro's trouble with Frémont, accompanied by a proclamation of March 8, requesting all citizens to place themselves under his orders[85]—a move perceived in the south as an attempt to seize political power. What right had a soldier to appeal directly to the people! The *junta* at Monterey had, moreover, recognized Paredes as Mexico's president (he had assigned all provincial funds to the military) and protested the acts of his predecessor, Herrera (who had appointed Pico governor).[86] The *junta* had also concluded that Castro's presence in the north was indispensable. The governor should be invited to Monterey to help save the country; and if he would not come, the general should establish his headquarters at Santa Clara and proceed as it seemed best under the circumstances.[87]

Pablo de la Guerra was sent south to seek a meeting of the leaders and inform Pico of the critical condition of the country—provoking Stearns' riposte that the *gentleman at the north* must suppose the southerners were less well acquainted with public affairs than he.[88] Larkin too wanted the governor and some of the legislature to come to Monterey and offered to pay Stearns a hundred dollars toward his expenses and be his host for several weeks.[89] He thought the *junta* might declare California independent, though he believed it would be premature.

Meantime the assembly at Los Angeles—alarmed by the actions of the *junta*, disturbed by their inability to stop the influx of foreigners, dismayed by the prospect of new Mexican troops without funds for their maintenance, and unable to find a solution to their country's overwhelming troubles—themselves called a *junta* of all the towns of California to be held at Santa Barbara on June 15.[90] To consider the grave circum-

---

* Called earlier the *diputación* and *junta departmental*, it was officially named the *asamblea* in the Mexican constitution of 1843.

stances in which California was placed, it was also to discuss, according to citizen Stearns, the "Squandering away in a most Scandelous manner the publick funds" at Monterey, the security of the peoples' rights, and perhaps a declaration of independence.[91] It was to comprise eighteen representatives from the towns, seven from the assembly, and not to exceed five (each) military and ecclesiastical members. Pico's pronouncement reached Monterey by May 21 and was posted by the prefect.[92] Suspicions on both sides, however, and Castro's adamant and vehement opposition[93] to Pico's civil rather than military means (and perhaps to an audit of his books) soon caused the proposal to be abandoned.

A rumor meanwhile spread that the Santa Barbara *junta* meant to declare the country independent and propose an English, American, or French protectorate. Thirty years afterwards, Pico would state that independence was much discussed in Los Angeles at the time and he was urged to proclaim it.[94] He sent an emissary to Mexico, he said, to obtain means to fight invasion, failing which the English Navy was to be urged to assume a protectorate should a rebellion in California occur. He asked Castro to come south to help make an arrangement (but he may have feared imprisonment). Meantime, both Stearns and Warner believed the people, particularly the "most respectable part," would join the United States if they were sure of immediate protection.[95] As for Larkin, he regretted the cancellation of the meeting, where he would have found many opportunities to transact business.[96]

On May 25, Pico learned from Manuel Castro that a band of foreigners had been feted by Frémont on the Sacramento and were about to fall upon Monterey.[97] The reports of approaching war, he said, the ambitions of the United States, and Frémont's presence and his raising an American flag should persuade the governor how serious was the country's position. Though Pico wrote to Mexico the same day of "armed adventurers" in the north,[98] he and the assembly persisted in regarding every action of the *comandante* as a pretext for seizing power, deposing Pico, and attacking the south. The assembly authorized the governor on June 3 to take all necessary steps to save the country and (in secret) suspended General Castro until order could be restored;[99] they would take the offensive, adopting Castro's devices. Pico had concluded, he afterwards said, that both he and Castro could not exist together in the department.[100] On June 16 he set out from Los Angeles with a military force, eighty strong by the time he reached San Buenaventura and to receive another accretion at Santa Barbara on the 21st.[101]

In Pico's absence, reports came to Los Angeles (false as they proved) of Castro marching south with seventy men and news on June 22 of his declaration on June 8 of martial law.[102] A meeting of citizens was quickly called by subprefect Stearns (Larkin's confidential correspondent), who, with some eighty men—twenty-five of them foreigners—enunciated their resistance to Castro. The *ayuntamiento* of the pueblo then organized companies of artillery, riflemen, and cavalry for self-defense.

In the north, Castro had been trying to raise a force, as approved by the *junta*, without much success.[103] On June 8 he wrote a most extravagant letter to Pico,[104] railing against the unlawful *junta* announced for Santa Barbara. Probably the most virulently eloquent of all the documents of the period, Larkin thought it "certainly well wrote" but hardly expected between the two leaders under the circumstances.[105] "Oh execrable profanation!" it declaimed. "Unheard of unfaithfulness." And it concluded by saying that Castro had repeatedly represented to the governor the dangerous situation of the country and the necessity to take measures for its defense but had been unable to reckon upon his cooperation. He found himself, therefore, under the indispensable necessity to declare the department under a state of siege, to be maintained with all the vigor of martial law. This was the declaration that on June 22 had struck the southerners as a blatant attempt "to erect an absolute dictatorship to the prejudice of all guaranties." Even some of the northerners were suspicious. Each side was willing to perish under the ruins of *la patria* if not to subscribe to a common cause. But the Californians, though bellicose, were seldom sanguinary.

Then, suddenly—at Santa Clara on June 15, near Santa Barbara on the 23rd, and at Los Angeles on the 24th—the military and civil leaders, all poised to fall upon one another, received startling news from Sonoma. That post on the northern frontier had on the 14th been captured by armed Americans![106]

Who was behind the uprising? Frémont, Gillespie, Larkin?

Larkin had been carefully instructed by the U.S. Secretary of State to conciliate the Californians, impress upon them the advantages to be enjoyed under American rule, and subvert any schemes by Europeans to take possession. His relations with the natives were fundamentally amicable and peaceful, and both as consul and merchant he did not favor rebellion. Gillespie, "a Gentleman in whom the President reposes entire confidence," was expected to cooperate with Larkin in carrying out the consul's instructions; and he had been ordered to reveal to Frémont the nature of Larkin's confidential letter.

Larkin's peaceful role as consul and confidential agent was congenial to him as civilian and merchant, though as secret agent (and perhaps as trader) his relations with the Californians lacked something of candor and his reports to the Secretary of State and press of scrupulous exactness. "I am remarkably well situated with this government and its people," he had written in 1842.[107] He never meddled seriously in their politics or spoke against their laws, modes, or religion. In traveling among the people he had always found something both to praise and to blame. They appeared to be satisfied with him, he said; why should he not be so with them? No less ardent an American in 1846, he still professed as trader to "prefer everything as it is." The time and country were good enough for him (revolution, certainly, being unsettling to business).[108]

Of the other two U.S. agents, Gillespie was an officer of the Marines, Frémont of the Army, and the latter headed a tough and perhaps oversize band of explorer-fighters. Their habits and demeanor were more likely to be authoritarian than permissive, their disposition to fight instead of parley and to take action rather than refrain. Neither, when opposed, was an apt conciliator. All three men were independent and resourceful, else they would not have reached the far Far West; and each had characteristics and goals which colored every thought and action. They shared the same general objective in respect to the "change" which everyone expected. Their presence and behavior would powerfully affect the conflict to follow.

There were others who harbored similar aspirations. Lansford W. Hastings, for one, had thought to bring ten thousand immigrants from the United States and become president of a Pacific republic (he was out wheedling credulous immigrants to follow his new route).[109] Foreigners on the spot, including Sutter and Marsh[110] (who would embrace Oregon) hankered to make California another Texas and themselves Sam Houstons. Even T. J. Farnham, who wrote many outlandish things about California, expressed to his friend Marsh the strongest desire of his heart that a "Republic of California" should arise; but he would not be ready until the following winter when he and his family would return with "10 to 20 thousand emigrants" to "authorise" the proceedings.[111]

The influence of the newcomers was already evident. Frémont's coming with a military force in December 1845, his appearance at Monterey and departure from Gavilán, the arrival of a U.S. officer with dispatches in mid-April, the advent of the sloop-of-war *Portsmouth* and its anchorage at San Francisco—amid constant talk of war—caused a ferment among both foreigners and natives. Then Frémont and Gillespie came back from the north in May, advancing from Lassen's to Neal's rancho and, on the 30th, to the Buttes below. To Americans in the Napa and Sacramento valleys, as to many Californians, these events were portents.

War rumors had long been circulating in the United States, Mexico, and California.[112] Locally there were inflaming reports of forces afoot in the north and south; of fomenting Indians to destroy crops and drive off stock; of anti-foreign proclamations; of the expulsion of the Americans; and of the intent of the Californians to take over the immigrants' mecca, New Helvetia. And there was a real *bando*[113] announcing that only naturalized foreigners could hold land and that aliens without passports would be subject to expulsion from the country "whenever the government finds it convenient" (the final six words were crucial). Some of the flames were fanned by aggressive and footloose foreigners to gain support from the more law-abiding class, but many of the settlers doubtless accepted the reports as credible.

True, Frémont had not been attacked by Castro in March, and in May Larkin thought he might walk the streets of Monterey without restraint.[114] Former Governor Alvarado had in April invited officers of the U.S. warship *Cyane* to a dance at Monterey. And General Castro had on May 9 organized a day-long "picnik party" for Captain Montgomery and his men twelve or fourteen miles in the country, a courtesy Montgomery returned with a "vaile" in the Government House on May 15.[115] Repeatedly, Larkin had informed the Secretary of State, eastern newspapers, and his friends in several ports that the Californians were well disposed toward foreigners—particularly Americans—disenchanted with Mexico, and expected political change.[116] Even Gillespie, in April, was prepared to travel unattended cross-country from Yerba Buena to Lassen's, had horses not been so expensive.[117] Frémont himself would spike the guns at Fort Point on July 1 without interference, and next day Robert Semple and two Americans would roam the streets of Yerba Buena and capture a Mexican citizen without opposition.

A main article of the settlers' bill of complaint against the Mexican regime was that they had come to California—been "invited to the country," as Gillespie was pleased to report[118]—expecting not only to settle there with their families but to live under a republican government.

These promises were soon broken, and they were threatened with extermination if they did not depart. Insofar as this pertained to California (rather than, say, the Oregon country), it was of course the grossest fiction.

Admission to any Mexican territory was governed by regulations issued on May 1, 1828, requiring passports, *cartas de seguridad* for internal travel, and other documents.[119] A general colonization law of August 18, 1824,[120] as afterwards amended, controlled the granting of public land. In 1830 Governor Echeandía had been specifically directed to distribute land to foreigners who complied with the law[121] (requiring naturalization, acceptance of the Catholic faith, and other accommodations), though Americans and Russians were to remain a minority and away from the islands and coast. Two years later the government asserted the right to expel non-naturalized foreigners whose stay might be inimical to public order.[122] Orders were received during 1839 and 1840 emphasizing compliance by foreigners with the law,[123] and the Californians were actually moved in the latter year to expel a number of threatening individuals who were illegally in the country.[124] Next year it was ordered that immigrants without legal passports not be permitted to remain and that even settlers must depart if they did not procure *cartas de seguridad*.[125]

Emigration to California was widely publicized in the United States, and newspapers openly spoke of it as a step toward annexation. Such sentiments of course reached Mexico, causing instant alarm, and Mexican representatives abroad were instructed to announce that persons going there without the consent of the Mexican government would do so at their own peril. In December 1842, the Mexican minister in Washington affirmed the falsity of reports that Mexico would make large grants of land to aliens;[126] the government, he said, had never thought of colonizing California with foreigners, and the encouragement to emigrants was a scheme of land speculators who wished to take advantage of the credulity of the ignorant.

But even after the Graham affair in 1840, strangers arriving in a seemly manner had no difficulty obtaining the necessary passports to reside or travel.[127] Members of the Bidwell party of 1841 proceeded to the coast for their papers, were arrested at San José as a formality, but pleaded ignorance of the law as was commonly done. They were already in the country, could not be driven back, and were granted temporary passes until well-known citizens became bondsmen for their good behavior. The country had the dire alternative, *Comandante* Vallejo said, of consenting to what it could not prevent or commanding without being able to enforce.[128]

Nor did Commodore Jones' overreaction in 1842 raise the expected furor. Nevertheless, the Mexican government took notice and sent an order of July 14, 1843, to California and other northern states. It not being proper for natives of the United States to reside in the department, it read, they were to quit it within a reasonable period to be fixed by the local governor; and persons from the United States were henceforth not to be permitted to enter.[129] (Upon observing that the law was discriminatory, an insistent American minister in Mexico would be assured it did not apply exclusively to American citizens.)[130] Although Santa Anna was apparently in deadly earnest in decreeing on June 17, 1843, that foreigners taken with arms were to be immediately shot, all continued to be welcomed in California; and Micheltorena, the last Mexican governor, perhaps more than all his predecessors, was favorably disposed toward them.[131]

Early in September 1845, Mexican dispatches announced that war would be declared immediately, and Governor Pico published a proclamation to "fly to arms."[132] At mid-month came an order of July 10 prohibiting the immigration of families "from the Missouri and Columbia."[133] Another, of July 19, instructed General Castro to put all the towns in a state of defense[134] (whereupon the *comandante* petitioned for reinforcements).

Castro toured the north in November to ascertain the number and distribution of foreigners.[135] To representatives at Sonoma he read the July 10 order and asked for passports, which the newcomers did not possess, saying their destination had been Oregon. Upon stating their peaceful intentions and that they would obey the law and depart in the spring if their petitions to settle were not granted, they were permitted to remain. In a decree of November 6 he noted that since most of the immigrants were families and industrious people and Mexicans were distinguished by their sentiments of hospitality, he deemed it best to permit them to reside provisionally in the department. A similar arrangement was made at Sutter's Fort on November 11; and Larkin wrote next day that the subprefect at Yerba Buena had told him that any Americans who applied through Leidesdorff would be given temporary credentials.[136]

Nevertheless, the Californians realized their predicament. The alarming influx of foreigners could not be prevented. Assistance from the Mexican government was improbable, but if troops came without their own support, the condition of the people would be deplorable. Furthermore, the administration of justice was capricious; government orders were not respected; no force was at hand to support the authorities; and public funds were diverted—there was a complete state of disorganization. Angustias de la Guerra Ord, one of the notable señoras of Monterey, would recall with candor and forgiveness that the conquest did not bother the Californians, "least of all the women."[137] California was on the road to most complete ruin, she would say. The Indians were out of hand, and there was the greatest antagonism between north and south, the Californians and Mexicans. Worst of all was the plundering which was carried on generally. Castro maintained a corps of officers sufficient for an army of three thousand, of whom few offered their services when the need came.

There was of course an enduring, residual streak of loyalty to Mexico inbred in most of the Californians which irresistibly came to the fore, in spite of all vexations, when they were attacked or their allegiance questioned. The malicious and unprovoked threat to their lives and sovereignty by insurgents in the north comprised such a provocation.

Subsequently, Frémont would explain to Senator Benton that many in his camp and throughout the country thought he should not have retreated in March from Gavilán, and it was the opinion of the officers of the squadron that he could not again retreat "consistently with any military reputation."[138] Having, therefore, carefully examined his position and foreseen all the consequences, he determined by June 6 to take such anticipatory measures as would seem to him most expedient to protect his party and justify his character. He would lay great emphasis upon self-defense and protecting the settlers against Castro's attacks;[139] but if he were minded, as a responsible leader, to verify any of the rumors wildly circulating among the Americans on the frontier, he made no attempt to question Larkin, with whom he was expected to cooperate, or other dependable informants. His proper course, he independently concluded, was to observe quietly the progress of affairs and "take advantage of any contingency" which he could turn to the profit of the United States.[140]

Frémont rode down to the Buttes from Neal's rancho on May 30, finding the temperature at noon to be 90°, the game fat and abundant.[141] Neal and Samuel Hensley, who had brought the most stirring rumors to Frémont's ears, had gone ahead to arouse the settlers in their own defense, urging them to meet at Frémont's camp.[142] "Notice is hereby given, that a large body of armed Spaniards on horseback, amounting to 250 men, has been seen on their way to the Sacramento valley, destroying crops, burning the houses, and driving off the cattle. Capt. Fremont invites every freeman in the valley to come to his camp at the Buttes, immediately." So read the notice delivered to William B. Ide by an Indian on June 8. Frémont proposed, said Ide, who heard it from him personally, not a declaration of independence but what Ide called, with some insight, *neutral conquest*, to provoke General Castro to strike the first blow. And the inflammatory task of making depredations and capturing some of the prominent Californians would be committed to roving Americans who had nothing to lose and everything to gain. Frémont himself would have no part in the action—but the immigrants had suffered indignities enough, he said, to justify any measures they might take.[143] Announcing that he would wait two weeks at the most before returning to the States, he moved his camp another square toward Sutter's Fort.*

Like Polk, Frémont awaited good tidings from the field.

---

* Frémont had arrived at Lassen's on May 24, two days later was at Neal's rancho, moved on the 29th to Bear River and to the Buttes the following day, leaving there on June 8 and camping on the American Fork on June 12 (FRE-MONT-1 498, 502, 509, 518).

8

The Bears

HE STARS were propitious. *Comandante* Castro, who had been trying to organize a force at Santa Clara—Larkin thought against
Pico[1]—had gone across San Francisco Bay to Sonoma at the beginning of
June to see the commandant of the frontier, General Mariano Guadalupe
Vallejo.[2] From him he obtained about two hundred horses, and on the
8th Lieutenants Arce and Alviso, with an escort, began to drive them by
way of William Knight's place across the Sacramento, American, and
Cosumnes rivers toward Santa Clara. Knight and others of course hurried the news to Frémont, along with a rumor that Castro was advancing
to drive the settlers from the country. Here, then, was a ready-made
"opening to commence business."

Quickly, a small party set out from Frémont's camp in pursuit, headed
by the hard-bitten ex-trapper and naturalized Mexican citizen Ezekiel
Merritt (whom Frémont described as fearless and simple, and Josiah
Royce later characterized as a man "of no great reputation for all virtues").[3] Arce and his men stayed the night of the 8th at Sutter's Fort and
the 9th at Martin Murphy's rancho on the south bank of the Cosumnes.
There, the next morning, the Americans surprised the party and relieved
them of most of their animals. When Arce protested that they had been
taken unawares, Merritt offered to return the horses, let them make a signal when they were ready, and he and his men would "try them again"
(or such was Larkin's story).[4] The Californians were then released to
carry the news that the seizure of Sonoma and New Helvetia was the
next step in the revolution.[5] Frémont the spectator "highly applauded"
the act, according to Ide, who was on hand when they returned.[6]

Although Frémont did not take part in this guerrilla maneuver (one or
two of his mountain men may have been with Merritt's party), his pres-

ence gave a sufficient warrant to the more intrepid characters—and in a letter to Benton, a deposition to Congress, and indeed until his death, he would take personal responsibility for the action.[7] Arce of course reported the whole affair to Castro, who again invited the cooperation of the civil authorities to oppose what he now properly judged to be an overture to invasion.[8] Larkin too heard of the filibustering movement after it had happened and wrote the Castros on the 14th that he would be pleased to assist the authorities in recovering the animals if a feasible method could be pointed out to him.[9] He had been at Santa Clara on the 8th and 9th (where some fifty Californians were gathered), consulting the "great guns and big bugs," and he visited José Castro again before reporting to Secretary Buchanan on the 18th what he knew of the affair.[10]

Meanwhile, the captured horses had been taken to Frémont's camp;[11] and on the 12th Merritt and his party, now increased to twenty-one, set off for Sonoma, intent upon further inciting Castro, consolidating their position, and obtaining animals, arms, and hostages.[12] They did not take the main road by way of Suscol along the north shore of the Bay but a route up Cache Creek, through Berreyesa, Pope, and Napa valleys, and to Bale's mill (north of St. Helena) on the 13th.[13] William Todd, John Grigsby, and the Kelseys were picked up along the way, and the force had grown to over thirty by the time they climbed the ridge into Sonoma Valley and arrived before Vallejo's house about dawn of June 14. Though this was technically a garrison town on the *frontera del norte*, the soldiers had been dispersed in 1844, and the residue of cannon, musketry, and ammunition may have belonged to the government, though Vallejo had not surrendered it to Castro a few days before.

On a quiet Sunday morning General Vallejo was awakened to find his home surrounded by armed men whose aspect was not reassuring. They were disorderly, rumpled, and begrimed. Some wore buckskin pants, some blue pants reaching only to the knee; several had no shirts; and many were without shoes. A few wore coyote or wolfskin hats, others slouched hats full of holes or straw hats "as black as charcoal." A marauding band of horse thieves, trappers, and runaway sailors, as a native would observe, they were "about as rough a looking set of men as one could well imagine."[14]

When Vallejo had donned his uniform as an officer of the Mexican Army, he opened the door, but little progress was made until the American resident (and Vallejo's brother-in-law) Jacob P. Leese was summoned as interpreter. When Leese inquired why Vallejo was being arrested,

Robert Semple, "6 feet 6 inches high and about 15 inches in diameter"—whom Mrs. Leese afterwards styled the "least unhuman of that god-forsaken crowd"—plainly stated that their objective was to make California free and that General Vallejo had influence and a great deal of property and arms which they required. If he understood them rightly, Vallejo replied, they could consider him one of them, for foreigners had always had his protection, and they would find no opposition. He also knew that the Californians were on the eve of asking protection from the United States (or so Leese and Lieutenant Joseph Revere recorded).[15]

There seemed to be no leader among the mediators—Merritt, Semple, and Knight—and no plan, except to seize arms, animals, and hostages. Guaranties were at length drawn up. The Californians, who believed Frémont was somehow responsible, agreed not to take up arms. The Americans gave assurance that they would not molest peaceful citizens or take more property than was needed for their immediate purpose. Though Leese had expected to see U.S. troops, Semple and the others claimed no such authority, only opposition to Castro's threat to oust all foreigners.[16]

But to the impatient outsiders, negotiations in the house seemed to be interminable, and John Grigsby was elected captain and sent to investigate. He did not soon return, and Ide followed. Vallejo's brandy, with which he was proverbially generous, may have played a part in the intolerable delay (Ide said the bottles had well nigh vanquished the captors), and a barrel brought up by Olivier Beaulieu was very likely a catalyst to the growing impatience in the yard. When the capitulations were at last signed, the men refused to ratify them as they stood and insisted that General Vallejo, Lieutenant Colonel Victor Prudon, and Captain Salvador Vallejo not be released under oath but sent as prisoners to Frémont's camp. Probably the Californians deemed it safer to go, though fearing for their families. The insurgents then appropriated whatever munitions lay about, seized the always strategic supply of horses, and locked up the alcalde and such other citizens as could be found. But while there was much drinking and excitement, the men were apparently dissuaded by their natural leaders, particularly Semple and Ide, from wholesale plunder. That Merritt, Semple, and Grigsby left Sonoma on the 14th with the prisoners may have shown a not-too-subtle lack of confidence in the company; or they may have been deputized to encourage Frémont's move to Sonoma. Grigsby did resign from the party (according to Ide), declaring he had been deceived into believing the operation was under Frémont's orders.[17] And Vallejo, fearing for the noncombatants, privately

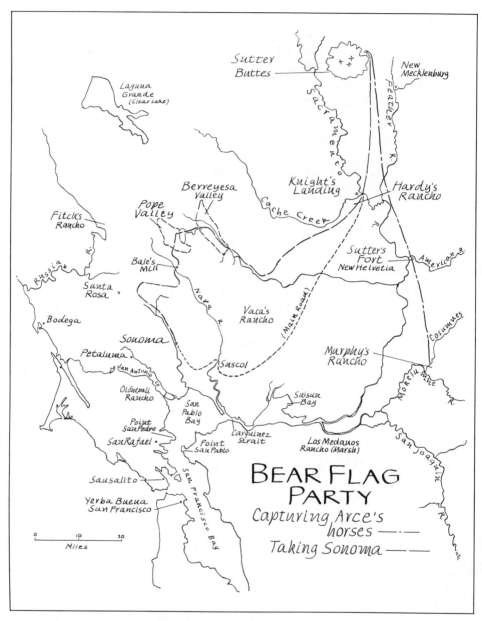

Route of the Bear Flag party from Sutter's Fort to Murphy's rancho and to Sonoma, a move to incite Castro, strengthen the settlers' position, and procure animals, arms, and hostages.

sent José de la Rosa to Captain Montgomery at Sausalito, requesting his protection.[18]

The first night out, at Vaca's rancho, some Californians under Juan Padilla aroused General Vallejo while the guard slept, offering to effect his escape, but he refused, expecting imminent freedom and fearing bloodshed.[19] The next night they stayed at Thomas Hardy's rancho on the Sacramento, buying there a "beav & other provisions" (for $12),[20] and on the 16th reached Frémont's camp at Sutter's landing (the main party being on the American River, some three leagues away).[21] Here Vallejo, anticipating immediate release or probation, was received in a most unsympathetic and aloof manner. Frémont, disclaiming any responsibility for the filibusters, hustled them all off—Leese now being found guilty by association—to be confined in Sutter's Fort.[22] Thus Vallejo, the settlers' friend, Leese, an American, and Prudon, who had been trying to induce the Californians to declare themselves favorable to annexation by the United States,[23] were the first victims of aggression. With Salvador Vallejo, José Noriega, Vicente Peralta, Julio Carrillo, Robert Ridley, and whoever else happened along, they would be held without charges or trial until released by U.S. naval officers in August in spite of Frémont's hard-line injunction. Taking the hint, Sutter declared himself in favor of the new movement and resigned his Mexican commission.[24]

The revolt at Sonoma was fast falling apart for lack of a rationale, the diversified motivations, opinions, and intentions of the crowd now showing through. Some were apprehensive about rebellion without Frémont's assured support—and he eighty horseback miles away. Among the insurgents[25] were farmers, hunters, and adventurers from the western frontier, some by way of Oregon, a few ex-sailors, and one of Frémont's men. Save one, they had arrived since 1841, almost half by a single migration, the Grigsby–Ide party of 1845. All now hailed from the Sacramento—from the environs of New Helvetia and Sonoma northward to Tehama. There were reckless and unprincipled fellows with nothing to lose but their lives who would as soon fight Californians as Indians to gratify a taste for violence, revenge, and personal advantage. Others, restless and careless of Mexican rights, were carriers of Manifest Destiny who sought by espousing independence and annexation to the United States to secure land and freedom, even power and wealth. Some were there only in self-defense; though ready to believe the worst about Mexicans they had probably seldom met, and to disapprove of any way of life they might devise, they were in their own ways peaceful, law-abiding individuals, living beyond the reach of the Californians' rule.

Grigsby having defected on the 14th, the man of the hour soon proved to be William B. Ide, the indispensable philosopher and rhetorician of an otherwise amorphous party. A man of austere Pilgrim descent who as a teacher, jack-of-all trades, and farmer had moved from Massachusetts to Vermont and then to Ohio and Illinois, he had arrived in California in the Grigsby–Ide party only the year before. Earnest and sincere, and with some advantages of education, he became the almost fanatical head of a movement which was in fact too tenuous and disorderly to accept solemnly his theoretical and ethical discourse and his pretensions as founding father. But Ide did have the idealism and declamatory flair required to draw the members together. "*Saddle no horse for me,*" he cried in the face of their indecision; "I will lay my bones here" before accepting the ignominy of commencing an honorable work and then fleeing "like cowards, like thieves. . . . In vain will you say you had honorable motives! Who will believe it? . . . Choose ye this day what you will be! We are robbers, or we *must* be conquerors!" The latter unimpeachable truth, arrayed in Biblical attire, may have been the clincher; for the men, now decreased to twenty-four, rallied around Ide and elected him their commander (or, it may be, as one participant remembered, they viewed it all as an amusing farce).[26]

Not surprisingly, their first two acts were to raise a banner and issue a proclamation. It would have been cheering but hardly lawful to fly the Stars and Stripes, to which certainly most of the rebels gave their allegiance. Instead, they concocted a flag with a whitish field supported by a red flannel stripe (reminiscent of the American flag) and a red star in the upper left-hand corner (remindful of Texas). To the right of the star appeared the flag's novel element, a rough representation of a grizzly bear— a ferocious animal, "an emblem of strength and unyielding resistance," well known in the country (some thought it looked like a pig). Below was rudely lettered in black, "California Republic." Such was the emblem of the *Bears*, raised on the 14th where only the Mexican flag had flown.[27]

Ide was no less compulsive than the Californians when it came to pronouncements. Some rhetorical or ritual statement of causes, purposes, and promises seemed, at least to him, to be as essential as a visual symbol, though some of the men disagreed.[28] He formulated it, sitting up all night, and dated it June 15, 1846. The "Proclamation to all persons, citizens of Sonoma"[29] was a long, windy document (and copies were issued in varying forms). It was also sophistic, that is fallacious or untrue, though salted with gems of reality. In it Ide pledged that peaceful citizens would not be disturbed. He claimed the settlers had been invited to the country by promises of land and a republican government, but had been denied the privilege even of buying or renting lands, been "oppressed by a military force of despotism . . . even threatened . . . with extermination" if they did not depart. All peaceful citizens were invited to join in perpetuating a government which would "encourage virtue and literature . . . and leave unshackled by fetters agriculture, commerce, and mechanism." Relying upon the "rectitude of his intentions, the favor of heaven, and the bravery of those who were bound to . . . him by the principles of self preservation, . . . the love of truth, and the hatred of tyranny," he hoped for success.

The paper bore the signature and impress of William B. Ide. Hubert Howe Bancroft, with some expertise in these matters, rates it below Castro's and Pico's proclamations in truthfulness and consistency as well as in orthography and literary merit, and about midway between the two in bombast and general absurdity. Its contemporary dignity, he notes, derived from the fact that it came from men who meant to fight as well as talk.[30] It made little sense to the Californians even in Spanish.

Other officers were elected (without salaries), and First Lieutenant Henry L. Ford, already a veteran of the Micheltorena campaign of 1844 and of the Arce raid, abstracted promises of implicit obedience. The alcalde, José de los Santos Berreyesa, was discharged and reappointed; import duties (at this inland seat) were reduced to one-fourth; provision was made to compensate (later) the owners of private property and to survey and distribute the national domain; and Ide was made captain-general. His paper nation was in good order.

On the day of the proclamation, the captain-general sent Todd on a mission to Captain Montgomery. He carried a letter that said California had been proclaimed a republic, and the "Spaniards," he had learned, were not only satisfied but pleased.[31] It was Ide's earnest desire to unite their "adopted and rescued" country to that of their early home. He did not ask outright for aid, only said that they had insufficient powder to work their cannon, and if they failed, they were destined for certain destruction.

Replying, Montgomery labeled Ide's action a hasty organization of the foreign population in opposition to constituted authority; and although

Commander John B. Montgomery of the U.S. sloop–of–war Portsmouth *had no authority, while representing a government at peace with Mexico, to furnish munitions of war.*

it was the privilege of all men to resist oppression, a just cause would always be characterized by a mild and humane regard for the privileges of others.[32] He added that as a representative of a government at peace with Mexico (as far as he knew), he had no authority to furnish munitions of war or even to identify himself with the popular movement.

At the same time, Montgomery responded to Vallejo's message of the 14th, brought by de la Rosa, disavowing the Bears on behalf of himself, his government, and Captain Frémont, and refusing to have anything to do with either party.[33] But he sent Lieutenant John S. Misroon to Sonoma to use his personal influence, without meddling in the revolt, to prevent violence to noncombatants.[34] Taking Todd and de la Rosa in the ship's launch, Misroon obtained from Ide a copy of the proclamation and a written pledge to prevent violence, which he delivered to the alcalde.[35] He then visited Vallejo's wife, who was allowed to send an open letter to the prisoners at Sutter's Fort, carried by her brother, Julio Carrillo (who was immediately locked up with the others).[36] Perhaps after reading the proclamation aloud to the garrison as a gesture of support, as Ide afterwards related,[37] the lieutenant left on the 17th, and in reporting to his superior gave the Bear Flag party high marks for orderly conduct. But Manuel Castro wrote the Mexican Minister of War two days later that the captain of the U.S. frigate *Portsmouth* had sent a launch full of ammunition to the invaders.[38]

A new, shorter, more moderate, and veracious proclamation was issued on the 18th[39] (it may be with Misroon's editorial assistance), and both versions were translated into Spanish and posted throughout California. While young Carrillo, with a passport from Ide, was imprisoned at Sutter's Fort, an American messenger with a certificate from Berreyesa put up one of the shorter manifestoes at Monterey and another traveled as far as Santa Barbara, where Pico forwarded it to the assembly in Los Angeles.[40]

Frémont, having established a base on the American Fork to be near the Fort, wrote Montgomery on June 16 of the movement to create "a settled and stable government" in California.[41] Unforeseen Mexican hostility, he said, having forced him to abandon his exploration of the Colorado, he would head for the Missouri about the 1st of July; and he asked that the *Portsmouth* remain at San Francisco to discourage hostile acts and keep communications open. Meantime, should anything be attempted against him, he would not permit a repetition of the recent insults he had received from General Castro. "I trust that our government will not severely censure any efforts to which we may be driven in defense of our lives & character."

Still believing Frémont disassociated from the settlers' affairs, Montgomery confessed that, though he was preserving a strict neutrality, his sympathies were "wholly with the gallant little band in arms for mutual defense"; and he undoubtedly encouraged Frémont by esteeming the capture of the horses and the surprise at Sonoma as "master-strokes" which should have been followed by a rush upon Santa Clara, where Castro could have been taken by thirty men.[42] Crediting Frémont's purpose to proceed immediately to the United States, he wrote the Secretary of the Navy on the 26th, detailing all the passing events and sent the letter to Frémont's camp for delivery.[43] That day Sutter sent an order to Leidesdorff for a small supply of brandy or aguardiente and sugar, since he was having visitors, "likewise some Gentlemen prisoners" whom he wanted to treat as well as possible.[44] And Leidesdorff, on his own behalf, begged Montgomery for a moderate-sized flag to hoist at Yerba Buena in case of trouble.[45]

At Santa Clara, General Castro learned about the taking of Sonoma a day after it happened and on the 17th composed two appropriate proclamations. The "contemptible policy" of the United States, one read, had induced a number of adventurers to capture the town of Sonoma.[46] "Banish from your hearts all petty resentments," he exhorted, hoping to unify north and south, "arise in mass, divine providence will guide us to glory." Another promised that foreigners living peaceably among them, occupied in their business, would be protected by the authorities, but any taking up arms against the country, forgetting the kind treatment they had received in former times, would be subject to the fortunes of war.[47]

The same day Castro, in apprehension and anger, asked Montgomery to explain the scandalous conduct of Captain Frémont in capturing Sonoma and taking Californians prisoner.[48] Montgomery replied in good faith that Frémont was in no way permitted to associate with the upheaval at Sonoma, and the general impugned his government's integrity by making such an accusation.[49] Again, after the *Portsmouth*'s launch returned from New Helvetia, Castro inquired why armed boats from the warship went about the Bay examining the trade in a port which belonged to Mexico.[50] Once more Montgomery forthrightly declared Frémont's neutrality as well as his own in sending boats to Frémont's camp; and he thought it proper to announce his intention to send another for the purpose of communication before Frémont's departure from California.[51] To Leidesdorff he likewise affirmed his role as a mere observer of passing events, looking out for the security and interests of his country and countrymen in an honest way.[52] (But the Old Man's "seat on the fence" was attributed by ordinary seaman Joseph Downey to an earnest desire to preserve his $2,500-a-year salary.)[53]

Nevertheless, Castro's eloquent charge of contemptibility and Flores' of "dissimulation and perfidy"[54] would not seem to them exaggerated; for in spite of Montgomery's protestations—and he was a just, honest, and religious man—it must have appeared that Frémont of the U.S. Army, aided by Montgomery of the Navy, and supported (or at least not redressed) by Consul Larkin, were at the heart of this filibustering business.

Larkin did not learn of the affair at Sonoma as soon as he might, for Leidesdorff was not prompt in relaying the information (he could not get a courier). But he knew about it by June 16 when James Stokes rode in from San José with the news, and a *bando* was posted on the 17th, calling upon all citizens to come in with their horses by 10 a.m. the next day.[55] Montgomery wrote him from Leidesdorff's house on the 16th, and next day Leidesdorff said it was "very strange" they should have taken Leese prisoner, who was known to be an American and a friend.[56] "I suppose there is something going on that we know nothing of."

The letters were received by Larkin on the 18th, and he too was puzzled.[57] The reason for the uprising he could neither give nor imagine, he told the Secretary of State[58]—yet he was thought to be "fully informed." Whether it was a personal affair, a robbery, or that foreigners, expecting two thousand more over the mountains in September, were taking government horses to meet them and "then change the Government," he could not tell. If so, he was two years behind in his expectations of things to come. "Captain Fremont and Mr Gillespie . . . are supposed by the Californians to be at the springing of this business and fanning it on."

Larkin also passed the news on to Stearns in Los Angeles,[59] as did British Vice-Consul Forbes, who thought foreigners on the Sacramento, like those in the south, were uniting with Pico against Castro.[60] Larkin advised Leidesdorff to admonish the insurgents not to injure innocent people or compel subjects of other nations to join their ranks.[61] To say he hoped it would end would be of no use, he added, for if "they have started the big Ball to roll . . . I can not stop it."[62]

Later, when the involvement of Gillespie and Frémont was well established, Larkin wished they had given him some previous hint of their "peculation." He had had no idea Gillespie would commence operations of any kind without his knowledge.[63] And when Montgomery learned the truth about Frémont from Gillespie at the end of June, he realized how peculiarly delicate and difficult his position was; having avowed not only his but Frémont's neutrality, he could hardly be supposed to have acted in good faith.[64] Meanwhile Larkin, Leidesdorff, and Frémont feared arrest, and the consul planned to pack his family off to Honolulu in the American bark *Angola* (but Mrs. Larkin would not go).[65]

Exhortations and warnings were quickly posted by alcaldes in the several towns, and General Castro appealed to Pío Pico on June 17 and again on the 21st, 25th, and 30th for cooperation.[66] If Pico did not intend to come, let him say so, that time and men would not be wasted in sending dispatches. It was Manuel Castro's notice of June 19,[67] a *violento extraordinario*, announcing the taking of Sonoma, which Pico received at Santa Barbara on June 23 as he was readying to march against the general. He responded with a vigorous proclamation.[68] A "gang of North American adventurers with the blackest treason that the genius of evil could invent" had taken Sonoma as they had stolen Texas, and he urged the Californians to "Fly . . . in all haste in pursuit of the treacherous foe." The North American nation could never be their friend, having laws, religion, language, and customs which were totally opposed. To Larkin he wrote directly on June 29 that the act of the insurgents tended "to excite the mind" and caused him to suspect that the government of the United States was somehow implicated. And he accused the consul of having witnessed with extraordinary coolness this act of aggression.[69] To this accusation of indifference, friend Larkin replied that he would not underrate the governor's good sense by supposing he believed a consular letter would have had any effect upon the persons in question.[70]

With some difficulty, especially at Monterey,[71] General Castro raised three divisions in the north, totaling some hundred and sixty men. One division of fifty or sixty under Joaquín de la Torre crossed the Bay from San Pablo to Point Quentín, probably on the 23rd, intending to attack Ide, and took the regular road to San Rafael. José Antonio Carrillo and Manuel Castro followed with similar forces but stopped at San Pablo. Meanwhile a party of about twenty-five probably younger, more rash, even desperate Californians—said to include Four-Fingered Jack—had been ranging the country west of Sonoma, awaiting developments and expecting reinforcements from Castro. Their leaders were a 22-year-old barber and saloonkeeper, Juan Padilla, and the rough-and-ready José Ramón Carrillo, whose horses may have been stolen by settlers from a ranch nearby.

About June 19, Ide sent Thomas Cowie and a man named Fowler to the Henry D. Fitch rancho on the Russian River to fetch a keg of powder; and with more bravado than good sense, they followed the main road toward Petaluma and Santa Rosa. Captured above the latter place by Padilla's men, they were killed or, as was widely reported, brutally murdered, though Carrillo, who wished to retain the prisoners, protested.[72] Two other Bears also seem to have been taken, including Todd. The killings created great alarm among the foreigners, and several more families came in to Sonoma, increasing their number to about two hundred.

On the 23rd, seventeen or eighteen men under Lieutenant Henry L. Ford rode out to rescue the prisoners, leaving a large force at Sonoma to repel Castro's expected attack. Not finding Padilla in the direction of Santa Rosa, they turned south toward his rancho.[73] Near the laguna of San Antonio, next morning, they charged the enemy but found only three or four men, whom they captured. Then, straggling along toward the Indian rancho of Olómpali after breakfast, they unexpectedly came upon what they took to be Padilla's twenty-five men. De la Torre, however, had arrived the previous evening with some of his party, bringing the Californians up to about seventy. But seeing a few men and a corral full of horses, the insurgents charged as they had done earlier in the day. Reaching the farmhouse, they surprised the whole force at breakfast and quickly took cover in a convenient woods. When the Californians attacked, the rifles of the Bears brought down at least two, one killed, and de la Torre backed off. After some long-range firing, the Californians retired toward San Rafael, and the Americans did not pursue. The prisoner Todd apparently escaped during the melee, and the insurgents, leaving, it may be, one or two dead, made their way back to Sonoma.

Even before Ford had set out, the Bears had been nervous. Castro was known to be preparing an attack, and their confidence in the eccentric Ide as general and father of a new republic was not rising. Ford had, therefore, sent an Irish sailor, John Neal, to Frémont's camp, where he arrived on June 20 to report Castro's planned assault. The same day Samuel Hensley and P. B. Reading came up from Marsh's rancho with similar reports.[74] Since the Californians now appeared to be on the offensive, and Frémont's plans were contingent upon such action, the captain prepared to move. Affairs had reached a critical state (or so he would in 1887 reason),[75] and it was unsafe to leave them to unfriendly or incompetent direction. "I represented the Army and the Flag of the United States. And the Navy was apparently co-operating with me." This gave his movement the national character which Mexico must respect. He would also say in his memoirs that he now drew up his resignation from the Army to be sent to Colonel Benton for acceptance if the government wished to disavow his action.

In answer to "urgent appeals made by the settlers for assistance," Frémont and some ninety men—his own party, Major Reading, six of Sutter's trappers, and settlers under Hensley—set off for Sonoma on June 23, leaving Edward Kern in charge at the Fort.[76] Arriving at 2:30 a.m. on the 25th, they were by noon of the following day, now 130 strong, on the way to San Rafael, where de la Torre and Padilla were reported to be and Castro was expected. Frémont now changed his mien—wrapping a common white handkerchief around his head to avoid recognition, an embittered Californian would afterwards maintain, not becoming a brave man. He wore a blue woolen shirt "of somewhat novel style," open at the neck, with a star worked on each side of the collar. Over this he pulled a deer-skin hunting shirt, trimmed and fringed, which had evidently seen hard service.[77]

No one was at the mission when they arrived (the enemy having just departed), so at 3 p.m. they occupied the now quiet buildings.[78] On Sunday the 28th a boat was espied crossing the Bay toward San Quentín, and Kit Carson with a few companions went to intercept it. Frémont's offhand instructions, according to Jasper O'Farrell (who said he was there) were that he had "no room for prisoners," a statement given credence at the time by the absent Kern. Three persons stepped from the boat, which then turned back toward San Pablo. They were Francisco and Ramón de Haro (twins, aged about 20) and José de los Reyes Berreyesa, their uncle, an old man whose son was alcalde at Sonoma and a prisoner of the Bears. One of the twins may have carried a message to de la Torre, though this was disputed, revealing the plans of Castro's two divisions at San Pablo, or instructing him, as it would be most unreliably asserted, to slaughter foreigners irrespective of age or sex. As the three approached, unarmed, to within fifty yards, Carson and his men shot them in cold blood, possibly in retaliation for the deaths of Cowie and Fowler. Frémont himself would ascribe the act to his Delawares "on a scout"; Gillespie, later, placed the blame upon Carson, with Frémont assenting; Godey would claim the men resisted arrest; Hargrave would say the killers had their orders before they started; while Larkin, still thinking of a more peaceful transition, feared that someone among the party would "commit reck-lessness" and deter others from joining.[79]

The same afternoon a scouting party intercepted a letter carried by an Indian, telling of de la Torre's intention to attack Sonoma the following day. Frémont and his force therefore hustled the twenty-five or thirty-miles back to headquarters by early morning of the 29th, creating a mighty stir in the garrison, since they were taken for the oncoming foe.

The Californians, however, had only been under too close scrutiny by Frémont at San Rafael and, by a false report, enticed him back to Sonoma while they escaped across the Bay from Sausalito in a borrowed schooner (or fled "in the most cowardly manner," in Gillespie's version).[80] Too late, Frémont discovered the subterfuge and the same day dashed back, but the enemy had departed. That evening Gillespie assured Montgomery that Sonoma could not be taken by three hundred "knaves such as these Californians" and begged some coffee and sugar for the captain.[81]

With twelve men on July 1, Frémont prevailed upon Captain William D. Phelps of the American bark *Moscow* to ferry them in the ship's launch across to the old fort at the Bay's entrance (which he would name the Golden Gate). Wading ashore, they climbed to the old *castillo* and, in the absence of any garrison, spiked the ten abandoned cannon—nearly all long brass Spanish pieces—without interruption.[82] (Phelps would subsequently bill the government $10,000 for this parlous venture and be awarded $50 upon Gillespie's testimony that no risk was incurred.)[83] Next day, another party made up of Robert Semple and ten Bears appeared in the streets of Yerba Buena, going "where they pleased," and took Robert Ridley prisoner, sending him to join the other captives at Sutter's Fort. Ridley, a naturalized Englishman and captain of the port, was, said Leidesdorff (who disliked him), more Mexican than the Mexicans and would get his just due one of these days.[84]

If things were not quite as Frémont represented them to his father-in-law, that "*de la Torre* was driven from the country, having barely succeeded in effecting his escape across the straits,"[85] the Californians *had* abandoned that part of the country. His measures, Frémont said, had freed from Mexican authority the territory north of the Bay from the sea to Sutter's Fort, a well-hedged boast General Ide would also make. While Castro "retrograded" toward his quarters at Santa Clara, Frémont and his men returned late on July 4 to Sonoma.

A great celebration took place on this first Independence Day, with many booming salutes, the reading of the Declaration of Independence, and a fandango, the San Rafael contingent returning in time for the ball. Next day Frémont called a public meeting at Salvador Vallejo's house, where, Ide said, the Bears were seated in one room and Frémont's men in another, with some officers of the U.S. Navy mixed in.[86] Frémont made an address, advising a course of action which was not, according to a resent-

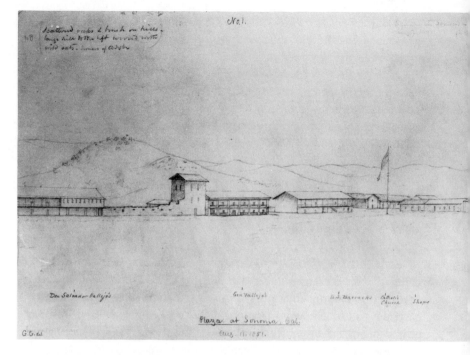

At Sonoma a great celebration took place on July 4, 1846, with many booming salutes, the reading of the Declaration of Independence, and a fandango.

ful Ide, to conquer California (and violate amicable relations with Mexico) but to take the usurper Castro, by whom he had been greatly affronted. Since all present had a common cause, he would accept the command if they would pledge obedience, proceed honorably, and not violate the chastity of women. The "people desired me to take charge," Frémont would later tell; and the movement might soon have collapsed without him.

A committee of one Bear and two of Frémont's men (Ide, John Bidwell, and Reading) was appointed to draw up a pledge or statement of purpose, and the majority agreed to date the era of independence not from the taking of Sonoma on June 15 but from July 5, enabling Frémont's administration to "begin at the beginning." The combined forces were then reorganized—Frémont becoming "Oso 1⁰," Gillespie, "Oso 2⁰"— and all vowed obedience and to remain in service until independence was assured.[87] That day the unsinkable Ide drew up conditions for annexation to the United States: equality in every respect to other states of the Union, California to retain its public lands, and the United States to pay the expenses of the revolution.[88]

Again parties were out collecting horses and cattle for the next phase of the revolution, some 700 mounts principally from the absent Vallejo, and 500 beeves from the government stock farm at Suscol. The force, now 224 strong, was divided into companies under Grigsby, Ford, and Granville P. Swift as captains.[89] Whatever else may have happened that day—and Ide would write a long and censorious account of Frémont's usurpation[90]—John Charles Frémont had abandoned his tandem role and avowal to return to the United States and taken over the filibusters' cause. Ide became "Oso de secunda clase."

Leaving Captain Grigsby with fifty men at Sonoma, the conqueror without portfolio headed back toward the Sacramento on July 6, hauling some small brass field pieces. In succoring the Bears, he had wished "rather to govern events than to be governed by them";[91] what was now his intention? He could advance upon Castro, who was retiring from Santa Clara by stages, and continue his march southward until it terminated in the complete conquest of the department (as he would afterwards imagine),[92] thus grasping victory in his own two hands. At Sonoma he had received a letter from Montgomery copying news that Sloat was expected at Monterey,[93] and he might have taken this as a portent of war and meant to hold his fire until formal hostilities began, thus mitigating his offense against the law of nations, bringing substantial support, and veiling or validating his private acts and motives. Montgomery told Captain Mervine at Monterey on July 2 that he would soon hear of a decisive blow on the part of the insurgents.[94] And Frémont would testify in 1848 that with 160 men he had set out around the head of the Bay to attack the general on the south side, where Americans from Santa Cruz and San José were prepared to join him.[95]

To the question, what was Frémont's proposed next move? there is not nor does there need to be a certain answer. He reached Sutter's Fort on July 10 and camped on the American River the following day.[96] That evening at about sunset a messenger from Revere at Sonoma brought the long foreseen and vastly comforting news that Commodore Sloat had taken Monterey four days before.[97] William Scott, the courier, also brought an American flag, to be hoisted at sunrise the next morning with a salute of twenty-one guns and the general rejoicing of the people. Even the prisoners of Frémont's little preemptive war, hearing the uproar, anticipated immediate liberation.[98]

By sheerest coincidence, Frémont's and Gillespie's conquest promised at once to become official. Happily, the captain had in hand an urgent request from the commodore to come at once to Monterey with a hundred well-mounted men, "accustomed to riding."[99] By taking anticipatory measures, he had justified his character and earned the mistrust and enmity of an alienated people.[100]

❧ 9 ❧

Sloat's Conquest (1846)

P RESIDENT POLK'S FORMULA for conquest was a simple and essentially practical one; and the equation was not entirely one-sided, for the conquered were to be treated fairly and offered their political freedom. Occupation + conciliation = acquisition + liberty and, of course, prosperity. What it lacked were all the factors not readily amenable to definition, particularly any allowance for human personality and Mexican history.

The Americans meant to have California, by purchase if they could. Mexico could not hold it, and it must fall to the United States and not some European colonizing power. The "Manifest Destiny" of the American Republic to possess the continent west to the Pacific had grown from political catchword to Presidential policy and an inexorable trend in North American history. By 1846, Texas having been annexed, only Oregon, New Mexico, and California remained outside the fold, and Polk had them on his agenda. He took Oregon by bluff and default (to England it was not worth the candle) and would get the rest by failed purchase and negotiation, doggedly followed by outright war. Acquiring territory without a fight would have been simpler, likely cheaper, less messy, and more benign, if it could have been done that way. But a comparatively rich, aggressive, and expanding nation like the United States had greater scope than its more impoverished and disorganized relations.[1] Always it could offer money to a poorer neighbor (this seemed the rational approach); have the law on it for its debts; be more persevering and relentless (because of being more stable); cozen it with demands and accusations; trespass its borders; tempt it toward the first hostile step; muster greater resources in wartime; and dictate the final settlement—a versatility particularly efficacious against a not too constant and effective opponent when other world powers would not interfere. Such was the developing scenario from which emerged paid agents of Army, Navy, and State and an autonomous emigration to enact the scenes which would bring California into the Union.

Hostilities between the United States and Mexico began just north of the Río Grande on April 25, 1846 (while Frémont, lacking that vital information, wandered up the Sacramento Valley with Gillespie in hot pursuit). The President had, in January, ordered Taylor into disputed territory south of the Nueces, without telling Congress but showing Mexico he meant business. Polk's directive of January 13 was received by the general on February 3, but he, being unprepared and a mite perverse (he was a Whig), did not leave Corpus Christi until March 8 or reach the Río Grande until the 28th. After some skirmishing and an American blockade of the river's mouth, General Arista crossed from Matamoros on April 24 and the following day captured two companies of reconnoitering U.S. dragoons, leaving several American dead.[2] Just two weeks later, on May 9, Polk received the long-awaited news and the next working day sent a message to Congress. A war resolution was rushed through the House (allowing only two hours for discussion), while a reluctant and truculent Senate debated it (for one day) in a "most animating and thrilling" way. "How do we know," shouted Calhoun, "that war exists?"; and Benton thought that "in the 19th century war should not be declared without full discussion. . . ."[3] The joint resolution was signed by the President on May 13, and his proclamation of the same day declared that "by the act of the Republic of Mexico, a state of war exists."[4] The requisite first clash would escalate.

Communication in 1846 was hardly instantaneous, and the news did not reach California for many weeks, though intimations of it seeped through. Such delay, dependent upon the fleetness of men, horses, and ships, had plagued military planning from the beginning, and the Cabinet necessarily took it into account. Almost a year beforehand—war on a distant coast being perforce a naval venture—the Secretary of the Navy had instructed Commodore Sloat of the Pacific squadron regarding the onset of hostilities. The President, Secretary Bancroft had said on June 24, 1845,[5] wished to pursue a policy of peace, and the commodore was to avoid any appearance of aggression. But if he should "ascertain beyond a doubt" that Mexico had declared war, he was immediately to occupy San Francisco and blockade or occupy such other ports as his force would permit, being careful to preserve, if possible, the most friendly relations with the inhabitants. The distance of the squadron made it necessary to disclose the government's views in the event of war, a contingency he was enjoined to do everything consistent with the national honor to avoid. Bancroft followed this with other letters, sending copies by various means, one, on October 17 (received the following March) altering the critical words *"declaration of war"* to "In the event of actual hostilities. . . ." Repeating his charge to conciliate the people, Bancroft advised him to communicate freely with the consul at Monterey. Sloat was also to discover the plans of the British and French and the attitude of the Californians toward Mexico and the United States. These (with some supplementary notes) would comprise the sum of Sloat's official instructions,[6] though other letters were dispatched which he himself would never see.

Sloat arrived at Mazatlán, via Panamá, Callao, and Hawaii, by November 19, 1845.[7] His instructions of June 24 had caught up with him at Honolulu, where he had gone for supplies, but he noted that the British had received communications from Washington by way of England three weeks ahead of his own newspaper accounts.[8] Returning from the Sandwich Islands, he had looked in at San Francisco but, with war on his mind, had not tarried for fear of raising suspicions.[9] He was confident, however, that he could destroy all of the places north of Acapulco and would have no difficulty occupying San Francisco and Monterey.[10] Since the earliest and best information could be had at Mazatlán, he decided to remain there. His instructions suited him exactly, he assured Secretary Bancroft, and he could be counted upon to put them into effect should offensive action be required, which he doubted. He had heard of the expulsion of Governor Micheltorena and his troops from California and believed the province to be virtually independent.

Lieutenant Gillespie reached Mazatlán in mid-February 1846 and within a few days was shipped in the *Cyane* to his destination, agreeable to the verbal orders of the President and Secretary of the Navy.[11] Sloat may have received a copy of his instructions of October 17 at this time, or perhaps a month later,[12] when he promised to carry out the orders to the best of his ability, though he was suffering from a liver complaint, rheumatism, and neuralgia. At Larkin's March 9 behest, he ordered the *Portsmouth* to Monterey on April 1, sending along copies of the constitution of Texas in Spanish, presumably for distribution as a handy reference.[13]

Sloat first heard news of the war accidentally. He had permitted Surgeon William Maxwell Wood to return overland through Mexico to the United States at his own expense, carrying written and verbal messages and a charge to acquire information useful to the government.[14] With him went the U.S. consul at Mazatlán, John Parrott. At Guadalajara they heard of a collision between American and Mexican forces on the Río Grande, and—recognizing its significance but fearing for their lives— they dispatched a rider the two hundred and fifty miles back to Mazatlán, where he arrived on May 17.[15] Next day, the commodore ordered Captain William Mervine to Monterey in the *Cyane*, with a letter to Larkin saying hostilities had apparently begun.[16] Sloat intended to visit Monterey at once and believed the consul could provide information which would enable him to pursue a proper course of action.[17] The squadron consisted of the flagship *Savannah*, the *Congress*, *Portsmouth*, *Cyane*, *Warren*, *Levant*, and schooner *Shark*. His movements were to be kept a profound secret (unlike Jones, the cautious commodore did not inform his officers), and if a report of war reached California, Larkin was to make light of it, saying it had been a mere skirmish between reconnoitering parties.

But Bancroft's conjecture that the flag would fly at Monterey and San Francisco within three weeks of Sloat's notification[18] did not come to pass. Remembering Jones' precipitate action in 1842, the anxious commodore waited. Two weeks elapsed, and on May 31 he recorded in his log: "Received report of Gen. Taylor's victory over the Mexicans on the 8th and 9th of May"[19] (at Palo Alto and Reseca de Palma in southern Texas). Determinedly he wrote to the Secretary, "I have received such intelligence as, I think, will justify my acting upon your order of the 24th of June, and shall sail immediately to see what can be done."[20] That day he apparently sent the *Levant* to Monterey, accompanying it for a time in the *Savannah*; but after idling in the Pacific four days he returned to Mazatlán, a maneuver meant to puzzle the British admiral.[21] On June 5, he learned that Taylor had captured Matamoros,[22] and he read his orders again, carefully. "I have upon more mature reflection," he advised Bancroft, "come to the conclusion that your instructions on the 24th June last, and every subsequent order, will not justify my taking possession of any part of California, or any hostile measure against Mexico . . . as neither *party have declared war*."[23] He would, therefore, in conformity with his instructions, avoid any act of aggression until one or the other party had done so, or the squadron in the gulf had commenced offensive opera-

Commodore John Drake Sloat of the U.S. Pacific squadron had been instructed to occupy San Francisco if he should ascertain beyond a doubt that Mexico had declared war.

tions. He found the situation "anything but pleasant," since he was unable to act, though it might appear to the world that war had actually begun. He promised, nevertheless, to proceed to California.

Sloat was a senior officer and had fought and vanquished pirates in his day,[24] but he was irresolute and distraught in this threatening situation. He was also 68 and ailing and had asked on May 6 to be relieved of his command because of failing health.[25] So another day passed. Then on June 7 he entered in his log, "News received of the blockade of Vera Cruz by the American squadron."[26] This was what he had asked for, and "At 2 p.m. got under way for Monterey." He apparently sailed in the *Savannah* the following day[27] and reached Monterey on July 1 or 2.[28] The *Warren* was left at Mazatlán to await hoped-for dispatches (and would bring

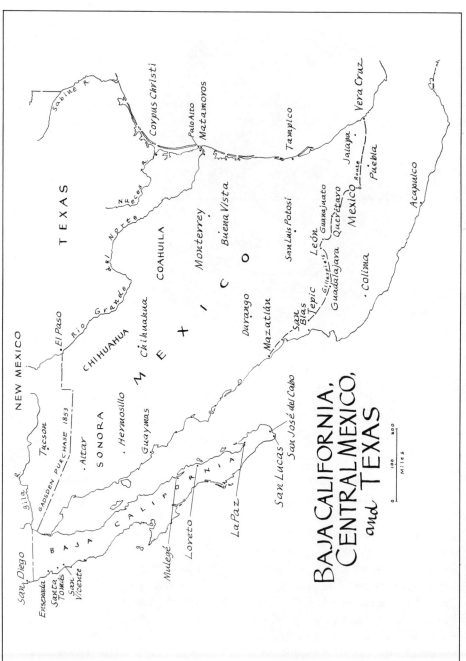

Baja California and central Mexico, to which Alta California was geographically and politically appended.

Polk's declaration of war on August 12).[29] Though belated, this action saved his reputation, for a letter from Bancroft of August 13 would bring a severe reprimand, and a second relieve him of his command of the Pacific squadron because of declining health "and for other reasons."[30] "The department willingly believes in the purity of your intentions. But your anxiety not to do wrong has led you into a most unfortunate and unwarranted inactivity." Happily, because of delayed transit, the commodore would have done all of the things required of him before the rebuke was penned.

Sloat brought the flagship around Point Pinos, even as Jones had done, and at 4 p.m. anchored quietly in the harbor beside the *Levant* and *Cyane* (the *Portsmouth* being at San Francisco). Having left Mazatlán fully determined to carry out the orders of the Navy Department—dictating action but enjoining the most friendly relations with the inhabitants—he now tendered the usual peacetime courtesies of a visiting foreign dignitary by offering to salute the Mexican flag. This formality, marveled at by his officers, was declined for want of powder with which to return the salutation.[31] On the evening of the 2nd he wrote to Larkin, asking whether his men might be sent ashore for twenty-four hours of liberty; they might make some noise but would spend $1,000 to $1,500, which would compensate for any annoyance.[32] The log says Larkin went aboard that day for a visit, still without any recent instructions, and was given the consular salute of nine guns upon departing.[33] On the morning of the 3rd the commodore wished to go on shore himself to take a ride with the consul, if it was convenient, and to call formally upon the authorities.[34]

The next day was the 4th of July, with the ships brightly dressed, and, as at San Francisco, a booming twenty-one-gun salute echoed over the town. The celebrations coinciding with the day of Our Lady of Refuge, patroness of the Bishopric of California, produced a "great fiesta" on board and ashore.[35] (Larkin, always busy, spent part of the 4th writing American officials in the Sandwich Islands that he still dreamed of persuading the Californians to call on the commodore for protection, "hoist his Flag & be his Countrymen, or the Bear may destroy them.")[36]

The 5th was Sunday, with religious services on board, and a launch arrived from the *Portsmouth* bringing official dispatches.[37] It also brought a letter of July 2 from Montgomery to Larkin, telling of Frémont's operations with the settlers, of spiking the guns at San Francisco, de la Torre's escape, and the capture of Robert Ridley.[38] Of the Bears he said the "country is undoubtedly theirs," and he warned that in less than fifteen days "they will be in your Midst."

Sloat had learned from Larkin at Mazatlán of Frémont's stand on Gavilán Peak[39] and now listened to disturbing reports of fighting between settlers and Californians and of Frémont's implication. His own instructions of October 1845, which he found to be similar to the consul's, emphasized peaceful and voluntary annexation; and Larkin certainly discouraged him from taking immediate, forceful possession, hoping the authorities would come to him for protection.[40] But Sloat was restive. He knew his orders should hostilities commence. He had known for six long weeks that actual fighting, if not a declared war, had begun. Now he heard reports of clashes in the north which might spread to Monterey and of the raising of a rebel flag. And he feared that the English admiral, Sir George Seymour, might appear in the eighty-gun ship-of-the-line *Collingwood* to intervene.[41] Probably he was being pressed by his own officers, who were not insensible to conditions.[42] To forestall anarchy and England, then, or usurpation by an indeterminate third force, immediate action was mandated. (And if, like Jones, he should prove to be premature, would not Captain Frémont of the Army now share the censure?)

The consul was summoned on board on the 6th. "We must take the place! I shall be blamed for doing too little or too much—I prefer the latter."[43] Larkin had been laboring mightily to bring the country into the American fold "through the will and voice of the Californians." He had had in his own hands for approval José Castro's plan to declare California independent in 1847 or 1848 when enough settlers were on hand to support it.[44] But the rising at Sonoma had interrupted all this. Though he preferred a peaceful transition, "more approved of by our Government," the "great Ball has been rolled. What can stop it?"[45] He had long prophesied the country's fate, and he was ready. He and Sloat conferred, drafted a summons to the military commander and a summons and invitation to Castro, composed a proclamation,[46] and readied a general order to Sloat's men—all sent off in suitable copies to Montgomery.[47] "I have determined to hoist the flag of the U. States at this place tomorrow," the commodore said. If Montgomery had a sufficient force or Frémont would join him, he was to raise the flag at Yerba Buena and take possession of the fort and that part of the country. Action?

The inhabitants of Monterey, being well primed by war rumors, knowing of American hostilities in the north, abetted apparently by a U.S. ship-of-war, and having for a week beheld three American warships bristling at anchor in the bay, could hardly have been surprised when the summons to surrender was brought ashore. Some thought the landing might have been slated for the 4th of July and were puzzled by the delay. "For days before," remembered one of Monterey's ladies, "it had been whispered that these ships were going to take the post on the 4th of July, and for this reason the priest was told to finish his afternoon devotions very early." [48] Hardly four years ago another such landing had been both well-mannered and stirring.

At 7 a.m. on July 7, Captain Mervine of the *Cyane* delivered the formal demand to the commandant of Monterey, handing it to Artillery Captain Mariano Silva (he who had surrendered to Jones). Because the Mexican government had commenced hostilities, the text read, the two countries were at war. The commodore therefore called upon the commanding officer to surrender all forts, stations, troops, arms, and public property of every description under his control. Immediate compliance would prevent the loss of life and horrors of war. To all of which Silva replied succinctly, at 8 a.m., that he was not authorized to surrender the place, having no orders to that effect, and the matter might be arranged with the commandant general, to whom the summons was being forwarded. He himself, withdrawing, was leaving the town "peaceful and without a soldier; nor, according to information from the treasurer, is there any public property or munitions. . . . God and liberty!" [49]

This taken care of, the commodore at 9:30 issued a general order to the three ships. [50] They were about to land on the territory of Mexico, with whom the United States was at war. "To strike her flag and hoist our own . . . is our duty." They must not only take California but preserve it as part of the United States, and it was therefore of the first importance to cultivate the good opinion of the inhabitants. Strict regulations regarding discipline, firearms, and the treatment of the people, particularly to avoid the "eternal disgrace which would be attached to our names . . . by indignity offered to a single female," were published, with the severest penalties prescribed for plunder.

Then, before 10 a.m., the ships' decks having been cleared for action, six boats from the *Cyane*, *Levant*, and *Savannah*, led by Mervine's gig and covered by the squadron's guns, proceeded in double file to the customhouse wharf, where at 10:20 some two hundred and fifty sailors and marines were unloaded. [51] Among those who marched to the front of that already historic building were some who had rehearsed with Commodore Jones. [52] Sloat's proclamation was read and posted in English and

Spanish, and the flag was raised amid cheers and twenty-one-gun salutes—that for nations—from each of the vessels in the bay.[53] No Mexican flag was this time struck, for none had flown in Monterey for some
months.[54]

Sloat's proclamation was short on rhetoric and persuasive (compared
with some by conquerors to follow).[55] Mexico had commenced hostilities, as Sloat believed, ushering in a state of war, and he would hoist
the American flag and carry it throughout California. "I declare . . . that
although I come in arms with a powerful force, I do not come . . . as an
enemy of California" but as its best friend; and henceforward California
would be a portion of the United States. Peaceable inhabitants would en-
joy a permanent government under which life, property, and religious
worship would be secured, rights which Mexico could not afford them.
Officers would be elected, import duties drastically reduced, and land titles guaranteed, and private property would not be taken without just
compensation—all straightforward and conciliatory answers to the natives' unspoken queries. Anyone not prepared to accept these privileges
would be permitted to dispose of his property and leave the country or
remain, observing strict neutrality.

By 11 a.m., the ceremonies ended, the boats returned, leaving Mervine
and the marines in charge of the town.[56] The occupying force began to
move in. They took over the customhouse and the old government building. A purser and surgeon from the squadron were appointed alcaldes
for the Californians, who would not serve. Police regulations were issued
and the streets patrolled, all shops being closed for two days and the retail of liquors strictly prohibited. A hundred marines with six musicians
paraded briskly for the diversion of the citizens (thirty-four more bands-
men would arrive on the *Congress*). Within six weeks the hill commanding the town was graded so as to rake the beach, a blockhouse and fort
were constructed and "Paixham, Corronades, and other Guns mounted,"
ready for action. Monterey was again in American hands.

On the day of the occupation, Larkin wrote Frémont at Sonoma that
the commodore wanted his cooperation and wished to know immediately whether he would come. The message was sent to James Stokes
and Charles Weber, foreigners at San José, for information, with a request to seal and deliver it and notify Marsh.[57] A copy also went to
Montgomery, hoping he could reach Frémont and ask him to come "that
the Commodore & myself may better understand the state of affairs in
the North" and any contemplated movements.[58] Uncertain about the in-

surgents at Sonoma, Larkin also addressed Ide, presuming he would now be inclined to desist from further action and remain passive at least for the moment.[59] Not until the 10th did he take time out to write the Secretary of State.[60] (Polk's earliest information would arrive on September 1 via the British legation.)[61] He renewed his request to Frémont on the 12th,[62] having assured a hesitant Sloat that the navy's work would be lighter if the captain could be used to curb horse-stealing and crimes in general as well as oppose any force sent against him. As an inducement, Frémont could promise his men $15 or $20 a month for their services.

Sloat too was aroused and active. To Montgomery he wrote (laboriously cloaked in numbers from the Naval Telegraphic Dictionary), "I hoisted the American flag here to-day at nine a.m.," asked him to post his proclamation in both languages, and repeated his instructions of the previous day.[63] In a letter to José Castro, Sloat called upon him to surrender, inviting him to Monterey to enter into articles of capitulation and receive assurances of safety.[64] He inquired of Larkin whether it would be well to post guards on the roads to Monterey to warn of an approaching force, though it should not be known they have "anything to do with us."[65] Meantime, he gave Purser Fauntleroy authority to raise a company of naval personnel and volunteers for this duty and to protect the inhabitants.[66]

To Pío Pico the commodore sent a copy of the summons to Castro and his proclamation and general order, assuring him that no improprieties had been committed and that business and social intercourse had not been disturbed in the slightest.[67] He had used every means in his power to stop the sacrifice of human life in the north. And he invited the governor to meet him at Monterey, where he would be received with all respect and "feel every confidence that an American officer expects when his word of honor is pledged."

Larkin too wrote Castro, a personal note from an old friend, encouraging him to see the commodore and assuring him of his safety whether or not there was agreement between them.[68] To Juan B. Alvarado, former governor and long-time associate, he expressed the belief that Castro could, with all honor to himself, enter into a convention that would be approved by his countrymen.[69] "Although we appear as enemies, I hope you two have known me a sufficient time to believe I would in the present as well as in other cases do all I could for you." To correspondent Stearns at Los Angeles he made long reports and hoped the general and commodore could settle their affairs satisfactorily.[70] He suggested the gover-

nor be diverted from any "Bumbastic proclamation" and invite the commodore to San Pedro, forgetting Mexico as Mexico had forgotten him.
"One great advantage," he reminded his American friend, "would be the
payment of debts."

Castro promptly replied to Sloat, openly locating his headquarters at
San Juan Bautista.[71] He first pointedly inquired whether the commodore
could explain to what government Mr. Frémont, a captain in the Army
of the United States, belonged, so that he would know how to act. Was he
under his command? In another note of the same date, he acknowledged
the summons to surrender and said he would need to consult His Excellency the Governor and the Honorable Assembly of the Department
(as had not always been his wont). But if the defense of the country was
his exclusive responsibility, he would spare no sacrifice to preserve it as
long as a single individual would join him in the cause. Pico would also
reply that he had not been able to discover that the occupation of the
country had been preceded by a declaration of war.[72]

Alvarado responded politely to Larkin, wishing he could accept his intimations—"and I would do it if I could dispense with my obligations,"
which he could not. He reminded Larkin of the efforts of the immortal
Washington to make his country independent of all foreign rule and
asked him to judge what he would do in circumstances like the present.[73]

Larkin was concerned about the feelings of the people, though as one
of the conquerors he could hardly comprehend the nature of their opposition. The families, he told Sloat, were fast becoming calm; those he
had visited denied fearing any danger.[74] By the 10th the military commandant and captain of the port had returned, reporting that over fifty
men had left Castro, who was going south.[75] The consul strongly recommended that Sloat appoint a Monterey schoolmaster from his own funds.
Opening a school as the first act of his administration would be placed to
his credit and help bring affairs to a happy conclusion. He offered to pay
a tenth of the cost.

Sloat's letter to Montgomery of the 7th was received at Yerba Buena in
the evening of the following day,[76] and Lieutenant Revere was immediately sent in one of the *Portsmouth*'s boats with flags to be raised
at Sonoma and Sutter's Fort. Then, early on the morning of the 9th,
Montgomery with seventy men—the sailors in white frocks, black hats
and shoes, the marines in their dress uniforms—rowed ashore at Clark's
Point in Yerba Buena Cove and, to the stir of one fife and a drum, hoisted

The town of Yerba Buena, renamed San Francisco in January 1847, showing the landing place at Yerba Buena Cove, soon to be choked by ships, wharves, and eventually landfill.

the flag in front of the customhouse in the public square.[77] A salute of twenty-one guns was followed by three cheers on shore and on board, in which the people, principally foreign residents, seemed cordially to join. On what would henceforth be known as Portsmouth Square, Montgomery (after whom a street on the waterfront a block away would be named) addressed a few words to the assembled people.[78] Sloat's "excellent proclamation" was read in both languages and posted on the flagstaff. Montgomery issued a brief proclamation, calling upon residents to enlist in a voluntary company to protect their homes and flag;[79] and a guard of thirty-two townsmen was enrolled under Lieutenant Henry B. Watson to hold themselves in readiness for any emergency.[80] Parties were sent to Mission Dolores, where they found an old lance and some public papers,[81] and to the old presidio and fort, where they observed three brass guns, "12s and 18s," old Spanish pieces made in 1623, 1628, and 1693, and seven others, all "lately spiked."[82]

With some qualms, Montgomery scrupulously acknowledged to the commodore having communicated with the belligerent parties in the north and accepted drafts on the Topographical Bureau for $2,199, which he hoped would be approved.[83] Later he sent copies of the correspondence, asking that enough of it be made known in Washington to offset the suspicion, rife in California, that he had compromised the neutrality of the flag by interfering in the affairs of the country.[84]

Montgomery also informed Frémont of Sloat's acts of possession and asked him to go to Monterey,[85] sending Purser Watmough to Santa Clara and San José to intercept him.[86] He invited Californians who had withdrawn during the "season of alarm" to return without fear.[87] In an exchange with Grigsby at Sonoma, he said the commodore would hardly countenance their living any longer "upon the ample stores" of the enemy.[88] He encouraged Grigsby's patriotic associates to cultivate relations with the people and reminded them that no man should be punished without trial (referring to Four-Fingered Jack, who seemed in danger of summary action).[89] Sloat felt it necessary to declare to the party at Sonoma that they were not regarded as enemies of the United States but as friends and brothers-in-arms fighting for independence, equal rights, and the freedom of republican institutions.[90]

Armed forces of the United States had occupied California soil, and the opposition was in full retreat. The commodore could announce his satisfaction that the flag was now flying at Yerba Buena, Sutter's Fort, Sausalito, and Bodega, and the United States was in quiet possession of the magnificent Bay of San Francisco and the country for a hundred miles around, to the manifest satisfaction of the inhabitants.[91] (Still, in Washington on July 6, President Polk was unwilling to reveal to Mexico and the world his plans to take California.)[92]

Near Sutter's Fort, Frémont—still unaligned—had requests from Sloat, Larkin, and Montgomery to hasten to Monterey. The commodore's letter was brought to him by Robert Livermore on July 11, and he headed down the valley the next morning with 160 men and two field pieces.[93] Before departing, he confirmed Kern in full command of the Fort, with instructions to iron and confine persons who disobeyed him and shoot any who might endanger the safety of the place.[94] In a bullish winning mood, he directed that, notwithstanding any other orders (and Vallejo's plea), the imprisoned Californians were to be retained despite the new banner flying overhead.[95] In time, the former Lord of New Helvetia would be commissioned second in command, with rank of lieutenant, and lament to Leidesdorff that it was "not very pleasant to have another as Commander in his own house."[96]

At the Mokelumne, Frémont sent the perdurable Gillespie ahead to Monterey to report.[97] Himself proceeding more leisurely, he crossed the San Joaquín River near Hills Ferry and the Coast Range, probably by Pacheco Pass, and arrived at San Juan Bautista on the 18th.[98] At the mission which he had earnestly scrutinized from Gavilán Peak four months before, he found nine large guns, nineteen kegs of powder, three of musket cartridges, two tons of shot, and one hundred and fifty muskets, all secreted by Castro.[99] Don José had been there as recently as the 9th, when he replied to letters from Sloat, then left for points south. San José, forty miles to the north, had been quietly occupied by nineteen settlers under Thomas Fallon on the 14th;[100] and shortly after Frémont reached San Juan, Fauntleroy appeared with a reconnoitering party, including Gillespie and naval Lieutenant Louis McLane, and bringing a flag, the last hoisted in the north.[101] The combined forces set out for Monterey on July 18. Going through the now familiar Gómez Pass, and spending the night at Gómez Creek, Frémont gave on the way "a marching salute" to the peak upon which he had made his defiant stand. Next day they reached Monterey.

It was a dramatic scene on that Sunday afternoon as Frémont's insurgents—one company of his own men and two of settlers—preceded by Fauntleroy's dragoons, swept into town. An eye-witness (who had read Fenimore Cooper) reported, "Here were true trappers. These men had passed years in the wilds. . . . A vast cloud of dust appeared first, and thence in long file emerged this wildest wild party. Frémont rode ahead, a spare active-looking man, with such an eye!" He was dressed in blouse and leggings, and wore a felt hat. After him came five Delaware Indians, a bodyguard. The rest, many of them blacker than the Indians, rode two and two, rifle held by one hand across the pommel of the saddle. The backwoodsmen wore long loose coats of deerskin tied with thongs in front, trousers of the same of their own manufacture. "The rest of the gang were a rough set; perhaps their private, public, and moral characters had better not be too closely examined." With three hundred extra horses in their train, the ground seemed to tremble under their heavy tramp. With their rifles, revolving pistols, and long knives glittering in the sun, their untrimmed locks flowing out from under their foraging

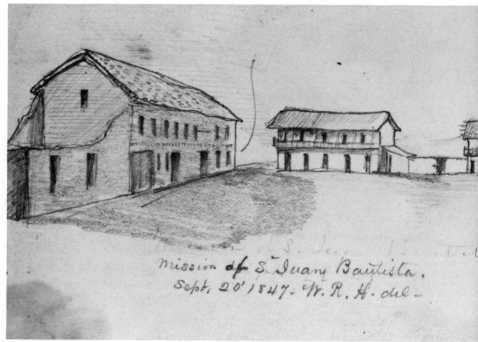

Mission San Juan Bautista, which Frémont had observed from Gavilán Peak in March 1846 and where in July he found nine large guns and other munitions recently abandoned by General Castro.

caps, and their black beards, with white teeth shining through, it was no wonder uneasy citizens looked out at them through grated windows.[102] And Frémont, who was not above posture (as Emerson noted after reading his *Report*), thought "our men made a strong impression" as they rode through the crowd on the way to camp.[103]

They stopped in an open space on the hills near the town, in messes of six or seven, and were visited by many curious men from the U.S. squadron, the British ship *Collingwood*, and the town. Their number, formidable appearance, and splendid marksmanship "astonished us all and made the Englishmen stare." Lieutenant James F. Schenck of the *Congress* was able to put into Frémont's hands a copy of his own report and to shake hands with Kit Carson,[104] while a son of Sir Robert Peel thought Semple was the most remarkable man he had ever met, knowing more about the history of his father and of England than he did himself.[105] Even Admiral Seymour came ashore to see the show, but not the commodore.

Gillespie had reported to Sloat a few days before but, not being authorized to make any statements, had listened without comment.[106] Now he
and Frémont went aboard together, finding the commodore glad to see
them and (perhaps misreading the cause of his tension) excited over the
gravity of the situation in which he was the chief figure.[107] "Mr. Gillespie
has told me nothing," Frémont remembered Sloat complaining; "he came
to Mazatlán, and I sent him to Monterey, but I know nothing." Full of his
own instructions to befriend and conciliate the inhabitants, the commodore asked by what authority they had taken up arms against the
Mexican people. "I informed him," said Frémont, "that I had acted solely
on my own responsibility, and without any expressed authority from the
Government to justify hostilities." Sloat was not comforted by this admission, but, still willing, it may be, to share his own uneasy burden, he
said (in Frémont's telling) that in taking Monterey he had acted upon his
faith in the captain's operations. Gillespie supposed Sloat was displeased

at having been anticipated, while Frémont, in his reconstruction, would wonder why the commander of a squadron would rely upon him for justification (though he would take credit for the commodore's aggressive action).[108] The interview ended abruptly, Sloat's eagerness for Frémont's cooperation and his readiness to embrace the unsavory rebels having vanished.

Sloat had in fact fulfilled his orders from the Secretary. He concluded that Fauntleroy's men could scout the enemy in the interior, and he would organize patrols of foreign residents to hold the towns and protect the people.[109] The company at Sonoma would be regularly enlisted to serve until Frémont left the territory.[110] But a younger, more decisive, and aspiring captain of the U.S. Navy, Robert F. Stockton, had arrived in the *Congress* on the 15th and was fidgety over the inaction.

Also swinging at anchor was the British ship-of-the-line *Collingwood*. Sir George Seymour, rear admiral and commander of H.B.M.'s squadron in the Pacific, had been for several months hovering on and off the coast near San Blas and Mazatlán (as earlier noted). With a dozen vessels on the station,[111] he had been attending to his official business—watching the French in the Pacific islands and British interests in Oregon—and being nervous about rival American activities in California. At Mazatlán in mid-May he had seen Aberdeen's instructions forbidding intervention in California's affairs but exhorting vigilance in preventing American ascendancy, and he had sent the *Juno* to encourage the Californians not to place themselves under the control of a foreign power.[112]

The *Juno* had brought visitors, one a German botanist, Karl Theodore Hartweg from the London Horticultural Society, collecting seeds and plants for introduction into England.[113] The other was the Reverend Eugene McNamara. Ostensibly representing the London Emigration Society, he wished to settle some thousands of Irishmen in the country as a bulwark to the Catholic religion against the "Methodist wolves" and to repel the wild Indians and North Americans. Originally conceived as colonies about San Francisco, Monterey, and Santa Barbara, the project was perforce transplanted to the interior valley.* "It does not require the gift of prophecy," McNamara had written to the Mexican President, to

---

* The site was described as lying between the San Joaquín River and the snowy mountains and extending from the Cosumnes River on the north to the extremity of the Tulares "in the neighborhood of San Gabriel" (McNamara to P.Pico 7 1 1846; P.Pico, grant 7 4 1846, in *512–75* 22–23, 23–25).

foresee that California would not long remain a part of the Mexican republic unless some defensive measures were adopted; and he sought one
square league (4,428 acres) for each family, without taxes and with the
assignment of duties from the port of San Francisco for a certain number
of years.[114]

Soon after the *Juno* reached Monterey on June 7, 1846,[115] Larkin
heard that the priest had been in Mexico City "all 1844" negotiating with
Herrera and Paredes, the latter objecting to the admission of any immigrants whose language was English since they would join the Yankees.
The vessel then went to Santa Barbara, Captain Blake to see Forbes, Mc-
Namara to call upon the governor; and Larkin urged Stearns to learn
more about his motives and movements.[116] Obtaining the governor's approval, probably on the 24th,[117] McNamara continued on to Los Angeles
to apply to the territorial assembly, which acquiesced on July 7 (with
some reservations).[118] The papers were then returned to the governor,
who had however left for the north and did not return until the 12th or
13th. The final decree, though signed by Pico, was dated July 4[119]—three
days before the assembly's endorsement and more than a week prior
to Pico's return, but pointedly predating Sloat's landing. McNamara
stopped again at Monterey and this time asked Larkin's opinion of the
title's validity under the American flag. The governor could not cede so
large an area, Larkin observed;[120] and by that time Mexican authority
over the territory had come at least provisionally to an end.[121]

Admiral Seymour was meanwhile on the way to Monterey. That he (if
not his men) expected to find the Americans already in control by seizure
or voluntary surrender[122] signifies there had been no race between him
and Sloat as has been alleged. This was confirmed forty years later
by Beauchamp Seymour, then Admiral Lord Alcester, but in 1846 flag-
lieutenant to his uncle on the *Collingwood*. "I see by my journal," he
wrote, "that we left Mazatlán (where the *Savannah* was) on the 24th of
May, 1846, arrived at San Blas . . . [about 150 miles] to the southward,
on the 27th, did not leave San Blas until June 13, and arrived at Monterey
July 16."[123] No rush!

On July 16, then, nine days after Sloat's landing at Monterey, a sail
hove in view, an English battleship. As Captain Samuel F. Dupont of the
Congress recorded,[124] "some surmise existed that the English would interfere"; so the vessels of the American squadron were signaled to pre-

pare for action, the decks being cleared and all men recalled on board. It was indeed the British admiral in the 80-gun *Collingwood*, which had that morning been becalmed off the coast but about 4:30 p.m. stood into the bay and anchored between the *Savannah* and *Cyane*. From the American flagship came the engaging strains of "God Save the Queen," to which the British ceremoniously responded with "Hail Columbia." Upon learning that Sloat had indeed occupied Monterey, the admiral is said to have answered, "I am sorry for it, but it is no business of mine"[125] (though Lieutenant Walpole of the crew said the men were astonished). Seymour took ample time to exchange courtesies with the American navy, witness Frémont's theatrical entry into town, and accept a set of topgallant masts and other spars from the U.S. commodore. He came to Monterey alone, it must be noted, not with "four other english men of war going into port," as alarmist Forbes reported.[126] The other vessels were American, and, altogether, they were a sight which "wild men of the West could not turn from, even to get their evening meal."[127]

After reading Sloat's proclamation, Seymour wrote (to Forbes with a copy to Sloat)[128] that whatever might be the commodore's expectations, he was not warranted by the law of nations, nor, he believed, by the Constitution of the United States, to declare that California had been annexed. The tenure which the U.S. forces at present held, he advised, should be regarded as provisional, pending future decisions or the issue of the war. Britain was an old hand at conquest.

Seymour also felt bound to explain to the Admiralty that his neutrality was caused by Aberdeen's orders and the legality of the American seizure, given a state of war.[129] In any event, he thought that California would probably become an independent state, since the Bear Flag revolt had caused so much anti-Americanism and the distance from Washington was so great. British control under these circumstances would not have been possible without large bodies of troops or loyal immigrants, and, lacking these, he preferred not to involve the British honor in a struggle for possession.

The officers exchanged visits, and Dupont thought Sir George a fine old gentleman, but he concluded that the Americans were equal to the British in efficiency "and worked smarter."[130] Larkin also visited Seymour, afterwards telling M. Y. Beach of the New York *Sun* that upon leaving the ship the admiral partly acknowledged the U.S. flag on shore by not giving him the customary consular salute.[131] Larkin's only apprehension was that should the United States lower the flag in California, the Bears would seize the country; or if several British ships remained on the coast, the inhabitants, who had not been consulted when Sonoma was taken, would declare for England "and we lose the Country." [132]

(He need not have worried, for Polk would say in December 1847 that he had no intention to undertake a costly war for nothing. [133] "The doctrine of no territory is the doctrine of no indemnity," he would argue with a divided Congress. Taking New Mexico and California would best suit the convenience of both parties, Mexico being too weak to retain them and they being contiguous to the United States. They were in our undisputed possession, had been the object of months of peaceful occupation, and, if they tried to rule themselves, would soon fall into the clutches of a more powerful state. His purpose and resolution, however worldly his reasoning, would provide the only continuity for the whole operation.)

However much and long the English threat had been feared by Americans in Washington, California, Mazatlán, and Honolulu, its final materialization in the shape of Admiral Seymour apparently did not cause much of a stir. The "Collingwood is here" was Larkin's full account of it to Buchanan on July 18; and he did not mention it in a long letter to the Secretary two days later. [134] Nor did Gillespie raise it as a topic of interest in an even longer epistle to Bancroft on July 25 (being more intent upon peddling his own view of California affairs to the Department). [135] Belatedly, Sloat advised Montgomery on the 23rd, "The Collingwood has been here for nearly a week, and is expected to leave to day; the admiral has been very polite and amiable." [136] To the New York *Sun*, Larkin reported that neither the admiral nor the English consul had made any protest. [137] As for Larkin's confidential correspondent in Los Angeles, when Stearns learned that some English men-of-war might call at San Pedro, he hoped that the report was true and they would want "a plenty of beef," for "John Bull is a lusty old fellow and has a stiff purse." [138]

The real significance of the visit was in good time revealed to Bancroft by Sloat after his departure from California, when he perhaps had the first opportunity to think on it. Admiral Seymour's visit had been very serviceable to the American cause in California, he said. [139] The inhabitants had fully believed he would take their part, and the conquest would have to be abandoned. But when they saw the "friendly intercourse subsisting between us, and found that he could not interfere in their behalf, they abandoned all hope of ever seeing the Mexican flag fly in California again." Probably just as decisive was the reply given by the admiral to Pico on July 23, answering the governor's letter of June 29 to Forbes, soliciting English protection: England would maintain a strict neutrality.[140]

The *Collingwood* sailed for Honolulu on July 23 (with McNamara aboard), the *Juno* having already departed for San Blas "with the News."[141]

❧10❧

Stockton's Conquest

C APTAIN ROBERT F. STOCKTON had been expected on the coast for
several weeks when he finally appeared at Monterey on July 15,
1846.[1] Having left Norfolk in the *Congress* in October 1845, he had
made a long, hard passage around the Horn. It was a voyage, Secretary
Bancroft noted, of which Stockton had volunteered to take the command,[2] and its first objective had been to land a new commissioner
and consul at the Sandwich Islands (where, by Stockton's account, he
"poured oil upon the waters").[3] He also carried sealed orders of even date
with those of Sloat and Larkin, which directed him to sail from the islands directly to Monterey.[4] There he was to deliver the original copy of
the Secretary of State's "secret instructions" of October 17, 1845, to the
U.S. consul, confer with him, learn all he could about Mexican affairs,
and do everything in his power to conciliate the good feelings of the people toward the United States. He also brought dispatches for Sloat and
was to attach himself to the commodore's squadron.

Finding Sloat in port, he went aboard the *Savannah*, to be quickly apprised of Sloat's intention to return home shortly, leaving the command
to him. Writing to the Secretary that he was an unwilling heir to his predecessor's cast-off honors and labors, he promised to try as a faithful stew-
ard "to improve the estate."[5]

Among Stockton's earliest informants was Lieutenant Gillespie, on the
17th. Larkin, knowing of this and of the lieutenant's hard-line views,
wrote Stockton a confidential note of caution.[6] But Stockton was entirely
his own man, a person of very considerable wealth and fame, energy and

imagination. Though short in stature, he was of somewhat lordly mien, self-centered and vain, with an appetite for adventure and a taste for glory. He too had fought pirates, served in the War of 1812, and earned the sobriquet of "Fighting Bob" through a propensity for dueling. In 1843–1844 he had supervised the development of an experimental low-lying, sail-and-steam-driven naval vessel, the *Princeton*, which carried among its armament two great cast-iron guns, one of which burst during a huge demonstration and show on board, killing the Secretaries of State and Navy.[7] Afterwards he had accompanied what was reputedly his own "navy" to Texas to foster annexation and urge its President (it has been alleged) to start a war with Mexico.[8]

Now Stockton was taking a flyer into the Pacific, with the prospect of falling in with some rewarding action. Larkin had wondered in May what object a commodore of Stockton's wealth, rank, and prospects had in leaving all and coming to the north Pacific—hardly to take charge of a squadron to see to whalers and some merchant ships, he reckoned.[9] According to a perennial hypercritic in Honolulu, Stockton's grand object there had been to flatter the missionaries, who would "sound the great advantage of [having] a Pious President to send Pious, pretending Commodores and Messengers of Peace," and pious American citizens would "vote for their Enthusiasms."[10] Stockton had indeed been admonished to nourish the good feelings of the Islands government toward the United States (and he had preached a sermon in the Rev. Mr. Armstrong's church on June 28).[11]

After Gillespie had left a disappointing interview with Sloat, he paid his respects to Stockton, whom he found not only ready to embrace the movements he and Frémont had made but just awaiting Sloat's departure to continue the operations which he said had been so happily commenced by them.[12] Since nothing could be done until Sloat surrendered the command, Gillespie hurried to San Juan to inform Frémont and, with him, made the triumphant entry into Monterey.

Frémont and Gillespie together now waited upon Sloat, then had a more promising but somewhat vague discussion with Stockton. Whereupon Frémont lightly remarked that he would make up his mind that night whether to stay in California or return to the United States (a stratagem he had used before).[13] Thus pressed, Stockton pledged to get in touch with them as soon as he was in command and asked them meanwhile to remain in the vicinity. He then wrote Sloat that it was very im-

Commodore Robert F. Stockton, a person of very considerable wealth and fame, energy and imagination, had volunteered for service in the Pacific, hoping to fall in with some rewarding action.

portant to seize General Castro or drive him out of the country, and he wished to send Frémont in the *Cyane* to head him off.[14] Had the commodore better not give him an order to take command at once and make his own arrangements? It would save a great deal of trouble.

Sloat was not yet ready to retire (perhaps awaiting orders from Washington, which would soon be on the way), but he was willing to surrender authority over the unwanted land forces and place the *Cyane* at Stockton's disposal. Therefore, on July 23 (the day of Admiral Seymour's departure), Stockton appointed Frémont to command the "California battalion of United States troops," with the rank of major—presumably in the horse-marines—and Gillespie captain and adjutant.[15] They were to volunteer the services of themselves and their battalion for as long as Stockton was in command and desired their support.[16] At the same time, Frémont was ordered to embark his troops on the sloop-of-war *Cyane*, to leave at daybreak on the 26th (though by the time his 165 "American Arabs of the West" got aboard it was 8 a.m.).[17] Once at San Diego, Frémont was to gather horses, camp so as to be in daily communication with the ship, and be prepared to march at a moment's notice. He was, by getting between Castro and the Colorado River, to prevent his escape. The men—to be increased to 300—were to be mustered under the military laws of the U.S. and receive ten dollars a month and rations. Stockton would soon sail in the *Congress* to San Pedro and notify Frémont of his movements.

Frémont was no ordinary subordinate. He had a direct line to the President, the Congress, and the American people through his father-in-law Senator Thomas Hart Benton, of Missouri, and he would make the connection useful. He had written Benton from the Sacramento River in May, and at Carmel he wrote again, the message to be taken to Washington by Sloat.[18] It was necessarily a selective account and would contain the particulars he wished to have known and remembered: his humiliation at Gavilán, his retreat from the snows of Oregon, Castro's truculence, raising the American flag, his commission under Stockton to command a battalion, and his impending departure for San Diego in the rear of Castro. (Benton would lay this letter before the President in November to show how, unwillingly, Frémont had been involved in hostilities against the Mexican authorities.)[19]

In a report to the Secretary of State on Monday of that week, Larkin had been speculating whether California might have been brought under the American flag by peaceful means. But by Friday he was urging Stockton to proceed to San Pedro.[20] The southern towns, particularly Los Angeles, where the governor resided, the sessions of the legislature were held, and the highest tribunal was convened, were still under the Mexican flag. If upon Stockton's arrival there, Castro and Pico proved not to be in arms, he could arrange affairs with them; and the consul offered his own cordial cooperation.

Larkin had long advocated the state of affairs which now obtained; and although his own approach to change had been abruptly aborted, there was no turning back. The "moment the stars fall . . . the Bear would take their place." There were advantages under the new regime which the Yankee merchant thought the natives would understand: the removal of a 21-cent duty on sheeting worth 6 cents in Boston, a sure rise in land values, an expanding market for local produce, and an end to hostilities among the Californians and with the detested Bears.[21] He would keep the welfare of the former owners of the country in mind from motives of friendship and humanity, he informed the Secretary of State. And he took great pleasure in writing to the New York *Herald* that now "I am in the U.S.A.—as well as yourself."[22]

On the morning of July 29, Commodore Sloat hoisted his broad pennant on the *Levant* and sailed for Panamá, leaving the entire squadron under Stockton's command. The United States was in quiet possession of "all 'Alta California' north of Santa Barbara," and he believed there would be no further opposition.[23]

The new commander-in-chief was ready to go. "This country has been trifled with long enough," he said (twenty days had passed since Sloat's landing), and he would not let Castro gather his forces but would take him or drive him out and give California a good government before he was done. Therefore, on the day of Sloat's departure, he issued an address to the people.[24]

"The Mexican government and their military officers have, without cause . . . been threatening the United States with hostilities," he noisily began. They had commenced the attack and been signally defeated. Castro had violated every principle of international hospitality by pursuing "with wicked intent" Captain Frémont of the United States Army, who had come to refresh his men. When, in order to redress these outrages, military possession had been taken of Monterey and San Francisco, the civil authorities had departed, leaving a state of anarchy. Stockton would end these lawless depredations, march against the "boasting and abusive chiefs" who would keep the country in a state of revolution and blood. The people were tired of the military usurpers. "They invoke my protection." He had come to succor the people, and as soon as the officers returned to their duties under a regularly organized government, the forces under his command would withdraw and the people be left to manage their own affairs.

Thus spake the newly invested chief, and he addressed a copy of the new doctrine to Bancroft that he might understand his position and why, as he thought, Commodore Sloat had raised the American flag.[25] When

Larkin sent the proclamation to the Secretary of State, he said he did not know where Stockton got the statements it contained (certainly not from him).[26] Montgomery at San Francisco apparently did not want to publish it; and the *Portsmouth*'s surgeon thought it "rather unintelligible" and perhaps preparatory to hauling down the flag.[27] Another American at Valparaiso, speaking for his countrymen, thought Stockton had taken a "step backwards," made a "'faux pas' . . . without any need whatever of having opened his face on the subject."[28] As for Sloat, he had tossed a copy into his desk as the *Levant* was getting under way from Monterey and did not read it until the 10th of August (after completing a businesslike report upon his California affairs).[29] Straightway he notified Bancroft that "It does not contain my reasons for taking possession . . . or my views or intentions towards the country; consequently it does not meet my approbation."[30] Stockton's special version of California history, and his subsequent interpretation of it for the Secretary of the Navy,[31] bore more than a casual resemblance to the explications advanced by Frémont and Gillespie. It also expressed something of his own conceit and grandiloquent rhetoric.

The day of his proclamation, the new commodore made Montgomery commander of the district of San Francisco and New Helvetia.[32] He also, upon Larkin's initiative, directed him to release General Vallejo and Julio Carrillo from confinement at Sutter's Fort, with such other prisoners of the Bears as might be worthy of conciliatory treatment.[33] Vallejo was to pledge either friendship for the United States or strict neutrality.[34]

Although Frémont would admit in 1848 having lost some freedom by joining Stockton's command, he was glad to have been relieved of his responsibility.[35] Forty years later he would dwell upon his reluctance to abandon the independent position in which he had left Washington. It had meant, he said, giving up a plan he had formed, "with the willing cooperation of Commander Montgomery," to continue the movement southward until he had completed the conquest of Alta California.[36] In his armchair version he had meant to travel down the coast through a country that would have been "of necessity friendly" and reach Los Angeles at the head of a strong, efficient, and increasing force, with a pacified country behind him.[37] Stockton's plan, in contrast, to land on a coast which the enemy could sweep clean of cattle and horses was no way to defeat a cavalry operating among its own people and familiar with every pass and trail. Nevertheless, he had had no choice but to embrace the situation into which circumstances had forced him. He had accepted the commodore's offer and would adhere to it loyally at the cost of his commission. Such were the consolations of retrospection.

When General Castro's force north of San Francisco had retired at the end of June, he was at Santa Clara, from where he sent Manuel Castro to make a reconciliation with Pico (who had set out from Los Angeles to oppose him).[38] On July 8 he received Sloat's call to surrender and, moving south to San Juan, replied the following morning.[39] He wrote Pico on the 11th from Los Ojitos (northwest of Paso Robles), sending Sloat's summons and his reply.[40] "There is still time," he entreated the governor, "the invaders have only occupied Monterey and San Francisco"; and he hoped Pico would recruit whatever force he could. But Frémont was on the way, under the squadron's orders. The general and governor met at Santa Margarita (north of San Luis Obispo) and, publicly embracing, began their cheerless march toward Los Angeles—the two armies traveling, it is said, twenty-four hours apart.

From San Luis Obispo, Pico wrote the Mexican Minister of Foreign Relations, mentioning Castro's resistance to the Americans, his own hasty march toward the north (not revealing its true purpose), and their resolve to defend the country. But their patriotism, without supplies of any kind, was inadequate to defeat the intruder.[41]

Governor Pico was again at Santa Barbara by the 16th, where he issued his war decree, ordering all citizens between 15 and 60, native or naturalized, to arms.[42] Every effort would be made to repel this "most unjust aggression of late centuries, undertaken by a nation . . . ruled by the most unheard-of ambition." By the time both forces reached Los Angeles, the assembly and *ayuntamiento* were in motion.[43] Subprefect Stearns threatened to fine the rancheros if they did not fly to their country's support; everyone was to defend the capital, and a commission would be sent as far as the frontier of Lower California to collect munitions.

But such a country with such a people and history did not find unanimity easy, even in crisis. Partisans of the north and south were hostile; the civil and military establishments were inflexibly opposed; personalities clashed; the general's regular forces and the governor's militia were incompatible; and the citizens' defense force at Los Angeles would not fight a foreign foe. Some were secretly in sympathy with the intruder, had little confidence in their leaders, or thought it all a bootless struggle. Both

officials and public were apathetic, and the government had little prestige, money, or credit. With all of Pico's exhortations, he raised fewer
than a hundred men to match the hundred-odd brought from the
north—and how were they all to be fed? By August even these were diminished by attrition to half their former number;[44] and on about the
4th, Castro moved with them to a camp on the mesa just south of town
(at Vernon), where he would shortly learn of Stockton's and Frémont's
approach.

When Frémont boarded the *Cyane* at Monterey on July 26, his motley
battalion entered the service of the United States to aid the Navy. "From
the character of the men, under so vigilant an officer," reckoned the editor of the newly established Monterey *Californian*, "we have every confidence of their success."[45] Some had never seen the ocean, let alone sailed
in a man-of-war, and the novelty of the voyage and prospects of action, if
not the seasickness, pleased them. Captain Dupont, now transferred to
the *Cyane*,* found her charts deficient, one by Arrowsmith being very
incorrect, though a rough plan of the coast picked up at the Sandwich
Islands was better.[46] Passing through the kelp beds, which he pronounced
as remarkable a sight as he could remember, they anchored at noon of the
29th at San Diego.[47] Here they captured the Mexican brig *Juanita* with
forty thousand percussion caps aboard, and Dupont proposed that the
town authorities hoist the American flag. When they declined, a party of
marines took possession, raising the flag at 4 p.m., and Frémont's force
debarked that evening and the following day. Upon the heights a few Californians could be seen reconnoitering.

Though the residents were unwilling to part with their horses, they
seemed well disposed. Juan Bandini, the chief citizen of the place, received them as friends[48] (a few days before having pleaded illness in ab-
senting himself from the assembly in Los Angeles).[49] Soon he would give
Frémont "an uncommonly beautiful horse," thoroughly trained—an elegant testimony of esteem (or propitiation) in that equestrian culture. Santiago Argüello, captain of the port, was also friendly, as was the Boston-
educated collector of customs, Pedro Carrillo; but the alcaldes would not
serve, fearing reprisals should the American flag come down.[50] The
women and children were joyful, according to Dupont, having been in
constant terror of Castro; and he would find San Diego a much more

* Dupont had come out on the *Congress* with Stockton and been assigned to
the *Cyane* when Mervine moved from that vessel to the *Savannah*.

Captain Samuel F. Dupont of the U.S. sloop–of–war Cyane *transported Frémont's California volunteers to San Diego in July 1846, where a party of his marines took possession.*

agreeable place than Monterey, where he had seen "no society whatever." Bandini was probably not pro-Yankee—having been the governor's secretary for a time, and extravagantly anti-Castro in feeling—but rather pro-winner, and he and Argüello, in an address to the people, explained their acceptance of the occupation and urged others to do likewise.[51] They argued Mexico's neglect, the inevitability of California's separation, the invincibility of American power, the necessity of self-preservation, and the improved prospects of the country under American rule.

Frémont's orders were to remain at San Diego until further notice. But he was impatient and unaccustomed to a subordinate role, had a personal grudge against Castro, and wanted to shorten the campaign and hurry home across New Mexico. He was about to set off toward Los Angeles with his topographical party, leaving the volunteers behind, when Dupont interfered. "I should not have put myself under the naval commander," Dupont conceded; but having done so, he must abide by the rules.[52] On August 8, the *Cyane*'s launch returned from San Pedro with the commodore's orders; the ship was to leave immediately for San Pedro and Frémont by land for the pueblo, while Gillespie and forty-eight men were to garrison San Diego.[53]

Stockton had left Monterey on August 1 with the consul aboard.[54] The *Congress* carried three hundred and sixty sailors and marines for land duty, with an armory of ninety muskets and bayonets and one small cannon from a merchant vessel (the commodore tended to belittle his own resources and overstate his opponent's). Going down the coast, he put in at Santa Barbara to take possession and raise the flag, leaving sixteen of his men under Midshipman William Mitchell.[55] On the 6th he anchored at San Pedro, twenty-five land miles from Los Angeles, and debarkation immediately commenced.[56]

On the way down Larkin composed letters to his erstwhile correspondent, Abel Stearns. He told of Frémont's "two hundred" volunteers at San Diego, who, with forces from all the ships, could mean "Near 2000 men . . . in motion to march through C[alifornia]."[57] Stockton wished no war measures but was determined to settle the fate of the country without further loss of time and "no half way measures." Stearns should go at once to the governor, the general, the assembly, and influential citizens and persuade them that the time to declare California independent of Mexico had come. And since the subject had been discussed for months in California, it should not take long to make a decision. Stockton would march within twenty-four hours, and if the Californians wished to avoid bloodshed and gather honor for themselves and peace and security for the country, they had better hurry. Stearns was to come with two others of note within twelve to fourteen hours, and "By no means fail coming . . . in preference to all other business." Stearns relayed an answer at once, received on the 7th, to which Larkin replied, "I am sorry it amounts to nothing," and he regretted that the prefect had not come in person.[58]

Stearns, for eighteen years a Mexican citizen and in California since 1829, was a shrewd and normally somewhat incautious fellow. Often tricky in petty dealings and notoriously fond of smuggling, he was in larger matters generally honorable and partial to the Californians, being a Mexican officer and married to Arcadia Bandini, one of Don Juan's beauteous daughters. Now, circumspectly, recognizing his ambivalent

The Yankee Abel Stearns, eighteen years a Mexican citizen and in California since 1829, was married to one of Juan Bandini's beauteous daughters and partial to the Californians.

role, he advised the consul to get in touch with the general. Impatiently, Larkin pointed out that Castro had already referred them to the governor, and Stockton would have no more correspondence on the subject. "The U.S. and M[exico] are at war," and Larkin had done all he could to prevent the visit of eight hundred soldiers to Los Angeles, with the evils which must attend such an operation.

From the mesa, Castro—whose forces were diminishing and who was therefore in a mood to treat—sent commissioners to Stockton, Pablo de la Guerra and José María Flores, both ardent Californian partisans.[59] On the way they sent a courier to the commodore, asking whether they would be received according to the rights of war. Stockton had sent an invitation and replied in the affirmative, appointing Larkin and Lieutenant J. F. Schenck emissaries.[60] Castro first proposed that all hostile movements be suspended before a conference began, else "there will not be negotiations."[61] This might have seemed a reasonable condition.

From Stockton's superior position aboard a man-of-war the view was different. He deplored the war, he said, but must prosecute it until the country ceased to be a part of Mexico.[62] This was his plain duty.* He would not halt his operations or negotiate on any other principle than that California declare its independence under the protection of the United States. "If . . . you will agree to hoist the American flag in California, I will stop my forces and negotiate the treaty." The price of negotiation was surrender.

Stockton's de facto refusal to negotiate with the Californians must have rankled in his conscience, for in February 1848 he was still laboriously trying to justify it to the Secretary of the Navy.[63] It was obvious, he would say, that Mexico had not been able to instruct its remote territory concerning the war and that local officers were acting upon their own authority. To negotiate with them would have recognized their right not only to carry on the war but to dispose of the public domain, which it had been one of his chief objects to prevent. Moreover, had he suspended hostilities it would have left the Mexicans in full control, and the extermination of the Americans would have been a certain outcome. Furthermore, the squadron would have had to reëmbark and the battalion be abandoned and perhaps sacrificed to "an exasperated and powerful enemy." He hoped these reasons warranted the President's approval.

Castro promptly expressed his "inexpressible surprise" at the commodore's insidious and degrading proposition.[64] He could not raise the American flag in the department under his command—"Never, never, never!" What would the commodore do if the proposal were reversed? Stockton's reply to this rebuke may have been aspersive, for he would tell the Secretary in September that he sent only a verbal message "which does not properly belong to history."[65]

Castro sent copies of the correspondence to the governor and the English vice-consul.[66] And to Pico he wrote from the "Field of the Mesa"

* The President's instructions, which Stockton had not seen, had been to occupy Los Angeles "if opportunity offer and the people favor" (Bancroft to Biddle, Stockton, or senior officer 8 13 1846, to Shubrick 8 17 1846, in 499–19 82, 92).

that he had tried to prepare a defense and oppose invasion, but could do neither. Though the governor had put the militia under his command, he could only count upon a hundred men, poorly armed and discontented, which made him fear that not even they would fight if the occasion demanded. Therefore, lacking every kind of resource to carry on a war, he would not jeopardize the safety of the people or his honor but would leave the country and report to the supreme government. He wanted to know what the governor expected to do, that he might be guided.[67]

With the letter went Castro's proclamation of August 9 to California's inhabitants.[68] A month and a half ago he had notified them of the war that "bandits, paid and led by . . . the United States," had brought to their soil. The government had now joined the horde at Sonoma in an iniquitous invasion. And "there is yet more! The American Government . . . wants us to betray our Mother Country. . . ." Whatever California's fate, never "belie . . . the glorious name of good Mexicans. . . . Death to the invaders!" Next day he issued a mournful notice of farewell.[69]

It was now the governor's turn to make a pronouncement, and he directed it, with some literary style, to his fellow citizens, compatriots, Mexicans, "My friends," and Californians all.[70] He called attention to America's ambitions to dismember the Mexican nation, citing Texas as an example. Now California had been invaded, and its defense was inadequate. Faced with ignominy or migration, he had chosen the latter and today separated himself from them. "Farewell! . . . I abandon the country of my birth, my family, property, and everything that a man holds most dear, all, to save the National Honor." (A skeptical Larkin correspondent in Los Angeles thought Castro's and Pico's stock in trade was "bombastic proclamations and fast legs.")[71]

Pico also addressed long announcements to the local British, Spanish, and French consuls.[72] Considering the power of the invading foe, it seemed prudent to suppress patriotic sentiments. Unable to prevent the present occupation, he was going to the capital to report to the Mexican government, leaving Alta California leaderless.

By August 10 the California establishment was in collapse, both the military and civil leaders having declared their intentions to depart. That night the assembly met, and the governor, presiding, proposed they adjourn so the enemy would find no one with whom to negotiate.[73] Each of the deputies made a patriotic speech, sorrowfully lamenting the fate that had been meted out to the country. Then, by a "decided plurality," it was resolved to dissolve the assembly and inform the people. They would not acquiesce in raising the American flag, though they could not prevent it.

In the night, both the general and the governor left the capital.[74] Disbanding his military force, Castro crossed to Altar in Sonora, where he vainly petitioned the central government for assistance.[75] Pico (whose safety, at Bandini's behest, Frémont had assured) stayed the night at Teodosio Yorba's Lomas de Santiago rancho (in Orange County), then lived in concealment until September 7, when he escaped into Baja California with his secretary. From Mulegé and Guaymas he repeatedly importuned the Minister of Foreign Relations for aid in the recovery of California and for his own relief, without avail.[76]

Stockton had written to Frémont from San Pedro the day of his arrival that there were perhaps 250 Californians at Stearns' Los Alamitos rancho (Long Beach), said to be badly equipped and leaving daily.[77] Unless he had better information, they were to meet at Temple's adjacent farm; and he sent a guide to lead Frémont to the meeting place. While successfully frustrating negotiations, the commodore had been briskly drilling his soldier-sailors in elementary land maneuvers.

(In Washington on August 10, President Polk was rationalizing to himself and the Congress the way of the United States with Mexico.[78] That country was indebted to the United States in a large sum which it could not repay, he began, and there was a dispute over the joint boundary. The nations were now at war, and the only way to obtain indemnity was by a cession of territory. The United States wanted Upper California and New Mexico, and perhaps other areas, for which he was willing to assume Mexico's American debt and pay an additional consideration. He was convinced the Mexican government would welcome such a solution. *Quod erat demonstrandum.*)

With negotiations abruptly ended, Stockton set out for Los Angeles on the 11th with some three hundred and fifty men.[79] Ahead went the band of musicians, followed by Captain Zeilin and his marines, then the sailors under Lieutenant Schenck, and afterwards four quarter-deck guns mounted on bullock carts and ready for instant action. The baggage and ammunition came next, drawn by four oxen, then the purser, doctor, and officers, some mounted on "rather sorry horses," the rest on foot. Late in the afternoon they learned the Californians had dispersed, and one hundred and fifty sailors were sent back to the vessel. The speed of the men was that of the oxen, and they camped the night at Temple's rancho. Next day, Larkin, a servant, and Midshipman Charles H. Baldwin went ahead with a flag of truce and the commodore's reply to Castro.[80] Finding no hindrance, they entered the empty streets of the town, occupied the Government House, and had it whitewashed and in order by the 13th when the army arrived, many of the inhabitants lending furniture at Larkin's behest.[81]

Two Americans, Benjamin D. Wilson and John Rowland, rode out to meet the advancing commodore, reporting Castro's and Pico's departure and bringing a favorite saddle horse as a gift from one of the Domínguez family.[82] With Stockton now well mounted, the party proceeded into town. Meantime, ten pieces of artillery had been found at the mesa, the guns ingeniously buried in one place, their carriages in another.[83] Frémont, after a pleasant march from San Diego, enjoying the fine beef of the country, had camped in the gardens within two miles of the pueblo, and the forces were happily joined.[84] At about 4 p.m., a formidable cavalcade paraded into Los Angeles, the band shrilling "Hail Columbia," raised the Stars and Stripes, and "quietly" occupied the capital. The navy settled into the Government House, Frémont's men camped near the river, and the commodore and his staff were regaled in the household of an American resident. The "filthy" condition of the town was redeemed, according to Dupont, by the surrounding vineyards, which he reported to be "very fine."[85]

Thus ended the "trying and hazardous march," as Stockton zestfully described it to the Secretary, "longer . . . perhaps, than has ever been made in the interior of a country by sailors after an enemy."[86] Because Frémont had not arrived in time, he carefully explained, "that bravado" Castro had escaped, but California was now entirely free of Mexican domination.[87] From San Francisco to San Diego, the country had surrendered to the inevitable without firing a gun—or so for the moment it seemed.

Stockton now issued a second proclamation to the people, adding to his title as commander-in-chief at this time that of governor.[88] Without fanfare or fantasy (he was a good winner), he announced that Castro had fled, the City of the Angels had been taken, and the flag of the United States was flying from every commanding position. California belonged to the United States and would soon be governed by officers and laws similar to those in the other territories. Meanwhile, military law would prevail. Persons adhering to the new order would be zealously protected; the military must swear not to take up arms; thieves would be put to hard labor; and the California battalion would be kept in service to prevent and punish aggression. The people were to meet and elect civil officers, and when this was not done, the commander-in-chief would make appointments. All persons must be in their houses from 10 p.m. until sunrise. Henceforth, California would be so governed and defended as to give security to the inhabitants and defy the power of Mexico.

What was not so evident, perhaps, even to nineteenth-century readers, was Stockton's injunction to the newly arrived Mormons. "You will see by my proclamation of the 17th," he wrote the President, "that I have my eye upon them."[89] An advance band of more than two hundred men, women, and children under Samuel Brannan had landed at San Francisco two weeks before,[90] and the commodore feared they would become a more serious problem than "our 'decided enemies.'" To this unsuspecting sect he had said, "Nor will any persons, come from where they may, be permitted to settle in the Territory, who do not pledge themselves to be in all respects obedient to the laws." Mormonism would make its home in Salt Lake City, some members would take part in the conquest of California, and those who came would prove to be sober and industrious, ready to work for anybody who would pay them (often at higher rates than their fellows). According to the master of New Helvetia at least, they were "the best people which ever I has had employed."[91]

Copies of the proclamation were sent to Montgomery and Gillespie to be translated and published,[92] and it was printed as a broadside in English and Spanish and in Monterey's newspaper, accompanied by Stockton's call for elections.[93]

From Los Angeles on August 26, Stockton made a direct appeal to the President, signing it "Your faithful friend and obdt. servt."[94] He expected to have his civil government in successful operation by October, he said. His "Organic Laws of the Territory" would be few and strong, a mix of old and new forms. As soon as he safely could, he would appoint Major Frémont governor and Captain Gillespie secretary of state. "I earnestly request you to confirm them in their places, as the most salutary arrangement that can be made for the good of the Territory." His work in California was about done, and he would be at San Francisco in October to receive the President's answer. "My word is at present the law of the land," he exulted. "My person is more than regal. The haughty Mexican Cavalier shakes hands with me with pleasure, and the beautiful women

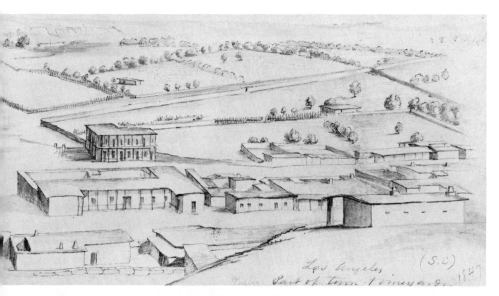

Los Angeles south of the plaza in 1847, with Abel Stearns' house facing Main Street and the Government House two town lots farther south.

look to me with joy and gladness as their friend and benefactor. In short, all of power and luxury is spread before me, through the mysterious workings of a beneficent Providence." This letter, with another for Bancroft, would go overland with Frémont's dispatches carried by Kit Carson[95] and find expression in reports of the Secretaries of War and Navy and the President's annual message. It would not receive a direct answer.

With his dispatch to the Secretary of the Navy, Stockton included an outline of a form of government—the "Organic Law of his Empire," as Larkin said he called it—by which Bancroft might see the sort of organization he had established and how he was proceeding.[96] It proposed offices of governor and secretary, with terms of four years (unless removed by the President), the former combined with that of commander-in-chief of the army. There would be a legislative council of seven persons, its acts subject to the absolute veto of the governor. Locally elected officers would function under the laws of Mexico until otherwise directed. That the Californians could not comprehend any more liberty than this "constitution" offered won it Larkin's approval. Stockton told Frémont that before his own departure he would name him governor and Gillespie secretary of state and would appoint the council and all necessary officers.[97]

For all of Stockton's subsequent defense of his prerogative to form a civil government, he made only a few appointments, named but did not install a council, set a day for its first meeting, and called elections. But though his "law" was sent to Montgomery at the end of September for suggestions, with a statement that he would promulgate it before he left the harbor[98]—and he would refer on January 16, 1847, to his "Laws established for the better government of this Territory, bearing date of September 2, 1846"—he apparently never published it in California.[99] Other matters intervened. Stockton wanted to be the father of his country and establish a line of successors (leaving to them the vicissitudes of office). He would explain to Bancroft in mid-September that his apparent haste in instituting laws was to show that California was completely in American hands and, a year later, that he wanted the territory to feel the benign influence of a free government as soon as possible.[100]

Unequivocal news of a formal declaration of war arrived by the *Warren* at San Pedro on August 17. Mexican newspapers, Polk's war proclamation, and Bancroft's letter to Sloat of May 13 all brought confirmation.[101] "The state of things alluded to in my letter of June 24, 1845, has occurred," read Bancroft's belated message. "You will therefore be governed by the instructions therein contained." To which Stockton could happily respond that all of his orders had been anticipated.[102] Dupont welcomed this vindication of Sloat's action and thought all honor should go to him, though probably "others will get it."

Expansively, Stockton declared all ports, harbors, bays, outlets, and inlets on the west coast of Mexico south of San Diego to be in a state of vigorous blockade; but to enforce this sweeping mandate he could assign only the sloops-of-war *Cyane* and *Warren*, each of twenty guns.[103] In a circular advising vessels of the state of war, he noted that California belonged to the United States, and a safe anchorage could be found in all seasons in the harbor of San Francisco.[104]

Frémont had meanwhile rounded up some of Castro's late troops, releasing them on parole, and many citizens were returning to their homes. Larkin noted the Californians were applying for justice in petty cases, which they had never thought of doing from their own alcaldes.[105] "This speaks volumes" concerning the political change in the country. They were also being paid for everything taken and were obtaining higher prices, and in dollars, than before. He thought Stockton tried to reconcile the people to the new system, being firm but kind to the natives. It was soon discovered that the archives had disappeared from Government House, and Frémont was ordered to seize the documents and other missing property if they could be found (he would himself take public papers and carry them to Washington).[106]

All of California was in American hands. In less than a month after he had assumed the command, Stockton jubilantly informed the Secretary, he had chased the Mexican army more than three hundred miles along the coast; routed and dispersed them; secured the territory for the United States; ended the war; restored peace and harmony among the people; and put a civil government into successful operation.[107] As soon as possible he would withdraw the squadron; and he ordered Frémont to increase his battalion to three hundred men to garrison the towns and guard against Indians and other enemies.[108] Frémont was to go north, see how many volunteers Fauntleroy and Montgomery could provide, and meet him at San Francisco on October 25. Larkin, too, was to be there, to make as he thought "some beginning and arrangements respecting the laws and statutes for California."[109] Stockton would gather his forces as he proceeded up the coast and be ready, when his business was completed, to "leave the desk and the camp, and take to the ship and to the sea."

The commodore craved larger and more conspicuous successes than California afforded. Though the country was high on Polk's list of war objectives, it was inferior in public perception, and military reputations were being made in assaults upon Matamoros and Vera Cruz. He must of course blockade the west Mexican ports and keep an eye out for privateers preying upon American commerce. So, while awaiting the President's reply, he would go to the Gulf of California, sail along the coast of Mexico and to the Sandwich Islands, and return to San Francisco by the end of October.[110]

But that was not all. His grand plan, with which he thought it unnecessary as late as October 1 to acquaint the department, was confidentially revealed to Captain Mervine on September 19.[111] With a large body of troops Frémont had been commissioned to assemble, he meant to land at Mazatlán or Acapulco and fight his way toward the Mexican capital. "I would that we might shake hands with General Taylor at the gates of Mexico," he gloated. He wrote anxiously to Frémont on September 28 to learn the prospects of recruiting his "thousand men, for a visit to Mexico."[112] An utter lack of enthusiasm among the settlers and immigrants, and Frémont's limited confidence in the enterprise (as he would after-wards tell),[113] plus a jarring surprise which the Californians had in store, made this play to the grandstand one he would never be called upon to fulfill.

On Stockton's last day in Los Angeles, he made Frémont commandant of the territory (subject to the governor and commander-in-chief) and di-vided the country into three military departments.[114] Gillespie was to head the southern department, including Baja California, with Lieu-tenant Maddox of the marines at Monterey and Montgomery at San Francisco.[115]

Stockton boarded the *Congress* at San Pedro on September 3, pausing at Santa Barbara two days later to pick up the men left there in August.[116] Here Midshipman Archibald McRea came aboard with dispatches, in-cluding one from Bancroft reiterating the importance of holding San Francisco.[117] He also brought a message from the Secretary of State to Larkin, the first he had received, he said, since October 1845.[118] On the 15th the commodore reached Monterey,[119] where everything appeared tranquil, though members of Castro's army were being required to pre-sent themselves and give parole. But an express from Montgomery on the 18th warned of an attack upon Sutter's Fort by a thousand Walla Wallas, revenging the murder of a young chief by an American a year before, as it was supposed.[120] Sending the *Savannah* ahead, Stockton left for San Francisco on the 24th, to learn the Indians had dwindled to forty in num-ber, all "friendly disposed"[121] (some would join Frémont's forthcoming march to Los Angeles).

Other news was more fateful. At the end of September a courier boarded the *Congress* at San Francisco bearing a simple message, "Be-lieve the Bearer," written in a very small hand on cigarette paper and bearing the seal of Lieutenant Gillespie. Juan Flaco ("lean John" Brown), after a six-day ride from Los Angeles, brought word that Gillespie was besieged in the Government House. In haste Stockton replied that the *Savannah* was under way, and if all was not well to send the courier back with a message.[122] To Larkin he said he would leave as soon as he could take on water, and to Mervine that the chief of the "Wallow-wallows" was expected and it would not do for him to depart.[123] Frémont was to hurry from the Sacramento with as many horses and men as he could muster.[124]

In truth, the commodore had a more diverting engagement. A great welcome was being prepared for him by the ebullient citizens of Yerba Buena (a "small miserable town," according to Dupont, much like a suburb of Honolulu).[125] At 10 in the morning of October 5 a procession assembled on Portsmouth Square. The chief marshal, with "Blue Sashes waving in the Wind," was followed by a military escort, including Captain John B. Montgomery and suite and an "excellent band of Music." In their wake came the magistrates of the district, representatives of the Russian, Hawaiian, and French navies, captains of ships in port, and a long line of citizens, among them General Vallejo (recently liberated from Sutter's Fort), followed by stragglers, Indians, and dogs. They moved in fine style down to the waterfront a block away. Here the "Governor General," alighting from his barge to the sound of guns, was conducted to the head of the line, where he was greeted by the orator of the day, Colonel William H. "Owl" Russell of Kentucky, former U.S. marshal of Missouri. Oratory was in flower. "You, sir," he hailed the commodore, "whose fortune it was to be born with . . . all the elegancies, comforts and endearments of domestic life, have chosen like the heroes and patriots of other days . . . to sacrifice their all on the altar of your country's good." Stockton had hoisted the Stars and Stripes. He had also, as the speaker happened to know, temporarily laid aside his sword and, in the character of legislator, formed a code of laws. And Russell gave voluble assurance of a hearty welcome on behalf of the proud citizens of Yerba Buena.

Stockton could reply in kind. "Colonel Russell: You have met me . . . at high-water mark . . . the tocsin of war was sounded . . . ease and luxury had no longer any charms for us. . . . We embarked with sealed orders . . . [and] it has turned up, sir, that California is our field of action. . . ." Commodore Sloat had handed him Monterey and San Francisco, and he was determined to conquer the whole country. He had landed at San Pedro; "the battle of good government against oppression was to be fought," and the question of possession forever settled. The Californians broke their camp, buried their guns, and fled; and he took possession. Now came news that two hundred armed men had attacked "our little band" at Los Angeles, left there for their protection under guarantees of peace and friendship. The *Savannah* was on her way, and the *Congress* would soon follow. He would go this time to punish as well as conquer; there would be no more insurrections. Ten thousand Sonorans could not shake his purpose. The "Sons of Liberty are on their way . . . but this is the time for fighting, not for making speeches—I am

done." The press said the address was replete with beautiful and energetic thought, calculated not only to kindle the imagination but sway the
judgment.[126]

Afterwards, an excellent collation was offered at the house of Captain
Leidesdorff, followed by the drinking of toasts, a reception "in all the
blaze and brilliancy of 100 Spermacitte Candles," and a ball lasting until
an early hour in the morning.

Eight days later, the *Congress* and the chartered merchant ship *Sterling*, with Frémont's hundred and sixty men—including "Owl" Russell,
Lansford Hastings, and Edwin Bryant—sailed for the southern coast.

11

Paradise Lost—
Gillespie's Fall

L IEUTENANT GILLESPIE, who had been left at San Diego on August 8 during the occupation of Los Angeles, was joined by Frémont on the 18th to discuss their proposed appointments as governor and secretary. By the 31st they were both in Los Angeles, where Gillespie received his commission as captain and military commandant of the southern district.[1] This arrangement made, Stockton set out for San Pedro on September 2, leaving Gillespie forty-eight men and $20,000 in scarce specie from the *Congress* for the military expenditures of the territory.[2] Frémont camped nearby until the 11th.

In his conqueror's proclamation of August 17, Stockton had declared that until the governor, secretary, and council were appointed and civil departments set up, martial law would prevail.[3] Persons found with arms outside their own houses were to be regarded as enemies, and all must be indoors from 10 o'clock at night until sunrise. Notwithstanding, being sensitive to political realities (and some of Gillespie's little quirks), the commodore gave instructions on tempering the "rigors of indispensable military law with appliances of peace."[4] His orders were to be strictly enforced except against those who might be exempted by Gillespie's writ. Whenever it was prudent, persons known to be friendly were to be allowed to go out themselves and to send their servants out before sunrise; and they were to be permitted to carry arms when needed for protection. Civil officers were to exercise their appropriate functions. Gillespie was to report to Stockton at every opportunity.

Years later Frémont would blame Stockton for instituting police reg-

ulations without respect to the feelings of the natives, citing the require-
ment to obtain permits from Gillespie, which "jarred against all the instincts of the people."⁵ Gillespie's own understanding was that he should
treat the natives with the "greatest kindness and lenity . . . but . . . be
very vigilant, firm and strict . . . and by no means . . . permit anyone to
escape" who might violate the commodore's proclamation.⁶ Not readily
would he moderate the chill wind to the shorn lamb.

Gillespie's qualifications for this assignment were not of the best.
Often he was neither a judicious leader nor a reliable witness. The information upon which he depended (and purveyed in long self-serving letters to the Secretary of the Navy) was commonly inadequate, for his vision was ever limited by his prejudices, which mounted to the level of
obsession. He served one lord mostly (and not always well), his own ambition, and since his cause had no other adherents, no one could keep the
faith but he. Such singularity of purpose bred a chronic suspicion of others (in Yerba Buena, spies beset him "at every turn") and fostered general
mistrust, leading to ill will and rancor. Every man, himself never excluded, was expected to do his duty precisely as the commandant momentarily saw it; but in appraising performance, he could not be counted
upon to judge dispassionately the evidence his eyes and ears presented.
Gillespie wanted to make and leave his mark, and he was vigorous and
valorous, in the vanguard of every fray. His tastes, he said, were entirely
in his profession, in which he anxiously desired advancement; and he did
not want to be sidetracked by Stockton's proffered appointment as secretary of state, though he would accept it temporarily out of duty, "having
commenced the work."

(Why did he write those interminable letters to the Honorable Secretary of the Navy, tendered to him as a close personal friend, one alone of
forty manuscript pages?⁷ Did he believe the great George Bancroft, histo-
rian, politician, and statesman, would read them from beginning to end
and take corresponding notice; or did he have faith that the written word
would somehow survive to bear testimony to his deeds and worth? More
than likely they expressed the hope, imparted to the Secretary at the beginning of his venture, that "should I be successful, I may not be forgotten."⁸ They tell more about him than he probably knew.)

This tall, red-headed American did not like the Californians. They
were not on his side, and they had no saving graces. They were "cowardly
and inert"; Castro was "devoid of principle," a "usurper and despot";
and the government was one of "Mexican tyranny and military despo-

tism." Not even his avowed friends could escape rejection. In April 1846 Larkin was in "every way worthy of the confidence reposed in him," a man of zeal, patriotism, and good judgment; but by July he was "entirely governed by his own Selfish views" and, when private business intervened, "willing to allow the Country to pass into other hands." [9] Even the "bold and chivalrous" Frémont, whom he eulogized as the Conqueror, would subsequently be charged with disobedience, a lack of courage, and wanting an understanding of military affairs. [10] There was of course reality behind all of these judgments, but whenever the humorless and magisterial captain felt that one extreme was true, the validity of any other view was irrelevant.

In Los Angeles he laid down needlessly oppressive regulations. According to Antonio Coronel, an influential citizen, no two persons were permitted to go about the streets together; under no pretext could people hold meetings in their homes; shops must be closed at sundown; liquor could not be sold without Gillespie's permission; and the commandant decided petty cases instead of leaving them to the *jueces de paz*. [11] Houses were searched for weapons, and persons imprisoned on mere suspicion. An American, Benito Wilson, reported that, having established very obnoxious regulations, Gillespie upon frivolous pretexts had the most respectable men in the community brought before him for no other purpose than to humiliate them, as they thought. [12] The people had given no just cause for such severity, which seemed altogether the result of Gillespie's vanity and want of judgment. When Larkin was later in the city, he heard from many that, had a proper person been left in charge, no disturbance would have ensued. [13] "It appears even from the Americans that Captain A H G punished fined and imprisoned who and when he pleased without any hearing." In short, Gillespie was a petty tyrant.

While the Angelenos had shown no disposition to oppose the new regime, a remnant of Castro's partisans—notably José Antonio Carrillo and José María Flores (Micheltorena's former secretary)—had retreated to southern California and formed a cell from which resistance might grow. Too, there had always been a turbulent element in the pueblo which even the Californians could not control (a revolt against Pico had occurred the previous November). Perhaps even before Frémont's departure, some Californians had gone as far north as Santa Barbara to recruit allies. [14] One Bonifacio Olivares (who had been banished to Los Angeles from Monterey in 1843) wrote to Salvador Vallejo at Sonoma on September 6, inviting him to help punish the sailors who had taken Los Angeles.[15] Since people were being branded as rebels before they had thought of rebellion,[16] some of the wilder spirits took advantage of the resentment to breed even greater excitement. Sérbulo Varela, a noted dissident who had opposed Pico the year before, became a kind of leader. With his fellows, each of whom could command a few followers, he raised a band of perhaps two dozen men, natives and Mexicans.

Gillespie had feared an attempt might be made to seize the money Stockton had placed in his charge (he could conceive of no other cause for dissidence), but the reinforcements from Frémont's camp until the 11th may have been a deterrent. On the 15th he sent a dozen men under Merritt to garrison San Diego[17] and later ten more, the most undisciplined of his crew, to Warner's ranch to get them out of town. He forwarded reports to Stockton and Frémont on the 20th, but the courier took the papers to the enemy instead.

At 3 a.m. on September 23, Varela's band made an assault upon the remaining Americans, of whom there were now only twenty-one. They may not have meant to fight but only to threaten or even capture the post by surprise, thus impressing both the conquerors and their countrymen. Among Gillespie's volunteers were some very reliable men, but others were unaccustomed to discipline, he said, and "perfect drunkards whilst in this Ciudad of wine & Aguadiente." But they were serviceable riflemen and gave a good account of themselves, routing the assailants.[18] Many residents had already fled (Stockton's election on the 15th produced twenty voters, one a Californian), and the renewed fighting and subsequent round-up by the excited Gillespie convinced them that war had again begun. Varela's band rapidly expanded, and some of the foreigners joined Gillespie's camp. Stockton had left no artillery, so the enterprising Gillespie set about fashioning cannon from four old guns lying in the government yard which officers of the *Congress* had pronounced unfit for service. And he collected scrapings of the blacksmith shops and a thousand pounds of pipe lead "for distilling" to make grape and round shot. On the 24th he fortified the hill above the town, strengthened the works about his quarters, and that night sent Juan Flaco to tell Stockton.[19]

The same day Varela issued a proclamation, signed by more than three hundred followers.[20] It was in character, with a kernel of substance to fit the current need. They beheld themselves "subjugated and oppressed by an insignificant force of adventurers" who were dictating despotic and arbitrary laws. All citizens were required to take up arms. The northern districts would be invited to adhere. The Californians had little ammunition but plenty of supplies, and a kind of siege was begun.

The following day two townsmen, Eulogio Célis and Francisco Figueroa, proposed a temporary cessation of hostilities, a proposition Gillespie thought should come from the enemy and to which he would willingly accede. At about sunset the proposal was returned, this time signed by José M. Flores, who had now been elected commander—though he and others had given their promise not to take up arms against the United States. Through field glasses Gillespie counted more than three hundred Californians in arms; the mediators estimated over four hundred; and Flores expected to have six hundred in very short order. With the foreigners who had recently joined, Gillespie could claim fifty-nine.

The enemy now demanded unconditional surrender and to be relieved from their parole, and they allowed Gillespie until sunrise of the next morning to make up his mind. Shades of Commodore Stockton! This time the Americans were affronted in the person of an officer of the United States "whose education had taught him to die at [his] post rather than permit his country's arms to be disgraced."[21] The initiative on the part of the Californians was rejected.

On September 26, after noon, another flag of truce was brought by Célis and Figueroa, proposing a conference at 4 p.m. As Gillespie hoped his courier to the commodore would get through, he consented, to gain time, and sent Dr. Gilchrist (surgeon of the *Congress*) and Nathaniel Pryor (a Kentuckian and long-time southern Californian) as his representatives. No headway being made, Flores was brought in at Dr. Gilchrist's request. With the "manners and address of a gentleman," he was reportedly apologetic and wanted only to make terms which would be suitable to Gillespie and induce him to depart. The conference was adjourned until 9 a.m. the next day. The American position in the Government House was again strengthened. After two hours of parley on the 27th, the conditions were still inadmissible: that the American force march out of town with the honors of war but in two parties, at different times, thus placing them at the enemy's mercy. Gillespie said he would negotiate on no other terms than that the Californians would retire to their homes. Flores sent him a note from Benito Wilson (who was being held prisoner).[22] It proposed that Gillespie and his men march out the following morning, unmolested by the Californians, proceed with their arms to San Pedro, and there embark. An immediate answer was demanded, and if it was nega-

Los Angeles from the hills, showing the settlement north and south of the plaza and the agricultural plots between it and the river.

tive, Flores would not be responsible for the conduct of his men, many of whom were drinking and eager for revenge.

Another act of defiance had meanwhile taken place at the Santa Ana del Chino rancho of Isaac Williams, thirty miles east of the pueblo. Before Stockton's departure, he had appointed Benito Wilson a captain of volunteers, with some twenty foreigners, to guard the Cajón Pass, "through which leads the 'Spanish trail' from New Mexico." [23] When Wilson learned that Castro had indeed fled to Sonora, he and his men went hunting. Upon hearing of the Californians' revolt "and that there was the devil to pay generally," they returned to Wilson's Jurupa rancho (at Riverside), then went on to Chino, where they expected to find ammunition but were disappointed. Mostly newcomers and contemptuous of the Californians' courage, the men decided to remain at Chino rather than escape to the mountains and later join the garrison at Los Angeles. They were sure the few shots left from their hunting trip would scare away any number of opponents.

On the evening of September 26, eighty to a hundred Californian horsemen appeared—"some of my own among them," Wilson noted—and by morning they were surrounded. Ammunition was scarce on both sides, but after one Californian had been killed, two of Wilson's men seriously wounded, and the asphalt and reed roof set on fire, the commander of the Californians, who proved to be Sérbulo Varela, proposed surrender. "You know I am your friend," he told Wilson, "neither you nor any of your friends shall be injured." Colonel Isaac Williams was also in the house, with his three children, and their grandfather, Antonio M. Lugo, had five sons in the attacking force.[24] The Americans all came out and were taken as prisoners to Los Angeles, Varela saving them from death on the way in revenge for the dead Californian. It was the insurgents' first victory. Wilson counseled Gillespie that it was in the interest of all Americans in the country that they capitulate.[25]

Even with Flores' new proposal in hand, Gillespie feared attack and on the 28th moved his whole camp, with twelve prisoners, to the hill above the town. There his position would have been secure except for a lack of water, the nearest supply being in a yard at the hill's base.[26] Another conference produced tentative terms by sunset which Gillespie thought honorable to both parties. Mindful of the distance from water, the Americans accepted the plan, and intermediaries went to work on the details. The articles of capitulation were completed at El Molino, near San Gabriel, on the morning of September 29, and at 1 p.m. brought for Gillespie's signature.[27] He would remind Bancroft that the treaty had been made by fifty-five men—deducting servants, fifty—opposing six hundred, at a place nearly six hundred miles from any relief. Should it meet the approval of the "kind friends" who had ordered him to the country, he would be fully repaid by their applause and the knowledge that he had maintained the honor of his country's flag.[28] Copies would find their ways into the archives of Mexico and the United States.

The articles of capitulation required that Captain Gillespie "retire from the plaza de Los Angeles" within the time necessary to ready his march to San Pedro, and that he remain at the port only long enough to make preparations to embark, "under word of honor not to protract that time." He would quit the plaza with all the honors of war. He would take the artillery mounted in the plaza, with the customary ammunition, leaving it at San Pedro. His private property could also be removed, but all U.S. stores were to be turned over to a Mexican official. Prisoners were to be exchanged, and such as would be taken thereafter were to be treated according to the laws of war (more hostilities were expected). The past conduct of all foreigners would be disregarded. As an addendum, the time for evacuating the plaza was set at 9 a.m., September 30th. Gillespie's force was not to be molested in any way, though Californian observers would march at a distance of one league. To all of these conditions the signators of both belligerents agreed, "giving their word of honor that they would be faithfully observed."

By 10 a.m. of the 30th, Gillespie was ready to move. An exchange of prisoners having been made the night before (a dozen Californians for the Chino captives),[29] the U.S. force of seventy-three, including servants and camp followers, marched past the Californians with flags flying. They left behind, Gillespie certified, no property of any value to the "insulting enemy."[30] By evening they were at the San Pedro anchorage, where they camped at 8 p.m.

"It is one of the articles of the Treaty," Gillespie wrote, "that I should embark for Monterey . . . but should have everything prepared before embarking."[31] The merchant ship *Vandalia* was in port, bound for Monterey, but was short of water, so some days were required to fill the casks by boat from a source three miles away. The ship's galley, too, was small, and it was necessary to build ranges on shore so the men could cook their provisions. Not putting any confidence in the Californians, Gillespie also built an "almost impregnable" fortification. All the while, he remarked, he fully intended to keep faith with the enemy, although the only justification, he felt, in dealing with men who had broken their parole was to save his party from defeat and their arms from "ignoble surrender."

Flores, meanwhile, believed Gillespie was stalling, and several communications passed between them.[32] Finally, on October 4, he charged the commandant with repairing his artillery and building entrenchments and asked, "Do these things belong to preparations necessary for departure?" Was this the conduct of troops under capitulation? Gillespie was ordered to embark "within two hours of this very day." To which Gillespie replied that although his preparations were not concluded, he would give in to the demands and go aboard by sunrise the next morning. But he and his officers had already decided they would not let the artillery fall into the hands of the enemy as the articles stipulated, for they believed it would be turned upon them while embarking.[33] They would therefore leave the night before, spike the guns on the beach, and quietly go on board the *Vandalia*, Captain Everett having assured them that water and bullocks could be had at the island of Catalina. "The sentinels were withdrawn, the Smith's hammers fell silently upon the Guns, every man was in the boats . . . & by 10 o'clock our whole force was safely on board." By next morning the Californians had moved back into San Pedro.

Gillespie was in fact not intending to sail. Counting upon his courier reaching the commodore, he determined to await the arrival of one of the ships from the north. On October 6, the cry of "Sail ho!" was heard, and the frigate *Savannah* (having picked up Colt's rifles at San Francisco)[34] rounded the north point of the bay and anchored nearby amid cheers and a two-gun salute. Gillespie and Gilchrist immediately went aboard, to find the impetuous Mervine eager to march upon Los Angeles. He had expected to hurry there to Gillespie's relief, but the commandant counseled caution, warning that he should not move without horses and artillery, advice echoed by the surgeon. Since Mervine had no field pieces on board, he was told of two six-pounders on the *Vandalia* which could be readily mounted. "But My dear Sir," Gillespie would inform the Secretary, "no attention was paid to either our advice or information."[35]

Captain Mervine craved a quick victory before Stockton appeared. He believed he had nothing to fear from the mounted Californians and that if he could force his way into the city, means of sustenance would be found. A little after sunrise on the 7th, therefore, about three hundred men—sailors, marines, and volunteers—were set ashore.[36] The prudent Gillespie recounts with self-satisfaction that his volunteers carried extra cannisters of rifle powder in their blankets (each with sixty to a hundred rounds), while Mervine's men had only what the cartridge boxes would hold. Nor would Mervine make preparations to carry the wounded; and he scorned taking a piece of artillery—"indeed! he was without reason." Stockton's instructions had been not to expose the ship and men unnecessarily but, if needed, to hazard both.[37]

The mode of advance was classic, the marines (ahead) and sailors (afterward) forming a square, with Gillespie's riflemen serving as skirmishers on either flank.[38] As they proceeded north from the San Pedro landing, with marshland on the right and the Palos Verdes hills to the left, they were menaced by a body of the enemy on the heights (under handsome six-foot-four José Antonio Carrillo). These Gillespie dispersed, by his own account, to avoid fire on the main body, but Mervine objected, "Capt . . . you are wasting ammunition. . . ." Then, entering the open plain covered with wild mustard, they came about 2:30 p.m. to rancho San Pedro of Manuel Domínguez (south of Compton), now deserted. Here they halted for the night to rest the weary men. By 8 a.m. of the 8th they were again on the march, quite as fatigued as before, by Gillespie's statement, since Mervine had responded throughout the night to every harassing tactic of the enemy. The Californians were soon discovered upon the road, 175 to 200 strong, and at 400 yards they discharged an ancient four-pounder (the "old woman's gun," a ceremonial piece from the plaza), the shot going over the Americans' heads. A charge was ordered, the marines and sailors now in a solid column, with volunteer riflemen in front and on the flanks. Gillespie, with greater experience (and writing with some hindsight), took cover in the bed of a dry creek, his men falling upon the ground to avoid fire, while the naval forces plunged ahead. A second artillery shot "touched" the tops of the bayonets and pikes, but the next and successive discharges dealt "dreadful havoc," with no attempt being made to check the loss of life. The Californians had been ordered to annoy the enemy with the field piece, not to engage them "furiously"; and by firing and dragging the cannon away with *reatas* attached to their saddles, they were able to deliver telling blows while exposing themselves to a minimum hazard.[39] "In truth," Stockton would later agree, "nothing short of a locomotive engine" could catch those well-mounted fellows.[40]

After three charges, in which several men were hit, Mervine called a halt. They could not overtake the flying artillery, and they returned to the abandoned rancho, where it was decided to fall back upon San Pedro. Making a cart for the wounded, they reached the landing by 3 p.m., losing another man by crossfire before the Californians' powder was spent. The casualties were perhaps four dead and four to six wounded.[41] The *Vandalia's* six-pounders had meanwhile been mounted, but the whole body of Americans embarked hastily upon the *Savannah*, and a council of officers decided to abandon San Pedro to the enemy. Very soon, dry goods, tallow, and hides belonging to Americans were being carted away "in broad day," while the frigate anchored in the roads and the *Vandalia* hustled off with a message for Commodore Stockton.[42]

At San Francisco on October 1, Stockton had sent a boat to Sonoma with a message for Frémont and his volunteers to come down.[43] While enlisting men for the Mexican coast had been difficult, fighting the Californians was more to the settlers' liking—though some wavered until it was known whether they would receive $25 a month or no.[44] Immigrants from the Rockies and Oregon were less choosy, their resources being exhausted; and after Kern (at Sacramento) had received a message from Frémont that "we want men," he began energetically mustering volun-

José Antonio Carrillo, six-foot-four captain of the Californian forces, who defeated Mervine and would frighten Stockton from San Pedro but later sign the Treaty of Cahuenga with Frémont as one of the Mexican commissioners.

teers and horses.[45] On the 10th, boats from the *Portsmouth* and *Congress* were ordered up-river to bring recruits to the chartered ship *Sterling*.[46] Troops were withdrawn from Sonoma, San José, Yerba Buena, and Monterey, alarming the inhabitants, who were authorized to enroll men for their own protection.[47] Thirty-five or forty volunteers under Charles Weber at San José were sent to blockade the passes below Monterey, stopping communication between the natives and "those who left."[48] This would be difficult.

Both Stockton and Frémont sailed from San Francisco on October 14.[49] The *Congress*, well stocked with nine field pieces,[50] was headed for San Pedro, where the commodore was to march upon Los Angeles. Frémont, in the *Sterling*, was to land at Santa Barbara, get horses, and make the three-day journey overland to the southern pueblo. South of San Francisco, however, Stockton spoke the *Barnstable*, bearing a message from Lieutenant Maddox at Monterey that the town was threatened and needed support.[51] Stopping there from the 15th to the 19th, the commodore left fifty men and two officers, with three pieces of artillery, before continuing down the coast.[52] In passing, he looked in at Santa Barbara, to find the *Sterling* had not yet arrived, though it should have been there several days before. (A closer inspection would have shown that place in the hands of the Californians. Theodore Talbot and nine men, left there by Frémont on his way north, had learned of the uprising from Juan Flaco and the "noble and disinterested" women of the town but, spurning surrender, would make an arduous thirty-four-day flight through the wilds to Monterey.)[53]

Stockton anchored at San Pedro on October 25 and, after two days of deliberation, determined to land the forces of the *Congress* and *Savannah* in the face of the "boasting insolence" of scattered enemy cavalry. The Californians had been routinely policing the port since the capitulation, with forces under Carrillo stationed at neighboring ranchos. For their own diversion, they had been playing games with the excitable Mervine, driving him to distraction. They raised the Mexican flag; chased cannon balls, holding them up for the enemy to see; sent a dog with a note warning of their approach and please have the coffee ready; and drove horses repeatedly up one ravine and down another to make their number appear greater than they were. Mervine was in a constant state of excitement, Gillespie reported.[54]

Gillespie's irregulars were to have gone ashore at 4 a.m. to surprise the foe and cover the general landing up a steep bank.[55] But they apparently failed to make the shore on schedule—"in consequence of a fancied force of the enemy," according to the cocky commodore.[56] Not so the sailors and marines, he boasted, who were ready in the boats and carried out the maneuver in a most gallant manner. "The commander-in-chief intends to lead on the attack, if there be one," his general order concluded. So, on the 27th the American flag was once more flying at San Pedro and a camp "of the strongest kind" established while they awaited word from Frémont.[57] Next morning Stockton himself went ashore, made some "bombastic speeches," it was reported, and read an order commending the determined courage of the sailors and marines.[58] Before noon, what appeared to be four hundred mounted Californians arrived to reinforce their fellows; and that night, without warning, Stockton ordered his troops to withdraw. Weary of "chasing and skirmishing," as the commodore would explain, and giving up (after three days) all hope of Frémont's cooperation, men and artillery were embarked before dawn.[59] "What will be said of this here and at home," the perplexed surgeon of the *Savannah* wrote in his journal.[60]

Although the commodore had perhaps seven hundred and fifty men and six pieces of light artillery with which to reoccupy Los Angeles, he sailed for San Diego on October 30, taking Gillespie's volunteers, transferred from the *Savannah*. Stockton's biographer would make it appear that he charged eight hundred Californians, forcing them to retreat, then decided that without horses his men would be worn down by fatigue.[61] San Pedro was an insecure anchorage, and though San Diego was farther from his objective by one hundred and fifty miles, it offered a superior harbor and more scope for action. He would make his headquarters there.

Stockton's ardor may have been dampened by a ruse perpetrated by the enemy, according to Benito Wilson, who, as an emissary from the Californians, was observing nearby.[62] Standing near the landing and looking back through an opening in the Palos Verdes hills, he saw a great cloud of dust and an "immense band of horses" which occupied several hours in passing. This exhibition, as already suggested, had been staged by the Californians driving mounted and riderless horses around and around a hill, visible to the anchored vessels.

Lieutenant Rowan afterwards remembered Stockton saying he had withdrawn because Frémont had turned back to Monterey, making it impossible for them to march at once upon Los Angeles;[63] but Frémont's movements were not known to him until November 1, after he had reached San Diego. Another reporter would relate in December, "the commander-in-chief lands, . . . goes back to the ship, and in the night sends orders to re-embark all the forces. . . . This order has not yet been explained."[64] According to Wilson, J. A. Carrillo, who produced the spectacular, wanted to propose a truce to Stockton to end the hostilities. He would let the commodore hold the landing, leave the fate of the country to higher authorities and more distant battlefields, and avoid hard feelings between peoples who would in all probability have to live together. Flores would yet make such a pacific overture.

About six weeks before, Ezekiel Merritt had arrived at San Diego with a dozen men from Gillespie's headquarters. After the revolt in Los Angeles, some Californians had been sent to retake the place, and Merritt,

The Palos Verdes Hills above the anchorage at San Pedro where Commodore Stockton had a vision of four hundred mounted Californians arriving to support their fellows.

with Bidwell (from San Luis Rey) and a few citizens, had taken refuge on the whaling vessel *Stonington* in the bay.[65] Bidwell then made a hazardous passage by boat to San Pedro for aid, and on October 13 Mervine sent down fifty sailors and volunteers in the *Magnolia* under Lieutenant George Minor.[66] With the help of a few natives, the Americans reoccupied the town; but the Californians continued to hover around, patrolling and cutting off supplies. Stockton reached the harbor on October 31 and, though the *Congress* stalled on the bar and was anchored outside, landed forty marines and Gillespie's volunteers.[67]

Next day the Mexican prize brig *Malek Adhel* arrived with a message from Frémont.[68] Two days out of San Francisco in the *Sterling*, he had spoken the *Vandalia* (Gillespie's temporary refuge) and learned of Mervine's defeat and that the enemy had driven off all animals along the coast. Exercising his discretion, he had turned back to Monterey, where he proposed to raise men, obtain guns, and retrieve horses left on the Cosumnes. He could thus check the insurrection in the north, obtain needed supplies, and be ready upon the arrival of reinforcements to march overland to Los Angeles. The captain of the *Malek Adhel*, Lieutenant W. B. Rushant, had learned from the *Sterling* of this change in plans and voluntarily carried the news to San Diego.[69]

By this chance proceeding Frémont had reaffirmed his independence and restored his initiative. He suggested that Stockton join him at Monterey, and by November 4 the *Congress* and *Savannah* were standing up the coast. Somewhere south of Monterey on the 9th, the commodore heard that Frémont would leave that day for Los Angeles, and he turned back to San Diego. Mervine, continuing on to Monterey, found that Frémont would not depart for a "week or two" and set about rendering aid.[70]

This time Stockton succeeded in getting the *Congress* into San Diego harbor and shortly established his headquarters at Señor Bandini's house on the plaza.[71] Volunteers under Captain Samuel Gibson were sent to Baja California in the *Stonington* to round up animals, marching back with some ninety horses, two hundred cattle, and many sheep (mostly Bandini's).[72] Jubilantly, Stockton wrote the Secretary that he would soon be a general of dragoons as well as a commodore, commander-in-chief, and governor.

More soberly, Captain Dupont of the *Cyane* deplored the navy's seizure of places other than Monterey and San Francisco, with perhaps a vessel at San Diego. They should have gone only where the ships could be taken and have defended only those occupied towns until land reinforcements came. Meanwhile, conciliation, a "friendly tone," evidence of the prosperity which might be expected, and a solicitation of the views of leading men would have done much to make the people feel they were a "friendly accession" rather than a fallen foe.[73]

Few were so indifferent to fame.

✂12✂

Advent of Kearny

I<small>N THE MIDST</small> of Stockton's preparations at San Diego—building fortifications, fighting off the Californians, scouring the country for animals, making shoes for men and harness for horses, and turning sailors
into soldiers—there was an unexpected interruption. On December 3
a messenger brought word that General Stephen Watts Kearny of the
United States Army had arrived with troops at Warner's Pass (in San Diego County). The letter apprised Stockton of Kearny's approach, said he
had come by order of the President, and asked him to open communications. That same evening Captain Gillespie, the commodore's man-
of-all-work, was dispatched to Kearny's camp with a flying column of
thirty-nine men and a brass four-pounder (the "Sutter" gun). He carried
intelligence from Stockton that a force of the enemy under Andrés Pico,
said to be a hundred strong, was at San Pasqual, and if Kearny thought it
advisable he should "beat up their camp."[1]

Kearny had left Fort Leavenworth on June 27 with the "Army of the
West" under orders of May 13 and 14 from the Adjutant General to protect American trade with Santa Fé and occupy that place.[2] On May 26
the President had discussed with his cabinet the importance of sending an
expedition to California to assure that it would be in the military possession of the United States when peace was made.[3] He had already stated
his purpose to acquire California and other northern provinces, and now
that the countries were at war, the prospects were "much better."[4] If
Kearny's troops in New Mexico were utilized for this operation, they
would be three weeks ahead of any new force which could be ordered
out. Instructions were therefore issued by General Scott and Secretary of
War Marcy to "press forward to California."[5] While Kearny was not required to set out from Santa Fé at once unless he considered the move-

ment seasonable, clearly there was to be no delay, for it was repeatedly stated that the President hoped he would reach the interior of California before winter and had no doubt every effort would be made to do so.

Kearny's 1st Dragoons were to be augmented by recruiting American settlers in New Mexico and California, and he was authorized to requisition men from the governor of Missouri and to muster as volunteers members of the great Mormon emigration then moving west.[6] Pointedly, his new rank of Brevet Brigadier General would be conferred upon him when his march to California began.[7] Another communication from Secretary of War Marcy of June 18 reported that arms, cannon, and provisions would be shipped around Cape Horn with a company of regular artillery (under Captain Tompkins) and that arrangements were being made to send a regiment of New York volunteers out by sea.[8] "These troops," Kearny was told in a crucial utterance, "and such as may be organized in upper California, will be under your command."

Kearny occupied Santa Fé on August 18, conquered and set up a government for New Mexico by September 22, and left on the afternoon of the 25th for California. His military force consisted of a personal staff, three hundred dragoons, a party of topographical engineers under Lieutenant William H. Emory, and experienced hunters and guides Antoine Robidoux and Jean Charbonneau.[9] He also started with two small howitzers "on wheels ten feet in circumference" and a number of wagons for baggage.

Mounted upon mules, some "devlish poor," they set out in great spirits as "men who had a duty to do & intended to do it."[10] Some animals gave out the first day—a bad prospect with San Diego 1,043 miles away.[11] Traveling some sixty-five miles down the Santa Fé River, they crossed the Río Grande del Norte at Albuquerque, passed the prettily situated town of Socorro, and thirteen miles below, on October 6, met a party of eight or nine men, charging down upon them and yelling like Indians. It was Kit Carson, Stockton's courier, on the way to Washington.[12] Kearny's instructions of June 3 had anticipated that U.S. naval forces might be in possession of the coastal towns of California and would cooperate in the conquest, but he now learned that he was "too late," California had surrendered without a fight, the American flag floated in every port, and Frémont was to be governor.

So, the war in California apparently being ended, Kearny's conquering force was reduced to a mere escort, companies C and K, with officers and aides totaling 121 men.[13] Carson, having just passed over the country

*Stephen W. Kearny, with the Army of the West, oc-
cupied Santa Fé in August 1846 and, under the President's orders, moved on to California to ensure the
military possession of that Mexican province by the
United States when peace with Mexico was made.*

they were to traverse, was induced much against his will to turn back as
guide. And Stockton's messages (one stating his intention to appoint Frémont governor)[14] were forwarded to Washington by Thomas Fitzpatrick,
another of Frémont's scouts. Two hundred dragoons turned back to
Santa Fé, and Lieutenant Emory sadly noted that many friends here
parted who would never meet again—"some fell in California, some in
New Mexico, and some in Cerro Gordo."[15] The two medical men drew
lots, and Dr. John S. Griffin was destined for California.[16]

Fourteen days c.. , on October 9, the road became so irregular and
broken that the baggage wagons were abandoned and pack saddles sent

for (the odometer being transferred to one of the howitzers).[17] Some 230 miles beyond Santa Fé on the 15th, the men left the Río Grande and headed west, up into the watershed of the Gila, first sighted on the 20th. A hundred yards before they reached the river, the roar of its waters let them know it would be different from the Del Norte, as "Clear and swift, it came bouncing from the great mountains." Though providing the most direct route to the distant Colorado, plenty of good water, and succulent trout, its often picturesque canyon made "damn bad roads," repeatedly forcing them to leave its course and traverse broken country. "The metallic clink of spurs," the rattling of mule shoes, the high black peaks, deep, dark ravines, and unearthly cactus all evoked the feeling they were "treading on the verge of the regions below."[18] Carson assured them it was a turnpike compared with some other routes, but a day's journey sometimes did not gain much in the direction of California, and the howitzers, the only wheeled vehicles, were often behind. On November 11 they passed the Pima villages, peopled by honest Indians cultivating fenced fields of cotton, corn, beans, and melons,[19] and by the 22nd neared the junction with the Colorado.

Being now on the road from California to Sonora, they came upon the trail of a large body of horses, thought at first to be Castro returning with troops to California or a Mexican force sent from Sonora to intercept them. Kearny ordered Carson to reconnoiter, "and we will fight them to night," but they proved to be refugees from a beleaguered coast.[20] From them they learned of the new revolt in Los Angeles and were advised to lose no time if they meant to aid their countrymen. Encountering five hundred horses and mules was a godsend to a now largely footsore battalion, and taking some of the Mexicans' stock—for which they paid, to the drovers' astonishment—they soon remounted, if upon largely unbroken and soon failing animals. Next day, another Mexican horseman was intercepted, carrying the mail from California, "which was of course opened."[21] Messages addressed to Castro and others in Sonora revealed details of the recent upheaval. The Americans had been expelled from Santa Barbara, the pueblo of Los Angeles, and other places, they read, and all spoke exultantly of throwing off the detested American yoke. One letter told of Mervine's defeat at San Pedro, attributed by Kearny to "Mexican braggadocio"; but that there was a disturbance of some kind there could be no doubt. One Mexican counseled them not to go to the pueblo with so small a force. Here for the first time they saw the use of the lasso, thrown with inimitable skill; "It is the saying in Chihua-

Dr. John S. Griffin, by drawing lots with another medical officer among Kearny's dragoons, was destined for California.

hua," Emory noted, "that 'a Californian can throw the lazo as well with his foot as a Mexican can with his hand.' "

The Colorado was crossed on November 25 about ten miles below the Gila.[22] The ford, some fifteen hundred feet wide, was narrow and circuitous, floating the mules in places, and its turbid waters and shifting sand islands reminded Emory of the Arkansas. By digging out an old well that night, they obtained sufficient "bad" water for drinking and cooking. But beyond, water and vegetation would be scarce or lacking, and they set out with bunches of grass tied to their saddles. The days became intensely hot, the sand deep, and the course winding, and the many failing mules provided a feast for the packs of wolves which followed. They continued until 9 p.m. on the 27th to reach a lake that proved to be salt. Next day they left at 4 a.m. and (having crossed Imperial Valley) encountered a dense fog blowing up from the Gulf.[23] Proceeding twenty-two miles, they camped on Carrizo Creek, finding a "magnificent spring," which, though highly impregnated with sulphur and salt, was the first drinking water in ninety miles. The last day of November they laid over at a little green place where the water was salty, the wind high, and the earth trembling, interfering with Emory's astronomical observations. They were at Vallecito—variously construed as "Bayou Cita" by Captain Johnston, "Vayeaw Chitoes" by the surgeon, and, a little later, "Bajiocito" by Captain Philip St. George Cooke of the oncoming Mormon Battalion.[24]

They noted the century plant and other shrubs and flowers, some new to their flora. On December 1, the "first day of winter," with snow on the high summits and all barrenness and desolation, they were still seeking confirmation of the glowing pictures painted of California. Their route over the next divide was "devious through narrow passes" (tortuous Box Canyon), after which they dropped down into the valley and former Indian village of San Felipe, where a warm stream flowed. Surmounting the next pass on December 2, they began to see fine oak trees and, along the mountain tops, clumps of lofty pine. From this vantage they descried in the distance the beautiful valley of Agua Caliente, waving with yellow grass, and at about 4 p.m. descended to Warner's rancho, very unexpectedly for the inhabitants, who mistook them for marauding Indians.[25]

Here they found themselves "near the heart of the enemy's stronghold" but in possession of the pass to Sonora. They camped at the junction of the roads to San Diego and Los Angeles and the following day began to appease their hunger. Seven of his men, Emory testified, ate a fat

General Kearny's route across the Colorado Desert to San Diego and, with Commodore Stockton's force, to Los Angeles, mapped by Lieutenant William H. Emory of the U.S. Topographical Engineers, a member of the party.

full-grown sheep at a single meal. He visited the thatched huts of the Indians and the "magnificent" hot springs, about three and a half miles north of Warner's house, and at night made his observations in spite of flying clouds and a trembling ground. Griffin noted ten or fifteen acres under cultivation near the house, with an acre and a half of vineyard. They also learned of a cache of mules and horses, driven by Antonio Coronel, who was on the way to Mexico for aid; and Kearny dispatched a party under Lieutenant John Davidson down the Los Angeles road to Aguanga to take them.[26]

Juan José Warner, owner of the Agua Caliente rancho (a naturalized Mexican citizen and Larkin's confidential correspondent), was a prisoner at San Diego; but that evening a neighbor from the Santa Isabel rancho, fifteen miles down the road to San Diego, was brought in. A short, stout man and former sailor, he appeared in a velvet hunting coat with matching trousers cut off at the knee and open on the outside to the hip; beneath, in true California style, were revealed drawers of spotless white, supported by leggings of black buckskin and heels armed with six-inch spurs. "Above the whole bloomed the broad merry face of Mr. Stokes, the Englishman."[27] Declaring himself to be neutral in the present controversy, he confirmed that Stockton held San Diego, while the rest of the territory was in the hands of the country people. He was going to San Diego on the morrow and would carry a letter from Kearny to the commodore. That day, Kearny sent a party back to pilot Captain Cooke and his Mormons across the desert[28] and the following morning proceeded down the San Diego road to Santa Isabel against a chilling wind and rain.[29]

Kearny's letter to Stockton, announcing his arrival, said he had taken possession of New Mexico, annexed it, established a civil government, and secured order.[30] He asked that a party be sent to meet him as quickly as possible, noting that he had intercepted Carson on the way, and the commodore's mail must have reached Washington at least ten days since.

Stockton acted at once, replying to Kearny at 6:30 p.m. on the 3rd and dispatching Gillespie.[31] The party consisted of thirty-seven volunteer riflemen, Midshipmen Beale and Duncan, ten Californians, native guide Rafael Machado, Mr. Stokes, and a field piece. Traveling by moonlight, they reached the Pedrorena rancho in El Cajon Valley at 3 a.m. Here they waited until daylight to negotiate the rocky approach to the mountains and, by sunset, made the Santa María Valley, where they stopped in some old adobe buildings in heavy rain. The morning of the 5th it poured in torrents as they ascended toward Santa Isabel; and after noon, when the weather had cleared, they met Kearny's advance and were received with great warmth and kindness by the general and his men. As directed, Gillespie reported upon the state of the country and a force of insurgents under Andrés Pico at San Pasqual, "six miles" distant, whom he might engage. Gillespie returned to Santa María for the night, while Kearny moved on to better grass two miles away. Rain was again falling in sheets, accompanied by a cold north wind. Gillespie had noted the exhaustion of the dragoons, who lay upon the ground despite the heavy rain, their strength and spirits seemingly expended.

News of the nearby enemy was nevertheless received with pleasure after a long and tedious march. Kearny ordered a reconnaissance, which, in council, Captain Benjamin D. Moore opposed, for if they were discovered, the element of surprise would be lost.[32] Gillespie suggested that his mountain men be allowed to reconnoiter, since they could proceed with more secrecy and security.[33] But Kearny ordered his aide-de-camp, Lieutenant Thomas C. Hammond, with six dragoons and the boy Rafael to scout the enemy. Down a long hill into San Pasqual Valley, within a half-mile of the Indian village, Rafael went ahead and learned in one of the huts that Pico's force was camped some distance away, their horses unsaddled. Before the boy could return, Hammond, impatient, came riding down with his men, their heavy swords clanging. A dog barked, and as they clattered back up the trail, the Californians rushed out shouting (according to Gillespie), "Viva California, abajo los Americanos" (while Griffin reported they gave three cheers). "By some accident," Emory wrote in his official report, the party was discovered and the enemy placed on the qui vive.[34]

Andrés Pico, in spite of the noise and warnings, believed the Americans were all at San Diego, except for Gillespie and his men, who were likely on a foraging expedition and could be ridden down by his well-mounted men.[35] Pico's followers were nevertheless uneasy at his inaction until a patrol brought in a blanket marked "U.S." and a dragoon jacket dropped in flight. A hurried order was given to round up the horses and mount the first ones caught.

Well before dawn on December 6, the reduced Army of the West, with Gillespie's force riding in the center, climbed over the pass above San Pasqual. As the weather cleared, the moon, close to setting, shone brightly, and a cold north wind blew down from the snow-covered ridge. So chilled were the men they could hardly hold their reins, and the doctor noted that although the arms had been out in the downpour, they had not been reloaded.[36] They were off in search of adventure. Beyond the summit Kearny addressed his force: their country expected them to do their duty, and they were to take the enemy alive, with their horses, if they were able.

Campfires glittered below as they moved down towards the Californians, who were already in the saddle. Although the alarm had been given, this was the road to San Diego,* and Kearny deemed it necessary to force a passage.[37] Gillespie had mentioned horses in the enemy's camp; and the general, a veteran cavalryman, coveted fresh mounts, which he would sorely need to fight his way to San Diego and Monterey. New Mexico had already been occupied without resistance, and Carson and Gillespie had probably assured him the Californians were cowardly and would not make a stand. After a monotonous cross-country march, the dragoons, too, were restive and spoiling for a fight. That it was a prudent or well-contrived maneuver for a brigadier general is not so surely said. Cold, weary, and poorly mounted, the little army relied upon powder that was not even dry.

First down the trail went the advance guard under Captain A. R. Johnston, about twelve men, mounted upon the best horses they had.[38] Next came the general's party, including Emory and William H. Warner of the engineers. Following were fifty dragoons under Captain Moore, upon tired mules, some ridden the thousand miles from Santa Fé. Then came about twenty volunteers under Captains Gillespie and Samuel Gibson, with the Sutter four-pounder and two mountain howitzers under Lieutenant John Davidson, supported by a number of dragoons. The remaining force under Major Thomas Swords, quartermaster, brought up and protected the rear and the baggage. There were not more than eighty-five men in the attacking force, the doctor estimated, many of whom would not get into the fray.[39] Moore was to direct the charge and had orders to surround the Indian village.[40] As they slogged ahead in the damp and cold, none anticipated that this would be the most lethal encounter of the California campaign.

Riding by twos, they were strung out in a long, tenuous line as they

---

* Another road led south from Santa María, probably the one Gillespie had taken.

Andrés Pico—Pío's brother—who had broken his parole after Castro's flight to Mexico, was in command of the Californians at San Pasqual and would later negotiate the Treaty of Cahuenga with Frémont which ended the fighting in California.

came down the dark trail, with Johnston's and Kearny's parties well in the lead. As the ground leveled off before reaching the village, the general ordered a trot; but Johnston, who apparently misunderstood, excitedly waved his sword and shouted "Charge!" The advance guard, on their good horses, galloped off into a layer of low cloud at full speed, opening a second gap in the long file.⁴¹ Plunging across a dry creek and around a little knoll, they met the enemy fronting them in a ravine, making a stand—the Californians did not know the strength of the American army, only a few of whom could be seen. Captain Johnston's advance immediately received a volley, which killed ther leader with a bullet through the head. As more dragoons on their broken-down mules appeared, the Californians broke their line, turned, and galloped on their fine mounts down the widening valley; and Moore, believing them in retreat, ordered

a second charge. They pursued the enemy in a most "hurly burly manner" for perhaps a mile, drawing farther away from the rest, some of
whom were still coming down the mountain path. Then, finding only a
scattered few of their pursuers close at hand, the Californians suddenly
wheeled and galloped back with their willow lances leveled for attack.
They spread as if herding cattle to encircle the oncoming line. (Pico had
not meant to risk a fight, he would afterwards say, but upon seeing the
disorder of Kearny's men could not resist the temptation.)[42]

"The enemy," Kearny would report, "well mounted and among the
best horsemen in the world, after retreating . . . rallied their whole force,
charged with their lances," and few of the Americans in front remained
untouched.[43] Moore, now in the lead, came face to face with Pico. He
shot at him with his pistol but missed, then charged with his saber but
was lanced by several of the enemy, unhorsed, and fatally wounded,
pierced sixteen times.[44] Nobody being able to reload fast enough—and
the American powder was damp, the Californians' in extremely short
supply—the battle resolved into a hand-to-hand fight with clubbed guns
and sabers against the long California lances. Some of the Americans
were pulled from their horses by the enemy's *reatas*, many received
thrusts from the rear as the skilled Californian riders fell upon them as
they rushed past. Lieutenant Hammond dashed to Moore's aid (they
were brothers-in-law), but he was struck down by a lance blow deeply
piercing his side. Moore died instantly, Hammond after two hours.

Now all was confusion. The Americans in the lead were far outnumbered. Many were dead. A few had fallen back. Kearny himself was
wounded in the back and though saved by Emory was out of the action
(he had defended himself valiantly, remained as "calm as a clock").[45] In
the disarray, cloud, and turmoil, some of the mountain men, dressed as
hunters, narrowly escaped death by their own comrades' hands.[46] Gillespie tells that he and his men—after warding off the enemy from the rear
and capturing the Californians' second in command—dashed forward
sword in hand when Hammond fell, crying, "Rally men, for God's sake
rally, show a front . . . face them."[47] Whether this exhortation was given
or heard above the uproar, Gillespie was at once recognized by the Californians, who fell upon him with dire vengeance. A skilled and dauntless
swordsman, he was nevertheless unhorsed and thrice wounded, once
over the heart (and would have been killed, it was said, had not his assail-
ant been eager to get away with his fine saddle and bridle).[48] But the un-
stoppable Gillespie somehow escaped to the rear to help bring one of the

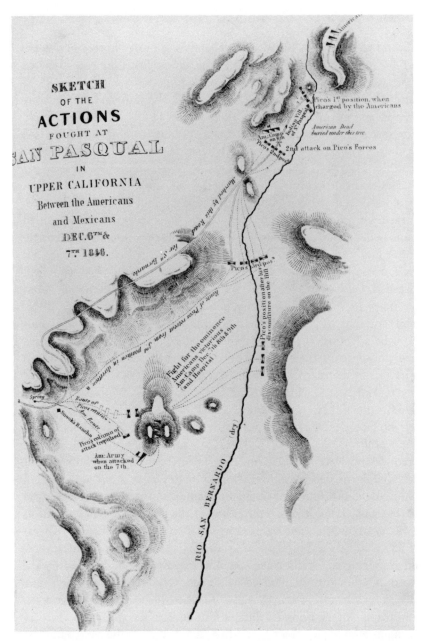

Lieutenant Emory's map of the action at San Pasqual, indicating battle sites, routes of the opposing forces, and the encampment on Mule Hill.

still unlimbered howitzers into action. As the volunteers appeared and more U.S. forces came to their aid, Midshipman James M. Duncan apparently unloosed the brass four-pounder, and the Californians retired—some of them making off jubilantly with one of the mountain howitzers which a pair of frightened mules hauled wildly through the Californians' line.[49] The intensive hand-to-hand fighting had lasted, it is supposed, about fifteen minutes.[50] Kearny wanted to make another charge but was restrained.[51]

It was a brief but costly battle. Surgeon Griffin reported eighteen dead and seventeen wounded—and not to exceed fifty men saw the enemy.[52] Besides Johnston, Moore, and Hammond, two sergeants were killed and two corporals, ten privates of dragoons, one of the volunteers, and a topographical engineer, a total of nineteen by Kearny's count, all by lances except two. Sergeant John Cox died three days later, Joseph Kennedy on the 19th, and the official roster of dead, prepared by Griffin, totaled twenty-one. The wounded were General Kearny, Captains Warner, Gillespie, and Gibson, Antoine Robidoux, a sergeant, a bugler, and nine privates of dragoons, each with from two to ten wounds, most of them when unhorsed and incapable of resistance. A lance nearly speared the surgeon but was warded off by his drawing an empty pistol. The number of Californian casualties was uncertain, the six left on the field, as intimated by Kearny, being unlikely, while Gillespie reported at least twenty killed and wounded. Andrés Pico admitted eleven casualties, none serious, and refused Griffin's proffered medical aid, claiming it was unneeded.[53] Captain Turner, with Lieutenant Davidson the only commissioned officers of dragoons to survive, temporarily assumed the command.

The Californians' success—a victory claimed by the Americans in official dispatches, since the enemy retired from the field—had followed the usual tactic of standing and retreating, to which the Americans were peculiarly vulnerable by virtue of their training, animals, and condition. "This was an action," Griffin laconically concluded, "where decidedly more courage than conduct was showed." Gillespie characterized it as a victory without any advantages; and an Irish dragoon in the advance party said it would have been well if the general had been killed, for "such another fight was unknown—it was a disgrace." As for Kearny, he assured his superiors that the great number of killed and wounded proved the officers and men had fully sustained the high character and reputation of the troops, though to his own wife he acknowledged, "We gained a victory . . . but paid most dearly for it."[54] (Another such victory, it was afterwards remarked, would have been disastrous;[55] but Kearny, Turner, Emory, and Gillespie would receive promotions for meritorious conduct in this action.)[56]

Following the battle, the Americans moved behind a natural breastwork, and Griffin did not finish dressing wounds until the sun was down. Since mules were too few to carry both the dead and wounded, and it was feared graves would be plundered for the clothes, burial was made in the darkness east of the camp under a willow tree, "with no other accompaniment" than the howling of wolves.[57]

Their provisions were exhausted, Emory recorded, their horses dead, their mules on their last legs; and the men, reduced by one-third their number, were ragged and worn. Since there were said to be wheeled vehicles at San Diego, thirty-nine miles away, Alexis Godey (another of Frémont's mountain men), Thomas H. Burgess (of the Bears), and one or two others were sent by a circuitous route to fetch transport. They carried a letter from Captain Turner to Stockton, telling of the battle and asking for a considerable force without delay to be sent by way of Soledad and San Bernardo.[58] Stokes returned on his own to San Diego to report upon San Pasqual, and Godey arrived the following day.[59] Meanwhile, the injured were carried in rude ambulances—willow poles covered with buffalo robes, dragged with one end trailing on the ground*—and they suffered terribly from the roughness of the road.[60]

December 7 dawned upon "the most tattered and ill-fed detachment of men that ever the United States mustered under her colors." But the enemy was ahead and pickets visible. The wounded were doing well, and the general, now able to mount his horse, resumed the command. The order to march was given, and they proceeded westerly over some low hills, the Californians retiring as they advanced. When above the San Bernardo rancho of Joseph Francisco Snook, a former English sea captain, they descended to the deserted house to water their animals and kill some chickens for the sick.[61] Then, as they drove many of the Englishman's cattle before them down the San Diego road, a cloud of enemy cavalry debouched from the hills behind them, bent upon stampeding their animals, while thirty or forty Californians dashed ahead to occupy an elevation the Americans must pass. Ordered to take the height on foot, the "brave, cool & deliberate" Emory, with a small party, boldly executed the command, though the Californians held their ground until ap-

---

* The litters were like the *travois* of the Plains Indians.

proached within gunshot. But the Americans had lost their cattle and realized they could go no farther encumbered by the ambulances, which required the attention of half the fighting force. They encamped that night on the rocky height, which they christened Mule Hill,* bored holes at its base for water, and killed the fattest of their lean mules for food.

Next morning they saw a commotion on the plain below, and shortly a flag of truce arrived with an offer to exchange prisoners. The Americans had only one to offer (Pablo Véjar) and were permitted to redeem Burgess, who with Godey and the rest of the party had been captured by the Californians as they returned from San Diego. The messenger also courteously brought some tea and sugar and a change of clothes for Gillespie, sent from San Diego by a friend. Emory, who negotiated the exchange, put in his journal that he found Andrés Pico a "gentlemanly looking and rather handsome man." Burgess' dismal news was that Stockton would not send further aid.[62] Much of the day was spent lightening the loads; and a great deal of serviceable property was destroyed, both public and private, "of great value in this country," the frugal Gillespie lamented.[63]

That night, Carson and Beale volunteered to go to San Diego for relief, with an Indian, Andrés, as guide. It was an expedition of some peril since all the passes were in the hands of the enemy—and it did indeed prove to be a dangerous, arduous, and tortuous journey through the cactus and sharp rocks in their bare feet.[64] (Carson may well have wished to explain his unexpected reappearance to the commodore.) That night Sergeant Cox, who just before leaving Fort Leavenworth had "married a pretty wife," died of his wounds and was buried on the hill.

The sick were still unable to travel, and the 9th was spent in camp, the naval officers believing Stockton would send relief. About that time Emory made his "Sketch [map] of the actions fought at San Pasqual in Upper California," clearly depicting the terrain and movements made.[65]

Next day, Dr. Griffin announced that all of the sick but two could get in the saddle (David Streeter and Joseph Kennedy), and the general issued orders to march the following morning. Meanwhile, the Californians made another foray, driving before them a band of wild horses in an attempt to stampede the Americans' remaining animals. The doctor saw them coming at full speed, "the wild devils with sheep skins & other

---

*Snook's house was just east of today's highway 395 and north of Lake Hodges. Mule Hill, formerly identified with Battle Mountain, is an unnamed height above bench mark 320 on the north shore of the lake, east of 395 (SCHREIER; COY).

things of that sort tied to their tails," but they were prepared. In the charge two or three of the fattest animals were killed and soon served "in the shape of gravy-soup" as an agreeable substitute for the poor steaks from their own worn-down animals.

Midway in a sleepless night—the men contemplating another encounter on the morrow—an outpost heard a man speaking English, and in a few minutes a column of a hundred tars and eighty marines under Lieutenant Andrew Gray of the *Congress* marched into camp. The men had left San Diego on Stockton's orders the evening of the 9th, their numbers augmented by marines and musketeers from the *Portsmouth*, just arrived from San Francisco. The whole day of the 10th they had remained "flat on their bellies" on top of a steep hill and renewed their march as soon as it was dark, expecting a fight. Having met only one enemy picket, they reached Kearny's camp about 2 a.m. "The jack tars seemed highly delighted playing soldier," and they busied themselves distributing clothes and provisions to threadbare and hungry dragoons, snatching some sleep until daylight.[66] While Stockton had refused Turner's request of December 6 (delivered the following day), he was perhaps more responsive to petitions from Carson and Midshipman Beale. Though he would subsequently testify that his troops were readied before they arrived,[67] he had replied to Turner that every serviceable horse had been sent with Gillespie, and he had no means to transport artillery or the wounded.[68] Godey had said they could defend themselves, and he would wait for further information. (The response, though intercepted by the Californians, had been accurately enough conveyed by Burgess.)[69]

Although Andrés Pico's force had been doubled to perhaps two hundred men, ready to charge the weakened and encumbered party when it reached the plain,[70] this sudden reinforcement completely surprised the enemy, who fled, leaving most of the cattle. These were reappropriated, and on the 11th, after four days on the hill, the body of troops marched twelve miles in close order to Los Peñasquitos rancho of Francisco María Alvarado. The owner was absent but had left plenty of turkeys, chickens, goats, and sheep, and two casks of wine. Señor Alvarado being "in the fight against us" (or, by another account, said to be a friend), the "havoc committed on the comestibles was immense."[71] The sheep not killed were driven on to San Diego, and a barrel of wine was taken "for our sick & wounded." Above the rancho they first sighted the Pacific Ocean, and the sudden view produced strange but agreeable emotions.

San Diego in December 1846 consisted of a few adobe buildings on a sand flat two miles wide, beyond which a long promontory ran into the sea.

"Lord!" one of the mountain men fancifully exclaimed, "there is a great prairie without a tree."

On Saturday, December 12, they followed down the deep Soledad Valley—green with wild oats like a new wheat field—ascended a steep hill to some tablelands, and dropped into a waterless valley which led to False Bay, two or three miles from San Diego.[72] Here they could see the fort overlooking the town and the barren waste which surrounded it. The settlement below consisted of a few adobe houses on a sand flat two miles wide, beyond which a long promontory ran into the sea. The mission was in view to the northeast, a fine large building, now deserted, and along the shore, abreast of the hide houses, the frigate *Congress* and sloop *Portsmouth* rode at anchor. Rain fell in torrents as they entered the town.

What remained of Kearny's fragmented Army of the West had reached the Pacific. Captain Dupont of the *Cyane*, for one, had long wished for Kearny's arrival, "that things might resume their proper place," the army in the interior, the navy on the coast, and some regular troops to replace Frémont's vagabond force.[73] Here Lieutenant Emory's military reconnaissance came to an end. He had accompanied the expedition to collect information on the unexplored regions through which the army might pass, insofar as this would not interfere with the more immediate military demands of the service.[74] There now being other claims, he was on January 28 separated from his topographical party and made acting adjutant general of the force.[75] His large, epoch-making map would be published by the United States Senate in 1847, of "towering significance" in the cartographic history of the west.[76] Kearny, meanwhile, moved in with the commodore until he could find other space, while it was Emory's "singular fate . . . as at Santa Fé, to be quartered in the calaboose."[77]

13

Paradise Regained

THERE WERE no titanic characters in the story of the reconquest of southern California by the Americans, nor was it a gigantic venture. We have met most of the actors, and they are human—the stalwart, arrogant, and impulsive Stockton; the umbrageous Gillespie; the strong-headed but elusive Frémont; and the hard-bitten, disciplined, but clement "old" general, Kearny. There were many of lesser standing, most of them loyal to one or another of the star performers. But if there were no epic heroes, neither were there infamous villains, and the story is laid in a paradise of a very prosaic sort.

The superstars among the Californians, José Castro and Pío Pico, had left the action some time before, and José María Flores (a Mexican, arrived in 1842) was running the show. He had taken the leading role during the revolt against Gillespie at the end of September, and broadened the action to include San Diego, Santa Barbara, Santa Inés, and San Luis Obispo (with Manuel Castro commanding in the north).[1] His act would be to harass the enemy, cut off supplies, exact participation of the Californians, and patrol the country against unlawful exploits. Guerrilla warfare was his most potent resource.

After the brief American occupation of Los Angeles in August and September, Flores had called the departmental assembly back into session, and it was reorganized on October 26, 1846, with Francisco Figueroa as president. Flores, already acting commander-in-chief, was elected to the dual office of governor and *comandante general* (ad interim), left vacant by Pico and Castro.[2] The country was declared in a state of siege, Pío Pico's sale of the missions was annulled,[3] and the properties were put up as security for loans to carry on the war. Representatives were sent to all the towns to raise volunteers or recruit by force.[4]

Prime attention was of course given to San Diego after Stockton's arrival there on October 31, and Californians under Leonardo Cota continued to hold the territory around the town. Flores issued an admonitory proclamation on November 4, noting the state of siege and requiring all male citizens from 15 to 60 to appear at the first warning—a cannon-shot, general alarm, and ringing of bells—under penalty of death as a traitor for any who did not comply. And he wrote to the independent and wayward San Diegan, Juan Bandini, urging his support, and asked Leonardo Cota to flatter him a little to see what could be obtained, especially arms and ammunition.[5]

There being no public funds, Captain Antonio Coronel (another Mexican, who came in 1834) was dispatched to Mexico near the end of November to solicit aid and convey the news; and with the usual band of horses he headed down the Sonora trail. Near the Colorado, he learned of the approach of a considerable number of American soldiers (Kearny's force) and, sending a courier on to Mexico, turned back to Aguanga, northwest of Warner's Pass. When news came to Los Angeles on December 4 of the capture of Coronel's horses by Americans, whose identity could not be surmised, Andrés Pico, with perhaps a hundred men, was ordered from the vicinity of San Luis Rey to investigate. And as Gillespie set out from San Diego on the 3rd to meet Kearny's oncoming troops, Pico's sister, from her adobe near the mission, saw the despised foreigners riding through the valley in the moonlight and quickly notified her brother. Indians brought a similar message, and on December 5 Pico and his horsemen reached the valley of San Pasqual.[6]

Now Flores was a Mexican, not a Californian, a member of *la otra banda*, and his prestige and success were envied by some. Among the restive was José Antonio Carrillo, his second in command, a veteran schemer who had lately distinguished himself by defeating Mervine. Between the Californians and Flores there had been recent and not unprecedented bickering, with some disobedience, and open criticism of Flores' schemes to obtain resources for the war and deal severely with Benito Wilson and other influential Americans. California's heritage of hospitality and insubordination could not be downed even by invasion; and on the night of December 3, a few natives under Francisco Rico engineered a revolt.[7] Flores was placed under arrest and charged with various misdemeanors, among them his intention to abscond with the (nonexistent) funds and send the Chino prisoners and Larkin as "trophies" to Mexico. Since Flores was willing to abandon the latter plan, and no evidence was forthcoming to support the first, he was on December 5 returned to power, in view of the critical condition of the country. (News of the approaching Americans had just been heard.) Rico and Carrillo were in turn jailed but soon discharged.

As soon as the attack against Gillespie was known in Monterey, Prefect Manuel Castro and other northern partisans hastened to offer their services, some ignoring their pledge not to take up arms, as Flores had done. The prefect was made commandant in the north on October 23,[8] with headquarters at San Luis Obispo, and reaching that place early in November, he managed to collect a force of more than a hundred men. Quickly learning of Frémont's return to Monterey in the *Sterling* to recruit cavalry and make a junction with Stockton, Castro determined to harass and delay the Americans' movements by seizing their horses and making sudden attacks. After issuing a proclamation on November 7, he and his men headed down the Salinas Valley and arrived near Soledad on about the 15th.[9] There he heard of American volunteers gathering at San Juan Bautista and that Consul Larkin had ridden out of Monterey with a single companion, bound for Yerba Buena.

Castro's aide José Chávez apparently conceived the idea of capturing the consul. Larkin was considered by Flores to be the most active of the enemies of Mexico,[10] and he was an important source of funds and credit for the enemy. Some regarded him as the cause of all the evils which had befallen the country and believed the campaign would be half over with him in their hands. He, himself, had long expected mischief. José Antonio Carrillo had meant to take him prisoner, he said, and another party had proposed to carry him off, hoping to precipitate the landing of the naval forces and hasten a final settlement. He had expected to be taken at the beginning of July when fifteen Californian troops came into town, but they apparently "did not think of it"; and in October he was warned that he was marked for destruction.[11] He saw himself as being valuable to the Californians in making a treaty or in some future exchange, and he accepted the eventuality with a certain lack of sobriety. He would not mind being taken prisoner, he wrote to Leidesdorff, providing he slept in a good bed, under cover, and had tea or coffee before starting out in the morning. He had made an account of his debts, prepared a will, and was pretty well ready for anything.

On the way to see his wife and sick daughter in Yerba Buena and to discuss a bread contract with Captain Montgomery, Larkin stayed the night of November 15 at Gómez' Los Vergeles rancho (near the foot of

Gavilán Peak). Sending his attendant on to San José, he intended to follow the next morning. But in the night he was awakened by Chávez and
ten men with guns, swords, pistols, and torches in their hands, shouting
"Vamos Señor Larkin," and was carried a few miles south to the advancing Californians' Salinas camp.[12]

Next morning, Manuel Castro's force of some 130 men, with a drum
and a Mexican flag, set out northeastward from Salinas with Larkin under guard. They meant to attack San Juan Bautista in the night and, by
their usual tactic, draw out the Americans in pursuit and cut off as many
as they could. But, as some of them had feared, Larkin's capture had
given their position away. From San Juan, two parties of Frémont's
assembling volunteers under Bluford "Hell Roaring" Thompson and
Charles Burroughs (with perhaps 100 men and 370 horses) arrived at
Gómez' rancho on the way to Monterey and sent a patrol ahead to reconnoiter. South of Gavilán in mid-afternoon they encountered an advance
guard of Californians under de la Torre;[13] and when the latter attacked,
some Indians rushed back to the rancho to give the alarm, while the
American scouts posted themselves in a grove of oaks. Behind de la Torre
came two companies of Californians under Castro and Chávez (the latter
with Larkin in tow). Though soon surrounded, the few American rifles
had the advantage over the Californian muskets, and only sporadic firing
occurred until the main body of Americans came into view.

While detachments on both sides remained in the grove, the fighting
now moved into the open, perhaps fifty Americans with rifles and plenty
of ammunition against sixty-five skillful horsemen with indifferent arms.
After an initial exchange, the Americans charged wildly, and the Californians feigned retreat, then returned to attack, while twenty or thirty of
their number in the grove apparently rushed the Americans from the
rear. Several were killed in hand-to-hand fighting at the periphery of each
force, including Burroughs; but the Americans, forced into a more compact group, renewed the fire, and the enemy fell back, with a number of
casualties.

The action at rancho La Natividad lasted some twenty or thirty minutes, according to Larkin, who was a spectator. At least four or five
Americans were dead and six or seven wounded, the Californians admitting only two dead and seven injured, including Chávez, though there
may have been more. Larkin told of a Californian who, seeing a relative
shot down, came toward him at full speed with his gun leveled, crying,
"this man caused it all"; but Larkin parried by moving beside another

rider.[14] The Californians gradually dispersed, while the Americans took refuge among the trees, both remaining within a mile of each other until dusk. Afterwards, Rico hastily set off with Larkin and a small party for Los Angeles, where Manuel Castro and a remnant of twenty-five or thirty men, abandoning their northern position, later appeared.

The Californians had enjoyed a long winning streak, from late September to mid-December—capturing the Americans at Chino, expelling Gillespie, defeating the navy at San Pedro, affrighting Stockton, taking Consul Larkin, and exacting a grim toll at San Pasqual and La Natividad. Stockton, the conqueror, would admit no part in these American reverses; they were charged to the incapacity of subordinates or colleagues in other services. Kearny named his bloody engagement a victory. And Gillespie might have cited Larkin's calculation that he should have had three or four hundred enlisted men in the south instead of the forty-eight volunteers allowed him by a sparing commodore.[15] As for Mervine, he wrote no long letters to Washington nor published books to justify his actions, though Stockton was at pains to document his fiasco and the "defeat" at San Pasqual. The "truth must be upheld," insisted the commodore, "let who may suffer."[16]

But revolt in the north was nearly over. There was one other local disturbance, the "Battle of Santa Clara," in January, after Frémont's departure from San Juan.[17] Perhaps a hundred Californians under Francisco Sánchez dramatized their resentment over the plundering of the ranchos, begun by Weber and Frémont's men, by capturing Alcalde Washington A. Bartlett of Yerba Buena (and the *Portsmouth*) and five or six Americans on a foraging expedition. With Captain Marston's marines and volunteers in pursuit, there was some rapid marching about by night and day and one brief skirmish on January 2 on the plain of Santa Clara. An armistice was then arranged, and American assurance given that property would not be taken without proper formalities. "Since that day," reported British Vice-Consul Forbes, a neutral (if never impartial) member of the negotiating party, "we have seen the commencement of a different treatment of these people," and he hoped it would produce a beneficial feeling in the Californians' favor.[18]

There would now be a brief interlude, an *entr'acte*, while the next scene of the war shifted into position. Since this interval had a highly significant bearing upon the development of the plot, it must be admitted as part of the action.

There were three main characters around whom the emerging drama was generating—Stockton, Kearny, and Frémont—each powerfully motivated by his own ego, aims, and experience. How do a general and a commodore cooperate under the best of circumstances? And to whom does an ambitious underling give precedence? The U.S. government had, to be sure, admonished the naval participants that it would expect the armed forces to cooperate with each other in the most friendly and effective manner.[19] But this little discourse was written to Sloat on July 12, 1846, and was not received by him or even by Stockton but by their successor, Commodore Shubrick, who did not reach California until January 1847. The only instructions received by Stockton had to do with taking possession, according protection, and preserving friendly relations with the people, much being left to his discretion.[20] Nothing was said of the army or of civil government, nor of the fact that land forces might be involved in the occupation. Not until Sloat had taken Monterey and Kearny been ordered to California did the department in Washington think to direct the commodore to establish a government and cooperate with the army.[21] Neither of these orders reached their distant addressees while they had any useful meaning.

Naval officers were the first to be alerted about hostilities on the Mexican west coast—they were already there. But moving an army was an explicit war measure, and General Kearny did not receive his marching orders until the end of May 1846.[22] These instructions, to proceed to California and occupy some of its principal points, in cooperation with the Navy, were amplified by the Secretary a few days later. Should he "conquer and take possession of New Mexico and California, or considerable places in either," he was to establish a temporary government.[23] Having set up a civil organization at Santa Fé, the general approached California with a like objective in view.

Stockton could only say to Kearny in disputing his claims to precedence that he had already conquered California before the general's arrival (with some recent annoying reversals) and set a government in motion. As conqueror, he was entitled by the "law of nations" to occupy and govern.[24] When asked a year later under oath what orders he had had concerning the formation of a government, he would truthfully reply, as he had not earlier been ready to do, "Well, I do not think I had any."[25]

Maybe Stockton and Kearny should have known enough, without detailed supervision, not to get into a squabble, but the Army and Navy, headed by forceful personalities, had vied with each other before and would again. Both men were adult and experienced, aged 51 and 52. Each was determined. And neither intended to give in. Frémont was 33, the third member of an all-but-classic triangle, to be wooed and won or rejected and caught at last in a trap largely of his own setting.

The quarrel probably began with Kearny's letter to Stockton from Warner's Pass on December 2,[26] announcing that he had been sent by the President and had already annexed New Mexico and set up a government there. Stockton was readying himself for a march upon Los Angeles, and Kearny's advent was an interruption, even an intrusion (had he not already sent his outline of government to Washington to show how he was proceeding?)[27] Certainly it would not speed up his process of preparation. But Stockton could spare Gillespie (who always played end man), and he sent his volunteer force, suggesting the general intercept a party of Californians on the way. The Battle of San Pasqual followed, and Godey reported the debacle to Stockton, who declined sending further aid until Midshipman Beale brought a second appeal. It is not hard to believe the commodore took some gratification as well as vexation from the necessity to extricate the general from his extremity; his repeated references to Kearny's "sad defeat" in official correspondence are too emphatic to mistake.[28]

So, on December 12, Kearny reached San Diego with a remnant of his dragoons. He could muster under a hundred—and many of the best were dead—while the commodore's force numbered above six hundred, with more on the way. Although Kearny, as brigadier general by brevet, outranked Stockton's assimilated grade of colonel (he may have supposed himself inferior to the commander of a squadron),[29] he was dependent from a military point of view because of a lack of matériel and men. And he had just been rescued, perhaps from annihilation, by Stockton's aid and was not yet recovered from his wounds. The commodore had arrived on the scene first, was commander-in-chief not only at San Diego but north to Sonoma and Sutter's Fort, called himself governor, and was already organizing an expedition against the enemy.

Pointedly, the commodore advanced on foot to welcome the general—every horse fit for use had been sent to rescue Kearny—and conducted him to his quarters. Although Stockton, as conqueror, believed he should be commander-in-chief, he offered this honor to the general (twice, he would say)[30] because of Kearny's standing in the army, his long experience, and the importance of military science in the movements which were about to begin. To this Kearny replied with courtesy or realism that

Stockton commanded the squadron and the major military forces in California, and he would go as his aide-de-camp. But on December 13, before moving to his own quarters, Kearny brought the commodore his instructions from the War Department; and Stockton on the 16th exhibited some of his dispatches.[31] If the commodore overlooked the implication that Kearny should be governor, and the general did not note with pleasure how well Stockton had anticipated his orders from Washington, charge it to single-mindedness or perversity.

In a subsequent conversation with Stockton, Kearny politely voiced the belief that under the President's instructions he was to be governor of California,[32] a view which "amazed" the commodore, since the general had twice refused his offer to be commander-in-chief. Kearny bowed to superior strength but meant, when his force was increased, to assume the command;[33] while Stockton, who intended to preserve his authority and transmit it to his partisan, would brook no interference while awaiting a reply from Washington to his announcement that he would appoint Frémont governor.[34]

Sincerely, officiously, or with pure malice, Kearny wrote to Stockton on December 22, suggesting they march toward Los Angeles to join Frémont or create a diversion in his favor, perhaps surprising the enemy at San Luis Rey.[35] "I do not think Lieut. Col. Fremont should be left unsupported to fight a battle upon which the fate of California may for a long time depend." He offered to accompany such an expedition and render aid, "either of head or hand."

Now the two men had discussed military maneuvers only the day before, and the commodore repeated with some asperity that he meant to march with part of his force upon San Luis Rey.[36] He wanted to go on to the pueblo, but that would depend upon circumstances. It might be necessary to "stop" the pass of San Felipe or march back to San Diego. If the general's object was to allow the enemy to get in his rear and cut off communications, he wanted to be excused from such advice. He would march upon San Luis Rey in a day or two, as soon as he could get the dragoons and riflemen mounted.

Kearny surely knew of the plan to march upon Los Angeles.[37] Likely he had heard of it from Gillespie as early as December 5 and from Stockton as recently as the previous morning. That very day his Captain Turner had been offered a choice of animals for some contemplated journey and had written his wife on December 21 that arrangements were then being made by Stockton to leave for Los Angeles, probably the following week.[38] Kearny's own offer to serve as aide-de-camp must have been made for some anticipated campaign. But the general answered that if he had so understood, he would not have written such a letter.[39]

There might have been a misunderstanding. Stockton may have spoken only in general terms, or Kearny might have thought the commodore irresolute, purposing to go only to San Luis Rey, while he wanted to march to Los Angeles. But it is also believable that Kearny was deliberately compiling a record for future reference. Soon afterward he would write to Washington that the march upon Los Angeles was reluctantly consented to by Commodore Stockton on his urgent advice, "correspondence to prove which is now with my papers in San Diego."[40] And still later, in November 1847, he would testify in Washington that the expedition "was organized in consequence, as I believe, of a paper which I addressed to Commodore Stockton."[41] He conceived there would be a day of reckoning, and he intended to be prepared.

There had been a good deal of activity at San Diego in the two months since October 30, when Stockton had vacated his uncomfortable berth at San Pedro. The town had been fortified. Saddles and harness had been collected or manufactured and carts assembled to convey the baggage and wounded. Forays for animals had been made two hundred and forty miles south of San Diego. Gillespie had been ordered into the field to give the enemy a foretaste of what was to come.[42] The *Portsmouth* was being brought from San Francisco and the prize schooner *Julia* (under Lieutenant Selden) sent to aid Frémont.[43] Men from the squadron were being drilled in land combat (with tactics simplified and orders reduced to "form line—form square—fire—repel charge—charge").[44] With supplies desperately wanting, Kearny had sent Quartermaster Swords to the Sandwich Islands in a trading vessel chartered for the purpose.[45] And when the general was sufficiently recovered, he exercised the men in field movements, repeatedly expressing his admiration for the manner in which his "jacks" performed. The commodore, a "gassy" old fellow, would collect a crowd around him and mark out the exact route he would follow, the maneuvers he meant to execute, and the "sure way" in which the Californians were to be beaten. To the Navy Department, Stockton wrote that he had in truth made an army out of the mechanics and sailors from his ships and taken his horses and beef from the enemy. A mind less strong than the commodore's, an ordinary seaman concluded, would have quailed at the prospect.

At San Francisco in October, Montgomery had been ordered to sail the *Portsmouth* to the Mexican coast as soon as the storeship *Warren* brought provisions.[46] But the *Portsmouth* was out of bread, and when the *Warren* appeared early in November it also needed that staple food. Although Larkin had a contract to supply bread to the navy, the ten thousand pounds he was ready to deliver fell far short of the quantity required.[47] Montgomery meanwhile sent the *Warren*'s launch to New Helvetia on November 13 with money to pay the garrison, and in the twelve or fourteen days allotted, it had not returned. Nor had it in seventeen or eighteen, when two vessels from up-river reported it had not been seen.[48] Since his eldest son commanded the boat and his youngest, as clerk, was aboard, with Daniel Hugunin, pilot, and a crew of nine, Montgomery postponed his departure. Soon his sailing orders were renewed, this time to meet the commodore at San Pedro or San Diego and bring $50,000 from the *Warren* (another staple the vessel did not possess). Raising $9,000 on government bills,[49] and not daring any more delay, Montgomery ordered "All Hands up Anchor" on December 5, and the *Portsmouth* reached San Diego four days later. Concerning his great personal anxiety, he only wrote the commodore it was "proper to report" that Hugunin and his clerk had been left behind (subsequently it was learned the officers had been murdered by the crew).[50]

The *Portsmouth* brought provisions to San Diego, but they were heavily levied upon by forces on shore—not excluding all the boarding pikes, leaving for the ship's defense only one old Californian carbine and a cutlass. Stockton had even converted the storeship *Erie* into a man-of-war; and Lieutenant Misroon wrote uneasily to Montgomery, now "Gov. of San Diego," that the *Portsmouth*'s supplies were low, and would he somehow call the attention of the distracted commodore to the serious state to which the squadron was being reduced.[51]

Whether it was the general's prodding or the commodore's final readiness, on the day after Kearny's letter, Stockton issued an order that on Monday the 28th the line of march would be taken for Los Angeles.[52] The more than six hundred men were organized into four companies.[53] One was composed of marines, musketeers, and carbineers from the *Portsmouth*, *Cyane*, and *Congress*, under marine Jacob Zeilin; another, of Kearny's dragoons, naval musketeers, and six pieces of artillery, commanded by Turner; a third, of sailor-musketeers from the *Savannah* and *Congress*, with naval Lieutenant William B. Renshaw as captain; and a body of "$25 men," volunteer skirmishers, including thirty "noble" California horsemen, all under Gillespie. The latter were to be the only ones mounted, save Hensley's "Life Guards" who rode ahead. Stockton expected to be joined by a hundred Indians who would, with the mounted volunteers, make a forced march back to San Diego if the enemy tried to get in their rear.[54]

The commodore assured Kearny on the 24th that he would be gratified to have him present on the march, which he hoped his health would permit. He also wrote Frémont that he had enough men to conquer the country and cautioned him not to attack the Californians: "let the enemy do the charging and your Rifles will do the rest."[55] On the 26th the command was mustered; the sick, lame, lazy, and those who thought they could not stand the fatigue were picked out and replaced by volunteers from the *Portsmouth*.[56] Dr. Griffin, who recorded several cases of "fever" on hand, of which one man had died, also mentioned "a fine ball last night, quite a turn-out of good looking women."[57]

The morning of the 29th (a day late), the troops were paraded before departure. The general at this juncture announced his wish to command the force—or was it, as he would affirm, at Stockton's request that he "kindly consented" to take the command?[58] He had helped drill the troops, and his decision may not have been the surprise Stockton affected, for surgeon Griffin had entered in his journal on December 26 that "Genl. Kearny it is now said will take the command at which the naval gentlemen seemed much pleased."[59] Stockton then convened the officers to inform them of Kearny's request and that he had appointed him to lead the men, with himself as commander-in-chief. This was of course an advantageous arrangement for the commodore, to whom land maneuvers were something of a mystery. Kearny was an experienced field man, wholly competent, as Stockton saw it, to take over "nearly all of the execution of details." To Kearny it gave greater authority than as aide-de-camp.

There is no doubt about this relationship between the two men, though both would later claim to have exercised full responsibility.[60] Kearny was invested with the command of the troops, subject to the commander-in-chief, who did on several occasions send messages which Kearny chose to regard as suggestions, but the sender transmitted as commands.[61] Major Bidwell of the commissary would later say he received orders from both men and obeyed them insofar as he was able.[62] That no open break occurred is also apparent; their relations seemed cordial and respectful, whatever resentment and indignation smoldered beneath. If Stockton maintained the upper hand, Kearny nursed his woes and waited.

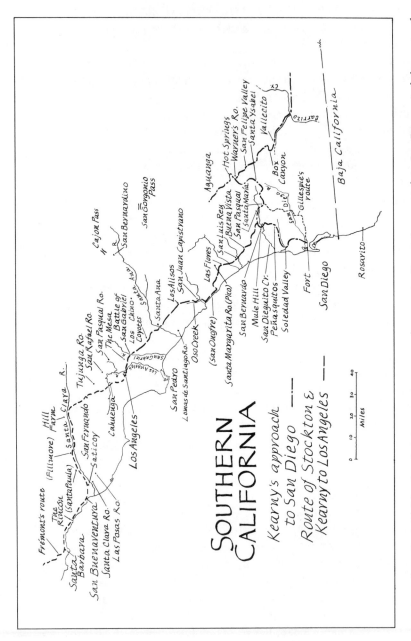

Map of southern California, showing contemporary place names, Kearny's approach to San Diego, and the route of Stockton and Kearny to Los Angeles, December 1846–January 1847.

With all the preliminaries on the 29th, the expedition got a late start.[63] The commodore and general rode to the center of the square, the band playing a quickstep, the "much revered" voice of General Kearny gave the order, and with a cheer the troops defiled before the two commanders. The men appeared more like veteran infantry, boasted Gillespie, "than sailors just ashore by accident." And one of the seamen gave full credit to "Fighting Bob . . . a Brave Officer and the Sailor's Friend"; no one less acquainted with the sailor's character could have succeeded. For the men had in a manner "unsexed themselves," becoming in an emergency what the sailor hates most: soldiers.

Carson and his scouts rode ahead. In the train could be seen artillery of various caliber (two of nine pounds, two of six, one of four, and a howitzer), hauled by poor mules, accompanied by some ten ox-carts of the country with wheels two feet in diameter and a four-wheel carriage, all heavily laden and drawn by oxen of the poorest sort. As they moved slowly north, it rained "like the devil," carts broke down, packs slipped off the mules. But they marched until 8 p.m., when they reached the first watering place, at Soledad, just north of San Diego. Thus early, Adjutant Emory concluded, the sailor's habit of discipline made him, when properly handled, a very good infantry soldier.[64]

Next day progress was better, and they fell in with a drove of sheep, which they captured as "prisoners of war." That night they camped three miles north of rancho Peñasquitos—following in reverse Kearny's route to San Diego. Next evening, the last of the year, they stopped at San Bernardo, near the foot of "Mule Hill" (which Griffin climbed again, to find the body of Sergeant Cox partly exposed). Stockton, with his staff, marines, and a piece of artillery, went on to the Snook ranch to spend the night under cover. The commodore, mused the surgeon, had a most enlarged view of the hardships of a soldier's life, having a fine tent well supplied with furniture and bedstead, while "our old Genl." had only his blankets, bearskin, and a common tent.[65]

In three days they had covered thirty miles; but on New Year's day, which was most beautifully clear, they traveled about fifteen and stopped at the Indian *ranchería* of Buena Vista, the sailors having begun to suffer from sore feet. They saw wild geese and a herd of antelope and noted cattle in all directions which the enemy had not driven away. But the most exciting scene was the lassoing of horses and cattle by Stockton's California *vaqueros* for the use of the troops. It was only six miles to San Luis Rey Mission, and here they spent the night of January 2, the Indian alcalde delivering it into their possession. Griffin and Emory greatly admired the Moorish-like structure and beautiful grounds—an extensive building, five hundred feet long, beautifully ornamented, the whole presenting "a most grand appearance." Here the Englishman John Forster, a California resident since 1833 and brother-in-law of the two Picos, came in, reporting Frémont's departure from Santa Barbara on the 27th (he had arrived that day) and that Andrés Pico had left Los Angeles with six hundred men to meet him. The same day Kearny spotted a naval officer making a cat-o'-nine-tails to discipline his men, and he cut it in pieces, saying "you shall punish none of My Jacks with any such articles."[66]

Whatever may have been Stockton's scruples about going beyond San Luis Rey, they now evaporated. There had been no opposition, and he knew something of Frémont's position, so they set out early on the 3rd and marched to Pío Pico's Santa Margarita rancho (Camp Pendleton). On a height above the Pacific about 2 p.m., Griffin saw whales spouting, and they camped within three-quarters of a mile of the sea near the abandoned *asistencia* of Las Flores. That day Stockton sent a dispatch to Frémont by George W. Hamley, master of the whaler *Stonington*, who had accompanied them from San Diego.[67] He said he hoped to be in Los Angeles in five or six days and suggested that Frémont join him on the road to the pueblo. The Californians, he warned, had gained a great deal of confidence from Mervine's and Kearny's defeats; and in the art of horsemanship, dodging, and running, it was futile to compete with them.

Next morning the road followed the top of a high embankment above the sea, and here about 11 a.m. they met three "Hostiles" on fine horses, bearing a flag of truce. They were William Workman, Charles Flügge, and Domingo Olivas—an Englishman, German, and Californian—bringing a letter from Flores.[68] The "governor and commandant general of the department and commander-in-chief of the national troops" wished to say to the commander of the forces of the United States that since the differences between the two countries had probably by now been settled, perhaps they could come to an honorable agreement. But if Stockton would not consent to a truce, the Californians had proven they could defend their rights and would fight to end the "tyranny and ominous discretionary power" of agents of the United States. According to Griffin, Stockton was so enraged by Flores' assumption of the titles of commander-in-chief and governor that he sent word, without consulting Kearny, that he would have nothing to do with him. Flores was a rebel, and he would shoot him if he could. The envoys pleaded, but Stockton

Mission San Luis Rey was delivered into the hands of the Americans: a Moorish–like structure five hundred feet long and beautifully ornamented, it presented a most grand appearance.

would accept only unconditional surrender. He had come to do his best, and please God he would!

Nine miles out the road descended to the beach, where fifty- to a hundred-foot cliffs intruded upon the shore (San Onofre Bluff). The tide was out, providing a narrow, hard road, and they kept scouts upon the hills; but the column stretched a great distance, and the enemy could have made the passage a formidable obstacle, as Emory observed. But they passed the eight-mile narrows without incident and camped late on an open plain at the mouth of San Juan Creek, two miles below San Juan Capistrano mission.

On the 5th they ascended to the mission, once a fine strong building,

with an arched cupola, thrown down by an earthquake in 1812.[69] It belonged to Forster and was used, or had been, as a stable. To this place the
Californians had come after the battle of San Pasqual, and four were still
there, by Griffin's account, suffering from severe wounds. Many families
had also taken refuge; and Stockton, fond of show, ordered up the band
and marched past "in all the pride of Military Display," the air resound-
ing with "Life on the Ocean Wave." Workman either accompanied the
army or returned that day and induced Stockton to issue a proclamation,
offering a general amnesty if the Californians would surrender Flores and
return to their ranchos.[70] This made Griffin uneasy, fearing they might
accept, then pitch into the Americans when they were off guard. But the
Californian Miguel de Pedrorena, an aide to Stockton, wrote his friend
J. A. Estudillo at San Diego that he was confident the proclamation
would open the eyes of the people and end the war.[71]

The army followed Oso Creek and stopped at rancho Los Alisos (past
El Toro), finding good wood and water and scores of "unfortunate"
chickens. Here they received a supply of fresh horses from Forster. About
them everything was green, but there was snow on the mountains, and
the nights were "devlish cold."

During a nineteen-mile march over a dead level on the 6th, they passed
the San Joaquín rancho of José Sepúlveda, seeing a vast number of cattle
in all directions, and came to the town or ranch of Santa Ana, belonging
to Bernardo Yorba. They were now near the enemy, and the place gave
evidence of it, not a soul being seen except a few old women who bolted
their doors. Finding a defensible position between the river and town,
they anticipated an undisturbed night's rest, but the wind "blew a hur-
ricane," and Emory (having never experienced a *Santa Ana*) thought it
something unusual in these parts.[72]

Though rumors had been drifting in, the enemy made their first appearance on the 7th, and hopes for a fight brightened.[73] The "rascals are
much better mounted than anything we can muster, and they know it,"
lamented Griffin, and they were impudent, capturing three of the army's
vaqueros and taking Forster prisoner. The battalion crossed the Santa
Ana River, a fine, dashing stream, watering many vineyards and corn-
fields, and at 3 p.m. camped at rancho Los Coyotes of the Nietos. Here
they learned from a "rich widow lady" that the enemy would give battle
the following day. Indeed, as the Americans arrived, some of the Californians were reconnoitering so close it was uncertain to which camp
they belonged. Stockton circumspectly wrote Montgomery to send the

Stonington to San Pedro with ammunition, two weeks' provisions for six hundred men, and boats to help them board if it should prove necessary.[74] (And Montgomery would warn Cooke of the Mormon Battalion, now approaching Warner's ranch, that the Californians were a subtle and mischievous enemy, heretofore underrated.)[75] That night, the commodore, passionately fond of dancing, ordered the band to Los Coyotes, and the California ladies were "soon whistling around in the giddy mazes of the waltz," their taper waists encircled by arms which would the following day be dealing death blows upon friends and relations.[76] Such were the Californians.

On the 8th the bugle sounded at dawn, and by 8 a.m. the Americans were marching across an undulating country which dipped gently toward the sea, plainly visible to the south and west. The resourceful Forster caught up with them again to report the enemy ambushed in willows and tall mustard at the lower ford of the San Gabriel River on the most direct road to the pueblo (the information having come from a Californian, likely Ramón Carrillo).[77] So Stockton diverted his force northeasterly to the upper crossing at the Paso de Bartolo, and as they neared the river at about 2 p.m., small squads of horsemen showed themselves on either flank. Clearly they meant to dispute the passage.

The plain bordering the river was about two miles wide, making a gradual descent to the crossing, while on the other side it rose to a small embankment, beyond which was a level place, backed by a higher bluff. At the onset of the plain they took their dinner, during which the enemy could be seen reconnoitering the near side. Within a quarter-mile of the stream the American line of battle was formed, and as they approached the river's edge, the Californians showed themselves in great force on the opposite bank, with a hundred or more crossing the river, threatening their advance. The Americans had that morning been reminded it was the 8th of January, the anniversary of Andrew Jackson's glorious victory over the British at New Orleans.

The Californians had for some time been anticipating Frémont's arrival from the north, where they knew he had been recruiting since the end of October. When, therefore, news came on January 3rd or 4th that he had passed Santa Barbara, several hundred horsemen were mustered at San Fernando mission and a hundred more sent out to meet him.[78] Then Flores learned on the 6th or 7th of Stockton's nearer approach and ordered all of his forces at once to the San Gabriel River, posting them in brush at the lower crossing.[79]

Lieutenant Edward O. C. Ord's map of the Los Angeles plains, locating the upper and lower crossings of the San Gabriel River on the way to Los Angeles.

Meanwhile, dissension, hardship, and failing hope had reduced popular enthusiasm for the war, and many Californians were ready openly or secretly to capitulate. Not a few had placed themselves under American protection at Monterey and San Diego, and others were deterred only by fear of reprisal from their fellows. Some had deserted, including most of the presidial company at Santa Barbara on the night of January 7.[80] The Californians had not harried the Americans on the road, attacked them at the narrow passage on the beach, or driven off the cattle. Their remaining inducements to action were recent successes, a stubborn pride, and an antipathy to foreigners, fomented from day to day by sometimes dispirited leaders. They had determined, however, to make a resolute, perhaps decisive stand at the San Gabriel, and about five hundred of them were soon hustled to the upper ford and posted on the high bluff.

The approaching Americans could see the Californians' lances and sabers glittering in the sun.[81] Above them on the right were two squadrons of horsemen under Andrés Pico (who two days before had challenged Frémont at Buenaventura)[82] and a few hundred yards to the left another body under José Antonio Carrillo. Their artillery, in the center, commanded the crossing. From the Americans' rear, a party of mounted skirmishers came down the plain "in beautiful style," passed between their advance guard and the river, crossed the ford, and joined the enemy.

On came the U.S. forces, arranged in their habitual marching order when near the enemy, a hollow square, to receive a charge of cavalry. In front was Turner's 2nd division, dragoons, and an artillery company of sailors with three guns, accompanied by Hensley's advance guard of mounted volunteers. On the right was the 1st division under Zeilin, marines, musketeers, and carbineers from the vessels. The left was composed of the 3rd division under Captain Renshaw, with companies of musketeers from the *Savannah* and *Congress*. And in the rear came Gillespie's 4th division of mounted volunteers and Californians, with two pieces of artillery. Some Californians also served as mounted skirmishers on the front, flanks, and rear. In the center of this moving square were all the baggage carts, cattle, spare oxen, and mules, comprising what the sailors brightly called a "Yankee corral." It was 3 p.m., and the time for action had come.

As Walter Colton would afterwards observe,[83] the war in California was on no great scale, but it impinged at certain points with terrific energy and had to be carried out with consummate tact, coolness, and courage. The "Old General" passed along the line, giving advice and encouragement to the men, and though no answer was heard, "the looks that flashed from an hundred eyes told . . . what was the inward resolve of all." The river was thirty to forty yards wide, knee-keep, and flowing over quicksand. Each bank was fringed with undergrowth, the near side level, the enemy's, above the small rise, flat and favorable to the movement of cavalry. Beyond, on the fifty-foot embankment which paralleled the river for miles, the Californian artillery was ranged at point-blank cannon distance, covering the ford. The party of volunteers under Hensley dismounted and went ahead as scouts. As the Americans neared the thicket, the Californian skirmishers retired, and a scattering fire was received from enemy sharpshooters. Four pieces of artillery could be counted on the height.

After Kearny had completed arrangements, the order "Forward" was heard. The first cannon shot from the enemy fell short and brought a shout of nervous derision from the troops. A second flew over their heads, and again there was laughter and jest. The advance, midway in the stream, was greeted by grape and round shot which skimmed the surface but was ineffective because its force was spent (San Gabriel mission powder was not of the best). The dragoons crossed—the commodore in front—and took possession of the lower bank. Kearny ordered Turner's artillery to unlimber and fire from the near shore, providing cover, but Stockton, calling impetuously for them to cross over, dashed in, dismounted, and seized the drag rope. The guns were heavy, a pause in the quicksand and all would be lost; "pull for your lives, your commodore is here . . . don't for the love of God lose these guns. . . ."[84] The men moved, they cheered, and over went the artillery while grape flew all about. Two nine-pounders, backed by Zeilin's marines, reached the breast-high embankment, behind which they established a new front, driving the enemy before. Stockton, primarily a gunner, took charge of the artillery, and his superior skill and powder and fondness for exercising the "big guns" now appeared to advantage. One of the first shots dismounted a California cannon, bringing a loud cheer from the men, "astounding the enemy," and making their fire more wild and uncertain.

Meanwhile, the main body of troops was advancing, with the "Old Fellow" on his mule leading the way, crying "steady my Lads, steady. Keep perfectly cool. . . ." In midstream his mule stopped still and the general, gathering his pistol in one hand, proceeded leisurely to dismount "as though he were . . . at his own door" and, keeping the same old pace, reached the bank at the head of the column. There they were deployed right and left in single file and covered themselves from the fire by lying down close under the first rise while the artillery battered away over their heads. "Fighting Bob," with telescope in hand, his face glowing with animation, sighted first one gun, then another and gave the orders to fire.

In about half an hour the enemy's guns fell silent, and ranks of horsemen could be seen on the hill. At Kearny's order the Americans rose to their feet and formed the now familiar pattern, then swarmed over the bank and moved shouting toward the next, some two hundred and fifty yards hence. When they were halfway across, the enemy began a charge. The "sight was a Glorious one, down they came in one long line, their Red Blankets, Black Hats and Bright Lances glittering . . . and death seemed to stare us in the face, for what could stay the power of that tide of Horse and Human Flesh." "Steady my Jacks, reserve your fire," the general's loud voice was heard above the uproar. Then, "front rank kneel to receive cavalry." The columns halted. Quickly each man dropped upon his knee and placed his spear-tipped musket or pike at an angle of 45 degrees, with the butt firmly buried in the earth; the body of men was encased in solid, gleaming steel. Simultaneously the files in the rear cocked their muskets in preparation. "There was no quail, no blanch." Carson could be seen with his eternal pipe in his mouth, never removing it except to fire. On they came and in a moment the word "Fire," and a sheet of flame flew along the line. "Oh that volley was so deadly, so destructive" that the cavalry paused, turned before another could be received, and regained the safety of the hill. The first enemy attack had been on the left front and rear; another was made on the right but veered off, and there was still a third. But in every direction they met the same wall of fire and steel. Kearny now shouted charge, "Charge and take the hill!" Up they went, with the commodore and general, a pistol in each hand, in the lead, the one mad with excitement, the other "cool as a Julap." It had already been assaulted by Hensley's skirmishers and was now found abandoned.

In an hour and twenty minutes the troops, artillery, and baggage train had all passed the river, the enemy's guns had been silenced, and the hill occupied. Many of the men did not fire a gun, the doctor recorded. In celebration the navy band blared "Hail Columbia" and "Yankee Doodle," which carried out over the plain.

The Californians encamped within sight, about a mile distant, but as the Americans had no means of pursuit against their well-mounted opponents, they settled down for the night farther down the river, where the mesa neared the water. The officers reviewed the battleground and agreed it had been a close affair. The steadiness of the troops and of the formation—which enclosed oxen, forty pack mules, and two hundred head of cattle—had not allowed one animal to escape. At some time Emory, the topographer, drew a "Sketch [map] of the Passage of the Rio San Gabriel, Upper California, by the Americans, discomfiting the opposing Mexican Forces, January 8th 1847."[85] Because of the proximity of the enemy, all fires were extinguished early that night.

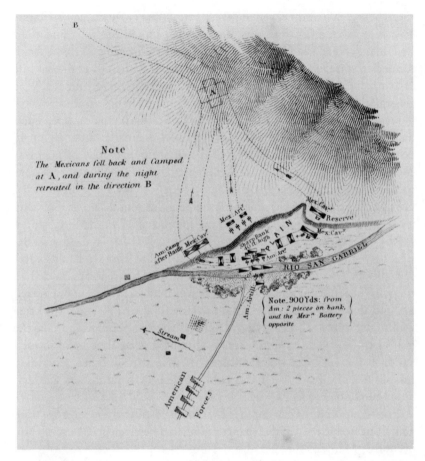

Lieutenant Emory's map of the battle of San Gabriel, showing the river, the sharp bank and hills beyond, and the placement of the Californian and American forces.

An alarm at midnight raised the camp, but no attack followed, and by morning the enemy had disappeared. Lorenzo Soto, whom Stockton had sent out several days before, came in with a white flag, saying Frémont was at San Fernando, and they all anticipated meeting him near the pueblo in the evening.

On the 9th at 9 a.m. the march across the mesa toward Los Angeles was resumed in the same order as before.[86] Scattered horsemen and reconnoitering parties hung upon the American flanks, and, five or six miles out, the enemy's line was discovered on the right, along the crest of a deep indentation in the plain, behind which their artillery was sheltered. Inclining a little to the left so as not to give Flores the full advantage of his position, the Americans' march was continued. The commodore had advised the men to keep their eyes upon the Californians' big guns and when they saw the flash to fall down and not rise until the ball whistled over their heads. At about 2 p.m., as they drew abreast of the enemy, they were fired upon at long range, and every man performed as directed, which seemed to astonish the enemy, who cheered lustily but were silenced when the Americans rose again and moved forward in as good order as before. A number of charges were made but were repelled, while Stockton, with "his pets," pelted the enemy with deadly aim.

Then the Californians deployed in a horseshoe formation and extended their line until the Americans were completely surrounded, apparently resolved to make a last desperate assault on all sides. Stockton's artillery was drawn inside the square as they marched on toward the town. At the sound of a gun, the Californians' "noble cavalry" advanced, constantly increasing in velocity as they came, charging with horrible yells. As they approached within range, the American volleys began, but on they rode until, within fifty yards, it seemed it would be hand-to-hand. But they could come no farther, the fire was too lethal, and they turned to take shelter in a nearby ravine. As the Americans departed, the Californians, always admired for their horsemanship, stripped the dead horses on the field without dismounting and carried off most of the saddles and bridles, their dead and wounded on horseback. It was perhaps 4:30, and the ambulatory engagement had lasted some two and a half hours.

The battle of Los Angeles or of the Mesa was ended, and the pueblo was in view. From a distance, prisoner Larkin (who would be released by Flores that night) observed the American forces marching toward the town in a compact square, cannons at each side.[87] But since the pueblo was known for its wine and aguardiente, the officers decided not to enter it until the morning. Having left the main road to avoid enemy artillery, they continued westerly, crossed the Los Angeles River, and camped upon its edge about two miles below the settlement. Emory produced another map, showing the maneuvers of the Californian and American forces in relation to the camp, the river, and the town: "Sketch of the Battle of Los Angeles, Upper California, Fought between the Americans and Mexicans, Jany. 9th, 1847."[88] American casualties during the two grueling

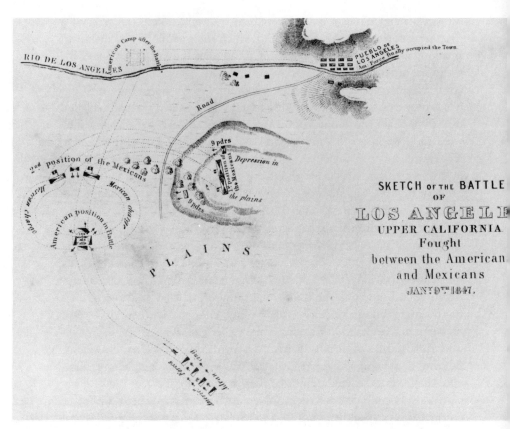

Lieutenant Emory's plan of the battle of Los Angeles, or of the Mesa, indicating the movements of the opposing forces, the site of the American camp after the fight, and the pueblo of Los Angeles.

days were twelve wounded (four severely; eight, mercifully, by spent balls) and three killed—among them, as Rowan mournfully noted, being "Smith, of the mizzen top (the one 'with a good eye in his head'),'' shot by accident.[89] Of the Californians, three were apparently killed, with up to a dozen wounded more or less seriously. The American volunteers' unmounted horses fell into enemy hands.

As the Americans settled down by the river, some four hundred of the Californians with their artillery drew off in an orderly manner toward the town, while about sixty moved down-river across from the camp. It appeared they were "not yet whipped" and might attack in the night. There was an alarm, and all hands were up and armed; but no assault followed, and from a distance the town seemed quiet. At about 9 in the morning of the 10th, after the camp had been raised, a flag of truce appeared, brought by Workman, Eulogio Célis, and Juan Avila, who proposed to surrender "their dear City of the Angels" if property and persons would be respected.[90] To this the commodore agreed; but, not altogether trusting Flores, they proceeded in battle array. Stockton having selected the "plainest and broadest road," they approached along the river, and as they left the cultivated lands and crossed a little ravine (the *zanja madre*, or irrigation ditch), the band "struck up" and carried them triumphantly into the plaza.*

Vigilance was not unwarranted, for the streets were full of "desperate and drunken fellows" who brandished their arms and saluted with every term of reproach.[91] The crest of the hill overlooking the plaza (Fort Hill, now mostly vanished) was teeming with horsemen, equally uncongenial. A scuffle broke out on the height, and a native, disarmed, attempted flight by rolling down the steep incline, with the others firing upon him. Believing it might be one of their *vaqueros*, the Americans fired a volley, and in answer to gunfire from the hill, the riflemen were ordered to clear it, "which a single fire effected." Two hundred men and two cannon were placed on the ridge, the remainder quartered in the town. And, having received the order, Captain Gillespie hoisted upon the Government House the same flag he had hauled down in September.

So Los Angeles was retaken. Parties of soldiers were soon all over the town, and "woe betide the house that had no occupants."[92] Surgeon Griffin, who savored the local wines—particularly the white—grapes, and other fruits, proclaimed it "decidedly one of the most desirable places" he had ever been.[93]

On the 11th, during a torrential rain, which helped dampen the populace, Kearny ordered a site for a fort selected to accommodate a hundred men. Emory speedily concurred; for Los Angeles, with some fifteen hundred residents and an equal number in its dependencies, was the center of wealth and population of Mexican California and the hub of military power. Here all the revolutions had had their origin, he said, and against it any Mexican force from Sonora would be directed. A rapid reconnaissance was made of the hill and a fort sketched to command the town and its principal approaches.[94]

---

*The route approximated present-day Alameda Street, turned left at Aliso, crossed the *zanja* into Los Angeles Street, and swung right a block into the plaza (*517*–41 121; KELLEHER).

The same day Stockton issued a general order, congratulating the troops upon their courage, which had perhaps "never been surpassed," and their cool determination, which had "extorted the admiration of the enemy." [95] It was signed by the commodore as governor and commander-in-chief and did not mention Kearny or his men; and when Emory carried it to the general, asking whether it should be read, he answered in the negative. [96]

14

War and Peace

B UT WHERE was Frémont? After the recapture of Los Angeles, no
word was received from him on January 10th, the 11th, or the day
after. There were only rumors: that he had turned back, was at San Gabriel, had fought a battle with Pico and Flores.[1] Three months before—a
long time under the circumstances—he and Stockton had left San Francisco in the *Sterling* and *Congress*, he for Santa Barbara to collect horses
and make the three-day march to Los Angeles.[2] Since then, the commodore had gone to San Pedro, moved on to San Diego, rescued Kearny's
Army of the West, readied an expedition of six hundred men for Los Angeles, fought the battles of San Gabriel and the Mesa, and retaken the
pueblo. Stockton had last heard from Frémont on November 2, in a note
from Monterey, telling of his return there because animals could not be
found.[3] It was now mid-January.

After Frémont had spoken to W. D. M. Howard of the *Vandalia* in
October, just off San Luis Obispo, and learned the bad news in the south,
he had turned back to Monterey to get the horses he had left on the Cosumnes, some cannon, and as many recruits for the battalion as possible. Upon
approaching the harbor, the *Sterling* was becalmed for several days, and
Frémont sent some captains ashore in a longboat, among them the immigrant Charles Burroughs, ordered to the Sacramento upon "very urgent
business for the government." Frémont and his men landed on the 27th
and 28th, when he wrote Stockton, suggesting that he too return to Monterey, where they could advance upon the southern pueblo together.[4]
This Stockton did not quite do (and Frémont would grumble about the
commodore's impatience and say that waiting would give a man of
Stockton's temperament some useful schooling.)[5] The battalion's arrival
at Monterey was opportune, for Lieutenant William A. T. Maddox of

the marines had gone off to San Juan with thirty men. A large number of Californians were reputedly in the hills ready to fall upon the town. Frémont began at once to prepare for the campaign, and the *Californian* assured its readers that "No half-way measures will be pursued."[6]

Immediately after Frémont and Stockton had left San Francisco, Montgomery had heard from Monterey of a general rising of Californians and wrote to Edward M. Kern, in command at Sutter's Fort.[7] Kern was to send expresses to hasten the approaching immigration and press into service anyone within reach. The ship's boats would bring them down to be assembled at San José, and enlistment was to be for three or six months at $25 a month. Kern was also to disarm the Californians within his reach and permit none to leave, since the "utter extermination" of foreigners was threatened.[8]

Some Americans began to raise volunteers on their own account—among them Edwin Bryant, Andrew Grayson, and Richard T. Jacob[9]—riding off in any direction from which immigrants were expected. "Every one who can raise among the emigrants 30 or 40 men becomes a captain," explained Walter Colton. Soon, down the river came the "rag tag and bobtail of all Creation," with or without coats, trousers, boots, moccasins, or shoes, but invariably with very good rifles. Some were decked out on the *Portsmouth* in red annd blue naval flannels, white frocks, pea jackets, and blue silk handkerchiefs, and given blankets, tobacco, arms, and ammunition (to be charged against future pay). They were then packed into the schooner *Dobey* for the Santa Clara landing, where they were to be mounted and join Frémont's force.[10] Kern's efforts were very successful, Montgomery thought, about ninety arriving from the Sacramento and Sonoma by November 8, with seventy or eighty more reportedly on the way, and two hundred Oregon and California Indians. With another forty-five from San José and Yerba Buena, the volunteers would number at least six hundred, enough, he doubted not, to disperse the enemy in the south.[11] Maddox brought a beautiful brass field piece and a *caballada* of horses from San Juan Bautista,[12] and several hundred animals were collected by Burroughs on the Sacramento.

With the threatened withdrawal of forces from Monterey and other points to suppress insurrection, local inhabitants began to fear attacks by Indians, Californians, even Americans (a guard was needed at San José, it was said, to keep new arrivals as well as the natives in order).[13] The people claimed to be entitled to protection under the American flag. Montgomery therefore authorized the recruiting of volunteers for local defense, sending James Griffith to Sonoma and Lansford Hastings to San José, where Charles Weber was already busy. The Californians were meanwhile engaged in the same activity, impressing their countrymen and commandeering animals for their own use and to prevent their falling into the enemy's possession.[14]

With Frémont's return, recruiting was greatly intensified. Weber's high-handed methods became particularly obnoxious to foreigners and Californians alike—seizing all their arms, horses, saddles, bridles, and accoutrements, "making a clean sweep of every thing of the kind," with few receipts given.[15] Ranchers were left without horses for plowing (it was seeding time), to herd their roaming cattle, or catch beef to eat. Yerba Buena was rapidly running out of meat, and it was obtained with difficulty anywhere.[16] At San José a wedding party was seen going through the streets on foot,[17] a thing never before known in California, a fine saddle horse lately purchased by the groom having been pressed into military service. Americans there even abused the alcalde, and Montgomery attempted to impose restrictions upon Weber's conduct.[18] He was to manifest some regard for the feelings and interests of the people, round up animals himself, and never take all of a man's horses, measures Weber regarded as impractical. They plundered the Californians to procure the means of fighting them, Colton noted.[19] Charles E. Pickett, a newly arrived lawyer from Oregon, likened Frémont's use of "scamps" to England's employment of mercenaries against the American colonists; and Larkin observed a "very reckless spirit among our new comers."[20] Frémont was raising a band of Walla Walla Indians, and Lieutenant Louis McLane, now captain of volunteers, thought this a bad policy, there being "too much of the blood hound about them," to which the Monterey editor agreed.[21]

Reports concerning the disposition of the Californians varied. Around San Francisco Bay they were said to be tranquil, while on the *contra costa* they were ready to descend upon the settlements as soon as the volunteers departed.[22] At San José it was believed the Californians would not join the insurrection unless driven to it by harsh treatment; yet the principal men at San Juan Bautista had all reputedly left for Los Angeles.[23] Some held that the natives did not like to be ordered around by their fellows and were ready to declare their independence or to surrender to the invader to avoid defeat.[24] One Californian bluntly acknowledged that if they had meant to drive out the Americans, they should have united when the Bear first raised its head—now it only aggravated their troubles.[25] Generally, the *Californian* concluded, citizens of property were at home cultivating their farms, while those with nothing to lose were in arms; California's revolutions always began in November, when farmers should be planting their crops.[26]

Nevertheless, emissaries from the south were getting through, stirring up revolt.[27] A force under Manuel Castro, riding toward San Juan (as already noted) had kidnapped Larkin and engaged a body of Americans at La Natividad.[28] The same night an Indian brought Frémont the news, and, with three hundred men, he set out from Monterey on November 17. Finding that the enemy had fled, Captain McLane and some of his flying artillery turned back to John Gilroy's ranch, commandeered a forge, and reappeared on the 28th with an ammunition wagon and "3 guns well mounted."[29] Many were still foraging among the ranchos, taking whatever was useful in the shortest possible time. It was with regret, the *Californian* assured its readers, that the United States took private property, but there was no remedy. By the law of nations, when anything useful belonging to the enemy could be "come at," it was taken.[30]

As recruits continued to gather, Frémont's battalion was organized into eight companies of cavalry and McLane's artillery, 428 men, including Indians and servants (rated an effective force of 350).[31] Some 1,900 horses and mules had been marshaled, many of them "miserable, sore-backed skeletons," and 300 head of cattle. A single bugle composed the band, "and a sorry one" it was, played by first-class musician Bill Miller, transferred at Frémont's request from the *Savannah*.[32]

Before leaving San Juan Bautista, Frémont wrote Mervine—in an unaccustomed mood of conciliation—that all military and civil authorities in the north were to abstain from further offensive action against the Californians, the greater part of whom he now conceded were of a peaceable disposition.[33] Weber's proceedings he arraigned as "little honorable to the United States," and he disclaimed them as disgraceful. In a burst of humility, he begged Mervine's compliance more as a favor than a command, believing that his title, Military Commandant of California, was little respected by Stockton's officers, and he would be "humiliated" to attach it to his name. He signed only as "Lt. Col. U.S. Army Commdg. California Battalion U.S. Troops." He was thoughtful or politic enough to leave a considerable number of horses to be divided among the farmers.[34] (Frémont was running for office.)

Now as Lieutenant Colonel, Mounted Riflemen, a rank he had found awaiting him at Monterey,[35] Frémont rode with his troops out of San

Juan on November 29.[36] They were a motley array in respect to race, language, weapons, and especially dress, but a formidable foe. There were Frenchmen and Germans, Englishmen and Canadians, Californians and Indians, and they represented every section of the United States: New England, central, south, and west. They varied greatly in temperament, character, experience, and education, integrity, intelligence, and motivation. Their leaders were for the most part a seasoned lot, fitted for the responsibilities of discipline and command. Certainly their chief had all the qualifications of habitude, disposition, and purpose to exact loyalty and obedience.

Not following the main road through the Salinas Valley, they proceeded instead up the San Benito River, the first day making about ten miles. From the start it rained, and McLane thought this a good reason to take the mission road,* but Frémont was determined to strike through the hills. They laid over the next two days to round up cattle—thirteen of which would be slaughtered every afternoon for food and cooked over every man's fire, the only sustenance for most of the way.[37] On the 3rd a little sun, and the battalion formed a hollow square and renewed its march up the San Benito and over the range into the Salinas Valley (near present-day King City). Parties of Indians (natives, Delawares, and Walla Wallas under Captain Richard Jacob) camped each night without fires one to three miles ahead and at the rear as scouts. No one left the camp without permission, and Frémont would say they passed through the country without giving any reasonable cause for complaint.[38] Though there were shenanigans and murmurs, a court-martial, reductions in rank, and several desertions, their behavior was perhaps remarkable under the circumstances.

By December 10 they reached San Miguel Mission, a hundred miles south and near the end of the Salinas Valley. "We have had infernal hard work. . . . Up one hill & down another," wrote the irritable captain of artillery (the McLane and Frémont clans were not on good terms). He was dragging three heavy guns and a wagon and would have taken the better road. They could be tracked by their broken-down animals, for already several hundred had been lost by reason of the cold rains, muddy

---

* El camino real, or main road, connecting the missions and presidios: below Monterey it passed through Soledad, San Antonio, San Miguel, San Luis Obispo, and Santa Inés, through the Gaviota Pass to Santa Barbara and San Buenaventura, up the Santa Clara River and to San Fernando, Los Angeles and San Gabriel, San Juan Capistrano, San Luis Rey, and San Diego (thence to Baja California).

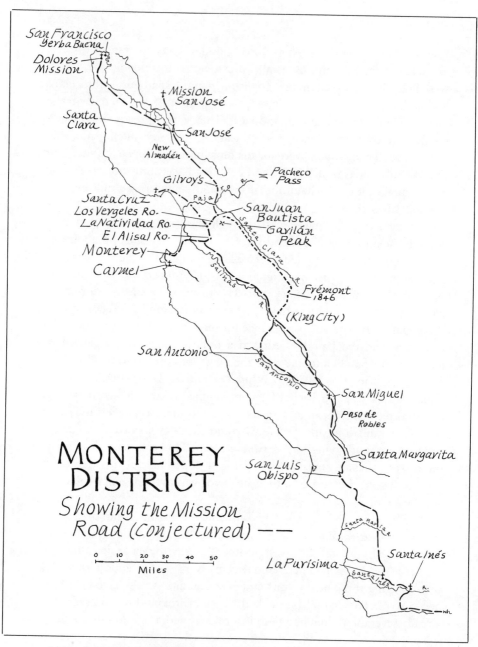

Map of the Monterey district, with contemporary place names, showing the mission road and the route of Frémont's march toward Los Angeles in November and December 1846. (For routes in Southern California, see page 204.)

trails, old washed-out grass, and the new growth without substance. On the 12th it rained again, and the men walked while the animals recuperated. Next day they caught and shot an Indian spy; and Larkin Stanley, a recently arrived immigrant, died of typhoid. On to Santa Margarita, "it blew a gale & rained torrents," but a feast with a roasted rib made McLane forget his troubles. Bryant affirmed the California beef to be generally fat, juicy, and tender, surpassing in flavor any other he had ever tasted.

On the 14th, wet and cold, they crossed the Cuesta Pass between the Salinas River and the coastal watershed, emerging above San Luis Obispo. Expecting to find enemy troops quartered there, they made observations from a hill overlooking the mission, then about 9 p.m. surrounded the buildings "in great confusion" and captured a few people.[39] The men were billeted in the church, the horses in the mission buildings. Scouts brought in some thirty Californians, among them José de Jesús Pico (nephew of Andrés and Pío), *juez de paz*, late commandant there, and more recently a conspicuous participant in the fight at Natividad. Having broken his parole, he was tried and sentenced to death but pardoned by Frémont, as Midshipman Wilson would say, "from some peculiar circumstances attending his case."[40] Frémont would afterwards explain that this clemency was due to the tearful appeals of Pico's wife, their fourteen children, many women in town, and some of Frémont's own men whom Pico had earlier befriended.[41] It also accorded with the colonel's new strategy of pacification. "Frémont intends taking him below," McLane recorded; and indeed Jesús Pico would stay with and aid his savior until Frémont's departure from California some months hence.

After some rest for men and animals on the 16th, and with plenty of grain from the mission, they moved south again in fine, sunny weather and reached the Nipomo rancho of William G. Dana (south of Arroyo Grande) on the 18th. A naturalized Bostonian and California resident for twenty years, Dana was married to the "still handsome" Josefa Carrillo (age 36) and had a "fine property & really a beautiful daughter."[42] Dana may have warned of an ambush by the Californians at Gaviota Pass, a narrow but almost level passage by the main road through the mountains to Santa Barbara (between Buellton and the sea); or Frémont might have thought to surprise the inhabitants of the town by taking an arduous and little-used way.[43] Keeping to the east of the accustomed route, they came early on the 20th to William Foxen's Tinaquaic rancho, where they laid

Frémont made observations from the hill behind San Luis Obispo Mission, then, about 9 p.m., surrounded the buildings in great confusion and captured a few people.

over, cleaning their guns in readiness for action. They were strong enough, some of them thought, to disperse any number of Californians, but Frémont was again taking "one of his damned short cuts" against the wishes of many of his fellows, who labeled him a "coward, old woman, etc. etc." [44] With a guide they proceeded on the 21st over a steep ridge to the valley of Santa Inés and stopped within a few miles of the mission. [45] Here they struck off up Santa Inés Creek, which was running full, rocky, and difficult to ford. Next day, with light rain and three crossings, they made only four miles and camped at the foot of the San Marcos Pass. There was little grass, but McLane, who cared for his horses, had packed some grain.

On the morning of December 24, Frémont rode ahead, leaving McLane a hundred extra men to get the guns over the mountain. It was the hardest day yet, but they reached the springs near the summit, their guide assuring them the worst was over. It rained all night and was still pouring on Christmas day, but by starting at 6 a.m., they climbed the last ridge by 9 o'clock and began the perilous descent. Yesterday's work was a pastime compared to this. The road was a gully worn by hauling lumber, with sandstone ledges over which they were obliged to lower the guns by hand. On one side the angle of slope was about 45°, on the other "as near up & down as possible." A heavy storm was blowing, the rain changed to sleet, and the guide took a wrong turn. By 4 p.m. they recognized the impossibility of getting the artillery down by nightfall, and the animals were so numbed they would not go ahead. So the guns were hauled to one side, the saddles and packs hidden in the bushes, the animals turned loose. While some of the men found whatever shelter there was among the rocks, the rest descended to the Goleta plain and by 10 p.m. made fires, cut brush to stand on, since the bottom was "knee deep" in mud and water, and waited till dawn without blankets. The torrent continued until 2 a.m., when Bryant, for one, arose, built a fire and a small platform, and by daylight had his clothes dry.[46]

The day after Christmas broke bright and clear. The men worked all day getting the guns and baggage down and recovering horses (among them "Old John," McLane's pack mule which had twice crossed the Rocky Mountains). But the destruction of horseflesh had been frightful, estimated at a hundred and fifty. It was 2 p.m. the following day before the battalion was ready, and so great had been the loss of animals that one or two companies proceeded on foot. They camped on a stream about half a mile from Santa Barbara.

Entering the town on the 28th, they found it almost empty, except for some Americans and a few of the town's "compassionate ladies," who particularly welcomed Talbot's men, whom they had presumed dead.[47] They remained a week, collecting horses, repairing damage, and "setting the not very well disposed people to rights." There was some searching of Californians' homes suspected of concealing arms.[48] McLane noted that the mission was large, in good repair, and leased by an American and a little Irish doctor (Daniel Hill and Nicholas Den) who were kind to him, as they had been to Consul Larkin when he had passed that way. The observant artilleryman greatly admired the irrigation system and the local women, particularly the daughters of American and English settlers who had married in the country. A letter from Flores was intercepted here, telling of Kearny's defeat at San Pasqual. Years later, Frémont would remember a visit with an old lady at Santa Barbara who urged him to make a just and generous peace which would be acceptable and enduring, and she would influence her people. In retrospect this seemed the beginning of the capitulation which followed.[49]

While they were here, the prize schooner *Julia* came in, a "swift vessel" (Leidesdorff's favorite, of which he had been master).[50] Its commander, Lieutenant Edward A. Selden, brought a long brass four-

Frémont remained in Santa Barbara a week, collecting horses, repairing damage, and setting the not very well-disposed people to rights.

pounder from Mervine for McLane's arsenal, a sister to one he already had. The vessel was to proceed to the Rincón, south of Santa Barbara where the cliffs came down to the sea, and stand by to assist if the Californians made a forced passage necessary,[51] then report to Stockton. Frémont wrote the commodore, telling of his position and intentions: he would leave on the 4th, march directly to the pueblo, and if not met by the enemy would attack them in the town.[52]

On January 3, 1847, they raised camp in fine weather, the country beginning to look green. It was reported that the Californians would dispute their passage at the Rincón, where the road narrowed to about fifty yards. If Flores could get his men to stand, thought McLane, they could empty a good many American saddles. The following night they camped on the beach, the *Julia* in view, and next day Frémont sent eighty rifles to the hills above the shore "to take our *friends* in the rear," while the artil-

lery led the column below. Here Selden came in with a boat to say he had seen a large enemy force. Flores had indeed sent a considerable body of men to the Rincón,[53] who had thrown up a breastwork across the road; but when they discovered the flanking movement along the hills, "they were off like birds." Removing the barricade, the Americans continued to Buenaventura Mission, where they camped in the garden. When their pickets were annoyed, McLane mounted a six-pounder on a little knoll, and as several Californians came near, the gunner fired, and in "10 seconds" they were gone.

The morning of the 6th it was blowing a gale, the men choked and blinded by dust. Scouts reported Californians approaching from the Santa Clara River below, and, as Frémont advanced, some of them skirmished at long shot. Andrés Pico wished to entice the Americans toward the lower ford of the river, where a large number of horsemen were concealed under an embankment. Some of Frémont's men favored an attack; they were in good spirits, had had no real encounter with the enemy, and might thereby resolve the affair at once. But they proceeded upstream along the edge of the hills instead, injuring the "Moral force" of the company, McLane thought. Crossing the river, they camped at the upper ford (near Saticoy). The Californians, scattering to avoid cannon-shot, waved their swords and banners, performing a great variety of equestrian feats.[54]

All night the wind blew, and it was fresh and cold in the morning as they traveled upstream. Flores had sent a second party of about twenty men under José Carrillo over the San Fernando Pass to the upper Santa Clara, and they came down to Juan Sánchez' Santa Clara rancho, where some of Pico's force also apparently retreated. About fifty strong, they challenged Frémont's advance guard but could not get between them and the column, so retreated to nearby Las Posas rancho.[55] The Americans camped that night on Carlos Antonio Carrillo's Sespe rancho.* "Night very cold."

They traveled another twelve or fifteen miles on the 8th against strong winds and over barren terrain, stopping in a grove of willows near a rancho. Ice formed two inches thick, but they found plenty of corn and *frijoles*. Here on the morning of the 9th Pedro Carrillo (who had lived in Boston and Honolulu) came in with George Hamley and a letter from Stockton. Hamley had left San Diego in the *Malek Adhel*, landed at San Buenaventura on the 8th, and gone through the enemy lines at night. The message told of Mervine's and Kearny's defeats and the Californians' elation, advised Frémont how to fight, and said Stockton expected to reach Los Angeles by the 8th or 9th.[56]

They climbed the narrowing river valley onto a fertile, well-watered plain and camped on the 9th at the "Hill farm" (near Castaic), where they again found corn, wheat, and beans in abundance. Once more they discharged, cleaned, and reloaded their arms in preparation. Then, crossing the plain by the San Fernando trail, they spent their last night in the mountains at the mouth of a narrow canyon, beyond which lay the San Fernando and Cahuenga plains. The Californians, they had heard, meant to stop them here, and enemy horsemen could be seen spread along the ridge ahead. So the guard was doubled, but they were not disturbed.[57]

* The distances traveled vary in the several accounts. After Saticoy they may have stopped on the 7th at Santa Paula or Fillmore and the following night near Fillmore or Piru.

The American force divided on the 11th. The main body advanced over a steep ridge to the right of the main road, while the artillery, horses, and baggage followed the rough but more direct route through San Fernando Pass. McLane wondered why they were not opposed: nature had "done everything—man need only stand & fight." That afternoon they camped at San Fernando Mission, with its extensive gardens and buildings in good repair. On the way they met two Californians with news of the battles of the 8th and 9th and the occupation of Los Angeles, and a courier arrived with a message from Kearny.[58] Had Frémont come down the mission road, McLane sourly lamented, "instead of backing & filling in those infernal Mountains," the Californians would have met them instead of the commodore, who would magnify his successes into battles of great note. With a "nicety of calculation or felicity of luck that excites wonder," they had arrived at the scene of action the morning after it had ended.[59]

After the engagement on the Mesa, the disoriented natives had collected in bunches, a hundred at Verdugo's San Rafael rancho, others for a time at nearby rancho San Pasqual (north of the pueblo), with Manuel Castro and Flores not far away.[60] The day Frémont reached San Fernando, he sent his reprieved California friend Jesús Pico to San Rafael. Arriving late, Don Jesús was detained, but he reported the kind treatment he had received and advised negotiations. The news was carried to rancho San Pasqual, where it was suggested to Flores and Castro that they see what guarantees could be obtained.[61] But Flores was of a different mind and, turning the command over to Andrés Pico, left with Manuel Castro and some others for Sonora.

José Carrillo and Agustín Olvera set off with Jesús Pico next morning for Frémont's quarters with the terms under which the Californians were willing to capitulate.[62] (Frémont would afterwards picture himself bidding the Californians lay down their arms or fight, riding fearlessly into the enemy's camp, and dealing directly with Pico.)[63] Both sides appointed commissioners, and Frémont proclaimed a one-day armistice while negotiations were completed.[64] The Californians, it was said, were ready to abandon the strife to which they had been driven by taunts of cowardice, but they would not yield to Stockton's harsh demands.[65] While several hundred Californians gathered off the road at Pedro López' Tujunga rancho,[66] Frémont's battalion moved to the Féliz adobe north of Cahuenga Pass, where Carrillo, Olvera, and the American commissioners, McLane, Pierson B. Reading, and William H. Russell, assembled. McLane entered in his journal that Russell was for unconditional surrender and as "obstinate as a king," but he and Reading prevailed, and articles which differed materially from Pico's were finally arranged.[67] The seven "Articles of Capitulation" entered into on the morning of January 13 were signed by the commissioners and by Frémont as "Military Commandant" and Pico as "Chief of the National Forces."[68]

The Treaty of Cahuenga required the Californians to surrender their public arms and return to their homes, obey the laws of the United States, and not renew hostilities while the war continued. It guaranteed the protection of life and property; relieved the inhabitants from taking an oath of allegiance until the final treaty was concluded; permitted them to leave the country without hindrance; and vouchsafed equal rights with citizens of the United States. The capitulation was not to preclude further guarantees which might in justice be required by either party, and an additional article was approved on the 16th, canceling paroles given by either side and freeing all prisoners. (Six supplementary provisions were also suggested by Carrillo and Olvera on the 18th which may have received Stockton's approval—calling for the retention of incumbents in office, popular elections, the protection of priests, recognition of the public debt by the United States, and payment for destroyed property and back salaries.)[69] In good time, copies would find their ways into the government archives at Washington and Mexico City.[70]

It was a generous compact. The Californian troops were dismissed to their homes, taking their arms, except such as were left as a sign of surrender. For these, Russell acknowledged receipt from Andrés Pico on the 18th: two pieces of artillery (one taken from Kearny at the battle of San Pasqual) with six charges of grape and six muskets.[71] With it, hostilities were ended, wrote Frémont, and the territory left peaceably in American hands. As, long ago, he had inaugurated warfare in California without mandate or warrant, so now, deliberately, without authority, and in his own right, he brought it to an end.

There were no formal arrangements for carrying the news from Los Angeles. Neither the Monterey *Californian* nor Yerba Buena's new *California Star* had reporters in the field. They were wholly dependent upon voluntary contributors and each other, and the Monterey editor admitted that he was "often deceived." Six days after Los Angeles was retaken, the *Californian* reported no news "from below," though there were plenty of rumors which the editor did not much believe. But he would not be surprised, he added, if the first tidings came through the washerwomen near Monterey. They had first known of Stockton's conquest of the pueblo in August, of its recapture by the Californians, and of Mervine's subsequent defeat. It was the most singular mode of news-gathering with which he was acquainted, excelling the carrier pigeon and the magnetic telegraph. By their most recent report, the commodore had taken Los Angeles three days before Frémont's arrival; most of the Californians had come in and given up their arms; and the colonel was close on the trail of those who had fled. "So runs the rumor, as it comes drifting over the suds. . . ."[72]

Monterey editor Robert Semple was brusquely challenged by Sam Brannan's *California Star*, whose management believed its scuttlebutt more credible. But it reported Kearny and Frémont joining forces; a hundred Californians under Pío Pico and José Castro killed; and Frémont surrendering his command to Kearny, then heading for Yerba Buena to take up his duties as governor![73]

The first news directly from the seat of war did not appear until January 28, in an extra of the *Californian*. In an account contributed by Stockton's purser, William Speiden, Kearny was mentioned only as leading a detachment of dragoons (and losing the battle at San Pasqual), a deception the editor tried to set straight on February 13. The *Star* echoed this report but allowed that others must have deserved some commendation.[74]

The treaty had of course been concluded by a lieutenant colonel within a few miles of two officers superior in rank and position. Kearny had received a copy of the truce of January 12 and, baffled, had written Stockton that Frémont must be ignorant of their presence and might capitulate and retire to the upper country. He offered to take two hundred and fifty or three hundred men and form a junction, but Stockton, probably believing he had won the war, did not take so dim a view.[75]

Three days before, just after Los Angeles had been re-taken, Kearny had sent Frémont an informal message.[76] "Dear Fremont: We are in possession of this place, with a force of marines and sailors." He was to join the general if he could, or Kearny would march to his assistance; avoid charging the enemy and please acknowledge receipt of the message. Although it was received by Frémont on the 11th, he made no reply. Another, more importunate note was written by the general on the 12th.[77] "I am here in possession of this place. . . . Acknowledge the hour of receipt of this, and when I may expect you." Still no answer. Frémont was busy negotiating with the enemy. Next day Kearny wrote twice, briefly at noon. "We are in force in this place . . . and know nothing of you further than your armistice of yesterday"; and at 2 p.m., more demanding, he had been here since the 10th, had written several letters, and Frémont was to come at once or let him know, and Kearny would go to him.[78]

Then, on the 13th of January, with a peace treaty of uncertain validity in his pocket, Frémont responded, giving his whereabouts as "On the march" (he was at Cahuenga).[79] "I have the honor to report to you" (it would prove a fatal expression) "my arrival at this place with 400 mounted riflemen and six pieces of artillery, including . . . two pieces lately in the possession of the Californians." Pico's forces had laid down their arms and surrendered to his command. He unabashedly signed the note as "Lt. Col. U.S.A.," a rank he understandably esteemed, and "military commandant of the territory of California" (which title, under less auspicious circumstances, he had been too "humiliated" to claim).

Frémont had been aware of the approach of Kearny's army since mid-November, when Montgomery had written of their departure from Santa Fé; and Stockton, on January 3, had mentioned the general's defeat.[80] Kearny had likewise known of Frémont's proximity with a force of volunteers which he meant to take under his command. None of the general's messages had mentioned the commodore's presence.

Stockton, having gone to great lengths to maintain his position as commander-in-chief vis-à-vis the general, could hardly applaud a devious and unauthorized treaty made by his creature, Frémont. When, after the reoccupation, Benito Wilson took Andrés Pico to see the commodore in the Avila house, Stockton did not hesitate to say, "and very positively," that neither Pico's nor Frémont's courses were in order. Wilson brought rumors from the street that Frémont did not intend to recognize the commodore and general, whereupon Stockton broke out, "What does the damned fool mean?"[81]

After the capitulation, Frémont did not come to Los Angeles at once but sent a scout on the 13th, William H. Russell.[82] He carried Frémont's "report" of that date to Kearny and was to discover Kearny's object in coming to the country and make the capitulation known to whoever might be chief in command. As Russell afterwards testified, he went first to Kearny to ask whether he had superseded Stockton.[83] Kearny replied that Stockton was acting as governor and commander-in-chief, and the capitulation should be delivered to him,[84] which Russell, after an hour of conversation, did. Russell also reported that Kearny accepted the treaty but said that Stockton did not; and the general suggested arguments with which Russell might respond to Stockton's objections. The same day Russell paid a second visit to the commodore, who had meanwhile read the treaty and concluded to ratify it; and on both occasions Stockton declared his intention to appoint Frémont governor as soon as he arrived in Los Angeles.[85] Spending the night with Kearny and Turner, Russell gathered from conversation that the general, too, greatly admired Frémont and meant to appoint him governor when he himself should leave for the United States after obtaining the supreme command.

Next morning Russell rode out to meet Frémont, finding the battalion some five or six miles from the pueblo. Both Kearny and Stockton, he said, were anxious to confer upon him the office of governor, and Frémont's only problem would be to choose between them. As to who was superior, Kearny had specific instructions from the President, which Russell had seen. But while Stockton claimed to have brought out "full and plenary instructions," * he would not exhibit them "like slaves did their papers." Russell was nevertheless impressed by Stockton's confident manner and concluded that although Kearny was a better friend of Frémont than Stockton, possessed some funds, had instructions from the Secretary of War, and shortly expected the arrival of troops, he admitted serving under Stockton and considered himself outranked by the commander of a squadron (which Kearny afterwards denied).[86] Russell therefore regretted that they must look to Stockton as commander-in-chief, since he was exercising these functions, and Frémont came to the same conclusion.

The battalion crossed the Cahuenga Pass in heavy rain, passed several springs throwing up mineral tar (which Edwin Bryant thought might one day be valuable) and entered the city of the Angels.[87] Frémont was conducted to quarters assigned by Stockton in the Government House, where Russell and Reading were also billeted, and the battalion went on to San Gabriel mission. As already determined, Frémont reported first to Stockton, then, as he would later explain, "called on" General Kearny. That day Kearny wrote to Washington that Frémont had arrived with four hundred volunteers, but he had heard nothing more about the

---

* Bancroft's order of October 17, 1845, saying nothing about government (RICHMAN 529).

troops expected from New York and New Mexico. Upon their arrival, he would have the management of affairs and would endeavor to carry out the President's instructions.[88]

Meanwhile, Lieutenant Emory, without the burdens of high office, "drank . . . the wine of the country, manufactured by Don Luis Vignes, a Frenchman . . . truly delicious, resembling more the best description of Hock than any other. . . ."[89]

Stockton also reported Frémont's arrival to the Department but was sorry to say that Flores had escaped to Sonora because of the colonel's delay.[90] A copy of the treaty was enclosed. Though he had himself refused to make it, he thought he should give his approval. And he was pleased to remind the Secretary they had recovered the gun taken from Kearny at San Pasqual. California was again tranquil, the civil government founded by him was in operation, and he would soon withdraw his men and sail to the coast of Mexico. Frémont would be appointed governor and Russell secretary of state[91] (as a lawyer, Russell being better qualified than Gillespie, who preferred to command the battalion).

Orders in an army are like holy writ in a cloister, to be obeyed, and Kearny had his instructions. "These troops and such as may be organized in upper California," the Secretary of War had said, would be under his command.[92] Now that Frémont had reported, and Stockton was about to make Gillespie major of the battalion,[93] Kearny decided the time for obedience had come. Early on the 16th, Emory sent a directive to "Lieut. Col. J. C. Frémont, Mounted Riflemen, Commd'g. California Vol."—the only army rating to which he was entitled.[94] It ordered that no change be made in the organization of the battalion without Kearny's approval; and an extract of the letter from the Secretary of War was enclosed.

Then Kearny turned his attention to the commodore. Russell had consulted Kearny and other friends about accepting the commission as secretary, and the general knew Stockton's intention to make Frémont governor[95] (a matter of ordinary knowledge throughout the city, Russell would remember). "I am informed that you are now engaged in organizing a civil government," Kearny wrote.[96] "As this duty has been specifically assigned to myself . . . I have to ask if you have any authority" from the President, the Secretary of War, or any other source to form a government and make appointments. If he had and would show it to him, Kearny would cheerfully acquiesce, otherwise he demanded that Stockton's proceedings cease.

The argument had been joined, and Stockton reacted the same afternoon. As he had told Kearny at San Diego, he had conquered California, put a civil government into operation, and sent a copy of the laws and the names of the officers to the President before Kearny's arrival. "I will only add, that I cannot do anything nor desist from doing anything, or alter anything on your demand, which I will submit to the President & ask for your recall." In the meantime, Kearny was to consider himself suspended from the command of the U.S. forces "in this place"[97]—excluding, Stockton would afterwards concede, Kearny's own dragoons.[98] (Less earnest men might have noticed the proceedings were more than a little absurd.)

Frémont and Russell were called into the commodore's headquarters and handed their commissions.[99] The text of Frémont's appointment proved to be an aggressive restatement of Stockton's position.[100] Having, by authority of the President and Congress and by right of conquest, taken possession, and having established laws for the government of the country, "*I, Robert F. Stockton*, governor and commander-in-chief . . . in obedience to the aforementioned laws," appoint J. C. Frémont governor and commander-in-chief of the territory of California until the President of the United States shall otherwise direct. Stockton, by whatever authority he could muster, but chiefly as conqueror, had done this thing, and only the President and no general of the army could interfere.

On Sunday, January 17, Kearny wrote Frémont that he wished to see him on business and upon his arrival inquired whether he had received Emory's directive. He had, and that morning had written such a reply as the brief time for reflection had permitted.[101] It had been left with his clerk (Talbot) to copy and was shortly brought in by Carson. Frémont looked over the manuscript, added his signature, and handed it to the general. Asking Frémont to be seated, Kearny perused the letter carefully. Having finished reading it, he said he was a much older man than Frémont, had a great regard for his wife and a long friendship with his father-in-law, and that these considerations induced him to advise that the letter be taken back and destroyed. Frémont stiffly declined, declaring that Stockton would uphold him in his position. Kearny assured him the commodore could not support him in disobeying his senior officer and that if he persisted he would unquestionably ruin himself. Frémont had had little experience with the hierarchy, and, by the interposition of an influential father-in-law, it had thus far all been good.

Frémont's letter stated that in July 1846 he had found Stockton in possession of the country and governing it, had accepted from him the commission of military commandant, and had exercised the responsibilities of that position to the present time. Upon his arrival in Los Angeles he had found Stockton still functioning as civil and military governor, with apparent deference from all, including the general, and Kearny himself had acknowledged Stockton's supremacy on the march from San Diego. "I feel, therefore . . . that until you & Commodore Stockton adjust between yourselves the question of rank, where I respectfully think the difficulty belongs, I shall have to report and receive orders, as heretofore, from the Commodore." Obedience in the army, however, would not prove to be negotiable.

Frémont also mentioned that Stockton would appoint him governor and wondered whether the general would do the same. Kearny said he would leave California as soon as the country was quiet, perhaps in a month or six weeks, would probably organize a government, and knew of no objection to appointing him governor. Frémont then stated (or such would be Kearny's allegation) that unless the commodore appointed him at once, he would not obey orders. Frémont wrote subsequently to Senator Benton that both the commodore and general had offered him the commission, the first immediately, the latter within four to six weeks;[102] so this much of the testimony is accurate. That he bargained for the position seems unreal: it had been promised to him by Stockton; the actual commission may have been delivered the previous day; and to threaten to disobey an officer whose authority he would not otherwise acknowledge seems brazen even for the ward of a famous senator. Frémont would maintain that Kearny had attempted to seduce him with the governorship, but proof for so substantial a charge is at best elusive. Frémont urged Kearny to see the commodore, hoping everything could be adjusted between them, and the general was willing but would not make the first move.[103]

That January 17 was "a most beautiful clear day," Surgeon Griffin appreciatively observed, and he wished he could say the same about their political affairs, which seemed to be in the greatest state of confusion.[104]

Later in the year, Kearny would contend before a panel of army officers that although Frémont had served under Stockton, he was an officer of the army and had reattached himself to Kearny's command by reporting to him. To which Frémont would respond that reporting his arrival at Los Angeles was for information only, not a resumption of duty—it was a familiar, private note in answer to familiar, private, and apparently most affectionate notes sent to him by the general.[105] The army would call it mutiny and insubordination.[106]

The general now wrote the commodore again.[107] Because of the enemy's recent defeat by troops under Kearny's command and capitulation to Frémont, the country could now for the first time be regarded as conquered. Having fulfilled this part of his instructions, Kearny was prepared to form a government, which Stockton opposed. To prevent a collision, therefore, and possibly civil war, he would remain silent for the present, allowing the commodore to do that for which he had no authority. A separate note announced he would withdraw the next day with the party which had escorted him to California. Carefully, he sent copies to Washington[108]—Emory's directive, Frémont's response, and Kearny's just-completed letter to Stockton. The latter may have in truth been a summary of Kearny's case intended primarily for the Department's files. (And Polk, reading it in April, would take Kearny's side, nor change his mind after a full conversation with Carson.)[109]

Both Stockton and Kearny were uncomfortable in their positions, though neither would let on. "I must go away," the commodore told Benito Wilson, and let Kearny settle the matter with Frémont. And Kearny, who was unaccustomed to defiance in high places, expressed actual fear of Frémont's large force of undisciplined men and asked Wilson to stand by and keep him posted.[110] Griffin, a loyal if often uneasy ally, feared that unless a military force arrived from the United States quickly, there would be a revolution. And it could all be attributed to "Fremont's thirst for glory, and Stockton's—I wont say what—but I only wish I could marry a Senators daughter."[111]

Kearny, his staff, and the remaining dragoons—with Wilson conscripted as far as the Santa Ana River—set out for San Diego on Monday, January 18. The general wished to put a safe distance between himself and Frémont's men or to make contact with Cooke's oncoming battalion, but some of the party thought it a dangerous journey. The Californians had not surrendered their arms, nor did they carry themselves as a people "conquered or even overpowered," as the surgeon noted.[112] At San Juan Capistrano on the 20th, Kearny was overtaken by the commodore, who, after setting up his government and making Gillespie major of the battalion,[113] had left Los Angeles the previous day with thirty men[114] and sent an express ahead, hoping the general would wait. Further along, Kearny met William P. Hall, a newly elected congressman from Missouri who had come out with Cooke's Mormon Battalion and hurried ahead to apprise him of their approach. Again overhauled by Stockton, they exchanged only a "passing salute," and late on the 23rd Kearny and his men tramped into San Diego in heavy rain.

Since the commodore had sent Lieutenant Gray ahead to San Diego with dispatches for the Secretary of the Navy, Kearny felt impelled to forward his version of the affair to Washington and detached his adjutant for this duty.[115] Emory reached San Diego ahead of Kearny, having encountered on the way parties of armed Californians just returned from the wars, one of which had supplied a plentiful meal of roast beef and a "good deal of bonhomie." Taking leave of his men and of the animals which had given so much good service, he and Lieutenant Gray boarded the *Malek Adhel* for Panamá on the 25th—Emory carrying with him his "Notes of a Military Reconnoissance, from Fort Leavenworth . . . to San Diego, in California." [116] Kearny sailed in the *Cyane* for Monterey on the 31st.

Stockton reached San Diego on the 22nd and the same day wrote to Bancroft. His civil government was in operation, and he was readying his ship for the Mexican coast. His courier, he pointed out, was the officer who had relieved Kearny at San Pasqual and could give particulars concerning that "unfortunate and disastrous affair." [117] Two weeks later, Stockton again recited to the Secretary the "extraordinary conduct" of General Kearny and wanted the President to have him recalled to prevent the consequences of "such a temper and such a head." The letter was a succinct, insinuating, one-sided account of their relationships from Carson's meeting with the general in New Mexico to their recent confrontation in Los Angeles. There followed a long, detailed narrative of the march on the pueblo in which Kearny was twice mentioned, once as being among the officers, again as having been sent an order by the commodore.[118]

Suddenly, Stockton was no longer governor, having surrendered that authority to Frémont on January 19, nor commander of a navy,* a new commodore, William B. Shubrick, having arrived at Monterey on the 22nd and notified him of his succession.[119] His impetuous reign had ended, and he could only await confirmation of his acts by the President. Captain Dupont may have spoken for more than one when he wrote in

---

* At this time a naval captain was given the unofficial title of commodore when commanding a squadron.

January that they were anxiously awaiting Shubrick's arrival. "Everything requires the presence of an officer with administrative qualities, and above all with the usual system of commanding squadrons. . . ."[120]

Frémont's career, too, had taken a new and gratifying turn—with imposing new quarters in the great Bell adobe on Los Angeles Street.[121] As military commandant, he had on January 17 sent Captain Maddox at Monterey a copy of the articles of capitulation, with orders to abide by them and forward copies to all commanders of U.S. forces in the north.[122] Two days later, after Stockton's departure from Los Angeles, the battalion was paraded and Frémont's appointment as governor read.[123] As both civil and military chief, he issued a circular on the 22nd, proclaiming peace and order restored.[124] It required the release of all prisoners, the return of civil officers to their duties, and the obedience of the military to civil authority. Published in the *Californian* two weeks later, it followed an editorial caveat that at the time the circular was issued, the arrival of Stockton's successor had not been known. Larkin sent a copy to the *Star*, where it appeared as "Glorious News!"; and J. B. Hull, Montgomery's successor, declared all military restraints upon the rights of citizens revoked and invited civil authorities to return to their duties.[125] In another issue, the *Star* editor headed a column "The Love of Power," citing Stockton's repudiation of Sloat's salutary regulations, framing a civil government, and "puffing and blowing around the country like a stranded grampus ever since."[126]

Though Stockton had named a legislative council and fixed the date of its meeting, he left Frémont to distribute the commissions—to Alvarado, Vallejo, David Spence, Larkin, Bandini, Santiago Argüello, and Eliab Grimes.[127] General Vallejo, as a leading Californian nominee, was urged by Frémont and Larkin to accept, while Lieutenant Revere at Sonoma advised against it because he thought Frémont's course would not be sustained.[128] At Los Angeles, Larkin was ordered by the governor to take the *Julia* to Monterey, pick up the northern delegates, and return to San Pedro by March 1.[129] (The council would never meet.)

As commander-in-chief (Stockton's line), Frémont authorized raising men for a second artillery company, and Captain J. K. Wilson and Major McLane of the navy were ordered to recruit.[130] McLane accepted reluctantly, for with a general of the army in the country he thought it was a wrong move. Moreover, the instructions were badly worded—but Frémont was "very touchy about his composition." Frémont further exercised his professed authority by convening a general court-martial and accepting the resignation of three captains and five lieutenants from the battalion (all to be charged against him as usurpation of authority).[131] Sometime during his incumbency, he extracted from the government archives the original papers relating to the McNamara affair—which he would claim to have thwarted—and would deliver them to Secretary Buchanan.[132]

Frémont's most stubborn administrative problem was financial. Not only did he negotiate loans locally at the "most usurious rates"[133] but in a moment of desperation made an appeal to the Secretary of State, who deftly passed it on to Marcy of War because California's government derived from the war-making power.[134] Although Stockton directed the purser of the *Congress* to give Frémont any money left over after the bills were paid, William Speiden had to report insufficient funds to liquidate his own accounts.[135] Frémont then applied to Shubrick for a "considerable sum," to learn that the amount brought out would be barely sufficient for the squadron.[136] The following month, battalion paymaster Reading was sent to solicit at Mazatlán, Lima, "or any other place," with powers to set rates of interest and do everything necessary to raise the amounts required.[137] Yet the same day Frémont agreed to pay Francis Temple $5,000 for Bird Island—Alcatraz—in San Francisco Bay as soon as funds could be obtained.[138] He would estimate his accumulated debt in 1848 to be about $600,000.[139]

Frémont wrote a long and reassuring letter to Senator Benton on February 3, undoubtedly meant for the President's eyes.[140] In all his intercourse with the people, he avowed, he had been motivated by the desire to win California by a voluntary expression of the popular will. There was now, therefore, only a feeling of satisfaction and gratitude to him among the population. He pleaded original ignorance of the controversy between Stockton and Kearny, but he had contracted with the commodore, and it would have been neither right nor honorable to withdraw his support. (His views were by June 7 in Polk's hands, but the President would nevertheless continue to believe Frémont "greatly in the wrong.")[141]

Before Shubrick, as commander of the naval forces, had learned of Kearny's arrival, he had written to Frémont of the army, offering cooperation. Nor had he apparently heard of Frémont's appointment as governor, and he was quickly apprised of that.[142] Frémont also mentioned Kearny's advent with outdated instructions, claiming the supreme command, a position it had been Frémont's duty to deny him. The President had been acquainted with these circumstances, but there had as yet been no reply. Frémont also reproved the Hon. Willard P. Hall for using his position to question the legitimacy of the new governor's tenure, hoping he would see that anything done to embarrass him would be inexpedient and improper. (And Benton would vow to finish Hall's career for making anti-Frémont speeches.)[143]

Frémont diligently pursued a policy of reconciliation, inviting former leaders in the south to serve as advisers. He appointed teams to survey losses of property during the occupation, permitted a Mexican vessel owned by Californians to trade on the coast, and treated the inhabitants generously.[144] Surgeon Griffin heard of his politeness to the natives and attendance at balls "of all descriptions," making himself thereby acceptable, a sentiment echoed by the *California Star*.[145] Leading Los Angeles citizens said he had gained the confidence of the people, and Larkin several times testified to his popularity in the southern region.[146]

There was dissent. He "wears the sombrero . . . and makes himself ridiculous," said a naval gentleman.[147] A later critic would hear that he gave rowdy balls and became popular with the lower classes, "but the best families *could* not attend them."[148] Others would recall his affinity with some of the local señoritas.[149] However it was, it would be reported upon his departure with the battalion in May that the city looked "gloomy and deserted," lacking the spirited fandangos which had enlivened the place at night, at which the natives, male and female, were in full attendance.[150]

Thus, during an interim of uncertain and conflicting authority, Frémont essayed not only to preside over the civil government but to assume the highest military office, acts which, in the awkward circumstances into which he had thrust himself, not even his supreme confidence and dramatic flair could long bring off.

~~15~~

Fight On—
Kearny Prevails

G ENERAL KEARNY had critics not only in Stockton's camp but among his own partisans. Naval Lieutenant McLane (who disliked Frémont) thought the general had shown a great want of moral courage and unfitness for command in not asserting his position and rights.[1] Stockton, he believed, would certainly crush a man of Kearny's weak character, although he recognized the general's behavior had been calculated to avoid civil war. One of Kearny's own officers, Lieutenant Henry Turner, who was easily provoked and considered Stockton a "low, trifling, truckling politician," confided to his wife that the general had not displayed his usual firmness and decision in dealing with Frémont, and his explanation was that he stood in awe of Senator Benton.[2] Although it was noised about that Kearny would prefer charges against the colonel, Turner did not believe it. Kearny's more mature friend, Captain Dupont of the *Cyane*, recognized how awkwardly placed the general was in respect to Senator Benton, his long-time intimate and only friend in the political world.[3] And Dr. Griffin accepted that Kearny, having no force at his command, must yield, though he had been "most outrageously used" by both Frémont and Stockton.[4]

Under wartime conditions one would expect to find the Army in control on land and the Navy at sea. So did the Polk administration when it got around to reflecting upon it. At the beginning the President only counseled harmony; but reciprocity in the armed services is based upon parity, not brotherhood. Equivalence in military terms is a compound of rank and substance (as it may be among civilians), and if either is lacking to a conspicuous degree, precedence flows to the strongest branch. Until the arrival of the Army of the West, the navy had enjoyed an exclusive jurisdiction in California; and when it was supposed that Colonel Stevenson's 1st New York Volunteers (coming by sea) might precede Kearny to the Pacific, Stevenson's orders were that in any joint action, the naval officer, if superior in rank, would organize a government.[5] But the dutiful Kearny reached California first, bringing with him a sufficiency of rank but a minimum of armed support—compared to the Navy, it was one to ten. Other factors interposed: Stockton's precedence in time and his command of military resources from San Diego to New Helvetia; his ebullient posture of success, disregarding all reverses, compared with Kearny's defeat and debilitating wounds; and his jaunty obstinacy, contrasted with the general's restrained but utterly determined resolution. Stockton knew, and Kearny suspected, the latter held the strongest hand—Marcy's instructions—but whatever the commodore's cards, he would play them aggressively to the end.

Kearny was nothing if not deliberate; and whether he was scheming or forearming himself depends upon one's assumptions. At San Diego he was uncertain how to begin. Indecision, lack of military support, "want of moral courage," deference, forbearance, or impaired physical vigor kept him from accepting the initially offered preferment. When he laid down his cards, Stockton would not show his. As the general's strength or prescience grew, he thought better of his earlier decision and gained control of the troops on the march to Los Angeles under Stockton's superior command. There was cooperation between them as long as Kearny would submit or the course was urgent. But when a lull occurred after the pueblo was reoccupied, Kearny thought he might gather Frémont's volunteers under his command (using his authority from Washington); and he demanded that Stockton show his orders or give in. To this the commodore responded in kind, suspending him from the lately bestowed command. Kearny backed off to avoid a clash with vastly superior force, and Stockton withdrew, delegating his civil authority to Frémont. It was not a draw; Stockton had played his trump card and left Frémont in his stead.

A domineering commodore might match a brigadier general, but could a lieutenant colonel (though married to a senator's daughter) do as well? Kearny still had only fifty or sixty men he could call his own, but others were on the way, and he was in no hurry. On January 30, 1847, he wrote the Secretary of War of the trouble he had been having and asked for support.[6] "Is it possible that a Naval & Military officer can find countenance in Washington . . . for such conduct. I will not believe it!"

Away back, in June 1846, when Kearny's orders were being readied, the Polk Cabinet had authorized taking a few hundred Mormons into the service as volunteers.[7] A very large body of this "singular sect" was then on its way westward, and Polk's object, he said, was conciliation, to "attach them to our country" and prevent them from assuming a hostile attitude toward the United States upon their arrival. But since American immigrants at Sutter's Fort were already alarmed at their coming, he wanted to be sure they did not reach California before Kearny's arrival and constitute the only U.S. forces in the country. Kearny's instructions of June 3 therefore directed him to recruit Mormons up to one-third of his command; and at Fort Leavenworth (Kansas) on the 19th he instructed Captain James Allen to raise four or five companies, each of up to a hundred men.[8] Elder J. C. Little, who had visited Polk in June to learn his attitude toward the migration,[9] was pleased with the prospect of moving so many of his people westward at government expense (though some believed it a plot to hasten the Saints' destruction).

The Mormons who enlisted at Council Bluffs on July 16[10] reached Santa Fé on October 9 and 12, where General Doniphan, an old Missouri friend, saluted them with a hundred guns. Kearny had already departed, but upon learning of Allen's death on October 2, he ordered Captain Philip St. George Cooke to assume the command and open a wagon road by the Gila route to the Pacific.[11] They were three hundred and forty strong when they set out from Santa Fé on October 19, leaving the families and feeble behind. On January 29, 1847, three months and over a thousand miles later, the Mormon Battalion reached San Diego, where Cooke was breveted lieutenant colonel by Kearny to increase his emoluments.[12] But although they had, as the congratulatory Cooke declared, with "crowbar and pick and axe in hand . . . marching half-naked and half-fed," discovered and made a road by which to bring wagons to the Pacific,[13] their appearance at that time in history was for Kearny a dubious good.

In August 1846, when one hundred and seventy Mormons had arrived in the *Brookline* at San Francisco, the *Californian* had reported them to be "gentes sencilla y industrioso"[14] (approbation directed to both Spanish and English readers), but reports had preceded them from Missouri and Illinois that they were a lawless and abandoned set, affrighting the Californians. The following month Larkin told Buchanan the country was "in some excitement" over the expectation of too many Mormons, and parties of natives had formed to oppose them. "Nothing in the world can equal the antipathy of a Californian to the Mormon tribe," William Garner wrote in November, though he himself had found them in his short acquaintance to be well educated, upright, and sociable.[15] Circumspectly, Kearny ordered Cooke's battalion to secluded San Luis Rey. It was a start toward the thousand men he told the Secretary would be needed to keep the peace—the Californians, he added, were "quiet from fear, not love of us."[16]

Kearny had sailed from San Diego in the *Cyane* on January 31 with Captain Dupont, accompanied by Captain Turner, Lieutenant William H. Warner of the Topographical Engineers, and Consul Larkin. He wanted to examine the environs of Monterey and San Francisco to determine where to station Colonel Stevenson's New York regiment and Captain Christopher Tompkins' company of artillery which were soon expected. Upon their standing into Monterey Bay on February 8, expecting to find only the "little *Dale*" at anchor, two other vessels appeared faintly. With an exchange of signals, they proved to be the razee *Independence*, one of the fastest and most powerful in the service, with Commodore William B. Shubrick on board, and the transport *Lexington*, bringing Tompkins' artillery. The latter, with one hundred and twelve men, could already be seen in a row of neat white tents upon the heights above.[17] Kearny's strength was increasing.

Shubrick had arrived on January 22 (the *Lexington* on the 27th), his ship a "frowning mass of thunder," having made a noble run out, the shortest to the coast by a vessel of war.[18] He had left Boston on August 29 to relieve Sloat at the end of his three-year term and by both seniority and orders succeeded Stockton in command of the squadron. Having already asked Stockton to come to Monterey, he now invited Kearny aboard, saluting him with thirteen guns. Shubrick had written the general on January 28[19] (a letter not received), telling of his readiness to cooperate, and they straightway compared notes. Kearny showed his orders of June 3 and 18, 1846, and the new commodore acknowledged him as commander of all the troops in California, which Stockton and Frémont had refused to do.[20] A good beginning.

Shubrick then presented his instructions, a letter from Bancroft to Sloat of July 12, 1846, which he had found in December at Valparaiso.[21] These told of sending a company of artillery in the *Lexington* to be used in establishing such posts as the commodore might find expedient, to be under his authority in the absence of an army officer of higher rank than captain. The United States meant to be in possession of Upper California when peace with Mexico was made. "This will bring with it," the next paragraph began, "the necessity of a civil administration. . . ." Kearny read on with increasing anxiety. "Such a government," the Naval Secretary plainly told the commodore, "should be established under your protection." Kearny's earlier orders were enclosed. Shubrick's new instructions were to be communicated to the general, who was to be informed that "they have the sanction of the President." If Kearny felt any consternation, he made no demonstration. The orders, he saw, post-dated his own—the Lord giveth, and the Lord taketh away.

Kearny immediately told the commodore that he cheerfully acquiesced and offered any assistance in his power. They agreed upon their separate duties, and Kearny was off in the *Cyane* to San Francisco on February 11, taking Turner, Warner, and Lieutenant Henry W. Halleck of the Engineers,[22] the latter having come out in the *Lexington* (with Lieutenants William T. Sherman and Edward O. C. Ord) to inspect the defenses. A site for fortifications must soon be selected, for heavy guns from the *Lexington* (24-pounders) must be landed.

After Kearny's departure, Shubrick wrote Bancroft that he would have accompanied the general had he not been daily expecting Stockton's arrival; it was important that he receive his predecessor's reports before proceeding further.[23] He had learned from the general of an "unfortunate difference" between himself and Stockton and of Frémont's refusal to acknowledge his authority, and it was his opinion that Stockton had named a governor who would not be acceptable to the people. Nevertheless, since his predecessor had made the arrangements and communicated them to the President, he would await the government's answer. He had written to Frémont before he had known of Kearny's arrival and would write again, saying he and the general had consulted about measures to be taken, and he hoped the President's wishes would soon be revealed.[24]

Shubrick made a more detailed report to the Department on February 15, giving the position of each vessel and news of the insurrection in the south.[25] Upon Tompkins' appearance with the artillery, he had withdrawn the seamen left on shore by Stockton and discharged the volunteers (whereupon the *Star* expressed great relief,[26] the inhabitants asked for protection,[27] and the volunteers demanded their pay).[28] He also enclosed a copy of his general order of February 11,[29] removing for six

Commodore William B. Shubrick, arriving at Monterey in the U.S. razee Independence *in January 1847, invited General Kearny aboard and pledged his willingness to cooperate.*

months all import duties from a list of staples—beef, pork, bread, flour, butter, cheese, sugar, and rice—prompted by the squadron's own pressing needs. It was hailed by the *Californian* as a blessing of American liberty; "Leave our ports free for five years," chanted the hopeful editor, "and California will not only be rich, but one of the most lovely spots on earth."

Further cooperating with the Army, the commodore ordered naval Commander Joseph B. Hull at San Francisco to acquaint Kearny with military affairs in his jurisdiction and turn over to him all horses and munitions which had been purchased or pressed into service.[30] Dupont wrote home that Shubrick was making a favorable impression. His affability, courtesy, and fairness had set an example to every officer.[31] And he described as perfectly refreshing the machinery of Shubrick's administration, clearly in contrast to his predecessor's offhand and peremptory reign.

The commodore's presence was also felt on shore. Within a week he had alleviated the harsh, often "disgraceful" restrictions under which the inhabitants of Monterey had been suffering during the preceding months. The war in California was over, martial law was ended, the civil authorities were performing their functions, and people were again free to travel "where gain or pleasure calls. . . . What a contrast between this week and last!" exulted resident William Garner on behalf of the populace. And he added that if there had been "*six Walter Coltons*" appointed as magistrates in as many towns (this one named by Stockton the previous July), great trouble and expense would have been avoided.[32]

Signalizing the changing aspect of government, Larkin gave a ball in his handsome residence, perhaps honoring the new commodore. "It has seldom been our lot to attend a more pleasant entertainment," applauded the *Californian*'s editor.[33] Among those present he listed the commodore, the consul of France, about thirty officers of the Army and Navy, Don Juan Alvarado, and most of the leading Californians, but best of all, "a large number of beautiful *ladies*," whose smiling faces made him feel he was no longer in the wilderness. Mr. Larkin provided an excellent supper, and it was hoped such parties would be repeated.

The *Cyane*, with Kearny aboard, drew into San Francisco Bay on February 12 in thick weather just ahead of the U.S. storeship *Erie* and anchored near Yerba Buena.[34] The *Erie* (its captain, Charles Turner, was Henry Turner's brother) had been sent by Stockton to Callao in September for "100,000$" and to carry his secretary, J. Parker Norris, to Panamá with "glorification dispatches" for Washington. But the vessel did not reach its most southern goal, returning instead with Colonel Richard B. Mason and Lieutenant James M. Watson on board, the latter with dispatches for Kearny and Shubrick.[35]

Mason, it proved, was dangerously ill and first received a visit from the *Cyane*'s surgeon (storeships not carrying medical officers). Then Kearny was rowed over to visit his former associate in the 1st Dragoons. He returned "radiant with the news" Mason had given him—new instructions from General Winfield Scott dated November 3, 1846.[36] In addition to communicating the emphatic approbation of the President, Scott directed that he establish defenses at Monterey and San Francisco and muster the California volunteers into service that they might be paid. Then, as a guide to California's governor, Kearny was to consult his letter from the Secretary of War of June 3, 1846, containing the now familiar phrase, "Should you conquer . . . New Mexico and Upper California . . . you will establish temporary civil government therein."[37] When he had done these things and assured the tranquility of the country, he could turn his duties over to Colonel Mason and return to Missouri (as he had earlier requested). Should he find Lieutenant Colonel Frémont in California, he was not to detain him against his wishes any longer than the necessities of the service demanded.

Another dispatch, of which Kearny received a copy, was addressed to Stockton.[38] It now advised Shubrick that under no circumstances was he to relinquish possession of Upper California. J. Y. Mason, the new Secretary of the Navy (Bancroft was now Minister to Great Britain), then explained that the President deemed it best for the public interest that the chief of the land forces should administer the civil government. "You will relinquish . . . the entire control over these matters." Port regulations and import duties were to be the responsibility of the Navy; and the importance of harmony between the two branches was earnestly reaffirmed. The two dispatches found in Kearny an attentive reader.

With other communications, Mason brought an order setting up the 9th and 10th Military Departments,[39] the latter comprising Oregon and as much of the Californias as might be subject to American rule. Its headquarters were to be "in the field," and General Kearny was in command, settling all doubts concerning his dual role.

The exuberant Jim Watson, "whom everybody knows," carried Shubrick's instructions by boat to Santa Clara, then by horse to Monterey on the 17th.[40] As soon as they had been read by the commodore, he wrote Kearny that he was ready to cooperate.[41] He also informed Frémont that naval officers on duty with his volunteers were to return immediately to the squadron unless General Kearny—who, "I am instructed, is the Commanding Military Officer in California, and invested by the President with the administrative functions of Government"—should want their services.[42] This was probably Frémont's first hint of the new instructions from Washington, but he paid them no heed, perhaps presuming they were not newly received. Nor did he communicate the commodore's wishes to the naval officers because they had not reached him through Stockton and for "want of courtesy" on Shubrick's part.[43] (Frémont may have meant to dash to Monterey at this point to see what was in the wind, for he issued orders on March 3 to be observed in his absence and countermanded them two days later.)[44]

Kearny and Mason left San Francisco for Monterey in the *Savannah* on February 26 and shortly took up residence in Larkin's house.[45] Both newspapers announced Kearny's appointment as governor, and the general and commodore issued a joint circular dated March 1, informing the people of the arrangements.[46] The President wanted the inhabitants to share the good government enjoyed by citizens of the United States and had invested the commodore and general with separate and distinct powers. The naval commander would regulate the import trade and establish port regulations, and the military chief would direct land operations and administer the civil government. The public documents of the week, the Monterey editor surmised, would be read with great interest.[47]

Another of the week's public announcements, dated at Monterey, the "capital of California," March 1, 1847, was signed by Kearny as general and governor.[48] His position now being vindicated, he was quick to make his news and views known. He would take charge of the government, protect the religious institutions of the country, and safeguard the persons and property of peaceable citizens. A free government would be provided with the least possible delay, but until then such laws as existed, which were not in conflict with the U.S. Constitution, would remain in force. The inhabitants were absolved from allegiance to Mexico and would be regarded as citizens of the United States unless they took up arms against the government. Officeholders were to continue at their posts. Losses suffered because of the war would be investigated and restitution made. The "poisoned fountains" of civil disorder were dried up; Americans and Californians were one people, and as a band of brothers they should emulate each other in improving their happy and prosperous home. (It was more mellifluous yet in Spanish.) Though hardly a "constitution for the future government of California," as one contemporary asserted, it was heralded by the editor of the *Star* as probably the best state paper ever issued in California.[49] And so rapidly would the present fade into the past that within a few months it would be remembered as the only U.S. document issued in California affecting the rights of the people.[50]

Commodores seemed to be coming in on every man-of-war, and James Biddle now appeared in the *Columbus* on March 2,[51] in time to give the joint circular his blessing. Senior to Shubrick in terms of service, he outranked him in this "monthly exchange of commodores." A small but vivacious man with a "perfect contempt for all humbug" (a young lieutenant thought him old and unfit at 64), he had an immediate understanding with Kearny concerning their joint duties. As long as either was in com-

Commodore James Biddle anchored the ship-of-the-line Columbus *at Monterey in March 1847; a small but vivacious man with a perfect contempt for all humbug, he came to an immediate understanding with Kearny.*

mand, the general reported, there was no possibility of disharmony; and Biddle would say it was his "duty" not to recognize Frémont.[52]

Good will between conqueror and conquered continued in vogue. The band was sent ashore on Sundays. Ex-Governor Juan B. Alvarado was invited to visit the *Columbus* and *Independence*—six battleships were now anchored in Monterey Bay—and he, Kearny, Mason, Colton, and other citizens were greeted by two commodores, an honor guard, the band, and a salute of eleven guns. (An hour after these felicitations began, Don Juan, overwhelmed or despondent, asked to be put ashore.)[53]

To the Californians, the quarrels among the new leaders and the succession of commodores were all too reminiscent of Mexican times, when rivalries were explosive and new commanders-in-chief heralded that some revolution had occurred. Stockton, indeed, did not rejoice upon the advent of a successor and would not report to him until despairing of

Presidential vindication. Shubrick, too, was deeply mortified to learn that the Secretary, when appointing him, had also asked Biddle to come and take the command.[54]

With four commodores afloat in the Pacific, Bancroft had been writing to all of them. Biddle had been for some time on the Chinese coast, commander of the East India squadron and special commissioner to the Emperor and government of China.[55] But with war looming, the Secretary had in May 1846—three months before Shubrick had been dispatched—put Biddle in command of the Pacific station and endeavored to get a message to him through Sloat to sail at once to the Mexican coast.[56] On August 13 (the day Sloat was relieved) Bancroft had also written desperately to Biddle, Stockton, or whoever was in command to take immediate possession of Upper California, addressing the recipient as commander-in-chief. A few days later an almost identical order went to Shubrick, also appointed to command in the Pacific, but with the provision that as long as Biddle remained on the Mexican coast, Shubrick was to serve under him.[57] Since the commodores appeared at Monterey in the order of their seniority, insofar as the Californians knew, the newcomer always won.

As it happened, Shubrick had left Boston in the *Independence* at the end of August 1846 and reached Valparaiso by December 2. There he met the *Columbus*, reported to Biddle, and showed him his instructions. From them Biddle first learned of his own new command, and he wrote Bancroft that he would proceed to California. Meantime, while Biddle called at Callao for dispatches, Shubrick was sent on to Monterey to carry out the Department's instructions as if the two had never met.[58]

Shubrick made a quick passage, by January 22, 1847. In reporting to the Department, he wrote on February 15 of Biddle's intention to come to California and on March 4 of his arrival and assumption of the command "by order of the Department, as I suppose."[59] Upon being shown Biddle's original orders of May 16, 1846 (picked up at Callao), Shubrick tendered his congratulations but, since he had been led to believe the assignment was meant for himself, asked permission to return to the States. He also wrote directly to Secretary Mason.[60] Having understood that he might find Biddle at Callao, touching on the coast to see whether his help was needed, he had agreed to serve in such a contingency as second in command. That Biddle had been ordered to remain had been carefully concealed from him, and he asked to be sent home.

Shubrick would become more tolerant of his position and duties. He left Monterey on April 10 to enforce the blockade against Guaymas and Mazatlán; and four days later Biddle received orders to turn the squadron over to him if his ship could be spared.[61] Upon Shubrick's return in mid-July, therefore, Biddle retired—carrying off, it was lamented, precious stores and all the canvas sent out for the squadron.[62] Before reconstituting the blockade in October 1847, Shubrick heard that a successor, Thomas ap Catesby Jones, was on the way, and he now feared being replaced before his work was done. So he volunteered in May to continue under Jones' command, and when instructions finally came in January 1849 to sail for home, he would return with apparent reluctance to Hampton Roads in May.[63]

Why these confused orders from Washington? The war in California was waged by a process of continuous improvisation in which distance, time, personality, and coincidence played heavy roles. To a remote commander-in-chief (with no general staff), throwing in all of his effective resources doubtless seemed less hazardous than staking everything upon a single course.

Similar complexities hampered the formation of a government for California. The need for civil organization was not immediately perceived by a President occupied with the contingencies of war. Not for a year after his initial instructions to Sloat did Polk direct Kearny to set up a temporary government.[64] Then, should the general not reach the coast in time, he repeated the order to Sloat and also to Stockton[65] (who, not receiving the dispatch, nevertheless arrogated the powers of governor to himself). When, four months after Kearny's departure for Santa Fé, Polk finally thought to dispel the confusion, he reminded the general and notified the commodores that it was in the public interest to have the chief of the army in charge on shore.[66]

By the end of February 1847, General Kearny was indubitably governor and the capital back at Monterey. Whatever the propriety of Stockton's civil regime—and Frémont and his capital still persisted in Los Angeles—it had been bypassed, and Kearny prepared for its foreclosure. However Stockton might wish to respond to the new instructions (whenever he might hear of them), he was in no position to interfere.

Kearny wrote Frémont on March 1, enclosing Military Department Orders No. 2 and sent them next day by Captain Turner to Los Angeles.[67] Certain duties, the general said, were required of him. He was to bring all the public documents to Monterey with the least possible delay.[68] His

California volunteers were to be mustered into the regular service in order that they might be paid, and any who were unwilling were to be conducted to Yerba Buena and discharged. Cooke was to command the southern district and post the volunteers and Mormon Battalion as he saw fit; and Frémont himself would not be detained but could leave as soon as the instructions were obeyed. It was not difficult for Frémont to comprehend that he was being divested not only of his civil power but of jurisdiction over the southern district and the battalion.

Turner arrived in Los Angeles on March 11 and the following day met Frémont, who agreed to go to San Gabriel and muster his men. Then riding on to San Luis Rey to deliver the orders to Cooke, Turner wrote that Frémont "quietly submits now and promptly acts on the instructions I handed him." [69] But even the skeptical Turner was too sanguine. Russell, Frémont's secretary of state, wrote on the 16th that the volunteers had declined without exception to be mustered into the service. [70] But what encouragement was offered to them is uncertain. Frémont did forward to Lieutenant Loker of the battalion the act of Congress regulating the enlistment of volunteers, and he, as an officer, was willing to enlist, since it would not affect his pay. [71] But the men demanded $25 a month (instead of the permissible $11), and Frémont improperly advised them that if they accepted the lawful rate they would forfeit all claim to more. Kearny was not unaware of this dilemma, knowing Stockton had promised wages in excess of what the auditor's office would support. [72]

Russell also told Cooke the "governor" considered it unsafe to discharge the battalion, and this he "will not do." And Cooke's regulars would not be needed at San Gabriel while the volunteers remained in service. When this reply reached San Luis Rey, Turner accurately appraised it as a refusal to obey Kearny's orders and dashed off to Monterey to report the disobedience. [73]

Frémont was not insensitive to his awkward position, and a day after Turner arrived at Monterey, Frémont also appeared. But before leaving the south, he explicitly instructed Captain Owens, who was temporarily to command the battalion, to make no move except to repel invasion, obey no order not coming from him, and surrender no public arms. Further, he ordered Santiago Argüello at San Diego to collect and hold all government horses south of Los Angeles subject to his will. [74]

When it became known that Frémont meant to go north, several prominent citizens of Los Angeles wrote him a letter. [75] It was not only inadvisable for him to leave, it read, but it would jeopardize the security of the southern country. The people still resented the conquest, and, with no one to calm their anxiety, they might get out of hand—consequences not easily seen "from the beaches of Monterrey." Frémont had the public confidence, and they urged him to remain. Among the signers were Benito Wilson, Abel Stearns, Alexander Bell, Juan Temple, and William Wolfskill, and Frémont replied on the 20th, gratified at their approbation.[76] They were aware, he explained, of the extensive debts he and Stockton had contracted, and he was going to Monterey to see that Kearny assumed the obligation. Otherwise, he could not surrender the government.

Frémont departed on March 22, full speed, for Monterey, perhaps meaning to overhaul the general's messenger. He had not mustered the volunteers or dismissed those who had declined; had told Cooke he needed none of his assistance; and had firmly instructed his subordinates to honor no order but his. He took no public documents. Accompanied by his devotee Jesús Pico and his black servant and *vaquero* Jacob Dodson, Frémont made his famous four-day ride to Monterey, sleeping only near Santa Barbara, at San Luis Obispo, and in the Salinas Valley on the way.[77] "Lieut. Col. Fremont and Captain Jose Jesus Pico arrived at my house yesterday," the 25th, reported Larkin, "three and a half days from . . . los Angeles. . . . Fremont came on business with General Kearny."[78] Frémont and Larkin made a courtesy call that evening. (Although the general paid for board and room, and his host relished being in the midst of things, Larkin would profess that the arrangements were "disagreeable," complaining that "Uncle Sam's Navy have taken possession of my wharf, and his Army my table and house.")[79]

Frémont had an interview with Kearny the following morning.[80] Colonel Mason being present, Frémont intimated he would like to see the general alone, but Kearny said the colonel had been sent to relieve him, and there was no conversation on public affairs that it was improper for him to hear. Kearny then reminded Frémont that on March 1 he had sent Captain Turner with orders; and before there was any further conversation, he wanted to know whether Frémont intended to obey. As Frémont hesitated, the general said that if he needed an hour or a day for consideration he could have it. After an hour's absence, Frémont agreed to comply. Kearny then repeated his orders and said he would send a ship for the men who would not be mustered, while Frémont, being prone to seasickness, could come by land. Late on the 26th, the colonel was on the road again and reached Los Angeles after noon on the 29th. Having been gone eight and a half days and in the saddle about a hundred hours, he had traveled perhaps seven hundred and fifty miles.

Why all the haste? Indeed what was the purpose of the expedition? Frémont would state at the end of the year that, after a period of tranquility under his rule, suddenly at the beginning of March armed bands were galloping about the country, the population was in commotion, there was a growing tendency toward violence—and he had dashed to Monterey to tell the general.[81] This state of affairs he attributed to the approach of the Mormons, Kearny's proclamation (ignoring the treaty of Cahuenga), the nonpayment of government debts, and the prospect that Frémont might be deposed. There *was* feeling against the Mormons, though Griffin noted in March that it was on the decline.[82] The southern Californians *were* restless, but rumors of invading Mexicans proved to be groundless (all "for Buncombe," the doctor reckoned, so Frémont would not have to go north).[83] And while Kearny's proclamation disregarded the capitulation, Frémont had not seen it before his departure. It promised restitution for proven losses, but uncertainty over the payment of government debts *was* an unsettling force.

Frémont's impetuous ride may have been meant to mitigate Turner's charge of disobedience, learn whether Kearny's recent orders were based upon new authority or old pretensions, and persuade the general to assume the accumulated debts. Later, Kearny would not recall that the topic of indebtedness came up (his memory would be erratic); and when questioned about Frémont's business at Monterey, he would testify, "I never knew; and it has frequently been a topic of conversation between myself and others as to what brought Lieutenant Colonel Frémont to Monterey."[84]

Support for Frémont's governorship was actively promoted in both north and south. Solicitations were made in San Diego in February, creating excitement; and shortly after Frémont's departure from Los Angeles, Russell set out with Carson and a party of fifteen, bearing dispatches and a "minister extraordinary" for Washington. Both Larkin and Cooke believed a southern California petition was included, and it was so reported in the *Californian* (which declared the candidate unqualified).[85] Another paper was circulated in the north in May, which Larkin believed would not contain the names of many well-known people. It was perhaps misleading, for it was reported at a public meeting in San Francisco that, while pretending to favor the return of Frémont to California to pay his debts, it contained statements endorsing his governorship. Printed petitions were likewise circulated against his appointment, of which Larkin thought the first article was perverted and the others "contained too much truth."[86] Frémont's acceptance in the south was not echoed in the north, where the remembrance of times past was still too green. With one general and three colonels above him[87] and no presidential hand outstretched in confirmation, his star was not ascending.

On March 23, during Frémont's absence, Lieutenant Colonel Cooke arrived in Los Angeles with one company of dragoons and four of the Mormon Battalion to establish his headquarters there.[88] By Kearny's orders he was to reconcile the unfriendly inhabitants, guard the pass near Warner's ranch and the road to Sonora, and keep an eye on San Diego. Upon approaching the town, he met a horseman who proved to be Gillespie (now relieved from duty).[89] Whatever his other propensities, Gillespie was loyal to the system and had come to pay his respects to the new commander.[90] Reporting Frémont's temporary absence, he conducted Cooke to the Government House south of the plaza and offered to go with Lieutenant John Davidson to Frémont's quarters to inquire whether it was rented upon public or private account. The dragoons were posted in the government building, the Mormons at the edge of town.

The next day Cooke and Davidson rode out to San Gabriel.[91] Calling upon Captain Richard Owens, Cooke asked to see the battalion's artillery standing in the mission yard. Davidson at once recognized two howitzers, one of them lost at San Pasqual and both now ordered by Kearny returned to Company C. Cooke said he would send men to fetch them, but Owens answered that he had Frémont's orders not to let them go. Cooke reasoned with him, read Shubrick's and Kearny's joint circular and departmental orders, and asked whether he did not acknowledge the authority of the United States. One of Frémont's trappers and no soldier, Owens answered with "perfect temper" that he considered Frémont the chief military authority in the country and asked Cooke to await his return, since no one would suffer from it in the meantime. Though Captain J.K. Wilson, in charge of the ordnance, had intimated he would surrender the guns if so directed, he stated next day that his commanding officer would not permit him to comply.[92] "The general's orders are not obeyed," wrote the incredulous colonel.[93] The President himself in person would fail to get the artillery. "I denounce this treason, or this mutiny, which jeopardizes the safety of the country." But he felt the public good required silence, and did not attempt to crush the resistance.

On March 27, the day after Frémont's departure from Monterey,

Lieutenant Colonel Philip St. George Cooke, who had, with the Mormon Battalion, pioneered a wagon road to California, made his headquarters at Los Angeles, with orders from Kearny to reconcile the inhabitants, guard the pass near Warner's ranch, and keep an eye on San Diego.

The American fort on the hill above Los Angeles as seen from Nathaniel Pryor's house, where Colonel Richard B. Mason and Colonel Philip St. George Cooke resided in April 1847.

Kearny sent Mason to the southern district with authority to attend to all matters, civil or military, which might be of public concern. He carried a letter to Frémont outlining his powers.[94] It also suggested that Frémont arrange his accounts for future settlement and send his topographical corps to Monterey for return to the United States. He was to be in Monterey twelve days after embarking the volunteers at San Pedro, as it might be necessary for him to go to Washington—now suggested for the first time. Meanwhile, Frémont and Jesús Pico galloped into Los Angeles on March 29 (the overtaxed Dodson having given out on the final day).[95]

Arriving at San Pedro in the *Warren*,[96] Mason took up residence in the pueblo on April 5 at Nathaniel Pryor's house, where Cooke also stayed. Gillespie thought his arrival fortunate. Although he "follows out his instructions, which are harsh under the circumstances," he was gentlemanly and reasonable and engendered a better feeling than had any other officer of Kearny's command.[97] Frémont did not take to him so kindly or with as keen an ear to practical consequences. He stood upon his dignity. At his interviews with Mason, Cooke was always present, by which Frémont was offended and would charge that he took notes on Frémont's replies (which Cooke denied). Later, Frémont would complain that he was in town a week without Cooke's having called, to be reminded that the regulations required him to report to Cooke as commander of the post.[98]

Mason wasted no time, requesting to see Frémont the first evening. On the 6th he rode to San Gabriel to review the battalion, and the troops were paraded. None would continue in service, and they claimed the right to be mustered out at San Gabriel rather than Yerba Buena upon a pledge made by Frémont, to which Mason agreed.[99] Kearny had given no instructions regarding their wages, so they departed without pay.[100]

Thus the California Battalion—that not very delicate instrument of Frémont's desire and power—expired leaving him only a disintegrating remnant of his topographical corps.[101] "I loaded my gun when I started from Sonoma," a dauntless member said, packed it through the war without firing it off, then tossed it into San Francisco Bay. And, "by God, I expect it lays on the bottom . . . loaded yet!!"[102]

After a meeting on the 12th, Mason asked to see Frémont's civil and military records. He had appointed only two collectors, he said, and sent over the few papers concerning the battalion which he could "at present find."[103] Since he was denounced as a usurper, he could hardly expect to be called upon for documents relating to his acts, and they had been forwarded to the United States. There was a dispute over Frémont's orders to Argüello not to surrender public property at San Diego (which Frémont denied),[104] and more of a delay than Mason thought meet in sending a list of horses and equipment.[105] Insistence and resistance were building to a precarious impasse.

When Mason wished to question Frémont on the 14th, he found it necessary to send twice. (Pryor would say there was a young woman in the case, and a sentry the governor kept always at his door turned Mason's messenger away.)[106] When the two men did meet, both were edgy and the dialogue strained. Frémont evidently expressed some hint of disobedience or defiance, whereupon Mason flared, "None of your insolence, or I will put you in irons!" Affronted, Frémont withdrew and that evening sent a note asking an apology for the language used. Mason answered that he could say nothing more until the impression he had received was removed, and Frémont unrelentingly replied that Major Reading would arrange a meeting requiring personal satisfaction, the ritual challenge to a duel. The receiver selected the weapons, and Mason, caught up in this hazardous sport, returned a not-so-sporting answer: they would be double-barreled shotguns with buckshot at twenty paces.[107] Writing a formal acceptance the next morning, Mason said he must first settle his affairs at Monterey, to which Frémont agreed. Kearny learned of the affair from former members of the battalion and forbade both parties "at this time, and in this country." Biddle too advised Mason that personal collisions would injure the public interest; even Stockton at San Diego wanted to make up the quarrel. Why Kearny did not arrest both men as the rules of war required went unexplained, though presumably he did not wish to remove his successor at so critical a stage.

In line of duty, Mason also learned while in Los Angeles that masters of vessels were buying volunteers' claims at about 30-percent discount and, with Frémont's sanction, using them at face value to pay duties.[108] He took steps to halt the depredations of the southern Indians.[109] He inspected the Mormon Battalion and found them in want of clothing and short of ammunition but going through a stiff course of instruction. Even Kearny's dragoons, he wrote, were inefficient because of a lack of everything needful. Shortly after his final interview with Frémont, Mason left for Monterey with an armed guard and reported to the general on the 26th.[110]

In Mason, Frémont had met his peer.

16

Kearny's Rule

IN THE ASSAULT STAGE of armed aggression, the one thing most needed may be armed aggressors, and the war in California produced appropriate men. Frémont and Stockton were authoritative, egotistical, and combative. Self-centered, they were sensitive to forces affecting their interests and could utilize the available resources to attain their ends. Frémont could manipulate the Bear Flag men into open revolution; discipline and command a motley force of immigrants and frontiersmen into a volunteer battalion; and propitiate a southern California population of overwhelmed but vengeful enemies into appreciative if something short of loyal citizens. Stockton, too, could command, deploy, and reconcile, though his wilful determination ofttimes overran his judgment. He would accept volunteer horsemen into the navy, recognize the utility of a brigadier general among his troops, and be liberal to a conquered people as only a domineering winner can. But neither was patient, well-balanced, or disinterested enough to rightly govern.

Then, time and the army produced the man. Kearny rode into the west with a small battalion but a large share of restraint and good judgment, sensibility and pertinent experience. And he arrived early enough in the conquest to supply background and continuity for the more peaceful period which was to follow. His fund of zeal and willpower matched that of the other main contenders. Years of army life, much of it in the west, and his occupation and organization of New Mexico prepared him to inaugurate California's new order. His strong good sense, as observed by Captain Dupont, lack of thirst for notoriety, abiding sense of duty, conciliatory spirit, and prepossessing exterior eminently qualified him, as the editor of the *California Star* declared, to discharge the important duties assigned to him by the President.[1] That he expected subordinates to obey his orders in wartime is hardly surprising; and if in peace he would not let bygones be bygones, mark it up to a lifetime of order and discipline.

Much of an administrator's job is routine, however crucial its function—which explains a critical flaw in Stockton's and Frémont's performances. From Kearny's methodical acts can be perceived something of his disposition and strategy.

CIVIL GOVERNMENT

As soon as the vague and arbitrary powers of California's alcaldes and governor encountered the American settlers' concept of "natural law," there quickly developed among the newcomers a strong hankering for home rule. To the few whose California memories ran back to July 7, 1846, Commodore Sloat had promised a government under which life, property, and the constitutional rights to worship the Creator would be enjoyed. Six weeks later, Stockton had added that as circumstances permitted, the country would be governed by officers and laws similar to those by which other U.S. territories were regulated and protected.[2] In January 1847 he created a legislative council with unprescribed duties but which Larkin thought was to help form a constitution and laws for the country.[3] Soon, however, there were both naval and army officers on the coast who could annul anything Stockton or Frémont might do, as Larkin noted, and the question of who was in charge was not quickly settled.

Although the council would not meet in Los Angeles on March 1 as advertised, nor in the north in the fall (because Kearny would persuade Biddle not to provide transportation),[4] it would remain very much alive, particularly in northern minds. In February 1847 the editor of the *California Star* heralded the council as inaugurating a new era and suggested it be enlarged to twenty members and call a convention on May 1 to form a constitution, legislature, and code of laws. Sections of the population, particularly newcomers, were not represented at all,[5] and soon public meetings were held in Sonoma, Santa Clara, and San Francisco, asking formal representation. Almost every person who came to town, the *Californian* claimed, brought proceedings of meetings to nominate delegates.[6] While Kearny's proclamation of March 1 assured the people that the United States wished to provide a free government with the least possible delay, he obviously concluded the time was not yet. He would not act precipitately on any subject, the *Californian* said. To inquiries he replied, "I will thank you . . . to say . . . that I have not called for any such council, nor do I at present contemplate doing so."[7] Whatever else he may have intended, he did not mean to identify himself with the regimes of Stockton and Frémont. Although Larkin believed the people would approve Kearny's "laws" when issued, the general did no more than sanction Mexican usages which were not in conflict with U.S. law.[8] (He would govern only a hundred days.)

APPOINTMENTS

Kearny appointed and instructed alcaldes, port collectors, and Indian agents. The local alcalde, as the Americans quickly discovered, was the only judicial officer in the country below the governor, his office alone having survived the downfall of all the uncertain governmental institutions of the Mexican period. But, as Josiah Royce observed, if the alcalde had endured, such Mexican law as had been transmitted to California had not; and the officers appointed or elected after the conquest characteristically "followed the devices of their own hearts."[9] Kearny may have recognized this, but he was not long enough in the territory to do more than validate the existing legal framework and give it some direction. By announcing in his proclamation of March 1 that the laws in existence not conflicting with the U.S. Constitution would remain in force until changed by competent authority, he meant only to retain the status quo ante until peace could be made and a legal government established, which he supposed might happen any day. Edwin Bryant, appointed alcalde at San Francisco in the spring of 1847, characterized civil proceedings as a mixture of "common law, equity, and a sprinkling of military despotism."[10]

Kearny directed Alcalde John Burton at San José not to accept cases which had already been decided by the former courts of the country and, indeed, not to retry suits in which he had already made decisions, it being necessary for litigants to await the establishment of higher tribunals.[11] He recommended to Alcalde Bryant that he sustain agreements entered into by his predecessors without inquiring into their expedience, provided they were not contrary to U.S. law.[12] In replying to Alcalde Henry D. Fitch at San Diego about assistance in enforcing the law, Kearny suggested he call upon the nearest military officer;[13] but a few days later he had to say to Mariano Bonilla at San Luis Obispo that in the absence of the military he hoped a sufficient number of citizens could be found to help implement his decrees.[14]

In confirming port collectors (a civil function), he directed that they accept nothing but specie, treasury notes, and drafts—though he excused David Alexander at San Pedro for taking $1,731 in government paper, a mistake he had been led into by others.[15] Having no records from his predecessors, Kearny asked what instructions they had previously received and fixed their salaries, if the amounts did not exceed their collections.[16]

INDIAN AFFAIRS

Much correspondence had to do with the Indians, their incursions, the white man's part in fomenting these affairs, and the need for troops and arms to protect both whites and reds. Kearny reacted prudently if traditionally in these situations, as had Captain Montgomery before him.[17] He appointed Vallejo and Sutter sub-agents for the north side of San Francisco Bay and the rivers.[18] Reminding them of the trouble the Indians had given the frontier inhabitants, he hoped that good advice and prudent counsel, with a quantity of Indian goods he hoped to send, might redeem them, else they would be punished by an armed force. In his best frontier manner, he said the Indians must now look to the President of the United States as their great father who takes care of his good children; that the agents were acting under his orders; and that offenses against Californians or Americans were the same, since they were now one people. Vallejo and Sutter were to receive $750 a year and report to the governor. Perceptively, only Sutter was cautioned not to spend any public money or contract indebtedness against the United States.

LANDS

In order not to inhibit the growth of San Francisco, Kearny released to the town in March 1847 all title and interest of the United States and territory of California in the beach and water lots around Yerba Buena Cove.[19] He decreed that certain mission properties remain in the care of the priests until proper tribunals were established.[20] He assured Vallejo that lands and privileges authoritatively granted to him by Figueroa would be recognized by the United States.[21] Reversing a decision of the alcalde at Sonoma, he declared in favor of an occupant of disputed property, leaving the final disposition to courts yet to be set up.[22] And he ruled that once a land case had been decided, it could not be returned to an alcalde's court.[23] The governor even authorized proceedings in a suit for the separation of man and wife.[24] But unless the case was urgent, he preferred to sustain the status quo until a new order could supplant it.

ADMIRALTY COURT

Exigency prompted Kearny in March to appoint Walter Colton, alcalde at Monterey,[25] judge of a court of admiralty for California; and within five days he was sitting in judgment upon the "United States and Captors vs. English Schooner William, her Hull, Cargo, Tackle. . . ." (The *William*, owned by a firm domiciled in a hostile state, had arrived at Monterey on March 22 and been seized by Commodore Biddle as a lawful prize.) Other cases would follow, and the Secretary of the Navy would in time regard the establishment of the court as justifiable, though making its awards subject to departmental approval (the Supreme Court subsequently ruling it illegally constituted).[26]

THE MAIL

On April 1, 1847, Kearny announced that mail would be carried between San Diego and San Francisco, commencing on the 19th.[27] He was not the first to propose such a service.[28] In the first issue of the Monterey *Californian*, August 15, 1846, the editor had suggested that regular communication be established between the Sacramento Valley and the extreme south—his newspaper depended upon it—noting that a single route would suffice since the population resided principally along the coast. A week later he solicited proposals to cover the portion from Monterey to Yerba Buena, the mail to be carried on horseback between Saturday morning and Tuesday night. He hoped persons from Santa Cruz, San José, and Yerba Buena would join him, taking their pay for the present from the postal receipts. Then he discovered that a weekly military express between Yerba Buena and New Helvetia had been inaugurated by Lieutenant Misroon, touching at intermediate points. Making a tour to promote the service, the editor returned from San Francisco in mid-October with assurance that Stockton would make the vital arrangements.

Stockton indeed told the Secretary of the Navy in October that he was arranging a weekly mail from one end of California to the other, to cost not more than $4,000 a year. Hostilities, however, interfered, and not until Los Angeles had been retaken and Shubrick published his notice of the peace on February 6, 1847, did editor Semple take up the subject again, devoutly wishing that someone who "has the POWER" would open communications. It was a melancholy sight for the editor to look over the packages of eight weeks of "his little paper" and see no possible means of getting them to his subscribers. Two issues later, and still no mail, he named persons in San José, Yerba Buena, San Rafael, Sonoma, New Helvetia, and the Sacramento Valley who would not only receive subscriptions but letters to the editor "or *any other person*" and forward them to any part of California, the Sandwich Islands, or the United States. He would also keep the *Californian*'s bags open for each departing vessel. The *Star*, too, announced in January that its bags for the States were available for the use of citizens; and two months later it would regard it as "singular" that no post office had been opened in (what was by then called) San Francisco,[29] the most important settlement in California.

General Kearny apparently took note of these rumblings. According to his proclamation, the mail would be carried between San Francisco and San Diego by two soldiers on horseback, starting every other Monday from each terminus. They would meet the following Sunday at Dana's Nipomo rancho (south of San Luis Obispo) to exchange loads and return to their starting places. Letters and papers would be carried free, and the schedule of arrivals at San Luis Rey, Los Angeles, Santa Barbara, and Monterey was given. Quartermasters were to serve as postmasters under the supervision of the responsible commandants. By April 24, the *Californian* could report the service in operation, and though far from perfect, it had brought the editor several communications. By September 1847, settlers on the Sacramento and its tributaries were demanding a post, saying they were beings of intellect and their Americanism was thorough and unbounded. Still, the following February a dissatisfied editor would offer a hundred dollars a year toward a weekly mail from San Diego to Sutter's Fort and wonder whether anyone else would second his proposition.

(With interruptions, the express would continue until superseded by the U.S. mail. Service would be suspended in August 1848 when the military force in the south was reduced, reinstated the following January with the arrival of two companies of dragoons under Major L. P. Graham, and limited in March to a monthly delivery south of Monterey. With the Gold Rush in 1849, Governor Riley would announce in May a semi-monthly express from Monterey to Sutter's Fort by way of San Francisco, Benicia, and Stockton, and south to San Diego with stops at the chief settlements. It would be thought prudent to explain on occasion that this was no regular mail, postal routes being the responsibility of Congress, but pending their establishment citizens could utilize the military express for letters and papers. As the Post Office Department opened routes in the spring of 1849, the military riders would continue to serve areas beyond their range, as would private agencies, advertising expresses by land and water. Yet in August 1849 a Sacramento editor would call the regular mail a "regular humbug," and not until June 1850 would a daily service be announced between that place and San Francisco.)

INSURRECTION

Kearny received information at the end of April 1847, brought from Sonora to Los Angeles, that General Anastacio Bustamente had been appointed commander-in-chief of the northwestern Mexican provinces and, with fifteen hundred men, was on his way to California.[30] The news had come from Mr. Pryor, who had heard it from Abel Stearns, to whom it had been imparted by Señor Sales, who had it directly from Andrés Pico. Cooke also reported that "Lemantura's vessel" (recently seized by Commander Hull at San Pedro) had sailed from Acapulco with arms and military stores and landed them at San Vicente or Santo Tomás in Baja California. Stockton was asked to investigate, and a party under naval Lieutenant Stephen C. Rowan spent several days south of Ensenada but found nothing.[31] Bustamente had received $600,000 from the Mexican government, it was alleged, and J. Y. Limantour, a French trader, brought military commissions of high rank for several Californians. Locally, an American patrol had found horses concealed in a canyon, and someone at Santa Barbara had encountered twenty armed men displaying a Mexican flag. In Los Angeles all the males had disappeared, "remaining absent considerably long" (at an unlicensed horse race at Santa Ana, as it proved); and Frémont, who had announced his departure, was inexplicably detained. There was apprehension of an immediate insurrection.[32]

Cooke did not credit "a fourth part" of the reports, but he had already sent a company of Mormons to the Cajón Pass on April 11 and now dispatched dragoons to patrol the Sonora road[33] and began work on the fort above town. Kearny too was skeptical, but the rumors had "much excited the excitable Californians," and it might be prudent, as Cooke opportunely noted, to reinforce the command at Los Angeles. Colonel Stevenson's New York Volunteers had recently arrived at Monterey,[34] and Kearny determined to go himself with two companies to the pueblo.

Like most good rumors, this one had a factual base. The Mexican government had never entirely forgotten Upper California but had thought of defending that remote territory on more than one occasion. In December 1845 the prefect of Los Angeles had been assured that "all kinds of aid" would be sent at once by Señor Limantour.[35] About the same time, perhaps six hundred troops with supplies and ships had been gathered at Acapulco under General Ignacio Iniestra for transportation to California but had been swept up in a revolution against Mexico's President Herrera.[36] Nevertheless, rumors of their approach continued to be heard. Manuel Castro was told in August 1846 that a force was ready to march,[37] and not long after it was said "some measures" had been taken to protect that far-off state.[38] After José Castro's flight into Sonora, he had written the Minister of Foreign Affairs and been assured, in October 1846, that General Bustamente's march was being expedited.[39] Pío Pico also sent a series of letters from Lower California, Guaymas, and Hermosillo, to learn eventually from General Santa Anna that Upper California was too distant and aid doubtful if it interfered with his own campaign.[40] Although Bustamente himself said in April 1847 that help would not be provided,[41] the Minister of War was still insisting in mid-June that the Supreme Government was "meditating exclusively" upon means to carry out an expedition.[42] In Los Angeles a new round of reports in September and October 1847 would sustain the excitement, though disturbances sometimes seemed as much aimed at despoiling merchants as defying American power.[43]

Kearny, meanwhile, left Monterey with Stevenson and his men in the *Lexington* on May 5 and reached Los Angeles on the 9th. However much the commotion might be laid to truth or invention, the general was soon writing to Washington that he found the people quiet, notwithstanding rumors to the contrary, "circulated (and I fear originated) by some of our own officers, to further their own wicked purposes."[44] Stevenson expected the new fortifications above the town to produce an impression of strength and power and predispose an otherwise unquiet people toward law and order.[45]

From the hill the view was not all of turmoil and dissension, and Colonel Cooke, the young Virginian, took time in April to record his impressions of the little white-walled pueblo revealed below.[46] Its meadows and bright stream, he noted, were intersected by many live-fence enclosures of vineyards, gardens, and orchards. On the right the mesa extended twenty miles to the sea, while in front and to the left smooth green hills swelled into mountains having the "rich blue tinge of a pure atmosphere," capped with snow.

Cooke believed that Frémont's lingering in the south contrary to Kearny's orders had a disquieting influence upon the people. Frémont would say he had meant to depart in April but was dissuaded by dangers on the road and what he took to be a lack of urgency in Kearny's orders.[47] He now asked permission to join his regiment in Mexico, which the general denied. Then he wished to return home from Los Angeles by a more direct route, and this too was refused. Kearny repeated his earlier instructions to proceed to Monterey, and Frémont and his topographical party set out on May 13. That day, Kearny revealed to the Adjutant General for the first time that Frémont's conduct had been such that he would be compelled to arrest him when they reached Missouri.[48]

Kearny would recall that he had first determined to arrest Frémont in Los Angeles after reading his letter of January 17, declaring that until the two leaders settled the question of rank between themselves, he would report to the commodore.[49] Although this resolve did not leak into any of the general's correspondence, both Dupont and Turner knew by mid-February that Frémont would return under charges.[50] Notwithstanding, Kearny told Frémont on March 1 that he would be permitted to leave the country as soon as he had complied with his instructions, and he so informed Benton in mid-month.[51] He gave a first vague hint of his intention to Frémont on March 28,[52] informed the Adjutant General on May 13, and would announce it bluntly to Frémont at Fort Leavenworth in August.

Returning to Monterey in the *Lexington* on May 27, Kearny assured Biddle that the southern part of the territory was quiet, and there was no probability of a disturbance unless it was stirred up by others. Moreover, the general now had over a thousand troops, enough to send two companies to Lower California, as he had been directed.[53]

Frémont too had arrived and camped on the Salinas River by May 19, and he expected to be ready to march homeward in about a week.[54] Ten days later a departmental order announced that Kearny would leave for the United States on the 31st, surrendering the command and governorship to Colonel Mason.[55] He was to be accompanied by Frémont, several officers (including Cooke and Turner), and a Mormon escort of thirteen men. That same day the topographical party was paraded and those who wished to remain asked to step out of line, an "exhibition" the resentful Frémont would call degrading. Frémont was not permitted to go to San Francisco for his geological and botanical specimens and was required to give up his topographical instruments for the use of Lieutenant Warner.[56] (But Kearny did not obtain copies of Frémont's correspondence with

Colonel Jonathan D. Stevenson of the New York Volunteers, once characterized by Captain Dupont as a fish out of water, with no military experience, who had come to California to recommence his political existence, was afterwards praised by his superior for maintaining excellent discipline among his men and harmony among the Californians.

Montgomery* of the previous June, acknowledging the commander's assistance, saying Frémont did not contemplate hostilities against the Californians, and declaring his intention to return at once to the United States).[57]

Both Kearny and Frémont were pressed to take certain action upon their return to the States. Larkin wanted the general to lay the many claims of the Californians before the President, requesting an immediate settlement—he was himself paying 2 percent a month on a "large sum." [58]

---

* Montgomery, having left San Diego for the Mexican coast in January 1847, had just come back to Monterey and would return from a similar voyage in August, then sail via Valparaiso for Boston, which he would reach by May 5, 1848 (MONTGOMERY).

Frémont had invited suggestions and received from Abel Stearns a list of things desired by "all good Citizens": a permanent government, a judiciary, a steamer between California and Panamá, a number of Catholic clergymen of liberal principles and good moral character, and additional troops.[59] As a merchant, Stearns wished Frémont to say there was a great scarcity of goods on the coast, and well-assorted cargoes would return a sure profit.

While in Santa Fé the previous September, Kearny had inquired of Washington whether, after taking California and establishing a government, he might return with his dragoons to Fort Leavenworth, a question repeated the following January.[60] Replies were received from both Scott and Marcy, one permitting his return to St. Louis with an escort, the other suggesting he march from Santa Fé with any surplus troops toward positions occupied by General Taylor.[61] With conflicting instructions and a new turn of events, he wrote in May that he would proceed to St. Louis and Washington, where he would be ready for any duty.[62] Colton testified that townsmen and neighbors would miss this generous and amiable man, in whom they had found "nothing of the ruthless invader. . . ."[63]

Kearny made his exit from Monterey on May 31 with a party of sixty-four, counting his Mormon escort and Frémont's and Emory's men.[64] Riding fifteen miles, they camped on the Salinas River. Stopping next day near Gilroy's, they decided not to cross the Carquinez Strait because of exceedingly high water, and rode eastward to Pacheco's rancho through luxuriant wild oats and grass. So they moved up the San Joaquín Valley, swimming the swollen rivers from the San Joaquín to the American, where they camped two miles above Sutter's Fort. Here Kearny was saluted by the "big guns," and dined at the fort the following day.[65] Frémont again asked permission to go his own way, without avail.[66]

After jerking beef and making other preparations, the party continued northward on June 16 toward Johnson's ranch, at the end of the emigrant trail. Here they were joined by Edwin Bryant and Congressman William P. Hall, who were returning to the States.[67] On the morning of the 19th, they began to ascend the California mountains, with Fallon as guide, reaching Truckee (Donner) Lake two days later, with snow up to twenty-five feet deep. At the Donner cabins, Major Swords was ordered to collect and bury the remains of the preceding winter's tragedy (a deed sometimes ascribed to Frémont).[68] Passing down the Truckee River—with its twenty-seven crossings,[69] the road was too broken to follow—they entered the desert on the 27th and reached the sink of the Humboldt after a laborious forty-two-mile day. Twice more did Frémont seek to take an independent route.[70] They were at Fort Hall on July 15 and a week later crossed the Green River, where they were seen to be "going ahead at rail road speed."[71] Traversing South Pass, they skirted Fort Laramie and reached Fort Leavenworth and the Missouri River on August 22, having gone 2,152 miles by Swords' reckoning in eighty-three days.[72] Turner had counted nine hundred and forty-one wagons and more than thirty-five hundred emigrants on the way.[73]

At Fort Leavenworth, Kearny summoned Frémont from his camp some two miles away and handed him an order of August 22.[74] It required him to turn over property held by the topographical party and arrange the accounts of the remaining nineteen men. The next paragraph read: "Lieut Col. Fremont, having performed the above duty, will consider himself under arrest, & will then repair to Washington City & report himself to the Adjutant General of the Army."

The time had come. Months before, young officers of the army and navy had doubted it would ever happen. No matter "how outrageous may be his conduct," Captain Turner had written, Kearny had not and would not arrest him—"the whole army is disgusted."[75]

In Washington, Kearny called upon the President on September 11. "I received him kindly," Polk recorded, "for I consider him a good officer." Frémont also paid the President a visit, on the 25th, and neither mentioned the arrest and charges.[76] The famous court-martial would follow, from November 1847 through January 1848, and Frémont would be charged with mutiny, disobedience, and conduct to the prejudice of good order and military discipline.[77] He would be found guilty on all counts but be recommended for clemency. That the President would confirm guilt only on the second two and order his return to duty, and Frémont would resign rather than admit the justice of the decision against him[78] is no part of this story. Although Polk knew no reason why the trial should differ from that of any other officer, except that Benton intended to make it so,[79] it became one of the celebrated uses of the courtroom as a public platform and exalted the defendant to presidential candidacy, a generalship in the army, and everlasting fame.

Nor is Kearny's further history specifically relevant, though he would serve briefly as military governor of Mexico City and head the 6th Military Department after the war, dying on October 31, 1848, of yellow fever contracted on Mexico's tropical east coast. "The gallant General Kearny, well known in California, is dead," the *Alta California* would report in January 1849.[80] With others in the California theater, he had captured the grand prize for which the war with Mexico was fought.

Stockton was the last of the triumvirate to depart. He had been at San Diego since January 22, 1847, though at the end of the month his successor had asked him to come to Monterey as soon as conditions permitted. Shubrick began looking for him daily;[81] but Stockton had but three days' bread on board, no money, and—more important—was awaiting the return from Washington of his secretary, Norris, with a hoped-for Presidential endorsement. "I shall therefore remain here," Stockton told Frémont, "until I get money, Bread and Despatches." Norris arrived at Monterey in the *Preble* on April 23, and Juan Flaco was sent as a courier to meet him.[82] But Stockton sailed for Baja California on the 27th, looking for enemy stores, and Norris went in pursuit.[83]

Stockton's importunate letter to the President of August 26, 1846, seeking confirmation of Frémont as governor,[84] never received a direct reply. But Norris brought an answer to that of September 19, requesting general approval of his proceedings for publication in the *Californian*.[85] In it Navy Secretary J. Y. Mason assured Stockton that his measures were believed to have been warranted by the laws of war; but in lieu of further approbation, the commodore was treated to a full-length statement of the principles which governed the conduct of officers in such circumstances. Such a tardy and impersonal review of official policy could have given Stockton little encouragement or satisfaction—and it reiterated the message of November 5 that the chief army officer was to head the government.

Having received only qualified support—with no mention of Frémont—Stockton at last turned toward Monterey, stopping at San Pedro to pick up Gillespie, and on May 26, after four months of procrastination, brought his vessel into Monterey Bay. There, Biddle was the reigning commodore, and Kearny sardonically observed that the *Congress* "is now in Port, where I think she will be kept . . . until *all* hands on board . . . learn their proper positions. . . ."[86]

Back in March, when Norris had not returned in the *Erie* as expected, Stockton had resolved to go to Washington himself as the only way to hear from the government. Accordingly, he asked Gillespie how many men, horses, and mules would be required to take them home "comfort-

ably and with the proper dignity as Conquerors of the Country." [87] Gillespie had been separated from the California Battalion by Kearny on the 1st
of the month, an action seconded by Commodore Biddle, who ordered
him to report on the *Columbus*. [88] After settling his accounts in Los Angeles, Gillespie joined the *Congress* on May 14 on its way to Monterey. [89]
Being on special duty, he was told by Biddle he could return to the United
States at his pleasure; but before he could leave for the north to make
arrangements for Stockton's journey, he was detained at Kearny's behest
(to preserve the peace, as the general claimed, or to prevent him from
testifying in Washington as Frémont contended). [90] Released within three
days, he set out for the Napa Valley, pledging, on Stockton's word, to say
nothing about Kearny. [91]

Stockton thought Norris might bring him permission to sail the *Congress* home, but he learned (by the *Erie*) that he could take the *Savannah*—only he was not ready. [92] Orders by Norris confirmed the *Savannah*,
but it had sailed for the United States some weeks before. [93] Dupont reported that Stockton gave a "grand entertainment" for Biddle aboard the
Congress at Monterey, during which he inquired whether the frigate he
had commanded so long might take him to Callao. "Oh, no! that could
not be," was Biddle's laughing reply, "it was time she was doing something." [94] Then the *Portsmouth*? But this too elicited a decisive "No." If
this was an actual conversation (as related by the upright Montgomery to
his honorable friend Dupont), Stockton had done well to plan an alter-
nate course.

The *Congress* anchored at San Francisco on June 19, and nine days
later the "thundering of the 'big guns'" from the frigate announced
Stockton's departure for the northern country and the United States. [95]
Following the salute, his seamen manned the rigging, giving three cheers
for their favorite commodore, then "three times three made the hills re-
sound. . . ." "California acknowledges her indebtedness to the gallant
Commodore," the local paper intoned, "and remembers him with gratitude among the first and bravest of her brave defenders." To which the
Monterey editor added a reflective note that if the departing commodore
had pleased everybody, he would have favored paying him divine honors.

Stockton took the road to Sonoma, then to "Camp Stockton, Nappa
Valley," as Gillespie called it. A passing observer recorded that it was
beautifully arranged. [96] Near the commodore's tent the flag was flying,
and Stockton's accoutrements were "very much after the style of the ancients, bedsteads, chairs, &c; . . . all those things," he thought, "would

do very well in the 'tent scene' on the Park Stage," but he doubted whether they would pay in the Sierra and Rocky Mountains. The party of forty—no one could go unless "under his pay"—was to cross the Sacramento at Hardy's near the mouth of Cache Creek on July 16 and proceed to Johnson's ranch, where the animals and provisions had been collected. Here he was visited by Captain Sutter, who presented him with the finest horse from his *caballada*.[97] On the 26th he was in Bear Valley, "in good spirits . . . two camps from the Summit,"[98] with the prospect of reaching Fort Hall in twenty days (a month behind on Kearny's trail). He was seen on August 9 a hundred miles beyond the sink of the Humboldt River,[99] traveling comfortably and with proper dignity, it is supposed, as earlier prescribed.

(As to who paid for the expedition, Stockton gave Gillespie $5,324.57 at San Francisco to buy animals and defray the cost of the journey and another $7,000 at St. Joseph, Missouri—for all of which Gillespie would account to the Navy and Treasury Departments in Washington.[100] Gillespie's own bill to the State Department as special messenger from November 1, 1845, to January 13, 1848, omitting time in the Battalion and not counting expenses—572 days at $8—was $4,576.)[101]

The commodore's visit with President Polk on November 25 was no stirring event: "Commodore Stockton of the Navy & a few other persons called today" was the Executive's only record.[102] More notable, before the year was out the commodore and general would, through an intermediary, make an amicable accommodation.[103]

17

Military or Civil— Mason Governs

To THE QUESTION, what law prevailed in California during the American conquest, military or civil? the most illuminating answer was given by General Kearny. The civil law, he said, "as far as the military authorities would admit of." [1] To the conqueror, government was a corollary of the conquest, a right of war, a means to secure possession and protect the inhabitants. Its authority derived not from the U.S. Constitution (except as it gave the President wide wartime powers), nor from any congressional act, but from the "law of nations" under which no political rights arising from the Constitution were conferred. California's wartime government was military, a mere emanation from the war-making powers, as Secretary Buchanan said. Its head was the army officer of highest rank, whose every word was law. [2]

Nevertheless, the President did not deem it improper or unwise for the inhabitants to help in selecting the officers who would make and execute the laws. This would ameliorate the despotic character of martial rule and provide checks based upon the will of the governed. As a war measure, the government was to conciliate the inhabitants and inspire confidence that American power would be maintained. Local officers were to continue to serve if they were favorable to the United States and would take the oath of allegiance. Kearny had said the United States wished to provide a free government with the least possible delay, when the people would exercise the rights of freemen by electing their own representatives to a territorial legislature. As a technique of conquest, it was one of soft-sell.

The government was thus indubitably military but performed such civil duties as were necessary to the enjoyment of the conquest. The governor was specifically instructed to abolish all arbitrary restrictions, insofar as it could be done with safety, and reduce customhouse duties. Moneys thus collected were to be applied to the purposes of the war, among which was the support of a temporary government. Although the ranking officer was expected to exercise the civil power, he could delegate that function, provided his appointee was subordinate to him and removable at his will. His administration was expected to be simple and economical, its cost not to exceed the revenues collected in the country.

Stockton's government had been brusque, declamatory, on paper; Frémont's expedient and appeasing; Kearny's cautious and empirical. None had been very explicit or comprehensible. All, for want of better, had abided such offices and usages as existed. What would Mason's be, now that hostilities had ended and peace and annexation were confidently expected? Clearly, the character of the government very much depended upon that of the governor.

Mason—a man of 50, tall, with light hair, coarse features, and rough and unpolished manners[3]—arrived in California in February 1847 with thirty years of military experience. His services had been entirely on the northern and western frontiers, where he had become second in command, then successor to Kearny as colonel of the 1st Dragoons. He had been ordered to California on November 3, 1846, to command the land forces until Kearny should arrive (outranking Colonel Stevenson, whom the President did not wholly trust).[4] An honest, intelligent, and determined officer, he was severe in manner "though not grim," possessed a wry humor, an elasticity and buoyancy of mind in social intercourse, and a large fund of good sense.[5] Himself devoted to duty, he expected much of others. Hard-pressed during his administration by conflicting interests among the population and unforeseen events arising out of the gold discovery, he exhibited a depth of feeling and good will, a tolerance of human foibles, and a knowledge of legal and political means which might have astonished a less critical and self-aggrandizing people.

Upon Kearny's departure, Mason produced no elaborate proclamation, only a modest statement that he "this day" entered upon his civil and military duties.[6] And he would have no superior in California until the arrival of General Persifor F. Smith in February 1849, to whom he would surrender the supreme military command but not the civil administration. Shortly, he left Larkin's house for the army barracks, where he

also installed his adjutant, William T. Sherman, the government translator, W. E. P. Hartnell (with the archives), and, in time, his secretary of
state, Henry W. Halleck.[7] It would be his headquarters for almost two
years.

California history took some decisive turns during Mason's incumbency. In July 1848 the war with Mexico ceased, and not only did hostilities and Mexican possession come to an end but the very rationale for
military rule. Meanwhile, late in January flecks of gold were picked up
above Sutter's Fort, modestly noted in the Monterey press as "Gold mine
found . . . on the American Fork."[8] The governor no doubt read this
news, and Quartermaster Folsom reported the rumor to him in mid-
April.[9] Soon, nearly three-quarters of San Francisco's males bolted to the
mines, and as the "sordid cry of 'gold! GOLD!! GOLD!!!'" emptied the
city streets, the *Californian* ceased to publish on May 29, the *Star* on
June 14. In July, the governor visited the Mormon diggings on the American River, where he found natives, foreigners, and Indians, some 4,000
he heard at the time. James W. Marshall, the discoverer, personally conducted him up the South Fork. "The truth," an astonished Mason reported, "would be miraculous to one who had not seen with his own
eyes" (and with his account he sent to Washington a number of identified
specimens and 230 ounces of dust locked in a Chinese tea chest).[10] Such
was the excitement that he could not get his compiled "Laws" printed or
raise a crew for the quartermaster's bark *Anita*.[11] Volunteer troops deserted in large numbers, as would the regular forces, along with sailors
from both naval and commercial vessels. It would be unsafe, he feared, to
bring ships into the ports "for some time." Yet throngs of gold seekers of
all races continued to pour in. Gold, peace, and U.S. sovereignty posed
formidable dilemmas for the military governor.

Mason's government would reflect his own judgment, conscience, and
personality. How did he conceive his powers?

THE GOVERNOR'S POWERS

"This is a military government," Mason wrote the alcalde at Sonoma on
June 2, 1847, the third day of his incumbency, "and the supreme power
. . . is vested in the senior military officer."[12] He appointed all officers[13]
and "regulated" or removed them from office,[14] called elections or declared them null and void.[15] He determined the scope of military and civil
jurisdiction, enforced the law, and interpreted or abrogated it.[16] Monitor-
ing the decisions of courts and referees, he approved, mitigated, or re-

*Colonel of dragoons Richard B. Mason, an honest,
intelligent, and determined officer, was severe in
manner though not "grim," possessed a wry humor, a
buoyancy of mind in social intercourse, and a large
fund of good sense; he would be California's military
governor from May 31, 1847, to April 9, 1849.*

jected the verdicts rendered.[17] He instructed judges and alcaldes and assisted them in making arrests, organizing tribunals, and executing their
judgments.[18] He made investigations, appointed special boards, courts,
and commissions,[19] ordered a prisoner to Monterey for trial,[20] and set
court fees.[21] He restricted immigration,[22] imposed or prevented the collection of military contributions,[23] and, with the cooperation of the naval
commander, regulated import duties.[24] He legalized the acceptance of
gold dust at the customhouse in lieu of specie[25] and launched an informal
census of the population and resources of the country.[26] Exercising his
discretion, he enforced or ignored regulations received from Washington.[27] All of these things he did.

But Colonel Mason was a just, not an arbitrary man, and he carefully reasoned and explained each decision. Even when insubordination rankled, he was forbearing if not lenient, conciliatory in the interest of peace, but rigorous in suppressing actual rebellion or curbing violence. When sedition was rumored, he professed always to have "a *halter*" for the necks of any who would attempt to overthrow the authority of the United States.[28] Should any prominent Californian be found guilty of such subversion, he was to be sent out of the country and not suffered to return.[29] For horse-thieves, he reminded the San José alcalde that the customary sentence had been a fine and hard labor, and he suggested that for flagrant cases fifty lashes would be salutary.[30] At the end of 1848 he wrote to the Adjutant General that although no court existed which could exact the death penalty, he would not disapprove the course taken at San José, where three prisoners convicted of killing and robbing men returning from the mines had been sentenced and hanged.[31] And he authorized the alcalde at San Miguel, after the murder of a family of ten, to carry out a sentence of death without referral to him if the evidence was clear and positive. It was no wonder, he thought, after the many atrocities recently committed, that the strict bounds of legal proceedings should have been a little overrun.[32] Crime was increasing with the flow of gold; there were no jails in the country where a criminal could be safely secured; and he would endeavor to assure that every man charged with a capital crime would receive a fair trial by a jury of his countrymen.

The governor was mindful of precedent. He would not revoke his predecessor's orders. Although he might not know what reasons had influenced Kearny's actions, he was bound to presume they were good and sufficient.[33] Nor would he instruct an alcalde to retry a case already settled by a predecessor;[34] once it had been decided, retrial must be before a jury.[35] And an appeal to the governor from an alcalde's decision must be sent officially authenticated by that court.[36] A settlement reached by arbiters could not be overruled, for the parties having agreed to accept a judgment stood pledged to abide by the verdict.[37]

When offenses of grave character devolved upon alcaldes, they were to be tried by juries of twelve men and the sentences, together with the testimony, forwarded to Mason for approval.[38] Cases involving amounts exceeding $100 were to go before juries of "six good and lawful men."[39] Although he appointed special courts in certain grave instances, he concluded that the precedent was not good and would not be followed except in extraordinary circumstances.[40]

Mason was empowered to appoint a civil governor subject to himself, but after ten months in office he reported to Washington that it was still too soon to separate the duties of commander and governor (and there were citizens who agreed).[41] He had not much changed the administration of justice but was readying the country for laws and a judicial system which Congress would in time provide—though he envisioned a lack of honest men to fill judicial offices.

LOCAL GOVERNMENT

What were an alcalde's powers as understood and sanctioned by the governor? After two days in office, Mason wrote to Boggs in Sonoma that he was not prepared to define the extent of an alcalde's authority and jurisdiction.[42] But for the time being he was to be governed by the customs and laws of the country as far as he could ascertain them and by his "own good sense and sound discretion." Three months later he could be no more explicit when asking William Fisher to accept the office at San José.[43] He was to observe the laws and usages "as they have heretofore existed" until others were established. The alcaldes were not authorities of the United States or of Mexico but were the civil magistrates of California within their jurisdiction, subject always to removal by the governor.[44]

There would be reminders that the supreme power was vested in the senior military officer. When Alcalde Nash refused to surrender the papers of his office at Sonoma to Kearny's appointee, Mason ordered the local commander to assist the new incumbent, then brought Nash to Monterey, where he soon agreed to comply.[45] Mason also intervened in the formation of the first town council at San Francisco, directing Alcalde Hyde to call an election and outlining the body's scope and duties.[46] When repeated petitions for Hyde's removal were received, and Mason asked the council for a report, he would not accept it for lack of substantiation,[47] and upon Hyde's resignation appointed a successor.[48] When an election was held at Los Angeles without his authorization, he declared it invalid and designated his own alcalde.[49] His intervention at Santa Barbara will be afterwards noted.

The alcalde's authority was between citizens; but when soldiers were concerned, the military took precedence, though Mason yielded in minor cases when the civil authorities evinced the proper motives.[50] Alcaldes, the governor learned, had "always" tried crimes committed aboard ships.[51] They were not to perform marriages when either party was a member of the Catholic Church, but when a priest entered into a contract with a citizen, he was subject to the alcalde's jurisdiction like any other man since an agreement "implies a reciprocity." [52] The first alcalde had general jurisdiction within a district, with auxiliary alcaldes having concurrent authority among themselves but being subordinate to him. [53] Suits could be appealed to the first alcalde, and defendants were bound to obey his decree. Much of the agitation to establish a civil government arose from the inability of the alcaldes to protect the rights and liberties Americans believed were guaranteed to them as citizens. [54]

Alcaldes had limited authority in the disposition of lands. It was the practice for alcaldes at Monterey and San Francisco to sell lots within the limits of the towns, and Mason authorized Boggs at Sonoma to do likewise, the proceeds to go to the municipality. [55] He referred to Vallejo's instructions from Governor Figueroa in 1835, which authorized 100-vara grants for house lots and gardens. [56] But a town could not dispose of its lands until it had been laid out and a town plat made. [57] Mexican law allowed the granting of municipal lands (*propios*) but not the common lands (*ejidos*), and Mason was probably referring to the latter when he stated that an alcalde had no authority whatever to sell or dispose of pueblo lands. [58] Town lands (*propios*) could be rented as well as sold, the proceeds going into the public treasury. [59] An alcalde could not make a final adjudication of land titles outside the towns but could try to settle matters among the parties and put persons in possession of the lands to which their deeds gave them title. [60] American authorities were bound to protect the rights of the Californians, and indeed the military government became their only shield against spoliation by settlers who expected to obtain land upon their arrival. [61]

The alcaldes could call for military aid to enforce their decrees and execute the laws, but while they were urged to be "vigilant, firm, impartial and decisive," they were also expected to be as mild and conciliating as the ends of justice would permit. [62] An official was cautioned that although his prisoners might have been plotting mischief, and would in all probability rob and steal when they had an opportunity, still he could hardly punish men for what it was supposed they intended to do. [63]

MILITARY VS. CIVIL AUTHORITY

As commander of the military forces, Mason instructed his officers to give the alcaldes such assistance as might be necessary. [64] They were to make arrests but not on their own authority. Civil authorities would no doubt be willing to turn over the unpleasant task of arresting and guarding their criminals, but this was not to be. The military were to oblige only when the alcaldes could not enforce their own decrees. When taking charge of a criminal, they were to be responsible only for his safety, not for executing the sentence, and this only when the general good required it. Costs were to be paid by the town. Not only was the army not an agent of the civil government, but when soldiers went in pursuit of horse thieves, Mason expected some of the inhabitants to join in recovering their own property.[65]

In distinguishing between martial and civil law, Mason said the former was a preventive code, to operate when the courts were interrupted and to keep soldiers from trampling upon the rights of the people.[66] Offenses committed by soldiers against citizens were to be tried by military commissions, but in dealings between citizens and soldiers, the civil law was to take its course. Army officers were not to be "too hasty" in interfering with the administration of justice, and threats of force or imprisonment were not to be used except under aggravated circumstances. Soldiers insulting a magistrate or peaceable inhabitant or committing a trespass were to be immediately arrested and reported to the commanding officer, who would bring them to trial.[67] Drunken soldiers were to be court-martialed. In support of such action, General Winfield Scott's orders (at Tampico) of February 19, 1847, were cited and published.

Scott's orders pertained to "grave offenses."[68] They created military commissions to try soldiers in enemy territory for atrocities which in the United States would be punished by civil courts. Martial law was declared to be an unwritten supplementary code under which the statutes of no particular state need be followed, but the sentence was to conform to known punishments in some one of the states. Courts were to aim at "substantial justice," avoiding learned technicalities and distinctions, while penalties were to be "just in themselves" and such as could be executed. The commissions were not to accept petty cases— and Mason demurred from the application of this drastic procedure by Captain Lippitt, who removed from the alcalde's court two civilians accused of using "seductive words" to camp women on the beach at Santa Barbara.[69] He also directed that the Indian Gerónimo be tried by the alcalde at Los Angeles, not by a military commission, since the crime was civil resistance and did not threaten military control.[70] He created a special civil court to try charges of counterfeiting gold coin, which he thought not appropriate for an alcalde nor proper for a military commission.[71]

WAR CONTRIBUTIONS

As a war measure, high import duties at American-held ports in Mexico were authorized in Washington in March 1847. President Polk had conceived this timely idea to help defray the cost of the war and place an additional burden upon the Mexican people, thus activating their desire for peace. The existing blockade was to be lifted and ports opened to the commerce of the world (except Mexican vessels). Such duties, not being authorized by the Constitution, were to be collected as an act of war. Appropriate regulations were issued by the Secretary of the Treasury at the end of March, apparently sent to California in May, and received in October. They were to apply immediately at San Francisco and Monterey.[72]

As a war measure against a hostile people this may have been justifiable retribution, but Mason and Shubrick instantly recognized its inappropriateness to California, where hostility had ceased and a large percentage of those penalized would be Americans. They therefore exercised their discretionary powers and on October 9 announced a delay in the imposition of duties for as long as the country remained tranquil.[73] A joint letter to the Secretaries of War and Navy was published in the *Californian*, clarifying their action; and meanwhile the regulations established by Shubrick on September 15 were to remain in force.[74] The following month Mason removed all duties upon lumber and California produce shipped from one local port to another.[75] He cited the order to General Kearny of June 3, 1846, that duties be reduced to a rate which would maintain the civil officers without yielding revenue to the general government. Promises had been made to the people, he said, some of whom had declared they were meant only to delude the Californians into submission; and to impose high duties now would make these individuals "pass for prophets" and, by a single blow, destroy the commerce of the country. Customs regulations were sent to commanders and issued for the information of shipmasters and merchants.[76] Mason was not unaware of the responsibility he had taken but believed he was fully justified. Larkin thought the action was a great stretch of authority, but the commerce of the country would have been ruined without it.[77] Under the new rules army collectors were to replace civilian personnel.[78]

The most famous war contribution levied in California was ordered by Mason on May 31, 1848, and the town of Santa Barbara was the victim. A "long six-pounder brass gun" (the descriptions varied) belonging to the brig *Elizabeth*, wrecked in the harbor, disappeared from the beach on April 5, and Captain Lippitt conceived the idea that it had been seized by the Californians to be used against him.[79] There had been rumors of an uprising in the town the previous July, which Mason, after a visit, had charged to the misbehavior of the New York Volunteers.[80] This time, ignoring in distant Monterey the captain's excitability and lack of tact and judgment, Mason associated the disappearance with renewed rumors of revolt and laid a contribution of $500 upon the town.[81] A per capita and property tax, it would be refunded whenever the culprits and cannon were disclosed. Thereby an inoffensive and for the most part friendly if wilful people, including some of California's most respectable and accomplished citizens, were placed under strict military censure and control. It was afterwards related how Colonel Stevenson (who disapproved of the action) brought the regimental band from Los Angeles and, with impartiality and melodious Spanish airs, succeeded in making the collections.[82] Much fruitless interrogation, correspondence, and indignation ensued[83] until, upon the promulgation of peace, the money was refunded.[84] The cannon would not be recovered for a decade, and a conspirator would recall that the Californians' success against Mervine at San Pedro had raised hopes for a similar blow at Santa Barbara.[85]

COMMERCE

Mason attempted not only to preserve the status quo and alleviate the impact of the war but through numerous concessions to stimulate California's economy. He continued the military express, of which citizens could avail themselves without charge, and permitted "light letters" to be sent to the United States with Carson's dispatches.[86] He granted temporary licenses to foreign vessels owned by resident U.S. citizens to engage in foreign and coastal trade until a proper register could be obtained from Washington.[87] Together, he and Shubrick issued regulations for the harbors of California, and Mason added to Shubrick's list of free imports.[88] He also exempted from duty a thrashing machine for Grimes' rancho on the Sacramento (the more wheat the cheaper the flour for the army)[89] and a steamship imported by Leidesdorff from Alaska (enterprise of this kind should be encouraged).[90] But many such requests he would not allow, for waiving duties, he pointed out, meant assuming the debt himself should these indulgences not be allowed at the Treasury.[91] Nevertheless, merchants, shippers, and editors raised objections, vastly preferring free trade.

With the influx of gold and the scarcity of currency, merchants were unable to pay duties exclusively in gold and silver coin as required by law. To an appeal from Monterey, Mason replied that if California gold could be wrought into convenient shapes, he would approve its reception at its intrinsic value (permission soon rescinded as manifestly illegal).[92] To San Franciscians he responded that the collector there would temporarily accept gold deposits at a rate low enough to encourage redemption, the payer being expected to redeem it in coin in from 90 to 180 days.[93] When money was required by government, the gold would be sold at auction, any profit going to the depositor. If, by throwing a large amount upon the market, it did not bring the required price, Mason noted that he would be held responsible because of his departure from orders. The export duty upon gold could likewise be paid in kind, a percentage of each shipment.[94] Mason recommended in August that a mint be established on San Francisco Bay so that millions of dollars in gold would not pass yearly into the hands of foreign capitalists.[95]

LAND

The governor made it clear at the start that he had no power to grant lands, this being the prerogative of Congress. Nor could existing titles be ratified until the formation of proper courts.[96] Meanwhile, he would not interfere with Mexican titles, and the alcaldes were to see that land rights were respected. If a grant was made before the flag was raised in California, "that is sufficient for us."[97] He considered it best not to stir up land titles by appointing special courts since their verdicts would only be temporary and breed litigation rather than end it.[98] He pointedly advised immigrants not to violate the rights of others if they wanted their own respected.

Mason recommended that surveyors be employed to lay off lands in accordance with deeds and deposit copies of papers in some office of record;[99] and he appointed several surveyors, among them William B. Ide, Jasper O'Farrell, Jacob R. Snyder, and Chester B. Lyman.[100] In boundary disputes he suggested that binding arbitration be entered into for the present.[101] He tried to get a copy of the papers relating to Alcatraz Island, which Frémont had agreed to buy for the United States.[102] At San Francisco, the presidio lands were claimed by private individuals (chiefly Larkin), and Mason thought it proper not to use them in any way that would injure the claimants' interests.[103] Even when a grantor was believed to have had no authority to convey title, recipients were allowed to continue in possession until tribunals were organized.[104] Grants by Flores, José Castro, and Pío Pico issued after the raising of the American flag were nevertheless regarded as illegal, and Colonel Stevenson was asked to establish friendly relations with the latter to see if a statement of the real facts in the case might be revealed.[105]

In February 1847 the *Californian* had promised to publish the "laws and precedents" pertaining to land titles as soon as they could be ascertained.[106] But it was no simple task to collect and examine the archives, and the compilation was not ready until March 1, 1849 (or published until the following year). Prepared at Mason's request, Secretary of State Halleck's "Report of the laws and regulations relative to grants or sales of public lands in California"[107] covered both public and mission lands and such as might be needed for government use. In forwarding the report to the Adjutant General, Mason observed that already much of what would probably constitute the public domain had been acquired by speculators who would endeavor to dispose of it to settlers at an exorbitant profit.[108]

Captain Dupont had noted in March 1847 that fortunes could be made in land.[109] Military officers who had gone inland came back "*California mad*," he said. The Santa Clara Valley had captivated Lieutenant Warner of the Topographical Engineers, the soil being rich beyond description. Grass and wild oats would hide a man on horseback; there were noble oaks with which no English park could compare; and the flowers were out—California poppies, iris, phlox, yellow violets. For $7,000 he could buy 65,000 acres with cattle swarming upon them. Not everyone, perhaps, was sensitive to the country's beauty, but few missed its opulent promise. Old-timers who owned land were acquiring more; and many newcomers, including army and navy personnel,[110] were speculating in town lots and ranchos. They were forerunners of what would be worse, and Dupont feared for the Californians, who he thought would be overwhelmed by the grasping avarice of an immense immigration.

MISSION LANDS

Mission properties were a special case. By a Mexican law of August 17, 1833, Upper California's twenty-one missions had been secularized—returned to the possession of the state—with only the churches, their adjacent buildings, and specified plots reserved to the priests.[111] The vast remaining lands were to be distributed under regulations of 1824 and 1828.[112] Governor Figueroa had authorized a partial conversion in 1834 (beginning with ten), turning their administration over to the government and specifying how grants were to be made.[113] Administrators could not alienate property without permission, and any allotted to the Indians would, if sold (which was illegal), revert to the nation.[114]

In 1843, Governor Micheltorena—still hoping to preserve some of the missions, make them self-supporting, and perhaps render a profit to the state—returned the remnant of twelve to the padres.[115] Nevertheless, nine which had been abandoned by the Indians or converted into pueblos were two years later offered for sale,[116] and ten more were to be rented at once or when their debts were paid.[117] Some months later, the assembly, wishing to prevent the "total ruin" of what still remained, sanctioned their bankruptcy or public sale.[118] Although an order received from Mexico in April 1846 suspended all such proceedings, Pico succeeded in disposing of twelve.[119] Finally, after the American occupation, an extraordinary session of the assembly on October 30, 1846, decreed Pico's sales unlawful and authorized one or more of the missions mortgaged to finance the war with the United States.[120]

Such was the complex status of the mission lands, as the conqueror came gradually to understand. They had been national property since 1833. Those which had become pueblos were subject to laws governing the same. Neither alcaldes nor commissioners could dispose of mission properties without governmental authority. Lessees must provide bonds to fulfill their obligations, and the government could eject anyone found guilty of injurious action. Lands for priests could not exceed two hundred varas, and within a pueblo not more than four hundred could be granted to an individual. Those not disposed of according to law remained the property of the state insofar as their identity and status could be ascertained.

But a new element complicated the picture. In October 1846, the editor of the *Californian* had informed persons newly arrived in the country that there were a number of missions, mostly unoccupied, where they might find shelter during the rainy season; and he named Carmel, San Juan Bautista, San José, Santa Clara, and San Rafael in the vicinity.[121] All of these, he said, were surrounded by public lands which could be cultivated without infringing upon the rights of others. By the following spring, however, General Kearny had found there were many claimants for missions San José, Santa Clara, Santa Cruz, and San Juan Bautista and decreed that they were to remain in the priests' hands until proper tribunals were established. Mason concurred in June, ordering unauthorized occupants at Santa Clara and San José to leave immediately, as they had done great injury to the premises and left no room for the padres. Backed by Captain Naglee, the alcalde was to enforce the decree.[122] This done, the humane governor interceded with the resident priest, Padre Real, proposing that occupants be permitted to stay until the harvest or longer if they paid rent, to which the padre assented.[123]

Neither alcaldes nor priests could dispose of mission lands. Mason found the laws so particular in forbidding their sale that he challenged Padre Real's assumed authority. The papers presented certainly gave him no right after July 7, 1846, Mason wrote, if indeed they did before, and he declared all sales made by his reverence null and void.[124]

Mason advised one claimant that his title seemed complete, and he had better make an arrangement with the priest at San Miguel until it could be examined by proper authorities.[125] Another, at San Buenaventura, was assured that he had nothing to fear in showing his documents if he had an honest title.[126] José Castro, who claimed the orchard at San Juan Bautista, was reminded that Kearny had placed that mission under the padre's care; but if the priest was willing, so was he.[127] Two Californians claiming Santa Inés were told they had not bought it at public auction as required, and if it had been purchased, how was it that they continued to pay rent? Their status as tenants was still intact.[128]

Mason inspected the northern missions and ordered Colonel Stevenson to examine those in the south and take measures for their preservation.[129] He hoped to restore San Luis Rey to something of its former prosperity.[130] Stevenson was also to visit Santa Barbara and San Buenaventura to see whether laws safeguarding the property and payment of rents were being observed.[131] A Californian at San Antonio, having been permitted to remove tiles from old buildings to re-roof a house purportedly burned by Frémont, was found to have despoiled substantial structures to cover a new one, an abuse strictly forbidden.[132] Nevertheless, Mason cautioned Stevenson to be certain that fraudulence was well established before wresting property from present holders.[133] Among the governor's last acts was an order to alcaldes, Indian agents, and others to assist in preserving the churches and in securing to the priests the possession of their houses and gardens. "Such was and is the supreme law."[134]

THE INDIANS

Secularization was an appointed stage in the process of colonization by which Indian lands were to be segregated from those of the Mexican nation, so that what remained could be conveyed to *gente de razón*.[135] But although generations of neophytes had lived and died in the missions, they were not ready to accept a responsible place in society, form pueblos, rule themselves, hold and cultivate land, and take advantage of community property, livestock, implements, and stocks of seed. The "monastic monopoly" had not been able to raise up self-governing citizens. The Indians had not become independent workmen; lands slipped quickly through their hands; and they became servants or slaves to the Californians or fled to the interior.

Mason wrote soon after Kearny's departure that the mission Indians had mostly joined the wild tribes and, with their intimate knowledge of the settlements, were able to do great mischief.[136] He hoped they might be reclaimed, placed between civilization and the wilderness, and, by treaty and discreet supervision, used as a barrier to incursions. But without a supply of Indian presents, the old frontiersman said, it would be useless to attempt anything of the kind, and he asked for useful gifts, not trinkets or baubles. He also wanted mounted troops.

Kearny had appointed Sutter and Vallejo Indian agents, and Mason added Captain J. D. Hunter in the south.[137] They were to reclaim the Indians to habits of order and industry, induce them to cease driving off horses and cattle, and report frequently to the governor. Dutifully, Sutter wrote to Mason from the upper Sacramento in July 1847 that a Californian and two foreigners from Sonoma had visited an Indian *ranchería*, been kindly received, then attacked the defenseless natives, killing thirteen and carrying off thirty-seven as slaves.[138] He also reported a chief's claim that two Californians had taken horses, whipped the chief, and abused the people; and he wanted to know how to proceed. Mason said a tribunal would be organized when the offenders were arrested, and if it approved the death sentence, he would have the men executed as a public example.[139] The safety of the frontier was not to be hazarded by a few lawless villains. Three men were in custody by mid-August and, with Vallejo and Boggs as judges, were apparently acquitted[140] (the only fault found with the proceedings by the governor being the exorbitant schedule of fees, which he revised drastically downward, not to set a precedent).[141]

The agents were responsible, according to Mason, particularly for the wild tribes but also for the neophytes of the missions and ranchos.[142] The latter were to be protected from ill treatment by their employers and be subject to the alcaldes and such regulations as might be made by agents with the governor's approval. Hostile groups were to be persuaded that the new government favored peace and would protect them from injury but punish them if they took matters into their own hands. Agents were also encouraged to collect information about the natives and suggest means to assure their security and happiness.

For their own preservation, Mason ordered both wild and mission Indians collected at San Luis Rey and encouraged others to cultivate the soil and abstain from aggression.[143] While assuring Vallejo that he would provide powder and lead for his protection, he supported the Indians' stand that whites should not intrude upon their lands.[144] Disapproving a lease to Sutter and Marshall by the "Yalesummy" tribe of a gold-bearing tract on the American Fork, because Indians could not legally dispose of land, he rightly surmised that should Indian titles be extinguished after the war, they would become part of the public domain.[145]

Contemporary records are replete with reports of vagrant Indians and their preference for a dissolute life over one of regular employment. This was no new determination in a country which had always depended upon the native population for labor. A hard-working, virtuous, inexpensive, and dependable body of workers is a boon to any organized society, and it would have been so in California could the employers have had their way. But the domesticated Indians were not prudent, frugal, and self-disciplined; they had been tamed under conditions of servitude and taught specialized functions which were beneficial to the system. Though often amiable, they were, when betrayed, ready to carry out retribution with their own hands. An early immigrant in the Sacramento Valley complained about the farmers' inability to retain their Indian laborers "even by the best and most conciliatory treatment," and he blamed the government for indulging Indian indolence and raising no obstacle to a dissolute mode of life.[146] It was not good for farming.

The government had done something. It had appointed agents. Then, to distinguish friendly Indians from horse thieves, it had ordered all persons hiring Indians to give each a certificate of employment.[147] Whereupon, any Indian outside his own town or rancho without identification could be arrested. An unemployed or wild Indian visiting a settlement was to carry a passport issued by the district agent. Yet, three months later, an editor could inquire, "why are our towns infested with idle, drunken, and thievish Indians . . . or why unprovided with certificates of locality?"[148]

Mason also forbade the sale of wine and liquor to Indians. The penalty was $50 to $100 and imprisonment for three to six months; and alcaldes had no choice, they went together.[149] Indians were declared to be competent witnesses, and the alcalde at Santa Barbara was told that although an Indian's testimony might have been in some respects improbable, the accused should have been subjected to trial; he must abide by the governor's order.[150] While Indians were liable to trial and punishment by magistrates of the nearest towns, in their internal government they were entitled by Mexican law to elect their own alcaldes, who should be assisted in promoting industry to save them from destruction.[151] Good intentions were also stirring in Washington, where the Secretary of War was about to appoint an Indian agent for all California.[152]

Mason counseled little kindness to horse thieves. "You may tell the people of your district, that if they catch Indians in the act of stealing . . . their horses . . . they should shoot them"; but if the Indians were merely loitering, they were to be sent to the alcalde, who would determine whether they were thieves.[153] If an Indian was caught killing or stealing a bullock, he should be "well (but not cruelly) flogged, like any other thief," white or red.[154] Local alcaldes or commanders were to organize parties of citizens, ready to move at a moment's notice when depredations were committed.[155] Mason would provide powder and lead but would not pay citizens to turn out for their own protection. As his troops diminished, the inhabitants would have to rely principally upon themselves, and he could apprehend no real danger, "however rife the rumor," while the people refused to volunteer to meet it.[156] A community nine-tenths American, he told the Adjutant General, ought to defend its own frontier.[157]

FUNDS

As Mason's predecessors had empirically discovered, no civil or military organization in California could long function without an external source of funds. Larkin had estimated Stockton's expenses at one or two thousand dollars a day, exclusive of the squadron;[158] and so large had Frémont's accumulation of debts become that it was having a prejudicial impact upon the conquest.[159] Stockton had brought some money in the *Congress* and sent the *Erie* to Callao for $100,000[160] (but it returned with only Mason on board). He had also established tonnage and tariff duties upon foreign vessels,[161] but revenue under wartime conditions was presumably minimal. Larkin had urged Stockton to come to Monterey and settle his accounts, something over $300,000, he said (of which Larkin's share was nearly $20,000).[162] Although there was apprehension that Stockton would leave California without authorizing payment, he apparently did settle claims for which he felt personally responsible, and meant to liquidate others.[163] He sought permission to go to Valparaiso or some other port and draw sufficient money upon his own responsibility to pay his and Frémont's debts, but Commodore Biddle thought it best to refer the matter to Congress.[164]

Kearny had shown little sympathy for his predecessors' predicament, having told inquirers to take their claims to whoever had originated them.[165] Mason, too, would not be held responsible for an incalculable financial burden and advised claimants to prepare written evidence for future examination.[166] Nevertheless, he wrote the Adjutant General that a speedy payment of these claims (estimated by Hensley and Reading at $700,000)[167] would be worth more in reconciling the Californians than ten times the money it would take to settle them.[168] Many of the volunteers were desperate, the planting season being past and their only resource being what was due them from the government.[169] Criticism and advice were generously offered by the press, the *Star*'s editor holding that Kearny's liability could be no less than his predecessors', and he could see no difference between the man who wrongfully took property and he who kept it.[170]

Army paymasters sometimes brought out hard cash to pay the troops, though they might bring only warrants for which no satisfactory market could be found. Navy regulations permitted the army to draw upon the purser of the flagship, and the naval commander was authorized to make drafts in an emergency upon Barings Brothers & Co. of London and hand the proceeds to the army paymaster.[171] But even the Navy had difficulty obtaining funds from foreign merchants at Mazatlán and other Pacific ports. Not until the end of 1848 did Washington respond to Mason's earnest request and begin to send regular couriers (each with about $100,000) to pay the rising cost of military operations.[172] Captain Cooke neatly pictured the situation in the spring of 1847 when he wrote that Kearny was "supreme" up the coast, Frémont in Los Angeles, Stockton at San Diego, and he at San Luis Rey—"and we are all supremely poor; the government having no money and no credit; and we hold the Territory because Mexico is poorest of all."[173]

The civil government was expected to be self-supporting by setting import duties at a level which would pay its costs, the War Department having no funds appropriated for the purpose.[174] Kearny had therefore directed the collector at San Francisco to turn over regularly to the assistant quartermaster such funds as were in his possession.[175] Mason, too, meant to keep his administration solvent. What must have been his first act upon becoming commander and governor was to separate the custom-house receipts from other public funds and apply them upon the governor's order to the uses of the civil department. It would not be necessary, he told the quartermaster, to open an account with the Treasury, for "that is a matter to be settled here."[176] And he reminded the commodore that moneys from customs belonged to the civil department and could not be used to pay debts of the general government.[177] Nor, as practice confirmed, could they be spent to care for sick and abandoned sailors, rescue immigrants from the Sierra Nevada, provide supplementary pay to military officers serving in a civil capacity, support survivors of a murdered man, or pay the costs of trials "not strictly legal."[178]

The "civil fund" would be used to cover the salaries of government officials, the costs of trials when prisoners were acquitted or could not pay, rewards for the apprehension of criminals, contributions toward the construction of jails, and the purchase of anchors and chains to buoy out rocks in San Francisco Bay. It would be spent for printing and advertising, supplies, travel, fuel, rent, and furnishings, and for expresses.[179] Although the fund was not meant to support the military, many thousands of dollars were "loaned" to the Army and Navy, particularly the former.[180] After the treaty of peace, Mason's authority to make collections would be challenged; and when Persifor Smith would arrive in 1849 to command the Pacific Division, he would claim but not obtain the right to the fund's administration.[181]

THE MINES

Soon after the discovery of gold, Mason expressed a belief that some "wholesome laws" should be made to secure personal rights and prevent discord in the mines (but no such provisions would appear in his code).[182] Perhaps, too, the district should be laid off in lots, with regulations to guarantee possession. A visit to the mines in July 1848 led him to ponder how the government might obtain some revenue from its mineral lands.[183] But considering the extent of the country, the peaceable character of the people, and the small and scattered military force at his command, he resolved not to interfere unless "broils and crimes" should require it. Still, the government was entitled to rent, and the longer the delay in making the collections, the more difficult it would become. Sur-

veyors could measure individual holdings and put the occupants in possession, then have a superintendent at Sutter's Fort grant licenses for $100
to $1,000 at his discretion. Better still, the entire district could be laid out
and sold at public auction in small parcels, twenty to forty acres. Nonetheless, after a second trip, to the Stanislaus River, he concluded that the
mining district should not be sold but thrown open to all and a small
percentage charged upon gold to be coined at a mint to be established.[184]
Meanwhile, he would impose a tax upon each lot exported, to be paid in
gold because of the difficulty of ascertaining the shipment's value.[185]
Soon, General Persifor F. Smith would be making his way up from Panamá, determining in his own stout heart to regard everyone not a citizen
a trespasser.[186]

The impact of the gold mania upon California's few communities was
awesome. It began softly, but whole towns were soon depopulated, beginning at Sonoma and San Francisco and moving progressively southward. In mid-May 1848, Bidwell wrote to Larkin that he had probably
heard a great deal more than was true about the richness of the placers,
stating the average earnings were ten dollars a day.[187] But gold was coming down the river on every vessel, and by the beginning of June Larkin
guessed that $20,000 in dust had been received for goods at San Fran-
cisco.[188] By then, San Francisco and San José were almost empty, three-
quarters of the houses in San Francisco being locked up, all work at a
standstill, the school closed, the men and their families departed. The
"Golden Yellow Fever" was not yet virulent in Monterey at the beginning
of the month, but at its end Larkin reported his renters had left, servants
and workmen were gone, brickyards, sawmills, and ranchos were un-
tended.[189] By July 20 there was no hotel or boardinghouse in the capital,
and the quartermaster was applying to eat at Larkin's table.[190] A few days
later, Stevenson reported from distant Los Angeles that a party was on
the way, and he was requiring passports to halt the departure of deserters.[191] As Talbott H. Green left Monterey for the mines at the end of September, he said he would not be surprised if the governor himself moved
to Sutter's Fort.[192]

DESERTIONS

Army, navy, and commercial vessels on the coast had been plagued by
desertions even before the discovery of gold. In October 1846 Montgomery had noted many defectors from whaling and trading vessels, for
which the condition of the country afforded "peculiar facilities," and in-

structed civil and military authorities to use every means for their apprehension.[193] Within a year, some two hundred fugitives from the naval
squadron were said to have gone to the redwood cuttings, and Shubrick,
believing they had been lured by seductive promises, issued a proclamation on September 6, 1847, offering a full and free pardon, "without
much success."[194] At the same time Mason warned that persons enticing
or concealing deserters would be subject to fines and imprisonment, and
local magistrates were made responsible for arrests and returning men to
their ships.[195] San Francisco produced its own ordinance, stipulating
penalties for soliciting and employing runaway soldiers and hard labor
for deserters caught in the town.[196] On one occasion Mason ordered the
commander at Santa Barbara to board a suspected vessel and if deserters
were found, the captain was to be fined a thousand dollars.[197] If he did
not pay, his papers were to be taken and the vessel stripped of its sails and
running gear. Some success in apprehending runaways was reported in
the press.[198]

By the end of May 1848, volunteer troops were deserting San Francisco for the new gold region, and Major James A. Hardie, in command
of the garrison, was mortified at so great a loss of his men. He dared not
send others in pursuit, he said; but Mason advised that some officers and
trustworthy men be dispatched with orders to shoot deserters who tried
to escape, otherwise bring them back in irons for trial.[199] After Mason's
first visit to the mining country, he threatened to have dragoons traverse
it in every direction, arrest deserters, and apprehend citizens who harbored them, trying them by a military commission according to the laws
of war.[200] If the people would not cooperate, he threatened to take military possession of the mines. Then, in the fall, he began experimenting
with two-month furloughs for soldiers wishing to dig gold, each carrying
a description of himself, his affiliation, and a statement of the exact period of release.[201] Stevenson had received stringent counsel, but ten of his
dragoons left Los Angeles by the end of September—and "so will all the
company go."[202] Why should soldiers remain? The war was over, and
those whose property they had stayed to protect were among the first to
set off for the placers.

Shubrick's successor, Commodore Thomas ap Catesby Jones—he of
1842—also discovered upon reaching Monterey in October 1848 the disposition of his men to desert, as eight of his crew rushed from the ship.[203]
With his "usual energy," he at once advertised "A new Gold Discovery,"
offering $40,000 for the return of deserters to the squadron—$500 each

for the first four and $200 for each one thereafter.[204] This produced not a single fugitive (only word from Washington that such "large efforts" were not advisable), and he promptly decided that no military or naval establishments could be maintained on the coast for years.[205] Still in December he was trying to recall some of his lost petty officers and seamen; and fewer desertions in the following months he would credit to good management and rigid discipline, though conceding that winter was not a favorable season for digging gold.[206] While Jones recommended keeping vessels at sea and discharging men on the coast, Mason believed that no soldier should be sent to California until Congress authorized adequate wages.[207]

As the mania worsened, army personnel had difficulty making ends meet. A common soldier receiving seven dollars a month could make ten or twenty a day in the mines.[208] Upon his arrival in February 1849, General Persifor Smith found that the wages of a good carpenter were more than the pay of the major general commanding the army (himself); and the salary of the Secretary of War (to whom he was writing) would not pay half the rent of the quarters to which a general officer was entitled by the regulations.[209] During a visit to the mines, he discovered that drivers of ox teams received more than double the pay and emoluments of any officer in the division. If his men were limited to the earnings fixed by law, he said, they must desert. They would therefore be given temporary employment by quartermasters at the going rate and be permitted to spend fixed terms in the mines (which tended greatly to allay the gold fever). Officers would be encouraged to seek employment surveying ranchos and towns, and Smith suggested that their salaries be pegged to the cost of living, from time to time fixing the rate according to an average of prices. Food should be shipped from the Atlantic and sold to them at the eastern rate so that while they might be "ruined," they would not also starve.[210] Officers and soldiers alike should be given public land to encourage them to stand by the colors.

Could a military government in California survive without an armed force?

ANNEXATION

∽18∾

End of the War— Mason's Dilemma

I NTIMATIONS OF PEACE with Mexico reached Mason on October 29, 1847, via the *Lexington*, and the end of the fighting was announced by the *Southampton* the following June.[1] But news of the treaty—dated February 2, 1848, ratified May 30, and proclaimed July 4—was not received from Mexico until the evening of August 6, via La Paz and Los Angeles.[2] Next day Mason issued a proclamation.[3] A new territorial government was probably on the way, he conjectured, but meanwhile the existing laws would remain in force, and civil officers should continue their functions if the sacrifice was not too great. Vacancies hereafter would be filled by regular elections, due notice being given. Instead of revolution there would be a stable government, administering impartial justice. And, for embellishment, "The arts and sciences will flourish, and the labor of the agriculturist, guided by the lamp of learning, will stimulate the earth to the most beautiful production." Mexican citizens were absolved from their former allegiance, and henceforth Americans and Californians would be "one . . . a band of brothers. . . ."

The military contributions act was replaced by the revenue laws of the United States; the reception of gold dust at customs was discontinued;[4] and the special levy upon Santa Barbara was ordered returned to its alcalde.[5] Although Mason had no authority to exact duties before a collections district was established, temporary civil collectors were nevertheless installed.[6] As General Smith would rationalize some months later, no duties could be imposed upon any vessels or goods, but if the interested parties preferred to pay rather than go away, they could deposit such amounts as were charged at ports of entry.[7] This procedure was in time supported by Commodore Jones, who said he would enforce the revenue laws whenever requested;[8] and shippers and importers necessarily went along. Sea letters continued to be issued to eligible American vessels, authorizing them to trade while awaiting official registry from Washington.[9]

The unavoidable was not averted, and the entire regiment of New York Volunteers was mustered out between August 15 and October 26, 1848, affecting detachments at Sonoma, San Francisco, San José, Santa Barbara, Los Angeles, and San Diego, and three companies from Lower California.[10] After being paid off, they formed themselves into parties for the mines.[11] Colonel Stevenson himself was discharged on October 25. A man lacking the President's confidence and characterized by Dupont as a *"fish out of water*, with no military knowledge . . . come here to recommence a political existence," Stevenson was highly praised by Mason for maintaining excellent discipline among his men and harmony among the Californians. Never had life and property in the southern district been so secure, Mason said, the magistrates so effectually supported, industry so encouraged.[12]

The release of the volunteers reduced Mason's force to two companies of regulars, one hundred and twenty-nine men, of whom fifty ablebodied soldiers were fit for duty.[13] Again there were widespread cries of alarm. Major Hardie foresaw serious consequences at San Francisco when the ranks of the evil-disposed were increased by "disorganizers" freed from the restraints of military discipline. "This is now a United States port," Captain Folsom protested; "we collect port charges . . . and in return we are under the most imperative obligation to protect trade."[14] Both thought a man-of-war should be sent for at once (there was none on the Upper California coast).

Transferring all regular troops to San Francisco and Monterey to guard large depots of munitions[15] meant closing posts from Santa Barbara to San Diego, creating the greatest excitement. From Los Angeles Stevenson reported that Indians had frequently shot down people in the roads and fields, and many feared the worthless of their own kind.[16] People who had been fast friends of the Americans in 1846 complained they were being abandoned. Mason offered arms which had been taken from the Californians during the war, but these were only forty-five old muskets, Stevenson had retorted, which had been repaired at the expense of the town.[17] Company C of dragoons was tentatively permitted to remain, but thirty-three men had already deserted at San Francisco, and if there were more, Los Angeles would have to be abandoned altogether.[18] Turning arms over to the inhabitants would then be the hazardous alternative.[19] Mason meanwhile advised Washington that if the Indians should rise, the people refuse to obey the authorities, or the merchants not pay the duties, he would have no force to compel obedience.[20]

Having abolished the collection of revenue as a military contribution and ordered the volunteers discharged, with all others whose service terminated with the war, Mason had exhausted his orders from Washington. And despite his positive public actions and utterances, he asked himself and the Adjutant General what right had he to exercise civil control in time of peace in a territory of the United States.

For the past two years no civil government had existed here, he noted, save that run by the military, and no civil authorities except the alcaldes appointed by himself. If he were to turn the management of the country over to the people, it would probably lead to endless confusion and anarchy. Likewise, if the customs were withdrawn and the ports thrown open, San Francisco would become a dumping-ground for all foreign goods in the north Pacific. So he continued the office of alcalde, appointed temporary collectors, and levied duties according to United States law. He was aware that in taking these steps he had no authority other than necessity, but the course seemed imperative until the arrival of dispatches from Washington. He did not anticipate rebellion, for men were so intent upon gold they had no time to think of mischief, but he earnestly advised that a government be provided as soon as possible. Though he needed troops, as sure as they came at seven dollars a month, they would desert with the certainty of making ten or twenty dollars a day in the mines.

While this defect in the civil order was being quietly perceived by the military authorities, there was a continuing public agitation for change. Disquisitions in the press by editors and contributors, signed "Lex," "Pacific," "Paisano," and "Leviticus," had been unending. The governor had done nothing, one had said, established no government, defined no supposedly existing law,[21] while another reminded American immigrants they had forfeited their inherent rights by living in an enemy's country.[22] It was not that the present government was evil, an editor conceded—it had placed no limitation upon a free press[23]—but if *he* had the affairs of state in hand, he would prescribe a code of laws and establish a temporary government. "A 'Jackson'" would do it, but a Mason "would rather be 'growled at' for doing *too little*, than . . . *too much*." Mason undoubtedly had the power to appoint a government and council to frame such laws as the country demanded, and if he would not assume the responsibility, the people should themselves take the necessary steps.[24] Winds of change were perceptibly rising.

The governor did bring forth some temporary laws. As early as March 5, 1848, he had spoken of having the duties of alcaldes, prefects, and judges clearly defined and published.[25] In April both newspapers assured the public that he would soon commence a judicial organization—though in subsequent issues the *Californian* said it was not so, and the *Star* objected to the delay.[26] Nevertheless, Mason sent his translator to San Francisco in May to oversee the printing of a Spanish edition of "some laws" and asked Captain Folsom to have copies in both English and Spanish struck off and stitched together for distribution.[27] On June 1 they were "in progress" at the *Star* office,[28] but with the exodus to the mines the paper ceased on June 10, though the job office remained open for business. The printing was apparently under way at the end of July,[29] and the first issue of the revived *Californian* announced on August 14 that a code of laws for governing the territory was ready.[30] But the same day there appeared in an adjacent column the "Glorious News" of the ratification of peace and the end of the war. Since the laws were for use during the military occupation of the country by forces of the United States (as the title-page stated), and it was now anticipated that Congress would provide a territorial organization, Mason never distributed the laws he had reluctantly devised.[31]

The *Laws for the better government of California*[32]—stillborn—were obviously American-made, though utilizing some offices in the existing judicial and law-enforcement system. They were probably compiled by California Secretary of State Halleck, drawing upon the statutes of Missouri and Texas and whatever other resources were available in Monterey.[33] The first article provided that the "laws and usages" which had prevailed would remain in force unless they conflicted with the new code. The provisions were workaday, beginning with "Administration" (and the administration of estates, that of William A. Leidesdorff, who had died in May,[34] being an urgent case). They called for superior and circuit courts, an attorney general and circuit attorneys, constables and sheriffs, clerks and recorders. They dealt with debts, crimes and punishments, the execution of judgments, appeals, venue, witnesses, juries, and habeas corpus. A treasurer and auditor were authorized, and there were sections on revenues, costs, fees and salaries, and on watercourses, marks and brands (nothing on mines). But like his predecessor, Mason had been loath to introduce a rigid code in so transient a situation. He had been ready to abide by Mexican law (suspended though never repealed by military rule)[35] until a new form of government could be instituted by "competent power."

Mason's procedure upon receiving news of the peace in August 1848 proved to be in keeping with the will of the U.S. government. Although President Polk had in July declared his inability to maintain civil organizations in the newly acquired territories after the war,[36] when Congress failed to act, he justified the preservation of the status quo much as Mason had done. But he would not propound this view to his Cabinet until October 3, 1848,[37] and the information would not reach Monterey until February 23, 1849, months after Mason's postwar crisis had begun. Congress did not establish a territorial government for California at its session ending August 1848—for "whatever" reasons, as Secretary Buchanan wrote—and the condition of the people was anomalous.[38] The military government no longer derived its authority from the laws of war. But there was an existing "government *de facto*" in full operation which would continue with the presumed consent of the people until Congress intervened. "The great law of necessity justifies this conclusion." Mason was to assure the inhabitants the President would "do what appertains to him" to remedy any inconvenience they might suffer, and he did not doubt they would remain quiet until a new organization was provided. This line of argument, and a scarcely concealed fear that California would declare its independence,[39] would be adhered to by Polk's Cabinet but not the administration to follow.

Meantime, the people were to be reminded that the Post Office laws had been extended to the new territory (though effective service would be a long time coming); that monthly steamers between Panamá and Astoria were required to deliver mails at San Diego, Monterey, and San Francisco (even if they proved to be highly irregular); and that Congress had appropriated funds to maintain a sufficient body of troops (but had not raised their pay and perquisites to reduce desertions). Above all, the people were now entitled to all the blessings and benefits resulting from the best form of government ever established among men.

RETURN OF THE NATIVES

Governor Mason's administration was further enlivened by the return of two personalities who had long months before been most prominent in

Lieutenant Henry W. Halleck of the U.S. Engineers, who had arrived at Monterey in February 1847 to inspect California's defenses, was appointed secretary of state by Governor Mason in August 1847 and would serve under Mason and his successor until the establishment of state government on December 20, 1849.

the country—José Castro and Pío Pico. Both had left Los Angeles when Stockton first occupied it in August 1846.[40] Castro with twenty men went directly to Sonora, committing his wife and children to the keeping of his neighbors. There he addressed the Mexican Minister of War and received expressions of sympathy and indignation, with assurances that General Bustamente would be marching that way.[41] Rumors spread in May 1847 that he was returning to California with a body of Sonoran Indians, but the skeptical and conciliatory Mason sent him a passport to come to Monterey, where he would be well received.[42] Later, word came of an approaching hostile force under Flores, Castro, and Pico, and Mason counseled vigilance.[43] Apprehension was heightened in December when an alarmingly large caravan of well-armed New Mexican traders appeared at the Cajón Pass, claiming to be American citizens and demanding admission.[44] Mason dispatched a guard to inspect the cavalcade and issued a proclamation forbidding the entrance of "Sonorenians" except under a flag of truce.[45] He authorized Colonel Stevenson to arrest any persons even suspected of exciting discontent.[46]

At this inauspicious moment Stevenson announced Castro's return to Los Angeles.[47] His arrival with only two companions tended to dampen local revolutionary ardor. But when he did not repair at once to Monterey, Mason sent word on February 7, 1848, that he had better come; his non-arrival had given rise to rumors "which create an excitement in the public mind. . . ."[48] Surely, having come so far and upon a passport from the governor, he would not violate his honor. It turned out that Castro had already written announcing his approach, and Mason sent another welcoming note.[49] Upon their meeting, the former *comandante*, unsolicited, gave the most solemn promise to abstain from all political activity and await the outcome of the war.[50]

Pío Pico, too, quit Los Angeles on August 10, 1846. Spending the night at Teodocio Yorba's Lomas de Santiago rancho (in Orange County), he concealed himself in the vicinity of his Santa Margarita rancho while gathering means to make the Mexican journey. With his secretary, José Matías Moreno, he crossed into Baja California on September 7, though Frémont had promised he would not be molested.[51]

At Mulegé on October 27, 1846, Pico began a long series of appeals to the Minister of Foreign Affairs in Mexico City. Having been overpowered by a superior force, he pleaded for assistance. The Californians were being seduced to declare themselves independent; and he named Bandini, Pedro C. Carrillo, and Santiago Argüello among those who had embraced the enemy's cause. Learning on November 11 that his countrymen had retaken Los Angeles, he hastened across the Gulf to Guaymas to relay the news.[52] Even a hundred men, he said, would assure the liberty of California if sent promptly. And he begged the government for "some amount" of his salary that he might continue on to the capital.[53]

Receiving no reply, he sent his secretary in January 1847 to inform the government, writing at the same time of three hundred North Americans (Cooke's Mormon Battalion) who had advanced along the Sonora frontier unmolested.[54] A long communication from Andrés Pico, telling of the outcome of the war and the Treaty of Cahuenga, was forwarded in April.[55] At Tepic, Moreno was persuaded to go no farther—Pico was no longer governor, a few troops could not oust the invader, and no aid would be given to that unfortunate state.[56] After Moreno's return, Pico wrote again, distraught that his homeland was being so passively abandoned.[57] In October the bombardment of Guaymas by the American squadron drove him inland,[58] where he sent still other letters, enclosing documents and pressing his appeal for aid as "an employee" dependent upon the central government. (Later, he would profess not to have needed such support, having won a good deal of money gambling in Guaymas.)[59]

In March 1848, after more than eighteen months of exile, Pico made a final entreaty. Self-esteem, he said, suggested that many of his communications had not been received, else they could not have been looked upon with such disdain. To a dozen anguished letters, the Foreign Minister had condescended to reply only in a laconic way that the government had "taken some measures" for California's aid. California was lost to the Mexican family, but let the republic "take leave of it with decorum," not as if it were a flock of sheep or a band of horses. And let the governor be treated with dignity.[60]

Under an armistice of February 29, 1848, Mexican officials were permitted to exercise their former functions, and in April the Californians were instructed to elect officials to administer that part of the Mexican republic. Believing this restored him temporarily to power, Pico requested Commander John Rudd of the *Dale* at Guaymas to carry him to Mulegé in his official capacity.[61] This the commander would not do, but Pico could go as a private citizen. He left Guaymas on May 22, Mulegé on June 3, and reached San Diego on July 6. A few days later he was at his Santa Margarita rancho and on the 15th at Workman's rancho La Puente, some eighteen miles east of Los Angeles.

Colonel Stevenson soon learned of his arrival at San Diego—where he did not report to the post commander—and wrote to Mason.[62] Pico was said to have come with full powers as governor and had only to show his credentials to have the administration turned over to him. At Workman's rancho he was visited by many Californians, and Stevenson heard that he did not intend to see him but to go to his brother's San Fernando rancho and communicate there with Mason. Conceiving that the Englishman Workman was just the man to encourage him not to report, Stevenson ordered Pico to appear immediately in person. A detachment of soldiers was to bring him in by force if he so much as hesitated to obey. But Pico had disappeared, and a second body of dragoons was sent with similar orders. Hugo Reid, a friendly Scot, came in on July 18 to say the fugitive was at San Gabriel and had been told he would certainly be arrested if he passed Los Angeles without seeing the authorities. Intending no disrespect, Pico appeared that evening, making his explanations. Though saying he had returned under the armistice, he denied meaning to resume his former functions and claimed he had advised his friends against revolution; no part of the conquered territory had been so well treated as California. He wished to go to San Fernando, where his secretary would prepare the required statement.

Pico and Mason not only spoke different languages, they represented disparate cultures; the intent of one could hardly be translated to the other. Pico now wrote both Stevenson and Mason that he had returned as Mexican governor of California "to establish in its towns the blessings of the . . . Armistice," and he asked that American forces raise no impediment to his establishing constitutional order.[63] He wanted Mexicans and Americans to look upon themselves as a fraternity. Pico was a man of ordinary intelligence, generous if sometimes reckless, disposed to be fair if not altogether trustworthy, an unexceptional man, as H. H. Bancroft observed, in a prominent position. He wished to take leave of his honored role "with decorum," and the happy event of the armistice seemed an opportunity to yield it legitimately and even, perchance, with ceremony.

But a long line of American conquerors had not taken and retaken the country as an exercise in civility. California had been subdued by the Departments of War and Navy, not State; they had ousted the Mexican commandant general and governor and fought the natives; and they were under Presidential orders to be in possession of the country when the war ended. Pico, in contrast, valued fame more than victory, esteem more than power, form more than substance, and he would settle with the United States or any other winner if it could be done with deference and decent recompense. He had never surrendered except to fate and now aspired to negotiate.

Pledging his neutrality—under penalty of imprisonment—Pico was given safe conduct to his Santa Margarita rancho to await Mason's answer.[64] It came. Translating Pico's pretensions as Mexican governor into overt rebellion, Mason ordered him immediately arrested and shipped to Monterey, permitting no communication with his countrymen and keeping it all a profound secret until he was safely confined.[65] Closer to events than his superior and more charitable, Stevenson made the former governor a prisoner in his own quarters, reminded Mason of his good advice to his fellows, and asked that the order be rescinded.[66] Fortunately for

Don Pío, news of the peace reached Monterey three days later, and Lieutenant Sherman wrote that if Pico was still imprisoned, he should be liberated.[67] With little peacetime charity, Sherman reminded the ex-governor that he might have been treated as a spy, and if he meant to stay in the country he had better be careful how he acted toward the authorities. So much for honor and dignity!

MASON'S DILEMMA

If Mason had been insensitive to Pico's lonely mission, his own was no more gratefully regarded by the people. Chief in a land where "forts were without soldiers," ordnance without guards, towns without men, a territory without laws or legislature, a colony deficient in communication with the home government, his lot was not an easy one. No military governor is likely to be popular in wartime, much less so in peace. Although once honored by a grand ball at Brown's Hotel in San Francisco,[68] Mason was more often violently criticized, as were his appointed officials. Were there not desperados abroad in the land, murders, drunkenness, and debauchery which he had failed to restrain? Immigrants were despoiling the missions, Indians organizing raids upon the ranchos, and bands of white men riding about, committing bloody assaults upon the people.[69] Mexican law and the want of democratic practices contributed to discontent. The revenue system, the conditional state of land titles, the lack of protective troops, and the inability or unwillingness of the authorities to put things to rights all stimulated opposition to the regime and to Colonel Mason, its most identifiable symbol. An American who did not take to him kindly thought him crude, unrefined, and far too narrow, despotic, and unconciliatory for his position; though he loved order and justice, every step he took gave rise to dissatisfaction, discontent, and, in the end, "complete anarchy."[70]

Mason was a military, not an elected ruler. He followed his orders from Washington when he thought they would work, bending them often in the peoples' direction, sometimes unpropitiously for his own good. "They failed to remember," remarked Bancroft, "that it required as much patience in him to govern them, as it did in them to be governed."[71] The newspapers sometimes took the offensive, often enough in the public interest though by their nature with the rhetoric distended. Public meetings, particularly in the north, sent him resolutions. And there was always a stream of correspondence—plaintive, entreating, contentious, demanding—to which Mason, with his secretary of state and adjutant, spiritedly responded. His comments sometimes had a burr, but they were carefully reasoned, often with authorities cited, and they made good sense and usually good law. His personality is perhaps best discerned in these communications.

The governor recognized the untenability of his position under California's highly unstable conditions. He had dwelt upon it at length in letters to the War Department, while accepting that some general agent of order was essential. Some of his officers were understanding. "Colonel Mason is in a tight place," Sherman wrote to Stevenson.[72] Most of the soldiers had deserted, he said, the Navy could not anchor for fear of losing its crews, and there was no civil organization in the country. The U.S. government had known all along that California would not be given up and the volunteers would be discharged. Yet it did nothing. People could scoff at promises of protection, good laws, and stable government. However Mason might be disposed, all the women of the country might be ravished, the men killed, horses stolen, and homes burnt, and "you couldn't get a dozen men to leave the Gold district to go to their aid."

Mason's predicament was in no way improved by the peremptory judgments of Senator Benton, widely published as a letter to the inhabitants of California and copied in San Francisco's new newspaper, the *Alta California*, in January 1849.[73] The people were now citizens of the United States, he declaimed, though without a government. Mexican law remained in force until altered by congressional authority; and the edicts of Mason and Kearny, "each an ignoramus," insofar as they were meant to change that law, were null and void. Having no lawful government or officers, and likely to get none except by their own efforts, they should call a convention, provide a cheap and simple government, and take care of themselves until Congress acted. (Benton then belabored Mason and Stevenson for reputedly defeating Frémont's claims in the Congress.)[74]

When Commodore Thomas ap Catesby Jones reached Monterey in October 1848, Mason had his first opportunity in months to consult with his peer in the Navy. Jones had left Norfolk in the *Cumberland* on November 3, 1847,[75] crossed the Isthmus, been picked up by the flagship *Ohio* at Valparaiso on January 20, and was off Mazatlán on May 6, where Shubrick was enforcing the blockade. According to Dupont, he was "elated, evidently," to get the command "on any terms."[76] Jones himself thought it might be his last sea service—he was 59—and he hoped to be allowed a full three-year cruise.[77] Characterized by Dupont as energetic, forthright, and assertive, he was, moreover, socially inclined, "not deficient in magnanimity," and did not require flattery or dislike a man because he disagreed with him. Although confident he could suppress desertion and on this voyage revive lost principles and practices under which the navy had prospered during the War of 1812, he was only moderately successful. Neither reward nor punishment, he would find, made any compact binding. His vision of repairing vessels on San Francisco Bay evaporated in the realization that for years no naval establishment could be operated economically on the California coast.[78] Enterprising in forwarding both his public and private interests, he was apt to get them mixed—whether in supplying San Francisco with beef, predicting the wants of immigrants, advocating Negro slavery in California agriculture, or championing Benicia.[79] (He would be asked to surrender his command to a successor on July 1, 1850, sooner than he expected,[80] and be convicted the following year of speculating in gold dust with government funds and suspended from the Navy for five years.)[81]

Jones received notice of the end of the war at Mazatlán on June 13 and began immediately to evacuate United States forces from that place and Baja California.[82] Never, he asserted, had he heard any resident, Mexican or foreign—with two hungry and mischievous exceptions—who did not deplore the return of peace and the loss of security they had enjoyed under the American flag. From July to mid-October he employed the whole squadron in bringing three companies of New York Volunteers and some 350 refugees and their baggage from La Paz and San José del Cabo to Monterey—without the expenditure "of a single dollar" from the national Treasury.[83] The refugees—men, women, and children, including the late governor of Baja California and its principal civil officers—had been induced to join the American cause by expectations the country would never be restored to Mexico and were now forced to flee with the wrecks of their fortunes. The quartermaster was directed to feed and house them for two months, and the commodore paid for their lost property from the military contribution collected in Mexico.[84]

Upon Mason's return from the gold region on November 15, he and Jones conferred upon their joint affairs.[85] They quickly agreed, under the rising tide of events, that if the sloop-of-war *St. Mary's* did not return from Panamá with notice of a territorial organization by Congress, they would recommend the election of delegates to frame laws and form a provisional government.[86] Unless a civil government was organized, Mason warned the Adjutant General, anarchy and confusion would result, and murder, robbery, and "all sorts of crime will be committed. . . ."[87]

To Mason this seemed like the beginning of the end, and since it would take several months to exchange notes with Washington, he wrote to Adjutant General Jones on November 24.[88] "The war being over, the soldiers nearly all deserted, and having now been from the States two years, I respectfully request to be ordered home." He felt no need to apologize, for only once before in his long career had he sought to be relieved, from recruiting in 1832 to join his company in the Black Hawk War.

As it happened, the War Department had already arranged for Mason's replacement. A letter had been written to him in October, announcing that a third military-geographic division was being created along the Pacific, embracing Departments 10 and 11 (California and Oregon) in order to facilitate their cooperation in case of need. Brevet Brigadier General Bennet Riley was to command in California, and General Persifor F. Smith was to head the division.[89] Mason was to consult fully with Riley and be relieved by him. Smith would become his military superior.

Governor Mason's days were numbered, but he maintained his position, "charged with civil affairs," until Riley appeared, still advocating to the Adjutant General the organization of a territorial government as soon as practicable.[90] Early in December the *St. Mary's* returned without news of congressional action, but Mason, at the end of his term, made no move, though public meetings at San José, San Francisco, and other population centers championed a provisional order.[91] New instructions were brought by General Smith on February 23, 1849, placing California under U.S. customs regulations but establishing no means for collections, and Mason asked the Navy to stand by to seize contraband goods and vessels.[92] Some postal routes were also authorized, and the President sent a message to the people by the Post Office agent, regretting the inaction of Congress, describing California's situation as anomalous, and exhorting the people to live peaceably under the existing government until a change could be made constitutionally.[93] Mason learned of his successor's approach at this time and, belatedly, that he was to preserve the status quo.[94] Unlooked-for troops under Major L. P. Graham, which had marched from Coahuila without Mason's knowledge, were in December temporarily quartered at Los Angeles.[95] By April 19, 1849, Riley was momentarily expected, and Mason thought it improper to make new appointments.[96] Three days later, the *Iowa*, with Bennet Riley and his troops aboard, sailed into Monterey Bay, "56 days from Valparaiso—all well."[97]

Thus, quickly, Richard B. Mason's broad powers were ended, after almost two years as California's supreme civil ruler and military commander.[98] He left the territory quietly by steamer on May 1, accompanied by no retinue or friends, and died of cholera the following summer at St. Louis.[99] "He possessed a strong native intellect," his one-time adjutant, William T. Sherman, said, "and far more knowledge of the principles of civil government and law than he got credit for." Stern and honest to a fault, he was the "very embodiment of the principle of fidelity to the interests of the general government."

ᔇ19ᔈ

Consent of the Governed— Riley's Rule

HE WAR with Mexico was indeed ended. Upper California was annexed; the tariff and postal laws of the United States had been extended over the territory; and the inhabitants were now entitled, as the
Secretary of State seductively observed, to all the blessings and benefits
provided by the best civil government ever established amongst men.[1] But
there was no civil government. The President and executive departments
could not initate it—they dared not—this being the privilege and responsibility of Congress. Yet, while Congress warily guarded this prerogative,
it would not act; its members were choosing up sides for the next war, the
one between the states. James K. Polk, the diligent war President (who
thought linking slavery to the acquisition of new territory was both mischievous and wicked),[2] would go out of office on March 3, 1849 (and die
June 15), to be succeeded by Old Rough and Ready, Zachary Taylor, hero
of the war he had done much to win and lose. A slave-owner who carried
eight southern states and seven in the north, he wished most of all to annex the newly acquired provinces while preserving the Union.[3] Boldly
favoring self-determination in respect to slavery in the new American
southwest, he urged California's unconditional admission. But southern
legislators would filibuster while California burned, and General Taylor
(whom Polk thought had no opinions of his own on any public ques-

tion)[4] would die of cholera two months before California achieved statehood under the Compromise Bill of 1850.[5]

In California, meanwhile, the inhabitants decried their military government. It was barely visible but when encountered was arbitrary, alien to their experience, and far too simple, there being too few layers of judgment between capricious local alcaldes and irrevocable power. Practically, it lacked the pervasiveness and persuasiveness of collective self-government, yet had not sufficient force to compel obedience. And it was too monolithic and transitory to react quickly and acceptably to rapidly changing conditions.

But greater elaboration was on the way. Back in October, a 3rd military–geographical division had been created, uniting Oregon and California under Brevet Major General Persifor F. Smith, introducing a new level of bureaucracy, and putting a ceiling upon the governor's martial powers.[6] Polk wanted a man of Smith's education, intelligence, and knowledge to be chief of staff, considering California's anomalous condition, with Brevet Brigadier General Bennet Riley—a "grim old fellow" and "fine free swearer"—civil governor and next in command.[7] The President, through his Secretary of State, sent a precautionary message to the people of California by a gentleman who had been ordered out to establish post offices and arrange for the conveyance of mail.[8]

Word had come to Polk at the end of September 1848 of a letter of August 27 from Senator Benton to the people of California, declaring their temporary government to be null and void and recommending they set up their own organization and not await the action of Congress.[9] The President believed they had no such right under the Constitution and hoped to counteract this erroneous doctrine before it reached its destination.[10] His advice, taken out by William Van Voorhies, an employee of the executive branch, would not reach San Francisco until February 28, 1849,[11] almost seven weeks after Benton's epistle had appeared in the local press. By the same vessel went General Smith, who had conversed with the President and held that only the de facto government was legal.[12] General Riley, to replace Mason, was not far behind and would be followed by other representatives of a burgeoning system.

General Persifor Smith "and lady," who had left New Orleans on December 18 and spent the month of January at Panamá (awaiting their steamer), reached Monterey on February 23, 1849, and San Francisco on the 28th.[13] While on the Isthmus Smith had written that from all he could learn of California, he did not see how it would be possible to live there.[14]

He came, nevertheless, as Mason's military superior, accepting that he had no civil authority. On the way he picked up certain preconceptions. Foreigners, he had learned, were ravaging the mining region and going off with large quantities of gold. The "rabble of the Pacific ports," bands of plunderers, were on their way and would comprise the worst kind of population, give a very bad foundation to society, and probably resist the administration of laws and government. He was disposed to regard all non-citizens who dug for gold upon public land as trespassers, subject to fines and imprisonment, and he notified the U.S. consul at Panamá to communicate this fact to his peers on the coast.[15] The government could disavow his action, he said, though he had not yet forbidden immigration, only threatened foreigners with the law. He reasoned that all entry upon public land was trespassing, but since Congress had made distinctions favoring citizens, forbearance might be justified for them. He recognized that he could only make arrests (if he had the means) and confine trespassers until courts were established. Indeed, in enforcing the law he would have to depend upon immigrants from the United States, whose "own interests must be involved to at least some extent."

The necessity to depend upon well-disposed citizens resulted from military desertions. No confidence could be placed even in regular troops, and he was sorry to see any go to California, for they would all defect. He was told that some of the most trusted marines had deserted from the British Navy, with their noncommissioned officers, a thing hitherto unknown. In fact, all vessels going to San Francisco lost their crews. He would post most of the troops at San Diego, it being farther from the mines and nearest the frontier. However, nothing would serve the interests of the United States like the organization of a regular government and the passage of laws to dispose of the public lands. Some evil beyond remedy, he feared, might make establishing a government difficult if not impossible, and he suggested that California be annexed as a judicial and collection district to Oregon. All that was necessary to give direction to the love of law and order "so general among our citizens" would be the institution of popular tribunals.

Smith would have some other notions fixed in his mind upon arrival.[16] He had heard on the way that many points about San Francisco Bay were more suitable for the collection of revenues than the town of that name. San Franciscans were eager to have the public offices, to enhance their property values, but he told the collector that since no port of entry had been established by law, vessels should be permitted to discharge at other

General Persifor F. Smith was a man of education, intelligence, and knowledge such as President Polk wanted to be chief-of-staff of a new military-geographical division uniting Oregon and California.

points, offering an equal chance to all.[17] Some weeks later he reported to Washington that the town of San Francisco was in no way fitted for military or commercial purposes.[18] There was no harbor, no landing place, bad water, an inclement climate, and it was cut off from the rest of the country—in time of war it could be isolated by a short line across the peninsula. And better harbors could be found inland.

Smith had particularly in mind the Strait of Carquinez, which he, with Commodore Jones, commissioners from Washington, and officers of the coast survey, would explore and recommend as a navy depot.[19] Near it was a favorable site, he noted, for a large town, where indeed a place called Benicia was already laid out (and he was speculating in a few lots).[20] By May 1 an army depot was established there, with two companies of troops for protection, and Smith had proposed to the Benicia entrepreneurs, Semple and Larkin, that an area adjacent to the town be ceded to the United States for quartermaster's stores and other purposes.[21] Henceforth, all shipments were to be made to "Benicia, bay of San Francisco." Jones also took strong exception to San Francisco's sandhills and its isolation near the end of an extremely sterile peninsula and recommended a customhouse at the more convenient port of Benicia (where he too reinforced his resolve by acquiring ten town lots).[22]

Postal agent William Van Voorhies arrived in San Francisco with letters of instruction from Postmaster General Cave Johnson and Secretary Buchanan.[23] As special agent for the department, he was to select postmasters for San Diego, San Pedro, Monterey, and other points where steam packets might touch (San Francisco's appointee, who never appeared, having already been selected in Washington). Postage was 40 cents a half-ounce from the Atlantic—mostly prepaid—and 12½ between places on the Pacific. Although large contracts had been awarded to bring mails by steamship to the coast, no routes to the interior had been authorized by Congress under the act of August 14, 1846, and any offices established there were required to be self-supporting. Compensation for carrying the local mail was to be from three to ten dollars a mile one way, and weekly and semi-monthly transportation by the cheapest mode was prescribed.

Voorhies may have been a rowdy, as Larkin's step-brother, Ebenezer Larkin Childs, alleged.[24] (This position of special agent, Childs claimed, had been created by Congress for himself but awarded to a law partner of Polk's brother, who had been "bolstered up" to chief clerk over the heads of thirty others.) But in disorderly California, Voorhies quickly perceived that no one seemed disposed to take upon himself the trouble of public office, "though it yield five times the compensation." Like General Smith, he was staggered by the prices asked and warned his superior that California might produce a heavy deficit, unmatched by receipts. And he advised that all California mail not intended for Monterey be sent to San

Francisco, since everyone was now likely to be there or in parts adjacent.[25] He departed for the upper country, where most of the inhabitants during the mining season "do congregate," but before his first reports could reach Washington in June, a new President and party would take office, and he would be displaced.[26]

Voorhies had an even more signal mission, to carry a message from the President to the people of California. Months before the peace with Mexico, Polk had worried about establishing more stable governments in California and New Mexico than the exigencies of war allowed; and when the treaty was transmitted to Congress on July 6, 1848, he had urged setting up territorial organizations to forestall confusion and anarchy.[27] But an aroused factionalism interfered. Attempts to compromise the convulsive slavery issue were made (a bill passed the Senate ʻbut not the House),[28] but the first session of the 30th Congress adjourned on August 14, 1848, without finding a solution. The authority over which Stockton, Kearny, and Frémont had so warmly contended and under which Mason operated until news of the peace, had ended, and there was nothing to take its place.

While Benton's mischievous advice to set up a local government would prove to be only premature, Polk thought it was meant to make Frémont governor and California an independent state. To forestall such an extremity, he assured the people he was guarding their interests and would press Congress at its session beginning December 4 to provide a government and extend U.S. laws over them.[29]

The letter to Voorhies of October 7, 1848, was signed by Secretary Buchanan.[30] The President congratulated the inhabitants upon the annexation of their "fine province" to the United States. Blessed with a mild and salubrious climate and fertile soil, rich in mineral resources, and extending over nearly ten degrees of latitude, with some of the finest harbors in the world, California's future wealth and prosperity seemed limitless. Getting down to basics, Polk regretted the failure of Congress to create a territorial government and recognized the people's condition as anomalous. Fortunately, he reassured them, there was an existing government in full operation, "and this will continue, with the presumed consent of the people" until Congress provided another. This consent was "irresistibly inferred," the argument continued, from the fact that no civilized community could possibly desire a state of anarchy. That there were alternatives, the people by their words and deeds would indicate, but the President counseled patience; Congress would probably act before local changes could be made. Mason received a copy for publication should it arrive before Voorhies. With Smith and Riley likewise briefed, Polk's official line seemed secure.

Colonel R. T. P. Allen, Voorhies' successor under the Taylor administration, reached San Francisco on June 13, 1849, and quickly alerted Washington that postal expenses would greatly exceed those at home. Income could scarcely match expenditures, however economic the management. He estimated receipts of $40,000 a year and expenses between $80,000 and $100,000. The incoming mail in May and June averaged 6,000 letters, and he supposed it might increase to 10,000 a month; but the August receipts were "near *eighteen thousand*," and he craved advice upon how they were to be handled.[31] By the end of August he had established offices and appointed postmasters in seven northern towns, and bids for carrying the mail to these points were due the first of September.[32]

Although the Postmaster General would inform Congress that supplementary funds would be required if there was to be even a limited service on the Pacific,[33] the department was meanwhile strictly governed by the means available. Consequently, when accounts from the agent began to arrive in Washington, showing the cost of transporting mail from San Francisco to Sacramento, Coloma, Stockton, and Monterey to be $62,400 a year (and contracts had not been made out in triplicate and submitted beforehand), he refused payment.[34] If mails to the interior could not be supported by the income from postage, they would not be delivered. Congress would get them to San Francisco, and the citizens could do the rest.

ADVENT OF RILEY

Brigadier General Bennet Riley, with troops of the U.S. 2nd Infantry, anchored at Monterey in the transport *Iowa* on the evening of April 12 and next day assumed the office of governor and commander of the 10th Military Department.[35] A large, bluff man in his mid-fifties, he would maintain his predominance in the civil sphere with sagacity and vigor, though his military superior would be Persifor F. Smith. He consulted freely with Colonel Mason and had the great good fortune to inherit his secretary of state, Captain Henry W. Halleck.

It will be remembered that Mason and Commodore Jones had agreed

Brigadier General Bennet Riley, a large, bluff man in his mid–fifties, reached Monterey on April 12, 1849, and next day assumed the office of governor; he would maintain his predominance in the civil sphere, though his military superior would be Persifor F. Smith.

in October 1848 that if the 30th Congress did not provide a territorial organization during its first session, they would recommend an election of delegates to form a provisional government.[36] That this radical proposal was made without the sanction of the President speaks to their apprehension about conditions over which they had a diminishing control. But although such a procedure was opposed by Polk except in an extremity,[37] it anticipated a policy adopted by the new President as the safest and most practicable course. Not until June 4, 1849, however, would President Taylor's emissary, Thomas Butler King, arrive at San Francisco with the word,[38] to be echoed by his Secretary of War, who would subsequently tell Riley it would not matter whether the first step was taken by the people or at the invitation of Congress.[39]

On April 10, 1849, Mason and Smith had sent another vessel to Mazatlán for news of congressional action.[40] If the tidings were not favorable, Riley was now determined to call an election of delegates to a constitutional convention and to fill vacant offices under the existing laws. If it had been done a year before, Halleck wryly observed, California would already have a regular government.[41] So, when the *Edith* returned on June 1, reporting another session ended without authorizing a territorial government, the governor, on his own, issued a proclamation.[42]

Riley had been sent out, he ingeniously began, not as a military governor but as the head of an existing civil organization. Military rule had ended with the war, but the government that remained was recognized by the laws of California, which said that in the absence of a properly appointed governor, the commanding officer was ex officio governor of the country. Thus unabashedly citing Mexican law, not the presumed consent of the governed, as his statutory base, Riley went on to describe the structure of the "present government" (taken from a translation and digest of pertinent Mexican law then being made).[43] Congress having provided no government, the existing law would be fully implemented; and he took the decisive step of calling an election to fill vacant offices and select delegates to frame a constitution for submission to the people and to Congress. The election would be held on August 1, and he named the offices to be filled, designated the number of delegates, fixed places of election, defined the election districts, and established the qualifications of voters. He also set September 1 as the meeting date of a constitutional convention to be held at Monterey.

Riley—and Halleck—had fused logic and logistics. It was well to adhere to established law until some authorized system could replace it, for many social and political relationships depended upon legitimacy. It was also hoped to arrest any drift toward separation from the United States and the creation of "another Texas" with which American authorities would have to deal. Though not in line with Polk's gospel according to Voorhies, the move would soon receive President Taylor's blessing. The pronouncement, notwithstanding, elicited a great deal of public opposition.

PRO PÚBLICO

Americans had long advocated popular sovereignty in the country. Before the conquest, the U.S. government had wanted the Californians to assert their independence under the protection of the United States. In June

1846 the Bear Flag party had declared California a republic. Sloat, a month later, had promised the inhabitants they could elect their own officers. The initial issue of California's first newspaper had argued that the people should form a government, draw up a constitution, and choose a legislature which could send a delegate to Congress.[44] Kearny had obligated the United States to set up a free government, and Mason had favored a provisional organization if Congress failed. As recently as January 4, 1849, readers of the *Alta California* had seen Benton's advice to call a convention and take care of their own needs; and Persifor Smith had noted at Mazatlán the following month that people were going out "armed" with Benton's letter to set up a representative government.[45] Virtually independent cells of government materialized throughout the mining region in the absence of any other viable form, and some of the newcomers had experience with home rule in Oregon and "Deseret." Americans wanted a visible, popular government based upon familiar law; and in some of the towns they set about organizing assemblies to make and enforce law, levy taxes, and provide justice. Likely they agreed with Sidney Smith's maxim, as expounded in the local press, that the "object of all government is roast mutton, potatoes, a stout constable, an honest justice, a clear highway, a free school."[46] Riley's arbitrary administration did not qualify, and they would have none of it.

The foundation of the governor's proclaimed authority was openly challenged. Stockton and Frémont had "swept away" Mexican law, an editor said.[47] Kearny did not promulgate it; Mason had not enforced it; the alcaldes had ignored it. If the governor had instructions to buttress his position, let him make them public. Whereupon, a letter of October 9, 1848, from Polk's Secretary of War was dutifully published, directing the commander to respect and assist the de facto government and not attempt to alter it until it was modified by competent authority.[48] Riley, the editor conceded, had carried out the letter of the law.

Increasingly the system did not work. Alcaldes ruled by whim,[49] were afraid to do their duty, or did not know what it was. Assault and murder were common, sometimes countered by lynch law. Property was not respected. There were Indian raids and reprisals. Gold attracted an immense immigration. Society's needs were not being satisfied: providing security, affording justice, quieting land titles, enforcing contracts, importing coin, standardizing the acceptance of gold dust, maintaining roads, delivering mail. The newspapers joined in propagating these views. "The present state of anarchy (we can call it nothing else) is much to be deplored"; and the *Alta California*'s editor declaimed at length upon the rights of the people and the lack of authority of the President, "a mere executive officer," to interfere.[50]

Public meetings favoring a provisional government began to be held at the end of 1848, first at San José on December 11, at San Francisco on the 21st and 23rd, and afterwards at Sonoma, Sacramento, Monterey, "Culloma," "Juba River," and San Diego.[51] (At Los Angeles, the Californians thought the "*juntas*" treasonable.)[52] Elected delegates were to meet at San José on January 8, postponed to March 5, May 1, and August 6 to allow the participation of more remote districts and await news from Washington.[53]

Meantime, to provide for local needs, Sonoma and Sacramento early in 1849 established legislative bodies.[54] San Franciscans, too, weary of wrangling among local officials and competing town councils, met in their "primary capacity" to set up a legislative assembly to enact laws not in conflict with the Constitution of the United States.[55] They abolished the obnoxious alcalde's office as the only remaining vestige of Mexican law, and elected three justices of the peace to serve a year or until superseded by other authority. Then they appealed to the military commanders, General Smith and Commodore Jones. Government by right of war had ceased, they said, and Mason (in their view) had withdrawn from the territory's affairs after the ratification of the peace. Having been advised by the President to submit for a time to the existing government, they had done this to a "certain degree" until the system had become too oppressive to bear. Since Riley's government rested upon the "presumed consent" of the people, the inhabitants, withholding that consent, might now organize as "they may think necessary" for their own protection.

General Smith, justifying Polk's confidence, returned a surprisingly soft answer, reiterating the President's stand.[56] By establishing even the best government upon a false basis, they were weaving an endless thread of litigation. However, he thought it not inconsistent for each district to make its own regulations for police and security, and he promised aid. He wrote to Washington in May that, unless driven to it, he would not employ military force to overthrow these "usurpations," but he asked that the Attorney General advise Riley what course to pursue.[57] Word was on the way.

Within a month after President Taylor had taken office on March 4,

1849, he had appointed Georgia Congressman Thomas Butler King agent of the United States in California. With the Senate evenly divided between slave and free interests, there was little likelihood any action would soon be taken upon California, and the 31st Congress would not meet again until December. King's instructions were dated April 3.[58] He had been made fully aware of the President's views, Secretary of State John M. Clayton said, and could suggest to the people measures to give them effect. The President would support the formation of any republican government which was the result of their own deliberate choice. Clearly, the new administration wanted a speedy application for admission by an already organized state which could be acted upon by Congress without undue debate (perhaps with territory enough to permit a subsequent division into free and slave areas).[59] Meanwhile, the existing laws would remain in force. Reputed attempts to launch an independent state were not much credited by the new Executive, but King was to be watchful and report upon this as well as the character and resources of the country.[60]

King arrived at San Francisco in the steamer *Panamá* on June 4, and on the 12th addressed the citizens in regard to "affairs respecting the territory, &c."[61] To further the movement toward statehood, he made an ostentatious tour of the mines, the most densely populated area, elaborately escorted by General Smith, Commodore Jones, and a detachment of U.S. Cavalry. As a congressman from Georgia, a direct representative of the President, and a highly visible and smooth-tongued political figure, King carried great weight with his hearers. Hubert Howe Bancroft refers to the "Pranks of T. Butler King,"[62] and contemporaries record his eccentricities. Making his "progress" through the mines, he would rise in the morning well after the sun was up and, after "making an elaborate toilet, having his boots blacked, and dressing as if going to the senate-chamber," would take breakfast. By the time he was ready to start, the sun was hot, marches were made in the worst part of the day, and the whole party was exposed to fever and sickness, as General Smith declared. (Upon his return, King almost died of dysentery in San Francisco.)[63] But he was a winsome speaker and tireless in espousing the proposed constitutional convention. In August he would requisition the steam propeller *Edith* from Commodore Jones[64] to take reportedly unenthusiastic southern delegates to Monterey and (with the quartermaster) charter the *Frémont* from San Francisco.[65] Because of illness he would not himself get to the convention, but his known pro-slavery leanings and open liaison with Washington, along with some irreparable deficiencies in judgment, would severely limit his influence with the delegates. Larkin would remember that the "very name of T. Butler King became unpopular" among the members.[66]

Riley was Smith's inferior in arms, but he was California's undaunted governor. Within a month of his arrival he suspended T. M. Leavenworth, the controversial alcalde at San Francisco and appointed a commission to investigate charges.[67] When, after the alcalde's reinstatement and almost immediate resignation, the legislative assembly seized the records, the governor declared they had usurped powers vested only in Congress and warned the people against abetting them or paying taxes.[68] The office of alcalde was established by law, he said, and should be sacred, and there was legal remedy for maladministration by individuals. Riley thereupon called for the election of a town council to replace the assembly, appointed judges and inspectors, outlined the relevant provisions of the law, and, for good measure, advised them regarding town lands.[69]

The day before the governor's warning (of June 4) reached San Francisco, the local assembly issued a long appeal to the people of California.[70] Congress had not only taxed them without representation but given them no government at all. Was there no form of organization which would harmonize with the Constitution, be acceptable to reasonable men, and not clash with those who claimed the powers of a de facto government? They called for a convention to meet at San José on the 20th of August to form a provisional government. If some delegates would not attend, it could be created by those who did; and if not everyone went to the polls for its ratification, the majority of voters would settle the question. (This appeal was written by Peter H. Burnett, former judge of the Oregon supreme court, and signed by Francis J. Lippitt, that doughty captain of volunteers at Santa Barbara.) Nothing daunted, Riley issued a list of polling places for the election to be held "the first of August next."[71]

This provoked another round of meetings, including the one on San Francisco's Portsmouth Square on June 12 at which King reassuringly spoke, a committee of correspondence was formed, and a motion to adopt Riley's dates was rejected.[72] The committee, headed by Burnett, issued its own address six days later.[73] While denying the governor the "least power" to appoint times and places, it nevertheless recommended, for the sake of unanimity, that his timetable be accepted, noting that it was already being acceded to by the districts of San José and Monterey.

And so the people would get what they wanted upon Riley's terms, and Burnett would reckon the whole controversy fortunate in hastening the state's formation.[74]

TROOPS

Riley generally perpetuated his predecessor's forms and policies. But while Mason had thought it best to station troops away from the mines to discourage desertion, Riley adopted a contrary procedure. By placing them as near the gold region as possible, he hoped both to maintain order and minimize defection.[75] "The gold mania is greater at a distance from the mines than in the immediate neighborhood," he informed General Smith's adjutant, Lieutenant William T. Sherman. Los Angeles and San Luis Rey were therefore abandoned as military posts and arms for defense supplied to uneasy farmers and other respectable persons.[76] Hazards to the people were greater from deserting infantrymen than from horse thieves, he asserted. Furloughs continued to be granted to soldiers, allowing them to labor for their own benefit when not required for duty. Nevertheless, he appealed to the people to assist the authorities in apprehending deserters, even recommended reviving the war penalty or adopting other drastic measures.[77] General Smith, too, regretted the removal of the death penalty for deserting, not that it should be inflicted often but that desertion had become less of a crime than formerly.[78] Other ailments than the gold fever also commonly afflicted the forces, and Riley appointed a medical director to collect information concerning prevalent diseases and the medical topography of the country in order to take preventive measures.[79]

Troops were sent to the Sacramento Valley to mediate between whites and Indians and, later in the year, were stationed at passes near San Bernardino and on the Colorado.[80] Controlling Indians was difficult because there was "no recognized Indian country" and therefore no means to prevent a too intimate contact of the races,[81] and Riley urged that Congress establish reserves over which the United States would have exclusive sovereignty. Because of the extraordinary immigration, land near the *rancherías* would no longer provide the aborigines with subsistence, and they must either perish or commit depredations upon their neighbors, which would be taken as a pretext for a war of extermination. Troops were likewise ordered to the northern and southern immigrant routes with supplies to relieve destitution.[82] With the limited forces at Riley's command, it was necessary to arm defenseless inhabitants,[83] and repeated requests were made to Washington for additional men, including staff officers (ordnance, medical, and topographical), with meager effect.[84]

THE MINES

Riley, too, made a visit to the mines, leaving Monterey on July 5, 1849, accompanied by Major E. R. S. Canby, Captain Halleck, and other officers.[85] The area was found to be generally peaceful, every little settlement and tented town having elected its own alcalde and constable. Only in some of the northern placers did he find that Spanish Americans had been forced out, their expulsion egged on by politicians willing to endanger the tranquility of the country. Farther south, the American population was disposed to protect this group, he noted (an inclination which would not last).[86] Asked his opinion about the rights of foreigners, he asserted that no one had a right to dig gold on public land; but until the United States should act, he would not countenance any group's claim to a monopoly.[87] This contrasted with General Smith's "no trespassing" policy, which he renewed in October, proposing mining licenses which would be available only to citizens of the United States.[88]

LANDS

Riley's views in respect to land titles complemented Colonel Mason's, both perhaps being founded upon the accumulated knowledge of Henry W. Halleck.[89] Adjudication of claims entailed the interpretation of Mexican law and the deferment of judgments until competent courts were established (a new Superior Court could settle questions of possession if not of title). Mission properties were vested in the government, with certain exceptions, and if they had not been legally conveyed, were still public property.[90] Riley took a strong stand in preserving government reserves against a multiplicity of claims.[91] In these views he was supported by General Smith, who realized the importance of quieting titles and perceived the differing Californian and American traditions, the voracious hunger for lands under the new regime, and the precarious state of Mexican claims. Smith recommended a board of commissioners to examine all titles held against the United States.[92]

In July, the Department of the Interior sent William Carey Jones, a specialist in Spanish land law and another son-in-law of Benton's, to examine the California and Mexican archives and report upon land titles.[93] Arriving in mid-September, he spent two months in San Francisco and Monterey, finding the Monterey records imperfect, in confusion, and with nothing earlier than 1839, then stopped a few days in Los Angeles and Mexico City. His report, issued the following year, presented the reassuring view, compared with Halleck's, that most of the titles were legitimate and would have been respected under continuing Mexican rule.[94] (A Board of Land Commissioners would be created by Congress in March 1851, which would hold—contrary to the promises of Larkin, Sloat, and Mason, and guarantees of the Treaty of Guadalupe Hidalgo that Mexican property rights would be "inviolably respected"—that all titles were invalid until proven otherwise. Many long-time landholders would be thereby despoiled, and decades of unsettled land titles ensue.)[95]

EXPLORATION

Riley also continued his predecessor's examinations of the country for military purposes and to compile information about its resources. In January 1849 Mason had sent Captain William H. Warner north of Sutter's Fort on such a mission and to Sonoma and the lake country twenty to thirty leagues beyond.[96] At the beginning of September, Riley ordered Lieutenant George H. Derby to lay out a military reservation at Johnson's ranch on Bear Creek (Camp Far West) and make a map of the Sacramento Valley,[97] then carry out a similar reconnaissance of the Tulare Valley and "Kerns Lake."[98] He asked Lieutenant A. J. Wilson to gather comparable information along the Kings River[99] and requested Major Emory, now with the U.S. and Mexican Boundary Survey, to collect data at the junction of the Gila and Colorado.[100] In October he sent Lieutenant E. O. C. Ord to examine the Cajón Pass and recommended at the beginning of the new year that he be permitted to explore a route for a "rail or other road" to the Río Grande by way of the Navajo country, upon which Ord had already made a preliminary report.[101] No other part of the frontier, Riley wrote the War Department, required so complete and minute an exploration as California.[102]

THE LAW

What were the "existing laws of California" to which military governors had repeatedly referred and American immigrants taken such exception? Commodore Sloat had only implied their existence in July 1846 when he asked that alcaldes and judges retain their offices and execute their functions "as heretofore. . . ."[103] Six weeks later, Commodore Stockton had been no more helpful in prescribing that the laws be administered "according to the former usages of the Territory."[104] This had not been good enough for the editor of the *California Star*, who asked in his first issue on January 9, 1847, "What laws are we to be governed by?" [105] He was of the opinion that the written laws of the country could be obtained and published, and for the convenience of the people it should be done.[106] He had accepted, however, that Stockton, as conqueror, had the right to impose military law and that his proclamation settled the matter for the time being: until a governor, secretary, and council were appointed, it had said, military law would prevail. General Kearny had added nothing more to public knowledge in March 1847 by recognizing "the laws now in existence, and not in conflict with the constitution of the United States." [107] Nor had Mason, who, while making it perfectly clear he was a military ruler, advised civil officers they were to be governed by the laws and customs of the country and their "own good sense and sound discretion." [108]

" 'Tis said," Larkin wrote to the New York *Herald*, "that Mexico had laws in C[alifornia], but they cannot be found and the oldest residents have no remembrance of them either in theory or practice." [109] They would therefore continue to live in "lawless blessedness," though there was now a fair supply of lawyers who could urge upon the alcaldes the laws of their native states as appropriate to any situation.

The *California Star* was right nevertheless. The laws of Mexico did exist if they could but be exhumed, translated, and published. But Mason had been too direct for that. If there was to be a code, Missouri and New York would be the model, not Mexico, and his *Laws for the better government of California* had been printed, then shelved in favor of "existing" law until it could be replaced "in a few short months" by a more orthodox procedure.[110]

When Governor Riley learned on June 1, 1849, that Congress had once again failed to provide a government for the country, he embraced the laws of California as the source of his civil authority, buttressed by the President's instructions and findings of the Supreme Court.[111] Though the allegiance of the people had changed, he said, the laws regulating their intercourse and conduct remained in force and could not be altered. But the elusive laws were this time about to materialize. They had been discovered at Monterey, translated, edited, and printed in three hundred copies for official use. On July 3 they were "soon" to be published, by August 10 were "in press," on the 17th were "ready for delivery in a few days," and were advertised in the *Alta California* as "just published" on September 20.[112] The *Translation and digest of such portions of the Mex-*

*ican laws of March 20th and May 23d, 1837, as are supposed to be still
in force and adapted to the present condition of California*[113] was edited
and translated by Jabez Halleck and W. E. P. Hartnell (doubtless engineered by the editor's brother, California's secretary of state). Long in
limbo, they now provided the framework for Riley's government, the local imprimatur for his authority, and he would abide by them in spirit
and in form (if not in detail) until the end of his civil rule. Their active life
would not close with his resignation, for the new constitution would stip-
ulate that all laws in force at the time of its adoption, and not inconsistent with it, would continue until altered or repealed by the legislature.[114]
Mexican law would merge and be submerged in the new American
system.

After the returns from the August 1 election were in, Riley issued formal appointments to the four justices of the Superior Court[115] and began
at once to speak of the "more thorough" organization of the judiciary
which had taken place, directing that appeals be referred there.[116] He also
notified prefects and judges of first instance of their appointments (sometimes distinguishing between civil and criminal jurisdiction)[117] and designated district attorneys for San Francisco and the San Joaquín[118] and a
fiscal or attorney general for California.[119] A legion of notaries-public
was commissioned as the legal order took root and spread.[120]

REVENUE

The "civil fund" of California, as earlier noted,[121] had its origin in instructions from the Secretary of War to General Kearny of June 3, 1846,
and January 11, 1847, directing that customhouse duties be used for purposes of the war, including a civil government. Kearny had ordered these
moneys turned over to the assistant quartermaster, and Mason had separated them from other public funds to be spent only upon his orders for
the use of the civil department. After learning of the peace, Mason had
continued upon his own authority to collect duties rather than open the
ports "free to the world" and had reported his decision to Washington.[122]
General Riley, having been instructed to receive the guidance of his predecessor,[123] continued to make collections and deposit them in the civil
fund, pointing out that he could not levy taxes and the cost of running
the government was substantial.

Riley made it plain that the civil funds were not to be used by the military without his written permission and required that sums already
loaned to the army be immediately refunded (which was unlikely) or

promptly reported to him.[124] Unused revenues accrued during and since the war would be kept separate, subject to the will of Congress,[125] and he appointed a state treasurer to take charge of them until the collections ceased.[126] When the Quartermaster General in Washington requested money for his subordinates in California, Riley assured him the civil fund was not adequate for his own use and asked that $500,000 be remitted to settle the army's outstanding debt.[127] Having made his point, he continued to transfer funds to the army for a variety of purposes, taking drafts upon Washington.[128]

Persifor F. Smith was not pleased by his lack of control over California's revenue and wrote Riley about it in mid-August.[129] In reply, the governor traced the history of the fund, emphasizing its civilian character and its indispensability to the civil order.[130] As governor, Mason had taken the responsibility of making the collections (a policy sanctioned by Smith at the time),[131] and this procedure had never been countermanded by the President or Congress. In following his lead, Riley had obligated himself to pay the civil officers, and he would redeem his pledge—Smith could not control his civil acts. Riley would surrender the collection of duties if necessary, but he alone was responsible for the moneys already in hand and would hold them until receiving orders from Washington. The governor sent copies of his reply to the Secretary of War and Adjutant General, with another to the treasurer of California to insure compliance.[132]

After the opening of the constitutional convention in September, Riley would ask the Adjutant General what to do with the funds remaining when the new state was set up.[133] He believed they belonged to the people of California and should be surrendered to the new government. But since the money had been collected by a federal agency, he would learn that it was subject to Congress and should be paid into the U.S. Treasury, with an account of all disbursements.[134] After James Collier arrived at San Francisco to take over as U.S. Collector on November 12, the collection of revenue for the support of the temporary government ceased, and Riley announced that accounts against the civil fund should be submitted before the end of the year. Since specie was short on the coast, surplus moneys were to be transferred to the quartermaster and commissary departments, taking drafts on services in Washington.[135]

Perhaps a full accounting of the civil fund was never made. In August 1849 Riley promised to send detailed reports to Washington "as heretofore,"[136] but upon surrendering his powers to the new state on December 20, he had to say that accounts from local collectors were not all in.[137] And in January 1850, after ordering the residue paid into the U.S. Treasury, he noted that it might still be several months before final returns were received. Congress had mandated a strict accounting of military contribution funds[138]—Riley's case was not unique—but the Secretary of War would tell the President in June 1850 that the governor's promises had not been fulfilled.[139] Collections of only $277,552.73 had been reported, with $978,736.67 turned over to the Army and Navy (the latter getting but $81,000). A special act for the relief of General Riley would pass Congress on February 3, 1853 (requiring an accounting and allowing the President to ratify his unauthorized disbursements), but he would die the following June.[140] There was agitation to refund the money to the state where it was collected, and remedy was sought in both the Senate and House, to no avail.[141]

INTIMATIONS OF CHANGE

Colonel James Collier, collector of customs for California, came overland from the United States with a military escort, a journey not lacking in hardship, danger, and delay. Crossing the Colorado River in mid-October 1849, he reached San Diego on the 29th, where he took ship for San Francisco.[142] Looking in at San Pedro and Santa Barbara on the way, he declared the former to be second only to San Francisco in commerce, the center of a large trade with the interior, and a place where much smuggling occurred. Upon his first day in office he received a welcoming letter from Commodore Jones, expressing the Navy's readiness to cooperate and accounting for some extra-legal measures he had taken.[143] Jones particularly recommended the licensing of foreign vessels in the coastal trade, else the mining population would be subject to the greatest extortion for life's necessities. Seventeen leading merchants also congratulated the collector upon his arrival and asked, in exchange for a strict enforcement of the revenue laws, that facilities like those on the Atlantic coast be provided, particularly warehousing.[144]

Collier declared himself "perfectly astounded" by the amount of business at San Francisco's port. With 312 vessels in the harbor and 697 arrivals since April, it equaled Philadelphia.[145] He was also astonished at the cost of living; salaries and rents were incredible—$2,400 a month for a two-story, four-room house, enough to startle a sedate, sober man. He asked that at least four cast-iron warehouses be shipped at once; nineteen vessels were now doing this duty, a costly, inconvenient, and hazardous practice.

The collector brought with him the law. Jones and the miners to the contrary notwithstanding, licenses for foreign vessels to trade in coastal and inland waters were promptly canceled. Though this might penalize his countrymen, it would benefit American shipbuilders as Congress intended.[146] California-built vessels were to be treated no better; not having been naturalized by the treaty, as were their owners, they too were foreign and illegal. Spirituous liquors could not be brought in cases of less than fifteen gallons, and ships and their cargoes were subject to forfeiture for infractions. Only recognized coins could be received for duties. But what about British ships cleared by the Hudson's Bay Company at Fort Victoria; vessels from Chile, which disregarded the treaty of reciprocity; and those from the Hanseatic republic concerning which he was uncertain? He was a young beginner, he wrote, eager to learn his duty, but was distant from authority, without courts nearer than Oregon and Louisiana, and greatly uncertain about his interpretations of a complicated and abstract law.

Bureaucracy was the first fruit of democracy. Visible and complex, it could be more exacting and unbending than what had gone before.

～20～

Constitutional Government— The Last of the Generals

C ALIFORNIA'S first constitutional convention convened at Monterey on September 1, 1849. The election had been duly held on the 1st of August,[1] and arrangements were made through the Army and Navy to transport the representatives by sea. Though the U.S. steam propeller *Edith* was most unfortunately lost on the way to San Diego to bring up the southern delegates, Foster, Stearns, J. A. Carrillo, and Manuel Domínguez reached Monterey on horseback in eight days. Except for the San José contingent, which came in an open wagon, members from the north arrived in the chartered vessel *Frémont*, which, with its "drunken" captain and inadequate provisions for thirty passengers, took five days and barely avoided destruction.[2]

The delegates had generally been selected from among the "common sense class," a contemporary said, seemed to be impressed with exalted ideas of their duty, and appeared intent upon executing their public trust and returning to their homes without unnecessary delay.[3] A great variety of personalities was present, among them some who meant to get themselves elected to office or gain other preferment. Of the final roster of forty-eight, seven proved to be Californians, six were foreigners claiming a decade or more in the country, and thirteen were newcomers with residence of a year or less. Except for the natives, Stearns of Los Angeles had been longest in the country, twenty years. Seventeen had come to California from slave states, twenty from the North. Nine were under thirty years of age. Fourteen were lawyers.[4]

The "center" of this assembly (as characterized by Josiah Royce)[5] was the Americans who had arrived before the gold discovery, acquired a strong vested interest in the country, and now feared the incoming population unless restrained by fixed law. The conservative "right" was made up of native Californians and some long-time foreign residents who loved the old order and were uneasy about the security of their land grants and the cost of government which might fall upon the landholders. (Southern Californians generally favored a separate territorial status wherein they could control their own destinies.) The "left" comprised the extreme Southern faction, ably led by William M. Gwin who wished to manipulate events toward an eventual division of the state should the southern portion prove amenable to slavery. There were observers present, among them John C. Frémont and Jessie, William T. Sherman (representing General Smith),[6] Peter H. Burnett (who came down a judge and returned a candidate for governor), John B. Weller, Colonel Russell, and Bayard Taylor. The last was looking for news, human interest, and experience.

Bayard Taylor of the New York *Tribune*, author, traveler, and journalist, had arrived at San Francisco on the *Panamá* in mid-August. After a quick trip to the diggings, he set off on foot for Monterey, having learned that in California a pedestrian had to carry his own hotel. In the capital, the convention already under way, he observed that most of the delegates had brought their blankets and found rooms wherever they were able.[7] Old-timers could stay with friends or relatives—Sutter and Stearns were stopping with David Spence—but other members found accommodation in the barracks, in a hotel which had been "extemporized," or under the trees. A few restaurants had sprung up, among them the Fonda de la Unión and Washington House. Larkin was inviting one member to lunch and another to dinner each day, and some of the natives were characteristically generous. The house of Doña Angustias Jimeno (daughter of the patriarch Juan José de la Guerra y Noriega of Santa Barbara) was a favorite resort for the leading delegates, she being a woman of vigor, intellect, and grace, and a splendid horsewoman, with a considerable skill with the lariat.[8] Taylor concluded that, except for Los Angeles (which he never visited), Monterey embraced the most pleasant society in the territory.

Taylor noted the natural refinements of the Californians and that the United States had many warm friends, particularly among the intelligent and influential.[9] But he perceived that the majority of the natives did not "rejoice" at the sudden change which had overtaken their country. The multitudinous immigrants had made them a hopeless minority, extinguishing their political importance; and the abrupt introduction of a new language, customs, and laws engendered bitterness even among many who were prospering under the new order. General Castro was seen at one of the restaurants, "gloomy and saturnine," and, according to a native, meditating the reconquest of the country. But Taylor believed that if the new government pursued a policy of impartiality, as the military authorities had done, differences of race and condition would be obliterated in a common citizenship.

The time for which the Americans at least had long been waiting was now at hand. The trustees of Colton Hall had invited the convention to assemble there. This two-story building, which Alcalde Colton had erected with the fines, fees, and the conscripted labor of felons,[10] had a meeting hall above and courts below. The upper room, measuring about thirty by seventy feet, had a railing at the center, dividing members and spectators. The delegates were arrayed at four long tables, with the president on a rostrum at the end. Over the raised platform were suspended American flags and an "extraordinary picture of Washington," evidently the work of a native artist. The appearance of the company was said to be exceedingly dignified and intellectual, and parliamentary decorum was strictly observed.

There was no quorum the first day, Saturday—only ten members—but a temporary chairman, Kimball H. Dimmick of San José, was elected.[11] On Monday Governor Riley transmitted the election returns, showing that thirty-seven delegates had been chosen from the ten districts. As the relative population of several of the areas had materially changed since his proclamation in June—particularly San Francisco, Sacramento, and the San Joaquín—Riley recommended through his secretary of state that additional representatives be received. He hoped that a spirit of harmony would prevail. "Your materials are good; let it never be said that the builders lacked skill in putting them together!"

Two days and part of a third were spent determining the membership of the house, and the number of representatives was authorized at seventy-three, though the delegates admitted and eligible to sign the finished document would turn out to be forty-eight.[12] Robert Semple from the district of Sonoma was elected president. That some members would be more vocal than others was apparent from the beginning. Among these were William M. Gwin (intellectually the "most admirable of all the unprincipled political intriguers in the history of California"),[13] Charles T. Botts, Henry Halleck, Edward Gilbert (of the *Alta California*), and M. M. McCarver—and as the days passed, Lansford Hastings, John McDougal, J. H. Jones, H. A. Tefft, E. O. Crosby, and Francis J. Lippitt. Members of this frontier assembly would prove to be generally respectful of their fellows and obedient to an accepted if diversified code of conduct; but they would not be dull. There would be artful maneuvering, genteel reproof, and not so gentle reproach; and the more experienced and loquacious politicians would show a marked resourcefulness in leading and misleading discussion. The division between newcomers and natives was sounded early by Gwin, who declared that it was not for the native Californians but for the "great American population," comprising four-fifths of the country, that the constitution was being made.[14] Having arrived only in June from New Orleans and Washington, with the already declared intention to return as a senator from California,[15] he had perhaps never faced native Californians or their exponents before, and he would seize several opportunities to explain this impropriety away.

Also present in the hall were the constitutions of the thirty states.[16] Iowa's, one of the newest and shortest, had been reprinted by Gwin for the use of members,[17] and, with New York's, proved to be most influential. The U.S. Constitution, Blackstone's *Commentaries*, Jefferson's and Cushing's manuals of procedure, and Webster's dictionary were also on hand.[18] Reporters present were admitted within the bar.[19] The ubiquitous J. Ross Browne (staying in a log hut with Halleck) was appointed convention reporter, Captain William G. Marcy (New York Volunteers) secretary with two assistants, the veteran William E. P. Hartnell interpreter and translator, and there were a sergeant-at-arms, doorkeeper, pages, and clerks.[20] There being no printing press available, the secretary brought together all the "handy writers" he could find to prepare working copies for daily use.[21] The local religious, Padre Antonio Ramírez and the Reverend S. H. Willey, conveniently alternated as chaplains. Not only the delegates but staff were counted upon to be well-mannered, and a clerk accused of incompetence and disrespectful language to a native member was summarily ejected.[22]

It was agreed by Thursday of the first week that a committee would prepare and report portions of the constitution for action by the main body, the latter functioning as a committee of the whole.[23] Expeditiously, a declaration of rights was presented the following morning, taken from the constitutions of Iowa and New York.[24] Among the articles added from the floor was a declaration that neither slavery nor involuntary servitude "shall ever be tolerated in this state," unanimously adopted.[25] Northerners were surprised by the readiness with which this strong language was accepted; and Alcalde Colton's assertion that "free white diggers won't dig with slaves" was a timely if oversimplified explanation. A provision outlawing capital punishment was rejected, as were proposals forbidding perpetuities, monopolies, and hereditary privileges, and guaranteeing the right to bear arms.[26] A declaration that "all men are entitled to equal political rights" was inserted but afterwards rescinded, and a provision making it obligatory to provide counsel to a prisoner was also turned down.[27] The bill of rights was received on Tuesday the 11th and laid on the table of the house.[28]

The committee next presented a draft of Article 2, the right of suffrage;[29] and to "every white male citizen of the United States" over 21 years old who would be entitled to vote was in time added "and every white male citizen of Mexico" who had elected to become a citizen under the treaty of peace. Extensive discussion made it abundantly clear that Indians were to be excluded from the franchise (though the Californians objected, Manuel Domínguez of the convention being a mestizo), as well as Africans and their descendants. In the provision's final form, the legislature would be able to admit Indians in special cases. There were to be no property qualifications, the majority as yet having few possessions.

A finance committee had been appointed on September 7 to determine how the expenses of the convention would be defrayed, a delicate matter, and an inquiry was forwarded to the governor. Replying, Riley considered himself authorized to use the "civil funds" for this purpose and said the necessary expenses would be paid.[30] But since his means were limited, and he was responsible for their use, he could not say beforehand whether he would pay all or what proportion. Reported to the house while a per diem for its officers was under discussion (with a proposal that the first legislature pay the bill), Halleck moved that the rates be reduced. On the present scale, the convention would cost $70,000 a month, which he knew Washington would not approve.[31] Few questions touching the interests of delegates received a simple answer, and this was no exception. California was abused by the general government; the laborer was worthy of his hire; they should not beg the governor to dole out such expenses as he thought necessary; the funds rightly belonged to California; and Riley's offer was unconstitutional. On the third day of discussion, the original proposal, in essence, was approved ($16 per day and mileage). Meanwhile, the committee had asked Riley whether he would place the sum of $70,000 at their disposal, to be informed that it was public money over which he could not surrender control. However, he would consider it his duty to pay the necessary expenses as far as his means would allow; and he outlined the procedure by which accounts were to be paid.[32]

The legislative department (Article 4) was next taken up,[33] the most extended arguments bearing upon the formation of corporations[34] and the exclusion of "free persons of color" as residents of the state.[35] The first, stemming from remembrance of the panic of 1837, prohibited any association from issuing paper which could circulate as money. The last, based certainly upon prejudice as well as experience in the mines, sought unsuccessfully to prevent free Negroes as well as slaves from settling in California.

On September 20th, provisions relating to the executive department were considered (Article 5) and accepted with some dispatch, a section authorizing the governor to suspend state officials being later stricken out.[36] A brief section on the militia was adopted without debate, though it would receive more attention upon second reading.[37] The state debt limit, proposed at $100,000, was upped to $300,000 and thus fixed in the constitution.[38] A mode for amending the basic law was accepted without discussion, but in subsequent debate a required two-thirds vote was replaced by majority rule.[39] Over some objection, provision was made for calling a new constitutional convention. Education occasioned much dispute, there being few children and potentially large sums of money at stake, and an aborted effort was made to permit the legislature to allocate the reserve fund to other purposes.[40] Several days of argument yielded a judicial department composed of a supreme court, district and county courts, and justices of the peace, with the legislature given power to set up municipal and other inferior courts.[41] There was controversy over whether the supreme and district courts should be established with criminal jurisdiction, what restraints should be placed upon the privilege of appeal, and what obligations the judge had in charging juries.

An article embracing miscellaneous provisions opened with the location of the state capital, San José and Monterey becoming the chief contenders (Benicia, San Francisco, Stockton, San Luis Obispo, and Santa

Barbara also being suggested).[42] San José won the distinction. Much feeling flared over setting penalties for dueling, but the article survived.[43] Other approved measures obligated the legislature to establish town and county governments,[44] permitted suits against the state, and taxed land according to its value upon appraisals made by local officials (the latter to protect owners of large ranchos in the south).[45] Other sections recognized the separate property of wives (God had made women "frail, lovely, and dependent," thought Virginian Botts, but their rights prevailed);[46] set punishments for bribery, forgery, perjury, and other high crimes;[47] and unanimously authorized the publication of state documents in both English and Spanish.[48]

A resolution that the new government commence operations promptly after the ratification of the constitution, without awaiting acceptance by Congress, elicited several hours of earnest discussion.[49] It gave rise to a long disquisition by lawyer Botts upon the illegitimacy of the existing military government. He viewed the changing policies in Washington as conflicts of opinion, charged that Riley's enunciation of Mexican law contradicted Supreme Court decisions, and declared that Congress had no authority over California in its unorganized state (thus magisterially challenging judgments of the Supreme Court). Halleck said he would himself vote for the proposition and was certain no opposition would be made in Washington or by "any party here," but a good deal of pent-up feeling was released before the resolution was unanimously adopted.

As a side issue, vehement debate also arose over the right of Washington to collect duties after the war, not having provided any government, and whether the civil fund now belonged to the people of California and should be paid into the new state treasury.[50] Halleck believed the funds would be turned over unless Riley received contrary orders, and a resolution claiming them would be only an embarrassment. It was laid on the table.

The first section of the "Schedule" continued in force all laws, rights, claims, and contracts not inconsistent with the new constitution, subject to action by the legislature.[51] Though opposed by some who thought the new state should spring newly reborn from the constitution, it was accepted by the delegates. It was further disputed whether, after ratification, the present governor should be requested or required to issue a proclamation calling an election.[52] Halleck was sure that whichever was done, the gentleman to whom they referred would do it. Debate ensued over how the constitution should be presented to the President, by the head of the existing government, or by duly elected representatives, and both were ultimately accepted.[53] The salaries of elected state officers were established, after the usual argument, the governor to receive $10,000, the lieutenant governor twice the pay of a state senator, legislators $16 a day plus travel, all others to be set by the legislature.[54]

Until the new legislature should divide the state into senatorial and assembly districts, apportionment was a controversial issue, occasioning a great struggle between north and south, permanence and transience, property and people.[55] Population was finally agreed upon as a basis, but in the absence of a census, Los Angeles and San Diego together were to have two senators; Santa Barbara and San Luis Obispo one; Monterey, San José, and Sonoma one each; San Francisco two; and the populous districts of the Sacramento and San Joaquín each four. By a similar calculus, San Diego and San Luis Obispo were each to elect one member to the assembly, Los Angeles, Santa Barbara, Monterey, and Sonoma two each, San José three, San Francisco five, and Sacramento and the San Joaquín each nine.

Disagreement over the preamble centered upon whether it should be brief or long and make reference to God; and the forces of brevity and deity won.[56]

The discussion that was fraught with the greatest diversity of opinion, fervor, and confusion arose over the eastern boundary of the new state.[57] Northern, western, and southern lines had been established by Oregon, the Pacific, and the treaty with Mexico, but the eastern border was undefined. Three lines were initially propounded, one drawn to embrace the "whole" of California to the province of New Mexico, cited as the original Spanish boundary, with the Rocky Mountains as its chief landmark. Another, "limited" line, following the ridge of the snowy mountains (Sierra Nevada) enclosed the most compact area. The third was to be drawn sufficiently beyond the Sierra to include the mineral and agricultural regions on the east side. Eight or ten proposals were in time presented to the body, with limits along the 105th, 107th, 114th, 115th, 116th, and 118th degrees of longitude and beginning on the north at the 117th and 120th meridians and running obliquely toward the Colorado River.

Argument did not necessarily support specific lines—they were imprecise enough upon the maps available—but principles derived from the problems of the day. The predominant objective was to gain admission into the Union, to pick a boundary which would not elicit congressional opposition and postpone or preclude the state's acceptance.

Closely entwined were some hopes, certainly by Gwin, that a large, un-
wieldly area might later be broken into other, potential slave states
(though analysis of voting records of Southern members shows no par-
tiality for a large state).[58] Some argued that if they designated a limited
area, Congress would approve it without question. But others held that
only by pushing the limits to the boundary of New Mexico as shown
upon Frémont's map of 1848[59] would opposition by allayed. Such a line
had already appeared upon at least three maps published by the government; and, more important, by accepting it Congress would be released
from deciding about slavery in this major portion of the newly acquired
domain. ("For God's sake leave us no territory to legislate upon in Congress," President Taylor's presumed spokesman, Thomas Butler King,
reputedly said.)[60] Moreover, law would thereby be extended over an area
where thousands resided near the Great Salt Lake and across which immigrants were making their perilous way.[61] To this the limited-boundary
faction opposed the excessive cost, and indeed the impossibility of governing so vast a region; the impropriety of including a population which
had taken no part in the constitutional convention; and the undesir-
ability, for some, of embracing the "peculiar" Mormon community. One
group held that the new state must set its own limits; another that no
eastern line should be drawn, leaving it to Congress; and there were those
who favored submitting a choice which could be negotiated by Congress
and the new legislature. Not until October 11 (the convention would adjourn on the 13th), and after the "center" had threatened to break up the
body rather than accept an oversized state, was essentially the present-
day boundary adopted. Southerners voted on both sides of every issue.

The first eleven articles of the constitution received their final reading
on October 10, the much-disputed section on the boundary and the
Schedule the following day.[62] Certified copies of the constitution in both
languages were forwarded to the governor, and 8,000 copies in English
and 2,000 in Spanish were ordered printed for circulation.[63] An address
to the people was prepared, recommending it to their consideration and
urging them to vote.[64] On the 12th a committee was designated to carry
the constitution to the "acting" governor, with a request that it be forwarded to the President at the earliest opportunity.[65] The same day Riley
issued a proclamation announcing the formation of a constitution which
was to be presented to the voters for ratification.[66] "The people are now
called upon to form a government for themselves" and elect officers
to execute the laws. If it should be ratified, he would "with pleasure,

surrender his powers to whomsoever the people may designate as his successor." [67]

Also on the 12th, Secretary of State Halleck rushed a copy of Riley's proclamation and the constitution in English to Treasurer Allen in San Francisco, with instructions to print them in a pamphlet for general circulation with the least possible delay. [68] Originally to have been published with English and Spanish in parallel columns, the texts were now, because of haste, to be issued separately, the work to be done by separate presses if expeditious. No effort was to be spared to effect a general distribution before the election on November 13. The Spanish translation went up by express on the 14th, with instructions for delivery of the finished product. [69] Both were printed by the *Alta California* office and ready by October 25, when the paper announced, "The constitution has been issued from our press in the English and Spanish languages and is now being distributed over the country, with all the speed of fleet California horses." [70] Bayard Taylor, returning to San Francisco, would encounter William G. Marcy and Henry A. Tefft, formerly secretary and secretary pro tem of the convention, returning with bundles of the new constitution strapped to their saddles. [71] Printed copies would be sent by Riley to the Adjutant General and by the commodore to the navy, carried by J. McHenry Hollingsworth and Edward F. Beale. [72]

Their labors completed, the delegates—each contributing $25—gave a ball to the citizens of Monterey on the evening of the 12th in return for one tendered to them earlier by the town. [73] Sixty or seventy ladies, as many males, and the members gathered in the upper story of Colton Hall, which had been cleared and decorated with young pines from the forest. General Riley appeared in full dress uniform, with the yellow sash won at the battle of Contreras; and the variety of dress, features, and complexions was striking. The "dark-eyed daughters of Monterey, Los Angeles, and Santa Barbara mingled in pleasing contrast with the fairer bloom of the trans-Nevadian belles." Handsome and aristocratic Don Pablo de la Guerra, the member from Santa Barbara, was the floor manager. The band, made up of two violins and two guitars, played alternately a waltz, contra-dance, and quadrille, and the music—each tune ending "in a funny little squeak"—made up in spirit what it lacked in skill. The gentleman gave the lady his hand to lead her to their place on the floor, both parties stood motionless during the pauses, and he led her "bravely . . . back to her seat" at the end. At midnight, supper was served in the courtroom below—turkey, roast pig, beef, tongue, and pâtés, with wine. The ladies began to leave at 2 o'clock, which by no means brought the dancing abruptly to an end.

On the next and final morning—with Sutter in the chair, the president being ill—the convention thanked General Riley for the kindness and courtesy which had marked their intercourse; and the address to the people was read and approved.[74] Magnanimously, they expressed the opinion that the head of the existing government, during his continuance in office, should receive a salary at the rate of $10,000 a year, his secretary at $6,000.

The signing of the constitution began a little after 3 p.m. "It was a day of beauty and sunshine." The flag had been hoisted in front of Colton Hall. And while some American ships in the harbor took no notice, on board the English bark *Volunteer* (from Sydney) the captain had run up the American flag "above those of every nation, making . . . a line of colors from the main truck to the vessel's deck."[75] The president, in feeble health (recovering from typhoid),[76] came in leaning upon the arm of his son: "R. Semple, President, and Delegate from Benicia," the irrepressible town promoter wrote.[77] As the ceremony began, the loud booming of cannon sounded through the hall as Captain Burton fired a salute of thirty-one guns from the fort—the last "for California." In something like alphabetical order, the other signatures were affixed to the freshly enrolled document Lieutenant Hamilton had been working upon night and day "with a lame and swollen hand."[78] Afterwards, the president made a few remarks, thanking the members for the honor they had done him and the courtesy they had always shown. Upon motion of Mr. Mc-Carver of Kentucky, Oregon, and Sacramento, the convention adjourned sine die, and the work was done.

But before scattering to their homes, the members proceeded in a body to General Riley's house.[79] John A. Sutter, the once-upon-a-time lord of New Helvetia, had been elected to address the general. Short and stout, with a broad forehead bald to the crown, blue-eyed, and with a "ruddy, good-humored expression of countenance," he stood before the general in an erect attitude, one hand to his breast as if making a report to his commanding officer on the field of battle. He expressed appreciation for the important services the governor had rendered to their common country. In response, General Riley (who had a defect in his speech) declared that he had never made a speech in his life. "I am a soldier," he said, "but I can *feel*," and he felt deeply the honor conferred upon him by the convention. After being interrupted by three cheers as governor and three

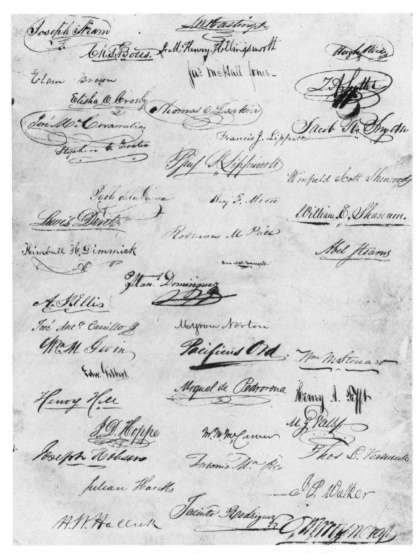

As the loud booming of cannon sounded through the hall, the members, in something like alphabetical order, affixed their names to the freshly enrolled constitution Lieutenant Hamilton had been working upon night and day with a lame and swollen hand.

more "as a gallant soldier, and worthy of his country's glory," he acknowledged the aid which had always been his from the secretary of state: "to him I have always appealed when at a loss myself; and he has never failed me." Wine flowed (the governor was credited with a rich supply), and many toasts followed.

Riley had written to Washington on October 1 that the convention meant to put the new government into operation as soon as might be convenient after ratification, without awaiting the approval of Congress.[80] "I have strong doubts of the legality of such a course," he had stated, but if it should be the will of the people, he would consider it his duty to surrender his civil powers to the new executive unless he received contrary orders from Washington. Before the Secretary of War could pen a reply, Riley wrote again on the 31st, saying the convention had ended and enclosing a printed copy of the constitution which had been submitted to the people.[81] As the Schedule indicated, the election would be held on November 13, he said, and it was proposed to inaugurate the new government on December 15, when he would surrender his powers. Whatever might be the legal objections, they must yield to the obvious necessities of the time. The authority of the existing government was too limited, its organization too imperfect, to provide for a country so peculiarly situated and for a population augmenting at so unprecedented a rate. And he told the Secretary he regarded it as his duty to pay the expenses of the convention. The price was high, "and by some may be considered extravagant," but the cost of government in California would for years be very large.

The Secretary would in time reply that since the arrangement Riley had described might already have been made, any instructions to the contrary might militate against the peace of the country and be productive of evil.[82] Moreover, officers of the Army would now be released from civil affairs, so inconsistent with their proper duties. That the change was not adversely regarded by the Cabinet was evidenced by that other emissary from Washington, William Carey Jones, who had written from Monterey at the end of September that a convention was in session, "engaged on precisely the work which I suppose will meet your views."[83]

The debates of the convention were reported in the *Alta California* by Edward Gilbert,[84] taken down in shorthand by Browne for official publication, and recorded (in journal form) by secretary's clerk J. F. Howe.[85] Not everyone had wished to see the proceedings issued, Mr. Botts for one having "no sort of fancy" to being thus exposed; there would be such haste that if they were correctly reported, it would leave the members in a very unenviable attitude before the country and do no credit to California.[86] The arrangement had nevertheless been approved and three candidates for reporter had appeared, correspondents of the New York *Herald* and New Orleans *Picayune* and J. Ross Browne, a writer and world traveler who had come out in the revenue service and found his job abolished. Since only Browne had mastered shorthand (and because he was a friend of Gwin), he had been appointed and in time was given $10,000 to print and publish 1,000 copies in English and 250 in Spanish.[87] (He would ship the money east in gold dust and with the income from this painstaking and toilsome venture enlarge his Washington home, subsidize his family and relations, and finance a year of further wandering in the Mediterranean.) The *Report* and *Relación* would be printed in New York in 1850 and 1851 and the requisite copies delivered to San Francisco. It would be popular in Washington, with copies purchased to place upon the desk of every member of Congress. Others, in Spanish, would be ordered, as anticipated, from Mexico and South America.

The election was held on November 13 and the constitution ratified by a vote of 12,061 to 811.[88] The turnout was smaller than expected, the 14,213 votes for governor representing about 13 percent of the supposed population.[89] But the season was extraordinarily rainy, and the mud, in San Francisco at least, where it had been "unfathomable" before, revealed a still "lower deep" (and the People's ticket had neglected to put the constitution on the ballot, thereby losing 1,130 votes).[90] On December 10 the returns were canvassed, and on the 12th transmitted by Halleck to the speaker of the new assembly.[91] Nearly all candidates had run as independents, for, except in San Francisco, there had been little organized party effort and the time between proclamation and election had been too short. Peter H. Burnett was elected governor (with 6,716 votes) and William Van Voorhies secretary of state.[92] On December 12 Riley proclaimed the constitution "ordained and established," ratified by an almost unanimous vote of the electorate.[93] And, as provided in Section 7 of the Schedule, he sent a certified copy to the President (by Captain A. J. Smith, U.S. Dragoons, formerly with the Mormon Battalion).[94] It would be laid before Congress.

Still precisely on schedule, the new legislature met in San José on December 15.[95] But there being no quorum (it was Saturday, the votes had just been counted, and the roads were in a dreadful state), it adjourned until Monday. One of the first bills introduced proposed the removal of the capital to Monterey.[96] The public buildings at San José, still incomplete, were less well adapted to their use than Colton Hall, and there were bitter complaints about the lack of accommodation and the exorbitant rates. Some "solicitude" was also expressed about the source of the legislators' mileage and per diem, and suggestions were heard that the "old governor" be retained in office so the legislature might be paid from the civil fund. On December 20 at 1 p.m., the ceremony of inaugurating California's first civil governor took place in the assembly chamber. Burnett "came alone," Gilbert of the *Alta* recorded, "—no pomp, no ceremony—no venal guards, no useless parade of armed men," only the people and their representatives.[97]

Earlier that day Riley had written the Adjutant General, "I shall this day surrender into the hands of the newly-elected Executive, all my powers as Governor of California," and after the inauguration he issued an appropriate proclamation.[98] "A new executive having been elected and installed into office . . . the undersigned hereby resigns his power as governor of California. . . . The principal object of all his wishes is now accomplished—the people have a government of their own choice. . . ." And his military order No. 41 confirmed the end of his administration and relieved Captain H. W. Halleck, Corps of Engineers, from his duty as secretary of state.[99]

The end of the old regime and the beginning of the new may have been a happy occasion, but the mode of transferring power was not auspicious. "It was a most unfortunate evidence of the 'want-wit' character of the legislature," Gilbert grumbled, that they should have forgotten to notify General Riley of the hour at which the inauguration would take place.[100] After obliging the "old hero" to make a journey of a hundred miles at this most inclement season, they forgot to give him the notice and thus deprived him and the ceremony itself of its highest honor and worthiest act, robbed him of an opportunity of publicly evincing satisfaction at the completion of a labor which had been his highest aim, and stripped the spectacle itself of its "most beautiful adjunct—the resignation of power by a deposed government, at the fiat of the people."

An "Elegant and Costly Present" had also been designed for presentation to the retiring governor, a "large and massive" snuff box.[101] Its sides encased products of the placer, "curiously joined," and in an oval on the back of the lid the initial *R* was set in pearls, an exquisite piece of workmanship of "novel beauty." But Gilbert further informed his readers that the gift had been made privately, which he had reason to believe was not the manner in which the subscribers, the general himself, or his friends would have preferred.[102] "This is another one of those carelessnesses which has led me so often into the belief that we have fallen upon evil times."

Riley would, however, receive some words of public praise from the new executive,[103] and before his departure from California on August 2, 1850,[104] his friends at Monterey—who had nominated him for governor, but he had declined[105]—would offer him both public and tangible proof of their local esteem.[106] This took the form of an enormous gold medal, weighing one pound, and a heavy chain of gold nuggets preserved in their native shapes, all presented at a great banquet in his honor.

By a solemn compact entered into by both conqueror and conquered, law west of the Sierra, if not civilization and order, had been democratically achieved. And while Mexico mourned its far northern inheritance, California would—reluctantly at last—be gathered into the North American Union,[107] which had meantime gone on to the consideration of more pressing business.

Notes

For brevity, major manuscript and printed sources are identified in the notes by key words printed in small capital letters (e.g., ROYCE; CONG.GLOBE). These refer to fuller information given in an alphabetical list of "Sources Cited," beginning on page 425. For multiple works by the same author, a hyphen and number are added to the name (ROYCE-1). This part of the citation may be followed by volume and page or item numbers (BANCROFT 1:69–81); and some citations, particularly to newspapers, may include both page and column numbers (CALIFN.3 27 1847 3/2). Correspondence, proclamations, and the like are identified in the notes by author, addressee, and date of composition (Kearny to Stockton 12 2 1846; Riley, proclamation to the people 6 3 1849); if capital letters follow the date of composition (7 12 1848A), more than one communication occurred between the author and addressee the same day. Microform copies of materials in the U.S. National Archives are listed under the abbreviation NA (NA45,M625,R283, signifying National Archives Record Group 45, Microfilm 625, Roll 283). Publications of the U.S. Congress are referred to by their U.S. Superintendent of Documents serial numbers (as in 573-17 282-83, meaning serial number 573, document 17, p. 282–83) listed separately, beginning on page 441.

CHAPTER 1. DRESS REHEARSAL—JONES' WAR

1. Larkin to J.G.Bennett 2 10 1843 (LARKIN 2:6).

2. Badger to T.A.C.Jones 4 26 1841 (422–166 44); Upshur to Jones 12 10 1841 (ibid. 46–50).

3. NILES 12 27 1842 63:243.

4. Some 20,000 to 30,000 troops, it was said, would be required to extend the boundary of Texas from the Río Grande to California and the Isthmus of Darien (CALLAHAN 3–4).

5. ADAMS,J. 4:437–38.

6. CALLAHAN 26; BOSCH GARCIA-1 14.

7. Forsyth to Butler 8 6 1835 (311–42 18–19).

8. Upshur to T.A.C.Jones 12 10 1841 (422–166 46–50).

9. T.A.C.Jones to Sect.Navy 5 21 1842 (ibid. 66–67).

10. T.A.C.Jones to Upshur 9 13 1842 (ibid. 68–69).

11. Parrott to T.A.C.Jones 6 22 1842 (ibid. 86–87); BOSCH GARCIA-1 343–45; Larkin to Atherton [10 1842] (HAWGOOD-1 119); inferred from statements from the Mexican Minister of Foreign Affairs to the U.S. Secretary of State and diplomatic corps.

12. T.A.C.Jones to Nicholas 9 6 1842 (NA45,M625,R282).

13. T.A.C.Jones to officers, and reply 9 8 1842 (422–166 84–86).

14. T.A.C.Jones to Dornin 9 8 1842 (ibid. 73–74); NILES 12 17 1842 63:243; BANCROFT 4:303 and n.9.

15. A.C.Jackson to Paige 11 3 1842 (JACKSON,A.C. 11–13); Anon. to W.C.Bryant 9 23 1842 (NILES 63:243); ANDERSON 41.

16. T.A.C.Jones to Upshur 10 24 1842 (*422–166* 69–73); ANDERSON [103].

17. Jackson to Paige 11 3 1842 (op.cit.); Alvarado to Micheltorena 10 19 1842 (*422–166* 20–21).

18. T.A.C.Jones to Upshur 10 24 1842 (op.cit.).

19. T.A.C.Jones to Upshur 9 13 1842 (*422–166* 68–69).

20. T.A.C.Jones, genl.order 10 18 1842 (ibid. 78–79); ANDERSON 41–42.

21. T.A.C.Jones to Upshur 10 24 1842 (*422–166* 69–73); BANCROFT 4:305–06. Jones had become a midshipman in 1805 at the age of 16.

22. T.A.C.Jones to governor 10 19 1842 (*422–166* 23–25).

23. Articles of capitulation (preliminary) 10 19 1842 (ibid.)

24. BANCROFT 4:295, 350.

25. Alvarado to Silva and reply 10 19 1842 (*422–166* 21).

26. Larkin to Atherton [10 1842] (HAWGOOD-1 119–22); T.A.C.Jones to Upshur 10 24 1842 (*422–166* 69–73); Articles of capitulation (final) 10 19 [i.e., 20] 1842 (*422–166* 30–31).

27. MEYERS 7 says 270 men.

28. Jackson to Paige 11 3 1842 (JACKSON,A.C. 11–13); MAXWELL 25; ANDERSON 43, 104–05; MEYERS 6–7; BROOKE.

29. T.A.C.Jones to the inhabitants 10 19 1842 (*422–166* 79–80).

30. T.A.C.Jones to Upshur 10 24 1842 (ibid. 69–73).

31. Parrott to T.A.C.Jones 6 22 1842 (ibid. 86–87).

32. T.A.C.Jones to Upshur 10 24 1842 (op. cit.).

33. T.A.C.Jones to Alvarado/ Silva 10 21 1842 (*422–166* 33).

34. T.A.C.Jones to Micheltorena 10 21 1842AB (ibid. 33–34, 40).

35. Alvarado to Micheltorena, Silva to Micheltorena 10 21 1842 (ibid. 32–33).

36. Micheltorena to Vallejo, to comdt., Santa Barbara, to S.Argüello, to Alvarado 10 25 1842 (ibid. 24–27); S.Argüello to Micheltorena 10 25, 11 8 1842 (ibid. 39, 28–29).

37. Micheltorena to Tornel 11 1842, 11 19 1842 (ibid. 18–20, 43); de la Canal y Castillo Negrete to Tornel 12 7 1842 (ibid. 17).

38. Jackson to Paige 11 3 1842 (JACKSON,A.C. 13); ANDERSON 43–44.

39. T.A.C.Jones to W.Thompson 10 22 1842 (*422–166* 89–90); BANCROFT 4:311–22.

40. Larkin to R.J.Walker 8 4 1844 (LARKIN 2:183).

41. Larkin to J.G.Bennett 2 10 1843 (ibid. 2:6).

42. T.A.C.Jones to Alvarado 10 26 1842 (*422–166* 43); Alvarado to T.A.C.Jones 10 29 1842 (ibid. 83–84); J.C.Jones to Larkin 11 5 1842 (LARKIN 1:310–11); Spear to Larkin 11 8 1842 (ibid. 1:314–15); T.A.C.Jones to Alvarado 10 24 1842 (*422–166* 81–82); Estrada to T.A.C.Jones 10 25 1842 (ibid. 82–83); T.A.C.Jones to Nicholas 11 7 1842 (NA45, M625, R282).

43. Larkin to Atherton [10 1842] (HAWGOOD-1 121).

44. T.A.C.Jones to Upshur 10 24 1842, encl. explanation of 10 23 and poll of 9 8 1842 (*422–166*:69–73, 87–89, 84–86), 11 16, 11 21 1842 (ibid. 90–93).

45. T.A.C.Jones to W.Thompson 10 22 1842 (ibid. 89–90).

46. Micheltorena to T.A.C.Jones 10 26 1842AB (ibid. 34–36).

47. Bocanegra to W.Thompson 11 16 1842 (ibid. 90–91).

48. T.A.C.Jones to Nicholas 1 9 1843 (NA45, M625, R282); JONES,T.A.C.

49. Micheltorena, proposition for a convention 11 19 1842 (*422–166* 36–37); WHITE; BANCROFT 4:319 n.

50. Upshur to T.A.C.Jones 1 24 1843 (*422–166* 66); BANCROFT 4:328 n.65.

51. Larkin began grumbling in November, though Jones did not leave until January. Larkin to S.Reynolds 11 18 1842, A.B. Thompson to Larkin 12 21 1842 (LARKIN 1:323–24, 347).

52. Interim appointment, Webster to Larkin 5 1 1843 (ibid. 2:358–60); Upshur, commission 1 29 1844 (ibid. 2:361–62); Upshur to Larkin 2 3 1844 (ibid. 2:75); Larkin to Sect.State 4 10 1844 (ibid. 2:91); Calhoun to Larkin 6 24 1844 (ibid. 2:143–44).

CHAPTER 2. ALTA CALIFORNIA

1. BANCROFT 3:667 (1836 estimates).

2. DANA 62–63, 70–71, 72, 203; for other views, SHUR 52, BANCROFT 3:668–69 n.2.

3. Brief biographical information, LARKIN 1:vi–ix.

4. BANCROFT-2.

5. BANCROFT 2:393, 653, 680–82, 3:402.

6. WAGNER 1:13–16; MADRIAGA 419–20; CORTES 298, 300; MATHES 103–05; Cortés' map of 1535 (WINSOR 2:442; WAGNER 1:17).

7. By Francisco de Ulloa (WAGNER 1:20–21, 32).

8. By Francisco Bolaños (ibid. 1:40–41).

9. RODRIGUEZ DE MONTALVO, 6 eds., 1510–1526; WINSOR 2:443 n.1.

10. WAGNER 1:41–42; *Relación* of voyage (BOLTON-1 13–39); BANCROFT 1:69–81.

11. HEIZER; HANNA; DRAKE'S PLATE; POWER; POWER-1; ZIEBARTH.

12. WAGNER 1:91.

13. Ibid. 1:91–92; CAUGHEY 72–75.

14. CHAPMAN 124–42; GRIFFIN,G.B. 63–73; MATHES-1; WAGNER 1:111–16.

15. RICHMAN 64–66; BANCROFT-1 1:29–31; WAGNER 1:156–57; HUTCHINSON 1–6.

16. RICHMAN 67–88; BANCROFT 1:113–70; CRESPI 59–273; COSTANSO.

17. RICHMAN 98–102, 105–08, 115–16; BANCROFT 1:220–24, 257–64, 279–92.

18. ACADEMY 1:20–29.

19. For Upper and Lower California, figures for 1773 (BANCROFT 1:211); CHAPMAN 290.

20. Concerning California's isolation, CHAPMAN 343, 346–50.

21. CHAPMAN 418–37; BANCROFT 2:43–57, 321–28, 330–31, 335–37, 338–39 n.38, 506–09; HARLOW-1 16–18.

22. BANCROFT 3:150–80.

23. Ibid. 4:122–39.

24. CHAPMAN 289–93, 394; BANCROFT 1:211–18, 237–38, 317–19, 333–38; HALLECK-1 appendix 134–39.

25. CHAPMAN 149–50, 388–91.

26. Ibid. 149–53, 385–88; RICHMAN 176–78, 219–27, 332–37; BANCROFT 1:575–99; ROBINSON,A. 24–26.

27. Not that the Indian's life in the wild was carefree, particularly for women (Boscana in ROBINSON,A. 237–341; concerning women's employment, 287–88).

28. CHAPMAN 391–92; ROBINSON,W.W. 33–43; BANCROFT 1:336–37, 610–11.

29. CHAPMAN 392–94; RICHMAN 346–48ff.; BANCROFT 1:661–63, 683 n.14; ROBINSON,W.W. 45–58; HALLECK-1 133–34.

30. CHAPMAN 397–415; BANCROFT 1:387–408, 426–49, 481–91, 501–49, 726–30, 2:20–42, 83–96; LANGUM.

31. CHAPMAN 438–54; BANCROFT 2:194–266, 430–49.

32. RICHMAN 229–38, 244–46, 248–64, 270–74, 278–82.

33. BANCROFT 3:15–16, 47–49.

34. The Híjar–Padres colony (HUTCHINSON, for make-up of colonists, 347–49; BANCROFT 3:259–91).

35. RICHMAN 231–33.

36. Form and practice varied; RICHMAN 234, 287–88, 469, 483–84; BANCROFT 2:675–77.

37. RICHMAN 293; FORBES,A. (1937) 185–86, 188–91.

38. MC WILLIAMS 50–55; CLARK; PITT 11–18; HEIZER-1 11–20. Some Mexicans in fact held office, received land grants, and were respected; and the "Dons" could not necessarily write their names.

39. HUTCHINSON 138; CLARK; HEIZER-1 138–42.

40. DANA 152.

41. BIDWELL-1 38; Dupont to Mrs.Dupont 8 4 1846 (DUPONT 45); ROBINSON,A. 93–94.

42. MURRAY 90–91; TALBOT 52; ROBINSON,A. 72, 73; SANCHEZ 375–78.

43. TAYLOR 141–42, 144.

44. BANCROFT 2:548, 678–80. The Híjar–Padres colony of 1834 included 22 teachers when there were only 3 elementary schools in the country (HUTCHINSON 172, 192–94, 322–24, 416).

45. CALIFN. 9 22 1847 2/1.

46. BANCROFT 4:2–41; ROBINSON,A. 180–84, 187–88; Barron to Larkin 6 3 1841 (LARKIN 1:87–88); Larkin to Sect.State 4 20 1844 (ibid. 2:100–01); Calhoun to Larkin 6 24 1844 (ibid. 2:144). Through the intervention of the British consul at San Blas, half returned the following year, entirely cleared of charges; see Chapter 3 below.

47. BANCROFT 4:273–75; RICHMAN 265–70, 272, 273, 276.

48. CHAPMAN 455–84; RICHMAN 229ff.; many illuminating details in BANCROFT 2:450–78, 510–38, 3:1–300, 414–607, 4:1–41, 192–205, 281–97, 350–67, 401–20, 455–545; for a contemporary view, ROBINSON,A. 69–70, 97–98, 118–25, 138–41, 173–86, 205–13.

49. Plan de independencia 11 7 1836 (ROBINSON,A. 175–76; DUPETIT-THOUARS 4:1–33; BANCROFT 3:470–71 n.28).

50. Previously joined in 1824, separated in 1829 (ibid. 2:676, 3:54, 532, 574).

51. Written 12 11 and 13 1841; RICHMAN 272–73; BANCROFT 4:204–05, 281–84.

52. CHAPMAN 480–83; RICHMAN 273–74, 278–81; BANCROFT 4:285–95, 350–67, 401–12, 418–20, 455–514.

CHAPTER 3. CALIFORNIA BY SEA—ALIEN ADVANCES

1. LA PEROUSE 2:194–235, 3:199–222, 266–67; BANCROFT 1:428–38.

2. VANCOUVER 2:1–51, 433–76, 486–501, 3:324–40; BANCROFT 1:510–15,

517–22, 524–29; BEAGLEHOLE 343–73. Vancouver's voyage provided the best available map of the coast (WAGNER 1:249, 252; 544–5 4–6) and charts of Trinidad and San Diego bays and the entrance to San Francisco.

3. SERVIN 225–29.

4. BANCROFT-1 1:381ff.

5. BANCROFT-1 1:29–31, 173–74, 185–92; OGDEN 3.

6. OGDEN 24, 32ff.; BANCROFT 1:539–40.

7. OGDEN 45–65.

8. LANGSDORFF; LANGSDORFF-1 2:148–217; BANCROFT 2:64–80, 4:158–89; RICHMAN 193–201, 268. Fort Ross was established in 1812 (BANCROFT 2:294–99); Otto von Kotzbue visited San Francisco in 1816 and 1824 (MAHR; BANCROFT 2:278–81, 645–46); and F.P.Lutke came in 1818 (SHUR 41), with many other vessels from the Sitka post.

9. OGDEN 66ff., 76ff.

10. CORNEY 19, 90.

11. BANCROFT 2:220–49; RICHMAN 211–13; CORNEY 121–25.

12. BEECHEY; BEECHEY-1 2:1–87, 319–21; MENZIES; BANCROFT 3:120–25.

13. DUHAUT-CILLY; BANCROFT 3:128–31.

14. BELCHER 1:114–37, 312–28; BANCROFT 4:142–46.

15. DUPETIT-THOUARS 2:77–144, 3:329–31, 4:1–33; BANCROFT 4:147–50.

16. LAPLACE 6:229–70; BANCROFT 4:152–55; BLUE.

17. DUFLOT DE MOFRAS 1:224–49; DUFLOT DE MOFRAS-1 1:251–518, 2:21–71; BANCROFT 4:248–55.

18. FORBES,A. part 2 relates to Upper California; BANCROFT 4:150–52.

19. HASKELL 2–5; STANTON.

20. WILKES 5:151–214, 244–56; WILKES-1 42–45; BANCROFT 4:240–48, 257–58 and n.3; ELDREDGE 339–42; HASKELL 31ff.; HARLOW-1 23–25, 72–73. A map of Upper California (to the Rockies) is found in Wilkes' *Narrative*, and one of the area between Monterey and the Sutter Buttes appeared in his *Western America* in 1849.

21. RICHMAN 293; BANCROFT 2:473 n.43, 3:117.

22. OGDEN 95–119. Wolfskill's license was issued in New Mexico (ibid. 109–10).

23. Ibid. 120–32.

24. Ibid. 151.

25. Micheltorena, decree 7 30 1844 (LARKIN 2:265–67); BANCROFT 4:428–29.

26. BANCROFT 4:140–41.

27. Ibid. 4:35–40; concerning the Graham affair, see Chapter 2 above.

28. 395–1 369; BANCROFT 4:258.

29. Upshur to T.A.C.Jones 12 10 1841 (422–166 46–50); T.A.C.Jones to Sect. Navy 5 21 1842 (ibid. 66–67).

30. See Chapter 1 above.

31. Sloat to Bancroft 11 19 1845 (NA45,M89,R32); Bancroft to Sloat 6 24 1845 (499–19 75).

32. Of the 148 ships in California ports in 1841–1845, 43% were American, Mexico followed with 10%, and Britain came third with 8% (BANCROFT 4:562–70 n.42).

CHAPTER 4. CALIFORNIA BY LAND—AMERICANS WEST

1. GILBERT 14–24; CHANNING 4:298–328.
2. WINSOR 7:479. In 1819 the boundary would be fixed at 42° from the Arkansas to the Pacific; see Chapter 5 below.
3. GILBERT 102.
4. SMITH,H.N. 17.
5. GILBERT 134–35, 140–42; SMITH,H.N. 17,21. The effective discovery was by a party under Thomas Fitzpatrick, of which Jedediah Smith was a member.
6. GILBERT 153–58, with a map showing Pike's route and others not here mentioned.
7. BOLTON 254; GILBERT 165–69; CLELAND-2 271.
8. GILBERT 170–91.
9. WHEAT 2:151–54, 242–44, 245; GILBERT 198–201.
10. GILBERT 135–36, 137–39. Smith's data appeared on maps by Brué in 1833 and 1834, by Gallatin and Tanner in 1836, and Bonneville in 1837 (WHEAT nos.401, 404, 417, 422, 423).
11. GILBERT 171–72; CLELAND-2 276–83.
12. GILBERT 175–85; FARQUHAR 53–58; _461_–174 105–290.
13. "Map of the exploring expedition to the Rocky Mountains in the year 1842 and to Oregon & North California in the years 1843–1844 . . . ," 1845; and after his third expedition, the "Map of Oregon and Upper California from the surveys of John Charles Frémont and other authorities . . . ," 1848. Both were by Charles Preuss and were landmarks in American cartography (WHEAT no.497, 2:194–200, 269, no.559, 3:55–62, 265).
14. On some maps shown flowing across the Sierra to the Pacific, this stream had been proven fictitious by Jedediah Smith in 1826 and was deleted by Gallatin and Bonneville in 1836 and 1837 (FARQUHAR 5, 58, 62 n.3; GILBERT 196–201; WHEAT nos.417, 423). Concerning Wilkes' 1841 survey, see Chapter 3 above.
15. FARQUHAR 54–57; GILBERT 181–82; _461_–174 220–46.
16. FARQUHAR 58; BANCROFT 4:439; Sutter to Larkin 3 28 1844 (LARKIN 2:85).
17. J.J.Abert to Frémont 2 12, 4 10, 5 14 1845 (SPENCE 1:395–97, 407–08, 422–23); Frémont to J.W.Abert 8 15 1845 (ibid. 2:11–12); _461_–174 [3]; POLK 10 24 1845 1:71–72; FREMONT-1 422.
18. GILBERT 185–87; FARQUHAR 58–61; FREMONT-1 439–41; BANCROFT 4:581–85, 5:2–3, 6–7.

CHAPTER 5. ANTECEDENTS TO CONQUEST

1. SMITH,J.H. 1:74–81, 424–32; KOHL; REYNOLDS; MORISON 36.
2. See Chapter 4 above.
3. WINSOR 7:497–500, 505; CHANNING 4:330–32, 5:336–39. For a Mexican view of boundary negotiations, BOSCH GARCIA 127ff.
4. PRIESTLEY 277–80; MERK-3 265–72.
5. PRIESTLEY 300.
6. MERK-1 106; GIBSON.
7. REEVES 100–03.
8. Ibid. 102–03.
9. PRIESTLEY 281–90, 299–300.

10. BINKLEY 21.

11. MERK-1 107; BINKLEY 32–33, 37, 43.

12. BINKLEY 93, 121.

13. MERK-1 133–48.

14. PRIESTLEY 303–05; POLK 12 29 1845 1:148.

15. J.B.Prevost to Sect.State 11 11 1818 (ANNALS 17th Cong., 1st sess., 1822 2136–40); COUGHLIN 19–20, 30 n.36.

16. Forsyth to Butler 8 6 1835 (*311*–42 18–19). The line appears on Duflot de Mofras' "Carte de la côte de l'Amerique," 1844 (DUFLOT DE MOFRAS-1 Atlas; WHEAT 2:180, 185).

17. PRIESTLEY 301; GIBSON 245.

18. Webster to W.Thompson 6 27 1842 (REEVES 102).

19. Alexander Forbes' widely disseminated volume of 1839 recommended that foreigners settle north and east of San Francisco Bay and along the Sacramento River and its tributaries, FORBES,A. (1937) 200.

20. COLLINS 225–29; HAUN 262–64; MERK-2 passim.

21. ELLSWORTH; HINCKLEY.

22. BENTON 631, 680, 710.

23. SMITH,H.N. 19–34; KOHL 74.

24. M.Y.Beach & Sons to Larkin 12 24 1845 (LARKIN 4:128–29).

25. Gillespie to Sect.Navy 2 18 1846 (NA45,M625,R283). After war had begun, an Englishman wandering through Mexico noted great hostility to foreigners, Texans, and Yankees, particularly in the *pulquerías* and barrios of the large towns (RUXTON 40–42, 68–69, 89).

26. DE VOTO 13.

27. PLETCHER 451–52.

28. MERK-1 278–79.

29. BANCROFT-1 1:234–38; MANNING 462.

30. England's claim harked back to Cook's voyage of 1778 and to Mackenzie and other traders, the American to Robert Gray's entry into the Columbia River in 1792, the Lewis and Clark expedition, and activities of the Missouri and American fur companies (BANCROFT-1 2:333–40, summary of approaches, 316–33).

31. Ibid. 2:340–42, 348–50.

32. The incipient "Monroe Doctrine"; MERK-1 106; BANCROFT-1 2:351–52 n.19, 354.

33. BANCROFT-1 2:354–60.

34. Ibid. 2:378–82.

35. Ibid. 2:397–414; POLK 10 24 1845, 1 10, 4 22, 4 23, 4 27 1846 1:70, 159, 344–45, 347, 360; MERK-3 326–29.

36. BANCROFT 3:160–62, 4:211–14; DOUGLAS 7–11.

37. DOUGLAS 1, 27; BANCROFT 4:211–18.

38. PLETCHER 44, 96; NILES 12 17 1842 63:243; BANCROFT 4:110–12, 260–61. The debt in 1840 was said to be $80,000,000, and the U.S. Department of State assured Congress in 1843 that no overtures were being made to cede California to England (*421*–127).

39. FORBES,A. (1937) xvii–xix, 92–93, 199–201.

40. BANCROFT 4:261 n.11; RICHMAN 296–97, 487 n.6.

41. ADAMS,E. 745–47; JACKSON,S.G.; JACKSON,S.G.-1.

42. ADAMS,E. 748–49.

43. Aberdeen to Bankhead 12 31 1844 (ibid. 752); Larkin to Buchanan 6 1 1846 (LARKIN 5:4–5).

44. MERK-1 114. England would have other opportunities to acquire California after war between the U.S. and Mexico had begun, one "an indirect offer of sale" by Mexican President Paredes in May 1846, "the first . . . from a responsible authority," another by President Herrera's minister in London in November 1847 to provide an excuse for British intervention; but by then California was hardly negotiable property (ADAMS,E. 761; PLETCHER 424–25, 542, 593).

45. Parrott to Buchanan 9 2 1845 (MANNING 8:748).

46. WILTSEE; NASATIR.

47. ADAMS,E. 754–56; see Chapter 9 below.

48. ADAMS,E. 756.

49. PLETCHER 430. A predecessor had raised the flag at Honolulu in 1843 and been disavowed for his trouble (ibid. 594).

50. Pico to J.A.Forbes 6 29 1846 (CAL.HIS.QT. 10:114–15); ADAMS,E. 758.

51. RICHMAN 493 n.42; Sloat to Bancroft 7 31 1846 (503–1 1008).

52. Seymour to Bankhead 8 27 1846 (SMITH,J.H. 1:531 n.1); PLETCHER 435–36.

53. Dupetit-Thouars, LaPlace, and Duflot de Mofras; see Chapter 3 above.

54. Larkin to Journal of Commerce 7 1845 (LARKIN 3:293).

55. BANCROFT 4:600–02 and n.25, 605; POLK 8 29 1845 1:9.

56. Buchanan to Wickliffe 3 27 1845 (BUCHANAN 6:130–32); STENBERG 46–48; PRICE 110–15; PLETCHER 197–200, 269–70; SMITH,J.H. 1:445–46; MERK-1 150–52.

57. MC COY 115–17; MERK-1 148.

58. For an assessment of Polk's responsibility, FEHRENBACHER 62–63; MC AFEE.

59. POLK 9 16, 11 10 1845 1:33–35, 93; MERK-1 153–54; Buchanan to Slidell 11 10 1845 (BUCHANAN 6:304–05).

60. POLK 9 16 1845 1:33–35; MERK-1 153–55. In exchange for the Río Grande boundary, the U.S. would assume the payment of claims plus 5 million dollars for New Mexico, 20 million for California north of Monterey, and 25 million for all Upper California.

61. Larkin to Buchanan 7 10 1845 (LARKIN 3:266); Parrott to Buchanan 9 2 1845 (MANNING 8:748); HUSSEY 46.

62. Bancroft to Sloat 10 14 [i.e., 17] 1845 (ROYCE-2 424), to Stockton 10 17 1845 (NA45,M625,R282); to Larkin 10 17 1845 (LARKIN 4:44–47).

63. Buchanan to Slidell 11 10 1845 (MANNING 8:180–81).

64. POLK 2 13, 16, 17 1846, 1 12, 14, 16 1847, 3 20 1847 1:223–25, 227–30, 233–34, 2:323, 325–27, 331, 432; Black to Buchanan 2 16, 24 1847 (MANNING 8:895, 897–98).

65. Buchanan to Slidell 3 12 1846 (BUCHANAN 6:402–06); KOHL 65.

66. MERK-1 158; KOHL 59–60, 63.

67. POLK 4 7, 11 1846 1:319, 322, 327.

68. MERK-1 158; MC CORMAC 409–10; WEEMS 103–04.

69. POLK 4 21, 25, 28, 5 9 1846 1:343, 354, 362–63, 384–85, 397, 438; PLETCHER 422–23.

70. POLK 5 9 1846 1:384–85; MERK-1 159; MC COY 96.

71. POLK 5 9 1846 1:386.

72. Ibid. 5 11 1846 1:391; *485–196* 3–4.

73. PECK 6, 14 n.

74. POLK 5 13 1846 1:395; Polk, proclamation 5 13 1846 (NA98,M210,R2; CALIFN. 8 15 1846 1/2).

75. POLK 5 13 1846 1:397.

76. Buchanan's statement in 1887 (PLETCHER 230).

77. BENTON 2:680.

CHAPTER 6. INCIDENT AT GAVILÁN

1. NEW HELVETIA 12 10 1845; BANCROFT 4:582–83; FREMONT-1 441.

2. *544–5* 15–18; FREMONT-1 442–50; KERN 57–58; BANCROFT 4:583–85; FARQUHAR 59–60.

3. NEW HELVETIA 1 15 1846; SUTTER 30; BANCROFT 5:3.

4. NEW HELVETIA 1 19 1846; SUTTER 30; FREMONT-1 451; *507–33* 372.

5. FREMONT-1 453; a house and garden at Montgomery and California streets which Leidesdorff bought from Robert Ridley early in 1847 (BANCROFT 5:678, block 9; BANCROFT-2 219, 303).

6. Frémont to Mrs. Frémont 1 24 1846 (FREMONT-1 452–53).

7. Ibid. 453–54; Larkin to Sect.State 3 27 1846 (LARKIN 4:270).

8. Sutter to Larkin 12 22 1845 (LARKIN 4:127). Sutter had also told Vallejo the day of Frémont's arrival (BANCROFT 4:583 n.24); Larkin to Sutter 1 20 1846 (LARKIN 4:168–69).

9. Larkin to Sect.State 3 6 1846 (ibid. 4:232–33).

10. Larkin to Stearns 3 19 1846 (ibid. 4:260).

11. The subprefect at Yerba Buena had forewarned Manuel Castro on 1 4 1846 of the arrival of what he took to be commissioners to fix the boundary between Mexico and the U.S. (BANCROFT 4:583 n.24).

12. Forbes to Olvera 1 28 1846 (FORBES,J.A. 3).

13. M.Castro to Larkin 1 29 1846 (LARKIN 4:185–86).

14. Larkin to M.Castro 1 29 1846 (ibid. 4:186–87).

15. FREMONT-1 454; *507–33* 372; Larkin to Sect.State 3 6 1846 (LARKIN 4:232–33).

16. Larkin to M.Castro 1 29 1846 (ibid. 4:186–87). General Castro would tell the Mexican Minister of War on 3 6 1846 that he had given Frémont permission to obtain provisions for his men who had been left in the mountains (BANCROFT 5:11).

17. *507–33* 373.

18. Larkin to Sect.State 4 2 1846 (LARKIN 4:275–77).

19. Larkin to Buchanan 3 6 1846 (ibid. 4:232–33).

20. BANCROFT 5:5.

21. Larkin to W.Rogers 3 6 1846, to Sect.State 3 6 1846 (LARKIN 4:233–34, 232–33).

22. KERN 57–58; FREMONT-1 455.

23. KERN 59–60; FARQUHAR 61; Talbot to mother 7 24 1846 (TALBOT 35–40).

24. Marsh to Larkin 2 15 1846 (LARKIN 4:199).

25. Frémont to Pacheco 2 21 1846 (SPENCE 2:68–70); BANCROFT 5:8.

26. Larkin to Sect.State 3 27 1846 (LARKIN 4:272–73); TALBOT 41.

27. FREMONT-1 456–57; *544–5* 33.

28. *507–33* 372; FREMONT-1 458.

29. Larkin to any commander 3 9 1846 (LARKIN 4:243–44).

30. Larkin to Frémont 3 8 1846 (ibid. 4:239–41).

31. NEW HELVETIA 2 19 1846; SUTTER 30.

32. Larkin to Sect.State 4 2 1846 (LARKIN 4:275–77).

33. Probably of 7 12 1844 (J.Castro to Mex.Min.War 4 1 1846, in NILES 11 21 1846 71:187–88); FREMONT-1 421–22, 461, 500.

34. J.Castro to Frémont [3 5 1846] (LARKIN 4:228–29); FREMONT-1 459; BANCROFT 5:10 n.18.

35. Frémont to Larkin 3 5 1846 (LARKIN 4:227–28).

36. M.Castro to Frémont 3 6 [i.e., 5] 1846 (LARKIN 4:229–30); BANCROFT 5:10 n.18.

37. Larkin to Frémont 3 5 1846 (LARKIN 4:228).

38. Talbot to mother 7 24 1846 (TALBOT 41).

39. J.Castro to Mex.Min.War 4 1 1846 (NILES 11 21 1846 71:187–88); FRE-MONT-1 459.

40. FREMONT-1 460. The flag may have been raised on hill 2146 some two miles north of present-day Fremont Peak (GUDDE-1 114/2) or upon the peak itself with his camp upon the flat just below.

41. Larkin to Sect.State 3 5 1846 (LARKIN 4:230).

42. Larkin to J. and M.Castro 3 6 1846 (ibid. 4:231).

43. M.Castro to Larkin 3 8 1846 (ibid. 4:238–39); JONES,W.C. 63–68; BANCROFT 5:12 n.24.

44. Larkin to Sect.State 3 9, 4 2, 4 17 1846 (LARKIN 4:242, 275–77, 288–90); FREMONT-1 422, 461, 500.

45. M.Castro to Larkin 3 8 1846. (op.cit.)

46. J.Castro to Mex.Min.War 3 6 1846 (CAL.HIS.QT. 4:375).

47. Larkin to Frémont 3 8 1846 (LARKIN 4:239–41).

48. J.Castro to M.Castro 3 7 1846 (BANCROFT 5:12 n.23); MARTIN 6–7.

49. J.Castro, proclamation 3 8 1846 (LARKIN 4:237).

50. Larkin to Frémont 3 8 1846, to Sect.State 3 27 1846 (ibid. 4:239–41, 270–73); BANCROFT 5:13–14.

51. Frémont to Larkin [3 9 1846] (LARKIN 4:245).

52. Larkin to Parrott 3 9 1846, to any commander 3 9 1846 (ibid. 4:244–45, 243–44).

53. Larkin to Sect.State 3 9 1846 (ibid. 4:242); BANCROFT 5:14 n.29.

54. Díaz to Larkin 3 10 1846, Larkin to Díaz 3 10 1846 (LARKIN 4:266, 247–48). Hartnell's translation of Frémont's phrase, "refuse quarter" as "give no quarter" caused the consul a good deal of anxiety in correcting the false impression (Larkin to Stearns 3 19 1846, to Frémont 5 31 1846, in LARKIN 4:260, 409).

55. Larkin to Sect.State 3 27 1846 (ibid. 4:270–73).

56. Larkin to Frémont 3 10 1846 (ibid. 4:248–49).

57. FREMONT-1 460.

58. MARTIN 6; BANCROFT 5:20 n.36.

59. Larkin to Sect.State 3 27 1846 (LARKIN 4:271); FREMONT-1 470.

60. J.Castro to Mex.Min.War 4 1 1846 (CAL.HIS.QT. 4:83–85), the report Senator Benton read to Polk in November and proposed to answer (POLK 117, 11 9 1846 2:219, 223–24; BANCROFT 5:19 n.35); J.Castro, Informe sobre . . . la invasión que el Captn. . . . J. C. Frémont hiso en este Departamento 4 1 1846 (MEX.SECT.DEFENSA, exp. 2163, reel 5).

61. Frémont to Mrs.Frémont 4 1 1846 (SPENCE 2:129–30).

62. ROYCE-3 781; Larkin to Buchanan 4 17 1846A (LARKIN 4:288-90).

63. Larkin to Sect.State 3 27 1846 (ibid. 4:271–72); FREMONT-1 460; BANCROFT 5:18 n.34.

64. Guerrero, circular 3 11 1846 (NA45,M625,R283), to Vallejo 3 11 1846, to M.Castro 3 14 1846 (CAL.HIS.QT. 4:381–82, 386–87).

65. J.Castro, proclamation 3 13 1846 (BANCROFT 5:19–20 n.35; NA45,M625, R283).

66. Larkin to Sect.State 3 27, 4 2 1846 (LARKIN 4:270–73, 275–77).

CHAPTER 7. FIRST IN WAR

1. *544–5* 18, 20–25; FREMONT-1 470–77; SUTTER 31.

2. For tribes probably encountered, COOK 10–11.

3. F.Guerrero to M.Castro 5 6 1846, M.Castro to governor 5 11 1846, Pico to Mex.Min.For.Rel. 5 25 1846A (CAL.HIS.QT. 13:103–05); MARTIN 8.

4. TALBOT 41–42; MARTIN 7; BANCROFT 5:22 n.39, 40.

5. MARTIN 7; BANCROFT 5:22 and n.41; SPENCE 2:124–25 n.6; CARTER 101.

6. FREMONT-1 478–86.

7. Frémont to Mrs.Frémont 1 24, 4 1 1846 (SPENCE 2:46–48, 129–30).

8. Frémont to Clyman ca. 4 2 1846 (SPENCE 2:131–32); CAMP 192–94.

9. Frémont to Benton 5 24 1846 (SPENCE 2:137–39).

10. Frémont to Benton 7 25 1846 (ibid. 2:181–85).

11. HINE 57–62; EGAN 464–77, 492–502.

12. FREMONT-1 486–88; *512–75* 30–31; NEW HELVETIA 5 29 1846; BANCROFT 5:24.

13. Gillespie to Bancroft 11 16 1845 (CAL.HIS.QT. 18:219); HUSSEY.

14. BANCROFT 5:26; *512–75* 30; Bancroft to Gillespie 11 1 1845 (HUSSEY 52).

15. POLK 1:83–84. In his accounts 4 15 1852 (GILLESPIE-3 373), Gillespie certifies that he was under confidential instructions from Polk and Buchanan and that his orders from the Navy were meant to conceal this arrangement; *512–75* 30.

16. Bancroft to Hooper 10 17 1845 (CAL.HIS.QT. 19:49).

17. Gillespie to Sect.Navy 12 13 1845, 1 16, 2 11 1846 (ibid. 18:219–22, 222–28, 17:125–26), 2 18, 4 15 1846 (NA45,M625,R283); Sloat to Mervine 2 1846 (ibid.); *512–75* 30; ROWAN 539–40; BANCROFT 5:27, 200.

18. Gillespie to Larkin 4 17 1846 (LARKIN 4:290); Buchanan to Larkin 11 1 1845 (ibid. 82).

19. Gillespie to Bancroft 12 13 1845 (CAL.HIS.QT. 18:219–22).

20. ROYCE 143–47; Buchanan to Larkin 10 27 1845, to Black 10 27 1845 (LARKIN 4:69).

21. Talbot to mother 7 24 1846 (TALBOT 42).

22. ROYCE 142; Benton to Buchanan 2 18 1848 (SPENCE 2:477); POLK 3 24 1848 3:399.

23. Frémont to Benton 5 24 1846 (SPENCE 2:138).

24. Buchanan to Larkin 10 17 1845, Larkin to Buchanan 7 10 1845 (LARKIN 4:144–47, 3:265–68).

25. Larkin to Buchanan 6 15 1846 (ibid. 5:28, 291).

26. MERK-1 132.

27. Larkin to Buchanan 6 15 1846 (LARKIN 5:28–29).

28. Larkin to Frémont 3 8 1846 (ibid. 4:239–41). Micheltorena had permitted Larkin to fly the American flag before his house, "a privilege granted to no

other consul in the Mexican Republic. . . ." (Alvarado to Larkin 4 30 1847, ibid. 6:134–36).

29. Larkin–Green, articles 1 1 1846 (ibid. 4:145–46), though Larkin could not leave mercantile affairs alone.

30. Larkin to Bennett 5 20 1846 (ibid. 4:382–84).

31. Larkin to Buchanan 4 17 1846 (ibid. 4:292–94).

32. Gillespie to Sect.Navy 4 18 1846 (CAL.HIST.QT. 17:137).

33. Larkin to Leese/Stearns/Warner 4 17 1846 (LARKIN 4:295–97).

34. ORD 58.

35. Gillespie to Sect.Navy 4 18 1846 (CAL.HIS.QT. 17:140).

36. GILLESPIE-3 262; *512–75* 30; Buchanan to Frémont 11 3 1845 (SPENCE 2:127 n.16).

37. Gillespie to Sect.Navy 4 18 1846 (CAL.HIS.QT. 17:135).

38. Larkin to Leidesdorff 4 19 1846AB (HAWGOOD-1 54; LARKIN 4:302).

39. MARTI 31.

40. Larkin to Gillespie 4 23 1846, Gillespie to Larkin 4 25 1845 [1846] (LARKIN 4:340–41, 346–47); BANCROFT 5:13.

41. Larkin to Leidesdorff 4 23 1846 (HAWGOOD-1 55–56).

42. Leidesdorff to Larkin 4 25 1846 (LARKIN 4:348).

43. NEW HELVETIA 5 28, 29 1846.

44. Sutter to Leidesdorff 5 11 1846 (LEIDESDORFF box 2).

45. Sutter to J.Castro [5 13? 1846] (CAL.HIS.QT. 6:82–83); BANCROFT 5:65.

46. *512–75* 30.

47. Buchanan to Frémont 11 3 1845 (SPENCE 2:127 n.16; CONG.GLOBE 30:1 1848, appendix, Senate 570/2).

48. FREMONT-1 489; *512–75* 12.

49. FREMONT-1 488; Gillespie to Sect.Navy 2 11 1846 (NA45,M625,R283); Bancroft to Sloat 10 17 1845 (ROYCE-2 424), of which Sloat did not acknowledge receipt, via Panamá, until 3 17 1846 (Bancroft to Sloat 8 13 1846A, *512–75* 71–72).

50. Bancroft to Sloat 6 24 1845 (*499–19* 75).

51. Marsh to Larkin 2 15 1846 (LARKIN 4:199).

52. Larkin to Gillespie 4 23 1846 (ibid. 4:340–41).

53. Gillespie to Sect.Navy 1 16 1846 (CAL.HIS.QT. 18:223).

54. Gillespie to Sect.Navy 2 18 1846 (NA45,M625,R283).

55. Gillespie to Sect.Navy 2 11, 18 1846 (ibid.)

56. Gillespie to Larkin 4 25 1846 (LARKIN 4:347).

57. *507–33* 373.

58. FREMONT-1 490–92; Gillespie to Larkin 5 24 1846 (LARKIN 4:393–94).

59. The nearest they came to Frémont's 1844 trail, which, some 30 miles north of here, turned east at Klamath Marsh to Summer Lake (GOODWIN-1 69; *461–174* 203–07).

60. FREMONT-1 492–97; Gillespie to Sect.Navy 7 25 1846 (CAL.HIS.QT. 17:273).

61. FREMONT 920.

62. FREMONT-1 535.

63. Ibid. 488–89.

64. Bancroft to Frémont 9 2, 3 1886 (CENTURY 41:923–24), written at age 86, with many inaccuracies.

65. FREMONT 922–23, 924, published in 1891, a year after his death; FRE-
MONT-1 489–90.

66. POLK 10 30 1845 1:84.

67. *512–75* 30; GILLESPIE-3 262, 266.

68. *512–75* 12–13.

69. Frémont, description of California expedition [1848?] (SPENCE 2:xxxi).

70. Talbot to mother 7 24 1846 (TALBOT 42).

71. *544–5* 25.

72. Gillespie to Larkin 5 24 1846 (LARKIN 4:393–94).

73. Frémont to Benton 5 24 1846 (SPENCE 2:137–39).

74. Larkin to Gillespie 4 23 1846 (LARKIN 4:340–41); Sloat to Montgomery
4 1 1846 (NA45,M625,R283); Montgomery to Stockton 5 30 1846 says April 23
(MONTGOMERY).

75. Larkin to Montgomery 5 31 1846 (LARKIN 4:406–07); Montgomery to
Frémont 6 3 1846 (SPENCE 2:143, 145).

76. Larkin to Gillespie 6 1 1846, to Frémont 5 31 1846 (LARKIN 4:407–09,
409–11).

77. FREMONT-1 503; Frémont, requisition 5 25 1846 (SPENCE 2:139–40).

78. FREMONT 925.

79. *512–75* 26; ROYCE 105; NEW HELVETIA 6 30 1846.

80. BANCROFT 4:1–41.

81. See Chapter 3 above.

82. Larkin to Stearns 12 30 1845 (HAWGOOD-1 45–48).

83. U.S.SUPREME COURT 221–53; BANCROFT 5:36–38.

84. BANCROFT 5:41–43.

85. J.Castro, proclamation 3 8 1846 (LARKIN 4:237).

86. U.S.SUPREME COURT 231; BANCROFT 5:39–42.

87. J.Castro, proceedings of *junta* 4 11 1846 (LARKIN 4:282–84).

88. Stearns to Larkin 5 14 1846 (ibid. 4:374–75).

89. Larkin to Stearns 5 1 1846 (HAWGOOD-1 60–62).

90. Pico, proclamation 5 13 1846 (LARKIN 4:370–74); F.Guerrero, decree
5 23 1846 (VALLEJO 209–09a); U.S.SUPREME COURT 222, 232, 237–38; BAN-
CROFT 5:44–47, 65–67.

91. Stearns to Larkin 6 12 1846 (LARKIN 5:18–20); Larkin to Stearns 5
21 1846, to Leese 5 21 1846, to Gillespie 5 31 1846, to Buchanan 6 1 1846, to
Forbes 6 12 1846 (ibid. 4:385–87, 407–09, 5:2–3, 18).

92. Larkin to Stearns 5 21 1846 (LARKIN 4:385); F.Guerrero, decree 5 23
1846 (VALLEJO 209–09a).

93. J.Castro to Pico 6 8 1846 (LARKIN 5:9–10); BANCROFT 5:45–46.

94. PICO 122–23.

95. Stearns to Larkin 6 12 1846(LARKIN 5:19); J.J.Warner to Larkin 6 16
1846 (ibid. 5:32–34).

96. Larkin to Forbes 6 12 1846 (ibid. 5:18).

97. M.Castro to Pico 5 11 1846 (CAL.HIS.QT. 13:104); Guerrero to M.Castro
5 6 1846 (ibid. 13:104–05).

98. Pico to Mex.Min.For.Rel. 5 25 1846A (CAL.HIS.QT. 13:103–04).

99. BANCROFT 5:48.

100. PICO 130.

101. BANCROFT 5:48–49.

102. Ibid. 5:50–51.
103. Larkin to Gillespie 6 1 1846 (LARKIN 5:1).
104. J.Castro to Pico 6 8 1846 (ibid. 5:9–10); U.S.SUPREME COURT 247–48.
105. Larkin to Stearns 6 14 1846 (HAWGOOD-1 67–68).
106. BANCROFT 5:53; U.S.SUPREME COURT 248.
107. Larkin to Atherton [10 1842] (HAWGOOD-1 121).
108. Larkin to Stearns/Leese/Warner 4 17 1846 (LARKIN 4:296).
109. BIDWELL 75–76; KELLY 17, 72; DE VOTO 45, 185, 313; BANCROFT 4:396–99.
110. LYMAN 263–67.
111. Farnham to Marsh 7 6 1845 (HAWGOOD-1 23–24).
112. BANCROFT 4:600–01 n.25, 5:33 n.5.
113. Guerrero, order 4 30 1846 (LARKIN 4:354).
114. Larkin to Buchanan 4 17 1846A (ibid. 4:289).
115. Goodsell to Larkin 4 19 1846, Larkin to M.Y.Beach 5 1846 (ibid. 4:301, 404–06); ROYCE-3 781.
116. Larkin to *Journal of Commerce* 8 1845, to Buchanan 7 10 1845, to M.Y.Beach 4 1846, to Sect.State 4 2 1846, to J.G.Bennett 5 30 1846 (LARKIN 3:292–96, 265–68, 4:355–56, 275–77, 402–04).
117. Gillespie to Larkin 4 25 1846 (ibid. 4:346–47).
118. Gillespie to Sect.Navy 7 25 1846 (CAL.HIS.QT. 17:272); Ide, proclamation 6 15 1846 (LARKIN 5:30).
119. BANCROFT 3:175–80.
120. HALLECK-1 120, 139–42.
121. BANCROFT 3:179–80.
122. *436–390.*
123. BANCROFT 4:114 n.7.
124. Ibid. 4:2–41.
125. BANCROFT 4:272–73.
126. Ibid. 4:379 n.1.
127. Ibid. 4:273, from the Honolulu *Polynesian.*
128. BANCROFT 4:266–72, 275 and n.31.
129. Tornel to Gov.Cal. 7 14 1843 (*436–390* 3).
130. THOMPSON 227, 232; Thompson to Bocanegra 12 23 1843, 1 4 1844, (*436–390* 2, 14–15); Bocanegra to Thompson 12 30 1843, 1 4 1844, to Gov.Cal. 1 4 1844 (ibid. 6–8, 14–15).
131. BANCROFT 4:381 n.2, 385–86.
132. Ibid. 4:602–03.
133. Ibid. 5:605 n.38.
134. García Conde to J.Castro 7 19 1845, Anaya to J.Castro 11 28 1845, Almonte to [J.Castro] 1 14 1846 (NA98,M210,R3).
135. BANCROFT 4:606–08.
136. Larkin to Yount 11 12 1845 (HAWGOOD-1 38).
137. Angustias de la Guerra (Jimeno) Ord (ORD 59).
138. Frémont to Benton 7 25 1846 (SPENCE 2:181, 182).
139. *512–75* 12.
140. FREMONT-1 508.
141. Ibid. 509; *544–5* 25.
142. *512–75* 33–34; FREMONT-1 509.
143. IDE 112-18; NILES 10 16 1847 73:110.

CHAPTER 8. THE BEARS

1. Larkin to Gillespie 6 1 1846 (LARKIN 5:1); Gillespie to Sect.Navy 7 25 1846 (CAL.HIS.QT. 17:274); *512–75* 26.

2. BANCROFT 5:105–09.

3. FREMONT-1 509; ROYCE 59.

4. Larkin, circular to Americans 7 8 1846 (LARKIN 5:119–21).

5. BANCROFT 5:108 and n.19.

6. IDE 118.

7. Frémont to Benton 7 25 1846 (SPENCE 2:181–85); Frémont, deposition [2 5 1848] (ibid. 2:471); ROYCE-4 33–34; BALDRIDGE 5, 21–22; HARGRAVE 4–5; LEESE 10–11.

8. BANCROFT 5:109 n.20.

9. Larkin to M. and J.Castro 6 14 1846 (LARKIN 5:20–21).

10. Larkin to Leidesdorff 6 8 1846A, to Stearns 6 14 1846 (HAWGOOD-1 67–69), to Buchanan 6 18 1846 (LARKIN 5:41–44).

11. Concerning their subsequent disposition, Folsom to Sherman 8 11 1847 (NA98,M210,R2).

12. BANCROFT 5:109–10; ROYCE 69; LEESE 8; CARTER 107. MARTIN 12–13 says Frémont now disbanded his official party, the men elected him leader, and he sent them off to Sonoma.

13. ROGERS-1 42.

14. LEESE,R. 2, 6; LEESE 6–10; CALIFN. 9 5 1846 1/1; BANCROFT 5:111–12.

15. LEESE 10; REVERE 65–66.

16. IDE 125–27; Montgomery–de la Rosa interview 6 15 1846A (CAL.HIS.QT. 1:79–80); BANCROFT 5:112–16 and n.24.

17. IDE 126–27.

18. Montgomery–de la Rosa interview 6 15 1846AB (CAL.HIS.QT. 1:79–81); BANCROFT 5:129–30.

19. LEESE 14–15; REVERE 65; BANCROFT 5:119–20.

20. Hardy, dr. to U.S. 6 16 1846 (FORT SUTTER 31).

21. *512–75* 27; FREMONT-1 520; Gillespie to Montgomery 6 16 1846 (NA45, M625,R283).

22. NEW HELVETIA 6 16, 19, 20 1846.

23. CARRILLO 7.

24. Montgomery to Leidesdorff 6 20 1846 (CAL.HIS.QT. 1:182–83); Gillespie to Montgomery 6 16 1846 (NA45,M625,R283). Frémont had told Sutter that if he did not like what was going on he could go join the Mexicans (BIDWELL-2 520).

25. For a list, BANCROFT 5:110 n.21.

26. IDE 127–28; BALDRIDGE 71–73; ROYCE 71–72.

27. There were many descriptions of the flag, and indeed several were described: Dupont to Mrs.Dupont 8 4 1846 (DUPONT 35); J.C.Montgomery to Mrs.Montgomery 10 20 1846 (NA45,M625,R284); Montgomery to Sect.Navy 5 6 1848 (MONTGOMERY); CALIFN. 2 13 1847 3/2; IDE 55, 130; FORD 12–13; HARGRAVE-1 2; BALDRIDGE i–iv; LEESE 41; CAL.HIS.QT. 10:113; BANCROFT 5:146–49 and n.1.

28. IDE 135–40, 163.

29. Ide, proclamation 6 15 1846 (LARKIN 5:30–31; NA45,M625,R283; CALIFN. 9 5 1846 2); BANCROFT 5:150–53.

30. BANCROFT 5:153.

31. Ide to Stockton [Montgomery] 6 15 1846 (CAL.HIS.QT. 1:82−83); IDE 141; BANCROFT 5:156.

32. Montgomery to Ide 6 16 1846 (CAL.HIS.QT. 1:84−85).

33. Montgomery−de la Rosa interview 6 15 1846A, Montgomery to Vallejo 6 15 1846 (ibid. 1:79−80, 80−81).

34. Montgomery to Misroon 6 15−16 1846 (ibid. 1:85−87).

35. Misroon to Montgomery 6 17 1846, to alcalde, Sonoma 6 17 1846 (ibid. 1:87−89, 89−90); Leidesdorff to Larkin 6 19 1846 (ibid. 1:178−81).

36. LEESE 17−18.

37. IDE 163−64.

38. M.Castro to Mex.Min.War 6 19 1846 (CAL.HIS.QT. 13:106−07).

39. Ide, proclamation 6 18 1846 (LARKIN 5:53−54); BANCROFT 5:159 n.9.

40. IDE 164; Pico to Forbes 6 29 1846 (CAL.HIS.QT. 10:114−15); U.S.SUPREME COURT 248; Flores to Pico 7 3 1846 (CAL.HIS.QT. 1:290−91).

41. FREMONT-1 518; Frémont to Montgomery 6 16 1846 (CAL.HIS.QT. 10:109−10); Gillespie to Montgomery 6 16 1846 (NA45,M625,R283).

42. Montgomery to Frémont 6 23 1846 (SPENCE 2:155, 157).

43. Montgomery to Bancroft 6 26 1846 (NA45,M625,R283).

44. Sutter to Leidesdorff 6 28 1846 (LEIDESDORFF box 2).

45. Leidesdorff to Montgomery 6 15 1846 (NA45,M625,R283).

46. J.Castro, proclamation 6 17 1846A (LARKIN 5:39; CALIFN. 9 12 1846 1/2).

47. J.Castro, proclamation 6 17 1846B (LARKIN 5:40; CALIFN. 9 12 1846 1/2).

48. J.Castro to Montgomery 6 17 1846 (CAL.HIS.QT. 10:105).

49. Montgomery to J.Castro 6 18 1846 (ibid. 10:105−06).

50. J.Castro to Montgomery 6 23 1846 (FREMONT-1 528).

51. Montgomery to J.Castro 6 24 1846 (CAL.HIS.QT. 6:278−79), to Frémont 6 26 1846 (FREMONT-1 527−28).

52. Montgomery to Leidesdorff 6 20 1846 (CAL.HIS.QT. 1:182−83).

53. DOWNEY 129.

54. Flores to Pico 7 3 1846 (CAL.HIS.QT. 1:290−91).

55. Larkin to Buchanan 6 18 1846 (LARKIN 5:41−44); Gleason to Paty 6 18 1846 (GLEASON 23); BANCROFT 5:134 n.18.

56. Montgomery to Larkin 6 16 1846, Leidesdorff to Larkin 6 17 1846 (LARKIN 5:35−36, 36−38).

57. Larkin to Leidesdorff 6 18 1846AB (HAWGOOD-1 73−76).

58. Larkin to Buchanan 6 18 1846 (LARKIN 5:41−44). There had been a rumor in April that some of Frémont's men were about to take a town north of the Bay (Larkin to Buchanan 4 2 1846, in LARKIN 4:276).

59. Larkin to Stearns 6 18 1846 (HAWGOOD-1 72−73).

60. Forbes to Stearns 6 26 1846 (ibid. 77−78).

61. Larkin to Leidesdorff [ca. 6 20 1846] (ibid. 76).

62. Larkin to Leidesdorff 6 18 1846B (ibid. 75−76).

63. [Larkin to Montgomery 7 5? 1846] (NA45,M625,R283), to Buchanan 7 20 1846 (LARKIN 5:143−46).

64. Montgomery, diary 6 28 1846 (ROYCE-3 782/1).

65. Larkin to Ten Eyck 6 21 1846 (LARKIN 5:61−63).

66. BANCROFT 5:134 n.18.

67. Ibid. 5:138, probably including the general's proclamations of June 17.

68. Pico, proclamation 6 23 1846 (ibid. 5:138 n.21; CAL.HIS.QT. 1:186−89).

69. Pico to Larkin 6 29 1846 (LARKIN 5:81−82).

70. Larkin to Pico 7 5 1846 (ibid. 5:104–05).
71. Larkin to Buchanan 6 24 1846 (ibid. 5:72); BANCROFT 5:134–35 and n.18. Alvarado may have mustered some 80 men (Gleason to Wyllie 7 3 1846, in GLEASON 27).
72. BANCROFT 5:160–61 and n.10; J.R.Carrillo to sister 6 22 1846 (CAL.HIS.QT. 1:184–85).
73. BANCROFT 5:164–68; CALIFN. 8 15 1846 4/1, 9 12 1846 1/1; Richardson to Montgomery 6 25 1846, Montgomery to Bancroft 6 26 1846 (NA45,M625,R283).
74. *512–75* 27, 34; FREMONT-1 522; BANCROFT 5:170.
75. FREMONT-1 520; JONES,W.C. 84–86.
76. FREMONT-1 525; SUTTER 36; NEW HELVETIA 6 22 1846; *512–75* 27; Bartlett to Montgomery 6 29 1846 (NA45,M625,R283); BANCROFT 5:170.
77. LEESE,R. 5; PHELPS 288–89.
78. Gillespie to Montgomery 6 29 1846 (NA45,M625,R283).
79. O'Farrell and Berreyesa statements, (Los Angeles) STAR 9 27 1856 2/2; SPENCE 2:186–87; BANCROFT 5:171–74 and n.2; Mason to Stevenson 2 28 1848A (STEVENSON); Talbot to mother 7 24 1846 (TALBOT 43); DUVALL,M. 53–54; HARGRAVE-1 3; GILLESPIE-3 448A; FREMONT-1 525; ROYCE-4 35; Larkin to Montgomery [7 5? 1846] (NA45,M625,R283).
80. FREMONT-1 525; *512–75* 28; Larkin to Commissioner, Sandwich Islands 7 4 1846 (LARKIN 5:101); Montgomery to Mervine 7 2 1846 (NA45,M625,R283), to Larkin 7 2 1846 (LARKIN 5:94–96); BANCROFT 5:174.
81. Gillespie to Montgomery 6 29 1846 (NA45,M625,R283).
82. PHELPS 290–91; Montgomery to Larkin 7 2 1846 (LARKIN 5:95); FREMONT-1 526, the number of guns varies; concerning the name Golden Gate, *544–5* 30 n.
83. *825–109* 71–72; ELDREDGE 2:712–13.
84. Montgomery to Larkin 7 2 1846 (LARKIN 5:95); Leidesdorff to Montgomery 6 29 1846 (NA45,M625,R283), to Larkin 6 30 1846 (LARKIN 5:86); Montgomery to Mervine 7 2 1846 (NA45,M625,R283).
85. Frémont to Benton 7 25 1846 (SPENCE 2:183).
86. IDE 197–202; ROGERS-1 55; FREMONT-1 526; Frémont to Benton 7 25 1846 (SPENCE 2:184); *507–33* 374; BIDWELL 103, 105; BIDWELL-2 522; BANCROFT 5:179.
87. LEESE 19.
88. TUOMEY 1:265–66.
89. *512–75* 28–29; BIDWELL 105; BANCROFT 5:184–85.
90. IDE 197–207.
91. FREMONT-1 520.
92. Ibid. 544.
93. Montgomery to Frémont 6 26 1846 (SPENCE 2:160–61); Larkin to Montgomery 6 20 1846 (LARKIN 5:58–59).
94. Montgomery to Mervine 7 2 1846 (NA45,M625,R283).
95. *512–75* 13; *507–33* 374; CALIFN. 3 20 1847 1/1.
96. NEW HELVETIA 7 10 1846; *512–75* 29; FREMONT-1 530 (says the 9th).
97. Montgomery to Frémont 7 9 1846 (*493–1* 651–52); CALIFN. 3 20 1847 1/1; Frémont to Benton 7 25 1846 (SPENCE 2:184).
98. Vallejo to Larkin 7 23 1846 (LARKIN 5:153–56).
99. Sloat to Frémont 7 9 1846 (SPENCE 2:168–70).
100. Larkin to Buchanan 7 20 [29] 1846 (LARKIN 5:180); ROYCE 79–82, 185.

CHAPTER 9. SLOAT'S CONQUEST

1. FEHRENBACHER 63.

2. DE VOTO 108–10, 132–34; PLETCHER 364, 373–77; WEEMS 97, 103–04, 107–08; MERK-3 362; Taylor's papers relating to the beginning of hostilities, *485–196, 485–197, 485–207, 486–209, 500–119.*

3. CALIFN. 8 15 1846 4/2; POLK 5 11, 12 1846 1:391, 394; MORISON 38–39.

4. Polk, proclamation 5 13 1846 (NA98,M210,R2; CALIFN. 8 15 1846 1/1–2).

5. Bancroft to Sloat 6 24 1845 (*499–19 75*). A letter of 5 5 1845, received at Callao in July, had cautioned him to be on his guard (CAL.HIS.QT. 2:162–63).

6. Bancroft to Sloat 8 5, 10 17, 12 5 1845 (CAL.HIS.QT. 2:165–67, 167–70, 171), 2 23 1846 (excerpt, *512–75 71*), 3 4 1846 (ref. in Sloat to Bancroft 4 30 1846, in NA45,M89,R32).

7. Sloat to J.Y.Mason 10 16, 21 1844, 11 20 1844, 1 3, 2 8, 4 25, 5 6, 7 29, 10 2 1845, to Bancroft 11 15, 19, 25 1845 (NA45,M89,R32).

8. Sloat to J.Y.Mason 7 29 1845 (ibid.).

9. Sloat to Bancroft 11 19 1845 (ibid.).

10. Sloat to Bancroft 11 25 1845 (ibid.).

11. Sloat to Bancroft 2 25 1846 (ibid.); Gillespie to Sect.Navy 2 18 1846 (NA45,M625,R283).

12. Gillespie to Sect.Navy 2 11 1846 (ibid.); FREMONT-1 488. Sloat acknowledged receipt via Panamá in Sloat to Bancroft 3 17 1846 (NA45,M89,R32).

13. Sloat to Montgomery 4 1 1846 (NA45,M625,R283).

14. Sloat to Bancroft 4 30 1846 (NA45,M89,R32); Wood's long report from Pensacola, Wood to Bancroft 6 4, 5 1846 (ibid.); WOOD 368–69; MC WHORTER 4–5, 6–7; BANCROFT 5:201–02.

15. By coincidence, the earliest date Bancroft conjectured Sloat might hear of the fighting (HOWE 290).

16. Sloat to Mervine 5 18 1846 (NA45,M625,R283), to Larkin 5 18 1846 (LARKIN 4:378).

17. Larkin would scour the country for dispatches he feared had not been received. Larkin to Montgomery 6 22 1846, to Leidesdorff 6 22 1846 (LARKIN 5:64–65).

18. HOWE 290.

19. DUNBAR 38.

20. Sloat to Sect.Navy 5 31 1846 (*512–75 70*).

21. Jackson to Paige 7 26 1846 (JACKSON,A.C. 21).

22. DUNBAR 38.

23. Sloat to Bancroft 6 6 1846 (*512–75 70–71*).

24. In the West Indies (BANCROFT 5:254 n.48).

25. Bancroft to Sloat 8 13 1846B (*512–75 73*).

26. DUNBAR 38.

27. Sloat to Bancroft 7 31 1846 (*520–60 258–60*).

28. The *Savannah*'s log records under July 1, "Standing in for the anchorage of the Town of Monterey . . . . At 4 p.m. let go starbd anchor . . ." (SAVANNAH 26); and in Sloat to Bancroft 7 31 1846 (*520–60 258–60*) the date is given as the 2nd, this being copied in the Secretary's annual report of 12 8 1846 (CALIFN. 5 6 1847 3/1). July 1 is given in Larkin to Buchanan 7 10, 18 1846, and to Ten Eyck 9 19 1846 (LARKIN 5:126, 141, 241), and Lieutenant Minor says 23 days from Mazatlán, or July 1 (BANCROFT 5:224 n.1). But July 2 is cited by DU-

VALL,R.C. 109, ROWAN 540, DUPONT-2 419, JACKSON,A.C. 25, Midshipman Wilson (*512–75* 40), and SWASEY 58. With most naval personnel agreeing on the 2nd, the day may have been reckoned from 12 noon rather than midnight.

29. CALIFN. 8 15 1846 1/1, 4/1.

30. Bancroft to Sloat 8 13 1846AB (*512–75* 71–73).

31. *512–75* 40–41.

32. Sloat to Larkin 7 2 1846 (LARKIN 5 : 96).

33. DUNBAR 39; DUVALL,R.C. 109; salutes as given by French, English, and American naval forces in the Pacific, CAL.STAR 4 10 1847 1/3.

34. L.W.Sloat to Larkin 7 2 1846 (LARKIN 5 : 98); DUNBAR 39.

35. ORD 59; Leidesdorff to Montgomery 7 3 1846 (NA45,M625,R283).

36. Larkin to U.S.Commissioner, Sandwich Islands 7 4 1846 (LARKIN 5 : 102).

37. ROWAN 540; DUVALL,R.C. 109 and SAVANNAH 28 say the 6th; Jackson to Paige 7 26 1846 (JACKSON,A.C. 25); *512–75* 41; BANCROFT 5 : 228–29.

38. Montgomery to Larkin 7 2 1846 (LARKIN 5 : 94–96).

39. Sloat to Bancroft 5 16 1846 (NA45,M89,R32); Larkin to Parrott 3 9 1846 (LARKIN 4 : 244–45).

40. Larkin to Buchanan 7 20 [i.e., 29] 1846 (LARKIN 5 : 181); BANCROFT 5 : 228 n.6.

41. Larkin to Buchanan 7 18 1846 (LARKIN 5 : 142), to Atherton 7 20 1846 (HAWGOOD-1 135).

42. Dupont to Mrs.Dupont 12 8 1846 (DUPONT 84–85); SWASEY 59; BANCROFT 5 : 229 n.10.

43. BANCROFT 5 : 228 n.6; DUNBAR 39.

44. Larkin to Buchanan 7 20 1846 (LARKIN 5 : 144).

45. Larkin to U.S. Commissioner, Sandwich Islands 7 4 1846 (ibid. 5 : 102).

46. Sloat to Commandant, Monterey, 7 7 1846, to J.Castro, 7 7 1846, to the inhabitants of California 7 7 1846 (*520–60* 260, 263, 261–62). Larkin submitted a suggested proclamation, a model not followed (LARKIN 5 : 125).

47. Sloat to Montgomery 7 6 1846 (SPENCE 2 : 164–65); DUVALL,R.C. 109.

48. ORD 59.

49. Sloat to Military Commandant 7 7 1846, Silva to Sloat 7 7 1846 (*520–60* 260–61).

50. Sloat, general order 7 7 1846 (ibid. 262–63; LARKIN 5 : 107–08); SAVANNAH 29–30.

51. BANCROFT 5 : 231; BAUER 151, 155; DUVALL,R.C. 109, 110 says 85 marines, 140 sailors.

52. JACKSON,A.C.; BAUER 152.

53. ROWAN 540.

54. BANCROFT 5 : 231; Larkin to Buchanan 7 10 1846, Paty to Larkin 3 17 1846, Larkin to Paty 3 18 1846 (LARKIN 5 : 126–27, 4 : 256, 257).

55. Sloat, proclamation 7 7 1846 (*520–60* 261–62; MANNING 8 : 877–78).

56. BANCROFT 5 : 231, 232; DUVALL,R.C. 111; Larkin to Stearns 7 8 1846 (LARKIN 5 : 115).

57. Larkin to Frémont 7 7 1846, to Stokes/Weber 7 7 1846 (LARKIN 5 : 111–12, 110–11).

58. Larkin to Montgomery 7 7 1846 (ibid. 5 : 112).

59. Larkin to Ide 7 7 1846 (ibid. 5 : 110).

60. Larkin to Buchanan 7 10 1846 (ibid. 5 : 125–27).

61. POLK 9 1 1846 2 : 108.

62. Larkin to Frémont 7 12 1846 (LARKIN 5:129–30).
63. Sloat to Montgomery 7 7 1846 (*503*–1 1015).
64. Sloat to J.Castro 7 7 1846 (ibid. 1012).
65. Sloat to Larkin 7 7 1846 (LARKIN 5:113).
66. Sloat to Fauntleroy 7 8 1846 (Society of Cal.Pioneers, Archives, Bancroft Library, p. 231).
67. Sloat to Pico 7 9 1846, with copy on the 12th (*503*–1 1013); U.S.SUPREME COURT 252–53.
68. Larkin to J.Castro 7 8 1846 (LARKIN 5:113–14).
69. Larkin to Alvarado 7 8 1846 (ibid. 5:114).
70. Larkin to Stearns 7 8, 14 1846 (ibid. 5:115–16, 132–34).
71. J.Castro to Sloat 7 9 1846AB (*503*–1 1012–13; 497–4 646–47).
72. Pico to Sloat 7 18 1846 (CAL.HIS.QT. 3:87), 7 25 1846 (STEARNS box 49).
73. Alvarado to Larkin 7 9 1846 (LARKIN 5:123–24).
74. Larkin to Sloat 7 8 1846 (ibid. 5:118–19).
75. Larkin to Sloat 7 10 1846 (ibid. 5:124).
76. Montgomery to Sloat 7 9 1846 (*503*–1 1015–16).
77. Montgomery to Leidesdorff [7 8 1846] (CAL.HIS.QT. 2:356–57); BAUER 155; DUVALL,M. 33–34.
78. Montgomery, address 7 9 1846 (*503*–1 1016–17).
79. Montgomery, proclamation 7 9 1846 (ibid. 1017).
80. Montgomery to Watson 7 9 1846 (ibid. 1021).
81. Misroon to Montgomery 7 11 1846 (ibid. 1021–22).
82. Misroon to Montgomery 7 9 1846 (ibid. 1018–19).
83. Montgomery to Sloat 7 9 1846 (ibid. 1016).
84. Montgomery to Sloat 7 20 1846B (CAL.HIS.QT. 9:85–86).
85. Montgomery to Frémont 7 9 1846 (SPENCE 2:166, 168).
86. Montgomery to Watmough 7 9 1846 (*503*–1 1018).
87. Montgomery, notice 7 11 1846 (NA45,M625,R283).
88. Grigsby to Montgomery 7 16 1846, Montgomery to Grigsby 7 18 1846 (*503*–1 1031–32).
89. Montgomery to Sloat 7 20 1846 (ibid. 1029–30).
90. Sloat, proclamation [7 18 1846] (CAL.HIS.QT. 1:291).
91. Sloat, general order 7 14 1846 (LARKIN 5:134–35).
92. POLK 7 6 1846 2:13–14.
93. CALIFN. 3 20 1847 1/1; BANCROFT 5:246–47.
94. Frémont to Kern 7 12 1846 (SPENCE 2:173); Stockton to Kern, appointment 7 25 1846 (FORT SUTTER 10).
95. Vallejo to Frémont 7 11 1846, Frémont to Kern 7 12 1846 (SPENCE 2:170, 172, 173).
96. Kern to Montgomery 8 18 1846 (NA45,M625,R283); Misroon to Kern 8 8, 16, 19 1846 (FORT SUTTER 27–29); Montgomery to Kern 8 26 1846 (ibid. 63); Sutter to Leidesdorff 8 14 1846 (LEIDESDORFF box 2). Sutter's commission paid $50 a month, one ration in kind, and an allowance of tobacco and ship's clothing.
97. Gillespie to Bancroft 2 16 1847 (CAL.HIS.QT. 17:282).
98. FREMONT-1 531–32; MC LANE 84.
99. MC LANE 84; Gillespie to Sect.Navy 7 25 1846 (CAL.HIS.QT. 17:277–78).
100. Montgomery to Fallon 7 13 1846 (*503*–1 1026–27); Fallon to Montgomery 7 16 1846 (NA45,M625,R283), to Sloat 7 16 1846 (CAL.HIS.QT. 8:75–76).

101. FREMONT-1 532; MC LANE 84; BANCROFT 5:247.

102. Gillespie to Sect.Navy 7 25 1846 (CAL.HIS.QT. 17:278); WALPOLE 215–16; Dupont to Mrs.Dupont 7 19 [1846] (DUPONT 32–33); COLTON-1 390–91.

103. DE VOTO 200; FREMONT-1 533.

104. CAL.STAR 7 3 1847 3/1; DUPONT 33; Jackson to Paige 7 26 1846 (JACK-SON,A.C. 27, 28); NILES 11 7 1846 71:160/2–3.

105. SWASEY 64.

106. Gillespie to Sect.Navy 7 25 1846 (CAL.HIS.QT. 17:277).

107. FREMONT-1 534; *512–75* 13.

108. Ibid. 535, 561.

109. Larkin to Frémont 7 24 1846 (LARKIN 5:158); Sloat to Montgomery 7 12 1846A (*503–1* 1023); Montgomery to Fallon 7 13 1846 (ibid. 1026–27); Sloat, proclamation 7 13 1846 (BANCROFT 5:235 n.13:28).

110. Sloat to Montgomery 7 23 1846 (*503–1* 1033).

111. WOOD 368.

112. Aberdeen to Bankhead 12 31 1844 (ADAMS,E. 753); PLETCHER 430, 435; Seymour to Bankhead 6 13 1846 (ADAMS,E. 758).

113. Larkin to Buchanan 6 18 1846 (LARKIN 5:41); Biddle to Bailey 12 5? 1846 (NA45,M89,R33); JEPSON 34, 53; ALDEN 47–48.

114. McNamara to Pres.Mexico, n.d., nos. 1, 2 (*512–75* 19–21).

115. ALDEN 48.

116. Larkin to Buchanan 6 18 1846, Stearns to Larkin 7 8 1846 (LARKIN 5:41, 117).

117. Figueroa/Botello to Governor 7 7 1846 (*512–75* 25).

118. U.S.SUPREME COURT 250–51; BANCROFT 5:215–23.

119. Pico, grant to McNamara 7 4 1846 (*512–75* 23–25).

120. Larkin to Buchanan 8 19 1846A (LARKIN 5:204).

121. The McNamara affair: Larkin to Stearns 6 14 1846 (HAWGOOD-1 68–69), to Buchanan 6 18 1846, 8 19 1846A, 8 23 1846AB (LARKIN 5:41, 204, 215, 218); Stearns to Larkin 7 8 1846 (ibid. 5:117); CALIFN. 9 29 1847 3/1-2; CAL.STAR 10 2 1847 1/2-3,2/1; BANCROFT 5:215–23. McNamara documents taken from the archives by Frémont while governor at Los Angeles and delivered to Buchanan in March 1848 (Frémont to Buchanan 3 1 1848, in SPENCE 2:480–81) are printed in *512–75* 19–25, 77–83.

122. PLETCHER 435; COLTON-1 393; WALPOLE 204.

123. Lord Alcester to C.R.Markham 5 19 1887 (CENTURY 40:794).

124. Dupont to Mrs.Dupont 7 18 1846 (DUPONT 30); *507–33* 269; SWASEY 62; FREMONT-1 532; Duvall,R.C. 112.

125. WALPOLE 204; Dupont to Mrs.Dupont 7 18 1846 (DUPONT 30).

126. Leidesdorff to Larkin 7 21 1846, Howard to Larkin 7 21 1846 (LARKIN 5:150); DUVALL,M. 37.

127. Dupont to Mrs.Dupont 7 19 [1846] (DUPONT 34).

128. Seymour to Sloat 7 22 1846, encl. Seymour to Forbes 7 22 1846 (FRE-MONT-1 555–56); confirmed by Washington, Marcy to Kearny 1 11 1847, J.Y.Mason to Stockton 1 11 1847 (*573–17* 244–45, 246).

129. Seymour to Bankhead 8 27 1846 (PLETCHER 435–36; SMITH,J.H. 1:531 n.)

130. DUPONT 30–31.

131. Larkin to Beach 7 29 1846 (LARKIN 5:172).

132. Larkin to Buchanan 7 20 1846 (ibid. 5:146).

133. Polk's annual message to Congress 12 7 1847 (*503*–1 9–12); POLK 10 12 1847 3:190; PLETCHER 554.

134. Larkin to Buchanan 7 18, 20 1846 (LARKIN 5:142, 143–46).

135. Gillespie to Bancroft 7 25 1846 (CAL.HIS.QT. 17:271–81).

136. Sloat to Montgomery 7 23 1846 (*503*–1 1033).

137. Larkin to Beach 7 29 1846 (LARKIN 5:171–72).

138. Stearns to J.Johnson 7 3 1846 (STEARNS box 62).

139. Sloat to Bancroft 7 31 1846 (*503*–1 1008).

140. Pico to Forbes 6 29 1846, Seymour to Forbes 7 22 1846, Pico to Forbes 7 29 1846 (CAL.HIS.QT. 10:114–15, 118–19, 116).

141. Larkin to Buchanan 8 19 1846, to Beach 7 29 1846 (LARKIN 5:204, 171–72).

CHAPTER 10. STOCKTON'S CONQUEST

1. Larkin to Buchanan 6 18 1846, to Montgomery 7 16 1846 (LARKIN 5:41, 136); Stockton to Bancroft 7 25 1846 (NA45,M625,R283); CALIFN. 5 6 1847 3/2.

2. Bancroft to Stockton 10 17 1845A (RICHMAN 528).

3. Stockton to Bancroft 7 25 1846 (op.cit.).

4. Bancroft to Stockton 10 17 1845B (RICHMAN 529).

5. Stockton to Bancroft 7 25 1846 (op.cit.), to J.Y.Mason 2 18 1848 (*573*–17 1038).

6. Larkin to Stockton 7 17 1846 (LARKIN 5:138).

7. BAYARD 87–93.

8. PLETCHER 197–200, 269; see Chapter 5 above.

9. Larkin to Stearns 5 24 1846 (LARKIN 4:392).

10. S.Reynolds to Larkin 6 28 1846 (ibid. 5:79).

11. CALIFN. 9 22 1847 3/3.

12. Gillespie to Sect.Navy 7 25 1846 (CAL.HIS.QT. 17:277).

13. FREMONT-1 544.

14. Stockton to Sloat 7 23 1846 (ibid. 543–44).

15. Stockton to Frémont 7 23 1846A (SPENCE 2:177), to Gillespie 7 23 1846 (GILLESPIE-3 15).

16. Stockton, memorandum [7 22 1846] (SPENCE 2:174).

17. Stockton to Frémont 7 23 1846B, Frémont to Gillespie 7 25 1846 (ibid. 2:178, 180); Dupont to Mrs.Dupont 8 4 1846 (DUPONT 35); DUVALL,R.C. 113.

18. Frémont to Benton 5 24, 7 25 1846 (SPENCE 2:137–39, 181–85).

19. Benton to Polk 11 9 1846 (NILES 11 14 1846 71:173–74); POLK 11 7, 9 1846 2:219, 224.

20. Larkin to Buchanan 7 20 1846, to Stockton 7 24 1846 (LARKIN 5: 143–46, 159–61).

21. Larkin to Buchanan 8 23 1846B, to Rogers 7 24 1846, to Stearns [8 6? 1846] (ibid. 5:218, 161, 185–86).

22. Larkin to Buchanan 7 20 [i.e., 29] 1846, to Bennett 7 26 1846 (ibid. 5:181, 169).

23. Sloat to Bancroft 7 31 1846 (*503*–1 1008); CALIFN. 8 15 1846 3/1 says the 28th; Larkin to Dimond 7 29 [i.e., 28] 1846 (LARKIN 5:171).

24. Stockton, address 7 29 1846 (LARKIN 5:175–77).

25. Stockton to Bancroft 7 28 1846 (*503*–1 1035).

26. Larkin to Buchanan 7 29 1846 (LARKIN 5:181).

27. DUVALL,M. 45.

28. F.D.Atherton to Larkin 12 3 1846 (LARKIN 5:290).

29. Sloat to Bancroft 7 31 1846 (*503*–1 1006–08).

30. Sloat to Bancroft 8 10 1846 (*537*–1 1034).

31. Stockton to J.Y.Mason 2 18 1848 (*503*–1 1037–54).

32. Stockton to Montgomery 7 29 1846AB (NA45,M625,R283).

33. Larkin to Leese 7 29, 9 21 1846, to Vallejo 7 29 1846 (LARKIN 5:178–79, 242–43).

34. Concerning the release of the prisoners: Vallejo to Frémont [7 11 1846] (SPENCE 2:170, 172); Stockton to Montgomery 7 27 1846 (NA45,M625,R283), to Vallejo 7 29 1846 (LEESE 67); Montgomery to Kern 7 29 1846 (FORT SUTTER 32); Montgomery, orders [8 1? 1846] (LEESE 72); Kern to Montgomery 8 2 1846 (NA45,M625,R283), 8 3 1846 (FORT SUTTER 76); Montgomery to Vallejo 8 3 1846 (LEESE 73); Prudon/S.Vallejo/Leese to Kern 8 5 1846 (NA45,M625,R283); Bartlett to Vallejo 8 6 1846 (LEESE 74–75); Ridley to Montgomery 8 7 1846, Vallejo to Montgomery 8 8 1846 (NA45,M625,R283); Leese to Larkin 8 12 1846 (LARKIN 5:195); Larkin to Vallejo 8 24 1846 (VALLEJO 233); Vallejo to Frémont 2 15 1847 (SPENCE 2:304–05).

35. *507*–33 374–75.

36. FREMONT-1 544.

37. Ibid. 561–62; regarding his actual march in November–December 1846, see Chapter 14 below.

38. See Chapter 7 above.

39. Sloat to J.Castro 7 7 1846, J.Castro to Sloat 7 9 1846AB (*503*–1 1012–13; 497–4 646–47; BANCROFT 5:143–44, 261–62.

40. J.Castro to Pico 7 11 1846 (CAL.HIS.QT. 3:185–86).

41. Pico to Mex.Min.For.Rel. 7 13 1846 (ibid. 13:109–10).

42. BANCROFT 5:263 n.9.

43. Ibid. 5:264 n.10.

44. J.Castro to Pico 8 9 1846B (CAL.HIS.QT. 13:118).

45. CALIFN. 8 15 1846 2/2.

46. Dupont to Stockton 7 29 1846 (DUPONT-1 2–3).

47. Dupont to Mrs.Dupont 8 4 1846 (DUPONT 34, 36–37), to Stockton 7 29 1846 (DUPONT-1 1); Larkin to Dupont 8 16 1846 (LARKIN 5:201).

48. Dupont to Stockton 7 31 1846 (DUPONT-1 4–5); FREMONT-1 563, 565.

49. BANCROFT 5:264 n.10.

50. Dupont to Stockton 7 29, 31 1846 (DUPONT-1 3, 4–5).

51. BANCROFT 5:282–83 n.35.

52. Dupont to Mrs.Dupont 8 4 1846 (DUPONT 40–41).

53. Dupont to Mrs.Dupont 8 12 1846 (ibid. 45–46); Stockton to Frémont 8 6 1846 (SPENCE 2:188–89); Gillespie to Bancroft 2 16 1847 (CAL.HIS.QT. 17:282).

54. Mervine to Montgomery 8 1 1846A (NA45,M625,R283). Larkin would afterwards submit an expense account of $376 for the expedition (Larkin, travel account 6 1 1847, in NA45,M625,R285).

55. W.Richardson to Montgomery 8 13 1846 (NA45,M625,R283); BAUER 167; BANCROFT-2 250.

56. Stockton to Bancroft 2 18 1848 (*503*–1 1040).

57. Larkin to Stearns 8 [6?] 1846AB (LARKIN 5:184–86). The crews of the *Congress, Cyane, Portsmouth*, and *Savannah* totaled 1,250 men, which, with the

Warren (at Mazatlán) and *Erie* (Sandwich Islands) and Frémont's 165 men, brought the number to 1,650, plus the marines.

58. Larkin to Stearns 8 7 1846 (LARKIN 5:187).

59. BANCROFT 5:268–69; BERNAL 4.

60. De la Guerra/Flores to Stockton and reply 8 7 1846 (*531*–31 3–4), Stockton to Larkin/Schenck 8 7 1846 (LARKIN 5:188).

61. J.Castro to Comd. U.S.Naval forces 8 7 1846 (*531*–31 4).

62. Stockton to J.Castro 8 7 1846 (ibid. 5).

63. Stockton to J.Y.Mason 2 18 1848 (*503*–1 1040–42).

64. J.Castro to Stockton 8 9 1846 (*531*–31 5–6).

65. Stockton to Bancroft 9 18 1846 (ibid. 2).

66. J.Castro to Forbes 8 9 1846, to Pico 8 9 1846A (CAL.HIS.QT. 10:119, 13:116–17).

67. J.Castro to Pico 8 9 1846B (ibid. 13:118–19); PICO 132. Pico would claim 400 volunteers but not enough munitions to last two hours (Pico to Mex.Min.For.Rel. 10 27 1846, in CAL.HIS.QT. 13:112).

68. J.Castro, proclamation 8 9 1846 (ibid. 13:117–18; another translation, ibid. 10:122).

69. J.Castro, proclamation 8 10 1846 (SHINN 396).

70. Pico, proclamation 8 10 1846A (CAL.HIS.QT. 13:122–23).

71. T.Frazer to Larkin 8 27 1846 (LARKIN 5:225).

72. Pico to Forbes/Lataillade/Gasquet 8 10 1846 (CAL.HIS.QT. 13:121–22).

73. Assembly, proceedings 8 10 1846, Pico to Mex.Min.For.Rel. 3 29 1848 (ibid. 119–20, 145–46); PICO 133–34.

74. Pico to Mex.Min.For.Rel. 10 27 1846 (CAL.HIS.QT. 13:114); BANCROFT 5:275.

75. BANCROFT 5:277–78 and n.25.

76. Ibid. 5:278 n.26; PICO 138–41; and see Chapter 18 below.

77. Stockton to Frémont 8 6, 9 1846 (SPENCE 2:188–89, 190); Dupont to Mrs.Dupont 8 12 1846 (DUPONT 45–46); FREMONT-1 566.

78. POLK 8 10 1846 2:76.

79. Larkin to Buchanan 8 23 1846AB (LARKIN 5:214–17); Stockton to Bancroft 8 28 1846 (499–19 166–67); PHELPS 300–03. Larkin and Stockton speculated that there were 500 of the enemy, with plenty of armament and powder.

80. Stockton to Larkin 8 11 1846 (LARKIN 5:194), to Bancroft 9 18 1846 (*531*–31 1–2).

81. Larkin to Buchanan 8 23 1846AB (LARKIN 5:215, 217).

82. WILSON 395–96.

83. SPENCE 2:191; Stockton to Bancroft 9 18 1846 (*531*–31 1–2).

84. FREMONT-1 565; Talbot to mother 8 29 1846 (TALBOT 49).

85. Dupont to Mrs.Dupont 8 17 1846 (DUPONT 50).

86. Stockton to Bancroft 8 22 1846 (NA45,M89,R33), 8 28 1846 (499–19 669).

87. Stockton to Montgomery 8 14 1846 (NA45,M625,R283).

88. Stockton, proclamation 8 17 1846A (499–19 107–08). He first signed as governor in Stockton to Montgomery 8 14 1846.

89. Stockton to Polk 8 26 1846 (SPENCE 2:193–95).

90. CALIFN. 8 15 1846 3/1, 8 22 1846 4/1; BANCROFT 5:544–54.

91. Spear to Larkin 8 30 1846, Leidesdorff to Larkin 4 15 1847, Sutter to Larkin 10 29 1847 (LARKIN 5:227, 6:102, 7:46–47).

92. Stockton to Montgomery 8 17, 24 1846 (NA45,M625,R283), to Gillespie 8 18 1846 (GILLESPIE-3).

93. CALIFN. 9 5 1846 2/1; CAL.STAR 1 9–23 1847 4/1, comment 1 16 1847 3/1-2; Stockton, proclamation 8 17 1846B (CALIFN. 9 5 1846 2/2).

94. Stockton to Polk 8 26 1846 (SPENCE 2:193–95).

95. Larkin to Sect.State 9 8 1846 (LARKIN 5:232–33); SPENCE 2:196 n.3.

96. Stockton to Bancroft 8 28 1846, [Form of govt. ca. 8 22 1846] (499–19 166–67, 109–10); Larkin to Buchanan 8 23 1846B (LARKIN 5:219–20).

97. Stockton to Frémont 8 24 1846 (SPENCE 2:192–93).

98. Stockton to Montgomery 9 29 1846 (NA45,M625,R284); Montgomery to Stockton 9 30 1846 (MONTGOMERY).

99. Stockton, proclamation 1 18 1847 (VALLEJO 260); BANCROFT 5:284–85. Stockton's proclamation to the people of 8 17 1846 (CALIFN. 9 5 1846 2/1) referred to a proposed governor, secretary, and council.

100. Stockton to Bancroft 9 19 1846 (NA45,M89,R33); *507–33* 182.

101. Dupont to Mrs.Dupont 8 17 1846 (DUPONT 49); Stockton to Bancroft 8 28 1846 (499–19 669); Polk, proclamation 5 13 1846 (CALIFN. 8 15 1846 1/2); Bancroft to Sloat 5 13 1846 (499–19 77); BANCROFT 5:289 n.1. The *Warren* had reached Monterey on the 12th.

102. Stockton to Bancroft 9 18 1846 (*531–31* 1–2).

103. Stockton, to whom . . . 8 19 1846 (*497–4* 670–71); CALIFN. 9 17 [i.e., 19] 1846 3/2; Stockton to Hull 8 20 1846, to Dupont 8 20 1846 (*497–4* 673, 674).

104. Stockton, circular 9 2 1846 (CALIFN. 9 17 [i.e., 19] 1846 3/2).

105. Larkin to Buchanan 8 22 1846 (LARKIN 5:213).

106. Stockton to Frémont 8 27 1846 (SPENCE 2:196, 198); Talbot to mother 8 29 1846 (TALBOT 50); Frémont to Buchanan 3 1 1848 (SPENCE 2:480–81).

107. Stockton to Bancroft 8 28 1846 (*497–4* 668).

108. Stockton to Frémont 8 24, 31, 9 1 1846 (SPENCE 2:192–93, 198, 199–200).

109. Larkin to Howard 3 1 1847 (LARKIN 6:32–33).

110. Stockton to Bancroft 9 18 1846 (*531–31* 1–2).

111. Stockton to Bancroft 10 1 1846, to Mervine 9 19 1846 (ibid. 13–14).

112. Stockton to Frémont 9 28 1846 (SPENCE 2:204–05).

113. FREMONT-1 572.

114. Stockton, general order 9 2 1846 (*520–60* 44), appointment, Frémont 9 2 1846 (*507–33* 110).

115. Stockton to Gillespie 8 31 1846 (*520–60* 43–44), proclamation 8 31 1846 (GILLESPIE-3 38); BANCROFT 5:290, 295.

116. Stockton to J.Y.Mason 2 18 1848 (*503–1* 1045).

117. Stockton to Bancroft 9 18 1846 (*531–31* 1–2); Bancroft to Sloat 5 15 1846 (*520–60* 235–36).

118. Larkin to Buchanan 9 8 1846 (LARKIN 5:232–33).

119. CALIFN. 9 17 [i.e., 19] 1846 2/1.

120. Stockton to Bancroft 9 19 1846B (*531–31* 9), to Montgomery 9 20 1846 (NA45,M625,R284); CALIFN. 9 17 [i.e., 19] 1846 1, 4.

121. CALIFN. 9 26 1846 2/1, 3/1, 10 10 1846 2/1; Stockton to Bancroft 10

1 1846 (*531*–31 113–14). *Concerning the Walla Walla "invasion"*: Kern to Montgomery 9 8 1846AB (NA45,M625,R284); Montgomery to Kern 9 10 1846 (FORT SUTTER 65), to Vallejo 9 10 1846 (VALLEJO 237); Sutter to Montgomery 9 18 1846, Stockton to Montgomery 9 20 1846, Kern to Montgomery 9 22 1846, Vallejo to Montgomery 9 23 1846, Kern to Montgomery 9 29 1846 (NA45, M625,R284); Stockton to Bancroft 10 1 1846 (*531*–31 13); Frémont to Kern 10 22, 11 20 1846 (SPENCE 2:209, 229–30).

122. CALIFN. 10 3 1846 3/1, 10 10 1846 2/1, 10 17 1846 2/2, 10 24 1846 2/1, 10 31 1846 2/2–3/1; Stockton to Gillespie 10 1 1846 (GILLESPIE-3 104); Gillespie to Bancroft 2 16 1847 (CAL.HIS.QT. 17:328–29); Stockton to J.Y.Mason 2 18 1848 (*503*–1 1045). There is uncertainty about the time of the courier's arrival (BANCROFT 5:304 n.15).

123. Stockton to Larkin 10 1 1846 (LARKIN 5:256), to Mervine 10 2 1846 (NA45,M625,R284).

124. Stockton to Frémont 10 1 1846 (SPENCE 2:206), to Bancroft 11 23 1846 (*531*–31 10), to J.Y.Mason 2 18 1848 (*503*–1 1045); FREMONT-1 573. Frémont picked September 30, when he was "transferred to the military," as the date of his separation from the Topographical Service (SPENCE 2:361 n.1).

125. Dupont to Mrs.Dupont 12 8 1846 (DUPONT 83).

126. CALIFN. 10 24 1846 1, 4, 2/1; BRYANT 330–32; DOWNEY 149–51; DU-VALL,M. 60; contemporary program reproduced in KEMBLE,E.C.-1 53; GREEN-WOOD item 86; BANCROFT 5:295–96.

CHAPTER 11. PARADISE LOST—GILLESPIE'S FALL

1. Stockton, proclamation 8 31 1846 (GILLESPIE-3 38); Gillespie to Bancroft 2 16 1847 (CAL.HIS.QT. 17:283); TALBOT 48–49.

2. Gillespie to Bancroft 2 16 1847 (CAL.HIS.QT. 17:284, 325).

3. Stockton, proclamation 8 17 1846 (*499*–19 107–08).

4. Stockton to Gillespie 8 31 1846 (*531*–31 7–8).

5. FREMONT-1 573–74.

6. Gillespie to Bancroft 2 16 1847 (CAL.HIS.QT. 17:283–84).

7. Gillespie to Bancroft 2 16 1847 (the original in NA45,M625,R284; CAL.HIS.QT. 17:281–84, 325–46).

8. Gillespie to Bancroft 11 16 1845 (CAL.HIS.QT. 18:219). Ironically, no portrait of this earnest and egocentric character seems to have survived.

9. Gillespie to Sect.Navy 4 18, 7 25 1846 (ibid. 17:136–37, 139, 279–80).

10. GILLESPIE-3 448B.

11. BANCROFT 5:306–07 n.19; ROYCE 188 n.1.

12. WILSON 397–98; WARNER 32; Dupont to Mrs.Dupont 12 8 1846 (DUPONT 87, 90–91).

13. Larkin to Mrs.Larkin 12 14 1846 (LARKIN 5:311–12); Gillespie's actions would be lauded in CAL.STAR 6 19 1847 2/3.

14. GARCIA 9.

15. Olivares to S.Vallejo 9 6 1846 (LARKIN 5:232); BANCROFT 5:308 n.20.

16. BANCROFT 5:305–08.

17. Ibid. 5:317.

18. Gillespie to Bancroft 2 16 1847 (CAL.HIS.QT. 17:325).

19. Ibid. 17:326–27, 328–29; John Brown, receipt for $30, 9 24 1846 (GILLESPIE-3 88).

20. BANCROFT 5:310 n.22; *531*–31 15–16.

21. Gillespie to Bancroft 2 16 1847 (CAL.HIS.QT. 17:327–29).

22. WILSON 401.

23. Frémont to Gillespie 9 7 1846 (SPENCE 2:202–03); WILSON 397–401; BANCROFT 5:311–14.

24. FOSTER 25–26.

25. WILSON 402; Gillespie to Bancroft 2 16 1847 (CAL.HIS.QT. 17:330).

26. CAL.HIS.QT. 17:331.

27. Flores/Gillespie, articles of capitulation 9 29 1846 (RICHMAN 493–94 n.48; MEX.SECT.DEFENSA, exp. 2199, reel 5, 179–201; NA45,M625,R284).

28. Gillespie to Bancroft 2 16 1847 (CAL.HIS.QT. 17:331–32).

29. BANCROFT 5:315.

30. GILLESPIE-3 91 lists U.S. property left at Los Angeles.

31. Gillespie to Bancroft 2 16 1847 (CAL.HIS.QT. 17:332).

32. Flores to Gillespie 10 4 1846, Gillespie to Flores 10 2, 3, 4 1846 (RICHMAN 494–95 n.48, summaries).

33. Gillespie to Bancroft 2 16 1847 (CAL.HIS.QT. 17:333–34).

34. DUVALL,R.C. 115.

35. Gillespie to Bancroft 2 16 1847 (CAL.HIS.QT. 17:334); Marston to Graham 5 1 1851 (NA45,M625,R284); CRAVEN-1 30.

36. Mervine to Stockton 10 25 1846 (NA45,M89,R33); DUVALL,R.C. 115; H.W.Queen, adjutant's report 10 7–8 1846 (NA45,M625,R284); DRIVER 340–49.

37. Stockton to Mervine 10 2 1846 (NA45,M625,R284).

38. Gillespie to Bancroft 2 16 1847 (CAL.HIS.QT. 17:335–38); Marston to Graham 5 1 1851 (NA45,M625,R284); DUVALL,R.C. 116–18; BANCROFT 5:319–20.

39. DRIVER 343.

40. Stockton to Bancroft 11 23 1846 (*531*–31 11).

41. DUVALL,R.C. 118; DUVALL,M. 62; Mervine to Stockton 10 25 1846 (NA45,M89,R33); Marston to Graham 5 1 1851 (NA45,M625,R284); CALIFN. 10 24 1846 2/1, 2 13 1847 2/2–3/1; BANCROFT 5:319 n.38).

42. Mervine to Stockton 10 9 1846 (NA45,M89,R33).

43. Stockton to Frémont 10 1 1846 (SPENCE 2:206).

44. Watson to Montgomery 10 20 1846 (NA45,M625,R284).

45. Frémont to Kern 10 4 1846 (FORT SUTTER 78); Kern to Montgomery 10 20 1846 (NA45,M625,R284).

46. Stockton to Montgomery 10 10 1846 (NA45,M625,R284); FREMONT-1 574–75.

47. Vallejo to Montgomery 10 15 1846, Colton to Montgomery 10 13 1846, Griffith to Montgomery 10 15 1846, Weber to Montgomery 10 17, 18 1846 (NA45,M625,R284).

48. Weber to Montgomery 10 21, 23 1846 (ibid.).

49. DUVALL, M. 61; *512*–75 41; FREMONT-1 577.

50. Dupont to Mrs.Dupont 12 8 1846 (DUPONT 89).

51. Stockton to Bancroft 11 23 1846 (*531*–31 10); DUVALL,M. 61.

52. CALIFN. 10 17 1846 3/2, 10 24 1846 3/1.

53. Talbot to mother 1 15 1847 (TALBOT 51–55); Talbot et al. to Frémont 2 4 1847 (SPENCE 2:287–90); *512*–75 52–53; CALIFN. 11 14 1846 2/1; BENTON-1 998/2–3 n.; BANCROFT 5:316–17 and n.31–34.

54. GARCIA 9–11; DUVALL,M. 64.

55. Zeilin, general order 10 26 1846 (*531–31* 16–17).
56. Stockton to Bancroft 11 23 1846 (ibid. 11).
57. Gillespie to Bancroft 2 16 1847 (CAL.HIS.QT. 17:339–40).
58. DUVALL,M. 63–64; Zeilin, general order 10 28 1846 (*531–31* 17).
59. Stockton to Bancroft 11 23 1846 (*531–31* 11), to J.Y.Mason 2 18 1848 (*503–1* 1046).
60. DUVALL,M. 64.
61. BAYARD 129.
62. WILSON 404–06.
63. ROWAN 544.
64. Dupont to Mrs.Dupont 12 8 1846 (DUPONT 89).
65. ROWAN 544–45; BIDWELL 108–09.
66. ROWAN 545; DUVALL,R.C. 119; Dupont to Mrs.Dupont 1 2 1847 (DUPONT 98); BANCROFT 5:324–25 and n.44.
67. Gillespie to Bancroft 2 16 1847 (CAL.HIS.QT. 17:340); DUVALL,R.C. 120; BANCROFT 5:326.
68. DUVALL,M. 65; Frémont to Stockton [10 27 1846] (SPENCE 2:211–12); FREMONT-1 579–80; *512–75* 41–42; *507–33* 378. The vessel had been captured by the *Warren* at Mazatlán in September.
69. Rushant to Montgomery [10] 27 1846 (NA45,M625,R284); Stockton to Bancroft 11 23 1846 (*531–31* 11–12).
70. DUVALL,M. 66; Mervine to Frémont 11 14 1846, Frémont to Mervine 11 14 1846 (SPENCE 2:224, 225–26); CALIFN. 11 14 1846 2/1.
71. Gillespie to Bancroft 2 16 1847 (CAL.HIS.QT. 17:340); Dupont to Mrs.Dupont 1 2 1847 (DUPONT 98); BANCROFT 5:327.
72. Stockton to Bancroft 11 23 1846 (*531–31* 12), to J.Y.Mason 2 18 1848 (*503–1* 1048); *507–33* 233; *512–75* 35).
73. Dupont to Mrs.Dupont 12 17 1846 (DUPONT 91–92).

CHAPTER 12. ADVENT OF KEARNY

1. Kearny to Stockton 12 2 1846, Stockton to Kearny 12 3 1846 (*531–31* 26–27); Stockton to J.Y.Mason 2 18 1848 (*503–1* 1048–49); Gillespie to Stockton 12 25 1846 (GILLESPIE-3 140), to Bancroft 2 16 1847 (CAL.HIS.QT. 17:340).
2. *517–41* 386; R.Jones to Kearny 5 13, 14 1846 (NA98,M210,R2); POLK 5 30 1846 1:439.
3. POLK 5 26 1846 1:429.
4. Ibid. 5 13, 30 1846 1:397, 438.
5. Scott to Kearny 5 31 1846, Marcy to Kearny 6 3 1846 (*499–19* 84–85, 5–7); POLK 5 30 1846 1:439.
6. See Chapter 15 below.
7. POLK 6 29 1846 1:493; Marcy to Kearny 6 3 1846 (*499–19* 7).
8. Marcy to Kearny 6 18 1846 (*573–17* 240); POLK 6 16, 20 1846 1:473, 481.
9. *517–41* 32–45; CLARKE 148–61.
10. GRIFFIN-1 17.
11. By Emory's odometer (*517–41* 176–78).
12. GRIFFIN-1 20; *517–41* 572; BENTON-1 978–79; Kearny to R.Jones 12 12 1846 (*503–1* 513–14). *Chief sources on the crossing:* *517–41* 45–105 (Emory), 567–613 (Johnston); TURNER 76–124; GRIFFIN-1 17–41.
13. Turner, orders 10 6 1846 (*507–33* 331); TURNER 80, 144–45; *517–41* 53, 572; BANCROFT 5:336–37.

14. Stockton to Bancroft 8 28 1846 (*499*–19 166–67); Larkin to Buchanan 9 8 1846 (LARKIN 5:232–33); GRIFFIN-1 20.

15. *517*–41 53.

16. GRIFFIN-1 20. Dr. Griffin would become a long-time resident of Los Angeles, dying there in 1898.

17. *517*–41 55–56, 574; Swords to Jessup 10 8 1847 (*503*–1 226–27); GRIFFIN-1 22.

18. *517*–41 61, 66, 579; GRIFFIN-1 25.

19. *517*–41 83–84, 599–601; Kearny to R.Jones 12 12 1846 (*503*–1 513–14); GRIFFIN-1 32–34.

20. GRIFFIN-1 36–37; *517*–41 94–95, 608.

21. *517*–41 96–97, 608–09; GRIFFIN-1 37.

22. *517*–41 99, 610; GRIFFIN-1 38.

23. *517*–41 102, 611; GRIFFIN-1 39; HOOVER 52–53.

24. *517*–41 559, 612; GRIFFIN-1 40; COOKE 185. In the 1850s, Vallecito would become an overland stage station.

25. *517*–41 104–05, 613.

26. *517*–41 106–07; GRIFFIN-1 43, 44; see Chapter 13 below.

27. *517*–41 106; Wm.B.Dunne, in GRIFFIN 61.

28. GRIFFIN-1 44; *517*–41 557–58; BIGLER 43, 45. They would reach Warner's on January 21.

29. *517*–41 107; GRIFFIN-1 44.

30. Kearny to Stockton 12 2 1846 (*531*–31 26–27).

31. Stockton to Kearny 12 3 1846 (ibid. 27); Gillespie to Stockton 12 25 1846 (GILLESPIE-3 140), to Bancroft 2 16 1847 (CAL.HIS.QT. 17:340); *507*–33 204.

32. CLARKE 198–99.

33. Gillespie to Stockton 12 25 1846 (GILLESPIE-3 140).

34. *517*–41 108; GRIFFIN-1 45.

35. CLARKE 201.

36. GRIFFIN-1 45.

37. CLARKE 204.

38. Kearny to R.Jones 12 13 1846 (*503*–1 515); GRIFFIN 60.

39. GRIFFIN-1 45, 47.

40. Gillespie to Stockton 12 25 1846 (GILLESPIE-3 140).

41. Kearny to R.Jones 12 13 1846 (*503*–1 515); Dupont to Mrs.Dupont 1 2 1847 (DUPONT 101–02); Turner to Mrs.Turner 12 21 1846 (TURNER 145); GRIFFIN-1 45–46.

42. BANCROFT 5:353 n.28.

43. Kearny to R.Jones 12 13 1846 (*503*–1 515).

44. Turner to Mrs.Turner 12 21 1846 (TURNER 145); CLARKE 208.

45. CLARKE 214.

46. GRIFFIN-1 46; Gillespie to Stockton 12 25 1846 (GILLESPIE-3 140).

47. Gillespie to Stockton 12 25 1846 (GILLESPIE-3 140), to Bancroft 2 16 1847 (CAL.HIS.QT. 17:342).

48. BANCROFT 5:352–53 n.28.

49. GRIFFIN-1 46; *507*–33 46–47.

50. Turner to Mrs.Turner 12 21 1846 (TURNER 145); CARTER 112–15.

51. GRIFFIN-1 47.

52. Ibid.; Griffin to Lawson 2 14 1847 (GRIFFIN-2); Gillespie to Stockton 12 25 1846 (GILLESPIE-3 140); *517*–41 108; Kearny to R.Jones 12 13 1846

(*503*–1 515); Turner to Stockton 12 6 1846 (*531*–31 27–28); *576*–24, tables B, D; Bancroft 5:346 n.19.

53. Gillespie to Stockton 12 25 1846 (GILLESPIE-3 140), to Bancroft 2 16 1847 (CAL.HIS.QT. 17:343); Flores to J.de J.Pico 12 7 1846 (BENTON-1 984/1); GRIFFIN-1 52; BANCROFT 5:347 n.20.

54. GRIFFIN-1 47; Gillespie to Stockton 12 25 1846 (op.cit.); Wm.B.Dunne (GRIFFIN 60); Kearny to R.Jones 12 13 1846 (*503*–1 516); CLARKE 220.

55. COY 12.

56. ALTA 1 25 1849 3/1, 2 22 1849 1/4.

57. *517*–41 109; Gillespie to Stockton 12 25 1846 (GILLESPIE-3 140). The bodies were later removed to San Diego (Sherman to Stevenson 4 13 1848 in NA98,M210,R1; Stevenson to Mason 6 14 1848 in NA98,M210,R3; BANCROFT 5:346).

58. Turner to Stockton 12 6 1846 (*531*–31 27–28).

59. Stockton to Bancroft 2 4 1847 (ibid. 24).

60. GRIFFIN-1 47–49; *517*–41 109; Gillespie to Stockton 12 25 1846 (GILLESPIE-4 140); CLARKE 221.

61. *517*–41 108–10, including Emory's map of the battle (cf. U.S.G.S. SE/4 Escondido, Calif. quadrangle, 7.5 min. series); Gillespie to Stockton 12 25 1846 (GILLESPIE-3 140), to Bancroft 2 16 1847 (CAL.HIS.QT. 17:343); Turner to Mrs.Turner 12 21 1846 (TURNER 146); Dunne (GRIFFIN 61); GRIFFIN-1 47.

62. GRIFFIN-1 47; Stockton to Turner 12 7 1847 (CLELAND 118–19).

63. Turner, orders 12 9 1846 (GRIFFIN-2 3); Gillespie to Bancroft 2 16 1847 (CAL.HIS.QT. 17:344).

64. *517*–41 111; CLARKE 224–25; CARTER 115; GRIFFIN-1 47, 55.

65. *517*–41 108; COY 9, 13–17; SCHREIER 3–4.

66. *517*–41 112; DOWNEY 170, 173–74; GRIFFIN-1 48.

67. *507*–33 188–89.

68. Stockton to Turner 12 7 1846 (CLELAND 118–19).

69. *517*–41 110; GRIFFIN-1 93 n.72; Flores to A.Pico 12 10 1846 (CLARKE 225); BANCROFT 5:351 n.26.

70. Pico had been reinforced by horsemen under Leonardo Cota (BENTON-1 984/1); BANCROFT 5:351; Turner to Mrs.Turner 12 21 1846 (TURNER 147).

71. DOWNEY 174–75; *517*–41 112; GRIFFIN-1 48.

72. Kearny to R.Jones 12 13 1846 (*503*–1 516); *517*–41 113.

73. Dupont to Mrs.Dupont 1 2 1847 (DUPONT 99).

74. *517*–41 7.

75. Ibid. 114; *507*–33 162.

76. "Military reconnaissance of the Arkansas, Rio del Norte, and Rio Gila . . . ," 1847 (*505*–7); WHEAT 3:4–5, 6–7, 260, no.544.

77. *517*–41 113.

CHAPTER 13. PARADISE REGAINED

1. BANCROFT 5:320–21 and n.40.

2. Ibid. 5:321–22 and n.41.

3. Assembly, decree 10 30 1846 (*573*–17 167); MEX.SECT.DEFENSA, exp. 2199, reel 5 (including Flores' military and economic report), 536–51.

4. GARCIA 9.

5. BANCROFT 5:330 n.5.

6. Ibid. 5:329–34, 341–42; CLARKE 193.

7. WILSON 403–04; Larkin to Mrs.Larkin 1 11 1847 (LARKIN 6:3); Flores, account of conspiracy of 12 3 1846 (MEX.SECT.DEFENSA, exp. 2479, reel 37); BANCROFT 5:331–33 and n.8.

8. BANCROFT 5:361–62. Manuel Castro may not have been one of those captured and paroled (BANCROFT-2 93).

9. BANCROFT 5:362–63 and n.6.

10. Larkin to Buchanan 1 14 1847 (LARKIN 6:10); BANCROFT 5:364–65.

11. Larkin to Leidesdorff 7 1 1846 (LEIDESDORFF box 2); Gleason to Wyllie 7 3 1846 (GLEASON 28); Larkin to Commissioner, Sandwich Islands 7 4 1846 (LARKIN 5:102); Bartlett to Montgomery 10 26 1846 (NA45,M625,R284); Larkin to Mrs.Larkin 11 25 1846 (LARKIN 5:288).

12. CALIFN. 11 21 1846 2/1, 2 27 1847 1/1; Larkin to Maddox 6 11 1847 (LARKIN 6:210–11); GARNER 123; Larkin to Leidesdorff 2 11 1847 (HAWGOOD-1 88–89).

13. Reports of the action at La Natividad: CALIFN. 11 21 1846 2/1-2, 2 27 1847 1/2; CAL.STAR 8 21 1847 1/2-3 to 2/1; MC LANE 90; FREMONT-1 594; Montgomery to Stockton 12 7 1846 (NA45,M625,R284); Frémont to Kern 11 20 1846 (SPENCE 2:229–30); BRYANT 360–63; SWASEY 67–71; KEMBLE,E.C.-1 57–82; BANCROFT 5:365–72.

14. Larkin to Mrs.Larkin 12 14 1846, 1 11 1847 (LARKIN 5:310, 6:3).

15. Larkin to [Stockton] 10 21 1846 (ibid. 5:262).

16. Stockton to Gillespie 3 11, 4 1 1847 (GILLESPIE-3 194, 208).

17. *Concerning the engagement at Santa Clara:* CALIFN. 1 16 1847 2/1, 2 6 1847 1/1; CAL.STAR 1 9 1847 2/3, 1 23 1847 2/2; DUVALL,M. 73–83; CRAVEN 140; Hull to Kearny 2 22 1847 (NA98,M210,R2); BANCROFT 5:377–83 and n.44; REGNERY.

18. Mervine, abstract of orders 1 5 1847 (CAL.HIS.QT. 10:124); Forbes, account, Battle of Santa Clara 1 15 1847 (ibid. 10:125–26).

19. Bancroft to Sloat 7 12 1846 (499–19 82); for the government's résumé of instructions and admonitions, Marcy to Kearny 5 10 1847, J.Y.Mason to Comdg. Officer 6 14 1847 (NA98,M210,R5).

20. Bancroft to Sloat 6 24 1845, 5 13, 15 1846 (499–19 75, 77, 79–80); Bancroft to Stockton 10 17 1845B (RICHMAN 529); *507–33* 198.

21. Bancroft to Sloat 7 12 1846 (499–19 81–82), to Stockton 8 18 1846 (NA45,M625,R283).

22. Scott to Kearny 5 31 1846 (499–19 84–85).

23. Marcy to Kearny 6 3 1846 (ibid. 6). Senator Benton also wrote Kearny that he was to be the civil and military governor (*507–33* 69), while Colonel Stevenson of the New York Volunteers would be told that if he reached California ahead of Kearny, the naval officer of highest rank was to form a government (Marcy to Stevenson 9 11 1846, in 499–19 13).

24. Stockton to Kearny 1 16 1847 (SPENCE 2:264), to Bancroft 2 4 1847 (*531–31* 25).

25. *507–33* 197–98.

26. Kearny to Stockton 12 2 1846 (*531–31* 26–27); and see KEARNY,T.

27. Stockton, [Form of government ca.8 22 1846] (499–19 109–10).

28. Stockton to Bancroft 1 11, 15, 22, 1847, 2 4 1847 (*531–31* 17–19, 20–21, 23, 24–26).

29. *507*–33 117, 264–65. Regulations concerning comparable ranks were sent in Bancroft to Shubrick 8 17 1846 and Scott to Kearny 11 3 1846 (*499*–19 92–93, 14–15).

30. Stockton to J.Y.Mason 2 18 1848 (*503*–1 1050); *507*–33 189.

31. Stockton to J.Y.Mason 2 18 1848; Stockton to Kearny 12 16 1846 (*531*–31 189); *507*–33 190.

32. *507*–33 79, 82, 190.

33. Ibid. 82, 165, 171, 325.

34. Stockton to Polk 8 26 1846 (SPENCE 2:193–95), to Bancroft 8 28 1846 (*499*–19 166–67).

35. Kearny to Stockton 12 22 1846 (SPENCE 2:241, 243). Neither knew Frémont's exact position, that day on Santa Inés Creek marching south (see Chapter 14 below).

36. Stockton to Kearny 12 23 1846 (*507*–33 111–12).

37. He would not, at the end of 1847, remember Stockton having told him so (ibid. 84–85).

38. Turner to Stockton 12 23 1846 (ibid. 190); Turner to Mrs.Turner 12 21 1846 (TURNER 147–48).

39. Kearny to Stockton 12 23 1846 (*507*–33 112).

40. Kearny to Adj.General 1 17 1847 (ibid. 94–95).

41. Ibid. 47.

42. Stockton to Bancroft 2 5 1847 (*531*–31 30–31); DOWNEY 167, 169, 176; Dupont to Mrs.Dupont 1 2 1847 (DUPONT 98); Gillespie to Bancroft 2 16 1847 (CAL.HIS.QT. 13:344); Stockton to Gillespie 11 15 1846 (GILLESPIE-3 119).

43. FREMONT-1 600; GARNER 157, 166.

44. DOWNEY 176, 181; Stockton to Bancroft 2 5 1847 (*531*–31 35–36).

45. Swords to Jessup 10 8 1847 (*503*–1 228).

46. Stockton to Montgomery 10 7 1846 (NA45,M625,R284).

47. At 12¢ a pound; *concerning bread contracts:* LARKIN 5:273–74, 287, 6:47, 48, 51–52, 60, 111, 112, 121, 149, 157, 202–03, 290, 298, 304, 310, 315, 319, 321, 337.

48. Montgomery to Kern 12 3 1846 (FORT SUTTER 75), to Stockton 12 7 1846 (NA45,M625,R284); Maury to Kern 12 9 1846 (FORT SUTTER 59); Hull to Shubrick 9 30 1847, Shubrick to J.Y.Mason 9 30 1847 (NA45,M625,R285); Bartlett to Montgomery 2 1848 (ibid.); DOWNEY 163–66; CALIFN. 1 23 1847 2/1-2, 3 27 1847 2/2; CAL.STAR 1 23 1847 3/1, 2 13 1847 3/1, 6 12 1847 3/3; ROGERS 87–92; BANCROFT 5:384.

49. Mervine to Montgomery 11 14 1846, Montgomery to Stockton 12 7 1846 (NA45,M625,R284).

50. Woodworth to Lanman 6 5 1848, Lanman to T.A.C.Jones 6 20 1848 (NA45,M89,R34); T.A.C.Jones to J.Y.Mason 7 27 1848, J.Y.Mason to T.A.C. Jones 2 15 1849 (NA45,M625,R286); ROGERS 87–92.

51. Misroon to Montgomery 12 26, 27, 28 1846 and others (NA45,M625, R284).

52. Zeilin, general order 12 23 1846 (*507*–33 113); Stockton to Kearny 12 24 1846 (SPENCE 2:246–47); DOWNEY 181.

53. *517*–41 115; Zeilin, roster 12 22 1846 (NA45,M625,R284); DOWNEY 182–84; Stockton to Bancroft 2 5 1847 (*531*–31 31); Turner to Stockton 12 23 1846 (*507*–33 190); GRIFFIN-1 55; BANCROFT 5:385–86 n.1.

54. Stockton to Kearny 12 24 1846 (SPENCE 2:246–47).

55. Stockton to Frémont 12 24 1846 (ibid. 2:247). The message, sent by a bearer, said he hoped to see Frémont on the 30th at San Luis Rey—but Frémont would not leave Santa Barbara until January 3.

56. DOWNEY 181.

57. GRIFFIN-1 54.

58. Kearny to R.Jones 1 12 1847 (*503–1* 516–17); *507–33* 47, 61, 116–17, 121, 191, 210, 322.

59. GRIFFIN-1 54.

60. Kearny to R.Jones 1 12 1847 (*503–1* 516–17); *507–33* 194, 199–200; BANCROFT 5:420–21 and n.13.

61. *507–33* 192–93, 199, 211, 322–23.

62. CLARKE 242.

63. GRIFFIN-1 55; DOWNEY 185–86; *517–41* 115; Gillespie to Bancroft 2 16 1847 (CAL.HIS.QT. 17:344).

64. *517–41* 115; see map, Emory's "Military reconnaissance . . . made in 1846–7 with the advance guard of the 'Army of the West'" (WHEAT 3:7–8, 260; GRIFFIN-1 43; TANNER.

65. DOWNEY 190–91; *517–41* 116; GRIFFIN-1 55.

66. GRIFFIN-1 56–57; *517–41* 116–17; DOWNEY 192–94.

67. Stockton to Frémont 1 3 1847 (*507–33* 272–273); ibid. 85, 229, 272. Captain Hamley's name was variously spelled Hamlin, Hamlyn, Hamblin, Hanly, Hawley (BANCROFT 5:401 n.19).

68. Flores to Stockton 1 1 1847 (*531–31* 19–20); Rowan to Dupont 1 14 1847 (DUPONT 439); *517–41* 117; DOWNEY 195–96; GRIFFIN-1 58–59.

69. Emory said in 1822 (*517–41* 118).

70. Stockton, proclamation 1 5 1847 (MEX.SECT.DEFENSA, exp.2479,f.30,reel 37).

71. Pedrorena to Estudillo 1 5 1847 (NA45,M625,R284). Another prominent Californian, Santiago Argüello, was also present: Stockton to Argüello 4 27 1847, to Pedrorena 11 25 1846, 4 27 1847, Speiden to Argüello, to Pedrorena 5 11 1847, Pedrorena to Mason 6 24 1847 (NA98,M210,R5).

72. *517–41* 118.

73. GRIFFIN-1 60; *517–41* 118–19; DOWNEY 199–201; Rowan to Dupont 1 14 1847 (DUPONT 439).

74. Stockton to Montgomery 1 7 1847 (NA45,M625,R284).

75. Montgomery to Cooke 1 14 1847 (MONTGOMERY).

76. DOWNEY 201.

77. BANCROFT 5:388–89 n.8, 390 n.10; CLARKE 245.

78. CALIFN. 3 6 1847 1/1; see Chapter 14 below.

79. The upper and lower crossings are shown on Edward O. C. Ord's "Topographical sketch of the Los Angeles plains and vicinity," 1849 (*558–47* 8), and A.F.Waldemar's "Sketch of a portion of Los Angeles County," 1861 (ROBINSON,W.W. 36, 39).

80. BANCROFT 5:390–91 n.10.

81. *Chief sources on the battles of San Gabriel and the Mesa:* DOWNEY 202–13; CARSHAW; *517–41* 119–21, including Emory's maps of the battles; GRIFFIN-1 61–62, 65; Rowan to Dupont 1 14 1847 (DUPONT 439–41); Stockton to Bancroft 2 5 1847 (*531–31* 32–35); Gillespie to Bancroft 2 16 1847 (CAL.HIS.QT. 17:344–45); CALIFN. extra 1 28 1847 1–2; BANCROFT 5:390–96.

82. MC LANE 100, 108.

83. COLTON 131.
84. DOWNEY 203–06; Stockton to Bancroft 2 5 1847 (*531*–31 33).
85. *517*–41 119.
86. For sources, see note 81 above.
87. Larkin to Mrs.Larkin 1 11, 17 1847 (LARKIN 6:3–4, 12).
88. *517*–41 120.
89. Griffin to Emory, statement 1 11 1847, Emory to Stockton 1 11 1847, Stockton to Bancroft 2 5 1847 (*531*–31 37, 36, 34–35); GRIFFIN-1 61–62; Rowan to Dupont 1 14 1847 (DUPONT 441); BANCROFT 5:395–96 n.12.
90. *517*–41 121.
91. *517*–41 121–22; GRIFFIN-1 62–63; Stockton to Bancroft 2 5 1847 (*531*–31 35).
92. DOWNEY 216.
93. GRIFFIN-1 64.
94. *517*–41 122.
95. Stockton, general order 1 11 1847 (*503*–1 1066–67); CALIFN. extra 1 23 1847 1/1; CAL.STAR 2 6 1847 3/1-2.
96. *507*–33 162; CARSHAW (NA45,M625,R284).

CHAPTER 14. WAR AND PEACE

1. GRIFFIN-1 64.
2. Stockton to Bancroft 11 23 1846 (*531*–31 10).
3. Frémont to Stockton [10 27 1846] (SPENCE 2:211–12), received at San Diego 11 2 1846; Stockton to Bancroft 11 23 1846 (*531*–31 11–12); FREMONT-1 579–80; see Chapter 11 above.
4. *507*–33 378; *512*–75 41–42; Frémont to Montgomery 10 22 1846 (NA45,M625,R284); MC LANE 88–89 (dates several days off); CALIFN. 10 31 1846 2/2, 3/2; BANCROFT 5:357.
5. Mervine to Frémont 11 14 1846 (SPENCE 2:224); FREMONT-1 580; see Chapter 11 above.
6. CALIFN. 11 7 1846 2/1.
7. Montgomery to Kern 10 15 1846 (FORT SUTTER 70), to Frémont 10 29 1846 (SPENCE 2:212–13); Kern to Montgomery 10 20, 27, 28 1846 (NA45,M625, R284); Montgomery to Stockton 12 7 1846 (ibid.).
8. Revere to Kern 10 17 1846 (FORT SUTTER 42). Frémont authorized Kern to provide for volunteers' families (Frémont to Kern 10 22 1846, in SPENCE 2:209; Kern to Gillespie 3 11 1853, in FORT SUTTER 99).
9. Bryant et al. to Kern 10 28 1846 (FORT SUTTER 51); BRYANT 347ff.; BANCROFT 5:358 n.2.
10. DOWNEY 154, 158–59; Montgomery to Frémont 10 29, 11 4 1846, 1 26 1847 (SPENCE 2:213, 215–16, 280–81); Watmough, muster roll 10 30 1846 (NA45,M625,R284).
11. Montgomery to Kern 11 8 1846 (FORT SUTTER 73).
12. CALIFN. 10 31 1846 2/2.
13. Colton to Montgomery 10 13 1846, Vallejo to Montgomery 10 15 1846, Pickett to Montgomery 10 30 1846 (NA45,M625,R284).
14. Stockton to Montgomery 10 8 1846 (ibid.); Montgomery to Weber 10 15 1846 (LEIDESDORFF box 2); Griffith to Montgomery 10 15 1846 (NA45, M625,R284); Montgomery to W.E.Taylor [10 15 1846] (LEIDESDORFF box 2);

Weber to Montgomery 10 17, 18, 21 1846, Kern to Montgomery 10 20 1846 (NA45,M625,R284); Hull to Kearny 2 22 1847 (NA98,M210,R2); GARNER 95, 118.

15. Pickett to Montgomery 10 30 1846, Murphy to Montgomery 11 2 1846 (NA45,M625,R284); Hull to Kearny 2 22 1847 (NA98,M210,R2); BANCROFT 5:358–59 n.2; for receipts, HIST.RECORDS, entries 20, 26ff.

16. Bartlett to Montgomery 11 5 1846AB, 11 6 1846 (NA45,M625,R284).

17. Pickett to Montgomery 10 30 1846 (ibid.).

18. Montgomery, note about Weber ca.11 3 1846 (ibid.).

19. BANCROFT 5:358 n.2.

20. Pickett to Montgomery 10 30 1846 (NA45,M625,R284); Larkin to Stockton 10 21 1846 (LARKIN 5:261).

21. MC LANE 91; CALIFN. 11 21 1846 2/2.

22. Richardson to Montgomery 11 1 1846, Watson to Montgomery 11 18 1846 (NA45,M625,R284).

23. Weber to Montgomery 10 21 1846, Pickett to Montgomery 10 30 1846 (ibid.).

24. GARNER 133, 157; CALIFN. 12 12 1846 2/2.

25. CALIFN. 11 21 1846 3/1–2 (Spanish), 12 12 1846 1, 4 (English).

26. Ibid. 12 5 1846 2/1, 12 19 1846 2/1–2.

27. Bartlett to Montgomery 11 5 1846B, 11 18 1846, Watson to Montgomery 11 18 1846 (NA45,M625,R284).

28. See Chapter 13 above.

29. MC LANE 90; a roster of his men includes 38 names (HIST.RECORDS, entry 52).

30. CALIFN. 11 7 1846 2/1.

31. Frémont to Stockton 1 2 1847 (SPENCE 2:249); *512–75* 61–63; MC LANE 91; BRYANT 366–68; BANCROFT 5:360–61 n.5. A roster of 12 19 1846 gives 394 men plus 9 staff, *vaqueros*, and other "ineffectives" (HIST.RECORDS, entry 48).

32. Mervine to Frémont 11 15 1846 (SPENCE 2:226); BRYANT 366.

33. Frémont to Mervine 11 27 1846 (SPENCE 2:233–34).

34. To be whisked away by marauding Indians shortly afterward (GARNER 170–71); CALIFN. 12 25 1846 2/1–2.

35. CALIFN. 10 31 1846 2/2; Polk, commission, Frémont [6 26 1846] (SPENCE 2:159); Mrs.Frémont to Frémont 6 16 1846 (ibid. 148, 149); Montgomery to Frémont 10 29 1846 (ibid. 213); Frémont to Montgomery 11 10 1846 (ibid. 221).

36. Departure date varies in accounts (BRYANT 365; MC LANE 91; TALBOT 55; CUTTS 160; BANCROFT 5:373).

37. BRYANT 369; they would eat mutton at San Miguel (ibid. 372).

38. FREMONT-1 598.

39. Ibid.; MC LANE 93; BRYANT 374.

40. *512–75* 42.

41. FREMONT-1 598–99; *507–33* 378–79; BRYANT 376.

42. MC LANE 94.

43. TOMPKINS 14–17; HOOVER 59–60; BANCROFT 5:377.

44. MC LANE 95; MC CHRISTIAN 6.

45. HOOVER 59–60.

46. MC LANE 95–97; BRYANT 379–82.

47. *512–75* 53–54; see Chapter 11 above.

48. NIDEVER 68–69.

49. FREMONT-1 600; SPENCE 2:237 n.

50. Stetson to Larkin 9 28 1846 (LARKIN 5:253); Frémont to Montgomery 11 10 1846, Montgomery to Frémont 11 13 1846 (ibid. 221, 223); Frémont to Mervine 11 14 1846, to Seldon 1 2 1847 (ibid. 2:225, 248).

51. MC LANE 97; BRYANT 386–87; Mervine to Frémont 11 21 1846 (SPENCE 2:232).

52. Frémont to Stockton 1 2 1847 (ibid. 2:249).

53. MC LANE 99–100; BRYANT 386–87; GARCIA 12.

54. Concerning the march to San Fernando: MC LANE 100–03; BRYANT 386–91; NIDEVER 71–73; GARCIA 12–14; OUTLAND; GIFFIN.

55. GARCIA 12–14.

56. Stockton to Frémont 1 3 1847 (*507–33* 272–73); ibid. 229; FREMONT-1 600–01; see Chapter 13 above.

57. Seeing their camp down a ravine, Flores' men from Las Posas departed for San Fernando (GARCIA 14).

58. Kearny to Frémont 1 10 1847 (SPENCE 2:250).

59. MC LANE 102; SMITH,J.H. 345.

60. GARCIA 14–16.

61. De la Guerra/Carrillo to Castro/Flores 1 11 1847 (BANCROFT 5:403 n.23); Flores/Pico reply 1 11 1847 (ibid. 5:403–04 n.24); [Larkin] 1 17 1847 (CALIFN. extra 1 28 1847 2/1; CAL.STAR 2 6 1847 3/2).

62. MC LANE 102.

63. *507–33* 379; FREMONT-1 601.

64. Frémont, cessation of hostilities 1 12 1847 (SPENCE 2:251).

65. Dupont to Mrs.Dupont 1 20 1847 (DUPONT 114–15).

66. GARCIA 15–16.

67. MC LANE 102–03.

68. Frémont/A.Pico, articles of capitulation 1 13 1847, and additional article 1 16 1847 (SPENCE 2:253–54, 259).

69. BANCROFT 5:405 n.26.

70. NA45,M89,R33; MEX.SECT.DEFENSA, exp.2278,reel 7; A.Pico to Mex. Min.War 4 5 1847 (CAL.HIS.QT. 13:133).

71. GARCIA 16; BANCROFT 5:405 n.26.

72. CALIFN. 1 16 1847 2/1, 2 13 1847 2/1; for note on washerwomen, DU-VALL,M. 2–3, SANCHEZ 373.

73. CAL.STAR 1 16 1847 2/2, 1 30 1847 3/2.

74. CALIFN. extra 1 28 1847 1/1–2 to 2/1, 2 13 1847 2/1–2 to 3/1; with reply by Stockton reluctantly published 5 22 1847 1/2–2/1; CAL.STAR 2 13 1847 1/1–2, 2/3.

75. Kearny to Stockton 1 13 1847 (SPENCE 2:252, 253 n.).

76. Kearny to Frémont 1 10 [1847] (ibid. 2:250).

77. Kearny to Frémont 1 12 1847 (ibid. 2:252). Frémont had earlier complained that his own officers would not report their positions, Frémont to Montgomery 11 10 1846 (ibid. 2:220–21).

78. Kearny to Frémont 1 13 1847AB (ibid. 2:255, 257).

79. Frémont to Kearny 1 13 1847 (ibid. 2:257–58).

80. Montgomery to Frémont 11 13 1846 (ibid. 2:223); Stockton to Frémont 1 3 1847 (ibid. 250).

81. WILSON 411, 413.

82. *507–33* 86–87, 324.

83. Ibid. 243–45, 257–70, 320–21.
84. Ibid. 324.
85. Ibid. 244, 258.
86. *507–33* 264–65,321–23.
87. BRYANT 393, 411–12. Russell and Kearny said in the morning, Bryant at 3 p.m. (*507–33* 257). They passed the tar pits at La Brea.
88. Kearny to R.Jones 1 14 1847 (ibid. 80).
89. *517–41* 122.
90. Stockton to Bancroft 1 15 1847 (FREMONT-1 654).
91. *507–33* 257–58, 259.
92. Marcy to Kearny 6 18 1846 (ibid. 32–33).
93. Ibid. 77–78, 203.
94. Emory to Frémont 1 16 1847 (SPENCE 2:265).
95. First learned in New Mexico in October 1846 when he interrupted Kit Carson on his way to Washington (see Chapter 12 above).
96. Kearny to Stockton 1 16 1847 (SPENCE 2:263).
97. Stockton to Kearny 1 16 1847 (ibid. 264). It would appear that Kearny's order concerning the reorganization was written in the morning, before Stockton's letter of dismissal, but delivered after Frémont's "lights were lit" (*507–33* 78, 118, 163–64).
98. *507–33* 200.
99. That evening, according to Stockton, no later than mid-afternoon in Russell's memory (ibid. 196, 197, 257–58, 263).
100. Stockton, appointment, Frémont 1 16 1847 (SPENCE 2:267).
101. Kearny to Frémont 1 17 1847 (ibid. 2:268); *507–33* 38–39, 76, 163, 228, 381–83; Frémont to Kearny 1 17 1847 (SPENCE 2:268–69).
102. *507–33* 39, 89, 392–93; Frémont to Benton 2 3 1847 (SPENCE 2:283); GRIFFIN-1 70.
103. *507–33* 87.
104. GRIFFIN-1 70.
105. *507–33* 80–81, 405.
106. Ibid. 4–20, 337–38.
107. Kearny to Stockton 1 17 1847AB (SPENCE 2:270–71; *507–33* 195).
108. Kearny to Adj.Genl. 1 17 1847 (*507–33* 94–95).
109. POLK 4 30, 5 4, 6 7, 6 8 1847 2:493, 3:10–11, 52–53, 54.
110. WILSON 413–14.
111. GRIFFIN-1 70.
112. Ibid. 70–71; *517–41* 123; WILSON 413–14.
113. BANCROFT 5:433; Stockton, proclamation convening legislative council 1 18 1847 (VALLEJO 266); Stockton to Gillespie 1 18 1847 (GILLESPIE-3 147).
114. Having loaded his sailors onto the *Stonington* at San Pedro (MC LANE 109; Dupont to Mrs.Dupont 1 20 1847, in DUPONT 117).
115. *517–41* 123–24, 126; *507–33* 99, 133, 165, 169; GRIFFIN-1 74.
116. Published in 1848 by the Senate (*505–7*) and the House (*517–41*), the former normally with the folding map, the latter with supplementary reports by J. W. Abert, Johnston, and Cooke (WHEAT 3:7).
117. A matter not lost sight of in other letters carried by Gray: Stockton to Bancroft 1 11, 1 15, 1 22 1847 (*531-31* 17–18, 20–21, 23).
118. Stockton to Bancroft 2 4, 5 1847 (*531–31* 24–26, 30–36).
119. Shubrick reached Monterey in the *Independence* (CALIFN. 1 23 1847 2/1;

Shubrick to Bancroft 1 20 [i.e., 22 or later] 1847, in NA45,M625,R284), and the news was carried to San Diego in the *Dale*, departing January 29 (CALIFN. 2 6 1847 3/2). Stockton had expected to be superseded by James Biddle (Stockton to Bancroft 10 1 1846, in *531*–31 113–14).

120. Dupont to Mrs.Dupont 1 2 1847 (DUPONT 108).

121. BELL-1 3; HOOVER 22.

122. Frémont to Maddox 1 17 1847 (CALIFN. 2 13 1847 1–2/1).

123. BRYANT 414; MC LANE 109; PHELPS 319.

124. Frémont, circular 1 22 1847 (SPENCE 2:275; CALIFN. 2 6 1847 2/2–3/1; CAL.STAR 2 6 1847 3/1, comment 2/1).

125. Tansil to Bartlett 2 17 1847 (CAL.STAR 2 20 1847 3/3); Hull, order 2 17 1847 (ibid.). Hull succeeded Montgomery as commander at San Francisco on November 19 (Hull to Kearny 2 22 1847, in NA98,M210,R2), and was superseded by Dupont on March 2 (DUPONT 141; CAL.STAR 2 20 1847 3/2, 3 6 1847 3/1).

126. CAL.STAR 2 20 1847 2/1.

127. Larkin to Vallejo 1 22 1847 (LARKIN 6:16); CAL.STAR 2 6 1847 2/2; GARNER 178; BANCROFT 5:433 and n.31.

128. Frémont to Vallejo 2 15 1847 (SPENCE 2:276); Larkin to Vallejo 1 22 1847 (LARKIN 6:16); Russell to Vallejo 1 22 1847 (VALLEJO 263); [Vallejo] to Frémont 2 15 1847 (SPENCE 2:304–05).

129. Larkin to Mrs.Larkin 1 22 1847 (LARKIN 6:15).

130. Frémont to Wilson 1 25 1847, to McLane 2 5 1845 (SPENCE 2:280, 291–92); MC LANE 110.

131. *507*–33 27, 62, 63; CAL.STAR 3 6 1847 2/2.

132. Frémont to Buchanan 3 1 1848 (SPENCE 2:480–81); Buchanan to Frémont 3 2 1848 (BUCHANAN 8:2); *512*–75 19–25, 77–83; see Chapter 9 above.

133. *From Temple:* Frémont, rcd. Temple 1 25 1847 (SPENCE 2:279); *from Cot:* Frémont, loan 2 4 1847 (ibid. 2:285–86); *from Célis:* Célis–Frémont, agreement 3 3 1847 (ibid. 2:409–11), ALTA 12 15 1849 3/2; *from Hüttman:* BANCROFT 4:465–66; *825*–109 40, 88–140; for other documents, SPENCE 2:407–21.

134. Frémont to Buchanan 2 6 1847, with endorsement 6 4 1847 (SPENCE 2:292–95).

135. Speiden to Frémont 2 4 1847 (ibid. 2:284–85 and notes).

136. Frémont to Shubrick 2 7 1847, Shubrick to Frémont 2 13 1847 (SPENCE 2:296, 303).

137. Frémont to Reading 3 2 1847 (ibid. 2:316).

138. Frémont, agreement to pay Temple 3 2 1847 (ibid. 2:317).

139. *512*–75 14–15.

140. Frémont to Benton 2 3 1847 (SPENCE 2:281–84).

141. POLK 6 7 1847, 8 19 1847 3:52, 128–29; *507*–33 379–80.

142. Frémont to Shubrick 2 7 1847, Shubrick to Frémont 2 13 1847 (SPENCE 2:295–97, 302–03).

143. Frémont to Hull 2 11 1847 (ibid. 2:300–01); Benton to Frémont 10 7 1847 (ibid. 2:403).

144. Frémont to Bandini 1 23 1847 (STEARNS box 27), to Stearns/Célis/Flügge 1 21 1847 (SPENCE 2:273), to all 3 9 1847 (ibid. 2:319); Kearny to Biddle 4 11 1847 (*573*–17 295–96); GARNER 178.

145. GRIFFIN-1 77; CAL.STAR 2 13 1847 3/3.

146. Citizens of Los Angeles to Frémont 3 18 1847 (SPENCE 2:325–26); Larkin to Gillespie 3 24 1847, to Frémont 3 16 1847 (LARKIN 6:70, 59).

147. DUVALL,M. 93.

148. In 1849, HUTTON 32.

149. FOSTER 21; (Los Angeles) STAR 9 6 1856 2/2; BELL 25.

150. CAL.STAR 5 29 1847 3/1.

CHAPTER 15. FIGHT ON—KEARNY PREVAILS

1. MC LANE 104.

2. Turner to Mrs.Turner 2 22 1847 (TURNER 155–56).

3. Dupont to Mrs.Dupont 2 20 1847 (DUPONT 128).

4. GRIFFIN-1 70–71.

5. Marcy to Stevenson 9 11 1846 (499–19 13).

6. Kearny to Marcy 1 30 1847 (KEARNY-1).

7. POLK 6 2 1846 1:444.

8. Marcy to Kearny 6 3 1846 (499–19 5); Kearny to J.Allen 6 19 1846 (BANCROFT 5:473).

9. POLK 6 3, 5 1846 1:445–46, 449–50.

10. BANCROFT 5:469–82; BIGLER 19ff.

11. *517–41* 551; CLARKE 165.

12. *517–41* 560; BANCROFT 5:428, 486; Montgomery to Stockton 1 29 1847 (MONTGOMERY); Kearny to Marcy 1 30 1847 (KEARNY-1).

13. Cooke, orders no. 1 (*547–2* 84–85).

14. CALIFN. 8 15 1846 2/2–3/1.

15. In May 1846, Pico had warned the assembly that 10,000 Mormons were on the way (GARNER 150 n.1). Larkin to Buchanan 9 22 1846 (LARKIN 5:247); CALIFN. 10 10 1846 2/1; GARNER 148–50; Dupont to Mrs. Dupont 2 21, 10 25 1847 (DUPONT 134–35, 259–60); GRIFFIN-1 79; Stevenson to Mason 7 23 1847 (*573–17* 347–48); *507–33* 233, 242, 243, 259–60, 262–63.

16. Kearny to Marcy 1 30 1847 (KEARNY-1).

17. Dupont to Mrs.Dupont 2 18 1847 (DUPONT 118–19); Kearny to Marcy 1 30 1847 (KEARNY-1); CALIFN. 1 23 1847 2/1, extra 1 28 1847 2/2, 2 6 1847 2/1, 2 13 1847 3/2.

18. *Independence*: sailing time 127 days (CALIFN. 1 23 1847 2/1); COLTON 159. *Lexington*: Tompkins to Kearny 1 27 1847 (NA98,M210,R2); Biddle to Bailey, orders 12 5? 1846 (NA45,M89,R33); CALIFN. extra 1 28 1847 2/2, 2 6 1847 2/1; SHERMAN 1:18.

19. Shubrick to Bancroft 1 20, 2 15 1847 (NA45,M625,R284), to Kearny 1 28 1847 (NA98,M210,R2).

20. Kearny to R.Jones 3 15 1847 (*573–17* 283).

21. Bancroft to Sloat 7 12 1846 (499–19 81–82).

22. Kearny to R.Jones 3 15 1847 (*573–17* 283); Shubrick to Bancroft 2 15 1847 (NA45,M625,R284); Dupont to Mrs.Dupont 2 19 1847 (DUPONT 122–23); CALIFN. 2 13 1847 3/2.

23. Shubrick to Bancroft 2 13 1847 (NA45,M625,R284).

24. Frémont to Shubrick 2 7 1847, Shubrick to Frémont 2 13 1847 (*507–33* 9–10, 417–18).

25. Shubrick to Bancroft 2 15 1847 (NA45,M625,R284).

26. Shubrick, general order 2 1 1847 (CALIFN. 2 6 1847 2/2); CAL.STAR 2 20 1847 3/1–2.

27. Burton et al. to Shubrick 2 19 1847 (NA98,M210,R2); Sill et al. to Comdr., New Helvetia 2 28 1847 (ibid.); Nash to Dupont 3 1 1847 (ibid.); Dupont to Shubrick 3 2 1847 (ibid.); Cooke, orders 3 2, 15, 18 1847 (ibid.); CAL.STAR 3 13 1847 1/1–2.

28. Oliver et al. to Biddle 3 8 1847 (NA98,M210,R2).

29. Shubrick, general order 2 11 1847 (CALIFN. 2 13 1847 3/2 and ff., comment 2 20 1847 2/1).

30. Hull to Kearny 2 22 1847, Shubrick to Kearny 2 23 1847 (NA98,M210,R2).

31. Dupont to Mrs.Dupont 2 21 1847, 2 18 1847 (DUPONT 133–34, 120).

32. GARNER 176–77; COLTON 17.

33. CALIFN. 2 20 1847 2/2.

34. CAL.STAR 2 20 1847 3/2, 2/2; Dupont to Mrs.Dupont 2 19 1847 (DUPONT 123–25).

35. Stockton to Bancroft 9 18 1846 (*531*–31 2); Larkin to Buchanan 6 30 1847 (LARKIN 6:226); for Mason's orders, Scott to Mason 11 3 1846 (NA98,M210,R2); Marcy to Mason 11 5 1846AB (ibid.; *573*–17 242). The *Erie* found Mason and Watson at Payta, south of Guayaquil, where they had gone in an English vessel from Panamá (CALIFN. 2 20 1847 3/2; Dupont to Mrs.Dupont 2 19 1847, in DUPONT 125); concerning Payta, WHITE 22–23, 36, 42.

36. Scott to Kearny 11 3 1846 (*499*–19 14–16).

37. Marcy to Kearny 6 3 1846 (ibid. 6).

38. J.Y.Mason to Stockton 11 5 1846 (ibid. 91), 1 11 1847 (NA45,M625,R284).

39. Freeman, orders no.49, 11 1 (or 3) 1846 (NA98,M210,R5); the 9th Department was New Mexico.

40. Shubrick to J.Y.Mason 3 4 1847 (NA45,M625,R285). Watson had earlier delivered Sloat's instructions at Honolulu (Sloat to Bancroft 11 25 1845, in NA45,M89,R32).

41. Dupont to Mrs.Dupont 2 20 1847 (Dupont 131); Shubrick to Kearney 2 23 1847A (NA98, M210, R2).

42. Shubrick to Frémont 2 23 1847 (SPENCE 2:308); MC LANE 112.

43. SPENCE 2:310 n.3.

44. Frémont to Gillespie 3 5 1847 (ibid. 2:318).

45. CAL.STAR 2 27 1847 2/1; CALIFN. 2 27 1847 2/1; Shubrick to J.Y.Mason 3 4 1847 (NA45,M625,R285); Larkin to McRae 3 17 1847 (LARKIN 6:63).

46. CALIFN. 3 13 1847 3/1; CAL.STAR 2 27 1847 2/1; Shubrick/Kearny, circular 3 1 1847 (SPENCE 2:313; CALIFN. 3 6 1847 2/1–2; CAL.STAR 3 6 1847 3/2); GREENWOOD 87.

47. CALIFN. 3 6 1847 2/2.

48. Kearny, proclamation 3 1 1847 (SPENCE 2:314–15; CALIFN. 3 6 1847 3/1–2, comment 3 13 1847·2/2; CAL.STAR 3 20 1847 1/1–2. It was dated March 1, went to the printer March 4, and was distributed in "many copies," probably the following day (*507*–33 100); GREENWOOD 88.

49. GARNER 195; CAL.STAR 3 20 1847 2/2, 3 13 1847 3/2; and the editor would submit a bill for $84 for the two documents, which Mason would declare exorbitant (Folsom to Mason 10 22 1847, in NA98,M210,R2); Sherman to Folsom 10 28 1847B (NA98,M210,R1).

50. Sherman to Riccord 10 25 1847 (NA98,M210,R1).

51. CALIFN. 3 6 1847 2/1; GARNER 195.

52. SHERMAN 34; CRAVEN 318; Kearny to R.Jones 3 15 1847 (*573*–17 284); Biddle to Kearny 4 11 1847 (NA98,M210,R5); POLK 7 22 1847 3:94–95, 96.

53. DUVALL,M. 92; GARNER 197; CALIFN. 3 13 1847 2/1.

54. Dupont to Mrs.Dupont 3 16, 4 20 1847 (DUPONT 144–46, 155–56).

55. CALIFN. 11 14 1846 2/2–1/3.

56. Shubrick to Biddle 3 5 1847 (NA45,M625,R285); Bancroft to Sloat 5 15 1846 (*499*–19 80).

57. Bancroft to Biddle, Stockton, or senior officer 8 13 1846 (*499*–19 82–84), to Shubrick 8 17 1846 (ibid. 92–93).

58. CALIFN. 1 23 1847 2/1; Shubrick to Bancroft 12 2, 12 1846 (NA45, M625,R284); Biddle to Shubrick 12 12 1846, to Bancroft 12 14 1846 (NA45, M89,R33).

59. Shubrick sailed December 14; Shubrick to Bancroft 1 20, 2 15 1847 (NA45,M625,R284), to J.Y.Mason 3 4 1847 (NA45,M625,R285).

60. Shubrick to Biddle 3 5 1847, to J.Y.Mason 3 6 1847 (ibid.).

61. Dupont to Mrs.Dupont 5 19, 6 7 1847 (DUPONT 172, 180); Shubrick to J.Y.Mason 6 15 1847 (*503*–1 1072).

62. Shubrick to J.Y.Mason 7 21, 8 3 1847 (NA45,M625,R285); CAL.STAR 7 31 1847 3/3; Dupont to Mrs.Dupont 10 5 1847 (DUPONT 241).

63. Shubrick to J.Y.Mason 9 28 1847AB (NA45,M625,R285); Dupont to Mrs.Dupont 10 2, 5, 28 1847 (DUPONT 236, 242, 254); J.Y.Mason to T.A.C. Jones 10 25, 11 1 1847 (NA45,M625,R285); T.A.C.Jones to J.Y.Mason 5 1848 (NA45,M625,R286); Shubrick to Sect.Navy 5 21 1849 (ibid.).

64. Bancroft to Sloat 6 24 1845 (*499*–19 75); Marcy to Kearny 6 3 1846 (ibid. 5–7); see Chapter 13 above.

65. Bancroft to Sloat 7 12 1846 (*499*–19 81–82), to Stockton 8 18 1846 (NA45,M625,R283).

66. Scott to Kearny 11 3 1846 (*499*–19 15); J.Y.Mason to Stockton 11 5 1846 (ibid. 91).

67. Kearny to Frémont 3 1 1847 (SPENCE 2:310); Turner, orders no.2, 3 1 1847 (ibid. 2:311–12); Turner to Mrs.Turner 3 16 1847 (TURNER 159); CAL.STAR 3 6 1847 3/1. He also sent the joint circular of 3 1 1847 (*573*–17 288; CALIFN. 3 6 1847 2) but not Kearny's proclamation of the same date (*573*–17 288–89), which was not printed until the 5th (*507*–33 100, 149, 421–22).

68. Including the Mexican archives taken to Los Angeles by Pío Pico in 1845 (GARNER 196).

69. Turner to Mrs.Turner 3 16 1847 (TURNER 159); *507*–33 148–49; COOKE 284.

70. Cooke to Frémont 3 14 1847 (SPENCE 2:320); Russell to Cooke 3 16 1847 (ibid. 2:323).

71. *507*–33 273; Cooke to Turner 3 25 1847 (ibid. 125); *512*–75 36–37; Hastings to Mason 2 13 1848 (NA98,M210,R3).

72. Kearny to Biddle 3 10 1847 (ref. in CLARKE 292–93), to Marcy 4 28 1847 (*573*–17 287).

73. Turner to Mrs.Turner 3 31 1847 (TURNER 161).

74. Frémont to Owens 3 15 1847 (SPENCE 2:320–21), to S.Argüello 3 18 1847AB (GRIFFIN-1 80).

75. Citizens of Los Angeles to Frémont 3 18 1847 (SPENCE 2:325–26).

76. Frémont to Workman 3 20 1847 (ibid. 2:327).

77. BANCROFT 5:443 n.11. Sherman and a party would, in May, require about fifteen days for the journey (SHERMAN 28).

78. Larkin to Bryant 3 26 1847 (LARKIN 6:73); CALIFN. 3 27 1847 2/2, 4 10 1847 3/2.

79. *507–33* 104; Larkin to Teschemacher 4 12 1847 (LARKIN 6:98); E.L. Childs to Larkin 9 25 1847 (ibid. 6:354).

80. *507–33* 34, 104, 105–07.

81. Ibid. 422.

82. GRIFFIN-1 79.

83. Ibid. 77; see Chapter 16 below.

84. *507–33* 105, 107.

85. GRIFFIN-1 75–76, 78; *507–33* 268; Larkin to Bryant 3 26 1847, to Buchanan 6 30 1847 (LARKIN 6:73, 225); Cooke to Turner 3 25 1847 (*507–33* 125); CALIFN. 6 12 1847 2/3. Russell and Carson reached Washington about the beginning of June (POLK 6 7 1847 3:52).

86. Larkin to Buchanan 6 30 1847 (LARKIN 6:225); CAL.STAR 6 19 1847 2/1–2, 2/3–3/1; CALIFN. 6 19 1847 3/1.

87. Larkin to Bandini 3 25 1847 (LARKIN 6:72).

88. COOKE 288; Kearny to Cooke 3 1 1847 (*507–33* 140–41); BANCROFT 5:445.

89. Kearny to Gillespie 3 1 1847 (GILLESPIE–3 170); Turner, orders no.2, 3 1 1847 (SPENCE 2:311–12); Biddle to Gillespie 3 31 1847, 5 4 1847 (*507–33* 221).

90. *507–33* 202.

91. Cooke to Turner 3 25 1847 (ibid. 124–26); ibid. 122, 135.

92. J.K.Wilson to Cooke 3 25 1847 (ibid. 123); Owens to J.K.Wilson 3 25 1847 (ibid.).

93. Cooke to Turner 3 25 1847 (ibid. 125); COOKE 292.

94. Kearny to Mason 3 27 1847, to Frémont 3 28 1847 (SPENCE 2:330, 331).

95. BANCROFT 5:443 n.11.

96. CALIFN. 4 3 1847 3/2; Mason to Frémont 4 5 1847 (SPENCE 2:332).

97. Gillespie to Larkin 4 7 1847 (LARKIN 6:88).

98. *507–33* 142–43.

99. Frémont to Mason 4 7 1847 (SPENCE 2:332–34); Loker to Mason [4 7 1847] (ibid. 2:333–34); Mason to Frémont 4 7 1847 (ibid. 2:334–35); Frémont to Mason 4 8 1847A (ibid. 2:336); Mason to Frémont 4 8 1847B (ibid. 2:338).

100. *Concerning pay:* Frémont to Gillespie 2 17 1847 (SPENCE 2:306–07); Loker to Frémont 4 7 1847 (ibid. 2:334); Mason to Frémont 4 7 1847 (ibid. 2:335); Reading to Frémont 5 29 1847 (ibid. 2:429); R.Jones to Marcy 8 21 1848 (NA98,M210,R5); and see Frémont's California claims, Chapter 17 below, n.159.

101. Mason to Frémont 4 9 1847, Frémont to Mason 4 9 1847B (SPENCE 2:340–41).

102. MC CHRISTIAN 8.

103. Mason to Frémont 4 12 1847, Frémont to Mason 4 13 1847 (SPENCE 2:345–46).

104. Mason to Frémont 4 8 1847AC (ibid. 2:337–39); Frémont to Mason

4 8 1847C, 4 9 1847A (ibid. 2:338–39, 340); but see Frémont to Argüello 3 18 1847AB (GRIFFIN-1 80).

105. Mason to Frémont 4 9 1847 (SPENCE 2:340–41).

106. FOSTER 19, 21; (Los Angeles) STAR 9 6 1856 2/2; BELL 25.

107. *Sources concerning this affair:* SPENCE 2:346–49, 350–53, 354–56, 357–58; *507–33* 108, 144; MC LANE 113; BANCROFT 5:447–48 n.21. The duel would be postponed again in May to some other time and sphere and never take place.

108. Russell to Alexander 3 21 1847 (SPENCE 2:328–29); Mason to Kearny 4 26 1847 (*573–17* 309); Kearny to Alexander 4 26, 5 12 1847 (ibid. 300, 305–06); Mason to R.Jones 6 21 1847 (ibid. 330); *507–33* 15–16.

109. Mason to Arquisola 4 11 1847, to the Indians 4 15 1847 (NA98,M210, R5).

110. Mason to Kearny 4 26 1847 (*573–17* 309); *507–33* 227.

CHAPTER 16. KEARNY'S RULE

1. DUPONT 135; CAL.STAR 2 20 1847 2/2.

2. Sloat to the inhabitants 7 7 1846 (*503–1* 1010–11); Stockton to the people 8 17 1846 (*499–19* 107–08).

3. Larkin to Mrs.Frémont 3 16 1847 (LARKIN 6:58).

4. Larkin to Bandini 3 25 1847, to Stockton 4 13 1847 (ibid. 6:72, 100); CAL.STAR 2 13 1847 2/3.

5. CAL.STAR 2 13 1847 2/1–2, 2 20 1847 3/1.

6. CALIFN. 3 13 1847 3/1.

7. Kearny to Nash 3 1 1847, to Bryant 3 4 1847, (*573–17* 290).

8. Larkin to Bryant 4 7 1847 (LARKIN 6:89); Kearny, proclamation 3 1 1847 (*573–17* 288–89; CALIFN. 3 6 1847 3).

9. ROYCE 201–02.

10. BRYANT 328.

11. Kearny to Burton 3 26, 4 10 1847 (*573–17* 292, 295).

12. Kearny to Bryant 4 19, 27 1847 (ibid. 297–98, 301–02).

13. Kearny to Fitch 4 27 1847, to J.J.Warner 4 27 1847 (ibid. 302–03).

14. Kearny to Bonilla 4 30 1847 (ibid. 303).

15. By Frémont; Kearny to Alexander 4 26, 5 12 1847 (ibid. 300, 305–06).

16. Kearny to Richardson 4 21 1847 (*573–17* 298), to S.Argüello 4 21, 26 1847 (ibid. 299, 300), to P.Carrillo 4 26 1847 (ibid. 301).

17. Montgomery, proclamation 9 15 1846 (CALIFN. 11 7 1846 2/2), as commandant, northern district.

18. Kearny to Sutter 4 7 1847, to Vallejo 4 14 1847 (*573–17* 294–95, 296–97).

19. Kearny, grant 3 10 1847 (ibid. 291); CALIFN. 3 27 1847 3/2; Kearny to Bryant 4 19 1847, to Pettit 4 27 1847 (*573–17* 297–98, 302).

20. Kearny, decree 3 22 1847 (*573–17* 291).

21. Kearny to Vallejo 4 6 1847 (ibid. 293–94).

22. Kearny to Nash 3 29 1847 (ibid. 293).

23. Kearny to Burton 4 10 1847 (ibid. 295).

24. Kearny to Burton 5 5 1847 (ibid. 305).

25. Appointed 7 28 1846 (COLTON 17), elected 9 15 1847 (CALIFN. 9 19 1846 3/1).

26. Kearny, appointment, Colton 3 24 1847 (*573–17* 291–92); CALIFN. 3 27 1847 3/1, 4 10 1847 3/1–2, 4 17 1847 1–2, 4 24 1847 1/1–2; GARNER 42; COLTON (1949) xxxvii; J.Y.Mason to T.A.C.Jones 10 25 1847 (NA45,M625, R285); BAUER 206.

27. *References to mail service:* Misroon to Kern 8 8 1846 (FORT SUTTER 27); Stockton to Bancroft 10 1 1846 (*531–31* 13); Kearny, arrangements for transporting the mail 4 1 1847 (CALIFN. 4 10 1847 1/1); Turner to Cooke, to Burton, to Hardie 4 2 1847 (NA98,M210,R1); Folsom to Kearny 4 7 1847 (NA98,M210,R2); Turner to Folsom 4 10 1847 (NA98,M210,R1); Folsom to Turner 4 18 1847 (NA98,M210,R2); Sherman to Burton 6 2 1847 (NA98,M210,R1); Cooke to Mason 6 16 1847 (NA98,M210,R2); Sherman to Stevenson 6 25 1847 (NA98,M210,R1); Folsom to Sherman 1 9, 2 20 1848 (NA98,M210,R3); Sherman to Folsom 2 24, 3 1, 12 7, 12 30 1848 (NA98,M210,R1), to A.J.Smith 8 11 1848 (*573–17* 638), to Graham 1 1 1849 (ibid. 877), to Folsom 1 9, 1 20 1849 (ibid. 878–79, 879–80), to W.G.Marcy 2 3 1849 (ibid. 885), to Folsom 2 3 1849 (ibid. 885–86); Mason, order no.10, 3 21 1849 (NA98,M210,R7); Canby to Graham 3 21 1849 (NA98,M210,R1), to Fitzgerald 5 7 1849 (*573–17* 906), 5 18 1849A (ibid. 910); Fitzgerald to Canby 5 12 1849 (NA98,M210,R4); Riley, orders no.21, 5 18 1849 (NA98,M210,R7; GREENWOOD 152), orders no.26, 6 20 1849 (NA98,M210,R7); Canby, sp.order no.31, 6 30 1849 (ibid.); Heintzelman to Canby 8 12 1849 (NA98,M210,R4); Canby, orders no.30, 8 14 1849 (NA98,M210,R7); Canby to Seawell 9 24 1849 (NA98,M210,R1); Riley to R.Jones 10 1 1849B (ibid.). Newspapers: CALIFN. 8 15 1846 3/1, 8 22 1846 3/2, 8 29 1846 4/2, 9 5 1846 3/1, 10 17 1846 2/1, 2 6 1847 2/1, 2 20 1847 2/2, 4 10 1847 1/1, 4 24 1847 2/1, 7 24 1847 2/2, 3/2–3, 9 22 1847 2/2, 2 23 1848 2/2, 3 15 1848 (BOGGS 16/1–2), 4 5 1848 (ibid. 17/2), 4 19 1848 (ibid.); CAL.STAR 1 30 1847 3/3, 3 27 1847 2/2–3, 4 17 1847 2/1, 9 18 1847 2/2, 9 25 1847 3/1–2, 3 11 1848 2/2; ALTA 6 28 1849 (BOGGS 28/2), 7 19 1849 (ibid. 30/1), 7 26 1849 (ibid.), 10 4 1849 (ibid. 34/1); (Sacramento) PLACER TIMES 8 25 1849 (ibid. 31/1); (Sacramento) TRANSCRIPT 6 6 1850 2/2, 6 25 1850 2/3, 7 29 1850 2/3; other sources in BOGGS.

28. Before the American period, a biweekly military express to which the people had access was operated between the presidios from San Francisco to San Diego, the couriers being soldiers, animals coming from the missions, and alcaldes and *comandantes* serving as postmasters (SANCHEZ 163–64; mention, BANCROFT 1:452, 453, 483).

29. The name was changed from Yerba Buena by ordinance of Alcalde Washington A. Bartlett (CAL.STAR 1 30 1847 4/3), and the new form was adopted by the *Star* 3 20 1847 (comment 2/1) following Kearny's use of the name in his decree granting beach and water lots to the town (ibid. 4/2).

30. Kearny to Marcy 4 28 1847 (*573–17* 286); Cooke to Turner 4 22, 25 1847 (NA98,M210,R2); Behn, memorandum 4 22 1847 (ibid.); Cooke to Turner 5 4 1847 (ibid.); GRIFFIN-1 77, 81–83.

31. Cooke to Stockton 4 24 1847, Stockton to Cooke 4 25 1847 (NA98, M210,R2), to Gillespie 4 26 1847 (GILLESPIE-3 225); ROWAN 549–50; GRIFFIN-1 81, 83.

32. COOKE 300, 302.

33. Ibid. 297, 301.

34. They came to San Francisco in the *Thomas H. Perkins, Susan Drew, Loo Choo,* and *Brutus* on March 6, 19, 26, and April 17 (CAL.STAR 3 13 1847 2/2–3, 3 27 1847 3/3, 4 24 1847 3/2, 3/3, 5 15 1847 2/3); four companies were taken to

Monterey in the *Lexington*, arriving April 4 (CALIFN. 4 10 1847 2/2–3/1; BIGGS 233).

35. Peña y Peña to Prefect 12 26 1845 (CAL.HIS.QT. 13:128–29).

36. INIESTRA; Anaya to J.Castro 11 28 1845 (NA98,M210,R3); Spence to Leidesdorff 6 14 1845 (HAWGOOD-1 23); Larkin to Marsh 7 8 1845 (ibid. 24–26), to Stearns 10 1 1845 (ibid. 36); Gillespie to Bancroft 1 16 1846 (CAL.HIS.QT. 18:223); additional information in MEX.SECT.DEFENSA, reels 6, 7, 36, 37, 65. The Mexican troops were initially meant to avenge and supersede Micheltorena (RICHMAN 281; BANCROFT 3:534, 4:527–29, 602–03, 5:33).

37. M.Castro to Min.For.Rel. 6 19 1846 (CAL.HIS.QT. 13:106–07); [Tornel] to M.Castro 8 18 1846 (ibid. 13:110–11).

38. Almonte to Min.For.Rel. 9 2 1846 (ibid. 13:111).

39. BANCROFT 5:278 n.25.

40. See Chapter 18 below; Santa Anna to Min.For.Rel. 12 30 1846 (CAL. HIS.QT. 13:129–30).

41. Gutierrez to Min.For.Rel. 5 3 1847 (ibid. 13:136).

42. Min.War to Min.Int. 6 17 1846 (ibid. 13:139–40).

43. Davis to Stevenson 9 17 1847 (NA98,M210,R2); Stevenson to Mason 9 22 1847 (ibid.); Sherman to Stevenson 10 6, 11 1847 (NA98,M210,R1); Stevenson to Sherman 10 19 1847 (NA98,M210,R2), to Mason 12 1 1847 (ibid.); Mason, proclamation 12 27 1847 (573–17 450); Sherman to Davis 12 29 1847 (NA98, M210,R1), to Stevenson 1 26 1848 (ibid.); Stevenson to Mason 2 8 1848A (NA98,M210,R3); CAL.STAR 5 15 1847 3/3, 5 22 1847 3/1, 5 29 1847 3/1, 12 18 1847 2/3.

44. Kearny to R.Jones 5 13 1847 (573–17 303–04), to Bailey [5 11 1847] (KEARNY 5); CALIFN. 5 6 1847 3/1.

45. Cooke to Turner 4 25 1847 (NA98,M210,R2); Stevenson to Kearny 5 23, 6 2 1847 (ibid.); Davidson to Stevenson 5 23, 6 15 1847 (ibid.); GRIFFIN-1 85.

46. COOKE 297–98.

47. Cooke to Turner 4 25 1847 (NA98,M210,R2); 507–33 233, 423–24.

48. 507–33 35; Kearny to R.Jones 5 13 1847 (573–17 303–04).

49. 507–33 41.

50. Dupont to Mrs.Dupont 2 20 1847 (DUPONT 128); Turner to Mrs.Turner 2 22 1847 (TURNER 156).

51. Kearny to Frémont 3 1 1847 (SPENCE 2:310), to Benton 3 17 1847 (BEN-TON-1 1038/2).

52. Kearny to Frémont 3 28 1847 (SPENCE 2:331).

53. Kearny to Biddle 5 28 1847 (NA98,M210,R1), to Marcy 4 28 1847 (573–17 286).

54. Frémont to Stearns 5 19 1847 (SPENCE 2:353–54); CAL.STAR 5 15 1847 2/1.

55. Turner, dept.order no.19, 5 29 1847 (SPENCE 2:358–59); BANCROFT 5:451–53.

56. 507–33 114, 274, 282, 283; BENTON-1 1009/3–1010/2, 1013/3. Colonel Abert in Washington also ordered Frémont to leave his instruments for Warner's use (J.J.Abert to Frémont 6 11 1847, in SPENCE 2:361).

57. Mason to Montgomery 5 30 1847, with reply (NA45,M625,R285).

58. Larkin to Kearny 5 29 1847 (LARKIN 6:177–78), to Stockton 5 8 1847 (ibid. 6:157).

59. Frémont to Stearns 5 19 1847, Stearns to Frémont 5 23 1847 (SPENCE 2:353–54, 356–57).

60. Kearny to R.Jones 9 16 1846 (*520–60* 175), to Marcy 1 30 1847 (KEARNY-1).

61. Scott to Kearny 11 3 1846 (*499–19* 15–16); Marcy to Kearny 12 10 1846 (*573–17* 242–43).

62. Kearny to R.Jones 5 1 1847 (NA98,M210,R1), 5 13 1847 (*573–17* 304), to Marcy 5 13 1847 (NA98,M210,R1), to R.Jones 5 30, 31 1847 (*573–17* 306, 304). Senator Benton, in pillorying Kearny in the Senate in July 1848, would say he went to California to steal honors for the conquest from those who had won them, then meant to return home on leave and spend the rest of the war with his family (BENTON-1 979/2).

63. COLTON 375.

64. Mason, to whom 5 31 1847 (*573–17* 332); TURNER 125–35; Swords to Jessup 10 8 1847 (*503–1* 229–33).

65. CAL.STAR 7 24 1847 2/3–3/1; SUTTER 39; NEW HELVETIA 50–51.

66. Frémont to Kearny 6 14 1847 (*507–33* 280–81).

67. BRYANT 453; CAL.STAR 6 5 1847 2/1.

68. TURNER 129; CLARKE 332–34.

69. BIGLER 106.

70. *507–33* 282.

71. CAL.STAR 9 18 1847 2/3, 9 4 1847 2/2.

72. Swords to Jessup 10 8 1847 (*503–1* 233).

73. Turner counted 941 wagons, 1,336 men, 789 women, and 1,384 children by the end of July, few destined for California (TURNER 133).

74. Kearny, orders 8 22 1847 (SPENCE 2:375); *507–33* 114–15.

75. MC LANE 104–05; Dupont to Mrs.Dupont 2 20 1847 (DUPONT 128); Turner to Mrs.Turner 2 22, 5 1 1847 (TURNER 155–56, 166).

76. POLK 3:168, 180.

77. *507–33*.

78. Ibid. 340–41, 447.

79. POLK 10 26 1847 3:205.

80. CLARKE 374–88; ALTA 1 25 1849 2/4.

81. Shubrick to Bancroft 2 15 1847, 2 13 1847 (NA45,M625,R284).

82. Stockton to Frémont 2 16 1847 (SPENCE 2:305), to Gillespie 4 1 1847 (GILLESPIE-3 208), 4 10, 23 1847 (SPENCE 2:343, 350); CALIFN. 4 29 1847 2/1, 3/2; concerning Norris, see Chapter 15 above.

83. GRIFFIN-1 82, 83; MC LANE 113. Norris reached San Diego in the *Julia* on May 5, sought out the *Congress*, returned to San Diego on the 11th, and the same day set out for Monterey by land.

84. Stockton to Polk 8 26 1846 (SPENCE 2:193–95); see Chapter 10 above.

85. Stockton to Bancroft 9 19 1846A (NA45,M89,R33); J.Y.Mason to Stockton 1 11 1847 (*573–17* 245–47; full text, NA45,M625,R284).

86. Kearny to Stevenson 5 30 1847 (STEVENSON); MC LANE 114.

87. Dupont to Mrs.Dupont 2 19 1847 (DUPONT 125); Stockton to Gillespie 3 11 1847 (GILLESPIE-3 194).

88. Kearny, orders no.2, 3 1 1847 (SPENCE 2:312); Biddle to Gillespie 3 31, 5 4 1847 (*507–33* 221); *507–33* 204.

89. *507–33* 204; Stockton to Gillespie 5 13 1847 (GILLESPIE-3 239).

90. *507–33* 214–15, 218–27, 307–08; MC LANE 114.

91. *507–33* (1973) 453 n.:p.206; BENTON-1 1015/1–1017/3.

92. Dupont to Mrs.Dupont 1 20 1847 (DUPONT 116); J.Y.Mason to Stockton 11 5 1846 (*499–19* 90).

93. J.Y.Mason to Stockton 1 11 1847 (NA45,M625,R284); CALIFN. 3 20 1847 3/2; Biddle to Mervine 3 17 1847 (NA45,M625,R285).

94. Dupont to Mrs.Dupont 6 23 1847 (DUPONT 187).

95. Montgomery to Mrs.Stockton 6 26 1847 (MONTGOMERY); MC LANE 114; CAL.STAR 7 3 1847 2/2, 3/3; CALIFN. 7 3 1847 2/1.

96. CAL.STAR 7 24 1847 2/3.

97. NEW HELVETIA 7 15 1847; SUTTER 41.

98. CALIFN. 8 21 1847 3/2.

99. CAL.STAR 9 4 1847 2/2.

100. Gillespie, receipts (GILLESPIE-3 242, 246, 319).

101. Gillespie to U.S.State Dept. 4 15 1852 (ibid. 373, 241).

102. POLK 11 25 1847 3:231.

103. Levin to Gillespie 12 4 1847 (GILLESPIE-3 253).

CHAPTER 17. MILITARY OR CIVIL—MASON GOVERNS

1. *507–33* 312.

2. Marcy to Kearny 1 11, 5 11 1847 (*573–17* 244–45, 250); J.Y.Mason to Stockton 1 11 1847 (ibid. 245–47); Buchanan to Frémont 6 11 1847 (SPENCE 2:362–63); GRIVAS 13–17, 79ff.

3. RYAN 1:283.

4. Scott to Mason 11 3 1846 (NA98,M210,R2); POLK 10 26 1846, 11 2 1846 2:209, 214; concerning Stevenson, ibid. 84, 103–04, 117–18, 147.

5. CAL.STAR 10 2 1847 2/2; SHERMAN 29.

6. Mason, to whom 5 31 1847 (*573–17* 332); CAL.STAR 6 19 1847 2/3ff.; GREENWOOD 95.

7. SHERMAN 1:39–40; Halleck would be appointed 8 13 1847 (*573–17* 377).

8. CALIFN. 3 15 1848 2/3.

9. BANCROFT 6:53.

10. Mason's long report to R.Jones 8 17 1848 (*503–1* 56–64); SHERMAN 1:75–84; Folsom to Halleck 8 14 1848 (NA98,M210,R6); Larkin to Buchanan 6 1 1848 (LARKIN 7:285–87).

11. Mason to Long 7 18 1848 (*573–17* 623–24); concerning the *Laws*, see Chapter 18 below.

12. Mason to Boggs 6 2 1847 (*573–17* 317–18).

13. His *secretary of state*: Mason, appointment, Halleck 8 13 1847 (ibid. 377); *alcaldes*: San Bernardino 6 1 1847 (ibid. 316), Santa Cruz 6 21 1847 (ibid. 332), San Juan Capistrano 7 14 1847 (ibid. 375), San José 8 30 1847 (ibid. 391–92), Sonoma 10 28 1847 (ibid. 413), San Luis Obispo 10 29 1847 (ibid. 413), San Juan Bautista 11 22 1847 (ibid. 432–33), San Luis Rey 11 24 1847 (ibid. 434), Los Angeles 12 10 1847 (ibid. 443), San Diego 12 10 1847 (ibid. 443), Benicia 1 3 1848 (ibid. 452), Santa Barbara 2 8 1848 (ibid. 473), Sacramento 11 28 1848 (ibid. 486–87); *sheriff*: 6 14 1847 (ibid. 322); *land surveyors*: 6 7 1847, 7 6 1847, 7 22 1847, 9 20 1847 (ibid. 320, 334, 377, 398); *Indian agent*: Hunter 8 1 1847 (ibid. 344–45, 384); *inspector of hides and tallow*: 8 13 1847 (ibid. 380); *auditor, customs*: 8 19 1847 (ibid. 385–86); *special com-*

missioners: Vallejo and Sutter 8 19 1847 (ibid. 384), Snyder 8 26 1847 (ibid. 146); *interpreter*: 1 22 1849 (ibid. 690); *collector and harbormaster*: 8 1 1847, 8 19 1847, 8 7 1848 (ibid. 379, 385, 654).

14. Mason to alcalde, Los Angeles 12 10 1847 (*573*–17 443), to Stevenson 12 29 1847, 6 11 1848 (ibid. 451, 563–64), to E.P.Jones/Leidesdorff 3 25 1848 (ibid. 499–500).

15. Mason to Hyde 7 15 1847 (ibid. 378–79), to Weeks 11 5 1847 (ibid. 417), to Sánchez 11 22 1847 (ibid. 433), to Stevenson 12 29 1847 (ibid. 451), to Blackburn 3 24 1848 (ibid. 498).

16. Sherman to Lippitt 8 25 1847 (ibid. 351–52), to L.Carrillo 8 25 1847 (ibid. 354); Mason, notice 2 12 1848 (ibid. 476–77).

17. Mason to White 3 16 1848 (*573*–17 494), to P.C.Carrillo 4 12 1848 (ibid. 509), to Ardisson 4 12 1848 (ibid. 508–09), to Reed 4 29 1848 (ibid. 546); Halleck to Lippitt/P.C.Carrillo 7 20 1848 (ibid. 570–71), to Stevenson/Foster 7 20 1848 (ibid. 571), to Lippitt 7 20 1848 (ibid. 571), to Foster 7 25 1848 (ibid. 574).

18. Mason to Weeks 12 20 1847 (*573*–17 445), to White 3 25 1848 (ibid. 498–99), 4 17 1848 (ibid. 551–54), 4 24 1848 (ibid. 542–43), to P.C.Carrillo 4 5 1848 (ibid. 507), to Foster 4 [18] 1848 (ibid. 540).

19. Mason to Vallejo 8 19 1847 (*573*–17 384); Sherman to Snyder 8 26 1847 (ibid. 146–47); Mason to S.F.Council 10 1 1847 (ibid. 361–62), to McKee 12 3 1847 (ibid. 439), to P.C.Carrillo 4 5 1848 (ibid. 505–06), to Foster 4 [18] 1848 (ibid. 540, 541).

20. Mason to Bonilla 6 16 1847 (ibid. 323).

21. Mason to Boggs/Vallejo 11 11 1847 (*573*–17 419–21), to Folsom 11 11 1847 (ibid. 421–22), to Carnes 4 5 1848 (ibid. 506–07).

22. Mason, proclamation 12 27 1847 (ibid. 450).

23. Shubrick/Mason, to the people 10 9 1847 (CALIFN. 10 27 1848 2/3–3/1); Mason to Lanman 10 15 1847 (*573*–17 408–09); Halleck to Alexander 8 7 1848 (ibid. 654–55); Sherman to Stevenson 5 31 1848C (ibid. 615).

24. Mason to R.Jones 11 11 1847 (*573*–17 399–401), to Folsom 2 22 1848 (ibid. 484), to Douglas 4 13 1848 (ibid. 509), to Stevenson 4 15 1848 (ibid. 511).

25. Mason to Howard 7 31 1848 (ibid. 664–65).

26. Halleck, circular 9 18 1847 (NA94,M182,R1); Stevenson to Halleck 10 4 1847 (NA98,M210,R6); Halleck to Stevenson 10 15 1847 (*573*–17 407–08).

27. Marcy to Kearny 6 3 1846 (499–19 6); Shubrick/Mason, to the people 10 9 1847 (CALIFN. 10 27 1848 2/3–3/1).

28. Mason to White 3 9 1848 (*573*–17 492).

29. Mason to Stevenson 7 14 1847 (ibid. 343).

30. Mason to Weeks 12 20 1847 (ibid. 445).

31. Mason to R.Jones 12 27 1848 (ibid. 653).

32. Mason to Dimmick 1 23 1849 (ibid. 691).

33. Mason to Grigsby 6 3 1847 (ibid. 318).

34. Mason to Vioget 10 28 1847 (ibid. 412).

35. Mason to Boggs 4 28 1848 (ibid. 545).

36. Mason to Thompson 8 27 1847 (ibid. 391).

37. Mason to J.F.Reed 4 29 1848 (ibid. 546).

38. Mason to Murphy 3 2 1848 (ibid. 488), to P.Carrillo 4 5 1848B (ibid. 505–06).

39. Mason, proclamation 12 29 1847 (ibid. 452).

40. Mason to McKee 12 3 1847 (ibid. 439).

41. Mason to Adj.Genl. 4 18 1848 (NA98,M210,R1); Boggs to Mason 5 8 1848 (NA98,M210,R3).

42. Mason to Boggs 6 2 1847 (*573*–17 317).

43. Mason to Fisher 8 30 1847 (ibid. 391–92).

44. Mason to P.de la Guerra/L.Carrillo 6 14 1847 (ibid. 321–22).

45. CAL.STAR 5 22 1847 3/2, 7 17 1847 2/2; Mason to Boggs 7 22 1847 (*573*–17 377–78), to Folsom 7 22 1847 (ibid. 344); Brackett to Mason 7 29 1847 (NA98,M210,R2); SHERMAN 1:31, 36–37.

46. Mason to Hyde 7 15 1847, 8 13 1847 (*573*–17 378–79; CAL.STAR 9 4 1847 2/3; GREENWOOD 91).

47. Mason to S.F.Town Council 10 1 1847 (CAL.STAR 10 9 1847 3/1-2), to Howard et al. 3 14 1848, 3 16 1848 (*573*–17 494–95), to E.P.Jones/Leidesdorff 3 25 1848 (ibid. 499–500).

48. Mason to Hyde 3 27 1848 (ibid. 500); Mason, appointment, Townsend 3 27 1848 (ibid.).

49. Mason, appointment, Foster 12 10 1847 (*573*–17 443), to alcalde 12 10 1847 (ibid.), to Stevenson 12 29 1847 (ibid.).

50. Sherman to L.Carrillo 8 25 1847 (ibid. 354).

51. Mason to Hardie 10 21 1847 (ibid. 404).

52. Mason to Burton 7 13 1847 (ibid. 335); Mason, circular 8 23 1847 (CAL.STAR 9 11 1847 3/3); Mason to Weeks 11 25 1847 (*573*–17 435).

53. Halleck to Serrano 10 31 1848 (*573*–17 675), to Bandini 8 12 1848 (ibid. 593), to Boggs 8 15 1848 (ibid. 595), to Lebrija et al. 1 21 1849 (ibid. 689).

54. CAL.STAR 12 25 1847 3/2.

55. Mason to Boggs 6 7 1847 (*573*–17 321).

56. CALIFN. 4 10 1847 1/2–2/2.

57. Mason to Blackburn 11 24 1847 (*573*–17 433–34).

58. Halleck to Marron et al. 5 15 1849 (ibid. 764); Mason to White 3 10 1848 (ibid. 492–93).

59. Mason to Foster 5 31 1848 (ibid. 558).

60. Mason to White 3 25, 4 24 1848 (ibid. 498–99, 543).

61. "Paisano," CAL.STAR 3 11 1847 1/2–3.

62. Sherman to alcaldes 7 3 1847 (*573*–17 340); Mason to P.C.Carrillo 4 12 1848 (ibid. 509).

63. Mason to White 3 2 1848 (ibid. 487).

64. Mason to Brackett 6 2 1847 (ibid. 325), to Naglee 7 10 1847 (ibid. 340–41); Stevenson to Salazar 8 4 1847 (NA98,M210,R2); Sherman to Stevenson 8 23 1847 (*573*–17 349–50); Halleck to P.C.Carrillo 7 19 1848 (ibid. 569–70); Mason to Sinclair 10 24 1848 (ibid. 677), to Burton 2 20 1849 (ibid. 890), to R.Jones 3 23 1849 (NA98,M210,R1).

65. Mason to alcaldes, Santa Cruz and San José 2 3 1848 (*573*–17 471).

66. Sherman to Lippitt 8 25 1847 (ibid. 351); Halleck to Lippitt 7 25 1848 (ibid. 575–76).

67. Mason, order no.36, 7 27 1847 (*573*–17 352).

68. Not covered by a congressional act of 1806 governing armies of the U.S.; Scott, general orders no.20, 2 19 1847 (ibid. 353–54); Sherman to Griffin 10 20 1847 (ibid. 402–03).

69. L.Carrillo to Lippitt 8 10 1847 (NA98,M210,R2); Lippitt to L.Carrillo 8 10 1847 (ibid.); L.Carrillo to Mason 8 16 1847 (ibid.); Sherman to L.Carrillo 8 25 1847 (*573–17* 354), to Lippitt 8 25 1847 (ibid. 351–52).

70. Stevenson to Mason 4 21 1848 (NA98,M210,R3); Sherman to Stevenson 5 8 1848 (NA98,M210,R1).

71. Mason to Stevenson 4 [18] 1848 (*573–17* 539–40), to Foster 4 [18] 1848 (ibid. 540, 541).

72. POLK 3 10 1847, 3 12 1847, 3 23 1847, 4 1 1847, 4 3 1847 2:416, 420, 437, 450, 454, modifications 6 11 1847, 10 12 1847, 1 2 1849 3:56, 189–90, 4:266; Polk to Walker, ex.order 3 23 1847 (RICHARDSON 4:523–24; NA98, M210,R6); Walker to Polk 3 30 1847 (RICHARDSON 4:524–29); Walker, tariff of duties 3 30 1847 (*515–8* 567–76); Polk to Sects.War/Navy 3 31 1847 (RICHARDSON 4:529–30); Walker, circular to collectors 4 7 1847 (NA98,M210, R6); J.Y.Mason to Comdg.Officer 4 3 1847 (ibid.), 5 10 1847 (NA98,M210, R5); Marcy to Kearny 5 10 1847 (ibid.); modifications: Walker to Polk 6 10, 11 5, 16 1847 (RICHARDSON 4:530, 531–32); Mason to Shubrick 12 11 [or 12] 1847 (*573–17* 444).

73. Shubrick/Mason, to the people 10 9 1847 (CALIFN. 10 27 1847 2/3–3/1).

74. Shubrick to collectors 9 15 1847 (NA45,M625,R285); Mason, circular 10 14 1847 (*573–17* 406–07).

75. Mason to R.Jones 11 11 1847 (*573–17*:399); Dupont to Mrs.Dupont 10 1 1847 (DUPONT 248).

76. Mason, circular 10 14 1847 (*573–17* 406–07), to Lanman 10 15 1847 (ibid. 408–09); Mason, extract of regs. 10 20 1847, as modified 11 5 1847 (MASON), to Folsom 10 14 1847 (*573–17* 405); Walker, circular 4 7 1847 (NA98, M210,R6, copy as modified for California).

77. Larkin to Buchanan 11 10 1847 (LARKIN 7:58).

78. Mason to Green 10 15 1847 (*573–17* 407), to Stevenson 10 20 1847 (ibid. 409), to Pedrorena 10 20 1847 (ibid. 409–10); Stevenson to Mason 11 2 1847 (ibid. 426).

79. Lippitt to Sherman 4 6 1848 (NA98,M210,R3).

80. Lippitt to Sherman 7 16 1847 (*573–17* 331); Mason to Hull 7 21 1847 (NA98,M210,R1); Hull to Mason 7 21 1847 (NA98,M210,R2); Mason to R.Jones 7 21 1847 (NA98,M210,R1); Sherman to Stevenson 7 25 1847 (STEVENSON); Mason to R.Jones 9 18 1847 (*573–17* 335–36).

81. Mason, order no.36, 5 31 1848 (THOMPSON & WEST 72); some were excepted who had aided the American cause. Papers relating to collections (NA98,M210,R6,7); Sherman to Stevenson 5 31 1848C (*573–17* 615); Stevenson to Lippitt 7 6 1848 and related documents (NA98,M210,R6); Halleck to Stevenson 7 21 1848 (*573–17* 573), to Ardisson 8 4 1848 (ibid. 589); BIGGS 119–25. Lippitt had little to say about the affair in his reminiscences (LIPPITT 74).

82. THOMPSON & WEST 72–74.

83. King to Lippitt 4 6 1848 (NA98,M210,R3); Lippitt to Sherman 4 6, 8 1848 (ibid.); de la Guerra to A.Pico 4 11 1848 (ibid.); Sherman to Stevenson 4 12 1848 (NA98,M210,R1), to Lippitt 4 12 1848 (ibid.), to Noriega 4 12 1848 (ibid.); Lippitt to Stevenson 4 12 1848 (NA98,M210,R3); A.Pico to Stevenson 4 13 1848 (ibid.); Lataillade to Stevenson 4 18 1848 (ibid.); Ayala to Stevenson 4 18 1848 (ibid.); Stevenson to Mason 4 18 1848 (ibid.); Lippitt, statement 4 18 1848 (ibid.); Alvarez, statement 4 18 1848 (ibid.); Rodriguez, statement 4 18 1848 (ibid.); Stevenson to Sherman 4 19 1848 (ibid.); Ruiz, statement 4 20 1848

(ibid.); Stevenson to Sherman [4 20 1848] (ibid.); Ignais et al., statements ca. 4 20 1848 (ibid.); Lippitt, statement 4 20 1848 (ibid.); P.C.Carrillo to Stevenson 4 20 1848 (ibid.); Stevenson to Mason 4 20 1848 (ibid.); de la Guerra to Sherman 4 20 1848 (ibid.); Foster to Mason 4 20 1848 (ibid.); Lippitt to Sherman 4 21 1848AB (ibid.); J.Carrillo, statement 4 23 1848 (ibid.); Lippitt to Sherman 4 25 1848 (ibid.); Sherman to Noriega 4 27 1848 (NA98,M210,R1), to Stevenson 4 27 1848 (ibid.); Mason to Stevenson 5 1 1848 (ibid.); Stevenson to Mason 5 16 1848 (NA98,M210,R3); Sherman to Stevenson 5 31 1848C (573–17 615); Mason, order 5 31 1848 (THOMPSON & WEST 72); Halleck to Stevenson 7 21 1848A (573–17 573); Stevenson to Mason 7 23 1848 (NA98,M210,R3); Halleck to Ardisson 8 4 1848 (573–17 589).

84. Halleck to Lippitt 8 7 1848 (573–17 591); Stevenson to Lippitt 8 20 1848 (NA98,M210,R6).

85. GARCIA 3–9; FOSTER 32–34; BANCROFT 5:586–87 and n.10–11.

86. See Chapter 16 above. Sherman to Folsom 2 24, 3 1, 12 7 1848 (NA98, M210,R1); CALIFN. 3 15 1848 2/3, 2/4. Both newspapers advertised mails to Independence, letters 50¢, papers 12½¢ (CAL.STAR 1 15 1848 2/2, 4 22 1848 2/4; CALIFN. 3 1 1848 2/1).

87. Mason, circular 12 10 1847 (573–17 442); Mason to R.Jones 11 11 1847 (ibid. 399), to Libbey 11 11 1847 (ibid. 428–29), to McKinney 11 13 1847 (ibid. 429), to Gray 11 23 1847 (ibid. 433), to Hinckley 4 14 1848 (ibid. 509–10).

88. Mason/Shubrick, police regs. for harbors 9 15 1847 (NA45,M625,R285); Shubrick to collectors 9 15 1847 (ibid.); Mason, Customhouse regs. 7 26 1848 (573–17 583–85); Shubrick, general order 2 11 1847 (CALIFN. 2 13 1847 3/2); Mason to R.Jones 11 11 1847 (573–17 399–401); circular 10 14 1847 (ibid. 406–07); MASON; GREENWOOD 89, 90, 92.

89. Grimes to Mason 2 12 1848 (NA98,M210,R6); Mason to Folsom 2 22 1848 (573–17 484).

90. Leidesdorff to Folsom 10 25 1847 (NA98,M210,R6); Sherman to Folsom 10 28 1847A (NA98,M210,R1).

91. Mason to D.Douglas 4 13 1848 (573–17 509), to Stevenson 4 15 1848 (ibid. 511).

92. Mason to Colton et al. 7 28, 8 18 1848 (ibid. 581, 589).

93. Howard et al. to Mason 7 22 1848 (CALIFN. 8 14 1848 3/3); Folsom to Mason 7 27 1848 (NA98,M210,R6); Mason to Howard et al. 7 31 1848 (573–17 664–65); Halleck to Folsom 9 10 1848B (ibid. 666); Folsom to Mason 11 7 1848 (NA98,M210,R6); BANCROFT 6:268–69 n.31).

94. Halleck to Folsom 8 1 1848 (573–17 586–87).

95. Mason to R.Jones 8 17 1848 (ibid. 534).

96. Mason to Abbisu 6 3 1847 (ibid. 319), to Semple 4 21 1848 (ibid. 542), to Spear 6 3 1847 (ibid. 319), to Adj.Genl. 4 18 1848 (NA98,M210,R1).

97. Mason to Blackburn 6 21 1847 (573–17 332–33), to Boggs 5 17 1848 (ibid. 551); Halleck to S.Smith 8 16 1847 (ibid. 380), to J.Black 8 16 1847 (ibid. 380–81).

98. Mason to Pickett 12 14 1847 (ibid. 440).

99. Halleck to S.Smith 8 16 1847 (ibid. 380), to J.Black 8 16 1847 (ibid. 380–81).

100. Mason, appointments, Ide 6 7 1847 (ibid. 320), O'Farrell 7 6 1847 (ibid. 334), Snyder 7 22 1847 (ibid. 377), Lyman 9 20 1847 (ibid. 398).

101. Mason to Weeks 11 24 1847 (ibid. 435).

102. Halleck to Graham 2 21 1849 (ibid. 695–96).

103. Larkin to Mason 6 1847 (LARKIN 6:228–29); Mason to Ross 3 23 1848 (573–17 497).

104. Halleck to Aquila 9 6 1847 (573–17 393).

105. Stevenson to Halleck 9 7 1847 (ibid. 179–80); Mason to Carnes 2 19 1848 (ibid. 479); Halleck to Stevenson 7 26 1848 (ibid. 668–69); Mason to Pico 2 21 1849 (ibid. 694); HALLECK-1 129.

106. CALIFN. 2 20 1847 2/1.

107. HALLECK-1.

108. Mason to R.Jones 4 13 1849 (573–17 118).

109. Dupont to Mrs.Dupont 3 17, 2 21 1847 (DUPONT 150–51, 134).

110. GATES; GATES-1.

111. HALLECK-1 125, 148–49; DWINELLE, addenda 26–27; a summary of regulations relating to the missions, Halleck to Stevenson 7 25 1848 (573–17 576–79); ELDREDGE 171–81.

112. Dated 8 18 1824 and 11 21 1828 (HALLECK-1 125, 139–42; DWINELLE, addenda 23–24, 25–26).

113. Dated 8 9 1834 (HALLECK-1 125–26, 149–53; DWINELLE, addenda 31–34; BANCROFT 3:342–44 n.4).

114. Supplementary rules by Governor Alvarado 1 17 1839 and 3 1 1840 (HALLECK-1 126, 154–60; DWINELLE, addenda 55–56, 57–60).

115. San Diego, San Luis Rey, San Juan Capistrano, San Gabriel, San Fernando, San Buenaventura, Santa Barbara, Santa Cruz, La Purísima, San Antonio, Santa Clara, and San José (HALLECK-1 126, 161–62; DWINELLE, addenda 83–84; BANCROFT 4:368–71).

116. Assembly regulation 5 28 1845: Purísima, San Rafael, San Francisco, Soledad, San Miguel, Carmel, San Juan Bautista, Capistrano, and Solano (HALLECK-1 126–27, 162–63; DWINELLE, addenda 88–89; BANCROFT 4:549–50).

117. Pico's regulations 10 28 1845: Santa Barbara, San Buenaventura, Santa Inés, San Fernando, Santa Clara, San José, San Antonio, San Rafael, San Luis Rey, and San Diego (HALLECK-1 127, 163–66; DWINELLE, addenda 90–92; BANCROFT 5:558–59).

118. 4 3 1846 (HALLECK-1 127, 166–67; BANCROFT 5:559).

119. San Juan Bautista, San José, San Luis Rey, San Rafael, San Buenaventura, San Diego, San Gabriel, Santa Barbara, Santa Inés, San Fernando, San Miguel, and Soledad, and the gardens of Santa Clara (BANCROFT 5:560–62 and n.8).

120. HALLECK-1 128, 167; BANCROFT 5:563.

121. CALIFN. 10 17 1846 2/1–2, 10 24 1846 2/1–2.

122. Kearny, decree 3 22 1847 (573–17 291; CALIFN. 3 27 1847 3/1); Mason, to all 6 24 1847 (573–17 3–4), to Naglee 7 10 1847 (ibid. 340–41).

123. Mason to Naglee 7 11, 19 1847 (573–17 341–42, 343), to Real 7 12 1847 (ibid. 334–35).

124. Mason to Real 11 16, 12 23 1847, 1 3 1848 (ibid. 429–30, 448, 453), to Blackburn 11 24 1847 (ibid. 433–34); Halleck to Stevenson 8 18 1848 (ibid. 596), to P.C.Carrillo 8 18 1848 (ibid.). Governor Riley would subsequently dismiss Real for having "shamefully neglected his duty" (Riley, to all 9 17 1849, in ibid. 829–30).

125. Halleck to W.Reed 9 18 1847 (ibid. 396).

126. Mason to Lataillade 3 29 1848 (ibid. 502–03).

127. Mason to J.Castro 3 6 1848 (ibid. 490).

128. Mason to Covarrubias/J.Carrillo 11 29 1847 (ibid. 436).

129. Mason to Stevenson 2 19 1848 (ibid. 479).

130. Sherman to Hunter 8 1 1847 (ibid. 344—45); Mason, appointment, Hunter 8 1 1847 (ibid. 384), to Hunter 8 2 1847 (ibid. 348—49), to R.Jones 9 18 1847 (ibid. 336—37).

131. Halleck to Stevenson 7 22 1848 (ibid. 574); Mason to Lataillade 3 29 1848 (ibid. 502—03).

132. Halleck to Soberanes 4 2 1849 (ibid. 702).

133. Mason to Stevenson 5 8 1848A (ibid. 549).

134. Halleck, circular 3 31 1849 (ibid. 701—02).

135. ELDREDGE 173—75, 180—81.

136. Mason to R.Jones 6 18 1847 (*573—17* 314—15).

137. Formerly of the Mormon Battalion; Kearny to Sutter 4 7 1847 (ibid. 294—95), to Vallejo 4 14 1847 (ibid. 296—97); Sherman to Hunter 8 1 1847 (ibid. 344—45, 384).

138. Sutter to Mason 7 12 1847 (ibid. 374).

139. Mason to Sutter 7 21 1847 (ibid. 376—77).

140. A.M.Armijo, "Growling" Smith, and John Egger; Mason to Anderson 7 21 1847 (ibid. 343—44), to Vallejo/Sutter 8 19 1847 (ibid. 384), to Hardie 8 19 1847 (ibid. 349), to Folsom 8 19 1847 (ibid.); Halleck to Hardie 9 10 1847 (ibid. 394), to Vallejo 9 15 1847 (ibid. 395); BANCROFT 5:610.

141. Mason to Boggs/Vallejo 11 11 1847 (*573—17* 419—21), to Folsom 11 11 1847 (ibid. 419—22).

142. Halleck to Sutter 8 16 1847 (ibid. 381—83), to Vallejo 8 16 1847 (ibid. 381), circular 8 16 1847 (ibid. 358—59).

143. Sherman to Hunter 8 1 1847 (*573—17* 344—45), to R.Jones 9 18 1847 (ibid. 336—37); Mason to Bonilla 11 30 1847 (ibid. 437—38), to Hunter 12 1 1847 (ibid. 438), notice 1 7 1848 (ibid. 454), to Comdg.Officer, S.F. 2 5 1848 (ibid. 472).

144. Mason to Vallejo 5 25 1848 (ibid. 556—57).

145. Mason to Sutter 3 5 1848 (ibid. 490); HEIZER-1 66—67.

146. CAL.STAR 12 11 1847 2/2.

147. Halleck, circular 9 6 1847 (ibid. 9 18 1847 3/3).

148. Ibid. 12 11 1847 2/2.

149. Mason, proclamation 11 29 1847 (*573—17* 437), circular 12 21 1847 (ibid. 447), to Longley 6 16, 17 1848 (ibid. 565—66).

150. Mason to P.C.Carrillo 7 20 1848 (ibid. 571—72).

151. Halleck, circular 3 31 1848 (ibid. 701—02).

152. Crawford to P.F.Smith 4 4 1849 (ibid. 275); and see HURTADO.

153. Sherman to Burton 9 6 1847 (*573—17* 355).

154. Mason to Sinclair 3 5 1848 (ibid. 489).

155. Mason to Price 3 21, 4 4 1848 (ibid. 496—97, 505), to Hardie 5 25 1848 (ibid. 557—58).

156. Mason to Vallejo 5 25 1848 (ibid. 556—57).

157. Mason to Adj.Genl. 5 19 1848 (NA98,M210,R1). *Grievances against Indians:* CAL.STAR 3 20 1847 2/1, 4 10 1847 2/2, 4/1—2, 4 17 1847 2/3, 3/2, 5 1 1847 2/2, 5 29 1847 3/1; Stevenson to Mason 6 28 1847, 7 12 1847A (NA98,M210,R2), 2 8 1848B, 4 21 1848 (NA98,M210,R3); Sherman to E.O.C.Ord 2 3 1848 (NA98, M210,R1); E.O.C.Ord to Mason 2 16 1848 (NA98,M210,R3); Stevenson to A.Pico 2 14 1848 (ibid.); Brackett to Sherman 2 25 1848 (ibid.); Lippitt to Sherman

3 9 1848 (ibid.); Sherman to Lippitt 3 21 1848 (NA98,M210,R1); Bonnycastle, orders 4 2 1848 (NA98,M210,R3); Stevenson to Lippitt 4 3 1848AB (ibid.); Brackett to Mason 4 14 1848 (ibid.); Sherman to Stevenson 5 8 1848 (NA98,M210, R1); Prieto to Stevenson 5 10 1848 (NA98,M210,R3); Rock to Leese 5 20 1848 (ibid.); Citizens of Sonoma to Mason 5 [22] 1848AB (ibid.); Leese to Boggs 5 [22] 1848 (ibid.); Hardie to Brackett 5 22 1848 (ibid.); Stone, affidavit 5 22 1848 (ibid.); Boggs to Mason 5 22 1848 (ibid.); Brackett to Mason 5 22 1848 (ibid.); Sherman to [Boggs?] 5 24 1848 (NA98,M210,R1); Hardie to Mason 5 28 1848 (NA98,M210,R3), to Sherman 5 28 1848AB (ibid.); Brackett to Hardie 5 29 1848 (ibid.); Hardie to Mason 6 1 1848 (ibid.); Hardie/Vallejo, treaty 6 1 1848 (ibid.); Brackett to Mason 6 1 1848 (ibid.).

158. Larkin to Buchanan 1 14 1847 (LARKIN 6:9).

159. *Frémont's California claims:* 512–75, 527–817, 698–49, 723–77, 751–8, 782–13, 821–63, 825–109; R.Jones to Marcy 8 21 1848 (NA98, M210,R5).

160. Larkin to Buchanan 6 30 1847 (LARKIN 6:226). The *Congress* sailed to Mazatlán in July 1848 for the "2d installment of $100,000 for the army," after Stockton's departure.

161. Stockton, circular 8 15 1846AB (497–4 673).

162. Larkin to Stockton 3 15 1847 (LARKIN 6:54–55).

163. GARNER 196; Stockton to Larkin 4 20 1847 (LARKIN 6:112); Speiden to Larkin 9 4 1847 (ibid. 6:314–15).

164. Larkin to Speiden 9 4 1848 (LARKIN 6:212–13); CALIFN. 6 12 1847 2/2.

165. Kearny to McKinstry 4 18 1847 (NA98,M210,R1).

166. Sherman to J.J.Warner 6 12 1847 (573–17 327), to Hardy 6 12 1847 (ibid.), to Stevenson 10 6 1847 (NA98,M210,R1); Hardy to Pedrorena 8 7 1848 (573–17 655).

167. 512–75 37.

168. Mason to R.Jones 6 18 1847 (573–17 315).

169. Bryant to Larkin 3 31 1847 (LARKIN 6:80–81).

170. CAL.STAR 3 27 1847 2/1, 2/3-3/1, 4 10 1847 3/1–2, 5 29 1847 2/1–2; SPENCE 2:xlv–xlvi.

171. Mason to Biddle 6 17 1847 (NA98,M210,R1), to W.H.Warner 6 17 1847 (ibid.); J.Y.Mason to Comdg.Officer 11 4 1846 (NA98,M210,R2).

172. Mason to Jessup 8 25 1848 (573–17 641); Jessup to Mason 12 8 1848 (NA98,M210,R4).

173. COOKE 283.

174. Marcy to Kearny 6 3 1846 (499–19 6), 1 11, 6 11 1847 (573–17 244, 250); J.Y.Mason to Stockton 1 11 1847 (ibid. 247); Riley to Hooker 8 30 1849 (ibid. 815).

175. Kearny to Richardson 3 29, 4 21 1847 (573–17 292–93, 298); with similar instructions to collectors at other ports.

176. Mason, circular 6 1 1847 (ibid. 316–17, to Folsom 7 16 1847 (ibid. 376).

177. Mason to Shubrick 8 16 1847 (ibid. 383).

178. Sherman to Leavenworth 9 30 1847 (ibid. 360); Mason to Ritchie 12 22 1847 (ibid. 448), to Folsom 11 11 1847 (ibid. 421–22), to Lataillade 1 24 1849 (ibid. 691), to Dimmick 1 23 1849 (ibid.). The sum of $70,000 would be loaned to the navy to bring emigrants from Baja California (Halleck to Allen 8 22 1849, in ibid. 813).

179. Mason to Carnes 4 5 1848 (*573–17* 506–07); Sherman to Folsom 10 23 1848 (NA98,M210,R1); Mason to Sinclair 10 24 1848 (*573–17* 677), to Foster 5 31 1848 (ibid. 558); Halleck to Folsom 2 3 1849 (ibid. 692); *578–72*.

180. Crawford to Taylor 6 26 1850 (*578–72* 3); Sherman to Folsom 11 25, 12 20 1847 (NA98,M210,R1), 8 3 1848 (*573–17* 641), to Davidson 11 24 1847 (NA98,M210,R1), to Carnes 4 14 1848 (ibid.); *578–72* 13.

181. Riley to Hooker 8 30 1849 (*573–17* 814–19); P.F.Smith to Freeman 12 30 1848 [i.e., 1849] (*561–52* 86–87).

182. Mason to Snyder 5 23 1848 (*573–17* 555–56). He had in February 1848 abolished the Mexican procedure for "denouncing" mines found on other peoples' lands (Mason [circular] 2 12 1848, in ibid. 476–77); Mason to White 3 9 1848 (ibid. 492).

183. Mason to R.Jones 8 17 1848 (ibid. 532–33).

184. Mason to R.Jones 11 24 1848 (ibid. 648). T.A.C.Jones to J.Y.Mason 11 25 1848 would echo these recommendations, but advocate an assay office rather than a more expensive mint (NA45,M89,R34).

185. Halleck to Folsom 8 1 1848 (*573–17* 586–87).

186. P.F.Smith to Marcy 1 7 1849 (ibid. 704), to Nelson 1 19 1848 (ibid. 716).

187. Bidwell to Larkin 5 15 1848 (LARKIN 7:260).

188. Semple to Larkin 5 19 1848 (ibid. 7:267); Larkin to Green 6 3 1848 (ibid. 7:290).

189. Larkin to Ten Eyck 6 3 1848 (ibid. 7:291), to Buchanan 6 28 1848 (ibid. 7:304).

190. Larkin to Buchanan 7 20 1848 (ibid. 7:321).

191. Stevenson to Mason 7 24 1848B (NA98,M210,R3).

192. Green to Larkin 9 28 1848 (LARKIN 7:367).

193. Montgomery to Kern 10 29 1846 (FORT SUTTER 73).

194. T.A.C.Jones to J.Y.Mason 7 28 1848 (NA45,M625,R286); Shubrick, proclamation 9 6 1847 (CALIFN. 9 8 1847 3/1; CAL.STAR 9 11 1847 3/2).

195. Mason, proclamation 9 6 1847 (CALIFN. 9 15 1847 2/3); CAL.STAR 9 18 1847 3/2).

196. S.F.ordinance 9 16 1847 (CAL.STAR 9 18 1847 2/3).

197. Sherman to [Lippitt] 8 24 1847 (*573–17* 350–51); Mason, customhouse and port regs. 7 26 1848 (ibid. 583–84).

198. CAL.STAR 9 25 1847 3/2.

199. Hardie to Sherman 5 28 1848B (NA98,M210,R3); Sherman to Hardie 6 1 1848 (NA98,M210,R1).

200. Mason, notice 7 25 1848 (*573–17* 580).

201. Mason, copy of furlough to dig gold 9 25 1848 (LANCEY 688).

202. Davidson to [Mason] 9 27 1848 (NA98,M210,R3).

203. T.A.C.Jones to J.Y.Mason 7 28 1848 (NA45,M625,R286), to R.B.Mason 10 19 1848 (NA98,M210,R3), to J.Y.Mason 10 25 1848 (NA45,M625,R286).

204. T.A.C.Jones, official notice 10 18 1848 (CAL.STAR & CALIFN. 11 18 1848 1/1).

205. J.Y.Mason to T.A.C.Jones 3 1 1849 (NA45,M625,R286); T.A.C.Jones to J.Y.Mason 11 2 1848 (ibid.).

206. T.A.C.Jones, notice 12 1848 (CAL.STAR & CALIFN. 12 23 1848 3/1), to J.Y.Mason 3 15 1849 (NA45,M625,R286).

207. Mason to R.Jones 12 27 1848 (*573–17* 650).

208. Mason to R.Jones 8 19 1848 (ibid. 598).

209. P.F.Smith to R.Jones 3 15 1849 (ibid. 713), to Crawford 6 20 1849 (ibid. 745), to Freeman 10 7 1849 (*558–47* 95–96); Riley to R.Jones 4 25 1849 (*573–17* 875); SHERMAN 1:102–05.

210. A recommendation approved, R.Jones to Gibson 6 22 1849 (NA98,M210, R4); Commissary General to See 8 6 1849 (ibid.).

CHAPTER 18. END OF THE WAR—MASON'S DILEMMA

1. News of a preliminary armistice of 8 24 1847, Lavalette to Shubrick or Mason 9 29 1847 (in Shubrick to Mason 10 1847, NA98,M210,R2; CAL.STAR 11 6 1847 1/3–2/1); of armistice of 3 9 1848, Mason to T.A.C.Jones 6 17 1848 (*573–17* 621).

2. Marcy to Mason 3 15 1848 (*573–17* 254–55); R.Jones to Mason 7 6 1848 (NA98,M210,R4), rcd. 1 29 1849; Lay to Mason 5 24 1848 (NA98,M210,R3); Sevier/Clifford [notification] 5 30 1848 (ibid.); Stevenson to Mason 7 31 1848 (ibid.); Mason to R.Jones 8 19 1848 (*573–17* 597); treaty and documents *521–69*.

3. Mason, proclamation 8 7 1848 (*573–17* 590–91); GREENWOOD 110, 111.

4. Halleck to Folsom 8 9 1848 (*573–17* 592); Mason to R.Jones 8 19 1848 (ibid. 597–98), to T.A.C.Jones 1 1 1849 (ibid. 685–86).

5. Halleck to Lippitt 8 7 1848 (ibid. 591); Stevenson to Lippitt 8 20 1848 (NA98,M210,R6); A.J.Smith to Sherman 10 1 1848 (NA98,M210,R3).

6. Mason to R.Jones 8 19 1848 (*573–17* 597–98); Polk's similar views (POLK 10 7 1848, 10 9 1848 4:147–48, 151); Walker, circular 10 7 1848 (*503–1* 45); Halleck to Pedrorena 8 7 1848 (*573–17* 655), to Alexander 8 7 1848 (ibid. 654–55), to Gilbert 8 21 1848 (ibid. 657–58), to Harrison 9 3 1848 (ibid. 660), 2 24 1849 (ibid. 694–95).

7. P.F.Smith to R.Jones 3 15 1849 (*573–17* 712–13), to Freeman 10 7 1849 (*558–47* 79–80); Halleck to Harrison 2 24 1849 (*573–17* 694–95).

8. Mason to T.A.C.Jones 2 26 1849 (*573–17* 696); T.A.C.Jones to C.V. Gillespie 2 26 1849 (ALTA 3 8 1849 2/4).

9. Mason to Aguirre 9 9 1848 (*573–17* 663–64), to Ross 9 10 1848 (ibid. 665–66); Halleck to Harrison 9 25 1848 (ibid. 671–74); Mason to Walters 11 15 1848 (ibid. 675–76), to R.Jones 12 28 1848 (ibid. 682–83); Burton to Mason 2 1849 (ibid. 693).

10. Sherman to Hardie 6 7 1848 (*573–17* 633), to Comdr. San José 8 7 1848 (ibid.), to Rich 8 7 1848 (ibid. 632), to A.J.Smith 8 11 1848 (ibid. 637–38); Mason to R.Jones 8 25, 12 27 1848 (ibid. 603, 650–51); BANCROFT 5:515–16.

11. Rich to Towson 10 23 1848 (HUTTON 85–86); Stevenson to Mason 10 26 1848 (NA98,M210,R3); BIGGS.

12. Dupont to Mrs.Dupont 3 17 1847 (DUPONT 147–48); Mason to R.Jones 12 27 1848 (*573–17* 651); Sherman to Stevenson 12 16 1848 (STEVENSON); BIGGS 223–30 passim.

13. Companies F, 3rd artillery, and C, 1st dragoons; Mason to R.Jones 8 19, 25 1848 (*573–17* 597, 603).

14. Hardie to Mason 8 14 1848 (*573–17* 612); Folsom to Sherman 8 14 1848 (ibid. 613).

15. Mason to R.Jones 8 19 1848 (ibid. 597).

16. Stevenson to Mason 8 20 1848B (ibid. 645–46).

17. Sherman to A.J.Smith 8 11 1848 (ibid. 637).

18. Sherman to Stevenson 8 26 1848A (ibid. 642); Mason to R.Jones 8 28 1848 (ibid. 643–44).

19. Halleck to Lebrija et al. 1 21 1849 (573–17 689); Mason to Garner 3 22 1849 (ibid. 896–97).

20. Mason to R.Jones 8 19, 28 1848 (ibid. 597–98, 644).

21. CALIFN. 7 17 1847 3/1; CAL.STAR 1 29 1848 3/1.

22. CALIFN. 7 24 1847 2/3.

23. Ibid. 2 16 1848 2/1; Captain Hull may have moved in that direction (CAL.STAR 1 16 1847 2/1); KEMBLE,E.C. 71–72.

24. CALIFN. 9 31 1848 2/1.

25. Mason to Sinclair 3 5 1848 (573–17 489).

26. CAL.STAR 4 22 1848 2/2, 5 20 1848 2/2–3; CALIFN. 4 26 1848 2/2, 5 3 1848 2/2.

27. Mason to Folsom 5 21 1848 (573–17 555), to Foster 5 31 1848 (ibid. 558).

28. Mason to Townsend 6 1 1848 (ibid. 559); a slip of 6 14 1848 announced that they had "stopped the paper."

29. Mason to Howard 7 28 1848 (573–17 581–82), to Hardie 8 1 1848B (ibid. 586).

30. CALIFN. 8 14 1848 2/2; Folsom to Halleck 8 8, 12, 16 1848 (NA98,M210,R6).

31. ALTA 6 14 1849 2/3; title-page note on Huntington Library copy; Mason to Hastings 10 24 1848 (573–17 677).

32. MASON-1; BYNUM; GREENWOOD 109.

33. Sherman to Griffin 10 20 1847 (573–17 403).

34. Mason to Larkin 5 20 1848 (ibid. 554–55); Sherman to Folsom 5 22 1848 (ibid. 613–14); Mason to Townsend 6 1 1848 (ibid. 559); Halleck to Hardie 8 1 1848B (ibid. 586); Riley, [notice] 7 1 1849 (ibid. 793); CAL.STAR 5 20 1848 3/1.

35. GRIVAS 14–16.

36. Polk, message 7 6 1848 (CALIFN. 9 23 1848 2/3–3/2).

37. POLK 9 30, 10 3, 7 1848 4:135–37, 140–43, 146–47.

38. Marcy to Mason 10 9 1848 (573–17 258–59); Buchanan to Voorhies 10 7 1848 (ibid. 6–9).

39. POLK 10 7 1848, 12 12 1848, 1 18, 3 5 1849 4:148, 231–32, 293–94, 375.

40. See Chapter 10 above.

41. BANCROFT 5:277–78 and n.25; J.Castro, proclamation 8 10 1846 (SHINN).

42. CAL.STAR 5 8 1847 2/1; Moreno to Mex.Min.For.Rel. 6 5 1847 (CAL.HIS.QT. 13:138); Mason, to all 6 17 1847 (573–17 323).

43. Davis to Stevenson 9 17 1847 (NA98,M210,R2); Stevenson to Mason 9 22 1847 (ibid.); Sherman to Stevenson 10 6 1847 (NA98,M210,R1).

44. Stevenson to Davidson 11 7 1847 (NA98,M210,R2); Davidson to Stevenson 12 12 1847 (ibid.); Stevenson to Mason 12 14 1847 (ibid.); Davidson to Stevenson 12 15 1847 (ibid.); Stevenson to Mason 5 3 1848 (NA98,M210,R3), preceded by Lieut. Stoneman's report.

45. Mason, proclamation 12 27 1847 (573–17 450); concerning the Sonorans, STANDART.

46. Sherman to Stevenson 10 11 1847 (NA98,M210,R1); Stevenson to Sherman 10 19 1847 (NA98,M210,R2); Sherman to Davis 12 29 1847 (NA98,M210,R1), to

Stevenson 1 26 1848 (ibid.); Mason to J.Castro 2 7 1848 (*573*–17 472); Stevenson to Mason 2 8 1848A (NA98,M210,R3); Sherman to Stevenson 2 9 1848 (NA98,M210,R1); Mason to Adj.Genl. 4 12 1848 (*503*–1 103–04).

47. Stevenson to Mason 1 9 1848 (NA98,M210,R3); CALIFN. 1 26 1848 2/2; CAL.STAR 1 22 1848 2/1–2, 1 29 1848 2/3.

48. Mason to J.Castro 2 7 1848 (*573*–17 472); Sherman to Stevenson 2 9 1848 (NA98,M210,R1).

49. Mason to J.Castro 2 9 1848 (*573*–17 474).

50. Mason to Adj.Genl. 4 12 1848 (*503*–1 104). Castro would depart for Lower California in 1853.

51. Pico to Mex.Min.For.Rel. 10 27 1846 (CAL.HIS.QT. 13:112–14); Pico, proclamation 8 10 1846 (ibid. 122–23); BANCROFT 5:278.

52. Pico to Mex.Min.For.Rel. 11 15, 16 1846 (CAL.HIS.QT. 13:125–26, 127–28).

53. Written 11 25 1846 (Pico to Mex.Min.For.Rel. 3 29 1848 in ibid. 13:147), reiterated 10 25 1847B (ibid. 13:142–43).

54. Pico to Mex.Min.For.Rel. 1 4 1847AB (ibid. 13:130–32), 3 29 1848 (ibid. 147). On December 18, near Tucson, Cooke wrote Sonora's governor (*517*–41 [563]).

55. P.Pico to Mex.Min.War,Marine 4 5 1847 (CAL.HIS.QT. 13:132–34).

56. Bustamente to Mex.Min.War 3 20 1847 (BUSTAMENTE); Pico to Mex.Min.For.Rel. 3 29 1848 (CAL.HIS.QT. 13:147); Moreno to Mex.Min.For.Rel. 6 5 1847 (ibid. 13:138).

57. Pico to Mex.Min.For.Rel. 3 29, 7 8 1847 (CAL.HIS.QT. 13:147–48, 140–41).

58. The *Congress* and *Portsmouth* fired 500 rounds into Guaymas on 10 20 1847 (BAUER 214–17; CRAVEN-1 76).

59. Pico to Mex.Min.For.Rel. 3 29 1848 (CAL.HIS.QT. 13:148), 10 25 1847B, 2 28 1848 (ibid. 13:142–43, 144); PICO 143, 144, 146.

60. Pico to Mex.Min.For.Rel. 3 29 1848 (CAL.HIS.QT. 13:146–47, 149); Almonte to Mex.Min.For.Affairs 9 2 1846 (ibid. 13:111); Lafragua to Pico 12 19 1846 (ibid. 128); Pico to Mex.Min.For.Rel. 8 7 1847 (ibid. 141).

61. BANCROFT 5:588 n.12; Pico to Mason 7 22 1848 (*573*–17 602).

62. Stevenson to Mason 7 20 1848 (*573*–17 598–600).

63. Pico to Stevenson 7 22 1848 (NA98,M210,R3), to Mason 7 22 1848 (*573*–17 602).

64. Halleck to Stevenson 7 21 1848C (*573*–17 572); Stevenson to Pico 7 27 1848 (NA98,M210,R3); Pico to Stevenson 7 29 1848 (ibid.); Stevenson, passport, Pico 8 5 1848 (ibid.); Stevenson to Mason 8 8 1848 (ibid.).

65. Sherman to Stevenson 8 3 1848 (*573*–17 631–32); Mason to R.Jones 8 23 1848 (ibid. 601).

66. Stevenson to Mason 8 14 1848AB (NA98,M210,R3).

67. Sherman to Stevenson 8 8 1848A (*573*–17 635).

68. CAL.STAR 10 2 1847 2/2.

69. Mason to R.Jones 12 27 1848 (*573*–17 652–53).

70. RYAN 1:283–84.

71. BANCROFT 6:274.

72. Sherman to Stevenson 8 26 1848B (STEVENSON).

73. Benton, to the people 8 27 1848, in N.Y.*Herald* 9 26 1848, copied from the *Courier-Enquirer* of 10 13 1848 (ALTA 1 11 1849 2/3–4). The *Alta California*,

heir to the *Californian* and *California Star*, began publication on January 4, 1849 (KEMBLE,E.C. 88).

74. Stevenson's reply, ALTA 1 25 1849 1/3–2; Mason's, ibid. 5 3 1849 1/3–4, 5 10 1849 1/3–4, 5 17 1849 1/3–4, 5 31 1849 2/1–3.

75. T.A.C.Jones to J.Y.Mason 11 4 1847 and ff. (NA45,M89,R34). Jones said he was at Monterey by the 9th (T.A.C.Jones to R.B.Mason 10 19 1848, in NA98, M210,R3), the *Californian* said by the 12th (CALIFN. 10 21 1848 2/2).

76. Dupont to Mrs.Dupont 1 7 1848 (DUPONT 301); CRAVEN-1 48.

77. T.A.C.Jones to J.Y.Mason 7 28 1848 (NA45,M625,R286).

78. T.A.C.Jones to J.Y.Mason 11 2 1848 (NA45,M89,R34).

79. T.A.C.Jones to Preston 9 24, 12 6 1849 (ibid.); T.A.C.Jones, Bay of San Francisco 12? 1849 (ibid.); T.A.C.Jones, N.Y. of the Pacific revisited 12? 1849 (ibid.); T.A.C.Jones, Wants of California immigrants 12 1849, and accompanying correspondence with J.B.Steinberger concerning food supplies (ibid.).

80. To Charles S. McCauley; Preston to T.A.C.Jones 5 10 1850 (NA45,M89,R34); T.A.C.Jones to McCauley 6 21 1850 (NA45,M625,R286); McCauley to Preston 6 24 1850 (ibid.); T.A.C.Jones, order 6 24 1850 (ibid.), to Preston 6 25 1850 (NA45,M89,R34), to W.A.Graham 8 26 1850 (ibid.).

81. ALTA 4 3 1851 2/2; BANCROFT 6:265 n.25; DICTIONARY 10:201–02.

82. T.A.C.Jones to J.Y.Mason 6 19 1848 (NA45,M89,R34).

83. CALIFN. 10 21 1848 2/2; T.A.C.Jones to J.Y.Mason 10 17 1848 and accompanying letters (NA45,M89,R34). He was, however, loaned $70,000 from the "civil fund" for this operation (Halleck to Allen 8 22 1849, in 573–17 813).

84. Mason to T.A.C.Jones 10 5 1848 (NA98,M210,R1), to R.Jones 11 24 1848A (573–17 648); HALLECK-2 68–74, 148–51.

85. CAL.STAR & CALIFN. 11 18 1848 3/1.

86. Ibid. 11 25 1848 2/1–3; CALIFN. 10 21 1848 2/1.

87. Mason to R.Jones 11 24 1848A (573–17 648–49).

88. Mason to R.Jones 11 24 1848B (ibid. 649).

89. R.Jones to Mason 10 2 1848 (NA98,M210,R4), received in February; Freeman, general order no.49, 8 21 1848 (NA98,M210,R5); R.Jones to Riley 10 5 1848 (NA98,M210,R6); POLK 10 7 1848 4:149–50; R.Jones, general order no.54, 10 10 1848 (NA98,M210,R6); Marcy to Riley 10 10 1848A (ibid.), 10 10 1848B (573–17 260–61); R.Jones to P.F.Smith 10 10 1848 (NA98,M210,R6); Marcy to P.F.Smith 11 15 1848 (573–17 265).

90. Mason to R.Jones 12 27 1848 (ibid. 653).

91. CAL.STAR & CALIFN. 12 16 1848 2/1, 3/2, 12 23 1848 2/3–4; see Chapter 19 below.

92. Mason to T.A.C.Jones 2 26 1849 (573–17 696).

93. Buchanan to Voorhies 10 7 1848 (ibid. 6–9); P.F.Smith to R.Jones 3 15 1849 (ibid. 712); see Chapter 19 below.

94. Mason to Riley 3 1 1849 (ibid. 892–93), to R.Jones 3 8 1849 (ibid. 654); Marcy to Mason 10 9 1848 (ibid. 258–59).

95. A.J.Smith to Sherman 12 2 1848 (NA98,M210,R3); Sherman to Folsom 12 13 1848 (NA98,M210,R1), to Graham 12 13 1848 (ibid.), to Stevenson 12 16 1848 (STEVENSON); Mason to R.Jones 12 27 1848 (573–17 649–50); Sherman to Graham 1 24 1849 (ibid. 882). Graham's force included 277 dragoons, 205 quartermaster's men, 92 wagons, and over 1,000 animals.

96. Mason to Haren 4 9 1849, to M.Scott 4 9 1849 (573–17 703).

97. Riley to R.Jones 4 10/13 1849 (ibid. 873).

98. Mason, order no.12, 4 13 1849 (NA98,M210,R7).

99. Mason sailed in the steamer *California* on May 1, 1849, and died at St.Louis July 25, 1850 (WILLEY 83 n.1; SHERMAN 1:92; DICTIONARY 12:373–74).

CHAPTER 19. CONSENT OF THE GOVERNED—RILEY'S RULE

1. Buchanan to Voorhies 10 7 1848 (*573–17* 9).

2. POLK 1 5 1847 2:308.

3. Taylor to House of Rep. 1 21 1850 (*573–17* 1–4).

4. POLK 11 8 1848 4:184.

5. Passed September 9, 1850, making New Mexico and Utah territories, abolishing slavery in the District of Columbia, enacting a stringent fugitive slave law, and admitting California as a free state (U.S. STATUTES 9:452–53, chap.50; BANCROFT 6:336–46).

6. R.Jones, order no.54, 10 10 1848 (ALTA 3 1 1849 2/4); L.Thomas, orders nos.55 and 61, 10 12, 17 1848 (ibid. 3/1); Marcy to Riley 10 10 1848 (*573–17* 260–61).

7. POLK 10 7 1848 4:149; FOSTER 17; BANCROFT 6:275.

8. Buchanan to Voorhies 10 7 1848 (*573–17* 6–9).

9. POLK 9 30, 10 3 1848 4:136–37, 140; Benton, to the people 8 27 1848 (ALTA 1 11 1849 2/3–4); see Chapter 18 above.

10. POLK 10 3 1848 4:142–43.

11. In the steamer *California*. Voorhies to Postmaster Genl. 3 13 1849 (*573–17* 958).

12. P.F.Smith to R.Jones 3 15 1849 (ibid. 712).

13. Mason to T.A.C.Jones 2 26 1849 (ibid. 696); P.F.Smith to Freeman 10 7 1849 (*558–47* 75, 78); ALTA 3 1 1849 2/3.

14. P.F.Smith to Marcy 1 18, 26, 2 15 1849 (*573–17* 707–10), to R.Jones 3 15 1849 (ibid. 712), to Freeman 10 7 1849 (*558–47* 75, 97–98).

15. P.F.Smith to W.Nelson 1 19 1849 (*573–17* 716); issued as a proclamation, Panamá *Star* 2 24 1849 (ROYCE 238).

16. P.F.Smith to Marcy 1 26 1849 (*573–17* 709), to R.Jones 3 15 1849 (ibid. 711–12).

17. P.F.Smith to Mason 3 6 1849 (ibid. 714–15); Halleck to Harrison 3 17 1849 (ibid. 698).

18. P.F.Smith to R.Jones 4 5 1849 (ibid. 717).

19. Marcy/J.Y.Mason, joint commission 11 30 1848 (ibid. 266–70); P.F.Smith to R.Jones 4 9 1849 (ibid. 721–23).

20. P.F.Smith to Larkin 3 2 [1849] (LARKIN 8:166–67); Semple to Larkin 3 6 1849 (ibid. 169–70); GATES-1.

21. P.F.Smith to R.Jones 5 1 1849 (*573–17* 739), to Semple/Phelps/Larkin 4 9 1849 (LARKIN 8:206).

22. T.A.C.Jones to Preston 6 16 1849 (*573–17* 950–51), 9 24 1849 (NA45, M89,R4), to Larkin 3 5, 5 18 1849 (LARKIN 8:167, 228–29); Larkin to [T.A.C. Jones] 5 21 1849 (ibid. 8:231); T.A.C.Jones, Wants of California immigrants 12? 1849, Bay of San Francisco and its harbors 12 1849 (NA45,M89,R4); GATES-1.

23. C.Johnston to Voorhies 11 1 1848 (*573–17* 956–58); Buchanan to Voorhies 10 7 1848 (ibid. 6–9).

24. Childs to Larkin 10 6, 11 29 1848, 4 17 1849 (LARKIN 8:4–5, 45–46, 216).

25. Voorhies to Postmaster Genl. 3 13, 3 14 1849 (*573–17* 958–60, 960–61).

26. Dismissed 3 30 1849, Voorhies would become California's first elected secretary of state; Collamer to Allen 3 31 1849 (*573–17* 961–62); DAVIS 659.

27. POLK 10 12 1847 3:189–90; Polk, messages 12 8 1846, 12 7 1847, 7 6 1848 (RICHARDSON 4:494, 542, 589–90).

28. Leaving slavery in the territories to be resolved by the courts; POLK 7 12, 16, 17, 19, 27, 28 1848 4:14, 20–21, 22, 23, 31, 33.

29. POLK 9 30, 10 3 1848 4:136–37, 140–43; see Chapter 18 above.

30. Buchanan to Voorhies 10 7 1848 (*573–17* 6–9); POLK 10 7 1848 4: 146–48.

31. Allen to Collamer 6 23, 8 2 1849 (*573–17* 969–70, 970–71).

32. Benicia, Sacramento, Stockton, San José, Vernon, Coloma, and Sonoma; Allen to Collamer 8 29 1849 (ibid. 971–72, 967–68, 973 [paging error]).

33. Postmaster Genl., report 12 3 1849 (*569–5* 785).

34. Collamer to Allen 12 10 1849 (*573–17* 974–76); concerning inadequacy of mail steamers: Riley to R.Jones 8 31 1849 (NA98,M210,R1), T.A.C.Jones to Preston 10 31 1849 (*573–17* 953–54); O.W.Pratt to A.D.Dodge 11 15 1849 (NA45, M625,R286).

35. Mason, order no.12, 4 13 1849 (NA98,M210,R7); Riley, order no.13, 4 13 1849 (ibid.), to R.Jones 4 10, 13 1849 (*573–17* 873).

36. CAL.STAR & CALIFN. 11 25 1848 2/1–3.

37. POLK 10 3 1848 4:143; Polk, message 12 5 1848 (*537–1* 12–13).

38. Smith wrote Riley of the new instructions 6 7 1849 (NA98,M210,R4), and they did not reach Monterey until the 10th (BROWNE 437).

39. Clayton to T.B.King 4 3 1849 (*573–17* 10); Crawford to Riley 6 26 1849 (ibid. 276).

40. Sherman to Folsom 4 10 1849 (NA98,M210,R4).

41. Gibbs to Riley 5 23 1849 (ibid.); Halleck to Stevenson 6 1 1849 (LEIDESDORFF).

42. Riley, proclamation 6 3 1849 (*573–17* 776–80); GREENWOOD 119, 120; Riley to R.Jones 6 30 1849A (*573–17* 748); BROWNE, appendix xviii; seconded by Smith, who recommended a convention such as had been "proposed in the U.S.Senate" (Smith to Riley 5 23 1849, in NA98,M210,R4; CONG.GLOBE 30:2 477/2).

43. The structure included a governor; secretary; territorial legislature; a superior court of four judges (one from each district); a *fiscal*; a prefect and two subprefects (marshals or sheriffs) for each district; a judge of first instance in each district (vested in the first alcalde); alcaldes; justices of the peace, and town councils. The powers of each were explicitly described in the existing laws. The four districts were comprised of San Diego/Los Angeles/Santa Barbara; San Luis Obispo/Monterey; San José/San Francisco; and Sonoma/the Sacramento/the San Joaquin (*573–17* 778; HALLECK,J.). Riley likened California's position to that of Louisiana upon its acquisition (BROWNE, appendix xxiv–xxvi).

44. CALIFN. 8 15 1846 3/1; echoed in CAL.STAR 2 13 1847 2/2.

45. P.F.Smith to Sect.War 2 15 1849 (*573–17* 710).

46. CALIFN. 9 22 1847 2/1.

47. ALTA 6 14 1849 2/3–4; cf. BURNETT 330–31.

48. Marcy to Mason 10 9 1848 (*573–17* 259); ALTA 6 21 1849 2/3-4.

49. He was "often himself the law" (COLTON 249; ROYCE 200–06).

50. ALTA 4 26 1849 1/3–2/1.

51. *Meetings at San José*: CAL.STAR & CALIFN. 12 23 1848 2/4; ALTA 1 4 1849

2/1–2, 1 25 1849 2/2, 6 21 1849 2/1. *San Francisco*: CAL.STAR & CALIFN. 12 23 1848 2/3–4; ALTA 1 4 1849 2/1–2, 3/2, 1 25 1849 2/2, 2 22 1849 2/3–3/1-2, 6 14 1849 3/1, 6 21 1849 2/3. *Sonoma*: ALTA 1 4 1849 3/2, 3 1 1849 1/3. *Sacramento*: ALTA 1 25 1849 1/2–3, 3 1 1849 1/3. *Monterey*: ALTA 2 1 1849 1/4, 2 22 1849 1/3, 4 24 1849 2/1, 7 12 1849 1/5. *Coloma*: ALTA 2 22 1849 1/3. *Yuba River*: ALTA 4 24 1849 2/1. *San Diego*: ALTA 7 26 1849 1/3.

52. GRIFFIN-3 14–16.

53. BROWNE, appendix xvi–xix; BURNETT 294–98.

54. ALTA 2 15 1849 2/3–4; BURNETT 294.

55. ALTA 2 15 1849 2/3, 2 22 1849 3/2; Dist.of S.F., minutes 2 12 1849 (*573–17* 729–35); BURNETT 307–10ff.

56. P.F.Smith to Creighton et al. 3 27 1849 (*573–17* 735–37).

57. P.F.Smith to R.Jones 5 1 1849 (ibid. 740).

58. Clayton to T.B.King 4 3 1849 (ibid. 9–11).

59. ROYCE 265–66; BANCROFT 6:283.

60. ALTA 7 12 1849 1/3–4, 7 19 1849 2/3; BURNETT 328–29. King's report to Congress was submitted in March 1850 (*577–59*) and privately printed under various titles (e.g., KING).

61. ALTA 6 14 1849 3/1; C.Ringgold to Preston 6 19 1849 (*573–17* 954–55); BURNETT 322.

62. BANCROFT 6:251, 281–83 and n.57.

63. Ringgold to Preston 8 31 1849 (*573–17* 955); T.A.C.Jones to Preston 9 1 1849 (ibid. 951–52).

64. T.B.King to T.A.C.Jones 8 13 1849 (ibid. 952); T.A.C.Jones to Preston 9 1 1849 (ibid. 951).

65. ALTA 9 13 1849 2/2–3.

66. *577–59* 6–7; Larkin to A.Hardy 8 2 1856 (LARKIN 10:291).

67. Gibbs to Riley 5 23 1849 (NA98,M210,R4); Riley suspends Leavenworth 5 6 1849 (*573–17* 759–60), appoints Green/Ward/Harrison a commission 5 6 1849 (ibid. 758–59), and restores Leavenworth 6 1 1849 (ibid. 771).

68. Riley, proclamation to the people, Dist.of S.F. 6 4 1849 (*573–17* 773–74); GREENWOOD 121; ALTA 6 14 1849 4/1–4, with comment 2/3–4.

69. Riley, notice of election 6 5 1849 (*573–17* 774); Halleck to Parker et al. 6 5 1849 (ibid. 774–76).

70. Lippitt, address 6 8 1849 (ALTA 6 14 1849 1/1–4); BURNETT 319; GREENWOOD 141.

71. Riley, to the people 6 22 1849 (*573–17* 785); ALTA 7 2 1849 1/2.

72. C.Ringgold to Preston 6 19 1849 (*573–17* 954); ALTA 6 14 1849 2/2, 3/1; GREENWOOD 140; the *Alta*'s advice to delegates (ALTA 7 2 1849 2/2–3).

73. S.F.Legislative Assembly, committee of corres., address 6 18 1849 (BROWNE, appendix xviii); BURNETT 325–26; ALTA 6 21 1849 2/3, 2/1, 7 12 1849 1/5.

74. BURNETT 332.

75. Riley to Sherman 4 16 1849 (*573–17* 899–901), to R.Jones 4 25 1849 (ibid. 873–76); Canby to Miller 5 4 1849 (ibid. 904); Canby, order no.16, 5 8 1849 (NA98,M210,R7); Graham to Canby 5 19 1849 (NA98,M210,R4); Canby to Wilson 5 20 1849 (*573–17* 911), to Lyon 5 21 1849 (ibid.); Riley to R.Jones 6 11 1849 (ibid. 915–17); Canby to Hooker 6 11 1849 (ibid. 921–22); P.F.Smith to Freeman 8 26 1849 (ibid. 746–47); Riley to Freeman 8 30 1849 (ibid. 935–36), 11 30 1849 (*561–52* 42–43).

76. Riley to Freeman 10 1 1849 (*573–17* 943); Canby to E.O.C.Ord 10 1, 10 5 1849 (NA98,M210,R1).

77. Riley, proclamation 5 6 1849 (*573–17* 760), to Crawford 8 30 1849B (ibid. 939–40); Canby, circular 8 12 1849 (NA98,M210,R1).

78. P.F.Smith to Freeman 10 7 1849 (*558–47* 98–99).

79. Canby to G.G.Turner 10 9 1849 (NA98,M210,R1).

80. Canby to Kingsbury 5 5 1849 (*573–17* 905–06), to Miller 5 7 1849 (ibid. 906–07); Riley to Hooker 7 22, 8 9 1849 (ibid. 925–26); Canby to Miller 8 23 1849 (ibid. 934), to Hooker 8 23 1849 (ibid. 933); Riley to Freeman 8 30, 9 20 1849 (ibid. 935–37, 941–43), to Hooker 11 2 1849 (*561–52* 74–75); Canby to I.Williams 9 3 1849 (NA98,M210,R1), to E.O.C.Ord 10 1 1849 (ibid.); P.F.Smith's revision of plan, Hooker to Riley 2 26 1850 (*561–52* 82–84).

81. Riley to Freeman 10 1 1849 (*573–17* 944), to R.Jones 10 15 1849 (NA98, M210,R1).

82. Canby to Gibson 9 3 1849 (NA98,M210,R1), to Allen 9 3 1849 (ibid.), to Heintzelman 9 26 1849 (ibid.); Riley to Freeman 10 1 1849 (*573–17* 944), 12 31 1849 (*561–52* 55–56), to Hooker 11 2 1849 (ibid. 74–75), 12 3 1849 (NA98,M210,R1); Canby to Heintzelman 11 1 1849 (*561–52* 73), to Emory 11 1 1849 (ibid. 73–74).

83. Riley, order no.16, 5 8 1849 (NA98,M210,R7); Canby to Williams 9 3 1849 (NA98,M210,R1), to E.O.C.Ord 10 1 1849 (ibid.), 10 5 1849 (ibid.).

84. Canby to Hooker 6 11 1849 (*573–17* 921–22); Riley to R.Jones 6 11 1849 (ibid. 916–17), to Freeman 8 30 1849 (ibid. 936–39); Crawford to Riley 12 11 1849 (ibid. 282–83).

85. Riley to R.Jones 8 30 1849 (*573–17* 785–89), to Freeman 9 20 1849 (ibid. 941–43); Lieutenant Derby's "Sketch of General Riley's route . . . July and Aug. 1849" (ibid. ff. 944).

86. PITT 55–64.

87. Riley to R.Jones 8 30 1849 (*573–17* 789).

88. P.F.Smith to Freeman 10 7 1849 (*558–47* 97–98).

89. Halleck to Esquer 5 9 1849 (*573–17* 761), to Marron et al. 5 15 1849 (ibid. 764–65), to E.P.Jones 6 18 1849 (ibid. 781), to Knight 10 4 1849 (ibid. 854–55), to Swart 10 4 1849 (ibid. 855), to Spence 10 19 1849 (ibid. 866), to A.M.Pico 12 4 1849 (*561–52* 33–34), to Galindo 12 4 1849 (ibid. 33).

90. Halleck to Avila 4 17, 5 15, 22 1849 (*573–17* 752, 766, 769–70), to Gómez 5 15 1849 (ibid. 766), to Majors 7 1 1849 (ibid. 794), to Heintzelman 8 13 1849 (ibid. 804–05), to Sternberger 8 13 1849 (ibid. 802), to Wescott 8 20 1849 (ibid. 810–11); Riley to R.Jones 8 30 1849 (ibid. 787), to whom 9 17 1849 (ibid. 829–30); Halleck to Spence 10 19 1849 (ibid. 866), to Father Gonzales 12 3 1849 (*561–52* 31–32).

91. Halleck to E.P.Jones 6 21 1849 (*573–17* 782); Canby to Keyes 8 9, 23 1849 (ibid. 927, 934–35), to Allen 8 14 1849 (ibid. 927); Halleck to Esquer 8 30 1849 (ibid. 820), to Geary 10 19 1849 (ibid. 865); Keyes to Canby 11 1 1849 (*561–52* 46–48); Riley to Hooker 11 15 1849 (ibid. 77–78), to Canby 11 16 1849 (ibid. 78–79); Canby to Keyes 11 16 1849 (ibid. 79–80); Halleck to Gray/ Witt 12 6 1849 (ibid. 36), to Brewster 12 6 1849 (ibid.); Keyes to Canby 12 10 1849 (ibid. 48–49); Canby to Keyes 12 26 1849 (ibid. 52); Riley to R.Jones 12 28 1849B (ibid. 44–46).

92. P.F.Smith to Freeman 10 7 1849 (*558–47* 99–101).

93. Butterfield to W.C.Jones 7 5 1849 (*573–17* 113–15); Ewing to Clayton

7 11 1849 (ibid. 112), to W.C.Jones 7 12 1849 (ibid. 116–17); Crawford to Comdg.Officer 7 13 1849 (ibid. 278); Riley to civil officers 10 4 1849 (ibid. 852).

94. 589–18; JONES,W.C.-1; HALLECK-1.

95. MORROW; BANCROFT 6:536–48; ROYCE 480–91; HARLOW 50–51; Treaty of Guadalupe Hidalgo, Article VIII (ROBINSON,W.W. 250–51).

96. Sherman to W.H.Warner 1 26 1849 (573–17 884); Canby to A.J.Smith 10 25 1849 (ibid. 868), 11 13 1849 (561–52 76); (Sacramento) *Placer Times* 2 16 1850 (BOGGS 42–45); R.S.Williamson, "Sketch of the route of Capt. Warner's exploring party," August–October 1849 (558–47). Warner was killed by Indians in September.

97. Canby to Derby 9 5 1849 (NA98,M210,R1); Riley to Hooker 9 1, 12 3 1849, 2 19 1850 (ibid.), to Freeman 9 20 1849 (573–17 941–43), 1 30, 2 14 1850 (NA98,M210,R1); Derby's report and map of "The Sacramento Valley from the American River to Butte Creek," September–October 1849 (558–47); FARQUHAR-1.

98. Riley to Hooker 11 4 1849 (561–52 76); Derby's report and map, "Reconnaissance of theTulares Valley," 1850 (621–110).

99. Canby to A.J.Wilson 9 11 1849 (NA98,M210,R1).

100. Canby to Emory 9 26 1849 (ibid.).

101. Canby to E.O.C.Ord 10 1 1849 (ibid.); Ord's reports (558–47 119–27); Riley to Freeman 10 1 1849 (573–17 943–44), 1 1 1850 (558–47 118–19).

102. Riley to Crawford 11 1 1849 (NA98,M210,R1).

103. Sloat, to the inhabitants 7 7 1846 (503–1 1011); CAL.STAR 2 13 1847 4/1).

104. Stockton, to the people 8 17 1846 (499–19 107; CALIFN. 9 5 1846 2/1); Stockton, address 7 29 1846 mentioned "existing laws" (503–1 1037).

105. CAL.STAR 1 9 1847 2/1.

106. Alcalde Walter Colton at Monterey said he had access to "the Mexican code as compiled in Frebrero and Alverez" (COLTON 249; BROWNE, appendix xxv), perhaps meaning ALVAREZ-1 (1828) or ALVAREZ (1842, which begins with "atribuciones de los alcaldes constitucionales") and FEBRERO.

107. Kearny, proclamation 3 1 1847 (573–17 288–89).

108. Mason to Boggs 6 2 1847 (ibid. 317), to Fisher 8 30 1847 (ibid. 392).

109. Larkin to Bennett 6 1 1847 (LARKIN 6:187).

110. MASON-1; Mason, proclamation 8 7 1848 (573–17 590); see Chapter 18 above.

111. Riley, proclamation 6 3 1849 (ibid. 776–77); Riley to R.Jones 6 30 1849A (ibid. 748–50); BROWNE, appendix xxiv–xxvi.

112. Halleck to Boggs 7 3, 8 10 1849 (573–17 795, 807), to Brackett 8 17 1849 (ibid. 809); ALTA 9 20 1849 3/1.

113. HALLECK,J.; BROWNE, appendix xxiv–xl; GREENWOOD 130.

114. BROWNE, appendix xii, Schedule, sec.1.

115. Halleck to Burnett 8 13 1849 (573–17 808), replaced by K.H.Dimmick 10 26 1849 (ibid. 859), to P.Ord 8 30 1849 (ibid. 820), to Dent 9 3 1849 (ibid. 821), replaced by R.A.Maupin 10 26 1849 (ibid. 869), to Covarrubias 9 3 1849 (ibid. 827); Riley, circular 7 2 1849, calling first meeting (ibid. 795).

116. Halleck to Forbes 8 20 1849 (ibid. 809), to Bellamy 8 20 1849 (ibid. 811), to Vallejo 8 22 1849 (ibid. 812–13), to Needa 9 4 1849 (ibid. 826), to Geary 10 3 1849 (ibid. 852), to Foley 11 3 1849 (561–52 21), to Spence 11 5 1849 (ibid. 22), to A.M.Pico 12 4 1849 (ibid. 33–34), to Galindo 12 4 1849 (ibid. 33).

117. *Prefects*: Sonoma 8 21 1849 (*573–17* 811), San Francisco 8 7 1849 (ibid. 797), Monterey 8 10 1849 (ibid. 807), San José 8 13 1849 (ibid. 806), San Luis Obispo 8 20 1849 (ibid. 808), San Joaquín 8 30 1849 (ibid. 827), Santa Barbara 9 6 1849 (ibid. 824), Los Angeles 9 18 1849 (ibid. 830). *Judges of first instance*: Sonoma 8 21 1849 (ibid. 811), San Francisco 8 6 1849, 9 21 1849, 9 24 1849 (ibid. 797, 832), Monterey 8 30 1849, 10 24 1849 (ibid. 820, 867), San José 8 13 1849 (ibid. 806); San Joaquín 8 30 1849 (ibid. 827), 11 28 1849 (*561–52* 28); San Luis Obispo 9 6 1849 (*573–17* 824), Santa Barbara 9 6 1849 (ibid. 825); Los Angeles 9 18 1849 (ibid. 830), 12 12 1849 (*561–52* 39); Sacramento 9 3 1849, 9 21 1849, 9 25 1849 (*573–17* 822, 832, 850), 11 16 1849 (*561–52* 24).

118. San Francisco: Hall McAllister 9 25 1849 (*573–17* 849); San Joaquín: T.V.VanBuren 10 31 1849 (*561–52* 19).

119. Frederick Billings 8 13 1849 (*573–17* 807).

120. For example, ibid. 804–05, 853–54.

121. See Chapter 17 above.

122. Mason to R.Jones 8 19 1848 (*573–17* 597–98); Halleck to Harrison 2 24 1849 (ibid. 694–95).

123. R.Jones to Riley 10 5 1848 (NA98,M210,R6); Riley to R.Jones 8 30 1849 (*573–17* 791).

124. Halleck, circular 5 3 1849 (*573–17* 756–57); Canby, circular 5 10 1849 (ibid. 907); Folsom to Canby 5 14 1849 (NA98,M210,R4); Halleck to R.Allen 10 2 1849 (*573–17* 851).

125. Riley to R.Jones 6 30 1849 (ibid. 751); Halleck, circular 7 2 1849 (ibid. 796).

126. Halleck to R.Allen 8 13 1849 (ibid. 802–03).

127. Riley to Jessup 8 15 1849 (ibid. 930).

128. Riley to R.Allen 9 5, 26, 10 2 1849 (ibid. 826, 850, 870), 11 3 1849 (*561–52* 21), to Hooker 9 5 1849 (*573–17* 824); Canby to R.Allen 10 6 1849 (NA98,M210,R1); Halleck to R.Allen 10 8, 10 17 1849 (*573–17* 857–862). He refused $60,000 to the navy, Halleck to Price 11 14 1849 (*561–52* 23).

129. Hooker to Riley 8 12, 29, 30 1849 (NA98,M210,R4).

130. Riley to Hooker 8 30 1849 (*573–17* 814–19).

131. P.F.Smith to R.Jones 3 15 1849 (ibid. 712–13).

132. Riley to Crawford 8 30 1849A (ibid. 814), to R.Jones 8 30 1849 (ibid. 791–92); Halleck to R.Allen 8 30 1849 (ibid. 820).

133. Riley to R.Jones 10 1 1849 (ibid. 819), 12 20 1849 (*561–52* 18–19).

134. Crawford to Riley 11 28 1849 (*573–17* 282), to P.F.Smith 4 8 1850 (*561–52* 15–16).

135. Collier to Meredith 11 13 1849 (*573–17* 25); Halleck, circular 11 19 1849 (*561–52* 26; ALTA 12 15 1849 3/3), to R.Allen 11 19 1849 (*561–52* 26).

136. Riley to R.Jones 8 30 1849 (*573–17* 792); Halleck to R.Allen 8 13 1849 (ibid. 802–03).

137. Riley to R.Jones 12 20 1849 (*561–52* 19), to Crawford 1 23 1850 (NA98,M210,R1).

138. U.S.STATUTES 9:412–14, chap.126.

139. Crawford to President Taylor 6 26 1850 (*578–72* 3).

140. U.S.STATUTES 10:154–55, chap.58; DICTIONARY 15:608–09.

141. *629–4; 652–27; 743–168*; ALTA 3 23 1850 2/1–2, 5 27 1851 2/2.

142. Riley to Hooker 11 2 1849 (*561–52* 75), 12 3 1849 (NA98,M210,R1); Harrison to Riley 11 12 1849 (NA98,M210,R7); Collier to Meredith 11 13 1849 (*573–17* 24).

143. T.A.C.Jones to Collier 11 12 1849 (*573–17* 34).

144. Mellus,Howard&Co. et al. to Collier 11 13 1849 (ibid. 28–29).

145. Collier to Meredith 11 13 1849 (ibid. 24–28).

146. Collier to Meredith 11 29 1849 (ibid. 29–33); BANCROFT 7:140–41 and n.27.

CHAPTER 20. CONSTITUTIONAL GOVERNMENT—THE LAST OF THE GENERALS

1. Election returns: ALTA 8 16 1849 2/1, 8 23 1849 2/1, 8 31 1849 2/1; Canby, special orders no.31, 6 30 1849, no.34, 7 24 1849 (NA98,M210,R7).

2. King to T.A.C.Jones 8 13 1849 (*573–17* 952); T.A.C.Jones to Preston 9 1 1849 (ibid. 951); McCormick to T.A.C.Jones 8 26 1849 (ibid. 953); Riley to T.A.C.Jones 9 3 1849 (NA98,M210,R1); T.A.C.Jones to Riley 9 7 1849 (NA98, M210,R4), to Preston 9 12 1849 (*573–17* 952); FOSTER 16; HANSEN 97; JONES, J.M. 12 (who also offers a firsthand account of electioneering in the mines and personal rivalries in the convention); ALTA 8 16 1849 2/1, 8 31 1849 2/3, 9 13 1849 2/2–3.

3. C.Ringgold to Preston 8 31 1849 (*573–17* 955).

4. BROWNE 478–79; WILLEY 93. *Delegates by district*: Sacramento and San Francisco 8 each, San José 7, San Joaquín and Monterey 6 each, Los Angeles 5, Sonoma 3, San Diego and San Luis Obispo 2 each, Santa Barbara 1, altogether, 14 from the mining districts and 34 others. The Californians were J. A. Carrillo, J. M. Covarrubias, M. Domínguez, P. de la Guerra, A. M. Pico, J. Rodríguez, M. G. Vallejo; the 6 long-time foreigners, J. Hanks, T. O. Larkin, M. de Pedrorena, P. Sansevain, A. Stearns, J. A. Sutter.

5. ROYCE 261–62.

6. SHERMAN 1:106.

7. TAYLOR 121, 139, 141; GUDDE 227; WILLEY 92; ROYCE 260.

8. TAYLOR 141–42; BROWNE,L.F. 129.

9. TAYLOR 144–45, 157–58.

10. COLTON 356; COLTON (1949) xl; the lower floor had been meant for an "academy"; TAYLOR 149.

11. BROWNE 7–8.

12. Ibid. 8–16, 19–20, 23–24, 26, 32, 121–23, 153, 164–65.

13. ROYCE 263.

14. BROWNE 11.

15. ELLISON 322; BROWNE,L.F. 121.

16. BROWNE 221; GOODWIN 230–41.

17. BROWNE 24; a copy of the *Pacific News* reprint is in the California State Archives.

18. BROWNE 16, 19, 48.

19. Ibid. 10; probably from the New York *Herald* and New Orleans *Picayune* and perhaps Bayard Taylor (BROWNE,L.F. 129).

20. BROWNE, *reporter*, 19, 26; *sect.,assts.*, 18–19; *clerks*, 29, 32; *translator and clerk*, 10, 18, 19, 95; *sergeant-at-arms, doorkeeper*, 19; *copy clerk*, 38; *pages*, 26; *salaries*, 95, 107.

21. Ibid. 38; WILLEY 94, the *Californian* had moved from Monterey to San Francisco in May 1847 (KEMBLE,E.C. 64, 80).

22. BROWNE 95.

23. Ibid. 21–22, 24–29.

24. Ibid. 30–54, 288–89, 292–98, 458, appendix iii–iv.

25. Introduced by W.E.Shannon of Rose's Bar; ibid. 43–44; GOODWIN 110–12; COLTON 374.

26. BROWNE 45–47; monopolies were opposed as granting privileges to some, to the exclusion of others.

27. Ibid. 43, 294, 297–98.

28. Ibid. 54.

29. Ibid. 61–76, 304–08, 323, 341, 458, appendix iv; HEIZER-1 95–104, 115–17.

30. BROWNE 30, 32; Riley to Botts et al. 9 11 1849 (573–17 828; BROWNE, appendix xli).

31. BROWNE 94–107, 289–92; $30 a day was first suggested, reduced to $16.

32. Riley to Botts et al. 9 13 1849 (573–17 829; BROWNE, appendix xli), to Crosby et al. 9 19 1849 (573–17 830–31; BROWNE, appendix xliv).

33. BROWNE 76–94, 108–21, 124–52, 308–15, 323–40, 458.

34. Ibid. 108–21, 124–36.

35. Ibid. 137–52, 330–40; GOODWIN 108–32; HEIZER-1 104–15, 117–19.

36. BROWNE 153–63, 341–43, 458.

37. Article 7, ibid. 165, 344–46, 458.

38. Article 8, ibid. 165–66, 458; not to affect the first legislature (ibid. 404).

39. Article 10, ibid. 166–67, 354–61, 459.

40. Article 9, ibid. 202–11, 458.

41. Article 6, ibid. 212–39, 458.

42. Article 11, ibid. 239–46, 362, 459.

43. Ibid. 246–55, 363.

44. Ibid. 256.

45. Ibid. 256–57, 364–76; other debate upon financial support for the new government, ibid. 43, 44–45, 201–02.

46. Ibid. 257–69.

47. Ibid. 272–73.

48. Ibid. 273–74.

49. Ibid. 274–88.

50. Ibid. 317–22.

51. Ibid. 380–81.

52. Ibid. 386–88, 397.

53. Ibid. 393–98, 399, 473.

54. Ibid. 400–02, 403–04.

55. Ibid. 400, 404–16, 461.

56. Ibid. 378–80, 416–17, 458.

57. Article 12, ibid. 123–24, 167–200, 417–30, 431–58, 461, appendix xi.

58. ROYCE 264–69; GOODWIN 168–74; WILLEY 104.

59. "Map of Oregon and Upper California, from the surveys of John Charles Frémont" (511–148).

60. BROWNE 184.

61. Ibid. 175, 433–37; regarding Polk's preferred boundary, POLK 4:254–55;

concerning Taylor's supposed wish to include the Mormons, GOODWIN 153–55 n.2.

62. BROWNE 458–59, 461.

63. Ibid. 288, 364, 462.

64. Ibid. 246, 465, 474–75.

65. Ibid. 473.

66. Riley, proclamation 10 12 1849 (*573–17* 858–59; BROWNE, appendix [iii]; ALTA 11 8 1849 1/1).

67. Concerning the convention: ROYCE 259–70; BANCROFT 6:284–304; GOODWIN 86–229; the Californians' participation, PITT 42–46; HARGIS.

68. Halleck to R.Allen 10 12 1849 (*573–17* 859–60).

69. Halleck to R.Allen 10 14 1849 (ibid. 860–61).

70. ALTA 10 25 1849 2/1; CALIF.CONSTITUTION; GREENWOOD 124, 125; the pamphlet editions are now very rare; text in BROWNE, appendix [iii]–xiii, *573–17* 862–64, 849–62 [error in paging], *563–68* 18–34; ALTA 11 8 1849 1–2/1.

71. TAYLOR 195.

72. Riley to R.Jones 10 31 1849 (*573–17* 850–51); T.A.C.Jones to Preston 10 31 1849 (ibid. 953–54).

73. TAYLOR 159–62.

74. BROWNE 474–77.

75. ALTA 11 22 1849 2/2; TAYLOR 163–64.

76. TAYLOR 193; BROWNE 476.

77. W.N.Davis,Jr., California State Archives, to author 1 10 1978; BROWNE, appendix xiii.

78. BROWNE 475; TAYLOR 163. Both the engrossed constitution, as of the third reading, and the enrolled document on parchment, signed 10 13 1849, are in the California State Archives, the signature of delegate Pedro Sansevain not however appearing as in the printed copies, he having been given a leave of absence on October 6 because of illness in the family (BROWNE 392).

79. BROWNE 476–77; TAYLOR 164–65.

80. Riley to R.Jones 10 1 1849A (*573–17* 819).

81. Riley to R.Jones 10 31 1849A (ibid. 850–51).

82. Crawford to Riley 11 28 1849 (ibid. 281–82), received in January; Riley to Crawford 1 23 1850 (NA98,M210,R1).

83. W.C.Jones to T.Ewing (Sect.Interior) 9 30 1849 (*573–17* 117–18).

84. ALTA 9 20 1849 1/3–5 to 2/1–4, 9 27 1849 1/1–5 to 2/1–4, 10 1 1849 extra, 10 11 1849 supp., 10 18 1849 supp., 10 25 1849 supp.; KEMBLE,E.C. 91.

85. BROWNE 465–66, 476; the official journal is in the California State Archives, signed by Marcy but in another hand.

86. BROWNE 163–64.

87. Ibid. 163–64; BROWNE,L.F. 121, 122–23, 129, 131, 133, 136–37; WALKER 29, 317–18.

88. ALTA 12 29 1849 3/1, for the steamer *Oregon* 12 31 1849 1/3–4; DAVIS 4.

89. Tri-wk. ALTA 12 26 1849 2/4; DAVIS 5–6; total population 107,000 (BANCROFT 6:305).

90. ALTA 11 15 1849 2/1.

91. DAVIS 5; Halleck to Speaker,Assembly 12 12 1849 (*561–52* 40).

92. DAVIS 5–6, 659; BURNETT 349; the first canvass showed the votes for Burnett to be 6,783.

93. Riley, proclamation 12 12 1849 (*561*–52 39; ALTA 12 22 1849 3/4).

94. Riley to Hooker 12 3 1849 (NA98,M210,R1), to Taylor 12 19 1849 (*561*–52 40), to whom 12 19 1849 (ibid. 41), to R.Jones 12 20 1849 (ibid. 19); Canby, special order no.68, 12 20 1849 (NA98,M210,R7).

95. Tri-wk. ALTA 12 19 1849 2/3; membership, ALTA 12 15 1849 2/3.

96. Tri-wk. ALTA 12 24 1849 2/2, 12 26 1849 2/3, 12 28 1849 1/2.

97. Ibid. 12 28 1849 1/3; Burnett's inaugural address (BURNETT 349–51; GREENWOOD 126, 127).

98. Riley to R.Jones 12 20 1849 (*561*–52 18), proclamation 12 20 1849 (ibid. 41; BROWNE, appendix xlvi).

99. Riley, order no.41, 12 20 1849 (tri-wk. ALTA 12 26 1849 3/2; BROWNE, appendix xlvi); Riley, order no.1, 1 1 1850 and suppl. memo. 1 17 1850, appointed Halleck acting aide-de-camp (NA98,M210,R7).

100. Tri-wk. ALTA 11 28 1849 1/2.

101. ALTA 11 29 1849 2/3.

102. Tri-wk. ALTA 12 28 1849 2/1.

103. BURNETT 359.

104. ALTA 8 2 1850 2/2; A.Spence to Larkin 1 24 1851 (LARKIN 8 : 372). Riley relinquished his command July 31, 1850 (Riley, order no.17, 7 31 1850, in NA98,M210,R7), was ordered to report to Washington, then to his regiment (R.Jones to Riley 4 17 1850, in NA98,M210,R5), and would die in Buffalo, N.Y., June 9, 1853 (DICTIONARY 15 : 608–09).

105. DAVIS 4.

106. BANCROFT 6 : 307 n.94.

107. Memorial requesting admission (BROWNE, appendix xiv–xxiii), with subsequent debate (*563*–68; GOODWIN 328–29).

Sources Cited in the Text

*PRINTED AND MANUSCRIPT SOURCES**
Arranged by key words as cited in footnotes to the text.

ACADEMY   Academy of Pacific Coast History. *Publications.* Berkeley: University of California, 1909–1919. 4 v.

ADAMS,E.   Adams, Ephraim D. "English interest in the annexation of California." *American Historical Review* 14:744–63, July 1909.

ADAMS,J.   Adams, John Q. *Memoirs of John Quincy Adams, comprising portions of his diary from 1795 to 1848.* Philadelphia: J. B. Lippincott & Co., 1874–1877. 12 v.

ALDEN   Alden, Roland H., and Ifft, John D. *Early naturalists in the far west.* San Francisco: California Academy of Sciences, 1943. 59 p. (Occasional papers no. XX.)

ALTA   *Alta California.* San Francisco, Jan. 4, 1849–June 2, 1891. (Newspaper file on microfilm.)

ALVAREZ   Alvarez, José María. *Instituciones de derecho real de Castilla y de Indias.* Taos, N.M.: 1842. 168 p.

ALVAREZ-1   Alvarez, José María. *Manual de práctica arreglado a la forma forense de la república mexicana.* México: Imprenta de Galván, 1828. 302 p.

ANDERSON   Anderson, Charles R., ed. *Journal of a cruise to the Pacific Ocean, 1842–1844, in the frigate United States.* Durham, N.C.: Duke University Press, 1937. 143 p.

ANNALS   U.S. Congress. *Annals of Congress of the United States,* 1st to 18th sessions. Washington, D.C.: Gales and Seaton, 1834–1856. 42 v.

BALDRIDGE   Baldridge, William. The days of 1846. 1877. (Bancroft Library ms. C–D 36.)

BANCROFT   Bancroft, Hubert H. *History of California.* San Francisco: The History Co., 1886–1890. 7 v.

BANCROFT-1   Bancroft, Hubert H. *History of the northwest coast.* San Francisco: The History Co., 1890. 2 v.

BANCROFT-2   Bancroft, Hubert H. *California pioneer register and index, 1542–1848.* Baltimore: Regional Publishing Co., 1964. 392 p.

BAUER   Bauer, Karl Jack. *Surfboats and horse marines: U.S. naval operations in the Mexican war, 1846–1848.* Annapolis, Md.: U.S. Naval Institute, 1969. 291 p.

BAYARD   [Bayard, S. J.] *A sketch of the life of Com. Robert F. Stockton.* New York: Derby & Jackson, 1856. 210, 131 p.

BEAGLEHOLE   Beaglehole, J. C. *The exploration of the Pacific.* 2nd ed. London: Adam & Charles Black, 1947. xv, 411 p.

* Publications of Congress are listed separately in a following section.

BEECHEY   Beechey, Frederick W. *An account of a visit to California, 1826–'27 . . . performed in His Majesty's ship Blossom . . . in 1825, '26, '27, '28.* San Francisco: Printed at the Grabhorn Press for the Book Club of California, 1941. 74 p.

BEECHEY-1   Beechey, Frederick W. *Narrative of a voyage to the Pacific and Beering's Strait.* London: Henry Colburn and Richard Bentley, 1831. 2 v.

BELCHER   Belcher, Edward. *Narrative of a voyage round the world performed in Her Majesty's ship Sulphur during the years 1836–1842.* London: H. Colburn, 1843. 2 v.

BELL   Bell, Horace. *Reminiscences of a ranger, or early times in southern California.* Los Angeles: Primavera Press, 1933. 499 p.

BELL-1   Bell, Horace. *On the old west coast, being further reminiscences of a ranger.* New York: Grosset & Dunlap, 1930. 336 p.

BENTON   Benton, Thomas H. *Thirty years' view, or a history of the working of the American government for thirty years, from 1820 to 1850.* New York: D. Appleton & Co., 1854–1856. 2 v.

BENTON-1   Benton, Thomas H. "Substance of a speech . . . in the Senate . . . July 1848, on the nomination of General Kearny for the brevet of major general." *Congressional Globe,* 1847–1848, appendix, pp. 977–1040.

BERNAL   Bernal, Juan. Statement. (Bancroft Library ms. C-D 43.)

BIDWELL   Bidwell, John. *In California before the gold rush.* Los Angeles: Ward Ritchie Press, 1948. 111 p.

BIDWELL-1   Bidwell, John. *A journey to California, with observations about the country.* San Francisco: John Henry Nash, 1937. 48 p.

BIDWELL-2   Bidwell, John. "Frémont in the conquest of California." *Century Illustrated Monthly Magazine* 41 (n.s.19): 518–25, February 1891.

BIGGS   Biggs, Donald C. *Conquer and colonize: Stevenson's regiment and California.* San Rafael, Calif.: Presidio Press, 1977. 263 p.

BIGLER   Bigler, Henry W. *Bigler's chronicle of the west . . . as reflected in Henry William Bigler's diaries,* by Erwin G. Gudde. Berkeley and Los Angeles: University of California Press, 1962. 145 p.

BINKLEY   Binkley, William C. *The expansionist movement in Texas, 1836–1850.* Berkeley: University of California Press, 1925. 253 p.

BLUE   Blue, Verne. "The report of Captain LaPlace." California Historical Society *Quarterly* 18: 315–28, December 1939.

BOGGS   Boggs, Mae H. B. *My playhouse was a Concord coach, an anthology of newspaper clippings and documents.* Oakland, Calif.: Howell-North, 1942. 763 p.

BOLTON   Bolton, Herbert E. *The Spanish borderlands, a chronicle of old Florida and the southwest.* New Haven: Yale University Press, 1921. 320 p.

BOLTON-1   Bolton, Herbert E., ed. *Spanish explorations in the southwest, 1542–1706.* New York: Barnes & Noble, 1946. 486 p.

BOSCH GARCIA   Bosch García, Carlos. *Historia de las relaciones entre México y los Estados Unidos, 1819–1848.* México: Escuela Nacional de Ciencias Políticas y Sociales, 1961. 297 p.

BOSCH GARCIA-1   Bosch García, Carlos. *Material para la historia diplomática de México.* México: Escuela Nacional de Ciencias Políticas y Sociales, 1957. 655 p.

BROOKE   Brooke, George M., Jr. "The vest-pocket war of Commodore Jones." *Pacific Historical Review* 31: 217–33, August 1962.

BROWNE   Browne, J. Ross. *Report of the debates in the convention of California, on the formation of the state constitution, in September and October 1849.* Washington, D.C.: John T. Towers, 1850. 479, xlvi p. Also: *Relación de los debates de la convención de California.* New York: S. W. Benedict, 1851. 439 p.

BROWNE,L.F.   Browne, Lina F., ed. *J. Ross Browne, his letters, journals, and writings.* Albuquerque: University of New Mexico Press, 1969. 419 p.

BRYANT   Bryant, Edwin. *What I saw in California: being a journal of a tour . . . in the years 1846, 1847.* New York: D. Appleton & Co., 1848. 480 p.

BUCHANAN   Buchanan, James. *The works of James Buchanan, comprising his speeches, state papers, and private correspondence.* Philadelphia: J. B. Lippincott Co., 1908–1911. 12 v.

BURNETT   Burnett, Peter H. *Recollections and opinions of an old pioneer.* New York: D. Appleton & Co., 1880. 448 p.

BUSTAMENTE   Bustamente, Anastacio. A. Bustamente to Minister of War, Mexico, March 20, 1847. 6 p. (Huntington Library ms. 41840.)

BYNUM   Bynum, Lindley. "Laws for the better government of California, 1848." *Pacific Historical Review* 2 : 279–91, 1933.

CALIF.CONSTITUTION   *Constitution of the state of California.* San Francisco: Office of the Alta California, 1849. 19 p. (Also issued in Spanish.)

CAL.HIS.QT.   *California Historical Quarterly.* San Francisco: California Historical Society, 1922– . Title, California Historical Society *Quarterly* until v.50, 1971.

CALIFN.   *Californian.* Monterey, August 15, 1846–November 11, 1848. (Newspaper file, Huntington Library.) Published in part as *The Californian, volume one facsimile reproductions of . . . numbers . . . between August 15, 1846 and May 6, 1847.* San Francisco: John Howell, 1971. 164 p.

CAL.STAR   *The California Star.* Yerba Buena and San Francisco, January 9, 1847–June 14, 1848. (Newspaper file, Huntington Library.) Published in part as *The California Star, Yerba Buena and San Francisco, volume I, 1847–48.* Berkeley: Howell-North, 1965. 212 p.

CAL.STAR & CALIFN.   *California Star and Californian.* San Francisco, November 18–December 23, 1848. (Newspaper file, Huntington Library.)

CALLAHAN   Callahan, James M. *American foreign policy in Mexican relations.* New York: Macmillan, 1932. x, 644 p.

CAMP   Camp, Charles L., ed. *James Clyman, frontiersman: the adventures of a trapper and covered-wagon emigrant as told in his own reminiscences and diaries.* 2nd ed. Portland, Ore.: Champoeg Press, 1950. 352 p.

CARRILLO   Carrillo, Julio. Narrative of Julio Carrillo as given by him to Robert A. Thompson. (Bancroft Library ms. C-E 67 : 8.)

CARSHAW   Carshaw, William L. Diary of William L. Carshaw, sailing master's clerk, U.S. sloop of war Dale, on a cruise from New York to the north and south Pacific oceans and Gulf of California and return, June 6, 1846 to August 23, 1847. (Typed copy in the National Archives, NA45,M625,R284.)

CARTER   Carter, Harvey L. *"Dear old Kit": the historical Christopher Carson, with a new edition of the Carson memoirs.* Norman: University of Oklahoma Press, 1968. 250 p.

CAUGHEY   Caughey, John W. *California.* New York: Prentice-Hall, 1940. 680 p. (2nd and 3rd eds., 1955, 1970.)

CENTURY   *Century Illustrated Monthly Magazine*, v. 1–22, 1870–1881, n.s., v. 1–98, 1870–1930. New York: Scribner's & Co., 1870–1930.

CHANNING   Channing, Edward. *History of the United States.* New York: Macmillan, 1920–1925. 6 v.

CHAPMAN   Chapman, Charles E. *A history of California: the Spanish period.* New York: Macmillan, 1928. 527 p.

CLARK   Clark, Harry. "Their pride, their manners, and their vices: sources of the traditional portrait of the early Californians." California Historical Society *Quarterly* 53: 71–82, Spring 1974.

CLARKE   Clarke, Dwight L. *Stephen Watts Kearny, soldier of the west.* Norman: University of Oklahoma Press, 1961. 448 p.

CLELAND   Cleland, Robert G. *From wilderness to empire, a history of California.* New York: Knopf, 1969. 445 p.

CLELAND-1   Cleland, Robert G. *A history of California: the American period.* New York: Macmillan, 1927. 512 p.

CLELAND-2   Cleland, Robert G. *Pathfinders.* Los Angeles: Powell Publishing Co., 1929. 452 p.

COLLINS   Collins, John R. "The Mexican war: a study in fragmentation." *Journal of the West* 11: 225–34, April 1972.

COLTON   Colton, Walter. *Three years in California.* New York: A. S. Barnes & Co.; Cincinnati: H. W. Derby & Co., 1850. 456 p. (1949 ed.: *Three years . . . with extracts from . . . Deck and Port.* Stanford, Calif.: Stanford University Press, 1949. xvii, 376, xix–xl p.)

COLTON-1   Colton, Walter. *Deck and port; or, incidents of a cruise in the United States frigate Congress to California.* New York: A. S. Barnes & Co., 1850. 408 p.

CONG.GLOBE   *The Congressional Globe*, 23rd to 42nd Congress, Dec. 2, 1833–March 3, 1873. Washington, D.C.: Printed at the Globe office, 1834–73. 46 v. in 111.

COOK   Cook, Sherburne F. *The population of the California Indians, 1769–1970.* Berkeley and Los Angeles: University of California Press, 1976. 222 p.

COOKE   Cooke, Philip St. George. *The conquest of New Mexico and California; an historical and personal narrative.* New York: G. P. Putnam's Sons, 1878. 307 p.

CORNEY   Corney, Peter. *Voyages in the northern Pacific . . . from 1813 to 1818.* Honolulu: Thos. G. Thrum, 1896. 138 p.

CORTES   Cortés, Hernán. *Letters from Mexico.* New York: Grossman Publications, 1971. lxviii, 565 p.

COSTANSO   Costansó, Miguel. *The Portolá expedition of 1769–1770, diary of Miguel Costansó.* Berkeley: University of California, 1911. 167 p. (Academy of Pacific Coast History *Publications*, v.2, no.4.)

COUGHLIN   Coughlin, Magdalen. "Commercial foundations of political interest in the opening Pacific, 1789–1829." *California Historical Quarterly* 50: 15–33, March 1971.

COY   Coy, Owen C. *The battle of San Pasqual.* Sacramento: California State Printing Office, 1921. 18 p. Report of the California Historical Survey Commission.

CRAVEN   Craven, Tunis A. M. "Notes from the journal of Lieutenant T. A. M. Craven, U.S.N., U.S.S. Dale, Pacific squadron, 1846–49." U.S. Naval Institute *Proceedings* 14: 119–48, 301–36, 1888.

CRAVEN-1   Craven, Tunis A. M. *A naval campaign in the Californias—1846–1849, the journal of Lieutenant Tunis Augustus Macdonough Craven, U.S.N. United States sloop of war Dale.* San Francisco: Book Club of California, 1973. 124 p. (Slightly variant text of CRAVEN.)

CRESPI   Crespí, Juan. *Fray Juan Crespí, missionary explorer on the Pacific coast, 1769–1774.* Berkeley: University of California Press, 1927. lxiv, 402 p.

CUTTS   Cutts, James M. *The conquest of California and New Mexico, by the forces of the United States.* Albuquerque: Horn & Wallace, 1965. 264 p. (Facsimile of 1847 ed.)

DANA   Dana, Richard H. *Two years before the mast, a personal narrative of life at sea.* New York: Heritage Press, 1947. 346 p. (First published 1840.)

DAVIS   Davis, Winfield J. *History of political conventions in California, 1849–1892.* Sacramento: California State Library, 1893. 711 p.

DE VOTO   DeVoto, Bernard. *The year of decision, 1846.* Boston: Little, Brown, 1943. 538 p.

DICTIONARY   *Dictionary of American biography.* New York: C. Scribner's Sons, 1928–1958. 22 v.

DOUGLAS   Douglas, James. *James Douglas in California, 1841, being the journal of a voyage from the Columbia to California.* Vancouver, B.C.: The Library's Press, 1965. xxvi,56 p. (A similar text appears in California Historical Society *Quarterly* 8:97–115, June 1929.)

DOWNEY   Downey, Joseph T. *The cruise of the Portsmouth, 1845–1847, a sailor's view of the naval conquest of California.* New Haven: Yale University Library, 1958. 246 p.

DRAKE'S PLATE   *Drake's plate of brass, evidence of his visit to California in 1579.* San Francisco: California Historical Society, 1937. 57 p.

DRIVER   Driver, Les. "Carrillo's flying artillery: the battle of San Pedro." California Historical Society *Quarterly* 48:335–49, December 1969.

DUFLOT DE MOFRAS   Duflot de Mofras, Eugène. *Duflot de Mofras' travels on the Pacific coast,* trans. and ed. by Marguerite Eyer Wilbur. Santa Ana, Calif.: Fine Arts Press, 1937. 2 v.

DUFLOT DE MOFRAS-1   Duflot de Mofras, Eugène. *Exploration du territoire de l'Oregon, des Californies et de la Mer Vermeille.* Paris: Arthus Bertrand, 1844. 2 v. and atlas.

DUHAUT-CILLY   Duhaut-Cilly, Auguste. "Duhaut-Cilly's account of California in the years 1827–28." California Historical Society *Quarterly* 8:131–66, 214–50, 306–36, 1929.

DUNBAR   Dunbar, Edward E. *Romance of the age, or the discovery of gold in California.* New York: D. Appleton and Co., 1867. 134 p.

DUPETIT-THOUARS   Dupetit-Thouars, Abel A. *Voyage autour du monde sur la frégate La Vénus pendant les années 1836–1839.* Paris, 1840–1844. 5 v.

DUPONT   Dupont, Samuel F. *Extracts from private journal-letters of Captain S. F. DuPont, while in command of the Cyane during the war with Mexico, 1846–1848.* Wilmington, Del.: Ferris Bros., 1885. 444 p.

DUPONT-1   Dupont, Samuel F. *Official despatches and letters of Rear Admiral DuPont, U.S. Navy, 1846–1848, 1861–1863.* Wilmington, Del.: Ferris Bros., 1866. 531 p.

DUPONT-2   Dupont, Samuel F. "The war with Mexico; the cruise of the U.S. ship Cyane during the years 1845–48, from the papers of her commander." U.S. Naval Institute *Proceedings*, 8:419–37, 1882.

DUVALL,M. Duvall, Marius. *A navy surgeon in California, 1846–1847, the journal of Marius Duvall.* San Francisco: John Howell, 1957. 114 p.

DUVALL,R.C. Duvall, Robert C. "Extracts from the log of the U.S. frigate *Savannah*." California Historical Society *Quarterly* 3:105–25, July 1924.

DWINELLE Dwinelle, John W. *The colonial history, city of San Francisco: being a narrative argument in the circuit court of the United States for the state of California, for four square leagues of land.* 4th ed. San Francisco: Towne & Bacon, 1867. xlv, 34, 106, 391 p. (Facsimile ed., Ross Valley Book Co., 1978.)

EGAN Egan, Ferol. *Frémont, explorer for a restless nation.* New York: Doubleday & Co., 1977. 582 p.

ELDREDGE Eldredge, Zoeth S. *The beginnings of San Francisco, from the expedition of Anza, 1774, to the city charter of April 15, 1850.* San Francisco: Author, 1912. 2 v.

ELLISON Ellison, William H. "Constitution making in the land of gold." *Pacific Historical Review* 18:319–30, August 1949.

ELLISON-1 Ellison, William H. *A self-governing dominion: California, 1849–1860.* Berkeley: University of California Press, 1950. 335 p.

ELLSWORTH Ellsworth, Clayton S. "The American churches and the Mexican war." *American Historical Review* 45:301–26, January 1940.

FARQUHAR Farquhar, Francis P. *History of the Sierra Nevada.* Berkeley and Los Angeles: University of California Press, 1965. 262 p.

FARQUHAR-1 Farquhar, Francis P. "The topographical reports of Lieutenant George H. Derby." California Historical Society *Quarterly* 11:99–123, 247–65, 365–82, 1932.

FEBRERO Febrero, José. *Febrero méjicano, ó sea la librería de jueces, abogados, y escribanos . . . adicionada con otros diversos tratados, y las disposiciones del derecho de Indias y del patrio . . .* México: Imprenta de Galván, 1834–1835. 9 v.

FEHRENBACHER Fehrenbacher, Don E. "The Mexican war and the conquest of California." In Knoles, George H., ed. *Essays and assays: California history reappraised.* San Francisco and Los Angeles: California Historical Society, 1973, p. 55–63.

FORBES,A. Forbes, Alexander. *California: a history of Upper and Lower California from their first discovery to the present time.* London: Smith, Elder & Co., 1839. xvi, 352 p. (Also, San Francisco: T. C. Russell, 1919, xvi,372 p.; San Francisco: John Henry Nash, 1937, xxxi, 229 p.)

FORBES,J.A. Forbes, James A. James Alexander Forbes collection. (Bancroft Library ms. C-B 679.)

FORD Ford, Henry L. The Bear Flag revolution in California, 1846. (Bancroft Library ms. C-E 75B.) Written in 1851.

FORT SUTTER Fort Sutter papers. (Huntington Library ms.)

FOSTER Foster, Stephen C. Angeles, 1847–1849. (Bancroft Library ms. C-D 82.)

FREMONT Frémont, John C. "The conquest of California." *Century Illustrated Monthly Magazine* n.s.19:917–28, April 1891.

FREMONT-1 Frémont, John C. *Memoirs of my life.* Chicago & New York: Belford, Clarke & Co., 1887. viii,xix,655 p.

GARCIA García, José E. Historical episodes of California. (Bancroft Library ms. C-D 85.) Dictated in 1878.

GARNER   Garner, William R. *Letters from California, 1846–1847*, ed. by Donald Craig. Berkeley and Los Angeles: University of California Press, 1970. 262 p.

GATES   Gates, Paul W. "Carpetbaggers join the rush for California land." *California Historical Quarterly* 56:98–127, Summer 1977.

GATES-1   Gates, Paul W. "The land business of Thomas O. Larkin." *California Historical Quarterly* 54:323–44, Winter 1975.

GIBSON   Gibson, Joe. "A. Butler: what a scamp." *Journal of the West* 11:235–47, April 1972.

GIFFIN   Giffin, Helen S. "The California Battalion's route to Los Angeles." *Journal of the West* 5:207–24, April 1966.

GILBERT   Gilbert, E. W. *The exploration of western America, 1800–1850, an historical geography.* Cambridge, Eng.: University Press, 1933. 233 p.

GILLESPIE   Gillespie, Archibald H. [Account of Bear Flag affair.] (U.C.L.A. Library ms., Gillespie collection 133:19.)

GILLESPIE-1   Gillespie, Archibald H. "Gillespie and the conquest of California, from letters dated February 11, 1846, to July 8, 1848, to the Secretary of the Navy . . ." California Historical Society *Quarterly* 17:123–40,271–84,325–50, 1938.

GILLESPIE-2   Gillespie, Archibald H. "Further letters of Archibald H. Gillespie, October 20, 1845, to January 16, 1846, to the Secretary of the Navy . . ." California Historical Society *Quarterly* 18:217–28, September 1939.

GILLESPIE-3   Gillespie, Archibald H. Gillespie papers, 1845–1860. (U.C.L.A. Library ms., Gillespie collection 133:19.)

GLEASON   Gleason, Duncan. "James Henry Gleason: pioneer journal and letters." Historical Society of Southern California *Quarterly* 31:9–52, March–June 1949.

GOODWIN   Goodwin, Cardinal L. *The establishment of state government in California, 1846–1850.* New York: Macmillan, 1914. 359 p.

GOODWIN-1   Goodwin, Cardinal L. *John Charles Frémont, an explanation of his career.* Stanford, Calif.: Stanford University Press, 1930. 285 p.

GREENWOOD   Greenwood, Robert. *California imprints, 1833–1862; a bibliography* . . . Los Gatos, Calif.: Talisman Press, 1961. 524 p.

GRIFFIN   Griffin, John S. Copy of the journal of Dr. John S. Griffin, U.S.A. (Bancroft Library ms. C-E 76.)

GRIFFIN-1   Griffin, John S. *A doctor comes to California, the diary of John S. Griffin, assistant surgeon with Kearny's dragoons, 1846–1847.* San Francisco: California Historical Society, 1943. 97 p. (Special Publication no. 18.)

GRIFFIN-2   Griffin, John S. Documents for the history of California, 1846–7, and especially of the Battle of San Pasqual. (Bancroft Library ms. C-B 79.)

GRIFFIN-3   Griffin, John S. *Los Angeles in 1849, a letter from John S. Griffin, M.D., to Col. J. D. Stevenson, March 11, 1849.* Los Angeles: Privately printed, 1949. 19 p.

GRIFFIN,G.B.   Griffin, George B., ed. *Documents from the Sutro collection.* Los Angeles: Franklin Printing Co., 1891. 213 p. (Historical Society of Southern California *Publications* 2:pt.1.)

GRIVAS   Grivas, Theodore. *Military governments in California, 1846–1850, with a chapter on their prior use in Louisiana, Florida, and New Mexico.* Glendale, Calif.: A. H. Clark Co., 1963. 247 p.

GUDDE   Gudde, Erwin G. *Sutter's own story, the life of General John Augustus Sutter and the history of New Helvetia.* New York: G. P. Putnam's Sons, 1936. 244 p.

GUDDE-1   Gudde, Erwin G. *California place names.* Berkeley and Los Angeles: University of California Press, 1969. 416 p.

HALLECK   Halleck, Henry W. History of California. (Bancroft Library ms. C-B 421, box 9.)

HALLECK-1   Halleck, Henry W. "Report on the laws and regulations relative to grants or sales of public lands in California." 1849. (U.S. congressional publication 573–17 118–82.)

HALLECK-2   Halleck, Henry W. *The Mexican war in Baja California, the memorandum of Captain Henry W. Halleck, . . . 1846–1848.* Ed. by Doyce B. Nunis, Jr. Los Angeles: Dawson's Book Shop, 1977. 208 p.

HALLECK,J.   Halleck, Jabez, and Hartnell, William E. P. *Translation and digest of such portions of the Mexican laws of March 20th and May 23d, 1837, as are supposed to be still in force and adapted to the present condition of California.* San Francisco: Office of the Alta California, 1849. 26 p.

HANNA   Hanna, Warren L. *Lost harbor; the controversy over Drake's California anchorage.* Berkeley and Los Angeles: University of California Press, 1979. 459 p.

HANSEN   Hansen, Woodrow J. *The search for authority in California.* Oakland, Calif.: Biobooks, 1960. 192 p.

HARGIS   Hargis, Donald E. "Native Californians in the Constitutional Convention of 1849." Historical Society of Southern California *Quarterly* 36:3–13, March 1954.

HARGRAVE   Hargrave, William H. California in 1846. 12 1. (Bancroft Library ms. C-D 97.) Related in 1878.

HARGRAVE-1   Hargrave, William H. Statement of William Hargrave. 7 p. (Bancroft Library ms. C-D 268.) Related in 1886.

HARLOW   Harlow, Neal. *Maps and surveys of the pueblo lands of Los Angeles.* Los Angeles: Dawson's Book Shop, 1976. 169 p.

HARLOW-1   Harlow, Neal. *The maps of San Francisco Bay from the Spanish discovery in 1769 to the American occupation.* San Francisco: Book Club of California, 1950. 140 p.

HASKELL   Haskell, Daniel C. *The United States Exploring Expedition, 1838–1842, and its publications, 1844–1874, a bibliography.* New York: New York Public Library, 1942. 188 p.

HAUN   Haun, Cheryl. "The Whig abolitionists' attitude toward the Mexican War." *Journal of the West* 11:260–72, April 1972.

HAWGOOD   Hawgood, John A. *America's western frontiers, the exploration and settlement of the trans-Mississippi west.* New York: Knopf, 1967. 440 p.

HAWGOOD-1   Hawgood, John A. *First and last consul, Thomas Oliver Larkin and the Americanization of California, a selection of letters.* 2nd ed. Palo Alto, Calif.: Pacific Books, 1970. xxxviii, 147 p.

HEIZER   Heizer, Robert F. "Francis Drake and the California Indians, 1579." *University of California Publications in American Archaeology and Ethnology* 42:251–302, 1947.

HEIZER-1   Heizer, Robert F., and Almquist, Alan F. *The other Californians, prejudice and discrimination under Spain, Mexico, and the United States to 1920.* Berkeley and Los Angeles: University of California Press, 1971. 278 p.

HINCKLEY Hinckley, Ted C. "American anti-Catholicism during the Mexican War." *Pacific Historical Review* 31:121–37, May 1962.

HINE Hine, Robert V. *Edward Kern and American expansion* . . . New Haven: Yale University Press, 1962. 180 p.

HIST.RECORDS Historical Records Survey, California. *Calendar of the Major Jacob Rink Snyder collection of the Society of California Pioneers.* San Francisco, 1940. 107 p. (Mimeographed.)

HOLMES Holmes, Maurice G. *From New Spain by sea to the Californias, 1519–1668.* Glendale, Calif.: Arthur H. Clark Co., 1963. 307 p.

HOOVER Hoover, Mildred B., and Rensch, H. E. and E. G. *Historic spots in California.* Stanford, Calif.: Stanford University Press, 1948. 411 p.

HOWE Howe, M. A. DeWolfe. *The life and letters of George Bancroft.* New York: Scribner's, 1908. 2 v.

HURTADO Hurtado, Albert L. "Controlling California's Indian labor force; federal administration . . . during the Mexican War." *Southern California Quarterly* 61:217–38, Fall 1979.

HUSSEY Hussey, John A. "The origin of the Gillespie mission." California Historical Society *Quarterly* 19:43–58, March 1940.

HUTCHINSON Hutchinson, C. Alan. *Frontier settlement in Mexican California, the Híjar–Padres colony and its origins, 1769–1835.* New Haven: Yale University Press, 1969. 457 p.

HUTTON Hutton, William R. *Glances at California, 1847–1853. Diaries and letters.* San Marino, Calif.: Huntington Library, 1942. 86 p.

IDE Ide, Simon. *A biographical sketch of the life of William B. Ide.* Claremont, N.H.: Author, 1880. 239 p.

INIESTRA Iniestra, Ignacio. Disquisición del Coronel Ignacio Iniestra . . . y documentatión relacionado con la organización de fuerzas destinadas a la defensa de la Baja y Alta California, años 1845–46. (In MEXICO,SECT.DEFENSA, Archivo exp. 2202.) Film copy in The Bancroft Library, reel 6.

JACKSON,A.C. Jackson, Alonzo C. *The conquest of California. Alonzo C. Jackson's letter in detail of the seizure of Monterery in 1842 and his letter on the final conquest in 1846.* New York: Edward Eberstadt & Sons, 1953. 31 p.

JACKSON,S.G. Jackson, Sheldon G. "The British and the California dream; rumors, myths, and legends." *Southern California Quarterly* 57:251–70, Fall 1975.

JACKSON,S.G.-1 Jackson, Sheldon G. "Two pro-British plots in Alta California." *Southern California Quarterly* 55:105–40, Summer 1973.

JEPSON Jepson, Willis L. "The explorations of Hartweg in America." *Erythea* 5:31–35,51–56, 1897.

JONES,J.M. Jones, James M. *Two letters of James McHall Jones, delegate to the California Constitutional Convention, 1849.* Carmel, Calif.: T. W. Norris, 1948. 25 p.

JONES,T.A.C. Jones, Thomas ap Catesby. *Visit to Los Angeles in 1843. Reprinted from the Daily Alta California.* Los Angeles: Roxburghe–Zamorano Keepsake, 1960. 28 p. (Also Historical Society of Southern California *Quarterly publication* 17:123–34, December 1935.)

JONES,W.C. Jones, William C. "The first phase of the conquest of California." California Historical Society *Papers* 1:pt.1 61–94.

JONES,W.C.-1 Jones, William C. *Land titles in California. Report . . . together with a translation of the principal laws on that subject.* Washington, D.C.:

Gideon & Co., 1850. 60 p. (Also issued by U.S. Congress, 1851, 589–18.)

KEARNY   Kearny, Stephen W. Kearny collection. (Bancroft Library ms. C-B 633:5.)

KEARNY-1   Kearny, Stephen W. *A letter from . . . San Diego, Upper California, January thirtieth, 1847.* Carmel, Calif.: T. W. Norris, 1950. 8 p.

KEARNY,T.   Kearny, Thomas. "The Mexican war and the conquest of California: Stockton or Kearny conqueror and first governor?" California Historical Society *Quarterly* 8:251–61, September 1929.

KELLEHER   Kelleher, M. Map showing the location of the old zanza madre, ditches, vineyards and old town, etc. Los Angeles, May 7th 1875. (Los Angeles City Hall, room 803, map no. 172.)

KELLY   Kelly, Charles. *Salt desert trails, a history of the Hastings cutoff and other early trails which crossed the Great Salt Desert.* Salt Lake City: Western Printing Co., 1930. 178 p.

KEMBLE,E.C.   Kemble, Edward C. *A history of California newspapers, 1846–1858.* Ed. by Helen Harding Bretnor. Los Gatos, Calif.: Talisman Press, 1962. 398 p.

KEMBLE,E.C.-1   Kemble, Edward C. *A Kemble reader, stories of California, 1846–1848.* Ed. by Fred Blackburn Rogers. San Francisco: California Historical Society, 1963. 168 p.

KEMBLE,J.H.   Kemble, John H. *The Panama route, 1848–1869.* Berkeley and Los Angeles: University of California Press, 1943. 316 p.

KERN   Kern, Edward. "Journal of Edward Kern of an exploration of the Mary's or Humboldt River, Carson Lake, and Owens River and Lake, in 1845." (Reprinted in SPENCE 2:48–63.)

KING   King, Thomas B. *California: the wonder of the age; a book for every one going to or having an interest in that golden region.* New York: W. Gowans, 1850. 34 p. (Also published as *California, its population, climate, soil . . .* London: Kent and Richards, 1850, 105 p. Also issued by the U.S. Congress, 577–59; and reprinted in TAYLOR 2:199–247.)

KIRSCH   Kirsch, Robert, and Murphy, William S. *West of the west; the story of California . . . as described by the men and women who were there.* New York: Dutton, 1967. 526 p.

KOHL   Kohl, Clayton C. *Claims as a cause of the Mexican war.* New York: Faculty of the Graduate School, New York University, 1914. 96 p. A published thesis.

LANCEY   Lancey, Thomas C. U.S. sloop-of-war Dale, its cruise, together with gleanings by the wayside, including the conquest of California. 896 p. (Bancroft Library typed ms. C-E 106.)

LANGSDORFF   Langsdorff, Georg H. von. *Langsdorff's narrative of the Rezanov voyage to Nueva California in 1806.* San Francisco: T. C. Russell, 1927. 158 p.

LANGSDORFF-1   Langsdorff, Georg H. von. *Voyages and travels in various parts of the world during the years 1803, 1804, 1805, 1806, and 1807.* London: Printed for Henry Colburn, 1813–1814. 2 v.

LANGUM   Langum, David J. "The caring colony: Alta California's participation in Spain's foreign affairs." *Southern California Quarterly* 62:217–28, Fall 1980.

LA PEROUSE   LaPérouse, Jean F. G. de. *A voyage round the world, in the years 1785, 1786, 1787, and 1788.* London: J. Johnson, 1798. 3 v. and atlas.

LAPLACE Laplace, Cyrille P. T. *Campagne de circumnavigation de la frégate l'Artémise pendant les années 1837, 1838, 1839 et 1840*. Paris: A. Bertrand, 1841–1854. 6 v.

LARKIN Larkin, Thomas O. *The Larkin papers, personal, business, and official correspondence*. Ed. by George P. Hammond. Berkeley and Los Angeles: University of California Press, 1951–1968. 10 v.

LARKIN-1 Larkin, Thomas O. "Six new Larkin letters." Ed. by Doyce B. Nunis, Jr. *Southern California Quarterly* 49:65–103, March 1967.

LEESE Leese, Jacob P. Papers of the Bear Flag. (Bancroft Library ms. C-B 70.)

LEESE,R. Leese, Rosalía de. Narrative of Mrs. Rosalía Leese who witnessed the history of the bear flag in Sonoma, 1874. (Bancroft Library ms. C-E 65:10.) Related in 1874.

LEIDESDORFF Leidesdorff, William A. Leidesdorff papers. (Huntington Library ms. LE.)

LIPPITT Lippitt, Francis J. *Reminiscences . . . written for his family*. Providence, R.I.: Preston & Rounds Co., 1902. 122 p.

LYMAN Lyman, George D. *John Marsh, pioneer; the life of a trail-blazer on six frontiers*. New York: Scribner's, 1930. 394 p.

MC AFEE McAfee, Ward. "Reconsideration of the origins of the Mexican–American war." *Southern California Quarterly* 62:49–65, Spring 1980.

MC CHRISTIAN McChristian, Pat. Narrative. (Bancroft Library ms. C-E 67:7.)

MC CORMAC McCormac, Eugene I. *James K. Polk, a political biography . . .* New York: Russell & Russell, 1965. 746 p.

MC COY McCoy, Charles A. *Polk and the presidency*. Austin: University of Texas Press, 1960. 238 p.

MC LANE McLane, Louis. *The private journal of Louis McLane, U.S.N., 1844–1848*. Ed. by Jay Monaghan. Los Angeles: Dawson's Book Shop, for the Santa Barbara Historical Society, 1971. 120 p.

MC WHORTER McWhorter, George C. *Incident in the war of the United States with Mexico, illustrating the serices of Wm. Maxwell Wood, Surgeon, U.S.N.* Oswego, N.Y., 1872. 9 p.

MC WILLIAMS McWilliams, Carey. *Southern California country, an island on the land*. New York: Duell, Sloan & Pearce, 1946. 387 p.

MADRIAGA Madriaga, Salvador de. *Hernán Cortés, conquerer of Mexico*. New York: Doubleday Anchor Books, 1942. 554 p.

MAHR Mahr, August C. *The visit of the "Rurik" to San Francisco in 1816 . . .* Stanford, Calif.: Stanford University Press, 1932. 194 p.

MANNING Manning, William R. *Diplomatic correspondence of the United States: inter-American affairs, 1831–1860*. Washington, D.C.: Carnegie Endowment for International Peace, 1932–1939. 12 v.

MARTI Marti, Werner H. *Messenger of destiny: the California adventures, 1846–1847, of Archibald H. Gillespie, U.S. Marine Corps*. San Francisco: John Howell, 1960. 147 p.

MARTIN Martin, Thomas S. *With Frémont to California and the southwest, 1845–1849*. Ed. by Ferol Egan. Ashland, Ore.: Lewis Osborne, 1975. 48 p. Dictated in the 1870s.

MASON Mason, Richard B. *Extract from the regulations for collecting the tariff of duties on imports and tonnage*. Monterey, California. October 20, 1847. [San Francisco, 1847]. 4 p.

MASON-1 California. Laws, statutes, etc. *Laws for the better government of Cal-*

ifornia, the preservation of order, and the protection of the rights of the in-habitants, during the military occupation of the country by the forces of the United States. By the authority of R.B. Mason . . . San Francisco: Published by S. Brannan, 1848. 67 p. (The *Alta California* 6 14 1849 2/3 says 140 p., perhaps combining the English and Spanish texts as Mason originally directed.)

MATHES   Mathes, W. Michael. *The conquistador in California, 1535: the voyage of Hernando Cortés to Baja California in chronicles and documents.* Los Angeles: Dawson's Book Shop, 1973. 123 p.

MATHES-1   Mathes, W. Michael. *Vizcaino and Spanish expansion in the Pacific Ocean, 1580–1630.* San Francisco: California Historical Society, 1968. 186 p. (Special Publication no. 44.)

MAXWELL   Maxwell, Richard T. *Visit to Monterey in 1842.* Ed. by John Haskell Kemble. Los Angeles: Glen Dawson, 1955. 40 p. (From Bancroft Library ms. dictated 35 years afterward.)

MENZIES   Menzies, Archibald. "Menzies' California journal" [of the Vancouver expedition]. California Historical Society *Quarterly* 2:265–340, January 1924.

MERK   Merk, Frederick. *Manifest destiny and mission in American history; a re-interpretation.* New York: Knopf, 1963. 265 p.

MERK-1   Merk, Frederick. *The Monroe Doctrine and American expansionism, 1843–1849.* New York: Knopf, 1966. 289,ix p.

MERK-2   Merk, Frederick. *Slavery and the annexation of Texas.* New York: Knopf, 1972. 290 p.

MERK-3   Merk, Frederick. *History of the Westward movement.* New York: Knopf, 1978. 660 p.

MEXICO,SECT.DEFENSA   México, Secretaría de la defensa nacional. Archivo. (Bancroft Library film copy of mss., with calendar.)

MEYERS   Meyers, William H. *Journal of a cruise to California and the Sandwich Islands in the United States sloop-of-war "Cyane"* . . . *1841–1844.* Ed. by John Haskell Kemble. San Francisco: Book Club of California, 1955. 68 p.

MONTGOMERY   Montgomery, John B. Letter book of Capt. John B. Montgomery, 1844–1848. (National Archives, Record Group 45.)

MORISON   Morison, Samuel E.; Merk, Frederick; and Fridel, Frank. *Dissent in three American wars.* Cambridge: Harvard University Press, 1970. 104 p.

MORROW   Morrow, William W. *Spanish and Mexican private land grants.* San Francisco and Los Angeles: Bancroft-Whitney Co., 1923. 27 p.

MURRAY   Murray, Walter. Narrative of a California volunteer. 1878. (Bancroft Library ms. C-D 132.)

NASATIR   Nasatir, Abraham P., ed. "The French consulate in California, 1843–1856." California Historical Society *Quarterly* 11:195–223,339–57, 12:35–64,155–72,331–57, 1932–1933.

NA45,M89   U.S. National Archives microfilm publications. Letters received by the Secretary of the Navy from commanding officers of squadrons, 1841–1886. Record group 45, microcopy 89, rolls 32–34, Oct. 16, 1844–Aug. 26, 1850.

NA45,M625   U.S. National Archives microfilm publications. Area file of the Naval records collection, 1775–1910. Record group 45, microcopy 625, rolls 282–286, April 1814–May 1855.

NA94,M182   U.S. National Archives microfilm publications. Records of the Adjutant General's Office. Letters sent by the military governors and the Secretary of State of California, March 1, 1847–Sept. 23, 1848. Record group 94, microcopy 182, 1 roll.

NA98,M210   U.S. National Archives microfilm publications. Records of the United States Army commands, 10th military department, 1846–1851. Record group 98, microcopy 210, rolls 1–7, March 23, 1847–July 8, 1851.

NEW HELVETIA   *New Helvetia diary; a record of events kept by John A. Sutter and his clerks at New Helvetia, California, from September 9, 1845 to May 25, 1848.* San Francisco: Grabhorn Press, 1939. xxvii, 138 p.

NIDEVER   Nidever, George. *The life and adventures of George Nidever, 1802–1883.* Ed. by William Henry Ellison. Berkeley: University of California Press, 1937. 128 p.

NILES   *Niles national register, containing political, historical, geographical, scientifical, economical, and biographical documents, essays, and facts . . .* Philadelphia, 1811–1849. 76 v.

OGDEN   Ogden, Adele. *The California sea otter trade, 1784–1848.* Berkeley and Los Angeles: University of California Press, 1941. 251 p.

ORD   Ord, Angustias de la Guerra. *Occurrences in Hispanic California.* Trans. and ed. by Francis Price and William H. Ellison. Washington, D.C.: Academy of American Franciscan History, 1956. 98 p. (From a Bancroft Library ms. related in 1878.)

OUTLAND   Outland, Charles F. "Frémont slept where?" *Journal of the West* 5:410–16, July 1966.

PECK   Peck, John J. *The sign of the eagle, a view of Mexico—1830 to 1855 . . . letters of Lieutenant John James Peck, a United States soldier in the conflict with Mexico.* San Diego: Union–Tribune Publishing Co., 1970. 168 p.

PHELPS   Phelps, William D. *Fore and aft; or, leaves from the life of an old sailor. By "Webfoot."* Boston: Nichols & Hall, 1871. 359 p.

PICO   Pico, Pío. *Don Pío Pico's historical narrative.* Trans. by Arthur P. Botello, ed. by Martin Cole and Henry Welcome. Glendale, Calif.: Arthur H. Clark Co., 1973. 171 p. (From a Bancroft Library ms., dictated in 1877.)

PITT   Pitt, Leonard. *The decline of the Californios, a social history of the Spanish-speaking Californians, 1846–1890.* Berkeley and Los Angeles: University of California Press, 1968. 324 p.

PLACER TIMES   *Placer Times.* Sacramento, April 28, 1849–June 15, 1851. (Newspaper film, Huntington Library.) Afterwards *Placer Times and Transcript.*

PLETCHER   Pletcher, David M. *The diplomacy of annexation; Texas, Oregon, and the Mexican War.* Columbia, Mo.: University of Missouri Press, 1973. 656 p.

POLK   Polk, James K. *The diary of James K. Polk during his presidency, 1845 to 1849.* Ed. by Milo Milton Quaife. Chicago: A. C. McClurg & Co., 1910. 4 v.

POWER   Power, Robert H. "Drake's landing in California: a case for San Francisco Bay." *California Historical Quarterly* 52:101–30, Summer 1973.

POWER-1   Power, Robert H. *Francisco Drake & San Francisco Bay: a beginning of the British empire.* Davis: University of California, 1974. 29 p. (University Library Associates.)

PRICE   Price, Glen W. *Origins of the war with Mexico: the Polk–Stockton intrigue.* Austin: University of Texas Press, 1967. 189 p.

PRIESTLEY Priestley, Herbert I. *The Mexican nation, a history.* New York: Macmillan, 1938. 507 p.

REEVES Reeves, Jesse S. *American diplomacy under Tyler and Polk.* Baltimore: Johns Hopkins Press, 1907. 335 p.

REGNERY Regnery, Dorothy F. *The battle of Santa Clara.* San Jose, Calif.: Smith and McKay Printing Co., 1978. 154 p.

REVERE Revere, Joseph W. *A tour of duty in California.* New York: C. S. Francis & Co.; Boston: J. H. Francis, 1849. 305 p.

REYNOLDS Reynolds, Curtis R. "The deterioration of Mexican–American diplomatic relations, 1833–1845." *Journal of the West* 11:213–24, April 1972.

RICHARDSON Richardson, James D. *A compilation of the messages and papers of the presidents, 1789–1897.* Washington, D.C.: U.S. Government Printing Office, 1898–1899. 10 v.

RICHMAN Richman, Irving B. *California under Spain and Mexico, 1535–1847.* New York: Cooper Square Publishers, 1965. 541 p.

ROBINSON,A. Robinson, Alfred. *Life in California during a residence of several years in that territory.* New York: Da Capo Press, 1969. 341 p. (Facsimile of New York: Wiley & Putnam, 1846.)

ROBINSON,W.W. Robinson, W. W. *Land in California.* Berkeley and Los Angeles: University of California Press, 1948. 291 p.

RODRIGUEZ DE MONTALVO Rodríguez de Montalvo, Garci. *Amadís de Gaula,* [5th book]. *Les serges del virtuoso cavallero espládian hijo de Amadís de Gaula.* Rome: J. de Junta & A. de Salamanca, 1525. Translated as *Queen of California.* San Francisco: Colt Press, 1945. 46 p.

ROGERS Rogers, Fred B. *Montgomery of the Portsmouth* . . . San Francisco: John Howell, 1958. 145 p.

ROGERS-1 Rogers, Fred B. *William Brown Ide, Bear Flagger.* San Francisco: John Howell, 1962. 101 p.

ROWAN Rowan, Stephen C. "Recollections of the Mexican war: taken from the journal of Lieutenant Stephen C. Rowan . . . U.S.S. Cyane . . . 1845–1848." U.S. Naval Institute *Proceedings* 14:539–59, 1888.

ROYCE Royce, Josiah. *California, from the conquest in 1846 to the second vigilance committee in San Francisco, a study of American character.* Boston and New York: Houghton, Mifflin, 1886. 513 p.

ROYCE-1 Royce, Josiah. Royce Collection. (Huntington Library mss. 20132–46.) Letters from Royce to Henry L. Oak.

ROYCE-2 Royce, Josiah. "The Frémont legend." The *Nation* 52:423–25, May 21, 1891.

ROYCE-3 Royce, Josiah. "Montgomery and Frémont: new documents on the Bear Flag affair." *Century Illustrated Monthly Magazine* 41 (n.s.19): 780–83, March 1891.

ROYCE-4 Royce, Josiah. Notes of an interview with General Frémont at Staten Island, Dec. 6, 1884, with corrections by Jessie Benton Frémont. (Bancroft Library ms. C-B 386 I:4.)

RUXTON Ruxton, George F. *Adventures in Mexico and the Rocky Mountains.* London: John Murray, 1847. 332 p.

RYAN Ryan, William R. *Personal adventures in Upper and Lower California in 1848–9.* London: W. Shoberl, 1850. 2 v.

SANCHEZ Sanchez, Nellie V. *Spanish arcadia* . . . Los Angeles: Powell Publishing Co., 1929. 413 p.

SAVANNAH   Savannah (U.S.Frigate). Smooth log of the United States ship Savannah . . . 1846–1847. (Bancroft Library ms. C-F 70; NA45,x2021.)

SCHREIER   Schreier, Konrad F., Jr. A study of the location of Mule Hill, California: General Kearny's camp after the Battle of San Pasqual. Los Angeles: County Museum of Natural History, 1973. 26 p. (Typed ms.)

SERVIN   Servin, Manuel P. "Costansó's 1794 report on strengthening New California's presidios." California Historical Society *Quarterly* 49:221–32, September 1970.

SHERMAN   Sherman, William T. *Memoirs of General William T. Sherman.* 4th ed. New York: C. L. Webster, 1892. 2 v.

SHINN   Shinn, Charles H. "Some California documents." *Magazine of American History* 25:394–402, May 1891.

SHUR   Shur, Leonid A., and Gibson, James R. "Russian travel notes and journals as sources for the history of California, 1800–1850." *California Historical Quarterly* 52:37–63, Spring 1973.

SMITH,H.N.   Smith, Henry Nash. *Virgin land, the American West as symbol and myth.* Cambridge: Harvard University Press, 1950. 305 p.

SMITH,J.H.   Smith, Justin H. *The war with Mexico.* New York: Macmillan, 1919. 2 v.

SPENCE   Spence, Mary L., and Jackson, Donald, eds. *The expeditions of John Charles Frémont.* Urbana: University of Illinois Press, 1970–1973. 2 v.

STANDART   Standart, M. "The Sonoran migration to California, 1848–1856: a study in prejudice." *Southern California Quarterly* 58:333–57, Fall 1976.

STANTON   Stanton, William. *The great United States Exploring Expedition of 1838–1842.* Berkeley and Los Angeles: University of California Press, 1975. 433 p.

STAR   Los Angeles *Star*, 1851–1864, 1868–1879. (Newspaper film, Huntington Library.)

STEARNS   Stearns, Abel. Abel Stearns collection. (Huntington Library ms. SG.)

STENBERG   Stenberg, Richard R. "The failure of Polk's Mexican war intrigue of 1845." *Pacific Historical Review* 4:39–68, 1935.

STEVENSON   Stevenson, Jonathan D. J. D. Stevenson papers. (U.C.L.A. Library ms. 2040.)

STOCKTON   Stockton, Robert F. *Letter of Commodore Robert F. Stockton, dated Philadelphia, April 13th, 1848.* San Francisco: Thomas W. Norris, 1951. 8 p.

SUTTER   Sutter, John A. *The diary of Johann August Sutter.* Introduction by Douglas S. Watson. San Francisco: Grabhorn Press, 1932. 56 p. Written in 1856.

SUTTER-1   Sutter, John A. Personal reminiscences of General John Augustus Sutter. 95 p. (Bancroft Library ms. C-D 14.)

SWASEY   Swasey, William F. *The early days and men of California.* Oakland, Calif.: Pacific Press, 1891. 406 p.

TALBOT   Talbot, Theodore. *Soldier in the west, letters of Theodore Talbot during his service in California, Mexico, and Oregon, 1845–53.* Ed. by Robert V. Hine and Savoie Lottinville. Norman: University of Oklahoma Press, 1972. 210 p.

TANNER   Tanner, John D. "Campaign for Los Angeles—December 29, 1846, to January 10, 1847." California Historical Society *Quarterly* 48:219–41, September 1969.

TAYLOR   Taylor, Bayard. *Eldorado, or, adventures in the path of empire; com-*

prising a voyage to California, via Panamá . . . and experiences of Mexican travel. New York: G. P. Putnam, 1850. 2 v.

THOMPSON Thompson, Waddy. *Recollections of Mexico*. New York: Wiley and Putnam, 1846. 304 p.

THOMPSON & WEST Thompson & West, publishers. *History of Santa Barbara county, California, with illustrations and biographical sketches*. Oakland, Calif., 1883. 477 p.

TOMPKINS Tompkins, Walker A. "The Foxen–Fremont fable." *Noticias*, quarterly bulletin of the Santa Barbara Historical Society 26:14–17, Spring 1980.

TRANSCRIPT *Transcript*. Sacramento, April 1, 1850–June 15, 1851. (Newspaper film, Huntington Library.)

TUOMEY Tuomey, Honoria. *History of Sonoma County, California*. San Francisco: S. J. Clarke, 1926. 2 v.

TURNER Turner, Henry S. *The original journals of Henry Smith Turner, with Stephen Watts Kearny to Mexico and California, 1846–47*. Ed. by Dwight L. Clarke. Norman: University of Oklahoma Press, 1966. 173 p.

U.S.PRESIDENT U.S. President (Polk). *Message from the President of the United States to the two houses of Congress*. 1st annual message December 2, 1845 (*480–2*); 2nd message December 8, 1846 (*493–1* and *497–4*); 3rd message December 7, 1847 (*503–1* and *515–8*); 4th message December 5, 1848 (*537–1*). (Reprinted in RICHARDSON 4:385–416, 471–506, 532–64, 629–70.)

U.S.STATUTES U.S. Laws, statutes, etc. *The statutes at large and treaties of the United States of America*. Ed. by George Minot. Boston: Little, Brown, 1851– , v.9, December 1, 1845–March 3, 1851.

U.S.SUPREME COURT U.S. Supreme Court. *United States vs. J. R. Bolton. Appellant's brief*. [n.p., 1859?] xxxi, 260, 200 p. (Record of departmental assembly, Los Angeles, March 2, 1846–July 24, 1847, p. 221–53.)

VALLEJO Vallejo, Mariano G. Documentos para la historia de California, 1769–1850. 36 v. (Bancroft Library ms. C-B 12.)

VANCOUVER Vancouver, George. *A voyage of discovery to the north Pacific ocean and round the world . . . performed in the years 1790, 1791, 1792, 1793, 1794, and 1795*. London: G. G. and J. Robinson and J. Edwards, 1798. 3 v. and atlas.

WAGNER Wagner, Henry R. *The cartography of the northwest coast of America to the year 1800*. Berkeley: University of California Press, 1937. 2 v.

WALKER Walker, Franklin. *San Francisco's literary frontier*. New York: Knopf, 1939. 400 p.

WALPOLE Walpole, Frederick. *Four years in the Pacific in His Majesty's ship "Collingwood" from 1844 to 1848*. London: Richard Bentley, 1849. 2 v.

WARNER Warner, Jonathan; Hayes, Benjamin; and Widney, J. P. *A historical sketch of Los Angeles County, California, from the Spanish occupation . . . September 8, 1771, to July 4, 1876*. Los Angeles: O. W. Smith, 1936. 159 p. (Reprint, 1876 ed.)

WEEMS Weems, John E. *To conquer a peace; the war between the United States and Mexico*. New York: Doubleday, 1974. 500 p.

WHEAT Wheat, Carl I. *1540–1861, mapping the transmississippi west*. San Francisco: Institute of Historical Cartography, 1957–1963. 5 v. in 6. (Vol.2, 1804–1845, vol.3, 1846–1854.)

WHITE White, Philo. *Philo White's narrative of a cruise in the Pacific to South America and California on the U.S. Sloop-of-war "Dale," 1841–1843.* Ed. by Charles L. Camp. Denver: Old West Publishing Co., 1965. 84 p.

WILKES Wilkes, Charles. *Narrative of the United States Exploring Expedition, during the years 1838, 1839, 1840, 1841, 1842.* Philadelphia: Lea and Blanchard, 1845. 5 v. and atlas. (For other eds. and publications, see HASKELL.)

WILKES-1 Wilkes, Charles. *Western America, including California and Oregon, with maps of those regions.* Philadelphia: Lea and Blanchard, 1849. 130 p.

WILLEY Willey, Samuel H. *The transition period of California from a province of Mexico in 1846 to a state of the American Union in 1850.* San Francisco: Whitaker and Ray Co., 1901. 160 p.

WILSON Wilson, Benjamin D. "The narrative of Benjamin D. Wilson." In CLELAND-2 371–416. Dictated in 1877.

WILTSEE Wiltsee, Ernest A. "The British vice-consul in California and the events of 1846." California Historical Society *Quarterly* 10:99–128, June 1931.

WINSOR Winsor, Justin. *Narrative and critical history of America.* Boston and New York: Riverside Press, 1884–1889. 8 v.

WOOD Wood, William M. *Wandering sketches of people and things in South America, Polynesia, California, and other places visited during the cruise on board of the U.S. ships Levant, Portsmouth, and Savannah.* Philadelphia: Carey and Hart, 1849. 386 p.

ZIEBARTH Ziebarth, Marilyn, ed. "The Francis Drake controversy: his California anchorage, July 17–July 23, 1579." *California Historical Quarterly* 53:197–292, Fall 1974.

PUBLICATIONS OF CONGRESS *

Arranged by *serial number* as cited in footnotes to the text. (The U.S. Superintendent of Documents number precedes the dash, followed by the Senate or House document number. At the end of each entry will be found the number of the Congress and session, whether publication was authorized by the Senate or House, the type of document, and its number, e.g.: 25:1 H.ex.doc.42, or 30:1 S.rept.35.)

311–42 U.S. President (Van Buren). *Boundary, United States and Mexico. Message from the President . . . transmitting the information required by a resolution of the House . . . .* Oct. 3, 1835. 94 p. (25:1 H.ex.doc.42.)

395–1 U.S. President (Tyler). *Message from the President . . . to the two houses of Congress . . . .* Dec. 7, 1841. 494 p. (27:2 S.ex.doc.1.)

421–127 U.S. Secretary of State. *Cession of California to England . . . A report . . . in answer to a resolution of the House . . . .* Feb. 9, 1843. 1 p. (27:3 H.ex.doc.127.)

422–166 U.S. President (Tyler). *Taking possession of Monterey. Message from the President . . . in reply to the resolution of the House . . . calling for information . . . .* Feb. 22, 1843. 117 p. (27:3 H.ex.doc.166.)

436–390 U.S. President (Tyler). *Message from the President . . . communicating . . . copies of correspondence with the government of Mexico, in relation to*

* Congressional documents, arranged by serial number, have been issued in microprint by the Congressional Information Service, Washington, D.C., with separate printed indexes.

the expulsion of citizens of the United States from Upper California. June 14, 1844. 19 p. (28:1 S.doc.390.)

461–174 Frémont, John C. *Report of the exploring expedition to the Rocky Mountains in the year 1842 and to Oregon and north California in the years 1843–'44* . . . . Washington, D.C.: Gales and Seaton, 1845. 693 p. (28:2 S.doc.174.)

480–2 U.S. President (Polk). *Message from the President . . . to the two houses of Congress* . . . . Dec. 2, 1845. 893 p. (29:1 H.ex.doc.2.) (Polk's 1st annual message, with reports, documents.)

485–196 U.S. President (Polk). *Hostilities by Mexico. Message from the President . . . relative to an invasion and commencement of hostilities by Mexico.* May 11, 1846. 120 p. (29:1 H.ex.doc.196.)

485–197 U.S. President (Polk). *Despatches from General Taylor. Message from the President . . . transmitting despatches* . . . . May 12, 1846. 6 p. (29:1 H.ex.doc.197.)

485–207 U.S. President (Polk). *Official despatches from General Taylor. Message from the President . . . transmitting copies of all official despatches received from General Taylor* . . . . May 27, 1846. 7 p. (29:1 H.ex.doc.207.)

486–209 U.S. President (Polk). *Reports from General Taylor. Message from the President . . . transmitting offical reports* . . . . June 12, 1846. 37 p. (29:1 H.ex.doc.209.)

493–1 U.S. President (Polk). *Message from the President . . . to the two houses of Congress* . . . . Dec. 8, 1846. 704 p. (29:2 S.ex.doc.1.) (Polk's 2nd annual message, with reports and documents.)

497–4 U.S. President (Polk). *Message from the President . . . to the two houses of Congress* . . . . Dec. 8, 1846. 704 p. (29:2 H.ex.doc.4.) (House ed. of 493–1.)

499–19 U.S. President (Polk). *Occupation of Mexican territory. Message from the President . . . in answer to a resolution of the House* . . . . Dec. 22, 1846. 111 p. (29:2 H.ex.doc.19.)

500–119 U.S. President (Polk). *Message from the President . . . transmitting the correspondence with General Taylor . . . not already published.* March 1, 1847. 454 p. (29:2 H.ex.doc.119.)

503–1 U.S. President (Polk). *Message from the President . . . to the two houses of Congress.* Dec. 7, 1847. 1369, 249p. (30:1 S.ex.doc.1.) (Polk's 3rd annual message, with reports, documents.)

505–7 Emory, William H. *Notes of a military reconnoissance from Fort Leavenworth, in Missouri, to San Diego, in California . . . Made in 1846–7 with the advanced guard of the "Army of the West"*. . . . Washington, D.C.: Wendell and Van Benthuysen, 1848. 416 p. (30:1 S.ex.doc.7.) (Has the large map not in 517–41 but not the supplementary reports by J. W. Abert, Philip St.George Cooke, and A. F. Johnston.)

507–33 U.S. President (Polk). *Message from the President . . . communicating the proceedings of the court-martial in the trial of Lieutenant Colonel Frémont.* April 7, 1848. 447 p. (30:1 S.ex.doc.33.) *507–33* (1973), a facsimile ed., in SPENCE 2:part 2.

511–148 Frémont, John C. *Geographical memoir upon Upper California in illustration of his map of Oregon and California.* . . . Washington, D.C., 1848. 67 p. (30:1 S.doc.148.) (Includes large map not in House ed., *544–5.*)

512–75 U.S. Congress. Senate. *California claims . . . February 23, 1848 . . . Re-*

port the Committee on Military Affairs, to which was referred the memorial of John C. Frémont, praying an investigation of the claims of citizens of California against the United States, for money and supplies furnished by them. . . . 83 p. (30:1 S.rept.75.) (Frémont said depositions herein might be considered a report upon his California operations, SPENCE 2:480–81.)

515–8 U.S. President (Polk). *Message from the President . . . to the two houses of Congress.* . . . Dec. 7, 1847. 1369, 249 p. (30:1 H.ex.doc.8.) (Polk's 3rd annual message, with reports, documents.)

517–41 Emory, William H. *Notes of a military reconnoissance, from Fort Leavenworth, in Missouri, to San Diego, in California. . . . Made in 1846–7 with the advanced guard of the "Army of the West".* . . . Washington, D.C.: Wendell and Van Benthuysen, 1848. 614 p. (30:1 H.ex.doc.41.) (Lacks large map normally found in *505–7* but includes reports of J. W. Abert, Philip St.-George Cooke, and A. F. Johnston.)

520–60 U.S. President (Polk). *Message from the President . . . with the correspondence . . . between the Secretary of War and other officers . . . on the subject of the Mexican War.* Washington, 1848. 1277 p. (30:1 H.ex.doc.60.)

521–69 U.S. President (Polk). *Treaty with Mexico. Message from the President . . . transmitting a copy of the treaty of peace, friendship, limits, and settlement, between the United States and the republic of Mexico . . . on the 30th of May 1848.* July 22, 1848. 74 p. (30:1 H.ex.doc.69.)

521–70 U.S. President (Polk). *New Mexico and California. Message from the President of the United States, transmitting, in answer to resolutions of the House . . . of July 10, 1848, reports of the secretaries of State, Treasury, War, and Navy.* July 24, 1848. 49 p. (30:1 H.ex.doc.70.) (Similar to *531–31*, with additions.)

527–817 U.S.Congress. House. *California claims. August 8, 1848 . . . Report: the Committee on Military Affairs, to whom was referred the bill from the Senate, entitled an act for ascertaining and paying the California claims.* . . . 39 p. (30:1 H.rept.817.)

531–31 U.S. Secretary of the Navy. *Report . . . communicating copies of Commodore Stockton's despatches, relating to the military and naval operations in California.* Feb. 16, 1849. 37 p. (30:2 S.ex.doc.31.)

537–1 U.S. President (Polk). *Message from the President . . . to the two houses of Congress at the commencement of the second session.* . . . Dec. 5, 1848. 1275 p. (30:2 H.ex.doc.1.) (Polk's 4th annual message, with reports, documents.)

544–5 Frémont, John C. *Geographical memoir upon Upper California, in illustration of his map of Oregon and California.* . . . Washington, D.C., 1849. 40 p. (30:2 H.misc.doc.5.) (Senate ed., with map, *511–148.*)

547–2 U.S. Secretary of War. *Report . . . communicating . . . a copy of the official journal of Lieutenant Colonel Philip St.George Cooke, from Santa Fé to San Diego, &c.* March 19, 1849. 85 p. (31:special sess. S.doc.2.)

549–1 U.S. President (Taylor). *Message from the President . . . to the two houses of Congress at the commencement of the first session.* . . . Dec. 24, 1849. 852 p. (31:1 S.ex.doc.1.) (Taylor's 1st annual message, with reports, documents.)

557–18 U.S. President (Taylor). *Message from the President . . . communicating information called for by . . . the Senate . . . in relation to California and New Mexico.* Jan. 24, 1850. 952 p. (31:1 S.ex.doc.18.)

558–47 U.S. Secretary of War. *Report . . . communicating information in rela-tion to the geology and topography of California.* April 3, 1850. 127, 37 p. (31:1 S.ex.doc.47.)

561–52 U.S. President (Taylor). *Message from the President . . . in answer to a resolution of the Senate calling for further information in relation to the for-mation of a state government in California. . . .* Read May 22, 1850. 180 p. (31:1 S.ex.doc.52.)

563–68 U.S. Congress. Senate. *Memorial of the senators and representatives elect from California, requesting . . . the admission of California into the Union; accompanied by a certified copy of the constitution. . . .* March 13, 1850. 35 p. (31:1 S.misc.doc.68.)

569–5 U.S. President (Taylor). *Message of the President . . . to the two houses of Congress. . . .* Dec. 24, 1849. 851 p. (31:1 H.ex.doc.5.) (Taylor's 1st annual message, with reports, documents.)

573–17 U.S. President (Taylor). *California and New Mexico. Message from the President. . . .* Jan. 24, 1850. 976 p. (31:1 H.ex.doc.17; p.833–48 are omit-ted and p.849–64 duplicated.)

576–24 U.S. Secretary of War. *Military forces employed in the Mexican war. . . .* Jan. 24, 1850. 77 p. (31:1 H.ex.doc.24.)

577–59 U.S. President (Taylor). *T. Butler King's report on California. Message from the President . . . transmitting the report of T. Butler King . . . bearer of dispatches and special agent to California.* March 27, 1850. 32 p. (31:1 H.ex.doc.59.) (For commercial eds., see KING.)

578–72 U.S. President (Taylor). *California—customs. Message from the Presi-dent . . . respecting the amount of money collected from customs in Califor-nia.* July 22, 1850. 13 p. (31:1 H.ex.doc.72.)

589–18 U.S. Secretary of the Interior. *Report of the Secretary . . . communicat-ing a copy of the report of William Carey Jones, special agent to examine the subject of land titles in California.* Jan. 30, 1851. 136 p. (31:1 S.ex.doc.18.)

621–110 U.S. Secretary of War. *Report of the Secretary . . .communicating . . . a report on the Tulare Valley, made by Lieutenant Derby . . . .* Washington, 1852. 37 p. (32:1 S.ex.doc.110.)

629–4 U.S. Congress. Senate. *Joint resolution of the legislature of California, rel-ative to civil fund of California.* Dec. 8, 1851. 1 p. (32:1 S.misc.doc.4.)

652–27 U.S. Congress. House. *California civil fund. Resolution of the legisla-ture of California in reference to the civil fund of that state.* March 20, 1852. 2 p. (32:1 H.misc.doc.27.)

698–49 U.S. Secretary of War. *Report of the Secretary . . . communicating the report of a board of officers of the army, appointed to examine a report upon claims for funds advanced, and subsistence and supplies furnished or taken for the use of Frémont's California battalion. . . .* March 16, 1854. 17 p. (33:1 S.ex.doc.49.)

723–77 U.S. Secretary of War. *Volunteers serving under Captain Frémont in California . . . March 15, 1854. Letter . . . in reference to the pay &c., of the volunteers. . . .* 1 p. (33:1 H.ex.doc.77.)

743–168 U.S. Congress. House. *Payments of moneys into the treasury of Cal-ifornia.* June 10, 1854. 4 p. (33:1 H.rept.168.)

751–8 U.S. Secretary of War. *Report of the Secretary . . . communicating the re-port of the board of officers appointed to examine claims contracted in Cal-*

ifornia under Lieut. Col. Frémont in 1846–'47. Dec. 14, 1854. 18 p. (33:2 S.ex.doc.8.)

782–13 U.S. Secretary of War. *California claims contracted under Colonel Frémont. . . .* Dec. 15, 1854. 18 p. (33:2 H.ex.doc.13.)

821–63 U.S. Secretary of War. *Report of the Secretary . . . in compliance with a resolution of the Senate . . . calling for a final report of the board of officers relative to funds, subsistence, and supplies furnished or taken for the use of Frémont's California battalion in 1846.* March 5, 1856. 19 p. (34:1 S.ex.doc.63.)

825–109 U.S. President (Pierce). *Message of the President . . . communicating . . . copies of letters and vouchers in support of claims presented by and allowed to John C. Frémont. . . .* June 18, 1856. 144 p. (34:1 S.ex.doc.109.)

Index

Designer: Dave Comstock
Compositor: G & S Typesetters, Inc.
Text: Linotron 202 Sabon
Display: Phototypositor Erbar and Aster
Printer: Braun-Brumfield, Inc.
Binder: Braun-Brumfield, Inc.